The Christian Tradition

1. The Emergence of the Catholic Tradition (100–600)

2. The Spirit of Eastern Christendom (600–1700)

3. The Growth of Medieval Theology (600–1300)

4. Reformation of Church and Dogma (1300–1700)

5. Christian Doctrine and Modern Culture (since 1700)

The Christian Tradition

A History of the Development of Doctrine

Jaroslav Pelikan

5 Christian Doctrine and Modern Culture (since 1700)

The University of Chicago Press

Chicago and London

JAROSLAV PELIKAN is Sterling professor
of history at Yale University and a fellow of
the Medieval Academy of America. His many
publications include *From Luther to
Kierkegaard, The Riddle of Roman Catholicism,
Development of Doctrine,* and *Historical Theology.*
He has also been editor of the American
Edition of *Luther's Works* and of *The Collected
Works of Erasmus.*

The University of Chicago Press, Chicago 60637
The University of Chicago Press, Ltd., London
© 1989 by The University of Chicago
All rights reserved. Published 1989
Printed in the United States of America
98 97 96 95 94 93 92 91 90 89 54321

Library of Congress Cataloging-in-Publication Data

Pelikan, Jaroslav Jan, 1923–
   Christian doctrine and modern culture (since 1700) / Jaroslav
Pelikan.
      p. cm. — (The Christian tradition ; 5)
   Bibliography: p.
   Includes index.
   ISBN 0-226-65378-1
    1. Theology, Doctrinal—History—19th century. 2. Theology,
Doctrinal—History—20th century. 3. Theology, Doctrinal—
History—18th century. I. Title. II. Series: Pelikan, Jaroslav
Jan. 1923– Christian tradition ; 5.
BT21.2.P42 vol. 5
[BT28]
230'.09 s—dc19
[230'.09'03]   88-23658
                                                CIP

Contents

Preface

Christian Doctrine and Modern Culture is the fifth and
final volume of my history of the development of
Christian doctrine, and it has in many ways turned
out to be the "Sorgenkind," as my friends (including
Albert C. Outler and the late William A. Clebsch)
had been warning me, both in person and in print,
that it would be. I first began planning and outlining
The Christian Tradition (though not yet under that
title) in the 1940s, and my earliest drafts and sketches
for it go back to the 1950s. I was quite sure all along
that I wanted to begin the account in the first volume
only after the New Testament, but I was much less
sure just where to end the fifth volume, dealing with
the modern period. The Amsterdam assembly of the
World Council of Churches in 1948 gave me a
possible "terminus ad quem," as did the promulgation
of the assumption of the Virgin Mary by Pope Pius
XII in 1950. But by the time I was ready to publish
volume 1, which appeared in 1971, the actions of the
Second Vatican Council had made it clear that I ought
to conclude my history of church doctrine in the
modern period, and therefore the work as a whole,
with that event.

Only gradually, moreover, had I sharpened my
focus on the history of the development of church
doctrine, as distinguished from the history of Christian thought in general. My treatment of the modern
period is, of course, the one most affected by that
specification of focus. Over the years I have in fact
lectured and written far more about the history of
theology in these past two or three centuries than

about the history of church doctrine--more about the
Enlightenment than about Pietism, more about Kierkegaard than about Grundtvig, more about Tolstoy
than about Soloviev, and, for that matter, more about
Harnack than about Newman. As the editor of a
five-volume series of monographs entitled *Makers of
Modern Theology* and of a three-volume collection of
sources in translation entitled *Twentieth-Century Theology in the Making*, I would have been at least as ready
to write the history of modern theology (although not
in one volume) as the history of doctrine. Indeed,
when I began teaching, I was assigned a course called
"History of Dogma" in the curriculum and another
called "History of Modern Theology"; subsequently I
taught a three-course series called "History of Christian Thought." Thus I would have found it easy—all
too easy—to give the systems of the last two and one-
half centuries, and especially the theological trends of
the twentieth century (many of whose leaders I had
known personally and in some of whose developments
I had even had some part), considerably more than
their fair share of space.

Yet it was appropriate that the epigraph for the first
volume of this work should have linked the names of
Newman and Harnack. As my readers and critics have
frequently commented, the successive volumes of the
work do seem to oscillate between the methodologies
suggested by those two names, and this fifth and final
volume (in which Newman and Harnack themselves
appear for the first time as actors in the drama rather
than merely as playwrights) does so more explicitly
than did any of its predecessors. For the modern
period in the history of Christian doctrine may be
defined as the time when doctrines that had been
assumed more than debated for most of Christian
history were themselves called into question: the idea
of revelation, the uniqueness of Christ, the authority
of Scripture, the expectation of life after death, even
the very transcendence of God. It was also a time
when the relation between the three terms "believe,
teach, and confess," with which the first volume of
this work opened in defining Christian doctrine, was
basically revised: theologians often "confessed" more
than they "believed," perhaps more than they

"taught." But volume 5, too, bears the title *The Christian Tradition*, and that has had to determine the selection of topics and of authors. It has likewise dictated that the use of the Christian past—of tradition, creed, and dogma—by the church in the modern period bulks large in this narrative, much larger than it does in most histories of modern theology.

In his *Autobiography* Edward Gibbon has described, speaking for every subsequent author of a multivolume work of history, the bittersweet feeling that comes with the completion of the final volume: "I will not dissemble the first emotions of joy on recovery of my freedom," Gibbon acknowledged; "but my pride was soon humbled, and a sober melancholy was spread over my mind, by the idea that I had taken an everlasting leave of an old and agreeable companion." For me, the joy and the melancholy are more than matched by the gratitude I sense to all those who have made it possible for me to take on, and now to complete, this ambitious lifework: my departed parents, my other teachers, my colleagues and students both undergraduate and graduate over a period of more than forty years, devoted librarians literally all over Christendom, the University of Chicago Press and its staff, Yale University, and above all my wife, Sylvia, to whom the completed work is dedicated.

Primary Sources

Authors and Texts

Adm.	Karl Adam
Chr.	*The Christ of Faith* [*Der Christus des Glaubens*]. Düsseldorf, 1954
Kath.	*The Essence of Catholicism* [*Das Wesen des Katholizismus*]. 12th ed. Düsseldorf, 1949
Un.	*One Holy Catholic and Apostolic Church in Catholic Perspective* [*Una sancta in katholischer Sicht*]. Düsseldorf, 1948
Albrt.*Vind.*	Valentinus Albert. *Exegetical Vindication of Joel 2:28-29* [*Vindiciae exegeticae Joël II, 28.29*]. Leipzig, 1695
Allat.	Leo Allatius [Leone Allacci]
Enchir.	*Enchiridion on the Procession of the Holy Spirit* [*De processione Spiritus sancti enchiridion*]. Rome, 1658
Perp.cons.	*The Perpetual Consensus of the Eastern and Western Church both in Dogma and in Ritual* [*De perpetuo Ecclesiae Occidentalis atque Orientalis tam in Dogmate quam in Ritibus consensu*]. 2d ed. Rome, 1655
Purg.	*The Perpetual Consensus of Both the Eastern and the Western Church on the Dogma of Purgatory* [*De utriusque Ecclesiae occidentalis atque orientalis perpetua in dogmate de purgatorio consensione*]. Rome, 1655
Syn.Eph.	*Vindication of the Council of Ephesus and of Saint Cyril* [*of Alexandria*] *on the Procession of the Holy Spirit from the Father and the Son* [*Vindiciae synodi Ephesinae et S. Cyrilli de processione ex Patre et Filio Spiritus Sancti*]. Rome, 1661
Alph.Lig.	Alphonsus Liguori [Alfonso Maria de Liguori]
Gl.Mar.	*The Glories of Mary* [*Le glorie di Maria*]
Theol.Mor.	*Moral Theology* [*Theologia Moralis*]
Alt.*Eth.*	Paul Althaus. *Die Ethik Martin Luthers*. Gütersloh, 1965
Ambr.	Ambrose of Milan
Off.	*On Duties* [*De officiis*]
Spir.	*On the Holy Spirit*
Amrt.	Eusebius Amort
Brd.	*Reflections on the New System of Father Laborde concerning Infallibility* [*Animadversiones ad novum Systema P. La Bordii de infallibilitate*]
Ep.	*Epistles*
Gut.	*Legal Opinion* [*Gutachten*]

Indulg.

Rev.

Theol.eclec.

Theol.mor.

Thos.Kemp.

Amvr.Nov.Sobr.

Andrts.
Dogm.

Dok.symb.

Ek.pol.

Kyr.

Symb.

Anf.Pan.serm.

Ang.Sil.CTrid.

Ans.
Cur d.h.
Pros.
Apol.Conf.Aug.

Arb.
Des.myst.

Inst.

Art.Hist.Pi.VII.

Art.XXXIX.
Art.XXXIX. (1801)

The Origin, Progress, Validity, and Results of Indulgences [De origine, progressu, valore, ac fructu indulgentiarum]. 2 vols. Augsburg, 1735

Revelations, Visions, and Private Apparitions: Safe Rules from Scripture, the Councils, the Fathers, etc. [De revelationibus, visionibus, et apparitionibus privatis regulae tutae ex scriptura, conciliis, SS. patribus etc.]. Venice, 1750

Eclectic, Moral, and Scholastic Theology [Theologia eclectica, moralis et scholastica]. 4 vols. Augsburg, 1752

Moral Theology Midway between Rigorism and Laxity [Theologia moralis inter rigorem et laxitatem media]. 2 vols. Venice, 1757

Critical Proof . . . that Saint Thomas à Kempis Is the Author of the Books Entitled "The Imitation of Christ" [Deductio critica . . . Ven. Thomam Kempensem librorum de Imitatione Christi authorem esse]. Augsburg, 1761

Amvrosii of Novgorod. Collection of Instructive Words [Sobranie poučitelnych slov]. 3 vols. Moscow, 1810

Chrēstos Androutsos

Dogmatics of the Orthodox Eastern Church [Δογματικὴ τῆς Ὀρϑοδόξου ᾿Ανατολικῆς ᾿Εκκλησίας]. 2d ed. Athens, 1956

Comparative Symbolics from an Orthodox Perspective [Δοκίμιον συμβολικῆς ἐξ ἐπόψεως Ὀρϑοδόξου]. Athens, 1901

Church and State from an Orthodox Perspective [᾿Εκκλησία καί πολιτεία ἐξ ἐπόψεως ὀρϑοδόξου]. 2d ed. 2 vols. Salonika, 1964

The Validity of Orthodox Ordinations, from an Orthodox-Catholic Perspective [Τὸ κύρος τῶν ᾿Αγγλικῶν Χειροτονιῶν ἐξ ἐπόψεως ὀρϑοδόξου]. Istanbul, 1903

Symbolics from an Orthodox Perspective [Συμβολικὴ ἐξ ἐπόψεως ᾿Ορϑοδόξου]

Philippe Anfossi. Panegyrics and Sermons [Panegirici e sermoni]. Rome, [1817]

Angelus Silesius [Johannes Scheffler].

The Council of Trent before Trent [Concilium Tridentinum ante Tridentinum]. Nissa, 1675

Anselm of Canterbury

Why God Became Man [Cur deus homo]

Proslogion

Apology of the Augsburg Confession [Apologia Confessionis Augustanae]

Antonio Arbiol y Diez

Mystical Disappointments of Souls that Have Been Delayed or Deceived on the Road to Perfection [Desengaños misticos a las almas detenidas, ò engañadas en el camino de la perfeccion]. Madrid, 1764

Religious Instruction [La religiosa instruida . . . para todas las operaciones de su vida regular]. Madrid, 1765

Artaud de Montor. History of Pope Pius VII [Histoire du Pape Pie VII]. 2d ed. 2 vols. Paris, 1837

The Thirty-Nine Articles

American Revision of the Thirty-Nine Articles (1801)

Ath.   Athanasius of Alexandria
  Ar.   *Orations against the Arians*
  Ep.Afr.   *Epistle to the Bishops of Africa*
  Inc.   *On the Incarnation of the Logos*
  Syn.   *On the Synods of Ariminum and Seleucia*
Ath.Par.Epit.   Athanasius of Paros. *Epitome or Collection of the Divine Dogmas of the
                        Faith* [' Ἐπιτομὴ εἴτε συλλογὴ τῶν θείων τῆς πίστεως
                        δογμάτων]. Leipzig, 1806

Aug.   Augustine of Hippo
  Bapt.   *On Baptism against the Donatists*
  Cat.rud.   *On the Catechizing of the Uninstructed* [De catechizandis rudibus]
  Civ.   *City of God* [De civitate Dei]
  Doctr.christ.   *On Christian Doctrine*
  Enchir.   *Enchiridion*
  Ep.fund.   *Against the Epistle of Manicheus Called Fundamental*
  Ev.Joh.   *Exposition of the Gospel of John*
  Gen.ad litt.   *Exposition of Genesis according to the Letter* [De Genesi ad litteram]
  Gest.Pelag.   *On the Proceedings of Pelagius* [De gestis Pelagii]
  Haer.   *On Heresies*
  Pecc.merit.   *On the Merits and the Remission of Sins* [De peccatorum meritis et
                          remissione]
  Praed.sanct.   *On the Predestination of the Saints* [De praedestinatione sanctorum]
  Serm.mont.   *Our Lord's Sermon on the Mount*
  Soliloq.   *Soliloquies*
  Spir.et litt.   *On the Spirit and the Letter* [De spiritu et littera]
  Vera relig.   *On True Religion* [De vera religione]
Avkm.   Protopop Avvakum Petrovič
  Knig.tolk.   *Book of Interpretations and True Doctrines* [Kniga tolkovanij i
                          pravoučenij]
  Žiz.   *Biography* [Žizneopisanie]
Bas.   Basil of Caesarea
  Hex.   *Homilies on the Hexaemeron*
  Spir.   *On the Holy Spirit*
Bau.   Ferdinand Christian Baur
  Chr.   *Christianity and the Christian Church during the First Three
                          Centuries* [Das Christenthum und die christliche Kirche der drei
                          ersten Jahrhunderte]
  Chrpart.   *The Christ Party in the Congregation at Corinth* [Die Christuspartei
                          in der korintischen Gemeinde]
  DG.   *History of Christian Dogma* [Lehrbuch der christlichen Dogmenge-
                          schichte]. 2d ed. Tübingen, 1858
  Episk.   *On the Origin of the Episcopacy in the Christian Church* [Ueber den
                          Ursprung des Episkopats in der christlichen Kirche]
  Neun.   *Church History of the Nineteenth Century* [Kirchengeschichte des
                          neunzehnten Jahrhunderts]
  Röm.   *The Purpose and Occasion of the Epistle to the Romans* [Ueber Zweck
                          und Veranlassung des Römerbriefs]
  Vers.   *The Christian Doctrine of the Atonement in Its Historical
                          Development from the Earliest Times to the Most Recent* [Die
                          christliche Lehre von der Versöhnung in ihrer geschichtlichen
                          Entwicklung von der ältesten Zeit bis auf die neueste].
                          Tübingen, 1838

Baum.*Pred.*	Siegmund Jakob Baumgarten. *Sermons* [*Predigten*]
Beb.*Gl.*	Balthasar Bebel. *Complete but Brief Confession of Faith* [*Auszführliche doch kürtzliche Glaubens-Bekandnusz*]. Strasbourg, 1685
Bec.Lóp.	Becerra López de Osuna y Zarate
Nuev.Ab.	*The New Abraham* [*El nuevo Abraham de la Iglesia*]. Mexico City, 1739
Sab.prod.	*The Prodigal Savant* [*El sabio prodigo Christo Señor Nuestro sacramentado*]. Mexico City, 1752
Beng.	Johann Albrecht Bengel
Brüd.	*Brief Sketch of the So-Called Unity of Brethren* [*Abrisz der so genannten Brüdergemeinde*]. Stuttgart, 1751
Gnom.	*Guide to the New Testament* [*Gnomon Novi Testamenti*]
Bert.	Giovanni Lorenzo Berti
Aug.	*The Augustinian System of Grace . . . Vindicated* [*Augustinianum systema de gratia . . .vindicatum*]. 2 vols. Rome, 1747
Diss.hist.	*Historical Dissertations* [*Dissertationes historicae*]. 3 vols. Florence, 1753-56
Theol.disc.	*On the Disciplines of Theology* [*De theologicis disciplinis*]. 10 vols. Bassini, 1792
Bgn.*Luth.*	Johann Bugenhagen. *Funeral Sermon for Doctor Martin Luther* [*Eine christliche Predigt über der Leich und Begräbnis D. Martini Luthers*]. Wittenberg, 1546
Bianch.*Pot.*	Giovanni-Antonio Bianchi. *Two Treatises on the Power and Polity of the Church* [*Della potestà e della politia della Chiesa tratatti due*]. 6 vols. in 7. Rome, 1745-51
Bl.*Unfehl.*	Felix Anton Blau. *Critical History of the Infallibility of the Church* [*Kritische Geschichte der kirchlichen Unfehlbarkeit*]. Frankfurt, 1791
Blach.*Log.*	Elias Blachopoulos. *Church Sermons* [Λόγοι ἐκκλησιαστικοί]. Athens, 1882
Blgkv.*Prav.*	Sergii Bulgakov. *Eastern Orthodoxy: Outlines of the Doctrine of the Eastern Orthodox Church* [*Pravoslavie: Očerki učenija pravoslavnoj cerkvi*]. New ed. Paris, 1985
Blms.	Jaime Luciano Balmes
Escép.	*Letters to a Skeptic in the Matter of Religion* [*Cartas a un escéptico en materia de religión*]
Prot.	*Protestantism Compared with Catholicism* [*El Protestantismo comparado con el Catolicismo*]
Rel.	*Religion Demonstrated* [*La religion demonstrada al alcance de los niños*]
Blrd.*Brth.*	Henri Bouillard. *Karl Barth: The Genesis and Evolution of Dialectical Theology* [*Karl Barth: Genèse et évolution de la théologie dialectique*]. 2 vols. Paris, 1957
Blrt.*S.T.*	Charles-René Billuart.
	The Summa of Saint Thomas Accommodated to Present-Day Academic Procedures [*Summa S. Thomae hodiernis academiarum moribus accommodata*]
Reg.fid.	*On the Rules of Faith* [*De regulis fidei*]
Grat.	*On Grace* [*De gratia*]
Jur.just.	*On Law and Righteousness* [*De jure et justitia*]
Bltmn.	Rudolf Bultmann

Jes.   *Jesus.* Tübingen, 1964

Th.N.T.   *Theology of the New Testament* [*Theologie des Neuen Testaments*]. Tübingen, 1953

Bnhfr.*Theol.Gem.*   Dietrich Bonhoeffer. *Theology and Congregation* [*Theologie und Gemeinde*]

Bnl.   Benedetto Bonelli

Anim.cr.   *Critical Animadversions on the Nocturnal Congress of Witches* [*Animavversioni critiche sopra il notturno congresso della lamnie*]. Venice, 1751

Diss.apol.   *Apologetic Dissertation on the Martyrdom of Simon of Trent, Murdered by the Jews in 1475* [*Dissertazione sul martirio del beato Simone da Trento nell' anno MCCCCLXXV, dagli Ebrei ucciso*]. Trent, 1747

Bnyn.*Lw.Gr.*   John Bunyan. *The Doctrine of the Law and Grace Unfolded*

Bon.VIII.*Un.sanct.*   Pope Boniface VIII. *Unam sanctam*

Boss.*Hist.var.*   Jacques Bénigne Bossuet. *History of the Variations of the Protestant Churches* [*Histoire des variations des Eglises protestantes*]

Br.*Comp.*   Johann Wilhelm Baier. *Compend of Positive Theology* [*Compendium theologiae positivae*]

Brand.*Dr.Con.*   The Margrave of Brandenburg. *The Three Confessions* [*Die Drey Confessionen*]. Cologne, 1695

Brd.*Cln.Cont.mnd.*   Bernard of Cluny. *On Contempt for the World* [*De contemptu mundi*]

Brd.*Clr.Cant.*   Bernard of Clairvaux. *Sermons on the Song of Songs* [*Sermones in Cantica Canticorum*]

Brgs.*Theol.Symb.*   Charles Augustus Briggs. *Theological Symbolics.* New York, 1914

Brlth.*Euch.*   Yngve Torgny Brilioth. *Eucharistic Faith and Practice.* London, 1953

Brnt.   Gilbert Burnet

Art.*XXXIX.*   *Exposition of the Thirty-Nine Articles.* 2d ed. London, 1700

Rom.   *A Discourse wherein is Held Forth the Opposition of the Doctrine, Worship, and Practices of the Roman Church, to the Nature, Designs, and Characters of the Christian Faith.* London, 1688

Trp.   *A Letter to the Reverend Mr. Trapp.* 2d ed. London, 1717

Brth.   Karl Barth

Ev.Ges.   *Gospel and Law* [*Evangelium und Gesetz*]

K.D.   *Church Dogmatics* [*Kirchliche Dogmatik*]. Munich and Zurich, 1932-.

Krch.   *The Church and the Churches* [*Die Kirche und die Kirchen*]

Prol.   *The Doctrine of the Word of God: Prolegomena to Christian Dogmatics* [*Die Lehre vom Worte Gottes: Prolegomena zur christlichen Dogmatik*]. Munich, 1927

Prot.Theol.   *Protestant Theology in the Nineteenth Century* [*Die protestantische Theologie im 19. Jahrhundert*]. Zurich, 1947

Rcht.   *Justification and Justice* [*Rechtfertigung und Recht*]. 2d ed. Zurich, 1944

Röm.   *The Epistle to the Romans* [*Der Römerbrief*]. 2d ed. Zurich, 1940

Tf.   *The Church Doctrine of Baptism* [*Die kirchliche Lehre von der Taufe*]. 2d ed. Zurich, 1943

Bsst. *Kyr.Chr.*   Wilhelm Bousset. *Christ as Kyrios* [*Kyrios Christos*]. Göttingen, 1913

Budd.   Johann Franz Buddeus

Mod.	*On Moderation . . . in Controversies among Theologians* [*De moderamine inculpatae tutelae in certaminibus theologorum*]. Halle, 1720
Phil.Ebr.	*Introduction to the History of the Philosophy of the Hebrews* [*Introductio ad historiam philosophiae Ebraeorum*]. 2d ed. Halle, 1720
Bulg.*Kat.*	Nicholas Bulgaris. *Sacred Catechesis* [΄ Ιερά κατήχησις]. New ed. Athens, 1940
Bush.	Horace Bushnell
Chr.Nurt.	*Christian Nurture*
Nat.	*Nature and the Supernatural, as Together Constituting the One System of God.* New York, 1858
Vic.Sac.	*The Vicarious Sacrifice, Grounded in Principles of Universal Obligation.* New York, 1866
Byl.*Com.phil.*	Pierre Bayle. *Philosophical Commentary on the Words of Jesus Christ* [*Commentaire philosophique sur ces paroles de Jésus-Christ*]. 2d ed. Rotterdam, 1713
Caj.*Mos.*	Cajetan (Tommaso de Vio). *Illustrious and Outstanding Commentaries on the Five Books of Moses* [*Commentarii illustres planeque insignes in quinque Mosaicos libros*]. Paris, 1539
Calv.*Inst.*	John Calvin. *Institutes of the Christian Religion*
Camp.	Alexander Campbell
Ev.	*The Evidences of Christianity*
Mcla.	*Debate on Christian Baptism between the Rev. W. L. Maccala . . . and Alexander Campbell.* Buffalo, 1824
Prcl.	*A Debate on the Roman Catholic Religion . . .* [*with*] *John B. Purcell, Bishop of Cincinnati.* Cincinnati, 1875
Rce.	*A Debate between Rev. A. Campbell and Rev. N. L. Rice*
Syst.	*The Christian System in Reference to the Union of Christians and Restoration of Primitive Christianity as Pleaded by the Current Reformation.* 3d ed. Nashville, 1956
Canst.*Spen.*	Karl Hildebrand von Canstein. "Foreword" ["Vorrede"] to Philipp Jakob Spener. *Final Theological Opinions* [*Letzte Theologische Bedenken*]. Halle, 1711
Card.*Infall.*	Giuseppe Cardoni. *A Study of the Dogmatic Infallibility of the Roman Pontiff and of Its Definability* [*Elucubratio de dogmatica Romani pontificis infallibilitate eiusque definibilitate*]. Rome, 1870
Casp.*Beyl.*	Vincentius Casper-Sohn. *A Necessary and Useful Appendix* [*Nöthige und nützliche Beylage*]. Stockholm, 1724
Cat.Heid.	*Heidelberg Catechism*
Ces.	Antonio Cesari
Ep.	*Epistles*
St.eccl.	*Flowers from Church History: Selected Discussions* [*Fiore di storia ecclesiastica: Scelti ragionamenti*]. Turin, 1881
V.Ges.Cr.	*Lectures on the Life of Jesus Christ and on His Religion* [*Orazioni sopra la vita di Gesù Cristo e la sua religione*]. Turin, 1830
CFlor. (1438-45) *Decr.Arm.*	Council of Florence. *Decree on the Armenians*
Chan.	William Ellery Channing
Calv.	*The Moral Argument against Calvinism*
Cath.	*Letter on Catholicism*
Evid.Chr.	*Evidences of Christianity*
Evid.Rev.	*The Evidences of Revealed Religion*
Fén.	*Remarks on the Character and Writings of Fénelon*

Hon.	*Honor Due to All Men*
Lke.	*Likeness to God*
Un.Chr.	*Unitarian Christianity*
Chil.*Rel.Prot.*	William Chillingworth. *Religion of Protestants a Safe Way to Salvation.* 9th ed. London, 1727
Chom.	Aleksej Chomjakov
Crk.	*On the Church [O cerkvi]*
Égl.lat.Prot.	*The Latin Church and Protestantism from the Viewpoint of the Orthodox Church [L'Eglise latine et le Protestantisme au point de vue de l'Eglise Orthodoxe].* Lausanne, 1872
Chrys.	John Chrysostom
Jes.	*Homilies on Isaiah*
Matt.	*Homilies on the Gospel of Saint Matthew*
CLater. (1215).*Const.*	Fourth Lateran Council. *Constitutions*
Clem.*Q.d.s.*	Clement of Alexandria. *Who Is the Rich Man that Is Saved? [Quis dives salvetur?]*
Clrdge.	Samuel Taylor Coleridge
Conf.Fid.	*Confessio Fidei*
Const.	*On the Constitution of Church and State according to the Idea of Each*
Ess.	*Essays on His Times*
Inq.Sp.	*Confessions of an Inquiring Spirit*
Log.	*Logic*
Ly.Serm.	*A Lay Sermon*
Ref.	*Aids to Reflection*
Rev.Rel.	*Lectures on Revealed Religion, Its Corruptions and Political Views*
Clrk.*Darw.*	Rufus Wheelwright Clark. *Darwin's Theory of the Descent of Man.* Albany, 1873
Cmrda.	Antoninus Seraphinus Camarda
Const.ap.	*Accurate and Clear Synopsis of the Apostolic Constitutions and the Gregorian Ceremonial Pertaining to the Election of a Pope [Constitutionum apostolicarum una cum ceremoniali Gregoriano de pertinentibus ad electionem Papae synopsis accurata, et plana].* Rieti, 1732
Conc.	Daniele Concina
Rel.riv.	*On Revealed Religion [Della religione rivelata].* 2 vols. Venice, 1754
Theol.chr.	*Christian Dogmatic and Moral Theology [Theologia christiana dogmatico-moralis].* 10 vols. Naples, 1772-75
Conf.Aug.	*Augsburg Confession*
Conf.Belg.	*Belgic Confession*
Conf.Scot.	*Scots Confession*
Conf.Sig.	*Confession of the Faith of Johann Sigismund Elector of Brandenburg*
Coz.*Graec.*	Lorenzo Cozza. *Polemical History of the Schism of the Greeks [Historia polemica de Graecorum schismate].* 4 vols. Rome, 1719-20
Crnly.*Int.*	Rudolf Cornely. *Historical and Critical Introduction to the Sacred Books of Both Testaments [Historica et critica introductio in U. T. Libros Sacros].* 4 vols. Paris, 1885-89
Cstrpln.*Infall.*	Ludovicus a Castroplanio. *The Controversy over Infallibility [De controversia infallibilitatis].* Naples, 1870
CTrid.	Council of Trent
Can.	*Canons*
Decr.	*Decrees*

CVat. (1869-70)   First Vatican Council
CVat. (1962-65)   Second Vatican Council

CVat. (1869-70)	First Vatican Council
CVat. (1962-65)	Second Vatican Council
Ad gent.	Decree on the Church's Missionary Activity [Ad gentes]
Dei Verb.	Dogmatic Constitution on Divine Revelation [Dei Verbum]
Dign.hum.pers.	Declaration on Religious Freedom [Dignitatis humanae personae]
Gaud.sp.	Pastoral Constitution on the Church in the Modern World [Gaudium et spes]
Int.mir.	Decree on the Instruments of Social Communication [Inter mirifica]
Lum.gent.	Dogmatic Constitution on the Church [Lumen gentium]
Nostr.aet.	Declaration on the Relationship of the Church to Non-Christian Religions [Nostra aetate]
Or.eccl.	Decree on Eastern Catholic Churches [Orientalium ecclesiarum]
Presb.ord.	Decree on the Ministry and Life of Priests [Presbyterorum ordinis]
Sacr.Conc.	Constitution on the Sacred Liturgy [Sacrosanctum Concilium]
Unit.redint.	Decree on Ecumenism [Unitatis redintegratio]
Cypr.Ep.	Cyprian of Carthage. Epistles
Cyr.H.Catech.	Cyril of Jerusalem. Catechetical Lectures
Delmp.	A. D. Delēmpasē
Oik.	The Heresy of Ecumenism ['Η αἵρεσις τοῦ Οἰκουμενισμοῦ]. Athens, 1972
Syn.	Pan-Orthodox Synod [Πανορϑόδοξος Σύνοδος]. Athens, 1976
Deutsch.	Johann Deutschmann
Aug.Conf.	Apologia for the Augsburg Confession [Apologia Augustanae Confessionis]. Wittenberg, 1667
Gnad.	Brief Refutation concerning the Opinion Attributed to Him Regarding the Term of Grace [Kurtze Ablehnung wegen der ihm imputirten Meinung von Gnaden Termin]. [Wittenberg, 1701]
Luth.	Confession to the Pastor in the Christian-Lutheran Church [Der Christ-Lutherischen Kirchen . . . Prediger-Beichte]. Wittenberg, 1698
Dipp.	Johann Konrad Dippel [Christianus Democritus]
Hrt.	One Shepherd and One Flock [Ein Hirt und eine Heerde]. Amsterdam, 1706
Orth.	Beginning, Middle, and End of Ortho- and of Heterodoxy [Anfang, Mittel und Ende der Ortho- und Heterdoxie. n.p., 1699
Dmls.Arch.	Nikolaos Damalas. On First Principles [Περί ἀρχῶν]. Leipzig, 1865
Dmtr.Orth.	Andronikos K. Dēmētrakopoulos. Orthodox Greece ['Ορϑόδοξος 'Ελλάς]. Leipzig, 1872
Doc.Chr.Un.	Documents on Christian Unity
Döll.	Johann Joseph Ignaz von Döllinger
Ep.	Epistles
Gnos.	History of Gnostic-Manichean Sects in the Early Middle Ages [Geschichte der gnostisch-manichäischen Sekten im frühen Mittelalter]. Munich, 1890
Heid.Jud.	Paganism and Judaism: A Vestibule to the History of Christianity [Heidenthum und Judenthum: Vorhalle zur Geschichte des Christenthums]. Regensburg, 1857
Ppst.Conc.	The Pope and the Council [Der Papst und das Konzil]

Ppstfab.	The Papal Legends of the Middle Ages [*Die Papst-Fabeln des Mittelalters*]. Stuttgart, 1890
Ref.	The Reformation: Its Internal Development and Its Effects in the Context of the Lutheran Confession [*Die Reformation, ihre innere Entwicklung und ihre Wirkungen im Umfange des lutherischen Bekenntnisses*]. 3 vols. Regensburg, 1846-48
Vat.Dekr.	Letters and Declarations concerning the Vatican Decrees between 1869 and 1887 [*Briefe und Erklärungen über die Vatikanischen Dekrete 1869 bis 1887*]
Dör.Pet.	Paul Döring. The "Key" of Dr. Petersen, Which Closes More than It Opens [*Der mehr zu- als auff-schliessende Schlüssel Herrn D. Petersens*]. Dresden, 1718
Dost.Br.Kar.	F. M. Dostoevsky. The Brothers Karamazov
Drnd.	Barthélemy Durand
Diss.	Ecclesiastical Dissertations for both the Sacramental and the Polemical Forum [*Dissertationes ecclesiasticae pro foro tam sacramentali quam contentioso*]. Avignon, 1703
Fid.vind.	The Faith Vindicated [*Fides vindicata*]. Avignon, 1709
Drnr.	Isaak August Dorner
Pers.Chr.	History of the Development of the Doctrine of the Person of Christ [*Entwicklungsgeschichte der Lehre von der Person Christi*]. 2d ed. 2 vols. Berlin, 1845-53
Syst.	System of the Doctrine of the Christian Faith [*System der christlichen Glaubenslehre*]. 2 vols. Berlin, 1879-80
Dry.Apol.	Johann Sebastian von Drey. Apologetics as the Intellectual Demonstration of the Divinity of Christianity as a Phenomenon [*Die Apologetik als wissenschaftliche Nachweisung der Göttlichkeit des Christenthums in seiner Erscheinung*]. 3 vols. Mainz, 1838-47
Dtr.Lmp.	Peter Friderich Detry. Brief Illumination in Response to Friderich Adolph Lampe [*Kurtze Beleuchtung . . . Friderich Adolph Lampe*]. [Bremen], 1717
Dup.Souv.pont.	Félix Antoine Philibert Dupanloup. The Sovereignty of the Pope according to Catholic Law and according to European Law [*La souveraineté pontificale selon le droit catholique et le droit européen*]. 2d ed. Paris, 1860
Düss.Th.	Düsseldorf Theses [*Düsseldorfer Thesen*] of 1933
Dyob.	Kōnstantinos Dyobouniōtēs
Joh.Dam.	John of Damascus [Ἰωάννης ὁ Δαμασκηνός]. Athens, 1903
Myst.	The Sacraments of the Eastern Orthodox Church [Τὰ μυστήρια τῆς ἀνατολικῆς ὀρθόδοξου ἐκκλησίας]. Athens, 1912
Edw.	Jonathan Edwards
Brnrd.	The Life of David Brainerd
Dist.Mrks.	The Distinguishing Marks of a Work of the Spirit of God
Fr.Wll.	Freedom of the Will
Fthfl.Narr.	A Faithful Narrative of the Surprising Work of God
Orig.Sn.	Original Sin
Rel.Aff.	Religious Affections
Sm.Thts.	Some Thoughts concerning the Revival
El.	Richard T. Ely
Gr.	Ground under Our Feet: An Autobiography
Soc.Lw.	The Social Law of Service

Elrt.*Morph.*   Werner Elert. *The Structure of Lutheranism* [*Morphologie des Luthertums*]. 2 vols. Munich, 1931-32

Emer.   Ralph Waldo Emerson
   Div.   *Divinity School Address*
   Jour.   *Journals*
   Nat.   *Nature*
   Rep.Mn.   *Representative Men*
   Sup.   *The Lord's Supper*

Engsch.*Pet.*   Carl Gottfried Engelschall. *Dr. Petersen's Totally Incorrect Understanding of the Seventh Trumpeting Angel* [*Der den siebenden posaunenden Engel gantz unrecht verstehende Herr D. Petersen*]. Dresden and Leipzig, 1720

Epiph.*Haer.*   Epiphanius of Salamis. *Against Eighty Heresies* [*Panarion*]

Erhrd.*Kemp.*   Thomas Aquinas Erhard. *Attack against the Shield of Thomas à Kempis* [*Polycrates Gersensis contra Scutum Kempense instructus prodiens*]. Augsburg, 1729

Erkl.*Bek.*   *First Barmen Declaration* [*Erklärung über das rechte Verständnis der reformatorischen Bekenntnisse in der deutschen evangelischen Kirche der Gegenwart*]

Ern.*Opusc.*   Johann August Ernesti. *Opuscula*

Ess.Consist.   Consistory of Esslingen

Eug.Bulg.*Orth.*   Eugenios Bulgaris. *Orthodox Confession* [Ὀρϑόδοξος ὁμολογία]

Eus.   Eusebius of Caesarea
   H.e.   *Ecclesiastical History*
   V.C.   *Life of Constantine* [*Vita Constantini*]

FCC.*Const.*   Federal Council of Churches of Christ in America. *Constitution*

Felb.*Hnd.*   Jeremias Felbinger. *Christian Handbook* [*Christliches Hand-Büchlein*]. Baltimore, 1799

Fén.   François de Salignac de la Mothe Fénelon
   Aut.égl.   *Letters on the Authority of the Church* [*Lettres sur l'autorité de l'église*]
   Ep.   *Epistles*
   Gr.préd.   *Letters on Grace and Predestination* [*Lettres . . . sur la grâce et la prédestination*]
   Inst.   *Instructions and Advice on Various Questions of Christian Morality and Perfection* [*Instructions et avis sur divers points de la morale et de la perfection chrétienne*]
   Let.div.   *Letters on Various Subjects of Metaphysics and of Religion* [*Lettres sur divers sujets de métaphysique et de religion*]
   Man.piét.   *Manual of Piety* [*Manuel de piété*]
   Tr.ex.   *Treatise on the Existence and the Attributes of God* [*Traité de l'existence et des attributs de Dieu*]

Feod.*Prav.*   Archimandrite Feodor. *On Orthodoxy* [*O pravoslavij*]. St. Petersburg, 1860

Feof.*Proc.*   Feofan Prokopovič. *Treatise on the Procession of the Holy Spirit* [*Tractatus de processione Spiritus Sancti*]. Gotha, 1772

Fil.   Filaret, patriarch of Moscow
   Ent.   *Conversation between a Skeptic and a Believer concerning the Orthodoxy of the Eastern Church* [*Entretiens d'un sceptique et d'un croyant sur l'orthodoxie de l'église Orientale*]
   Knig.Bit.   *Commentary on the Book of Genesis* [*Zapiski . . . Knigi Bitija*]. 3 vols. Moscow, 1867

Gbts.*Ekkl.*	Athanasios M. Giebtits. *The Ecclesiology of the Apostle Paul according to Saint Chrysostom* [῾Η ἐκκλησιολογία τοῦ ἀποστόλου Παύλου κατὰ τόν ἱερόν Χρυσόστομον]. Athens, 1967
Gel.I.*Ep.*	Pope Gelasius I. *Epistles*
Gers.*Aufer.*	Jean de Gerson. *The Removability of the Bridegroom from the Church* [*De auferibilitate sponsi ab ecclesia*]
Gffrd.	Lord Arthur Gifford
Lect.	*Lectures*
Trst.	*Trust, Disposition, and Settlement*
Gib.	Edward Gibbon
Aut.	*Autobiography*
Dec.	*The History of the Decline and Fall of the Roman Empire*
Gldn.*Ch.Kng.*	Washington Gladden. *The Church and the Kingdom*
Gr.XVI.	Pope Gregory XVI [*Mauro Cappellari*]
Mir.	*Mirari vos*
Tr.	*The Triumph of the Holy See and of the Church* [*Il trionfo della Santa Sede e della Chiesa*]
Gr.Naz.	Gregory Nazianzus
Carm.	*Poems* [*Carmina*]
Or.	*Orations*
Grh.*Loc.*	Johann Gerhard. *Theological Loci* [*Loci theologici*]
Grig.Mont.	Louis Marie Grignion de Montfort
Am.sag.	*The Love of Eternal Wisdom* [*L'amour de la sagesse éternelle*]
Vr.dév.	*Treatise on True Devotion to the Blessed Virgin* [*Traité de la vraie dévotion à la Ste. Vierge*]
Grnvg.	Nikolai Fredrick Severin Grundtvig
Chr.Brnlr.	*Christian Fundamentals* [*Den Christelige Børnelaerdom*]
Chr.Snd.	*The Truth of Christianity* [*Om Christendommens Sandhed*]
Nrd.Myth.	*Nordic Mythology* [*Nordens Mythologi*]
Pr.	*Sermons* [*Praedikener*]
Ref.	*Continuance of the Lutheran Reformation?* [*Skal den lutherske Reformation virkelig fortsaettes?*]
Snd.Chr.	*True Christianity* [*Om den sande Christendom*]
Gth.	Johann Wolfgang von Goethe
Eck.	*Conversations with Goethe in the Last Years of His Life by Johann Peter Eckermann* [*Gespräche mit Goethe in den letzten Jahren seines Lebens von Johann Peter Eckermann*]
Fst.	*Faust*
Gtti.	Vincenzo Lodovico Gotti
Coll.	*Theological-Polemical Colloquies* [*Colloquia theologico-polemica*]. Bologna, 1727
Ver.eccl.	*The True Church of Christ* [*Vera ecclesia Christi*]. Venice, 1763
Ver.rel.	*The Truth of the Christian Religion* [*Veritas religionis Christianae*]. 2 vols. Venice, 1750
Gtz.	Georg Heinrich Götze
Bek.	*The Joyful Caution of Christians against the Wickedness of the Devil . . . in Refutation of Dr. Balthasar Bekker's "The Enchanted World"* [*Der Christen Freudige Fürsichtigkeit für des Teufels Boszheit . . . wieder D. Balthasar Bekkers "Bezauberte Welt"*]. Dresden, 1696

Unt. *Necessary Instruction about the Proud Speeches of the Pietists and Fanatical Enthusiasts [Nöthiger Unterricht von denen stoltzen Reden derer Pietisten und fanatischen Schwärmer].* Chemnitz, 1693

Gyar.*Infall.* Giovanni [János] Gyarmathy. *The Infallibility of the Roman Pontiff as a Belief that is Well-Grounded and Commendable [La infallibilità del Romano Pontefice credenza fondata e commendabile].* Rome, 1870

Hag.*DG.* Karl Rudolf Hagenbach. *History of Dogma [Lehrbuch der Dogmengeschichte]*

Han.Consist. Consistory of Hanover

Harn. Adolf von Harnack

DG. *History of Dogma [Lehrbuch der Dogmengeschichte].* 5th ed. 3 vols. Tübingen, 1931

Erf.Erl. *Research and Experience [Erforschtes und Erlebtes].* Giessen, 1923

Marc. *Marcion: The Gospel of the Alien God [Marcion: Das Evangelium vom fremden Gott].* 2d ed. Leipzig, 1924

Red.Auf. *Addresses and Papers [Reden und Aufsätze].* 2 vols. Giessen, 1904-6

Wes. *The Essence of Christianity [Das Wesen des Christentums].* 4th ed. Leipzig, 1901

Wiss.Leb. *From Scholarship and Life [Aus Wissenschaft und Leben].* 2 vols. Giessen, 1911

Wrk.Voll. *From the Workplace of the Departed [Aus der Werkstatt des Vollendeten].* Giessen, 1930

Hckng.*Reth.* William Ernest Hocking. *Rethinking Missions: A Laymen's Inquiry after One Hundred Years.* New York, 1932

Hcks. George Hicks

Cat. *A New Catechism.* London, 1710

Ltrs. *Several Letters which Passed between Dr. George Hicks and a Popish Priest.* London, 1705

Hdge. Charles Hodge

Darw. *What Is Darwinism?* New York, 1874

Ess.Rev. *Essays and Reviews.* New York, 1857

Rom. *Commentary on the Epistle to the Romans.* 2d ed. New York, 1886

Syst.Theol. *Systematic Theology.* Reprint ed. 3 vols. Grand Rapids, Mich., 1981

Hdly. Benjamin Hoadly

Def. *A Defence of the Reasonableness of Conformity.* London, 1707

Flt. *A Letter to Mr. Fleetwood: Occasion'd by His Late Essay on Miracles.* London, 1702

Kngdm. *The Nature of the Kingdom, or Church, of Christ.* 3d ed. London, 1717

Hef. Karl Josef von Hefele

Conz. *History of the Councils [Conziliengeschichte].* 7 vols. Freiburg im Breisgau, 1855-74

Hon. *The Case of Pope Honorius [Causa Honorii Papae].* Naples, 1870

Hfkntz.*Jüd.* Christian Hoffkuntz. *Description of the Christian Baptism of a Jew in Torgau [Beschreibung einer christlichen Jüden-Tauffe . . . zu Torgau].* Leipzig, [1706]

Hfmnn. Johann Christian Konrad von Hofmann.

Enc. *Encyclopedia of Theology [Encyclopädie der Theologie]*

Hil. Hilary of Poitiers

Const.	To Emperor Constantine [Ad Constantinum Augustum]
Trin.	On the Trinity
Hll.	Karl Holl
Luth.	Luther
Ost.	The East [Der Osten]
Wst.	The West
Hlr.Alt.	Friedrich Heiler. Autonomy in the Ancient Church and Papal Centralism [Altkirchliche Autonomie und päpstlicher Zentralismus]. Munich, 1941
Hnbrg.Vers.	Daniel Bonifacius Haneberg. An Essay on the History of Biblical Revelation [Versuch einer Geschichte der biblischen Offenbarung]. 2d ed. Regensburg, 1852
Hno.Theol.	Francisco Henno. Dogmatic, Moral, and Scholastic Theology [Theologia dogmatica, moralis, et scholastica]. 8 vols. Venice, 1785
Holb.Evol.Scr.	Arthur Holborow. Evolution and Scripture. London, 1892
Hon.I.Ep.	Pope Honorius I. Epistles
Hor.Ep.	Horace. Epistles
Hrbn.Crk.	Jozef Miloslav Hurban. The Evangelical Lutheran Church [Církev evanjelicko-luteránská]. Skalice, 1861
Hrlss.	Gottlieb Christoph Adolf von Harless.
Enc.	Theological Encyclopedia and Methodology from the Standpoint of the Protestant Church [Theologische Encyklopädie und Methodologie vom Standpunkte der protestantischen Kirche]. Nürnberg, 1837
Hrmnn.	Wilhelm Herrmann
Nt.	The Crisis of the Protestant Church Connected with Theology, and Its Solution [Die mit der Theologie verknüpfte Not der evangelischen Kirche und ihre Ueberwindung]. Tübingen, 1913
Wirk.	The Reality of God [Die Wirklichkeit Gottes]. Tübingen, 1914
Hrn.H.e.	Georg Horn. Ecclesiastical and Political History [Historia ecclesiastica et politica]
Hrom.	Josef L. Hromádka
Csty.	Paths of a Protestant Theologian [Cesty protestantského theologa]. Prague, 1927
Th.crk.	Theology and the Church [Theologie a církev]. Prague, 1949
Hrsn.Kngdm.	Benjamin Harrison. The Kingdom of Heaven
Hrth.	Hierotheos [Mētropoulos]
Ēs.	Commentary on the Prophet Isaiah ['Ερμηνεία εἰς τόν Προφήτην 'Ησαῖαν]. Athens, 1883
Herm.	Commentary on the Epistles to Timothy and Titus ['Ερμηνεία εἰς τάς πρός Τιμόθεον καί Τίτον ἐπιστολάς]. Athens, 1882
Log.	Church Addresses [Λόγοι ἐκκλησιαστικοί]. Athens, 1882
Myst.	The Mystery of Divine Fellowship [Τό Μυστήριον τῆς θείας κοινωνίας]. New York, 1942
Thrsk.	True Worship ['Η ἀληθής θρησκεία]. 2d ed. Athens, 1895
Hüg.	Friedrich von Hügel
Ess.	Essays and Addresses on the Philosophy of Religion. 2 vols. London, 1949-51
Myst.	The Mystical Element of Religion as Studied in Saint Catherine of Genoa and Her Friends. 2d ed. 2 vols. London, 1961
Real.	The Reality of God
Inn.XI.Cael.Past.	Pope Innocent XI. Caelestis Pastor

Innok.*Bog.oblič.*	Archimandrite Innokentij. *Polemical Theology* [*Bogoslovie obličitelnoe*]. Kazan, 1859
Iren.*Haer.*	Irenaeus. *Against Heresies*
Iv.	James Iverach
Chr.Evol.	*Christianity and Evolution.* London, 1894
Gd.Kn.	*Is God Knowable?* London, 1887
Thsm.	*Theism in the Light of Present Science and Philosophy.* New York, 1899
Jab.*Sal.*	Ernst Daniel Jablonski. *Excellent Addresses on the Last Words of Solomon in the 12th Chapter of Ecclesiastes* [*Vortreffliche Reden über die letzten Worte Salomons im 12. Kapitel seines Predigers*]
Jam.	John Jamieson
Acct.	*A Faithful Account of an Important Trial in the Court of Conscience.* [London, 1806]
McGl.	*Socinianism Unmasked . . . Occasioned by Dr. McGill's "Practical Essay on the Death of Christ."* Edinburgh, 1787
Sac.Hist.	*The Use of Sacred History, Especially as Illustrating and Confirming the Great Doctrines of Revelation.* 2 vols. Edinburgh, 1802
Serm.	*Sermons on the Heart.* 2 vols. Edinburgh, 1789-90
Vind.	*A Vindication of the Doctrine of Scripture . . . concerning the Deity of Christ.* 2 vols. Edinburgh, 1794
Jcksn.*Rem.*	John Jackson. *Remarks on a Book Intitled Christianity as Old as the Creation.* London, 1731
Jeff.	Thomas Jefferson
Ep.	*Epistles*
LJ	*The Life and Morals of Jesus*
PJ	*The Philosophy of Jesus*
Syl.	*Syllabus of an Estimate of the Merit of the Doctrines of Jesus, Compared with Those of Others*
Vir.	*Notes on Virginia*
Jer.*Niž.Uč.*	Jeremija of Nižni Novgorod. *Instruction concerning the Truths of the Orthodox-Christian Faith and Church* [*Učenie . . . ob istinach pravoslavno-Christovoj věry i cerkvi*]. St. Petersburg, 1864
Joan.Kv.*Jub.Shor.*	Joannikij of Kiev. *Jubilee Collection* [*Jubilejnij sbornik*]. St. Petersburg, 1899
Joh.D.	John of Damascus
Exp.fid.	*Exposition of the Faith* [*Expositio fidei*]
Hom.	*Homilies*
Jrms.*Kndtf.*	Joachim Jeremias. *Infant Baptism in the First Four Centuries* [*Die Kindertaufe in den ersten vier Jahrhunderten*]. Göttingen, 1958
Jwl.*Apol.*	John Jewel. *An Apology of the Church of England*
Kbl.	John Keble
Chr.Yr.	*The Christian Year.* Oxford, 1827
Nat.Ap.	*National Apostasy.* Oxford, 1833
Oc.	*Occasional Papers and Reviews*
Spir.	*Letters of Spiritual Counsel and Guidance*
Khns.*Dogm.*	Karl Friedrich August Kahnis. *Lutheran Dogmatics Presented by a Historical-Genetic Method* [*Die lutherische Dogmatik, historisch-genetisch dargestellt*]. 2 vols. Leipzig, 1861-64
Kierk.	Søren Aabye Kierkegaard
Afs.Uvid.Eft.	*Concluding Unscientific Postscript to the "Philosophical Fragments"* [*Afsluttende uvidenskabelig efterskrift til de Philosophiske Smuler*]

Begr.Ang.   The Concept of Anxiety [Begrebet Angest]
Ent.   Either/Or [Enten-eller]
Fr.Bv.   Fear and Trembling [Frygt og Baeven]
Ind.Chr.   Attack upon "Christendom" [Indøvelse i Christendom]
Phil.Sm.   Philosophical Fragments [Philosophiske Smuler]
Stad.   Stages on Life's Way [Stadier paa livets vei]
Syg.Dd.   Sickness unto Death [Sygdommen til Døden]
Klfth.   Theodor Friedrich Dethlof Kliefoth
DG.   Introduction to the History of Dogma [Einleitung in die Dogmenge-
                    schichte]. Parchin and Ludwigslust, 1839
Knt.   Immanuel Kant
Auf.   Answer to the Question: What Is Enlightenment? [Beantwortung der
                    Frage: Was ist Aufklärung?]
Krit.pr.Vern.   Critique of Practical Reason [Kritik der praktischen Vernunft]
Krit.rn.Vern.   Critique of Pure Reason [Kritik der reinen Vernunft]
Rel.   Religion within the Limits of Reason Alone [Religion innerhalb der
                    Grenzen der blossen Vernunft]
Kol.Káz.   Ján Kollár. Sermons and Addresses for Sundays, Holidays, and Other
                Occasions [Nedělní, svátečné a příležitostné Kázne a Řeči]. vol. 2.
                Budapest, 1844
Komn.Prosk.   Joannes Komnēnos. Guide to Worship on the Holy Mountain Athos
                [Προσκυνητάριον τοῦ ἁγίου ὄρους τοῦ ῎Αϑωνος]
Krb.Diar.   Johann Georg Korb. Diary of a Journey to Moscow [Diarium itineris
                in Moscoviam]. Vienna, [1700]
Krks.   Diomēdēs Kyriakos
Antipap.   Against the Pope [᾽Αντιπαπικά]. Athens, 1893
Dok.   Essay on Ecclesiastical History [Δοκίμιον ἐκκλησιαστικῆς
                    ἱστορίας]. Athens, 1874
Ekkl.Hist.   Ecclesiastical History from the Founding of the Church to Our Own
                    Times [᾽Εκκλησιαστικὴ ῾Ιστορία ἀπὸ τῆς ἰδρύσεως
                    τῆς ἐκκλησίας μέχρι τῶν καϑ᾽ ἡμᾶς χρόνων]. 3
                    vols. Athens, 1897-98
Ench.Pat.   Manual of Patrology [᾽Εγχειρίδιον Πατρολογίας]. Ath-
                    ens, 1898
Theol.diat.   Theological Lectures [Θεολογικαὶ διατριβαί]. Athens, 1898
Krmr.Mssge.   Hendrik Kraemer. The Christian Message in a Non-Christian World.
                New York, 1938
Krth.   Charles Porterfield Krauth
Cons.Ref.   The Conservative Reformation and Its Theology. Philadelphia, 1871
Rel.   Religion and Religionisms. Philadelphia, [1877]
Krtšv.Sob.   A. V. Kortašov. On the Road to an Ecumenical Council [Na putach k
                vselenskomu soboru]. Paris, 1932
Lacrd.   Henri Dominique Lacordaire
Conf.   Lectures at Notre Dame of Paris [Conférences de Notre-Dame de Paris]
Cons.   Considerations of the System of Monsieur de Lamennais [Considér-
                    ations sur le système de M. de La Mennais]
Dom.   Life of Saint Dominic [Vie de saint Dominique]
Égl.emp.rom.   The Church and the Roman Empire in the Fourth Century [L'Église et
                    l'empire romain au quatrième siècle]
Loi hist.   Discourse on the Law of History [Discours sur la loi de l'histoire]
Thos.Aq.   Discourse on the Transfer of the Head of Saint Thomas Aquinas
                    [Discours pour la translation du chef de Saint Thomas d'Aquin]

Lam.   Félicité Robert de Lamennais

Av.   *The Future [L'Avenir]*

Déf.   *Defense of the Essay on Indifference in the Matter of Religion [Défense de l'Essai sur l'indifference en matière de religion]*

Ep.   *Epistles*

Indiff.   *Essay on Indifference in the Matter of Religion [Essai sur l'indifference en matière de religion]*

Mx.égl.   *The Evils of the Church and of Society, and the Means of Remedying Them [Des maux de l'Eglise et de la société, et des moyens d'y remédier]*

Par.cr.   *Words of a Believer [Paroles d'un croyant]*

Réf.   *Reflections on the State of the Church [Réflexions sur l'état de l'Eglise]*

Rel.   *Religion Considered in Its Connections with the Political and Civil Order [De la religion considérée dans ses rapports avec l'ordre politique et civil]*

Lang.   Joachim Lange

Antibarb.   *Dogmatic and Hermeneutical Reponse to the Barbarism of Orthodoxy; or, the System of Evangelical Dogmas [Antibarbarus orthodoxiae dogmatico-hermeneuticus sive Systema dogmatum evangelicorum].* 2 vols. Berlin, 1709-11

Mittl.   *The Correct Middle Way [Die richtige Mittel-Strasze].* Halle, 1712

Nach.   *Correct Report concerning the Incorrectness of the So-Called "Innocent Reports" [Auffrichtige Nachricht von der Unrichtigkeit der so genannten Unschuldigen Nachrichten].* 10 vols. Leipzig, 1707-14

Paul.   *Historical and Hermeneutical Commentary on the Life and Epistles of the Apostle Paul [Commentatio historico-hermeneutica de vita et epistolis Apostoli Pauli].* Halle, 1718

Leo XIII.   Pope Leo XIII

Aet.Pat.   *Aeterni Patris*

Ap.cur.   *Apostolicae curae*

Mir.car.   *Mirae caritatis*

Or.dign.   *Orientalium dignitas ecclesiarum*

Prov.   *Providentissimus Deus*

Rer.Nov.   *Rerum Novarum*

Less.   Gotthold Ephraim Lessing

Bew.   *On the Proof of the Spirit and of Power [Über den Beweis des Geistes und der Kraft]*

Frag.   *Fragments of an Anonymous Writer from Wolfenbüttel [Fragmente eines Wolfenbüttelschen Ungenannten]*

Nath.   *Nathan the Wise [Nathan der Weise]*

Zw.   *On the Intention of Jesus and of His Disciples [Von dem Zweck Jesu und seiner Jünger]*

Leyd.*Jans.*   Melchior Leydecker. *The History of Jansenism [De historia Jansenismi].* Utrecht, 1695

Lid.   Henry Parry Liddon

Div.   *The Divinity of Our Lord and Savior Jesus Christ.* London, 1867

Pus.   *Life of Edward Bouverie Pusey.* 4 vols. London, 1893-97

Lmp.   Friedrich Adolf Lampe

Betr.   *Meditations on the Entire History of the Sufferings of Jesus Christ, according to All Four Evangelists [Betrachtungen über die ganze Leydensgeschichte Jesu Christi, nach allen vier Evangelisten].* 2 vols. Lemgo in Lippe, 1756

Brt. The Holy Bridal Decoration of the Wedding Guests of the Lamb [*Der heilige Braut-schmuck der Hochzeitgäste des Lams*]. 5th ed. Bremen, 1737

Dtr. Reasons for Not Answering Peter Friderich Detry [Ursachen warum auf Peter Friderich Detry . . . nicht geantwortet wird]. Bremen, 1717

Ew.Str. Two Treatises on the Eternity of Punishment [*Zwo Verhandlungen von der Ewigkeit der Strafen*]. Bremen, 1729

Ghm. The Mystery of the Covenant of Grace [*Geheimnis des Gnaden-Bundes*]. 2 vols. Bremen, 1719

Hist. Synopsis of Sacred and Ecclesiastical History [*Synopsis Historiae sacrae et ecclesiasticae*]. 4th ed. Utrecht, 1747

Theol.elench. Rudiments of Argumentative Theology [*Rudimenta theologiae elenchticae*]. Bremen, 1729

Theol.nat. Compendium of Natural Theology [*Compendium theologiae naturalis*]. Utrecht, 1734

Lnrgn.*D.Tr.* Bernard Lonergan. On the Divine Trinity [*De Deo trino*]. 2 vols. Rome, 1964

Lōl.*Symb.* Sophocles D. Lōlē. On the First Creed [Περί τό πρώτον Σύμβολον τῆς Πίστεως]. Athens, 1958

Lschr. Valentin Ernst Loescher
Del. Final and Faithful Words to His Beloved Congregation in Delitzsch [*Letzte und getreue Worte an seine geliebte Gemeinde zu Delitzsch*]. Leipzig, [1707]

Dr.Pred. Three Sermons on the Knowledge and Honor of the Son of God [*Drey Predigten von der Erkänntnis und Ehre des Sohnes Gottes*]. Dresden and Neustadt, 1733

Hör. Evangelical Sermon on the Various Hearers of the Word of God [*Evangelische Predigt von unterschiedlichen Hörern der göttlichen Rede*]. Dresden, 1734

Pens. Necessary Reflections on the Book "Free Thoughts about Religion" [*Nöthige Reflexionen über das . . . Buch Pensées libres sur la religion*]. Wittenberg, 1724

Unfehl. Fundamental Consideration of the Infallibility of the Roman Catholic Church as Null and Void [*Gründliche Vorstellung von der Römisch-Catholischen Kirche nichtigen Unfehlbarkeit*]. Frankfurt and Leipzig, 1724

Lub.*Hist.esp.* Henri de Lubac. History and Spirit [*Histoire et esprit*]. Paris, 1950
Luth. Martin Luther
Dtsch.Kat. Large Catechism [*Deutscher Katechismus*]
Kl.Kat. Small Catechism [*Kleiner Katechismus*]
Post. Christmas Postil [*Weinachts-Postille*]
Serm.Sacr. Sermon on the Sacrament [*Ein Sermon von dem hochwürdigen Sakrament des heiligen wahren Leichnams Christi und von den Brüderschaften*]

Lw. William Law
Bngr. Three Letters to the Bishop of Bangor
Chr.Perf. A Practical Treatise upon Christian Perfection
Dem.Er. A Demonstration of the Gross and Fundamental Errors of a Late Book
Reas. The Case of Reason, or Natural Religion, Fairly and Fully Stated
Ser.Cl. A Serious Call to a Devout and Holy Life

McGl.*Ess.*	William McGill. *A Practical Essay on the Death of Jesus Christ.* Edinburgh, 1786
Maj.*Mayr.*	Heinrich Majus. *Epistle to Friedrich Mayer* [*Epistola ad . . . Fridericum Mayerum*]. n.p., 1705
Mak.	Makarij, Metropolitan of Moscow
Kv.*Ak.*	*History of the* [*Spiritual*] *Academy of Kiev* [*Istorija Kievskoj akademij*]. St. Petersburg, 1843
Prav.*bog.*	*Orthodox-Dogmatic Theology* [*Pravoslavno-dogmatičeskoe bogoslovie*].
Rask.	*History of the Russian Schism* [*Istorija russkago raskola*]. 2d ed. St. Petersburg, 1858
Makr.	Apostolos Makrakēs
Anth.	*The Threefold Composition of Man* [Τό τρισύνθετον τοῦ ἀνθρώπου]. Athens, 1882
Herm.	*Commentary on the Entire New Testament* [᾽ Ἑρμηνεία ὅλης τῆς καινῆς διαθήκης]. 4 vols. Athens, 1891
Log.*kat.*	*Catechetical Addresses on the Creed* [Λόγοι κατηχητικοὶ ἐπὶ τοῦ συμβόλου τῆς πίστεως]. Athens, 1871
Mar.*Inst.symb.*	Philip Marheinecke. *Institutes of Symbolics* [*Institutiones symbolicae*]. 2d ed. Berlin, 1825
Marc.*Inst.*	Michel Angelo Cesare Marcelli. *Theological Institutes* [*Institutiones theologicae*]
Marit.*Thos.Aq.*	Jacques Maritain. *Saint Thomas Aquinas.* New York, 1958
Mayr.	Johann Friedrich Mayer
Anti-Spen.	*Against Spener* [*Anti-Spenerus*]. Hamburg, 1695
Ger.	*Opened Limitations of Judgment* [*Eröffnete Gerichts-Schrancken*]. [Hamburg], 1708
Hall.	*Mild and Thorough Answer to the Theological Faculty in Halle* [*Gelinde und gründliche Antwort auff der Theological Facultät zu Halle . . . Verantwortung*]. Leipzig, 1707
Mis.	*The Abuse of the Freedom of Believers* [*Mıszbrauch der Freyheit der Gläubigen*]. [Hamburg], 1692
Piet.	*Commentary on the Pietists of the Ancient Church* [*De Pietistis ecclesiae veteris commentatio*]. Hamburg, 1696
Pont.*rom.*	*On the Election of the Pope* [*De pontificis romani electione*]. Holmia and Hamburg, 1690
Red.	*Spiritual Addresses* [*Geistliche Reden*]. Berlin, 1702
Witt.	*Wittenberg's Innocence of a Double Murder* [*Das bey doppeltem Mord unschuldige Wittenberg*]. Wittenberg, 1686
Mchl.*Lit.*	Virgil Michel. *The Liturgy of the Church according to the Roman Rite.* New York, 1938
Mck.*Vor.*	Alexander Mack, Sr. *Brief and Simple Presentation of the Rules and Ordinances of the House of God* [*Kurze und einfältige Vorstellung der . . . Rechten und Ordnungen des Hauses Gottes*]. Germantown, Pa., 1774
Mel.*Loc.*	Philip Melanchthon. *Loci*
Mēn.*Did.*	Ēlias Mēniatēs. *Lenten Sermons* [Διδαχαὶ εἰς τὴν ἁγίαν καὶ μεγάλην τεσσαρακοστήν]
Mhlr.	Johann Adam Möhler
Ath.	*Athanasius the Great and the Church of His Time* [*Athanasius der Grosse und die Kirche seiner Zeit*]. Mainz, 1827
Ein.	*Unity in the Church; or, The Principle of Catholicism, Presented in the Spirit of the Church Fathers of the First Three Centuries* [*Die*

	Einheit in der Kirche, oder, Das Princip des Katholicismus, dargestellt im Geiste der Kirchenväter der drei ersten Jahrhunderte]. 2d ed. Tübingen, 1843
Ges.Schr.	*Collected Writings and Papers [Gesammelte Schriften und Aufsätze]*. 2 vols. Regensburg, 1839-40
Lehr.	*New Investigations into the Doctrinal Oppositions between Catholics and Protestants [Neue Untersuchungen der Lehrgegensätze zwischen den Katholiken und Protestanten]*. 2d ed. Mainz, 1835
Pat.	*Patrology, or History of Christian Literature [Patrologie, oder Christliche Literärgeschichte]*
Symb.	*Symbolics; or Presentation of the Dogmatic Oppositions of Catholics and Protestants according to Their Public Confessional Writings [Symbolik: oder Darstellung der dogmatischen Gegensätze der Katholiken und Protestanten nach ihren öffentlichen Bekenntnisschriften]*
Mich.Od.*Ev.*	Archimandrite Michail of Odessa. *On the Gospels and Gospel History [O evangelijach i evangelickoj istorij]*. Moscow, 1865
Mid.	Conyers Middleton
Ltr.Rom.	*A Letter from Rome, Showing an Exact Conformity between Popery and Paganism*. London, 1729
Mir.	*Free Inquiry into the Miraculous Powers which Are Supposed to Have Subsisted in the Christian Church*. London, 1749
Wat.	*A Letter to Dr. Waterland*. London, 1731
Milt.	John Milton
Areop.	*Areopagitica*
Doct.	*Two Books of Investigations into Christian Doctrine Drawn from the Sacred Scriptures Alone [De Doctrina Christiana Libri Duo Posthumi]*
Mmchi.*Orig.ant.*	Tommaso Maria Mamachi. *Christian Origins and Antiquities [Origines et antiquitates christianae]*. 5 vols. Rome, 1749-55
Mnkn.*Bl.*	Gottfried Menken. *Views of the Life of the Apostle Paul and of the Early Christian Congregations [Blicke in das Leben des Apostels Paulus und der ersten Christengemeinden]*. Bremen, 1828
Mnschr.*DG.*	Wilhelm Münscher. *History of Christian Dogma [Lehrbuch der christlichen Dogmengeschichte]*
Mntl.	Charles René Forbes, le Comte de Montalembert
Ang.	*On the Political Future of England [De l'avenir politique de l'Angleterre]*
Ans.	*Saint Anselm [Saint Anselme]*
Av.	*The Future [L'Avenir]*
Élis.	*History of Saint Elizabeth of Hungary [Histoire de sainte Elisabeth de Hongrie]*
Int.cath.	*Catholic Interests in the Nineteenth Century [Des intérêts catholiques au dix-neuvième siècle]*
Lib.égl.	*The Freedom of the Church [Liberté de l'église]*
Mor.*Luth.*	Thomas More. *Response to Luther*
Mos.	Johann Lorenz von Mosheim
Tol.	*Commentary on the Life . . . of John Toland [De vita . . . Joannis Tolandi commentatio]*. Hamburg, 1722
Vind.disc.	*Vindication of the Discipline of Ancient Christians against the "Nazarene" of John Toland [Vindiciae antiquae Christianorum disciplinae, adversus . . . Jo. Tolandi . . . Nazarenum]*. 2d ed. Hamburg, 1722

Mrce.*Sub.* Frederick Denison Maurice. *Subscription No Bondage.* London, 1835

Mrchn.*Sacr.Bib.* Giovanni Francesco Marchini. *On the Divinity and Canonicity of the Holy Bible* [*De divinitate et canonicitate Sacrorum Bibliorum*]. Turin, 1874

Mrck. Johannes à Marck

Apoc. *Commentary on the Revelation of Saint John* [*In Apocalypsin Johannis commentarius*]

Cant. *Commentary on the Song of Solomon* [*In Canticum Shelomonis Commentarius*]

Comp. *Didactic and Argumentative Compendium of Christian Theology* [*Compendium theologiae Christianae didactico-elencticum*]

Exeg.exerc. *Exegetical Exercises* [*Exegeticae exercitationes*]

Pent. *Commentary on Several Chief Parts of the Pentateuch* [*In praecipuas quasdam Partes Pentateuchi Commentarius*]

Scrip.exerc. *Scriptural Exercises on Twenty-Five Selected Passages* [*Scripturariae exercitationes ad quinque et viginti selecta loca*]

Syl. *Collection of Philological and Theological Dissertations on Certain Selected Texts of the New Testament* [*Sylloge dissertationum philologico-theologicarum ad selectos quosdam textus Novi Testamenti*]

Text.exerc. *Textual Exercises on Fifty Selected Passages* [*Textuales exercitationes ad quinquaginta selecta loca*]

Mrkrd. Jōannēs Nikolaos Alexandros Maurokordatus.

Off. *On Duties* [Περὶ καθηκόντων: *De officiis*]. Leipzig, 1722

Mrr. Christian Maurer

Mry. John Courtney Murray

Prob.Gd. *The Problem of God: Yesterday and Today.* New Haven, 1964

Trths. *We Hold These Truths: Catholic Reflections on the American Proposition.* Garden City, N.Y., 1964

Mtz.*Theoph.* Eusthatios Mētzēs. *Theophylact of Bulgaria* [᾿ Ερμηνεία εἰς τὰ τέσσαρα ἱερὰ Εὐαγγελία]. Leipzig, 1788

Mynst. Jacob Peter Mynster

Betr. *Considerations of the Doctrines of the Christian Faith* [*Betragtninger over de christolige troesluerdomme*]. 3d ed. 2 vols. Copenhagen, 1846

Luth.Kat. *On the Danish Editions of Luther's Small Catechism* [*Om de danske udgaver af Luthers lille katechismus*]. 2d ed. Copenhagen, 1837

Pr. *Sermons for All the Sundays and Feast Days in the Year* [*Praedikener paa alle Søn- og Hellig-Dage i Aaret*]. 4th ed. Copenhagen, 1845

Naud. Philippe Naudé [Naudäus]

Kouak. *Brief History of the Rise and Progress of Quakerism, with Some of Its Dogmas* [*Histoire abregée de la naissance et du progrez du kouakerisme, avec celle de ses dogmes*]. Paris, 1699

Myst. *Nonpartisan and Thorough Investigation of Mystical Theology* [*Unpartheyische und Gründliche Untersuchung der mystischen Theologie*]. Zerbst, 1713

Nbr. Reinhold Niebuhr

Ch.Lt. *The Children of Light and the Children of Darkness.* New York, 1944

Fth.Hist.	*Faith and History: A Comparison of Christian and Modern Views of History.* New York, 1949
Nat.Dest.	*The Nature and Destiny of Man.* 2 vols. New York, 1943
Neum.	Erdmann Neumeister
Adv.	*Christian Instruction on the God-pleasing Observance of Advent, Christmas, and New Year's [Christlicher unterricht wie die h. Adventszeit, das h. Christ-Fest und das Neue Jahr gotgefällig zu feiren sey].* [Hamburg], 1737
Bew.	*A Firmly Established Proof that Christ Jesus Has Rendered Satisfaction for Us and for Our Sins [Festgegründeter Beweis . . . dasz Christus Jesus für uns und unsere Sünden gnung gethan].* 2d ed. [Hamburg], 1730
Ev.Nach.	*Evangelical Echo [Evangelischer Nachklang].* 2 vols. Hamburg, 1726-29
Fünf.	*Continued Fivefold Church Devotions [Fortgesetzte fünffache Kirchen-Andachten].* 2 vols. Hamburg, 1726
Hnd.	*Verses of Praise of the So-Called Peasant Dog [Lob-Gedichte des so genannten Bauer-Hundes].* Hamburg, n.d.
Marp.	*Proof that the So-Called Scriptural Consideration of Doctrinal Argument by Marperg Is Not Scriptural [Beweis, dass die Marpergisch so genannte schriftmässige Betrachtung des Lehr-Elenchi nicht schriftmässig sey].* [Hamburg], 1727
Ps.	*Psalms, Hymns of Praise, and Spiritual Songs [Psalmen und lobgesänge und geistliche lieder].* n.p., n.d.
Rch.	*Spiritual Burnt Offering: Sermons on the Common Prayer of the Church [Geistliches Räuch-opfer; das ist, predigten über das gemeine kirchengebeth].* [Hamburg], 1751
Wied.	*Thorough Refutation of the Recently Published Brief Presentation of the So-Called Restitution of All Things by Ludwig Gerhard [Gründliche Wiederlegung des von M. Ludwig Gerhard neulich herausgegebenen Kurtzen Begriffe von der alsogenannten Wiederbringung aller Dinge].* Hamburg, n.d.
Newm.	John Henry Newman
Apol.	*Apologia Pro Vita Sua*
Ar.	*The Arians of the Fourth Century.* 6th ed. London, 1890
Art.XXXIX.	*Remarks on Certain Passages in the Thirty-Nine Articles*
Dev.	*An Essay on the Development of Christian Doctrine*
Gram.	*An Essay in Aid of a Grammar of Assent*
Id.Univ.	*The Idea of a University Defined and Illustrated*
Insp.	*On the Inspiration of Scripture*
Jour.	*Journal*
Min.Com.	*Thoughts on the Ministerial Commission*
Prim.Prac.	*The Present Obligation of Primitive Practice*
Proph.Off.	*Lectures on the Prophetical Office of the Church Viewed Relatively to Romanism and Popular Protestantism*
Scr.Prf.	*Lectures on the Scripture Proof of the Doctrines of the Church*
Univ.Serm.	*Sermons, Chiefly on the Theory of Religious Belief, Preached before the University of Oxford.* London, 1843
Vis.Ch.	*The Visible Church*
Nieb.	Helmut Richard Niebuhr
Ch.Min.	*The Purpose of the Church and Its Ministry.* New York, 1956
Chr.Cult.	*Christ and Culture.* New York, 1951

Rad.Mon.	Radical Monotheism and Western Culture. New York, 1960
Rev.	The Meaning of Revelation. New York, 1960
Soc.Srcs.	The Social Sources of Denominationalism. New York, 1929
Nmnn.	Johann Georg Neumann
Ehr.	Obligatory Defense of Honor [Abgedrungene Ehren-Rettung]. Wittenberg, 1699
Er.	Extensive Discussion of the Question of the Divine Term of Grace [Ausführliche Erörterung der Frage vom göttlichen Gnaden-Termin]. Wittenberg, 1701
Spen.	Forerunner against Spener [Prodromus Anti-Spenerianus]. Wittenberg, 1695
St.Ver.	A Steadfast Defense [Standhafte Vertheidigung]. Wittenberg, 1696
Term.	Discussion of the Question of the Peremptory Term of Salvation [Erörterung der Frage vom Termino Salutis Peremptorio]. Wittenberg, 1700
Nrs.	Henri Noris
Hist.pel.	History of Pelagianism [Historia pelagiana]
Syn.quint.	Historical Dissertation on the Fifth Ecumenical Council [Dissertatio historica de synodo quinta]
Vind.Aug.	Vindication of Augustine [Vindiciae Augustinianae]
Nsl.Bek.KO.	Wilhelm Niesel. Confessions and Church Orders of the Church Reformed in Accordance with the Word of God [Bekenntnisschriften und Kirchenordnungen der nach Gottes Wort reformierten Kirche]. Munich, [1938]
Nss.Dipp.	Heinrich Georg Neuss. Testing of the Spirit and Doctrine of Dippel [Probatio spiritus et doctrinae Democriti, Das ist, Prüfung des Geistes und der Lehre Christiani Democriti, sonst Dippel genannt]. Frankfurt and Leipzig, 1701
Nürn.Sen.	Senate of Nürnberg
Nvn.	John Williamson Nevin
Myst.Pres.	The Mystical Presence
Schf.	Introduction to Philip Schaf[f]. The Principle of Protestantism
Oik.Gr.Nyss.	Constantine Oikonomos, ed. Two Epistles of Gregory of Nyssa [Δύο ἐπιστολαί]. Athens, 1850
Or.	Origen of Alexandria
Cels.	Against Celsus [Contra Celsum]
Princ.	On First Principles [De principiis]
Ors.Ist.	Giuseppe Agostino Orsi. On the History of the Church [Della istoria ecclesiastica]. 20 vols. Rome, 1747-62
Ost.	Jean Frédéric Osterwald
Arg.ref.	Arguments and Reflections on the Books and Chapters of the Holy Bible [Argumens et reflexions sur les livres et sur les chapitres de la Sainte Bible]. 2 vols. Neuchâtel, 1720
Cat.	Catechism, or Instruction in the Christian Religion [Catechisme ou instruction dans la religion chrétienne]. Neuchâtel, 1747
Corrupt.	Treatise on the Sources of the Corruption Prevailing at the Present Day among Christians [Traité des sources de la corruption, qui règne aujour-d'hui parmi les Chrétiens]. 2 vols. Amsterdam, 1700
Dz.serm.	Twelve Sermons on Various Texts of Holy Scripture [Douze sermons sur divers textes de l'Ecriture sainte]. Geneva, 1722
Eth.	Compendium of Christian Ethics [Ethicae Christianae Compendium]. London, 1727

Pal.	William Paley
Ev.Chr.	Evidences of Christianity
Hor.Paul.	Horae Paulinae
Nat.Theol.	Natural Theology
Papad.Symb.	Chrysostomos Papadopoulos. Historical and Critical Study of the Creed of the Second Ecumenical Council [Τὸ σύμβολον τῆς Β' οἰκουμενικῆς συνόδου. ἱστορική καὶ κριτική μελετή].Athens, 1924
Pet.	Johann Wilhelm Petersen
Hchzt.	The Wedding Feast of the Lamb and His Bride [Die Hochzeit des Lammes und der Braut]. Offenbach am Main, [1701]
Myst.	Mystery of the Restitution of All Things [Μυστήριον ἀποκαταστεως πάντων, d.i. Geheimnis der Wiederbringung aller Dinge]. 3 vols. Frankfurt, 1700-1710
Pff.Hist.theol.	Christoph Matthäus Pfaff. Introduction to the Literary History of Theology [Introductio in historiam theologiae literariam]. 2d ed. 2 vols. Tübingen, 1724-26
Phds.	Blasios I. Pheidas
Ekk.hist.	Church History [' Ἐκκλησιαστική ἱστορία]. Athens, 1973
Kan.	Historico-Canonical and Ecclesiological Presuppositions of the Interpretation of the Sacred Canons [Ἰστορικοκανονικαί καί ἐκκλησιολογικαί προϋποθέσεις ἑρμηνείας τῶν ἱερῶν κανόνων]. Athens, 1972
Pent.	The Authority of the Pentarchy of Patriarchs [' Ο θέσμος τῆς πενταρχίας τῶν πατριαρχῶν]. 2 vols. Athens, 1969-70
Phot.Bib.	Patriarch Photius of Constantinople. Library [Bibliotheca]
Pi.IX.	Pope Pius IX
Ineff.	Ineffabilis Deus
Syl.	Syllabus of Errors
Pi.X.	Pope Pius X
Lam.	Lamentabili
Pasc.	Pascendi dominici gregis
Sacr.ant.	Sacrorum antistites
Pi.XI.	Pope Pius XI
Cast.con.	Casti connubii
Div.il.mag.	Divini illius magistri
Quad.	Quadragesimo anno
Pi.XII.	Pope Pius XII
Div.affl.Spir.	Divino afflante Spiritu
Hum.gen.	Humani generis
Mun.	Munificentissimus Deus
Myst.corp.	Mystici corporis
Piep.	Franz Pieper
Chr.Dogm.	Christian Dogmatics [Christliche Dogmatik]. 3 vols. Saint Louis, 1917-24
Plmp.Pan.	C. E. Plumptre. General Sketch of the History of Pantheism. 2 vols. London, 1878-79
Plmr.Russ.Ch.	William Palmer. Notes of a Visit to the Russian Church in the Years 1840, 1841. London, 1882
Plot.Rask.	K. Plotnikov. Brief Manual on the Schismatic Movement [Kratkoe rukovodstvo po raskolovedeniju]. St. Petersburg, 1902

Pnch.*Dict.*   Barthélémy Pinchinat. *Chronological, Historical, and Critical Dictionary on the Origin of Idolatry [Dictionnaire chronologique, historique, critique, sur l'origine de l'idolatrie etc.]* Paris, 1736

Pnnch.*Hon.*   Guiseppe Pennacchi. *The Case of Pope Honorius I at the Sixth Ecumenical Council, Addressed to the Fathers of the Vatican Council [De Honorii I. romani pontificis causa in Concilio VI. . . . ad patres Concilii Vaticani].* Regensburg, 1870

Poir.   Pierre Poiret
  Chr.ed.   *The Christian Education of Children, on the Basis of True Principles [De christiana liberorum e veris principiis educatione libellus].* Amsterdam, 1694
  Fid.rat.   *Faith and Reason Compared [Fides et ratio collatae].* Amsterdam, 1708
  Oec.div.   *The Divine Economy [L'oeconomie divine].* 2 vols. Frankfurt, 1705
  Théol.cr.   *The Theology of the Heart; or, Collection of Various Treatises Containing Divine Illuminations of Pure and Simple Souls [La théologie du coeur, ou recueil de quelques traités qui contiennent les lumières les plus divines des âmes simples et pures].* 2d ed. Cologne, 1690
  Théol.myst.   *Collection of Various Treatises of Mystical Theology [Recueil de divers traitez de théologie mystique].* Cologne, 1699

Polyc.*Ep.*   Polycarp of Smyrna. *Epistle to the Philippians*
Pont.Com.Bib.   Pontifical Biblical Commission [Pontificia Commissio de Re Biblica]
Prcl.   John B. Purcell
Prksch.   Otto Proksch
Prn.*Prael.*   Giovanni Perrone. *Theological Lectures [Praelectiones theologicae].* 32d ed. 10 vols. Turin, 1877-79
Prstly.*Soc.*   Joseph Priestley. *Socrates and Jesus Compared.* Philadelphia, 1803
Ptz.*Sed.inf.*   Giovanni Vincenzo Patuzzi. *On Seeking the Location of Hell on Earth [De sede inferni in terris quaerenda].* Venice, 1763
Pus.*Hist.*   Edward Bouverie Pusey. *An Historical Enquiry into the Probable Causes of the Rationalistic Character Lately Predominant in the Theology of Germany.* 2 vols. London, 1828-30

Qnl.   Pasquier Quesnel
  Arn.   *The Case of Arnauld, or Antoninus Arnaldus Vindicated [Causa Arnaldina, Antoninus Arnaldus . . . vindicatus].* Liège, 1699
  Aux.   *Sketch of the History of the Congregation on Aids to Grace [Abrégé de l'histoire de la Congrégation De Auxiliis].* Frankfurt, 1687
  Clém.IX.   *The Peace of Pope Clement IX [La paix de Clément IX].* Chambéry, 1700
  Déf.égl.rom.   *Defense of the Church of Rome and Its Sovereign Pontiffs [Défense de l'église romaine et souverains pontifes].* 2d ed. Liège, 1697
  Dx.rec.   *Two Collections of Many Acts, Declarations, and Other Pieces [Deux recueils de plusiers actes, déclarations, et autres pièces].* [Chambéry, 1700]
  Ex.piét.   *Exercises of Piety [Exercises de piété].* Paris, 1693
  Exp.apol.   *Apologetic Explication of the Sentiments of Father Quesnel [Explication apologétique des sentiments du Père Quesnel].* 2 vols. n.p., 1712

Reb.*Poen.*   Karl Ludwig Rebstock. *On Penitence [De poenitentia].* Frankfurt, 1708

Reim.*Apol.*	Hermann Samuel Reimarus. *Apology or Defense of the Rational Worshipers of God* [*Apologie oder Schutzschrift für die vernünftigen Verehrer Gottes*]
Remp.	Johann Rempen
Cour.	*An Extraordinarily Accomplished Courier* [*Ein extraordinair . . . abgefertigter Courrier*]. Hildesheim, 1698
Luth.	*The Immortal Luther* [*Unsterblicher Luther*]. Hildesheim, 1699
Rndt.	Eusèbe Renaudot
Diss.	*Unpublished Dissertation on Oriental Liturgies* [*Dissertatio inedita de liturgiis orientalibus*]
Lit.Or.	*Collection of Oriental Liturgies* [*Liturgiarum Orientalium Collectio*]. 2 vols. Paris, 1716
Rsch.	Walter Rauschenbusch
Chr.Soc.Cr.	*Christianity and the Social Crisis.* New York, 1907
Miss.	*Conceptions of Missions*
Theol.	*A Theology for the Social Gospel.* New York, 1917
Rtl.	Albrecht Ritschl
Fid.imp.	*Implicit Faith: An Investigation of Blind Faith, Knowledge and Faith, Faith and the Church* [*Fides implicita. Eine Untersuchung über Köhlerglauben, Wissen und Glauben, Glauben und Kirche*]. Bonn, 1890
Ges.Auf	*Collected Papers* [*Gesammelte Aufsätze*]. Freiburg im Breisgau, 1893
Piet.	*History of Pietism* [*Geschichte des Pietismus*]. 3 vols. Bonn, 1880-86
Recht.	*The Christian Doctrine of Justification and Reconciliation* [*Die christliche Lehre von der Rechtfertigung und Versöhnung*]. 3 vols. Bonn, 1882-83
Theol.Met.	*Theology and Metaphysics* [*Theologie und Metaphysik*]. 2d ed. Bonn, 1887
Unt.	*Instruction in the Christian Religion* [*Unterricht in der christlichen Religion*]
Rtschl.*DG.Prot.*	Otto Ritschl. *History of Protestant Dogma* [*Dogmengeschichte des Protestantismus*]. 4 vols. Leipzig and Göttingen, 1908-27
Rufin.*Symb.*	Rufinus. *Commentary on the Apostles' Creed* [*Commentarius in symbolum apostolorum*]
Sail.	Johann Michael Sailer
Ep.	*Epistles*
Mor.	*Manual of Christian Morality* [*Handbuch der Christlichen Moral*]. 3 vols. Munich, 1817
Past.	*Lectures on Pastoral Theology* [*Vorlesungen aus der Pastoraltheologie*]. 5th ed. 3 vols. Sulzbach, 1835
Sav.Conf.	*Savoy Confession*
Schbrt.*Bek.*	Hans von Schubert. *The Development of Confessions and Church Politics (1524-1534)* [*Bekenntnisbildung und Religionspolitik (1524-1534)*]. Gotha, 1910
Schd.*Jer.*	Johann Caspar Schade. *Pay Attention, Berlin! That Is, the Threefold Witness of the Lord Jesus about Jerusalem* [*Bedencke Berlin! Das ist, des Herrn Jesu dreyfaches Zeugnis über Jerusalem*]. Leipzig, 1696
Schf.*Prin.Prot.*	Philip Schaff [Schaf]. *The Principle of Protestantism*
Schl.	Friedrich Daniel Ernst Schleiermacher

Chr.Gl.   *The Christian Faith Systematically Presented, in Accordance with the Fundamental Principles of the Evangelical Church [Der christliche Glaube nach den Grundsätzen der evangelischen Kirche im Zusammenhange dargestellt]*

Chr.St.   *Christian Morality [Die christliche Sitte]*
Ein.N.T.   *Introduction to the New Testament [Einleitung in das Neue Testament]*
Gesch.   *History of the Christian Church [Geschichte der christlichen Kirche]*
Herm.   *Hermeneutics [Hermeneutik]*
Krit.   *Critique [Kritik]*
Leb.Jes.   *The Life of Jesus [Das Leben Jesu]*
Rel.   *On Religion: Addresses to the Cultured among Its Despisers [Über die Religion: Reden an die Gebildeten unter ihren Verächtern]*

Schlnk.Th.Bek.   Edmund Schlink. *Theology of the Lutheran Confessions [Theologie der lutherischen Bekenntnisschriften]*. 3d ed. Munich, 1948

Schltz.Röm.9,5   Hermann Schultz. *Romans 9:5 Explained in Its Exegetical, Critical, and Biblical- Theological Context [Römer 9,5 in exegetischer, critischer und biblisch- theologischer Beziehung erklärt]*

Schmdt.Bcht.   Johann Schmidt. *A Christian Sermon on the Way and Manner of Making Confession [Christliche Predigt von . . . der Art und Weise zu beichten]*. Strasbourg, 1662

Schmn.Prav.   Alexander Schmemann. *The Historical Road of Eastern Orthodoxy [Istoričeskij Put' Pravoslavija]*. New ed. Paris, 1985

Schpf.Luth.   Justus Schoepfer. *Luther Saved from Burning [Lutherus non combustus]*. Wittenberg, 1717

Schtz.Haer.   Friedrich Wilhelm Schütz. *Inaugural Disputation: On the Usefulness of Heresies in the Church [Disputatio inauguralis De haeresium in ecclesia utilitate]*. Leipzig, 1724

Schw.Gth.   Albert Schweitzer. *Goethe*. Olten, 1953
Schwrd.   Johann David Schwerdtner [Innocentius Deodatus Sincerus]
   Comm.   *Serious Scruples of Conscience about the Communion Held at Königsberg [Dringende Gewissens-Scrupel in der zu Königsberg . . . gehaltenen Communion]*. [Königsberg], 1707

Schwzr.   Eduard Schweizer
Scriv.   Christian Scriver
   Seel.   *The Treasure of the Soul [Der Seelenschatz]*
   Zuf.And.   *Occasional Devotions [Zufällige Andachten]*
Seem.   Sebastian Seemüller
Sem.   Johann Salomo Semler
   Baum.   *Introduction to Dogmatic Theology [Einleitung in die dogmatische Gottesgelersamkeit]*. In: Siegmund Jakob Baumgarten. *Evangelical Doctrine of Faith [Evangelische Glaubenslehre]*. 3 vols. Halle, 1759-60

   Calv.   *Also about the Alleged Calvinism in Göttingen [Auch über den vorgeblichen Calvinismus in Göttingen]*. Halle, 1788

   Erkl.   *Thorough Explanation of Several New Theological Propositions, Censures, and Complaints [Ausführliche Erklärung über einige neue theologische Aufgaben, Censuren und Klagen]*. Halle, 1777

   Erud.   *Brief Instruction in Liberal Theological Learning [Institutio brevior ad liberalem eruditionem theologicam]*. 2 vols. Halle, 1765-66

   Frag.   *Response to the "Fragments of an Anonymous Writer," Particularly "On the Intention of Jesus and of His Disciples" [Beantwortung der*

	Fragmente eines Unbekannten insbesondere vom Zweck Jesu und seiner Jünger]. 2d ed. Halle, 1780
N.T.Int.	*Apparatus for the Liberal Interpretation of the New Testament* [*Apparatus ad liberalem Novi Testamenti interpretationem*]. Halle, 1767
Rel.	*Final Confession of Faith about Natural and Christian Religion* [*Letztes Glaubensbekenntniss über natürliche und christliche Religion*]
V.T.Int.	*Apparatus for the Liberal Interpretation of the Old Testament* [*Apparatus ad liberalem Veteris Testamenti interpretationem*]. Halle, 1773
Sherl.	William Sherlock
Def.	*A Defence and Continuation of the Discourse Concerning the Knowledge of Jesus Christ.* London, 1675
Soc.	*Present State of the Socinian Controversy.* London, 1698
Vind.	*A Vindication of the Doctrines of the Holy and Ever Blessed Trinity, and of the Incarnation of the Son of God.* London, 1690
Shprd.Comm.	Massey Hamilton Shepherd. *The Oxford American Prayer Book Commentary.* New York, 1950
Shrlck.Bngr.	Thomas Sherlock. *Remarks upon the Lord Bishop of Bangor's Treatment of the Clergy and Convocation.* 3d ed. London, 1717
Sim.Thess.Lit.	Simeon of Thessalonica. *On the Sacred Liturgy*
Slp.	Josyf Slipyj
Ep.	*Epistles*
Posl.	*Messages* [*Poslanija*]
Taj.	*The General Doctrine of The Holy Sacraments* [*Zahalna nauka pro svjati tajni*]
Slv.	Vladimir Sergeevič Soloviev
Bogočlv.	*Lectures on Godmanhood* [*Čtennija o Bogočelovečestve*]
Duch.osn.	*The Spiritual Foundations of Life* [*Duchovnyja osnovy žizni*]
Id.russ.	*The Russian Idea* [*L'idée russe*]
Krit.	*Critique of Abstract Principles* [*Kritika otvlečennich načal*]
Rus.égl.	*Russia and the Universal Church* [*La Russie et l'église universelle*]
Soph.	*Wisdom* [*La Sophia*]
Vlk.spr.	*The Great Schism and a Christian Politics* [*Velikij spor i christianskaja politika*]
Smdt.	Karl Ludwig Schmidt
Sob.	Council [Sobor] of the Russian Orthodox Church in Moscow
Soc.Crd.	*The Social Creed of the Churches*
Socr.H.e.	Socrates Scholasticus. *Ecclesiastical History*
Söd.	Nathan Söderblom
Bid.	*A Study of the Christian Understanding of Faith in Revelation* [*Ett bidrag till den kristna uppenbarelsetrons tolkning*]. Uppsala, 1911
Chr.Fell.	*Christian Fellowship: The United Life and Work of Christendom.* New York, 1923
Kat.prot.	*The Problem of Religion in Catholicism and Protestantism* [*Religionsproblemet inom katolicism och protestantism*]. Stockholm, 1910
Liv.Gd.	*The Living God: Basal Forms of Personal Religion.* London, 1933
Rel.st.	*Religion and the State* [*Religionen och staten*]. Stockholm, 1918
Tl.	*Essays* [*Tal och essayer*]

Und.	*Jesus' Teaching about the Kingdom of God [Jesu undervisning om Guds rike].* 3d ed. Stockholm, 1933
Upp.	*Religion of Revelation [Uppenbarelsereligion].* 2d ed. Stockholm, 1930
Span.	Friedrich Spanheim (the Younger)
Cont.	*Controversies about Religion [Elenchus Controversiarum de religione]*
Ev.vind.	*Defenses of the Gospel according to Matthew [Evangelicae vindiciae]*
Exerc.acad.	*Academic Exercises [Exercitationes academicae]*
H.e.	*Church History [Historia ecclesiastica]*
Praescrip.	*On Prescription in Matters of Faith [De praescriptione in rebus fidei]*
Xen.	*The Gifts of Enemies Are Not Gifts: or; The Gifts of Roman Catholics Rightly Evaluated [' Εχϑρῶν δῶρα ἄδωρα seu Xenia Romano-Catholicorum juste pretio aestimata]*
Spen.	Philipp Jakob Spener
Albrt.	*Thorough Defense of His Innocence against the Preface of Dr. Valentinus Albertus [Gründliche Vertheidigung seiner Unschuld . . . gegen Herrn D. Valentini Alberti . . . Praefat].* Stargardt, 1696
Beant.	*Thorough Answer [Gründliche Beantwortung].* Frankfurt, 1693
Bed.	*Final Theological Judgments [Letzte theologische Bedencken]*
Gtts.	*The Theology Shared by All Believing Christians and Authentic Theologians [Die allgemeine Gottesgelehrtheit aller glaubigen Christen und rechtschaffenen Theologen].* Frankfurt, 1680
Mess.	*That Our Lord Jesus is the True Messiah or Christ [Dasz unser Herr Jesus der wahre Messias oder Christus seye].* Frankfurt, 1701
Stec.*Un.cons.*	Valentinus Steccanella. *Theological Disquisition against the Novel Doctrine of the Necessity of a Unanimous Consensus of Bishops [Adversus novam doctrinam de necessitate unanimis episcoporum consensus theologica disquisitio].* Rome, 1870
Stffr.*Th.N.T.*	Ethelbert Stauffer. *The Theology of the New Testament [Die Theologie des Neuen Testaments].* 3d ed. Stuttgart, 1947
Sth.	Robert South
Animad.	*Animadversions upon Dr. Sherlock's Book.* 2d ed. London, 1693
Trith.	*Tritheism Charged upon Dr. Sherlock's New Notion of the Trinity.* London, 1693
Stngr.*Ges.*	Johann Melchior Stenger. *Jesus Our Only Lord and Lawgiver [Jesus unser einiger Herr und Gesetzgeber].* n.p., 1693
Stod.	Solomon Stoddard
Apl.	*An Appeal to the Learned.* Boston, 1709
Conv.	*A Treatise concerning Conversion.* Boston, 1719
Gd.Chr.	*A Guide to Christ.* Boston, 1714
Sfty.	*The Safety of Appearing at the Day of Judgment in the Righteousness of Christ.* Boston, 1687
Strim.*Un.E*	Samuel Strimesius. *Two Treatises on the Church Union of Protestants [Tractatus duo, De unione Evangelicorum ecclesiastica].* Amsterdam, 1711
Strss.*Chr.*	David Friedrich Strauss. *The Christ of Faith and the Jesus of History [Der Christus des Glaubens und der Jesus der Geschichte]*
Strz.*Orth.*	Aleksandr Sturza. *Enchiridion of the Orthodox Christian [' Εγχει-ρίδιον τοῦ ' Ορϑοδόξου Χριστιανοῦ].* St. Petersburg, 1828

Stvr.*Orth.Ang.*	Basileios Stavrides. *Orthodoxy and Anglicanism* [' Ὀρϑοδοξία καί 'Αγγλικανισμός]. Athens, 1963
Swed.	Emanuel Swedenborg
Cael.	*Heaven and Its Wonders, and Hell, from Things Heard and Seen* [*De Caelo et ejus Mirabilibus et de Inferno ex auditis et visis*]. New York, 1890
Ver.Chr.	*The True Christian Religion* [*Vera Christiana religio*]. Amsterdam, 1771
Symb.Apost.	*Apostles' Creed* [*Symbolum apostolicum*]
Symb.Ath.	*Athanasian Creed* [*Symbolum Athanasianum*]
Symb.Nic.-CP	*Niceno-Constantinopolitan Creed* [*Symbolum Nicaeno-Constantino-politanum*]
Syn.Br.*Auf.*	Synod of the [Moravian] Brethren. *Declaration* [*Aufsatz*]
Terst.	Gerhard Tersteegen [Gerrit Ter Steegen]
Abr.	*Summary of the Fundamental Christian Truths* [*Abrisz christlicher Grundwahrheiten*]
Bros.	*Spiritual Crumbs* [*Geistliche Brosamen*]
Ep.	*Epistles*
Tert.	Tertullian
Apol.	*Apology* [*Apologeticum*]
Marc.	*Against Marcion* [*Adversus Marcionem*]
Praescrip.	*Prescription against Heretics*
Thdt.*H.e.*	Theodoret of Cyrrhus. *Ecclesiastical History*
Theol.Erkl.	[*Second*] *Barmen Declaration*: *Theological Declaration about the Present Situation of the German Protestant Church* [*Theologische Erklärung zur gegenwärtigen Lage der Deutschen Evangelischen Kirche*]
Theoph.*Apol.*	Theophilus [Alexander Mack the Younger]. *Apology, or Scriptural Reply concerning Certain Truths* [*Apologie oder schriftmäsige Verant-wortung etlicher Wahrheiten*]. Ephrata, Pa., 1788
Thom.	Gottfried Thomasius
Chr.	*The Person and Work of Christ* [*Christi Person und Werk*]. 2d ed. 4 vols. Erlangen, 1856-63
DG.	*The History of Dogma as the History of the Development of the Teaching of the Church* [*Die Christliche Dogmengeschichte als Entwicklungs-Geschichte des kirchlichen Lehrbegriffs*]. 2 vols. Erlangen, 1874-76
Thos.Aq.	Thomas Aquinas
Gent.	*Summa against the Gentiles* [*Summa contra Gentiles*]
S.T.	*Summa Theologica*
Thos.Kemp.*Im.Chr.*	Thomas à Kempis. *The Imitation of Christ*
Tin.*Chr.*	Matthew Tindal. *Christianity as Old as the Creation: or, The Gospel a Republication of the Religion of Nature*. London, 1730
Tlch.	Paul Tillich
Hist.Chr.Tht.	*A History of Christian Thought*
Prot.Theol.	*Perspectives on 19th and 20th Century Protestant Theology*
Syst.Theol.	*Systematic Theology*. 3 vols. Chicago, 1967
Tnnt.	Gilbert Tennent
Dang.	*The Dangers of an Unconverted Ministry*. 2d ed. Boston, 1742
Disc.	*Discourses, on Several Important Subjects*. Philadelphia, 1745
Nec.	*The Necessity of Holding Fast the Truth*. Boston, 1743
Serm.	*Twenty-Three Sermons upon the Chief End of Man*. Philadelphia, 1744

Tol.   John Toland

   Amyn.   *Amyntor: or, A Defense of "Milton's Life."* London, 1699

   Milt.   *The Life of John Milton.* London, 1699

   Myst.   *Christianity Not Mysterious.* [London], 1696

   Pan.   *Pantheisticon: or, A Formula for the Celebration of the Socratic Fellowship* [*Pantheisticon: sive, Formula Celebrandae Sodalitatis Socraticae*]. London, 1720

Tor.*Car.*   Bernardo della Torre. *The Characters of Unbelievers* [*De' caraterri degl' increduli*]. 2 vols. Naples, 1779

Törn.*Reg.*   Gustaf Törnvall. *The Spiritual and the Worldly Realms according to Luther* [*Andligt och världsligt regemente hos Luther*]. Lund, 1940

Trlsch.   Ernst Troeltsch

   Chr.Rel.   *Christianity and the History of Religions* [*Christentum und Religionsgeschichte*]

   Rel.Ind.   *Religious Individualism and the Church* [*Religiöser Individualismus und Kirche*]

   Soz.   *The Social Teachings of the Christian Churches and Groups* [*Die Soziallehren der christlichen Kirchen und Gruppen*]

Trtn.*Inst.*   Francis Turretini. *Institutes* [*Institutio theologiae elencticae*]. 2d ed. 3 vols. Geneva, 1688-89

TWNT   *Theological Dictionary to the New Testament* [*Theologisches Wörterbuch zum Neuen Testament*]

Ub.*Int.*   Ubaldo Ubaldi. *Introduction to Sacred Scripture* [*Introductio in Sacram Scripturam*]. 3d ed. 3 vols. Rome, 1886

Vinc.Ler.*Comm.*   Vincent of Lérins. *Commonitorium*

Vnzi.*Rec.*   Luigi Vincenzi. *A New Review of the Writings and Doctrine of Saint Gregory of Nyssa and of Origen* [*In S. Gregorii Nysseni et Origenis scripta et doctrinam nova recensio*]. 4 vols. Rome, 1864-65

Walt.*Mir.*   William Walton. *The Miraculous Powers of the Church of Christ Asserted through Each Successive Century.* [London], 1756

WCC   World Council of Churches

   Trad.   *Tradition and Traditions*

   Wys.Worsh.   *Ways of Worship*

Wer.   Samuel Werenfels

   Diss.   *Theological Dissertations* [*Dissertationes theologicae*]

   Misc.   *Miscellanies* [*Miscellanea*]

Wes.*Serm.*   Charles Wesley. *Sermons*

Wet.*N.T.*   Johann Jakob Wettstein. *Books for the Criticism and Interpretation of the New Testament* [*Libelli ad Crisin atque interpretationem Novi Testamenti*]. Halle, 1756

Wilb.   William Wilberforce

   Ep.   *Epistles*

   Pr.Vw.   *Practical View of the Prevailing Religious Systems of Professed Christians.* [London, 1797.] Philadelphia, 1798

Wlb.*Inc.*   Robert Isaac Wilberforce. *The Doctrine of the Incarnation of Our Lord Jesus Christ.* Philadelphia, 1849

Wlch.   Johann Georg Walch

   Pol.   *Introduction to Polemical Theology* [*Einleitung in die polemische Gottesgelahrtheit*]. Jena, 1752

   Rel.aus.   *Historical and Theological Introduction to the Religious Controversies that Have Arisen Especially outside the Evangelical Lutheran Church* [*Historische und theologische Einleitung in die Religions-*

	Streitigkeiten, welche sonderlich ausser der Evangelisch-lutherischen Kirche entstanden]. 3d ed. 5 vols. Jena, 1733
Spir.	*History of the Controversy of the Greeks and Latins over the Procession of the Holy Spirit* [*Historia controversiae graecorum latinorumque de processione Spiritus Sancti*]. Jena, 1751
Wlff.*Nat.Gott.*	Christian Wolff. *Natural Theology, Composed according to the Method of Proof* [*Natürliche Gottesgelahrtheit nach beweisender Lahrart abgefasset*]. 2 vols. Halle, 1744-45
WMC.*Co-Op.*	World Missionary Conference. *Co-Operation and the Promotion of Unity.* Edinburgh, 1910
Wms.*Res.*	Isaac Williams. *On Reserve in Communicating Religious Knowledge*
Wrds.*Dty.*	William Wordsworth. *Ode to Duty*
Wrns.*Myst.*	Gottlieb Wernsdorf. *A Correct and Biblically Based Opinion about Mystical Theology* [*Aufrichtige und in Gottes Wort gegründete Meinung von der Mystischen Theologie*]. Wittenberg, 1729
Wsly.	John Wesley
Ep.	*Epistles*
Hom.	*The Doctrine of Salvation, Faith, and Good Works, Extracted from the Homilies of the Church of England*
Jour.	*Journal*
Just.	*Justification by Faith*
Mid.	*A Letter to the Reverend Doctor Conyers Middleton, Occasioned by His Late Free Enquiry*
Pl.*Acct.*	*A Plain Account of Genuine Christianity*
Serm.	*Sermons on Several Occasions*
Wss.*Ur.*	Johannes Weiss. *Primitive Christianity* [*Das Urchristentum*]
Wsz.	H. F. Weisz
Zeis.*Unver.Gew.*	Philipp Christop Zeisen. *An Undespairing Conscience* [*Unversagtes Gewissen*]. Frankfurt and Leipzig, 1696
Zēz.*Hen.*	Jōannēs D. Zēzioulas. *The Unity of the Church* [ʽΗ ἑνότης τῆς ἐκκλησίας]. Athens, 1965
Zin.	Federigo Maria Zinelli
Infall.	*Concerning the Infallibility of the Pope* [*Intorno alla infallibilità del Romano Pontefice*]. Treviso, 1870
Un.suf.	*On the Unanimity of Votes for the Dogmatic Decrees of Ecumenical Councils* [*Della unanimità dei suffragi nei decreti dommatici dei concili ecumenici*]. Turin, 1870
Zinz.	Nikolaus Ludwig Graf von Zinzendorf
Aug.Conf.	*Twenty-One Discourses on the Augsburg Confession* [*Ein und zwanzig Discurse über die Augspurgische Confession*]
Beth.	*Some Addresses in Bethel* [*Einige Reden . . . in Bethel*]
Gem.	*Public Addresses to the Congregation* [*Öffentliche Gemein-Reden*]
Gespr.	*Remarkable Conversations between a Traveler and Various Other Persons, concerning All Sorts of Truths Connected with Religion* [*Sonderbare Gespräche zwischen einem Reisenden und allerhand andern Personen, von allerley in der Religion vorkommenden Wahrheiten*]
Hom.	*Homilies on the Litany to the Wounds of Christ* [*Homilien über die Wundenlitanei*]
Lond.Pred.	*London Sermons* [*Londoner Predigten*]
Off.Red.	*A Collection of Public Addresses* [*Eine Sammlung Offentlicher Reden*]

Penn.Nach.	*Reports from Pennsylvania about the Kingdom of Christ* [*Pennsylvanische Nachrichten von dem Reiche Christi*]
Red.	*Addresses in Berlin* [*Berlinische Reden*]
Rel.	*Nine Public Addresses on Important Matters Pertaining to Religion* [*Neun öffentliche Reden über wichtige in die Religion einschlagende Materien*]
Sieb.	*Seven Final Addresses* [*Sieben letzte Reden*]
Soc.	*The German Socrates* [*Der Teutsche Socrates*]
Zst.	*Addresses Delivered to the Synod of the* [*Moravian*] *Brethren in Zeyst* [*Die an den Synodum der Brüder in Zeyst . . . gehaltenen Reden*]

Editions and Collections

AAS	*Acta Apostolicae Sedis.* Rome, 1909-.
Adams	Adams, Dickinson W., ed. *Jefferson's Extracts from the Gospels.* Princeton, 1983.
Aland	Aland, Kurt, ed. Philipp Jakob Spener. *Pia desideria.* 2d ed. Berlin, 1955.
Alberigo-Jedin	Alberigo, Giuseppe, and Jedin, Hubert, eds. *Conciliorum oecumenicorum decreta.* 3d ed. Bologna, 1973.
Alexander	Alexander, Gerhard, ed. Hermann Samuel Reimarus. *Apologie oder Schutzschrift für die vernünftigen Verehrer Gottes.* 2 vols. Frankfurt, 1972.
Anal.Hymn.	*Analecta Hymnica Medii Aevi.* Leipzig, 1886-1922.
Argentré	Argentré, Charles Du Plessis d', ed. *Collectio iudiciorum de novis erroribus.* 3 vols. Paris, 1728.
ASS	*Acta Sanctae Sedis.* 41 vols. Rome, 1865-1908.
AUA	American Unitarian Association, pub. *The Works of William E.[llery] Channing.* Boston, 1901.
Baker	Baker, Frank, ed. *The Works of John Wesley.* Oxford, 1975-.
Baron	Baron, Hans, et al., eds. Ernst Troeltsch. *Gesammelte Schriften.* 4 vols. Tubingen, 1913-25.
Barth-Niesel	Barth, Peter, and Niesel, Wilhelm, eds. *Johannis Calvini opera selecta.* 5 vols. Munich, 1926-36.
Basler	Basler, H. S., ed. *Dr. Jablonski's Vortreffliche Reden über die letzten Worte Salomon's im 12ten Kapitel seines Predigers.* Philadelphia, 1849.
Battaggia	Battaggia, Giuseppe, ed. Mauro Cappellari [Pope Gregory XVI]. *Il trionfo della Santa Sede e della Chiesa.* Venice, 1832.
Becher	Becher, Ad., ed. *Gerhard Tersteegen's . . . gesammelte Schriften.* 8 vols. Stuttgart, 1844-45.
Begtrup	Begtrup, Holger, ed. *Nik. Fred. Sev. Grundtvigs udvalgte Skrifter.* 10 vols. Copenhagen, 1904-9.
Bek.	*Die Bekenntnisschriften der evangelisch-lutherischen Kirche.* 2d ed. Göttingen, 1952.
Bell	Bell, George Kennedy Allen, ed. *Documents on Christian Unity.* 4 vols. London, 1924-58.
Benrath	Benrath, Karl, ed. Karl Rudolf Hagenbach. *Lehrbuch der Dogmengeschichte.* 6th ed. Leipzig, 1888.
Berti	Berti, Giovanni Lorenzo, ed. *Henrici Norisii . . . opera omnia theologica.* 3 vols. Venice, 1769.

Bestmann	Bestmann, H. J., ed. J. Ch. K. von Hofmann. *Encyclopädie der Theologie*. Nördlingen, 1879.
Bethge	Bethge, Eberhard, ed. Dietrich Bonhoeffer. *Gesammelte Schriften*. 4 vols. Munich, 1958-61.
Beyreuther	Beyreuther, Erich, and Meyer, Gerhard, eds. Nikolaus Ludwig von Zinzendorf. *Hauptschriften*. 6 vols. Hildesheim, 1962-63.
Bihlmeyer	Bihlmeyer, Karl, ed. *Die apostolischen Väter*. Tübingen, 1924.
Blantēs	Blantēs, Spyridon, ed. Élias Mēniatēs. Διδαχαὶ εἰς τὴν ἁγίαν καὶ μεγάλην τεσσαρακοστήν. Venice, 1804.
Booty	Booty, J. E., ed. John Jewel. *An Apology of the Church of England*. Ithaca, N.Y., 1963.
Braaten 1967	Carl E. Braaten, ed. Paul Tillich. *Perspectives on 19th and 20th Century Protestant Theology*. New York, 1967.
Braaten 1968	Carl E. Braaten, ed. Paul Tillich. *A History of Christian Thought*. New York, 1968.
Bury	Bury, John Bagnell, ed. Edward Gibbon. *The History of the Decline and Fall of the Roman Empire*. 7 vols. London, 1896-1900.
Canstein	Canstein, Carl Hildebrand von, ed. *Herrn D. Philipp Jacob Speners Letzte Theologische Bedencken*. 3 vols. Halle, 1711.
Casanovas	Casanovas, I., ed. Jaime Luciano Balmes. *Obras Completas*. 8 vols. Madrid, 1948-50.
Cassirer	Cassirer, Ernst, et al., eds. *Immanuel Kants Werke*. 11 vols. Berlin, 1921-23.
CCSL	*Corpus christianorum. Series latina*. Turnhout, Belgium, 1953–.
Centenary	Centenary Edition of Ralph Waldo Emerson. *Works*. 11 vols. Boston, 1903-4.
Černecova	Černecova, V. I., ed. F. M. Dostoevsky. *Bratja Karamazovi*. Petrozavodsk, 1970.
Choma	Choma, Ivan, ed al., eds. *Opera omnia Card. Josephi archiepiscopi majoris*. Rome, 1968–.
Christophoros	Χριστοφόρος ὁ ἐξ ᾿Ιωαννινῶν, ed. Jōannēs Komnēnos. Προσκυνητάριον τοῦ ἁγίου ὄρους τοῦ ῎Αθωνος. Venice, 1856.
Coburn	Coburn, Kathleen, et al., eds. *The Collected Works of Samuel Taylor Coleridge*. Princeton, 1969–.
Coelln-Neudecker	Coelln, Daniel von, and Neudecker, Chr. G., eds. Wilhelm Münscher. *Lehrbuch der christlichen Dogmengeschichte*. 3 vols. Cassel, 1832-38.
Conzemius	Conzemius, Victor, ed. Ignaz von Döllinger. *Briefwechsel*. 4 vols. Munich, 1963-81.
Cotta	Cotta, Johann Friedrich, ed. Johann Gerhard. *Loci theologici*. 20 vols. Tübingen, 1762-89.
Cross	Cross, F. L., ed. *Athanasius de Incarnatione*. London, 1939.
CSEL	*Corpus scriptorum ecclesiasticorum latinorum*. Vienna, 1866–.
DAI	*Dopolnenija k Aktam istoričeskim*. St. Petersburg, 1846-72.
Dessain	Dessain, Charles Stephen, ed. *The Letters and Diaries of John Henry Newman*. London, 1961–.
Drachmann	Drachmann, A. B., Heiberg, J. L., and Lange, H. O., eds. Søren Aabye Kierkegaard. *Samlede Voerker*. 14 vols. Copenhagen, 1901-6.
Ed.Leon.	*S. Thomae Aquinatis opera omnia, iussu Leonis XIII edita*. Rome, 1882–.

Edwall   Edwall, Pehr, et al., eds. *Ways of Worship: The Report of a Theological Commission of Faith and Order.* London, 1951.

Ench.Bib.   *Enchiridion Biblicum: Documenta ecclesiastica Sacram Scripturam spectantia.* 3d ed. Naples and Rome, 1956.

Ferguson   Ferguson, Alfred R., et al., eds. *The Collected Works of Ralph Waldo Emerson.* Cambridge, Mass., 1971–.

Forgues   Forgues, E. D., ed. Hugues Félicité Robert de Lamennais. *Oeuvres complètes.* 15 vols. Paris, 1836-59.

Friedrich   Friedrich, Johann, ed. "Beiträge zur Kirchengeschichte des 18. Jahrhunderts, aus dem handschriftlichen Nachlass." *Abhandlungen der Bayerischen Akademie der Wissenschaften,* Historische Classe, 13-II:1-142. Munich, 1877.

Fritsch   Fritsch, Caspar, pub. *Io. Aug. Ernesti opuscula theologica.* 2d ed. Leipzig, 1792.

Gardner   Gardner, Edmund G., ed. Friedrich von Hügel. *"The Reality of God" and "Religion and Agnosticism."* London, 1931.

Gaudé   Gaudé, Léonard, ed. Alfonso Maria de Liguori. *Opera moralia.* 4 vols. Rome, 1905-12.

GCS   *Die griechischen christlichen Schriftsteller der ersten drei Jahrhunderte.* Berlin, 1897–.

Geischer   Geischer, Hans-Jürgen, ed. David Friedrich Strauss. *Der Christus des Glaubens und der Jesus der Geschichte.* Gütersloh, 1971.

Geiselmann   Geiselmann, Josef Rupert, ed. Johann Adam Möhler. *Symbolik.* Darmstadt, 1958.

Gendrot   Gendrot, Marcel, et al., eds. Louis Marie Grignion de Montfort. *Oeuvres complètes.* Paris, 1966.

Ges.Auf.KG.   Karl Holl. *Gesammelte Aufsätze zur Kirchengeschichte.* 3 vols. Tübingen, 1948-65.

Gilman   Gilman, William H., et al., eds. *The Journals and Miscellaneous Notebooks of Ralph Waldo Emerson.* 16 vols. Cambridge, Mass., 1960-82.

Glorieux   Glorieux, Palémon Jean, ed. Jean Gerson. *Oeuvres complètes.* 10 vols. Paris, 1960-73.

Gosselin   Gosselin, J. E. A., ed. *Oeuvres complètes de Fénelon.* 10 vols. Paris, 1848-52.

Gould   Gould, Marcus T. C., ed. *A Debate between Rev. A. Campbell and Rev. N. L. Rice.* Lexington, Ky., 1844.

Harrold   Harrold, Charles Frederick, ed. John Henry Newman. *An Essay on the Development of Christian Doctrine.* New York, 1949.

Hart   Hart, H. StJ., ed. Samuel Taylor Coleridge. *Confessions of an Inquiring Spirit.* London, 1956.

Harvey   Harvey, W. W., ed. *Sancti Irenaei . . . Adversus Haereses.* 2 vols. Cambridge, 1857.

Hayden   Hayden, John O., ed. William Wordsworth. *The Poems.* 2 vols. New Haven, 1981.

Henry   Henry, René, ed. Photius. *Bibliothèque.* 8 vols. Paris, 1959-77.

Holmes-Murray   Holmes, J. Derek, and Murray, Robert, eds. John Henry Newman. *On the Inspiration of Scripture.* Washington, 1967.

Hoskier   Hoskier, H. C., ed. Bernard of Cluny. *De contemptu mundi.* London, 1929.

Houben   Houben, H. H., ed. Johann Peter Eckermann. *Gespräche mit Goethe in den letzten Jahren seines Lebens.* Wiesbaden, 1959.

Hussey Hussey, R., ed. Socrates Scholasticus. *Historia ecclesiastica*. Oxford, 1853.

Jackson Jackson, Thomas, ed. *Works of the Rev. John Wesley*. 3d ed. 14 vols. London, 1829-31.

Jaki Jaki, Stanley L. *Lord Gifford and His Lectures: A Centenary Restrospect*. Edinburgh and Macon, Ga., 1986.

Janus Janus [Johann Joseph Ignaz von Döllinger]. *Der Papst und das Concil*. Leipzig, 1869.

JDT *Jahrbücher für Deutsche Theologie*. 23 vols. Stuttgart and Gotha, 1856-78.

Karsavin Karsavin, L. P., ed. A. S. Chomiakov. *O cerkvi*. Berlin, 1926.

Ker 1976 Ker, I. T., ed. John Henry Newman. *The Idea of a University Defined and Illustrated*. Oxford, 1976.

Ker 1985 Ker, I. T., ed. John Henry Newman. *An Essay in Aid of a Grammar of Assent*. Oxford, 1985.

Kirchner Kirchner, Johann Georg, ed. Siegmund Jakob Baumgarten. *Predigten*. 3 vols. Halle, 1756-59.

Kittel Kittel, Gerhard, et al., eds. *Theologisches Wörterbuch zum Neuen Testament*. 9 vols. Stuttgart, 1933-73.

Knopf Knopf, Rudolf, ed. Johannes Weiss. *Das Urchristentum*. Göttingen, 1917.

Kotter Kotter, Bonifatius, ed. *Die Schriften des Johannes von Damaskus*. Berlin, 1969–.

Lachat Lachat, P., ed. Jacques Bénigne Bossuet. *Oeuvres complètes*. 31 vols. Paris, 1862-66.

Leclercq-Rochais Leclercq, Jean, and Rochais, Henri, eds. *Sancti Bernardi Opera*. Rome, 1957–.

Lecoffre Lecoffre, Jacques, pub. *Oeuvres de M. Le Comte de Montalembert*. 9 vols. Paris, 1860-68.

Lequette Lequette, J. B. J., ed. Charles-René Billuart. *Summa Sancti Thomae hodiernis academiarum moribus accommodata*. 10 vols. Paris, 1874-76.

Leydecker Leydecker, Melchior, ed. Georg Horn. *Historia ecclesiastica et politica, cum notis et continuatione*. Leiden, 1687.

Lo Grasso Lo Grasso, Joannes B., ed. *Ecclesia et status: Fontes selecti historiae juris publici ecclesiastici*. 2d ed. Rome, 1952.

LPT *A Library of Protestant Thought*. New York, 1964–.

Manuzzi Manuzzi, Giuseppe, ed. *Delle lettere del P. Antonio Cesari dell' Oratorio*. 2 vols. Florence, 1845-46.

Marck Marck, Johannes à, ed. *Friderici Spanheimi opera omnia*. 3 vols. Amsterdam, 1701-3.

Masson Masson, Pierre Maurice, ed. *Fénelon et Mme. Guyon: Documents nouveaux et inédits*. Paris, 1907.

Merc. *Lancaster Series on the Mercersburg Theology*. Philadelphia, 1964–.

Metaxas Metaxas, Neophytos, ed. Ὀρθοδόξος ὁμολογία . . . παρὰ Εὐγενίου τοῦ Βουλγάρεως. Kemalige [Egin], 1828.

Miller Miller, Perry, et al., eds. *The Works of Jonathan Edwards*. New Haven, 1957–.

Minear Minear, Paul S., ed. *The Old and the New in the Church*. Minneapolis, 1961.

Moreton Moreton, G., ed. *The Works of the Reverend William Law*. 9 vols. Cambridge, 1892-93.

Moxon	Moxon, R. S., ed. Vincent of Lérins. *Commonitorium*. Cambridge, 1915.
Mozley	Mozley, Anne, ed. *Letters and Correspondence of John Henry Newman during His Life in the English Church*. 2 vols. London, 1891.
Neumeister	Neumeister, Erdmann, ed. *Pietismus a magistratu politico reprobatus et proscriptus*. Hamburg, 1736.
Niesel	Niesel, Wilhelm, ed. *Bekenntnisschriften und Kirchenordnungen der nach Gottes Wort reformierten Kirche*. Munich, [1938].
Nordland	Nordland edition of *The Collected Works of Georges Florovsky*. Belmont, Mass., 1972–.
Opitz	Opitz, H. G., et al., eds. *Athanasius' Werke*. Berlin, 1934–.
Owen	*The Evidences of Christianity; A Debate between Robert Owen and Alexander Campbell*. Cincinnati and Chicago, n.d.
Patterson	Patterson, Frank Allen, et al., eds. *The Works of John Milton*. 18 vols. New York, 1931-38.
Peschke	Peschke, Erhard, ed. August Hermann Francke. *Werke in Auswahl*. Berlin, 1969.
Peterson	Peterson, Merrill, ed. Thomas Jefferson. *Writings*. Library of America edition. New York, 1984.
PG	*Patrologia Graeca*. Paris, 1857-66.
Pii IX Acta	*Pii IX Pontificis Maximi Acta*. Pars Prima. 9 vols. Rome, [1854-78].
PL	*Patrologia Latina*. Paris, 1878-90.
Plitt-Kolde	Plitt, Gustav Leopold, and Kolde, Theodor, eds. *Die Loci communes Philip Melanchthons in ihrer Urgestalt*. 4th ed. Leipzig and Erlangen, 1925.
Pohl	Pohl, Michael Joseph, ed. *Thomae Hermeken a Kempis . . . Opera omnia*. 7 vols. Freiburg, 1902-22.
Poussielque	Poussielque Frères, pub. Henri Dominique Lacordaire. *Oeuvres*. 9 vols. Paris, 1872.
Prato	Alphonsus Maria de Liguori. *Le glorie di Maria*. New ed. Prato, 1898.
Pünjer	Pünjer, Bernhard, ed. Friedrich Daniel Ernst Schleiermacher. *Reden über die Religion*. Braunschweig, 1879.
Pusey	Edward Bouverie Pusey, ed. John Keble. *Occasional Papers and Reviews*. Oxford and London, 1877.
Radlov	Radlov, E., et al., eds. Vladimir Sergeevič Soloviev. *Sobranie sočinenija*. 9 vols. St. Petersburg, 1901-7.
Regopoulos	Regopoulos, Basileios, ed. Chrēstos Androustos. Συμβολική ἐξ ἐπόψεως ’Ορθοδόξου. 3d ed. Salonika, [1963].
Reimer	Reimer, G., pub. Friedrich Daniel Ernst Schleiermacher. *Sämmtliche Werke*. 30 vols. Berlin, 1834-64.
Reithmayr	Reithmayr, Franz Xaver, ed. *Dr. J. A. Möhler's . . . Patrologie oder christliche Literärgeschichte*. Regensburg, 1840.
Reischl-Rupp	Reischl, W. K., and Rupp, J., eds. Cyril of Jerusalem. *Opera*. 2 vols. Munich, 1848-60.
Reusch	Reusch, Franz Heinrich, ed. Johann Joseph Ignaz von Döllinger. *Briefe und Erklärungen über die Vatikanischen Dekrete 1869 bis 1887*. Munich, 1890.
RIB	*Russkaja istoričeskaja biblioteka*. St. Petersburg, 1872-1927.
Rilla	Rilla, Paul, ed. Gotthold Ephraim Lessing. *Gesammelte Werke*. 10 vols. Berlin, 1954-58.

Robert-Samuel	Wilberforce, Robert, and Wilberforce, Samuel, eds. *The Correspondence of William Wilberforce.* 2 vols. London, 1840.
Robinson	Robinson, Andrej Nikolajevič, ed. *Žizneopisanija Avvakuma i Epifanija: issledovanie i teksty.* Moscow, 1963.
Rouleau	Rouleau, François, ed. Vladimir Soloviev. *La Sophia et les autres écrits français.* Lausanne, 1978.
Ruhbach	Ruhbach, Gerhard, ed. Albrecht Ritschl. *Unterricht in der christlichen Religion.* Gütersloh, 1966.
Rusk	Rusk, Ralph L., ed. *The Letters of Ralph Waldo Emerson.* 6 vols. New York, 1966.
Ryhinerus	Ryhinerus, Petrus, ed. Samuel Werenfels. *Opuscula theologica, philosophica et philologica.* 3d ed. 2 vols. Amsterdam, 1772.
Salaville	Salaville, Sévérien, ed. Eusèbe Renaudot. *Dissertatio de liturgiis orientalibus.* 2d ed. Rome, 1938.
Sanford	Sanford, Elias B., ed. *Federal Council of the Churches of Christ in America: Report of the First Meeting* (1908). New York, 1909.
Saunders	Saunders, Dero A., ed. *The Autobiography of Edward Gibbon.* New York, 1961.
SC	*Sources chrétiennes.* Paris, 1940–.
Schaff	Schaff, Philip, ed. *Creeds of Christendom.* 6th ed. 3 vols. New York, 1919.
Schiel	Schiel, Hubert, ed. Johann Michael Sailer. *Briefe.* Regensburg, 1952.
Schmitt	Schmitt, F. S., ed. *Sancti Anselmi opera omnia.* Seckau, Rome, Edinburgh, 1938-61.
Scholder	Scholder, Klaus, ed. Ferdinand Christian Baur. *Ausgewählte Werke in Einzelausgaben.* 4 vols. Stuttgart, 1963-70.
Schütz	Schütz, Christian Gottfried, ed. *D. Joh. Salomo Semlers letztes Glaubensbekenntnisz über natürliche und christliche Religion.* Königsberg, 1792.
Sharrock	Sharrock, Roger, ed. *The Miscellaneous Works of John Bunyan.* Oxford, 1976–.
Shedd	Shedd, William Greenough Thayer, ed. Samuel Taylor Coleridge. *Complete Works.* 7 vols. New York, 1853.
Soč.Fil.	*Sočinenija Filareta Mytropolyta Moskovskago y Kolomenskago: Slova i reči.* 5 vols. Moscow, 1873-85.
Soudakoff	Soudakoff, Archiprêtre, ed. *Entretiens d'un sceptique et d'un croyant sur l'orthodoxie de l'église Orientale par Monseigneur Philarète.* Paris, 1862.
Steudel	Steudel, Paul, ed. Johann Albrecht Bengel. *Gnomon Novi Testamenti.* Stuttgart, 1891.
Stier	Stier, Heinrich, and Stier, Rudolf, eds. Christian Scriver. *Gesammelte Werke.* 7 vols. Barmen, 1847-54.
Stolpe	Stolpe, Sven, ed. Nathan Söderblom. *Tal och essayer.* Stockholm, 1974.
Svaglic	Svaglic, M. J., ed. John Henry Newman. *Apologia Pro Vita Sua.* Oxford, 1967.
Sylvester	Sylvester, Richard S., et al., eds. *The Complete Works of St. Thomas More.* New Haven, 1963–.
TheolEx	*Theologische Existenz Heute.* 1933–.
Thodberg	Thodberg, Christian, ed. *N. F. S. Grundtvigs praedikener 1822-26 og 1832-39.* Copenhagen, 1983–.

Tichon	Archimandrite Tichon, censor. Makarij of Moscow. *Pravoslavno-dogmatičeskoe bogoslovie*. 5th ed. 2 vols. St. Petersburg, 1895.
Tomassini	Tomassini, Franciscus Xaverius, ed. *Institutiones theologicae quas Fr. Michael Marcellius . . . concinnavit*. 7 vols. Foligno, 1847.
Tr.Tms.	*Tracts for the Times*. Oxford, 1833-41.
Trunz	Trunz, Erich, ed. *Goethes Faust*. 2d ed. Hamburg, 1968.
Velzen	Velzen, Cornelius à, ed. *Joannis Marckii* [*Opera*]. 23 vols. Amsterdam, 1689-1748.
Vi.Med.	*The Via Media of the Anglican Church Illustrated in Lectures, Letters and Tracts Written between 1830 and 1841 by John Henry Cardinal Newman*. 2 vols. London, 1901-8.
WA	*D. Martin Luthers Werke*. Weimar, 1883–.
Walker	Walker, Williston, ed. *The Creeds and Platforms of Congregationalism*. New ed. Boston, 1960.
Walther	Walther, Carl Ferdinand Wilhelm, ed. Johann Wilhelm Baier. *Compendium theologiae positivae*. 3 vols. Saint Louis, 1879.
Ward	Ward, Harry Frederick. *The Social Creed of the Churches*. New York, 1912.
Wayland	Wayland, Daniel Sheppard, ed. *The Works of William Paley*. 5 vols. London, 1837.
Weigle	Weigle, Luther A., ed. Horace Bushnell. *Christian Nurture*. New Haven, 1967.
Wolfe	Wolfe, Don M., et al., eds. *Complete Prose Works of John Milton*. 8 vols. New Haven, 1953-82.

"Alas, Theology, Too"

See vol. 1:40-41

See vol.3:291-92

Just as the *City of God* of Augustine was the premier literary statement of the central themes in the patristic "triumph of theology," and as the *Divine Comedy* of Dante Alighieri was the most celebrated poetic embodiment of the medieval understanding of "nature and grace," so the classic dramatization both of the positive and of the negative relations between "Christian doctrine and modern culture" (as the title of this volume has it) was almost certainly the verse drama *Faust*, by Johann Wolfgang von Goethe, who died in 1832—at the precise midway point of the period being covered in this volume.

In the opening scene of the drama proper, the aged philosopher, on Easter morning, begins by lamenting the fruitlessness of his quest for wisdom through knowledge, which has taken him through all four of the faculties of the medieval university: "philosophy, jurisprudence, and medicine—and alas, theology,

Gth.*Fst*.1.354-56 (Trunz 20)

Gth.*Fst*.1.1216-23 (Trunz 43-44)

too." He recognizes the "yearning for revelation" and the special place of the New Testament as the most noble and beautiful object of that yearning. This recognition moves him, as both seeker and scholar, to ponder the meaning of "the sacred original" of the prologue to the Fourth Gospel. Should the Greek

John 1:1

Gth.*Fst*.1.1224-37 (Trunz 44)

Gth.*Fst*.1.737-41 (Trunz 30)

Gth.*Fst*.1.765 (Trunz 31)

word "λόγος" there be translated "word [Wort]" or "thought [Sinn]" or "power [Kraft]" or "deed [Tat]?" he wonders. As the angelic choir chants the Easter message, "Christ is risen," he replies: "I hear the message all right; it is only the faith that I lack." His doubt does not, however, preclude an understanding of the nature of tradition. For to the fatuous observa-

1

Gth.*Fst*.1.570-73 (Trunz 26)

Gth.*Fst*.1.574-76 (Trunz 26)

Gth.*Fst*.1.682-83 (Trunz 29)

*Anal.Hymn.*50:193-94

Gth.*Fst*.2.12102-11
(Trunz 364)

Slv.*Soph*.int.1 (Rouleau 78)

Schf.*Prin.Prot*.2.5
(*Merc*.1:182-83)
Gth.*Fst*.1.1830-31
(Trunz 60)
Schf.*Prin.Prot*.2.5
(*Merc*.1:205)

Pus.*Hist*.1 (1828-I:4-5)

Kierk.*Fr.Bv*.2.3 (Drachmann
3:155)

See pp. 229-30 below

Harn.*Wes*.1 (1901:2)

tion of his pedantic servant that history is instructive because it teaches "what many a wise man has thought before us," so as to demonstrate "how we have carried things so much further," Faust replies sarcastically, "Yes, all the way to the stars!" and insists that the past is a book with seven seals, adding his own view of the function of tradition: "What you have as heritage, now take as task, for thus you will make it your own."

By an intuition no less evocative theologically than it was musically, Gustav Mahler in his Eighth Symphony, first performed in 1910, juxtaposed the closing lines of *Faust* with the medieval hymn *Veni Creator Spiritus*. For during the century or so that followed Goethe's death, the relation between tradition and doubt articulated in his *Faust* became a spiritual and intellectual presupposition for Christian thinkers of widely varying outlooks. The Russian Orthodox philosopher and theologian Vladimir Sergeevič Soloviev attached the closing lines of *Faust* (in Russian translation) to his book of 1876, *La Sophia* (written in French). While lamenting that "Goethe has his bright and dark sides both in this, that he is all nature" without the specificity of grace, the Reformed German-American historian Philip Schaff saw *Faust* as an exception, because it "moves rather in the medieval elements," and he applied the words of Mephistopheles that "a scoundrel who speculates is like an animal" to German Protestant theology and scholarship. Writing while Goethe was still living, the founding father of the Oxford Movement in Anglicanism, Edward Bouverie Pusey, called Goethe "one of the most philosophic observers of Germany," who had found in "the contest of faith and unbelief" a "great plan" and "the only and deepest theme of the history of the world and of man." To Søren Kierkegaard, Faust was "the doubter par excellence," an appropriate expression for an "age when indeed all have experienced doubt," although he was disappointed that Goethe's portrait of him lacked "a deeper psychological insight into the secret conversation of doubt with itself."

At the turn of the century, Adolf Harnack took the leitmotiv for his lectures on *The Essence of Christianity* from the words of Goethe, spoken just eleven days before his death, words also quoted by the liberal

Schw.*Gth*. (1953:75)

Adm.*Chr*.18 (1954:265)
Adm.*Kath*.2 (1949:31)

Gth.*Eck*.11.iii.1832
(Houben 584)
Harn.*DG*.
(1931-I:158;1931-
II:2;1931-III:2)

Brth.*Prot.Theol*.pr. (1947:v)

Gth.*Fst*.1.570-73 (Trunz 26)

See p. 300 below

Brth.*Prot.Theol*.1 (1947:5)

Emer.*Jour*.14.iv.1833
(Gilman 4:155)

Newm.*Jour*.4.iv.1833
(Dessain 3:272)

Newm.*Ep*.7.iii.1833
(Mozley 1:370)

Emer.*Rep.Mn*.7 (Ferguson
4:158)

Emer.*Rep.Mn*.7 (Ferguson
4:163)

Newm.*Id.Univ*.1.6.5
(Ker 1976:121)

Newm.*Id.Univ*.app.
(Ker 1976:473-83)

Protestant Albert Schweitzer and by the Roman Catholic theologian Karl Adam (who elsewhere called Goethe "the old master") in discussing the "ethical perfection of Christ's humanity": "Beyond the grandeur and the moral elevation of Christianity, as it sparkles and shines in the Gospels, the human mind will not advance." Harnack set various quotations from Goethe as epigraphs for each of the volumes of his *History of Dogma*. And although Karl Barth did not include a chapter on Goethe and Christian theology in his *Protestant Theology in the Nineteenth Century*, despite his having been "not altogether unprepared for it at the time" (indeed, having been perhaps better prepared than almost anyone else), he did invoke lines from *Faust* cited earlier, without even having to identify them, to warn his disciples no less than his critics that "anyone who is confident, unjustifiably confident, that 'we have carried things so much farther,' is in no position any longer to take seriously 'what many a wise man has thought before us.' "

In the spring after Goethe died, two young English-speaking Protestant theologians, presumably unbeknownst to each other, attended Maundy Thursday services on 4 April 1833 at the Basilica of Saint Peter in Rome: the Unitarian Ralph Waldo Emerson, who acknowledged that "these forms strike me more than I expected, and yet how they do fall short of what they should be"; and the Anglican John Henry Newman, who was thrilled to be in "the city to which England owes the blessing of the gospel" but troubled by "the superstitions, or rather, what is far worse, the solemn reception of them as an essential part of Christianity." Emerson was to find that Goethe had "said the best things about nature that ever were said"; "the Old Eternal Genius who built this world," Emerson exclaimed, "has confided himself to this man more than to any other." For his part, Newman called Goethe (along with Aristotle, Thomas Aquinas, and Isaac Newton) "a truly great intellect, and recognized to be such by the common opinion of mankind," even though he was "without the Catholic pale," and he appended quotations from a long discourse on Goethe to the 1852 edition of his *Idea of a University*. The ambivalence suggested by the statements of Goethe's

Faust about doubt and tradition and by the alternative reactions to it may be seen in the systems of these two nineteenth-century thinkers, who in turn may be seen as spokesmen for the relation of Christian doctrine to modern culture.

Dividing the history of the West into three periods—"the Greek, when men deified nature . . . the Christian, when . . . [they] craved a heaven out of nature and above it . . . [and] the modern"—Emerson defined "the modern," as distinguished from "the Christian," as the period "when the too idealistic tendencies of the Christian period running into the diseases of cant, monachism, and a church, demonstrating the impossibility of Christianity, have forced men to retrace their steps." Such a retracing of steps, he believed, would lead away from the tyranny of tradition. "Why should not we have a poetry and philosophy of insight and not of tradition?" he asked in the very first paragraph of his very first book. From insight would come integrity, a willingness to break with the public doctrine of the church in the name of personal conviction, as Emerson himself did when he explained that he was no longer willing to celebrate the Lord's Supper, even according to Unitarian ritual, because he had been "led to the conclusion that Jesus did not intend to establish an institution for perpetual observance when he ate the Passover with his disciples." Behind that conclusion, however, lay a growing doubt, which he shared with Goethe, about the entire insistence of historic Christianity on the particularity of Jesus Christ as Mediator in any other sense than "that only sense in which possibly any being can mediate between God and man—that is, an instructor of man." It was a view of Jesus to which he gave classic expression in his *Divinity School Address*, attacking "the traditionary and limited way of using the mind of Christ." Still speaking, so he claimed, in the name of the authentic teaching of Jesus, he not only rejected the orthodox dogmas of the Trinity and the person of Christ, as other Unitarians did, but ultimately broke with the traditional Judeo-Christian definitions of the historical revelation of God: "He speaketh, not spake."

Emerson's unknown fellow worshiper at Saint Peter's on that Maundy Thursday in 1833 was at least as

Emer.*Jour*.AZ.1849.59
(Gilman 11:201)

Emer.*Nat*.int. (Ferguson 1:7)

Emer.*Sup*. (Centenary 11:4-5)

Emer.*Sup*. (Centenary 11:18)

Emer.*Div*. (Ferguson 1:83-84)

Emer.*Div*. (Ferguson 1:89)

aware as he of the tension between doubt and tradition, but from that tension he would draw diametrically opposite conclusions. Like Emerson, Newman acknowledged as valid the "recognition of our impotence to solve momentous and urgent questions, which has a satisfaction of its own," and thus he, too, could speak of "the pleasures of doubt." No less than Emerson, he found the notion of a static tradition unacceptable: it was a universal principle, applicable to Christianity no less than to any other truth, that "the highest and most wonderful truths, though communicated to the world once for all by inspired teachers, could not be comprehended all at once by the recipients, but . . . have required only the longer time and deeper thought for their full elucidation." That implied for him a positive attitude toward history, as the medium for this development of Christian doctrine and therefore as the bearer of tradition. But it implied as well the acceptance of the churchly character of doctrine, and hence the affirmation of the authority of the church, past and present. "From the age of fifteen," he asserted, "dogma has been the fundamental principle of my religion: I know no other religion."

Newm.*Gram*.6 (Ker 1985:137)

Newm.*Dev*.int.21 (Harrold 28)

Newm.*Apol*.2 (Svaglic 54)

It was within such a tension between tradition and doubt or between dogma and relativism that the history of Christian doctrine developed during the eighteenth, nineteenth, and twentieth centuries; but it often did so while still employing the "form of sound words" developed by tradition. Thus for the Eastern Orthodox as well as for the Reformed, "believing" and "orthodox confession" were still inseparable; Roman Catholics went on insisting upon the distinction, which also prevailed among Anglicans, between school opinions and church doctrine; and the analogous distinction between "public doctrine" and "private study" was repeated by various kinds of Lutherans. "We believe, confess, and teach" was, therefore, the stock formula with which, through an entire book, an opponent of Pietism introduced his point-by-point attack on its doctrine. "We confess, believe, and teach" were likewise the words with which the chief interpreter of Pietism introduced his point-by-point response to such attacks. Going be-

2 Tim.1:13

Eug.Bulg.*Orth*.7 (Metaxas 27-28);Lmp.*Ghm*.16 (1719-II:1111-13)
Qnl.*Exp.apol*. (1712-II:16)
Brnt.*Rom*. (1688:39);
Pus.*Hist*.2.4 (1828-II:41-42)

Frnck.*Meth*.3.31 (1732:206);Sem.*Erud*. (1765-II:179-80)
See vol.1:1;vol.4:3-4

Deutsch.*Luth*. (1698)

Spen.*Gtts*.7 (1680:340-56)

yond the relatively narrow range of the doctrinal differences between these two—both of whom continued to affirm the orthodox tradition of the Nicene Creed and even of the *Augsburg Confession*—a younger British contemporary of theirs could, in almost the same words, declare that God had willed what all mankind should "believe [and] profess," but then he proceeded immediately to state that God had "given them no other means for this but the use of reason."

Tin.*Chr*. 1 (1730:6)

This is, then, preeminently the period in which tradition stood in tension not only with doubt but with reason, including "historical reason." That tension has produced some of the most fascinating and most profound systems in the entire history of philosophy, systems associated with such names as Descartes and Leibniz, Kant and Hegel. Yet these systems are not, as such, a part of the history of Christian doctrine; nor, for that matter, are the theological systems that developed alongside them, and often in dialogue with them or in dependence upon them. Like its predecessors, this volume concentrates on narrating the history of the development of church doctrine; it strives to be (invoking an analogy that can be helpful if used with care) a history of constitutionalism rather than a history of political theory. It does not present the history of systematic theology since 1700, much less the history of philosophical theology or of the philosophy of religion (all of which merit careful scholarly attention); but it deals with these subjects at best en passant, as they have shaped, or occasionally as they have been shaped by, the history of "what the church has believed, taught, and confessed on the basis of the word of God." It continues to concentrate on the chorus rather than on the soloists.

See vol. 1:1-10
Dipp.*Hrt*. 2
(1706:26);Sem.*Erud*.
(1765-I:159)

CVat. (1962-65).3.*Int.mir*.1.3
(Alberigo-Jedin 844)

But the soloists have frequently been in danger of drowning out the chorus. This has been especially true in a period in which all the churches have seen it as a "duty to preach the news of redemption with the aid of the instruments of social communication." Social though these instruments of communication have been, they have also sometimes permitted the trendy to crowd out the traditional. It has been a characteristic of modern theology, as its practitioners

Zinz.*Soc*.4 (Beyreuther 1-I:35)
Lam.*Ep*.12.x.1825
(Forgues 13:137)

Lschr.*Unfehl*.pr.
(1724: A4v-A5r)

Engsch.*Pet*. (1720:29)

See pp. 280-81 below

Bau.*Vers*.int. (1838:15-16)

See pp. 75-89, 267-69 below

See pp. 82-83, 116-17,
224-25 below
See pp. 114-16, 263-64
below
See pp. 150, 184, 232 below
See pp. 83-86, 150, 156
below

began to realize in the eighteenth and nineteenth centuries, to use journals as a polemical medium and to publish such theological "journals and brochures without number," which have been broadcast across the countryside in a veritable "war of the pen." At the same time, the history of theology has, in the modern period, frequently been employed as a prolegomenon by systematic theologians; some of the most far-reaching and brilliant contributions to it have come from such an interest. Yet this interest can also foreshorten the historical perspective by making some present-day system or other the norm for the history, as when a brilliant nineteenth-century theologian identified the three decades leading up to his own day as one of the three major periods in the history of the doctrine of the atonement, alongside the first fifteen centuries of the church and the three centuries after the Reformation.

Nevertheless, this has been as well the time when the history of doctrine, more particularly the "history of dogma," has become a historical and theological discipline in its own right. Its practitioners, too, have often been intent on justifying their own (sometimes implicit) theological systems, but the very relativism at work in some of those systems has frequently enabled them to do remarkable justice to historical positions for which they had little or no personal theological sympathy. In the present narrative, this latter way of doing the history of doctrine, for all its historicism, plays a considerably more prominent role than does the former, for all its brilliance; for it has, sometimes almost against its will, managed to listen to the chorus rather than to the soloists. Yet even that distinction between chorus and soloists requires further refinement. There have been a few soloists from various eras of Christian history whose life and teaching have made them, also in the modern period, major themes for the chorus, rather than primarily soloists in their own right. The outstanding among these have been, for the several traditions: Origen of Alexandria among the Greek fathers, with his countless more orthodox disciples; Augustine of Hippo among the Latin fathers; Thomas Aquinas among medieval thinkers; and Martin Luther among the Reformers.

Repeatedly, therefore, a history of church doctrine, no less than a history of individual systems, has had to turn to Origen and Augustine, Thomas and Luther, and to the subsequent careers of their teachings; but in doing so it must look at them as their work has been a factor in the development of the church's teaching. In the case of each of these four, moreover, even in the case of Origen, that treatment accords with his own estimate of his place as a "man of the church."

Lub.*Hist.esp*.2 (1950:47-91)

During this period, therefore, Faust's lament that "alas, theology, too" had been shown to be all too human, and consequently the recognition that in modern culture "tradition had lost its authority" in such a way that "history must then be pressed into service" determined the doctrinal agenda. But this could—and did—lead in turn to a more profound insight into the development of Christian doctrine and hence to a new recognition, historical and even theological, of the tradition on which that development rests but to which it stands in a dialectical relation.

Smith (1964) 55

See pp. 273-81 below

1

The Crisis
of Orthodoxy
East and West

Slv.*Rus.égl.*1.4 (Rouleau 164)

Plot.*Rask.* (1902:12-14)

During the convulsions of the Reformation and Counter-Reformation, the Christian church and its dogma in both East and West were facing another crisis, far more ominous in its implications. In 1667 the patriarchate of Moscow excommunicated the "Old Believers," who would go on evoking amazement by their zeal for martyrdom, for opposing changes in the Russian Orthodox liturgy and splitting away from the established church. At about the same time, Jansenism within the Roman Catholic Church, Pietism within the Lutheran and Reformed churches, and Puritanism within the Anglican Church were addressing a fundamental challenge to the forms of doctrine and of life that had come out of the Reformation settlements in the West. And both East and West were beginning to recognize that, beyond any of these challenges from within what still had to be accounted

Gal.6:10

"the household of faith" in some sense, the very existence of church and dogma would, from the seventeenth century onward, confront the "lamentable sight" of a growing attack by modern culture and secular thought.

Sherl.*Def.*int. (1675:1)

At the beginning of the eighteenth century, therefore, it may still have seemed possible for a Greek Orthodox bishop to commemorate the Feast of Orthodoxy, the first Sunday in Lent, by expressing wonderment at "the growth of the orthodox faith," because "heresy is declining and orthodoxy is triumphing"— evidence that "orthodoxy is altogether divine." Half a world away, ecclesiastically and doctrinally as well as geographically, German Baptists in Pennsylvania

See vol.2:145;Mmchi.
*Orig.ant.*1.1.10 (1749-I:74)

Mēn.*Did.*2.1 (Blantēs 92)

Mēn.*Did.*4 (Blantēs 214)

Mēn.*Did.*2.1 (Blantēs 97)

9

Mck.*Vor*.pr. (1774:A6v-A8r)

Mēn.*Did*.2.1 (Blantēs 98)

Mēn.*Did*.1.5 (Blantēs 61)
Mēn.*Did*.4 (Blantēs 214)
Drnd.*Diss*.pr.
(1703:A4r);Conc.*Rel.riv*.1.2
(1754-I:8-21);Mos.*Tol*.2
(1722:4-6)

Tin.*Chr*.11 (1730:165)

ap.Nmnn.*Spen*. (1695:10)

Byl.*Com.phil*.pr. (1713-I:91)
Ost.*Corrupt*.2.1
(1700-II:10-11)

Casp.*Beyl*.8.14 (1724:55)

Pet.*Hchzt*.5.16 (1701:172-73)

Sem.*Rel*.18 (Schütz 138)

Mayr.*Red*.3 (1702:343)

could celebrate "the beginning of this present [eighteenth] century" as the time when, through the creation, "alongside the conventional institution of the church, of private assemblies," as manifested in the mutual covenant of the eight persons who had begun their movement, God had once more revealed his grace. Yet everyone knew everywhere that orthodoxy of whatever confessional definition was under siege. Thus the same Eastern Orthodox bishop, even while proclaiming that "the faith is triumphing on all sides," had to lament that "on account of our sins" Constantinople, "the queen of cities" and capital of Byzantine Orthodoxy, had been conquered and sacked by the Muslims and that the Orthodox faith was still in grave peril.

In most countries of the West, there was a similar sense of crisis among the defenders no less than among the despisers of orthodoxy. "A deluge of every thing that's ill has overflowed Christendom, and does so still in most places," the most important publication of English Deism observed; "there is scarcely anyone who cares about any kind of Christianity, not to mention orthodoxy," was the Protestant version; in French-speaking territory, whether Roman Catholic or Protestant, "all orthodox believers in sound doctrine" were warned against those who "until our own time" had continued to "revolt against the faith" because of their conviction that "all the faiths are exhausted" and that "most of the Christian churches . . . [in] our century" were in a state of decline; and in Scandinavia it was necessary to protest against an attack on "scholasticism" that was in fact aimed at any orthodox systematic theology. Amid a general decline in the prestige of all the established orders of society, the clergy were in the worst condition of all. In spite of (perhaps because of) the unprecedented proliferation of theological "textbooks, catechisms, confessions of faith or of doctrine, symbolical books, hymnals, etc.," orthodox doctrine could not command universal respect any more. Preaching in the year 1700, one theologian warned that "Satan is using every device to exterminate the Lutheran doctrine of faith," and another that "today, and in this very place," none could say to his congregation as the

1 Thess.5:5
Frnck.*Pred.*Epiph.5
(1700:10-11)

Tol.*Myst.*con. (1696:175)

Wer.*Diss.*18 (Ryhinerus
1:329)

Dipp.*Orth.*6 (1699:93-94)

Qnl.*Clém.*IX.pr. (1700:xxxvi)

Rndt.*Lit.Or.*pr. (1716-I:A2r)

Sth.*Animad.*pr. (1693:i)

Lmp.*Gbm.*11;12
(1719-1;688;76?)
Gaz.*Prael.*1.1.2.3
(1831-I:44-45);
Conc.*Rel.riv.*2.2.1
(1754-I:239-44);Tor.*Car.*2.4
(1779-II:252)
Reim.*Apol.*1.1.4.8 (Alexander
1:133); Byl.*Com.phil.*pr.
(1713-I:97)
Span.*Exerc.acad.*1.1
(Marck3:529);Mos.*Tol.*11
(1722:52-55)
Pff.*Hist.theol.*prol.
(1724-I:36-37)
Spen.*Bed.*1.1.34 (Canstein
1:203)
Gtti.*Coll.*2.4.9 (1727:344)
Hrn.*H.e.*3.3.13 (Leydecker
1:396)
Nad.*Kouak.*2
(1699:9);Zinz.*Zst.*32
(Beyreuther 3-II:255)
Ost.*Cat.*ep.ded. (1747:v)

apostle Paul had: "You are all children of light and children of the day." In a tone of defiance (and in capital letters) John Toland declared in 1696, "I acknowledge no orthodoxy but the truth"; in the same year, a Swiss champion of Reformed orthodoxy criticized the excessive polemical zeal of those who regarded themselves as "the props of orthodoxy and the chief pillars of the Christian cause"; three years later, a radical Pietist critic attacked as "foolishness" the practice of "calling each other fellow believers merely because of a harmony in our confession of doctrine"; in 1700, a defender of Jansenism asserted his refusal to permit any "human authority to compel the human spirit to believe something contrary to the evidence"; and in 1716 a leading Roman Catholic student of liturgy warned that without a better grasp of Eastern Christendom it would be impossible to understand the continuity of the church, "uninterrupted since apostolic times in both faith and discipline."

Although all Christian denominations were, by the end of the seventeenth century, coming under attack for their doctrine, the orthodoxy of the Anglican communion experienced the crisis of being "impugned from without and betrayed from within" in special ways, and it responded to the crisis with statements of faith that spoke for most of the rest of the church as well. "Nowhere has the Reformed religion undergone more remarkable changes since it first arose," a Reformed professor in Holland commented, "than in England"; error had "made the greatest headway in the Church of England," which was the seat of Deism. Anglicanism had the reputation—praiseworthy to some, blameworthy to others—of ignoring more recent dogmaticians in favor of patristic writers, of tolerating different or even contradictory points of view (while being fanatically opposed to Roman Catholicism), and therefore of swinging from one doctrinal extreme to another. It was, some thought, "naturally inclined" to cultivate visions and private revelations. On the positive side, the Society for Promoting Christian Knowledge, established in 1698, earned the admiration of Europeans for a "zeal that does not restrict itself to the

Frnck.*Meth*.3.29 (1723:
187-88);Frnck.*Pred*.Oc.
(1700:14);Frnck.*Pred*.Trin.2
(1699:52-53);Zinz.*Soc.*
(Beyreuther 1-I:98-99)

See vol.4:2-3

Tin.*Chr*.13 (286-87)

Brnt.*Art.XXXIX*.pr.
(1700:ix-x);Hcks.*Cat*.pr.
(1710:v)

Frei (1974) 51

needs of England but reaches out to foreign lands,"
and English books contributed to Pietist devotion on
the Continent.

The English church resisted classification under the
rubrics of comparative symbolics, and "our clergy,
though their Calvinistical [*Thirty-Nine*] *Articles* continue the same, have varied both as to doctrines and
discipline." Thence arose the reputation that "we in
England differed only about forms of government and
worship, and about things that were of their own
nature indifferent," while leaving unresolved "matters
of great moment" in doctrine. Because "modern
theology began in England at the turn from the
seventeenth to the eighteenth century," Anglican
responses to the crisis of orthodoxy, dating from the
seventeenth century and occasionally even the sixteenth, had often anticipated the doctrinal emphases
that were to develop within other denominational
traditions only during the eighteenth century. By
employing as subtitles in this chapter the titles of
works that appeared in England even before the
acuteness of the crisis was generally recognized, we
shall be seeking to come to terms with that unique
position of Anglicanism and its offshoots, and at the
same time to examine within all the churches the
nature of the doctrinal crisis, in order thereby to
understand, in the subsequent narrative, the nature of
their responses to it.

Apologia for the Church

Writing his exposition of the *Thirty-Nine Articles of the
Church of England* just at the turn of the eighteenth
century, Gilbert Burnet, bishop of Salisbury, recalled
"the first and indeed the much best writer of Queen
Elizabeth's time," John Jewel, also bishop of Salisbury, "the lasting honor of the see in which the
providence of God has put me, as well as of the age in
which he lived." Not only because of its literary
quality but because of its churchmanship and doctrine, it is understandable that Jewel's *Apologia for the
Church of England* of 1562 was still seen as relevant to
the crisis of 1700. Its defense of the church had
anticipated many of the issues with which not only
Anglicanism but every kind of ecclesiastical Christi-

Brnt.*Art.XXXIX*.pr.
(1700:iii)

anity everywhere would be concerned in that crisis. And now even more than in the Reformation era, the church needed defending, not only this church or that church, nor even this church against that church, but the very idea that "we are united to Christ by our union with the catholic visible or invisible church, which necessarily includes our visible fellowship and society with that particular church wherein we live," even if that church as an institution was clergy-ridden and authoritarian, politically established and "Caesaropapist," supersitious in piety and orthodox in dogma.

The "Bangorian controversy," set off in 1717 by a sermon of the Anglican bishop of Bangor, Benjamin Hoadly, on "The Nature of the Kingdom, or Church, of Christ," seemed to his critics to involve not only the political question of church and state but the theological question of the validity and visibility of the institutional church as such. Hoadly attacked, as one of "the grossest mistakes in judgment about the nature of Christ's kingdom, or church," the tendency to draw analogies between it and "other visible societies." This brought upon him the charge of disparaging "the authority of the Church of England," although his defenders dismissed such charges as "much more consistent in the mouth of a professed papist than of a minister of a Protestant church, and particularly of the Church of England." He was attacked as well for "the freedom he takes with the fathers of the primitive church" and with the confessional tradition of the entire church, but he claimed only to be warning against "some professed Christians who contend openly for such an authority as indispensably obliges all around them to unity of profession, that is, to profess even what they do not, what they cannot, believe to be true."

Jewel had been concerned to define the church as "not shut up . . . into some one corner or kingdom, but . . . catholic and universal and dispersed throughout the whole world." The definition of the church was by the end of the sixteenth century—and continued to be at the end of the seventeenth—integral to any defense of it. Yet repeating Reformation definitions that had come out of a competition among versions of "orthodoxy" took on a different tone now

Hcks.*Ltrs*.5 (1705:84-85)

Sherl.*Def*.5 (1675:433)
Lang.*Mttl*.1.3 (1712:12)
Spen.*Pi.Des.* (Aland 15);
Lschr.*Pens.* (1724:19;24-26);
Dipp.*Hrt*.2 (1706:21)

Lw.*Bngr*.3 (Moreton 1:106)

Hdly.*Kngdm.* (1717:24)
Shrlck.*Bngr.* (1717:27)

Brnt.*Trp.* (1717:16)

Shrlck.*Bngr.* (1717:23)

Hdly.*Kngdm.* (1717:27-28)

Jwl.*Apol.*2 (Booty 24)

See vol.4:262-74

Zinz.*Gespr.*11 (Beyreuther
1-III:95)

*Art.XXXIX.*19 (Schaff 3:499)

Tin.*Chr.*13 (1730:319)
Ath.Par.*Epit.*prol.7
(1806:35);Bulg.*Kat.*27
(1940:55)

Eug.Bulg.*Orth.*7 (Metaxas 26)

Brnt.*Rom.* (1688:48)

Cypr.*Ep.*16.3 (*CSEL* 3:519)

Deutsch.*Luth.*1.3.1 (1698:19)

Dipp.*Hrt.*1 (1706:1-2)

Dipp.*Orth.*8 (1699:116-17)

Ost.*Cat.* (1747:58)
Ost.*Dz.serm.*6 (1722:210-13)

Wer.*Diss.*24 (Ryhinerus
1:416)

Sem.*Erkl.*3 (1777:267-71)

that there was a fundamental "distinction between church and religion" and the competition was, more and more, between all those versions of orthodoxy on one side and their radical rejection on the other. Taking up the definition in the *Thirty-Nine Articles*, that "the visible church of Christ is the congregation of the faithful, in which the pure word of God is preached, and the sacraments are duly administered in accordance with the institution of Christ," Tindal asked, "Yet is it [the church] not everywhere else taken for the clergy?" Even when the church was defined, in this case by Greek Orthodox theologians, as "strictly speaking, the gathering of the faithful," the net outcome of the definition was that "the one holy catholic and apostolic church" was equated, by another Greek Orthodox theologian, with "the bishops, presbyters, and deacons."

Yet the definition of the church as "a society of Christians united in the same faith, for worshiping of God jointly," did put the emphasis elsewhere than on its hierarchical and institutional structure. When a spokesman for orthodox Protestantism added to the patristic metaphor of the church as mother the specification that the church was to be the one who "instructs the believing children of God in theology and in all the articles of faith," this didactic and intellectualistic definition could not completely undo the meaning of the metaphor. Radical Pietists defined the church as "including only the living and holy believing members," therefore not the spiritually dead members who maintained a merely external connection with it, and they found "the true fellowship of the life of Jesus Christ" not in the established churches but in the "sectarians" of the Reformation and in "others among the silent in the land." Yet if the church was defined as "the assembly of the faithful who believe in Jesus Christ" and if this church was identified as the body of Christ, even a defender of orthodoxy had to acknowledge that erring believers, too, were still part of that mystical body; conversely, the status of "Christians who are outside the church" raised problems for any definition. The normative component of the definition was unavoidable for Roman Catholic ecclesiology, which defended the

Drnd.*Fid.vind*.4.3
(1709:536-38)
Bert.*Theol.disc*.22.5
(1791-IV:277-79)

Pnch.*Dict*. (1736:443-58)

Jwl.*Apol*.4 (Booty 65)
Span.*Xen*.8 (Marck
3:1131-32)

Tert.*Apol*.50.13 (*CCSL* 1:171)
Ors.*Ist*.7.1 (1747-III:133-36)

Spen.*Pi.Des*. (Aland 11)
See vol.4:373-74
Frnck.*Bcht*. (Peschke 100)

Lmp.*Ghm*.13 (1719-I:833-34)
Iren.*Haer*.3.3.1 (Harvey 2:9)
Gtti.*Coll*.2.6.1
(1727:366);Ors.*Ist*.4.45
(1747-II:286-87)

Ang.Sil.*CTrid*.pr. (1675:A4r)

See vol.4:117-18

See pp. 81-83 below

Dipp.*Hrt*.pr. (1706:B1v)

Dipp.*Hrt*.pr. (1706:B2v)
Gen.11:1-9

visibility of the true church but argued that "the true church is not present among heretics" such as Lutherans and Calvinists, who belonged rather to the history of schism.

When defining the church, Jewel had protested in response to Roman Catholic charges: "Surely we have ever judged the primitive church of Christ's time, of the apostles, and of the holy fathers, to be the catholic church." This identification of "the true primitive church" as both the ideal and the norm was a presupposition shared by all parties at the beginning of the eighteenth century. Tertullian's statement, proverbial by now, that "the blood of Christians is seed," which meant that persecution had produced firmness of faith in the ancient church, supported the contention of the new Reformation that prosperity and political acceptance had not been good for the church, which had been "in a better and more glorious condition before God" when it was persecuted. It was necessary only to read the history of the church, as written for example by Gottfried Arnold, to draw the contrast with the present. A review of how the church had been corrupted in each successive age led inevitably to the warning that such a fall of the church would happen again in this last age of its history. Citing early testimony, such as that of Irenaeus, for Roman primacy, expositors of Roman Catholicism equated "the true, uncorrupted, uncontaminated, and genuine church of Christ" with "that church which is in conformity with the primitive church of the first four centuries," namely, their own. Yet in many respects such a conformity with the primitive church, which had already been an issue in the ecclesiological debates before the Reformation, was beginning to belong more to the question than to the answer. As historical research probed the sources of knowledge about it, it appeared that the pattern of primitive Christianity had been forsaken by subsequent ages, perhaps even that it could no longer be identified, much less recovered.

Among the epithets used by radical critics for their accusation that the church had already fallen—including such titles as "our Baalite Israel"—the favorite was "Babel." The tower of Babel was the scene

Mayr.*Red.*1
(1702:22);Nmnn.*Spen.*
(1695:36);Gib.*Dec.*15 (Bury
2:25);Hrn.*H.e.*2.3.6
(Leydecker 1:279)

Rev.14:8;18:2 (Isa.21:9)

Mrck.*Apoc.*pr.14 (Velzen C1r)
See vol.4:256

Sem.*Rel.*20 (Schütz 157)
Zinz.*Soc.*25 (Beyreuther
1-I:257)

Pet.*Hchzt.*13.33
(1701:395-96)

Dipp.*Orth.*8 (1699:106)

Albrt.*Vind.*17 (1695:24);
Han.Consist.15.iii.1703
(Neumeister 103); Lschr.*Hör.*
(1734:30)
Spen.*Beant.*2.23 (1693:127);
Lang.*Mttl.*1.6 (1712:36)

Spen.*Pi.Des.* (Aland 40)

Spen.*Bed.*1.1.25
(Canstein1:138);Schd.*Jer.*2
(1696:E4r);Zinz.*Off.Red.*17
(Beyreuther 2-IV:138-43)

Frnck.*Zw.Anspr.* (1701:7)

John 10:16

Matt.25:32-33
Frnck.*Pred.*Mis. (1700:42)

Frnck.*Pass.Marc.*1 (1724:27)

Deutsch.*Luth.*2.7.3;2.7.9
(1698:129;132)

Beng.*Brüd.*1.3.30 (1751:235)

of the original confusion of tongues; in the New Testament "Babylon" was the code word for "Rome" (at least for the city, if not for the papacy); "Fallen is Babylon!" was the paean of the Apocalypse, in which the "lukewarm" church of Laodicea represented "Babel"; and Luther's widely quoted treatise of 1520, *The Babylonian Captivity of the Church*, had brought these biblical connotations together in a form that made the term (despite "the pathetic play on the words 'Bible' . . . 'Babel' ") an effective slogan for the demands of a new Reformation as well. The antithesis, formulated in the Apocalypse, between the harlot of Babylon and the pure bride of Christ had its counterpart now, and the radical Pietists found "Babel" a fitting name for all the orthodox churches.

The more conservative founders of Pietism were charged with following the same usage in their criticisms of orthodoxy, but they would not go that far. Philipp Jakob Spener expressed his sympathy for those Roman Catholics who had concluded "that there no longer is any pure church on earth, that the children of God are still captives in Babylon." He admitted that "today, too, we have a Babel" and asked, "Why should we not also have a Jerusalem that may be in ruins but is nevertheless distinct from Babylon?" Observing that "on any one day we can hear many invectives about 'Babel,' " August Hermann Francke warned that it would be "making the church of God into a Babel" if the biblical promise of "one flock, one shepherd" became the pretext for bringing sheep and goats together into one fold; and he urged anyone who "speaks only about 'Babel' and about outward corruption" to turn inward and "destroy the Babel within." Disavowing the epithet as an "extreme slander," defenders of the established churches insisted that they were "the true church of God . . . and must in no wise be regarded as 'Babel,' " which it was unwarranted to transfer from "the city of Rome" to "the Christian religions" as a whole.

Yet the Christian religions were obviously not a "whole" any more, not the one mystical body of the one Christ, but a host of church bodies, confessions, and denominations, competitive and mutually exclusive. Despite the continuing praise for Jacques Bé-

See vol.4:373

Rndt.*Lit.Or*.pr. (1716-I:I1r)

Drnd.*Fid.vind*.3.55
(1709:515)

See vol.4:374-85

Bert.*Aug*.4.1 (1747-II:15)
Bianch.*Pot*.1.1.14
(1745-I:116-21)

Jwl.*Apol*.3 (Booty 47)

Spen.*Bed*.1.1.51 (Canstein
1:277)
Lmp.*Ghm*.12 (1719-I:754);
Span.*Cont*. (Marck 3:891)
Hrn.*H.e*.3.1.21 (Leydecker
1:320-21)
Brand.*Dr.Con*.3
(1695:F2v-I1v)

Spen.*Pi.Des*. (Aland 63-64)

Wer.*Diss*.25.1 (Ryhinerus
1·434)

Lschr.*Pens*. (1724:36);
Schwrd.*Comm*. (1707:Ar,

Strim.*Un.Ev*.2.1 (1711:53)

Strim.*Un.Ev*.2.7 (1711:67)
Strim.*Un.Ev*.2.10 (1711:74)

Zinz.*Penn.Nach*. (Beyreuther
2-II:51-52);Tol.*Myst*.pr.
(1696:xxx);Spen.*Bed*.1.1.32
(Canstein 1:199)

Zinz.*Zst*.3 (Beyreuther
3-II:20-21)

nigne Bossuet, author of the polemical *History of the Variations of the Protestant Churches*, and the insistence that Roman Catholic theologians were "not divided in the matters that pertain to the faith and are accepted by the church as dogmas," it was possible even within Roman Catholicism to describe the competing theological viewpoints about the gifts of grace as "sects of Catholics" and to criticize Bossuet. Jewel had taken advantage of such diversity within Roman Catholicism to contend that although "unity and concord doth best become religion, yet is not unity the sure and certain mark whereby to know the church of God." After nearly two centuries of incessant controversy since the outbreak of the Reformation, the question of unity, at any rate within Protestantism, now seemed more urgent than that: "There could hardly be a greater blessing to the Evangelical [Protestant] church" than its reunion. Despite the "fruitless" efforts to achieve it (from the Colloquy of Marburg in 1529 to the Colloquy of Thorn in 1645), there was a desire for "a union of most of the confessions among Christians," coupled with the sense that "the primary way of achieving it, and the one that God would bless most, would perhaps be this, that we do not stake everything on argumentation."

When an irenic Reformed theologian charged that "the Reformed are somewhat closer to peace" while "the Lutherans are in the main further away from it," this was an accusation that confessional Lutherans took as praise. Reformed irenicism urged an "ecclesiastical tolerance" in which both sides would "acknowledge that they belong to the society of the same catholic church"; "those who are one in the foundation of the Christian faith" were also "one in Christian charity and churchly fraternity," with the "less fundamental dogmas" being left free. There was a widespread feeling, even among proponents of divergent viewpoints, that the confessional labels coming out of the Reformation were making less and less sense, now that all the churches were "sects" and the differences within the denominations were in many ways more profound than the differences between them. Even on the doctrine of the person of Christ, which the disputes over the real presence in the

See vol.4:352-59
Strim.*Un.Ev*.2.3
(1711:58-59)

See vol.4:357-58

Sem.*Calv.* (1788:29)

Span.*Cont.* (Marck 3:892)
Strim.*Un.Ev*.2.3
(1711:23-25);Lmp.*Theol.elench.*
2.19 (1729:20)
Spen.*Bed*.1.1.12 (Canstein
1:85);Wlch.*Pol.* 3.1.12; 5.5
(1752:579-80;1148)

ap.Deutsch.*Luth*.2.15.3
(1698:158)

Tin.*Chr.*13 (1730:299)

Jwl.*Apol.*4 (Booty 65)
Span.*Xen*.1 (Marck
3:1119-22)

Ang.Sil.*CTrid*.con.
(1675:S7v)

Brnt.*Art.XXXIX.*19
(1700:183);Hcks.*Ltrs.*2
(1705:43-44)

See vol.4:347

Mid.*Mir*.int.
(1749:cxi);Hcks.*Ltrs*.app.2
(1705:Aa3r-Aa5v)

Lschr.*Unfehl*.9 (1724:68-69)

Mrck.*Comp.*32.13 (Velzen
18:637)

Tol.*Myst*.pr. (1696:xvi)

Eucharist had made a central issue between Calvinists and Lutherans, there was now thought to be an agreement in essentials, or at any rate a recognition that certain christological issues, such as the communication of the ubiquity of the divine nature of Christ to his human nature, were not articles of faith but "merely theological opinion" and did not affect salvation. There was, in short, a "fundamental consensus among Protestants."

No such fundamental consensus was perceived to exist between Protestantism and either Roman Catholicism or Eastern Orthodoxy. Proponents of Protestant reunion were often the same ones who objected to the "remnants of popery" within those churches, such as the Anglican and Lutheran, that had, by drawing "popish conclusions from Protestant principles," retained more of medieval doctrine and practice than had others. "We have indeed put ourselves apart," Jewel had insisted, "not as heretics are wont, from the church of Christ, but, as all good men ought to do, from the infection of naughty persons and hypocrites." "Is the Lutheran or Calvinist church . . . ancient or new?" was a specious dilemma, and in response to the taunt, "Where was your church before?" Jewel's successor could respond: "It was where it is now, here in England, and in the other kingdoms of the world; only it was then corrupted, and it is now pure." Therefore William Chillingworth, who had moved from Anglicanism to Roman Catholicism and back, had "on this foundation . . . built the most solid and rational defense of the Protestant cause which has ever been offered to the public since the Reformation." Similarly, defenders of the *Augsburg Confession* accepted the label "Old-Catholic Lutheranism," and Calvinists laid claim to continuity "of doctrine and of discipline" with the ancient church.

Infallibility was the issue to which controversy between Protestants and Roman Catholics inevitably returned, although some critics could see "no difference between popish infallibility and being obliged blindly to acquiesce in the decisions of fallible Protestants." While there were some Protestant exegetes who could examine the central proof text, Matthew

See vol. 1:352-53;
vol.2:158-70; vol.3:46-47;
vol.4:115-16,270-73
Ost.*Arg.ref.*Matt.16
(1720-II:26)
Mrck.*Syl.*5.13
(Velzen15:173);Span.*Ev.vind.*
3.1-3 (Marck 3:345-440)

Lang.*Paul.*1.13 (1718:31)

Lschr.*Unfehl.*2 (1724:8)

Bl.*Unfehl.*2 (1791:11-20)
Bl.*Unfehl.*13 (1791:146)

Bl.*Unfehl.*10 (1791:123)
Hcks.*Ltrs.*1
(1705:27-33);Mrck.*Comp.*
32.22 (Velzen18:646)
Lschr.*Unfehl.*1 (1724:1)

1 Tim.3:15
Mrck.*Exeg.exerc.*44.3 (Velzen
9:705-6);Wlch.*Pol.*3.2.3.2
(1752:655-56)

Amrt.*Gut.*1753 (Friedrich 35)

Bert.*Theol.disc.*3.11
(1792-I:153)

Qnl.*Clém.IX.*pr. (1700:viii);
Qnl.*Déf.égl.rom.*1.5
(1697:96);Leyd.*Jans.*1.1.16
(1695:69)

Mos.*Vind.disc.*1.8.5
(1722:220-21)

Ors.*Ist.*3.20 (1747-II:56)
Pnch.*Dict.* (1736:31-46)

Mid.*Mir.*3 (1749:51)
See vol.1:109-15

Bl.*Unfehl.*10 (1791:110-14)

16:18-19, without polemics against papal claims, others made the "perversion" of the passage a major issue and, while acknowledging that there was "some sort of special respect for Peter himself" in such passages, repeated the identification of the "rock" on which Christ built the church as not the person of Peter or of his successors but "the doctrine that Peter confessed." Critics of papal infallibility within Roman Catholicism used the passage to prove that there had been no guarantee of infallibility to the successors of Peter. Besides, the Council of Nicea itself had not laid claim to infallibility, and the church fathers had argued for their doctrine on the basis of its "transmission by an unbroken succession of teachers" in Christian tradition rather than on the basis of a theory of infallibility. If there was to be such a theory of infallibility, as distinguished from indefectibility, was it to be predicated of the pope or of the consistory or of the general council? Fundamentally, also according to orthodox Roman Catholics, it was to be the true church as "the pillar of truth" (which Protestants applied to the elect, not to the "outward" institution) that the promise of indefectibility had been given, that "it would never err in faith and worship"; but that promise, according to Roman Catholic apologists, pertained to "the infallibility of the Apostolic See." The opponents of Jansenism were accused of advocating "a new [theory] of infallibility," by which, "as the church can decide with an infallible authority about matters of faith," the pope could decide also about matters of fact, with "the same infallibility as that of Jesus Christ."

The upsurge of historical scholarship during the eighteenth century, which compelled Protestants to acknowledge the antiquity of papal authority and compelled Roman Catholics to catalogue all the antipopes, gave added prominence to the various data of church history that seemed to refute the doctrine of the infallibility of the church or the pope: millennialism "even in the earliest ages, and within thirty or forty years after the apostles"; Origen's preface to *On First Principles*, one of the earliest and most systematic patristic discussions of authority in the church, which was silent about the infallibility of the church; the

See vol.4:107-9
Bl.*Unfehl*.16 (1791:225)
Mayr.*Pont.rom*.1.4
(1690:11-12);Cmrda.*Const.ap.*
2.35;2.40 (1732:254;265)
Drnd.*Fid.vind*.3.31
(1709:455)

Lschr.*Unfehl*.9 (1724:65-66)
See vol.4:108
Gaz.*Prael*.2.3.14.348-50
(1831-II:84)
See vol.2:150-53;
vol.4:108,342
Drnd.*Diss*.1.2 (1703:7)
Seem.*Ep*.31.iii.1775
(Friedrich 38)
Coz.*Graec*.2.17.830-97
(1719-I:339-59)

See pp. 250-52 below
Lschr.*Unfehl*.8
(1724:57);Span.*H.e*.7.9
(Marck 1:1227-28)
Lschr.*Unfehl*.8
(1724:56-57);Allat.*Purg*.3
(1655:3-9)

Allat.*Perp.cons.* (1655:590)

Pff.*Hist.theol*.3.6
(1724-II:32-37);Zinz.*Gespr*.14
(Beyreuther 1-III:122);
Hcks.*Ltrs*.7 (1705:151)

Rndt.*Lit.Or.pr.* (1716-I:O2r)

Mid.*Ltr.Rom.* (1729:50-51)

Mak.*Kv.Ak*.2.3;3.2
(1843:97-100;158)
Wlch.*Spir*.9.7 (1751:163)

Lmp.*Hist*.2.8 (1747:207)

history of canon law, including the forged decretals, as well as the familiar provision that the pope could be deposed if he fell into heresy; the contradiction (despite their being linked as authorities) between the Second Council of Nicea in 787, which had approved the use of icons, and the Synod of Frankfurt in 794, which had not; the error of Pope John XXII on the doctrine of the vision of God, which required exculpation; and the textbook case of Pope Honorius I, which, despite efforts to dismiss it on the grounds either that in condemning him the Council of Constantinople in 681 was not a legitimate ecumenical council or that the text of its *Acts* was corrupt, continued to stand, as it would at the First Vatican Council in 1870, as evidence that Honorius "had been and had remained a heretic and the pope at one and the same time."

As the use of similar argumentation against "the entire Greek church" by Roman Catholicism indicated, the condemnation of Honorius had been part of the "ill will" and separate histories through which Eastern and Western Christendom had gradually been alienated from each other. Now, a thousand years later, a deepening recognition of what that alienation had cost both sides, as well as of the new time of crisis into which they both had come, helped to bring some new awareness of affinities, though not automatically any new sympathy, on all sides. Those Roman Catholics who were sympathetic at least to Eastern liturgies criticized Protestants for their ignorance of these materials, which some Protestants were citing as evidence that pagan worship had survived there in Christian guise. Eastern Orthodox theologians such as Feofan Prokopovič, the archbishop of Novgorod who had briefly been a Roman Catholic, published defenses and descriptions of Orthodoxy in Latin, which evoked the admiration of Western scholars and made it easier for them to understand Orthodox doctrine, at a time when the knowledge of Greek was in decline and the knowledge of Russian was virtually nonexistent in the West.

At least some of the histories of the church coming out of Western scholarship paid tribute to Patriarch Photius as theologian and churchman, although oth-

Allat.*Perp.cons.* (1655:589)

Ath.Par.*Epit*.pr. (1806:v)
See vol.2:164-66
Eug.Bulg.*Orth*.8 (Metaxas 30-31)
See vol.1:13,353

See vol.2:169
Coz.*Graec*.1.3.21-34
(1719-I:5-7);Nrs.*Syn.quint.*10
(Berti 2:105)

Ath.Par.*Epit*.prol.8 (1806:41)

Eug.Bulg.*Orth*.8 (Metaxas 31-34)

Allat.*Enchir*.31 (1658:219-35)

Byl.*Com.phil*.1.6 (1713-I:220)
Spen.*Pi.Des.* (Aland 15);
Lschr.*Pens.* (1724:19;24-26);
Dipp.*Hrt*.2 (1706:21)

Span.*H.e*.9.8 (Marck1:1312);
Wlch.*Spir*.3.4 (1751:55)

See vol.2:183-98
Brnt.*Art.XXXIX.*5
(1700:70);Wlch.*Spir*.10.1
(1751:166);Baum.*Pred*.1.3
(Kirchner 1:68);
Terst.*Abr*.1.3.6 (Becher 2:50)
Coz.*Graec*.3.9
(1719-II:33-52);
Bert.*Theol.disc*.7.19;9.4
(1792-II:64-65;109-10)

Drnd.*Fid.vind*.1.16 (1709:52)

Allat.*Enchir*.8 (1658:37-40)

Ath.Par.*Epit*.1.2.7
(1806:162-203)

ers continued the polemic against him. Eastern scholars reciprocated by paying attention, specific though critical, to "the scholastics among the Latins." In opposition to papal claims of monarchy, they continued to stress the doctrine of pentarchy, including the original primacy of Jerusalem and the legendary founding of the patriarchal see of Byzantium-Constantinople by the apostle Andrew; Roman Catholic ecclesiology rejected all of this on both historical and theological grounds. "There is," spokesmen for the East insisted, "no monarchical administration in the church of Christ," as the Western papalists contended. Rather it was the shared authority of Rome, Constantinople, Jerusalem, Alexandria, and Antioch as the five patriarchal sees, and the authority of the seven ecumenical councils (though not of the Councils of Florence or Trent) that should prevail. Western scholars responded not only by claiming the authority of those ecumenical councils for their own positions, but by pointing out that the Caesaropapism of the secular powers in the East enabled, for example, the grand duke of Moscow to enact severe laws against dissidents. But "Caesaropapism" was an accusation that could be directed also against some forms of Protestant polity.

While recognizing the role that such questions of papal and conciliar authority had played in the controversy over the procession of the Holy Spirit "from the Father and the Son [ex Patre Filioque]," orthodox (and less than orthodox) Protestants continued to "receive the Creed according to the usage of the Western churches"; Roman Catholics, defending the addition of the phrase to the Nicene Creed both procedurally and doctrinally, recognized this as one of the few real points of difference and denounced the Greek view as "heresy." One of the most important questions was whether or not Western theologians were justified in citing the authority of the fourth-century Greek fathers for their position. The Greek Orthodox polemist Athanasius of Paros (whose life spanned most of the eighteenth century) regarded the Filioque as sufficiently important to be accorded the longest chapter in his *Epitome or Collection of the Divine Dogmas of the Faith*, attacking it as an "innovation"

Ath.Par.*Epit*.1.2.7
(1806:164;191)

Sherl.*Vind*.3 (1690:34)

Strz.*Enchir*.5.2 (1828:196)

Eug.Bulg.*Orth*.2 (Metaxas
13-15)

Allat.*Enchir*.13 (1658:65-69);
Allat.*Syn.Eph*.70 (1661:544);
Coz.*Graec*.3.9.226
(1719-II:50)

ap.Amrt.*Theol.eclec*.1.6.7
(1752-1-I:127)

See vol.2:193-94

Strz.*Enchir*.2.5
(1828:71);Eug.Bulg.*Orth*.2
(Metaxas 15);Zinz.*Gem*.33
(Beyreuther 4-II:82)

Mrck.*Comp*.5.11 (Velzen
18:105-6);Lmp.*Theol.
elench*.6.26 (1729:40)
Wlch.*Spir*.pr. (1727:A3v)

Sherl.*Vind*.2 (1690:17)

Jwl.*Apol*.5 (Booty 83)

Jwl.*Apol*.4 (Booty 65);
Hcks.*Ltrs*.10 (1705:233)

See vol.2:281-82
See vol.4:136-38
Span.*Ev.vind*.1.8;1.20 (Marck
3:25-27;78-83)
See vol.2:279-80
Brnt.*Art.XXXIX*.22
(1700:24-26)
Gtti.*Coll*.1.8.14
(1727:130-31);Allat.*Purg*.34
(1655:233-51);Coz.*Graec*.
6.15.877-78 (1719-IV:253);
Amrt.*Indulg*.2.2.20
(1735-II:40)

and going on to "accuse the Latins of introducing this altogether novel dogma into the common teaching of the faith."

In addition to this procedural objection to the Filioque, which was theological as well because of its opposition to "addition or subtraction" in the creed, Eastern Orthodoxy attacked it on theological-trinitarian grounds. In the Trinity, the Father "alone is the principle and the source and the cause"; therefore the Spirit did not proceed from the Father "after the Son," but rather "with the Son." Roman Catholic theologians denied that from the Filioque "it necessarily follows that there are two causes within the Trinity"; and in a communication to Peter the Great of Russia, they declared their approval of the compromise formula "from the Father through the Son" if this was correctly understood. Invoking the standard distinction between "theology" and "economy," Eastern and Western theologians continued to agree that the economic "sending" of the Spirit within time, as distinct from the eternal "procession," was indeed "from the Father through the Son." The Protestant theologians who agreed with the Western doctrine did not regard the whole question as one that affected salvation or that "ought to have made . . . a schism between the two churches."

When John Jewel, opposing the "high brag they [Roman Catholics] have made, how that all antiquity and a continual consent of all ages doth make on their side," had defined "the primitive church of Christ's time, of the apostles, and of the holy fathers," rather than the Roman Catholic Church, as genuinely "the catholic church," he was identifying himself no less with the Greek fathers than with the Latin. That identification pertained not alone to matters of church administration and authority, where Protestants had long appealed to the antimonarchical polity of the East in criticizing papal claims, but to other areas of doctrinal interest. The Protestant rejection of the doctrine of purgatory would sometimes include the argument that "the Greek church never received it," although Roman Catholics, who pitted the Greek fathers against "recent" Eastern theologians, claimed that it had taught both purgatory and indulgences. As

See pp. 108-9 below

Ath.Par.*Epit*.2.2.5
(1806:247-48)

See vol.2:170-83

Lmp.*Hist*.2.7 (1747:189-90)

See vol.2:105-17

Ex.20:4

Zinz.*Gem*.14 (Beyreuther
4-II:226-27)
Brnt.*Art.XXXIX*.7
(1700:104)

See vol.4:216-17
Strz.*Enchir*.3.2 (1828:91-93)

Ath.Par.*Epit*.4.2.8
(1806:388-89)

Brnt.*Rom*. (1688:13)

Ost.*Cat*. (1747:88)
Coz.*Graec*.5.15.953
(1719-III:237);Pnch.*Dict*.
(1736:3-4,183);Gaz.*Prael*.
2.3.5 (1831-II:52-55)

See vol.2:261-70
Eug.Bulg.*Orth*.12
(Metaxas 51);
Ath.Par.*Epit*.1.1.10
(1806:89-90)
Ath.Par.*Epit*.1.1.11
(1806:96-99)
Span.*H.e*.1.15 (Marck1:581);
Wlch.*Spir*.6.2 (1751:101)
Ors.*Ist*.1.59 (1747-I:115-16);
Amrt.*Theol.eclec*.1.2.3
(1752-1-I:22-24)
Bert.*Theol.disc*.2.5
(1792-I:98)

See pp. 80-83, 89-101 below

the defense of the Christian doctrine of creation became more demanding during the eighteenth century, the Eastern versions of "cosmogony," as its Greek exponents contrasted them with Western ones, acquired special appeal, also in the West.

Other theological origins of the schism between East and West, and particularly those associated with worship practice, continued to receive attention on all sides. The hostility of the Reformed churches to the use of images, while directed in the first instance against "idolatry" within Roman Catholicism, had to consider the East as well. It was there that "the abuse [of images] had grown in the church," precipitating the iconoclastic controversy. Disregarding the authority of the second commandment, which prohibited "graven images," the Roman Catholic Church (and the Lutheran) "threw it in as an appendix to the first, and then left it quite out in her catechisms"; the Eastern church, which (like the Reformed and Anglican) counted it among the Ten Commandments, proceeded to explain it away through the standard arguments developed by the Byzantine partisans of images. It was "sad . . . how great a part of Christendom worship God by images," and how even their supposed "usefulness for instruction" had become an excuse for "adoring" them. In response to continued Western polemics, the systematizers of Eastern Orthodoxy affirmed and defended their distinctive doctrine of divine energies and of the "uncreated light," as this had been developed by Gregory Palamas, and they quoted the authority of Dionysius the Areopagite for it, despite the aspersions upon the doctrine itself and upon that authority by Protestants as well as Roman Catholics, who dismissed Dionysius as "fictitious."

All of these statements of what each church defined as "orthodox" were much the same as they had been for the past century or two, and yet they also manifested signs of the crisis that was coming upon all the brands of "orthodoxy." The objective aspect of the crisis would become visible when the historical-critical reading of the New Testament and ancient Christian writers laid open to question the traditional accounts of how the church was established and the

Bert.*Theol.disc.*33.8
(1792-VII:122-24)
Mid.*Mir.*int.
(1749:lx);Allat.*Perp.cons.*
(1655:688)
Amrt.*Theol.eclec.*13.2.20.8
(1752-3-II:65)

sacraments instituted. Any supposition of a "perpetual tradition of the holy fathers" about church and sacraments, including the Eastern and Western conception of the Mass as sacrifice and the practice of private Mass, was in fundamental jeopardy if New Testament scholarship could show that the formulas of institution in the Gospels were not authentic and did not reflect the original intention of Jesus. Then the "fall of the church" would not be dated from the conversion of Constantine or the establishment of a

See vol.4:316,321-22

monarchical papacy, but from the very first generation of disciples. The dimensions of that new crisis in the eighteenth century gave poignant force to the words of Jewel's *Apologia* in describing the crisis of the six-teenth century: "This was a rueful state; this was a

Jwl.*Apol.*5 (Booty 99)

lamentable form of God's church."

Investigations into Christian Doctrine

Despite the reputation of England as a place where all the theological controversies were "only about

Brnt.*Art.XXXIX.*pr.
(1700:ix-x)

forms of government and worship," English apologists for the church at the turn of the eighteenth century did recognize that "we ought not to begin with the notion of a church, and from thence go on

Brnt.*Art.XXXIX.*19
(1700:179)

Brnt.*Art.XXXIX.*19
(1700:175)

to the doctrine," but rather that "we are first to examine the doctrine, and according to that to judge the purity of a church." It was English, American, and European Protestantism, rather than Eastern Orthodoxy or Roman Catholicism, that took the lead in the movement for reformation of doctrine—a movement that would, however, eventually make itself felt within all the churches. The second half of the seventeenth century and the first half of the eighteenth were a time when an apologia for

Zinz.*Zst.*13 (Beyreuther
3-II:85)

doctrine, not merely for this doctrine or that doctrine but for doctrine as such, became as urgent a need as the apologia for the church. Ultimately the two needs were identical, because it was specifically

Mos.*Vind.disc.*2.3.5
(1722:321)

church doctrine that was now being subjected to ridicule, the very definition of doctrine as not the private or idiosyncratic ideas of individual theologians, but as that which the church believed, taught,

See vol.1:1

and confessed, and as that which the church could and should enforce as its collective voice.

Mos.*Tol.*17 (1722:89)

Emblematic of both those needs was a book begun about 1655 and completed in fair copy about 1660, by England's internationally celebrated man of letters, the Puritan poet and theologian John Milton—begun about 1655, but not published until almost two centuries later, in 1825. It bore the title (in Latin) *Two Books of Investigations into Christian Doctrine Drawn from the Sacred Scriptures Alone.* Both the date of composition and the postponement of the date of publication furnish evidence about the development of Christian doctrine during this period. In his biography of Milton, published in the final year of the seventeenth century, John Toland, praising him as "a person of the best accomplishments, the happiest genius, and the vastest learning which this nation, so renowned for producing excellent writers, could ever yet show," identified as "his masterpiece, his chief and favorite work in prose" Milton's *Defense of the English People*; he added that while there had been in addition "some miscellaneous pieces much inferior to his other works," Milton had likewise written "a *System of Divinity*, but whether intended for public view or collected merely for his own use, I cannot determine; . . . and where [it is] at present is uncertain."

Milton himself called *Christian Doctrine* his "dearest and best possession," but he did not publish it. The reason for his own hesitation and for the delay also after his death was evidently that by "investigations into Christian doctrine drawn from the Sacred Scriptures alone" he in fact meant a critical examination—and where warranted a revision, or where necessary a repudiation—of doctrine in a way that was, as he himself acknowledged, "at odds with certain conventional opinions" about such central components of the orthodox dogmatic tradition as the doctrines of the Trinity and the person of Christ. In this he believed himself to be participating in "the reforming of Reformation itself." As the preface to the book *On First Principles* of his admired predecessor Origen had done for the early church, Milton's preface to *Christian Doctrine* and his introductory chapter formulated most of the basic issues involved in the investigations into Christian doctrine and in the crisis of orthodoxy that such investigations helped to precipitate.

Tol.*Milt.* (1699:149)

Tol.*Milt.* (1699:95)

Tol.*Milt.* (1699:141)

Tol.*Milt.* (1699:148)

Milt.*Doct.*ep. (Patterson 14:8)

Milt.*Doct.*ep. (Patterson 14:8)

Milt.*Areop.* (Wolfe 2:553);Milt.*Doct.*ep. (Patterson14:2)

See vol.1:109-17

Milt.*Doct*.1.1 (Patterson
14:20)

See vol.1:335-38;
vol.2:13-14; vol.3:13-17;
vol.4:176-77, 211-12,281-82

Felb.*Hnd*.pr. (1799:np)

Eug.Bulg.*Orth*.6 (Metaxas
25-26)

Amrt.*Theol.elench*.4.2.17
(1752-1-IV:64-67)

Wlch.*Pol*.3.1.8 (1752:574)

See pp. 208-9, 250, 279
below

When Milton professed that he did not intend to "teach anything new in this work," he was, as far as the words themselves went, asserting what every (or almost every) interpreter of Christian doctrine in every church had always claimed to presuppose. Yet the conclusions that each drew from this same presupposition identified the underlying differences among them and among their churches. Milton meant by the formula that he was seeking only to restate the authentic biblical message, regardless of whether or not this required the surrender of long-cherished traditions. Similarly, Jeremias Felbinger, a Silesian "semi-Socinian" who found refuge in Amsterdam, averred in the preface of 1651 to his enchiridion of Christian doctrine that "there is nothing new to be found here, but only what, long ago, the Son of God and his holy apostles taught and instituted"; but that disclaimer of novelty was also chiefly an exclusionary principle, directed against orthodox dogma and catholic tradition. In declaring their loyalty to the doctrines handed down by "holy tradition," Eastern Orthodox theologians included within such tradition "both that which is in Scripture and that which is outside of Scripture," but they denied the authenticity or even the possibility of "new" doctrine; they simultaneously asserted the legitimacy of earlier "development" and the illegitimacy of "development" now. Roman Catholic teachers of the time likewise eschewed doctrinal innovation and denied the Protestant allegation that they were ascribing to the church any authority to establish new articles of faith. Repeatedly they and their successors were to face the necessity of clarifying and refining that stand, when the history of dogma showed that "new" doctrines, including the Trinity and transubstantiation, had developed, and especially when, in 1854 and again in 1870 and yet again in 1950, "new" Roman Catholic dogmas about the Virgin Mary and about papal infallibility were promulgated.

By defining Christian doctrine as "the doctrine which, in all ages, Christ . . . taught by divine communication, for the glory of God and the salvation of mankind, about God and about worshiping him" and adding that "we may rightly insist that

Milt.*Doct.*1.1 (Patterson
14:16)

Poir.*Chr.ed.*31 (1694:42)

Amrt.*Theol.eclec.*4.2.prol.
(1752-1-IV:8)

Allat.*Perp.cons.* (1655:638);
Gtti.*Coll.*2.10.1 (1727:416)

Lw.*Dem.Er.* (Moreton 5:8-9)

Ang.Sil.*CTrid.*2
(1675:B12v-C5v)

See pp. 194-95, 207, 262,
276-77 below

Bl.*Unfehl.*28 (1791:591-93)

Sem.*Erud.* (1765-I:55)
Luke 2:1

Sem.*Rel.* (Schütz 80)

Sem.*Rel.* (Schütz 97)

Christians should believe in the Scriptures, from which this doctrine is drawn," Milton strove to locate his investigations into Christian doctrine within the context and the continuity of biblical Christianity and, in some sense, of ecclesiastical Christianity as well. Once again, however, such a definition of continuity could be misleading. When the Huguenot Pietist Pierre Poiret defined "faith" as "believing and trusting in those things that God has told us about divine matters," this did not mean the same as when his younger contemporary, the Roman Catholic theologian Eusebius Amort, defined "theological faith" as "assent yielded to an object [of faith] for the sake of the authority of God," since by "the authority of God" in his definition Amort was referring to the authority of the church as well as the authority of Scripture. All sides would agree with the requirement that differences of doctrine were decisive, not differences of ritual, and that "some knowledge of what God has revealed both in the Old and New Testament be required for a right understanding" of Christian doctrine, but not with the requirement that "Sacred Scripture is to be interpreted in accordance with the sense of the church" as expressed in its dogmas.

Yet this Roman Catholic definition of doctrine as "dogma" was also beginning to show signs of the crisis: to prove a dogma from tradition, it was important above all to cite "the fathers who lived in the first two centuries"; the trouble was, as later historians of dogma were to discover repeatedly, that "there are extremely few dogmas discussed in the writings of these fathers." One of the pioneers in the history of dogma pointed out that the Greek word "δόγμα" had not always referred to "parts of the faith of Christians," but (as its appearance within the Christmas Gospel showed) to a "decree" or command. From these and other historical considerations it was evident to him that a consensus on "dogma," even on such dogmas as the Trinity and the person of Christ, was not now, and never had been, necessary for authentic "participation in the Christian religion," and that it was nothing short of "a coarse atheistic presumption" for the church to enforce conformity to its dogmatic formulas. At the same time he argued

Sem.*Frag*.46 (1780:338)

Mrck.*Comp*.3.9 (Velzen 18:63)
Ptz.*Sed.inf*.1.5;2.9
(1763:19;127)
Mrck.*Comp*.3.12 (Velzen
18:65)

Brnt.*Art.XXXIX*.int.
(1700:6-7)
Wer.*Diss*.25.3 (Ryhinerus
1:442);Spen.*Beant*.2.8
(1693:99);Frnck.*Meth*.3.28
(1723:163)

Lw.*Bngr*.2 (Moreton 1:64)

Beng.*Brüd*.1.1.1 (1751:2)

Wer.*Diss*.18 (Ryhinerus
1:331)

Schwrd.*Comm*. (1707:Av)

Br.*Comp*.prol.27-34 (Walther
1:45-68)
Wlch.*Spir*.10.13 (1751:184)

Lang.*Antibarb*. (1709-II:489)

that this relativism should not be used to justify elimination "of the very teachings of Jesus" from a consideration of "the chief part of Christianity."

In the immense corpus of all that had been believed, taught, and confessed as Christian doctrine through all the centuries of Christian development, not everything could be on the same level: was, for example, the idea of the subterranean location of hell to be enforced as an "article of faith" and a binding tradition? Everyone, albeit with varying criteria, conceded some form of the "necessary distinction . . . between articles of faith and articles of doctrine: the one are held necessary to salvation, the other are only believed to be true"—or perhaps, as critics sometimes suggested, believed to be necessary not for salvation, but "for the integrity, connection, and neatness of someone's theological system."

Therefore "the truths of the Christian religion" remained true "whether we can persuade ourselves to believe them or not," and in the evaluation of a church's right to be called Christian "the primary concentration must be on doctrine," its correctness but also its completeness. Irenic theologians had to grant that "vague, general, and ambiguous formulas" intended to gloss over major doctrinal differences between the churches, though perhaps well-meaning, "have harmed more than they have helped." An orthodox Lutheran critic of irenic theology attacked a method that overlooked questions of doctrinal "truth" about the real presence in the Eucharist for the sake of expressing "love" by sharing in Holy Communion. The inherited distinction among articles of faith as "fundamental" or "nonfundamental" and, within the former category, as "primary" or "secondary" fundamental articles, was not to obscure the imperative to "love every divine truth, whether it is fundamental or not."

Such differences of definition between and within the several churches were, however, being played out now against the background of a deepening unease not only about the differences but about the very idea of such a definition. "We believe, confess, and teach," defenders of Lutheran orthodoxy could assert against Pietism, "that theological truths, divine truths, are and remain divine truths in and of themselves . . . at

Deutsch.*Luth*.1.2.10;1.1.4
(1698:18;4-5)

Mos.*Tol*.8 (1722:33-34)

Tol.*Myst*.pr. (1696:xiv)

Reim.*Apol*.2.5.1.1 (Alexander
2:423)

Reim.*Apol*.1.1.4.4 (Alexander
1:125)

Dipp.*Orth*.6 (1699:80-85)

Nss.*Dipp*.14 (1701:83)

Sem.*Rel*.19 (Schütz 149)

Frnck.*Meth*.3.20
(1723:110-11)

Frnck.*Bcht*. (Peschke 96)

See vol.4:3-4
Deutsch.*Luth*.1.2.10
(1698:18)

all times and in all places," but obtaining assent to such a proposition was more difficult now. It was, as his critics pointed out, an extreme expression of the unease when John Toland declared his resolve to "trouble myself about" only the points he called "the terms and doctrines of the gospel," which he saw as "not the articles of the East or West, orthodox or Arian, Protestant or Papist, considered as such, but those of Jesus Christ and his apostles"; but some such distinction between the original Christian message and the doctrines of orthodoxy, whether Protestant or Roman Catholic or Eastern Orthodox, was beginning to pervade the churches.

Another extreme critic had been led by his historical researches to the conclusion that "not everything by far that eventually became a fundamental article of Christian faith" was to be found in the writings of the evangelists and apostles, but that much of it had been "defined as orthodox only through the subsequent formulas of faith." And when yet another, while insisting that it was not his intention "to posit an indifference in matters of faith or to deny that an erroneous and hostile prejudice can often obstruct the work of regeneration and the kingdom of grace," urged that "saving faith" did not consist in assent to such dogmas as "the merit of Christ and its imputation" or to "the saving opinions of the Athanasian Creed," but in "simple obedience" and genuine discipleship, his conservative opponent warned him that "meanwhile it is nevertheless not wrong to defend the truth and purity of doctrine, though within appropriate limits." Less extreme critics had also concluded that doctrinal uniformity among Christians of different places and times was impossible and hence unnecessary. Some were drawing a contrast between the absolute authority of "theology" if understood as "the primitive nature of the dogmas, without the admixture of any human activity" and the relative authority of "theology" as it was understood in "this century, this nation," and they were denouncing the "dreadful abuse" of doctrine that had resulted from learning the formulas of the catechism by rote.

The stock Reformation formula, "We believe, confess, and teach," perhaps also the reversal of the usual

See vol.4:333

Pnch.*Dict.* (1736:127-28)
Pff.*Hist.theol.*3.8
(1724-II:205-6);Sherl.*Def.*2
(1695:146-50)
Wlch.*Pol.*4.2.4
(1752:1051-52)
Brnt.*Art.XXXIX*.int.
(1700:8)

Allat.*Purg.*3
(1655:8);Wlch.*Pol.*5.6
(1752:1148-49)

See vol.2:286-95

Wlch.*Spir.*9.4 (1751:157)

Pff.*Hist.theol.*3.7
(1724-II:63-85)

Ang.Sil.*CTrid.* (1675)

See vol.4:3

Ost.*Cat.* (1747:10)

Sav.Conf.pr. (Walker 438)

Milt.*Doct.*ep. (Patterson 14:4)

order of its two final terms, suggests how important the creeds of the ancient church and the confessions of the Reformation era were for the definition of orthodoxy, as well as for the crisis of orthodoxy, in all the churches. The use of a particular confession as a norm of orthodoxy, going beyond the ecumenical norms, made it possible for friend and foe alike to characterize the various churches: the Lutheran on the basis of the *Augsburg Confession* and *Book of Concord*; the Reformed on the basis of the *Heidelberg Catechism*, the *Belgic Confession*, and other standards; Arminianism on the basis of the *Remonstrant Confession*; and the Church of England on the basis of the *Thirty-Nine Articles*. But such use had come to occupy a decisive place as a criterion of orthodoxy also in the Eastern Orthodox and Roman Catholic churches. The *Orthodox Confession of the Faith of the Catholic and Apostolic Eastern Church* drawn up by Peter Mogila, metropolitan of Kiev, was, as inside and outside observers noted, "highly esteemed and followed as a norm" not in Russian Orthodoxy alone, but in the Greek Orthodox Church as well; and the *Canons and Decrees of the Council of Trent* together with the *Catechism of the Council of Trent* came to occupy a similar position, providing, for example, the German mystical poet and convert from Protestantism, Angelus Silesius (Johannes Scheffler), with the basis for an appeal to his sometime confrères to come back to the true church. A French Reformed catechism was speaking for all of these churches when, on the basis of Romans 10:9-10, it linked believing the truth of doctrine with making a firm confession of it, as was the preface to the *Savoy Confession* reaffirmed at Boston in 1680 when, quoting the same passage from Romans, it declared that there was not "a greater evidence of being in a state of salvation than such a confession."

Yet at the same time John Milton was speaking for a growing number of individuals within those same churches when he explained that he had "decided not to depend upon the belief or judgment of others in religious questions," but "to puzzle out a religious creed for myself by my own exertions." He set this method into explicit opposition with the "disgraceful and disgusting [phenomenon] that the Christian re-

Milt.*Doct*.ep. (Patterson 14:12)
Milt.*Doct*.1.31 (Patterson 16:298)

Hil.*Const*.2.5 (*PL* 10:566-67)

Tin.*Chr*.11 (1730:163-64)

Tin.*Chr*.13 (1730:286)

Bl.*Unfehl*.26 (1791:529)
Zinz.*Zst*.29 (Beyreuther 3-II:225-26)
Ess.Consist.24.vii.1709 (Neumeister 292)
Mayr.*Red*.5 (1702:399)

Lschr.*Hör*. (1734:32)

Deutsch.*Luth*.1.5.23 (1698:59)

Deutsch.*Luth*.1.5.3 (1698:45)

Brnt.*Art.XXXIX*.int.;9;17 (1700:8;116;168)

See vol.4:177,212

Sherl.*Vind*.3 (1690:31)

See vol.1:117
Bert.*Diss.hist*. (1753-II:27);
Bert.*Theol.disc*.22.6 (1792-IV:280-81)

ligion should be supported by violence" and coercion; "every trace of force or constraint" was to be eliminated. Quoting the misgivings of Hilary of Poitiers about creeds, Milton's biographer identified "the imposers of creeds, canons, and constitutions" as "the common plagues of mankind"; it was "plain from church history that creeds were the spiritual arms with which contending parties combated each other." Such criticism was directed not only against a particular creed, with the Athanasian Creed a favorite target, but against the very idea of "compulsion" in doctrine, since " 'church' and 'coercion' are mutually opposed concepts." The ordinance of a local consistory in opposition to Pietism that "subscription to the symbolical books should always be absolute, not conditional" was an effort to put into legislative form as Protestant canon law the regulation that the theologian be bound to the public statement of the church's faith, which was in turn bound to the word of God. Within Protestantism at any rate, the Lutheran enforcement of confessional subscription represented one end of the spectrum, where inconsistencies between the confessions assembled in the *Book of Concord* were not to be emphasized but reconciled, because "the symbolical books are the church books of God"; the other end of the spectrum was represented by the Anglican position that if an article of the *Thirty-Nine Articles* "can admit of different literal and grammatical senses, even when the senses given are plainly contrary to one another, both sides may subscribe the article with a good conscience and without any equivocation."

Although the three so-called ecumenical creeds had received the endorsement of all the major parties in the Reformation of the sixteenth century and were regarded as "a kind of secondary rule [of faith], as containing the traditionary faith of the church," it was no longer possible to take even their normative status for granted. In opposition to the doubts that Renaissance humanists had cast on Rufinus's report about the composition of the Apostles' Creed by the disciples of Christ shortly after Pentecost, Roman Catholic scholars were inclined to defend the traditional account. Protestants were more willing to call that

Lmp.*Hist*.2.2
(1747:75-76);Hrn.*H.e*.1.2.2
(Leydecker 1:137)

Sem.*Frag*.8 (1780:49)

Ost.*Cat*. (1747:29-30)
Poir.*Chr.ed*.43 (1694:55)

Drnd.*Fid.vind*.3.56
(1709:520)
Bert.*Diss.hist*.
(1753-III:234-35);
Brnt.*Art.XXXIX*.8
(1700:106)

Avkm.Žiz. (Robinson 142)

Symb.Ath.44 (Schaff 2:70)
Dipp.*Orth*.4;7 (1699:53;101)
Sherl.*Vind*.2 (1690:10-21);
Zinz.*Lond.Pred*.3.7
(Beyreuther 5-I:367)

See p. 197 below

See vol.1:339,343

Mayr.*Hall*. (1707:14)

Dipp.*Orth*.5 (1699:67)
Niss.*Dipp*.2 (1701:32,25);
Ors.*Ist*.12.37 (1747-V:53-57)
Sem.*Rel*.24 (Schütz 203-9);
see vol.4:322
Hrn.*H.e*.1.3.4 (Leydecker
1:176-77)

account a "figment" and to question whether there had been any creed or confession at all in the primitive church. Notwithstanding such questioning, they found in the Apostles' Creed "a summary [abrégé] of the doctrine that the apostles preached" and therefore a useful primer for the education of children. Although the Athanasian Creed was still occasionally attributed to Athanasius, almost everyone had to concede that it was not his, having been composed in Latin rather than in Greek; yet now it was sometimes being accepted in the East as an authentic work of Athanasius, for example by Archpriest Avvakum, leader of the Old Believers, who quoted it at length. Because of its concluding condemnatory formula, "This is the catholic faith; unless one believes it faithfully, one cannot be saved," it represented to radical Protestant critics "an irrational chaos" and a contradiction of the authentic teachings of Jesus; but more conservative Protestants went on defending it.

Of the three creeds, the Nicene alone had a genuine claim to the title "ecumenical," though only, as Eastern theologians repeatedly reminded their Western opponents whether Roman Catholic or Protestant, without the unilateral corruption of its text through the insertion of the Filioque. For Eastern Orthodox expositions of the Christian message, "the faith of the 318 fathers of the Council of Nicea" continued to serve as a summary of "holy tradition" and as a basis for defining its content. As the Credo in the liturgy of the Latin Mass, it was for Roman Catholic interpreters the prime example of the ancient principle that "the rule of prayer should confirm the rule of faith." The Pietists were accused of "an open hatred for the Nicene Creed and Constantine the Great," but the very challenge of rationalistic detractors to Nicene orthodoxy evoked from confessional Protestants and from Roman Catholics a defense of the Nicene Creed and of its key term "homoousios" (despite the familiar words of Luther disparaging the term) as a bulwark against heresy.

All of that assumed that "heresy" was still as definable and as identifiable as "orthodoxy." Milton was not so sure about either one: he denounced "irrational bigots who, by a perversion of justice, condemn anything they consider inconsistent with conventional beliefs and give it an invidious title— 'heretic' or 'heresy'—without consulting the evidence of the Bible upon the point," and he countered that "since the compilation of the New Testament, nothing can correctly be called heresy unless it contradicts that" explicitly. For Eastern Orthodoxy, heresy could arise either in contradiction to the mysteries of the faith concerning the divine being itself, in questions of "theology," or in contradiction to the doctrines based upon the history of salvation in Christ and the church, in questions of "economy." But in the seventeenth and eighteenth centuries the most conspicuous challenge to Eastern Orthodoxy was coming from the adherents of the schismatic Raskol of the Old Believers in Russia. They professed a complete "orthodoxy [pravoslavie]" in their loyalty to "everything in the church, handed down to us by traditions from the holy fathers, [as] holy and incorrupt" in both theology and economy, because they held steadfastly to "what the old printed books teach about the Deity and about other dogmas." But they were charged with "schism, sedition, and false doctrine" for "condemning the correction of the holy creed [svjatogo simbola ispravlenie], the joining of the first three fingers for making the sign of the cross, the correction as well as the correctors of [liturgical books], and the coordination of church singing [between priest and choir]." In the face of this ecclesiastical and doctrinal crisis, the standard distinction between "heresy" and "schism," as it had been formulated for Eastern Orthodoxy by church fathers such as Basil of Caesarea in the fourth century, appeared to have broken down.

Although various of the church fathers had located "heresy" within liturgy and ritual, Western writers, both Protestant and Roman Catholic, continued in their catalogues to define it as "error of doctrine" or as "an error of intellect concerning the faith, rooted in ignorance," or as a conscious opposition to the orthodox faith; thus Origen, Pelagius, and Theodore of Mopsuestia deserved to be labeled as "heretics." To radical critics, this rehearsal of stereotype formulas of condemnation amounted to saying that "whoever does not agree with our church and our confessions is

---

Marginal references:

Milt.*Doct*.ep. (Patterson 14:12);Milt.*Areop*. (Wolfe 2:543)

Ath.Par.*Epit*.3.4 (1806:300)

Avkm.*Žiz*. (Robinson 171)

Avkm.*Knig.tolk*.3 (*RIB* 39:532)

Sob.13.v.1666 (*DAI* 5:448)

See vol.1:69

Span.*Ev.vind*.2.20 (Marck 3:311-20)
Pnch.*Dict*. (1736:15-16)
Schtz.*Haer*.1.10 (1724:23)
Amrt.*Theol.mor*.3.2 (1757-I:253-54);
Amrt.*Theol.eclec*.16.2.2.5 (1752-4-II:69)
Wlch.*Pol*.int.6 (1752:9)
Nrs.*Hist.pel*.1.1;1.3;1.9 (Berti 1:2;27;85);
Nrs.*Syn.quint*.5;11 (Berti 2:29-31;124)

Dipp.*Hrt*.pr. (1706:A8v)

Gal.5:20;Tit.3:10;Jude19

Rom.12:6

Dipp.*Orth*.6 (1699:76-77)

Dipp.*Orth*.6 (1699:98)

Mid.*Mir*.int. (1749:lxxxvi)

Lmp.*Hist*.2.2 (1747:87)

Lmp.*Mttl*.2.1 (1712:106)

Sherl.*Vind*.3 (1690:22)
1 Cor. 11:19 (Vulg.);see
vol.4:245; p. 269 below

Schtz.*Haer*.2.20;2.3;2.17
(1724:67-68;34-35;62)

Frnck.*Id*.37 (Peschke 191);
Zinz.*Gem*.10 (Beyreuther
4-I:174);Zinz.*Aug.Conf*.15
(Beyreuther 6-II:267)

Hil.*Trin*.2.3 (*CCSL* 62:39)

Qnl.*Exp.apol*. (1712-I:51)

Qnl.*Clém.IX*.int.;1.3
(1700:2;36)

See vol.4:78

Sherl.*Vind*.2 (1690:17);
Wlch.*Spir*.10.12 (1751:182)
Gr.Naz.*Or*.21.35 (*PG*
35:1125)

Wer.*Misc*.1.4 (Ryhinerus
2:31)
Mrck.*Comp*.pr.;1.17
(Velzen 18:B1r;8)
Sem.*Frag*.10
(1780:57);Zinz.*Red*.4
(Beyreuther 1-II:49)
Tin.*Chr*.13 (1730:289);
Nss.*Dipp*.2 (1701:25)

obviously a heretic," when in fact the New Testament's definition of a heretic as "one who, still alienated from Christ and from his kingdom of grace, invents an 'analogy of faith' in accordance with reason and the letter of Scripture and then seeks to impose it upon others as saving truth," now applied "only to the orthodox" rather than to those whom the orthodox were condemning. In part, that criticism rested on the estimate that "there never was any period of time in all ecclesiastical history in which so many rank heresies were publicly professed [as] . . . within the first three centuries," a historical assumption that their opponents rejected as exaggeration, since "there have always been heretics from the beginning of the Christian church" to the present. The entire assault upon the orthodoxy of the creeds "makes faith a very useless, and heresy a very innocent and harmless thing," but the familiar words "There must be heresies," which meant that within the providence of God a betrayal of the faith could have beneficial side effects, were not to be used to justify toleration of false doctrine.

The critique of traditional doctrine concentrated with special vigor on its excessive preoccupation with terminology. The charge of logomachy had appeared repeatedly in the history of doctrinal conflict, as when Hilary had urged that "heresy lies in the sense assigned, not in the word written"; quoting these words, Pasquier Quesnel pressed for a distinction between the heretical and the orthodox meaning of ambiguous formulations. Such a stalwartly orthodox theologian as Peter Lombard, as well as later medieval thinkers including Duns Scotus, had consigned much of the dispute over the Filioque to the category of logomachy, a view that received new support in this period. Gregory of Nazianzus had observed that in the era of Athanasius "there was a danger of the whole world being torn asunder in the strife about syllables"; there were many who, perceiving the same danger now, pointed out that the trinitarian vocabulary as such was not indispensable and that it had itself undergone change in the course of orthodox development. Yet the caution against logomachy and "strange terms and sophistries borrowed from the

Milt.*Doct.*1.5 (Patterson 14:208)

stupidity of the schools" could easily become an attack on trinitarian orthodoxy, as Milton's doctrine of God showed. Confessional theologians warned that dismissing "the dispute between the Lutherans and Calvinists about the Sacrament" as "merely verbal" or as "a war of the grammarians" did violence not only to confessional orthodoxy but to the very nature of biblical language. The sixteenth-century controversy over whether original sin had become part of the "essence" of human nature was likewise more than a quarrel over terminology. Everyone would have agreed that some differences did not pertain to dogma at all and that ways of speaking did not affect salvation, but theologians ranging from radical to conservative also agreed that simply inventing new terminology was not the solution to the crisis of orthodox doctrine, since "it is easy to come together on words." The solution lay deeper, because the crisis lay deeper.

Tin.*Chr.*10 (1730:139)
Wer.*Diss.*10.5 (Ryhinerus 1:193)
Lw.*Dem.Er.* (Moreton 5:6);
Deutsch.*Aug.Conf.*
(1667:17-22)
See vol.4:142-45
Neum.*Marp.*2.5
(1727:141);Pnch.*Dict.*
(1736:162)
Allat.*Perp.cons.* (1655:641)
Sem.*Rel.* (Schütz 171)
Dipp.*Hrt.*2
(1706:34);Amrt.*Rev.*1.4
(1750:50)

Zinz.*Gespr.*5 (Beyreuther 1-III:37)

The Doctrine of the Law and Grace

See vol.2:146-70;
vol.4:262-74

See vol.2:181-83

See vol.4:8-9

See vol.4:374-85

More perhaps than any other doctrinal issue, even the question of authority, the Augustinian doctrine of grace, with its many permutations, demonstrated the continuity and yet the discontinuity between Eastern and Western Christianity, as well as between the Protestant Reformation and the preceding development of Christian doctrine within the West itself. The complexity of that continuity and discontinuity had already manifested itself in Roman Catholicism through the conflicts of the seventeenth century over grace, the gifts of grace, and the "aids to grace," but the complex relationship among the various positions was coming into sharper focus in the second half of that century. During that half-century, another English man of letters, John Bunyan, in addition to his best-known works *The Pilgrim's Progress* (1678 and 1684) and *Grace Abounding to the Chief of Sinners* (1666), also published in 1659 and revised in 1685 a treatise entitled *The Doctrine of the Law and Grace Unfolded.*

Bnyn.*Lw.Gr.*2 (Sharrock 2:187)

In celebrating "this glorious doctrine" and denouncing "a legal and old covenant spirit that secretly persuades the soul that if ever it will be saved by Christ, it must first be fitted for Christ," Bunyan was

Bnyn.*Lw.Gr.*2 (Sharrock 2:184)

Lw.*Chr.Perf*.9 (Moreton 3:134)

articulating a position that his successor in the next generation was to call "the absolute necessity of divine grace" as "a confessed doctrine of Christianity." "Confessed" though it was in one form or another by all who affirmed their loyalty to Christianity, the doctrine of grace was nevertheless a major source of contention and was now becoming a major component of the crisis of orthodoxy. One of the most decisive differences between Eastern and Western doctrine had long been the absence within Eastern Christian history of a controversy corresponding to that over nature and grace between Augustine and the Pelagians. In the course of that controversy, a synod of Greek-speaking bishops at Lydda-Diospolis in Palestine at the end of A.D. 415 had, much to Augustine's chagrin, declared that because Pelagius "anathematizes everything that is contrary to the church's faith,

ap.Aug.*Gest.Pelag*.20.44 (*CSEL* 42:99)

See vol.2:272

we confess him to belong to the communion of the catholic church"; unlike most of the Augustinian corpus, moreover, these proceedings had been preserved in Greek by Photius and were still circulating in that form among Eastern churchmen and theolo-

Phot.*Bib*.54 (Henry 1:42-44)

gians in the modern era. Despite the formal condemnation of Pelagianism as a heresy at the ecumenical

See vol.1:318

Council of Ephesus in 431, the technique of rehearsing the antithesis between Augustine and Pelagius as

Blrt.*S.T.Grat*.1 (Lequette 3:1-13)

the standard methodology for introducing the doctrine of grace enjoyed little or no popularity among Eastern theologians, being confined largely to Protes-

See vol.4:225-27;258-59
See vol.2:10-11

tants and Roman Catholics. Eastern theologians, who could speak of God's "granting a reward as a gift"—

See vol.4:259

See vol.1:300-301

thus transcending Reformation antitheses about grace—had been more likely to invoke the other pole of Augustine's conflict over the doctrine of grace, the defense of free will and responsibility, engaged as they were in a defense against various systems, whether Muslim or Manichean, that appeared to emphasize the arbitrariness of divine sovereignty at the cost of

See vol.2:216-42

human free will.

Leyd.*Jans*.2.1.14 (1695:289-90)

Conf.Aug.2.3 (*Bek*.53)

As the *Augsburg Confession*, following the precedent of Thomas Bradwardine, had, in condemning "the Pelagians and others," in fact been attacking positions of Roman Catholic scholastics and of certain Protestants that seemed to espouse an excessive optimism

See vol.4:139-40

Amrt.*Theol.eclec*.7.3.2
(1752-2-II:56-62)

See vol.4:225

Nrs.*Vind.Aug*.8 (Berti 2:456)
Poir.*Théol.cr*.pr. (1690-I:A4r)

Arb.*Des.myst*.5.1
(1764:598-606)
Inn.XI.*Cael.Past*. (Argentré
3:362-63)

Qnl.*Clém.IX*.1.3 (1700:37)

See vol.4:140

Brnt.*Art.XXXIX*.17
(1700:151)
ap.Leyd.*Jans*.2.1.10
(1695:262-69)
Bert.*Aug*.ded.;4.1
(1747-I:viii;64)

Hrn.*H.e*.1.3.30 (Leydecker
1:208)

Drnd.*Fid.vind*.3.2
(1709:363-66)
Pinch.*Dict.*
(1736:191-98;298-304);
Leyd.*Jans*.1.3.7
(1695:165-69)

about human capacity apart from grace, so in this period the same labels were easy to apply to perceived deviations from Augustinian orthodoxy. The language of the Synod of Dort, accusing Arminianism of "summoning the Pelagian error back up out of hell," was now repeated almost verbatim (though without attribution) by a cardinal of the Roman Catholic Church in his own vindication of the Augustinian doctrine of grace against Arminianism, as well as against various "Semi-Pelagian" movements within his own communion. According to a Protestant contemporary, "that infernal Pelagianism" was "the true atheism of the heart, which banishes from the human heart God and his Spirit, as well as his inner operations, and the illuminations of divine grace by which he rescues us from our infinite corruption." The "mystical errors" of Louis Molina, which had been condemned by Pope Innocent XI, were denounced by a defender of Jansenism as "the same as the errors of the Pelagians or the Semi-Pelagians." "Semi-Pelagian" would appear to have been less of a term of opprobrium when an Anglican described how, forsaking the extreme position represented by Luther's *Bondage of the Will*, "all the Lutherans have gone into the Semi-Pelagian opinions so entirely and so eagerly that they will neither tolerate nor hold communion with any of the other persuasion," i.e., Calvinists. Others continued to lump together "Manicheans, Lutherans, Calvinists, and Jansenists" as predestinarian opponents of free will.

The conflicts of the sixteenth-century Reformation as well as the post-Reformation controversies in both Protestantism and Roman Catholicism had already made necessary a new and more complex taxonomy of doctrines of grace than the simplistic distinction between Augustinianism and Pelagianism, even with the addition of "Semi-Pelagianism" as a separate species. Such developments of the seventeenth and eighteenth centuries as Jansenism, Molinism, and Quietism in Roman Catholicism, Puritanism and then Methodism in Anglicanism, and Pietism in Continental and American Protestantism (including the interactions among various of these movements) now added to the complexity. When a Roman Cath-

Span.*Cont.* (Marck
3:850-55);Wlch.*Pol.*4.2.2
(1752:1048-50)

Pnch.*Dict.* (1736:75)

Poir.*Oec.div.*2.17
(1705-II:571-72)

Nmnn.*Term.* (1700:33-36);
Nmnn.*Er.* (1701:33)
Albrt.*Vind.*1.13
(1695:21-22);Mayr.*Piet.*6.9
(1696:108-10)
Amrt.*Ep.*1749 (Friedrich 54)
Bert.*Aug.*4.1 (1747-II:125)
Qnl.*Exp.apol.* (1712-I:43)

Qnl.*Clém.IX.*pr.
(1700:xxxv-xxxvi)

Bert.*Aug.*1.1 (1747-I:91)
Bert.*Theol.disc.*17.1
(1792-III:210)

Drnd.*Fid.vind.*3
(1709:359-530)

Ors.*Ist.*19.1
(1747-VIII:247-49);
Qnl.*Exp.apol.* (1712-I:121)

Bert.*Aug.*ded. (1747-I:iii)

See vol.4:374-85
Leyd.*Jans.*2.1.3 (1695:229)

olic reference book on heresy could acknowledge that four of the five main doctrinal points of Arminianism, as usually listed in Protestant polemics, were "orthodox" in the light of "the faith of the church"; or when a Pietist, while also condemning Pelagianism, could group "Calvin, the Jansenists, and the Thomists" on the doctrines of grace and predestination; or when some orthodox Lutherans reciprocated by accusing the Pietists of espousing Calvinist doctrines regarding the divine decrees, while others identified Pietism with Pelagianism, and yet others with Manicheism; or when some Roman Catholics took it as "an ignorant slander" or "an atrocious calumny" to be called a Jansenist, while to others it was an "honor," despite the ambiguity of the label, which was in fact a way of attacking genuine Augustinianism; or when an orthodox Roman Catholic could seek to make distinctions between Jansen, Baius, and Quesnel on some questions while classifying them together on others—the resultant confusion in all quarters made it obvious that the categories were in need of some basic reconsideration. The entire third book of *The Faith Vindicated* by the French Franciscan Barthélémy Durand was given over to the refutation of those "heresies that have arisen in opposition to the grace of God and his glory."

In part, the history of the doctrine of grace itself compelled such reconsideration, as became clear through the historical and theological study of two of its more important stages: the theology of Augustine, in relation on the one hand to that of Thomas Aquinas and on the other hand to that of Luther and Calvin; and the doctrinal decrees of the Council of Trent. The first of these was, theoretically, the common property of the entire Christian tradition, although in fact it belonged almost completely to the West alone; the other was a predominantly Roman Catholic concern.

Augustine was believed to have been destined by Providence itself to be "the doctor of grace," to whom, as "the most brilliant light of the church and the most glorious conqueror of the Pelagian and other heresies," it was appropriate to dedicate a systematic defense of the doctrine of grace. The heavy verbatim borrowings from Augustine in Jansen's *Augustinus*,

Qnl.*Exp.apol.* (1712-I:117)

Bert.*Theol.disc.* 17.3
(1792-III:215)
Nrs.*Vind.Aug.* 3.3 (Berti
2:305)
Qnl.*Exp.apol.* (1712-I:46;65)

Bert.*Aug.* 3.1 (1747-I:340-43)

Leyd.*Jans.* 2.2.14 (1695:377)

See vol.4:221-29

Nrs.*Vind.Aug.* 1 (Berti 2:274)

Leyd.*Jans.* 1.3.10
(1695:183-88)

Lmp.*Ghm.* 12 (1719-I:752);
Hrn.*H.e.* 3.3.68 (Leydecker
1:516)

Bert.*Aug.* 4.1 (1747-II:58)

Bert.*Theol.disc.* 14.8
(1792-III:130,134)

Bert.*Aug.* 4.2 (1747-II:216)

Amrt.*Theol.eclec.* 7.3.4
(1752-2-II:73)

Qnl.*Exp.apol.* (1712-I:54)

ap.Nrs.*Vind.Aug.* 2 (Berti
2:281-86)

Nrs.*Hist.pel.* 1.23 (Berti
1:205)
Bert.*Theol.disc.* 4.6
(1792-I:176-78)

Boss.*Hist.var.* 5.1 (Lachat
4:65)

Hcks.*Ltrs.* pr. (1705:A8v-B1r)

Lschr.*Unfehl.* 8 (1724:59)

which the censors had apparently not recognized and therefore had condemned, made it necessary for opponents of Jansenism to counterpose "the Jansenist thesis" and "the Augustinian antithesis." If Thomas Aquinas was "the great disciple of Augustine" and "his faithful interpreter," their views of predestination and grace should agree. Yet the claim of the followers of Calvin to be "Augustinian, in fact Pauline," but emphatically not Thomistic, in their doctrine of grace and predestination continued to be so effective that their Roman Catholic opponents perceived a danger in using Augustine against them.

Despite the "hereditary hatred of the Jansenists for the Reformed," Calvinists found in Jansen's *Augustinus* a doctrine of "the irresistible power of the grace of God that is correct and in accordance with the Reformed doctrine." The Jansenists shared with them a refusal to acknowledge any "aids to grace" that were not efficacious, which seemed to have led both of them to a doctrine of irresistible grace and consequently to a denial of free will. Their opponents contended that it was authentically Augustinian to distinguish between "sufficient grace," as the grace "that grants the ability but not [necessarily] the will," and "efficacious grace," as "the supernatural illumination of the mind or the motion of the will," which was then joined with human assent; but the Jansenists did not find the distinction particularly useful. In reponse to the charge that Augustine had simply contradicted himself on the relation between the doctrines of grace and free will, it was obligatory to explain that at some stages of the Pelagian controversy he had been constrained to defend grace and at other stages free will, but that in principle he had consistently affirmed both. In this respect as in others, Thomas Aquinas had been his faithful disciple.

Protestants were able to invoke the historical authority of Bossuet (whom they acknowledged as a "fair and generous opponent") to argue that before Luther's time "the grace of Jesus Christ had not been proclaimed as it should have been," which had helped to bring about the Reformation. The confusions in the response of the sixth session of the Council of Trent to the Reformation's doctrine of grace were a major

CTrid.6.*Cap*.3
(Alberigo-Jedin 672)

See vol.4:237-39
Pnch.*Dict.* (1736:403-16)
Qnl.*Exp.apol.*
(1712-I:150;176-77)
Span.*Cont.* (Marck 3:851-52)
Drnd.*Fid.vind.*2.7 (1709:223)

CTrid.6.*Can*.4
(Alberigo-Jedin 679)

Bert.*Aug*.4.3 (1747-II:347)

Pnch.*Dict.* (1736:272-89)

CTrid.6.*Can*.22
(Alberigo-Jedin 680)

Qnl.*Arnau*.pr.3 (1699:vii)

Qnl.*Aux.* (1687:19-27)
Qnl.*Arn*.pr.23;26
(1699:xxxv;xxxix)

Qnl.*Exp.apol.* (1712-I:110)
Leyd.*Jans.*2.2.3
(1695:321-77)

Qnl.*Déf.égl.rom.*1.3
(1697:35-59)

Wer.*Misc.*1.4 (Ryhinerus
2:33)

Baum.*Pred.*2.4 (Kirchner
2:124-35);Zinz.*Gem.*26
(Beyreuther 4-I:348-49)
Mrck.*Comp.*4.42 (Velzen
18:94-95)

source of the continuing ambiguity. Its declaration that "though [Christ] died for all, yet all do not receive the benefit of his death, but only those to whom the merit of his passion is communicated" could be taken to mean that Christ had died only for the elect, as the Jansenists (despite papal condemnation) taught while claiming Trent, and as the Calvinists taught while opposing Trent. Its condemnation of the position of the Protestant Reformers "that man's free will, moved and aroused by God, by assenting to God's call and action in no way cooperates toward disposing and preparing itself to obtain the grace of justification" had left open to continuing debate the question of whether by "the grace of justification" here it had been referring to sufficient grace or to efficacious grace.

Perhaps most troubling of all was Trent's dual rejection of the Pelagian and Manichean extremes: the heresies "that the one justified either can without the special help of God [speciale auxilium Dei] persevere in the righteousness received, or that with that help he cannot." This made it possible for Jansen, as well as his predecessors and followers, to represent themselves as teaching a "doctrine of efficacious grace" that was not only "Augustinian" but "papal." In the tangled proceedings of the papal congregations that had dealt with the question of aids to grace, the popes had not, as some maintained, favored the Molinist views but had continued to follow Augustine and Thomas "as the two chief guides" on the orthodox Roman Catholic doctrine of grace. The outcome of this historical development was a lack of clarity on the doctrine of sufficient grace, well summarized by one Reformed observer: "The Jesuits . . . affirm it, but the Jansenists deny it. Yet there have also been others, called 'neo-Thomists,' who, while speaking in the same way as the Jesuits, believed exactly what the Jansenists did."

As all sides in all these controversies would have agreed, this lack of clarity in the doctrine of grace resulted in part from a problem of definition: "Wherein does the grace of the New Testament consist?" While agreeing that the word "grace" had various meanings in Scripture, Bunyan took the

Rom.6:14

Bnyn.*Lw.Gr*.2 (Sharrock 2:83-84)

Nmnn.*Term*. (1700:17-19)
Bert.*Aug*.4.1
(1747-II:131-32)

Luke 1:28 (Vulg.)

Mēn.*Did*.5.11 (Blantēs 306)
Grig.Mont.*Vr.dév*.200
(Gendrot 618-19)

Luke 1:38 (Vulg.)

Edw.*Rel.Aff*.1 (Miller 2:119)

Edw.*Rel.Aff*.3.1 (Miller 2:234)

Edw.*Rel.Aff*.3.1 (Miller 2:210)

Span.*Exerc.acad*.1.3 (Marck 3:534-38);Span.*Ev.vind*.2.1 (Marck 3:221-25)

statement "You are not under law but under grace" to be referring to "the free love of God in Christ to sinners, by virtue of the new covenant, in delivering them from the power of sin, from the curse and condemning power of the old covenant, [and] from the destroying nature of sin, by its continual working." "To explain the word and to distinguish" among its various meanings, one Protestant enumerated seven kinds of "grace": justifying, assisting, prevenient, preparatory, operating, arousing, and perfecting. Even that catalogue, whose distinctions were not universally accepted, did not include the distinction over which so much of the controversy within Roman Catholicism had been swirling, between sufficient grace and efficacious grace. The emphasis on the need for human assent to efficacious grace found its supreme exemplar in the Virgin Mary as "full of grace," which meant that the grace she received from God was "boundless" and was "the infallible mark of her predestination," yet not at the cost of the free assent expressed in her words to the angel of the annunciation, "Let it be done to me according to your word." It was still correct to identify as the two "extremes" that of "discarding all religious affections, as having nothing solid or substantial in them" and that of "look[ing] upon all high religious affections as eminent exercises of true grace, without much inquiring into the nature and source of those affections, and the manner in which they arose." Yet now it had become urgent to identify "the seal of the Spirit" as not the "revelation of any fact by immediate suggestion" but as "grace itself in the soul," in opposition to the "many kinds of false religious affections, which multitudes are deluded by, and probably have been in all ages of the Christian church," but which in this age were in danger of becoming dominant in all the branches of the Christian church.

As Bunyan's title, *The Doctrine of the Law and Grace*, suggests, the doctrine of grace had, since the Old as well as the New Testament, stood in dialectical relation to the doctrine of the law, hence to both the doctrine of creation and the doctrine of sin. Bunyan emphasized that despite its designation as "new," the covenant of grace, not the covenant of law or of works,

Bnyn.*Lw.Gr*.2 (Sharrock
2:93-94)
Bnyn.*Lw.Gr*.2 (Sharrock
2:167)
Heb.9:15;12:24

Grig.Mont.*Am.sag*.3.35
(Gendrot110)

See p. 109 below

Wlff.*Nat.Gott*.250;338
(1744-I:253;335)

Jab.*Sal*.14 (Basler 165-66)

Edw.*Rel.Aff*.1 (Miller
2:118);Mrck.*Comp*.15.26
(Velzen18:309)

Lmp.*Ew.Str*.2 (1729:292-93)
Mrck.*Scrip.exerc*.21.7
(Velzen10:998);Zinz.*Red*.10
(Beyreuther 1-II:138)
Poir.*Oec.div*.2.15 (1705-I:539)

Reim.*Apol*.2.5.2.2 (Alexander
2:452-55)

See vol.4:139-40

Theoph.*Apol*.12 (1788:31)
Drnd.*Fid.vind*.4.19
(1709:588-92)
Lang.*Mttl*.1.9
(1712:96);Hrn.*H.e*.1.3.30
(Leydecker 1:210)
See vol.1:316-18
Theoph.*Apol*.4 (1788:12)
Drnd.*Fid.vind*.2.5
(1709:217-20);
Bert.*Theol.disc*.12.13
(1792-III:43)
See vol.1:315-16
Rom.6:23

Feld.*Hnd*.1 (1799:5)

represented the original relation between Creator and creature, and that this "covenant is not broken by our transgressions" since "it was not made with us" but with "the Mediator of this new covenant." The doctrine of the creation of man by God as "the living image of his beauty and his perfections, the grand vessel of his graces, and the admirable treasure of his riches" was the foundation of authentic wisdom about creation and about grace. At a time when the crisis in the doctrine of creation evoked from some of its defenders a kind of pantheism as a counterpoise to Deism and from others a doctrine of annihilationism, it seemed necessary to assert "with greater precision the distinction between God and our soul" as a creature, and to declare that if the Epicurean doctrine of annihilation was being taught by some Christians, "they are not worthy of the name 'Christian.' "

Most of the theologians who did call themselves by that name were "generally agreed that sin radically and fundamentally consists in what is negative, or privative, having its root and foundation in a privation or want of holiness," and that therefore sin did not have any "being" of its own. Despite the continuing—and sometimes intensified—Protestant doctrine that all who were descended from Adam were sinners, it was one of the ironies of the changing situation during this period that the sharpest critique of the Augustinian doctrine of original sin was coming not from the East, but from Protestant theology, which during the Reformation had begun by attacking late medieval scholasticism as a "Semi-Pelagian" defection from the severity of that doctrine. The opposition among certain Protestants to the "erroneous" practice of infant baptism, which, since Pelagius had also accepted it, had been a principal support of the Augustinian doctrine of original sin, led them to speak of unbaptized infants as "innocent before God, in genuine innocence, and for the sake of Jesus Christ, the only Mediator." Some of the more radical Protestants were also beginning to revive the Pelagian interpretation of death as not the punishment and "wages of sin" inherited from Adam, but a natural occurrence. Eastern theologians went on characterizing sin as "a boundless poison, a boundless evil,

Mēn.*Did*.2.2 (Blantēs 108)
Eug.Bulg.*Orth*.3 (Metaxas 16-17)

Ath.Par.*Epit*.2.2.9 (1806:269)

Mēn.*Did*.1.7 (Blantēs 75)

Span.*Ev.vind*.1.15 (Marck 3:52-54)

Bnyn.*Lw.Gr*.pr. (Sharrock 2:17)

Bnyn.*Lw.Gr*.2 (Sharrock 2:199)

Rev.22:17

Strz.*Orth*.pr. (1828:2)

Mēn.*Did*.1.1 (Blantēs 5)

John 15:5

Conf.Aug.20.39
(*Bek*.81);*Apol.Conf.Aug*.4 256
(*Bek*.210);*Conf.Scot*.
13 (Niesel 96);*Conf.Belg*.14
(Niesel124);*Heid.Cat*.127
(Niesel 180-81)
Qnl.*Exp.apol*. (1712-I:93)

Mēn.*Did*.1.5 (Blantēs 51)

Ath.Par.*Epit*.1.1.19
(1806:130-33)

Drnd.*Fid.vind*.1.30
(1709:98-100)

Amrt.*Theol.eclec*.6.3.1
(1752-2-I:50)

Wlff.*Nat.Gott*.156
(1744-I:161)

a boundlessly oppressive weight," but also as "an ancestral sin distributed to everyone from Adam." Not only death as the consequence of sin, but "the transgression of the ancestor Adam has been handed on and is being handed on to the entire human race." Yet they likewise went on emphasizing its "voluntary" character.

That emphasis was a reminder that in addition to the dialectic between grace and law, the other dialectic that had figured prominently in the history of the doctrine of grace was the one between grace and merit or grace and reward, whose foundation was in turn the dialectic between grace and free will; this included, in Bunyan's formula, the doctrine of the "common providences" of God extended to all, as distinct from his other doctrine of the particular divine providence of election, predestination, and the final perseverance of the saints. As an enchiridion of Eastern Orthodox doctrine was to put it, quoting the words of the final chapter of the Bible, "Let him who desires take the water of life without price," there had to be such "desiring," because "the beautiful and ardent desire of the soul is demanded before everything else." It was a refrain of Eastern Orthodox preaching that "God wills, and if man also wills, man has been predestined." The very words of Jesus, "Apart from me you can do nothing," which the Lutheran and Reformed confessions of the sixteenth century had quoted to prove that free will in relation to God was a delusion and which Jansenists were still quoting that way, meant to Eastern Orthodox interpreters not only that "the grace of God is necessary," but that the cooperation of the human will was necessary also. Otherwise, they maintained, God would have to be, as in the thought of Calvin, the author of evil.

Roman Catholic interpreters, too, accused Calvin, as well as Luther and Zwingli, of making God the cause of sin, although in making the accusation they explained that God was indeed the cause of a sinful act insofar as it was an act but not insofar as it was sinful. Concerning the foreknowledge of an omniscient God, everyone would agree that it extended also to the "free choices" of the soul before they were made; yet those who followed Thomas Aquinas in his reading of

Bert.*Theol.disc.*4.3
(1792-I:168)
See vol.3:114-16
Bert.*Aug.*4.1 (1747-II:66-73)

See vol.4:259
Amrt.*Theol.eclec.*7.3.5
(1752-1-II:74-75)
Grig.Mont.*Am.sag.*6.72
(Gendrot 130)

Brnt.*Art.XXXIX.*17
(1700:45)

Brnt.*Art.XXXIX.*pr.
(1700:vi)

Scriv.*Seel.*3.8 (Stier 5:57)
Scriv.*Zuf.And.*65 (Stier
1:88-89)

Brnt.*Art.XXXIX.*pr.
(1700:vi)

See vol.1:319-24

Brnt.*Art.XXXIX.*17
(1700:149)

Mēn.*Did.*1.1 (Blantēs 1)

Wlch.*Pol.*5.3 (1752:1145)

See vol.4:365-66
Bert.*Theol.disc.*6.3
(1792-I:235)

Augustine rejected "the false conclusion of the Gnostics and Hussites that from foreknowledge there follows a necessity of contingent actions and the elimination of freedom," and they continued the medieval quest for a "harmony" between grace and free will. The medieval proposition that "to one who does what lies within him, God does not deny his grace," meant that "no one does what lies within him except by a grace that is extrinsically supernatural," and yet the reason some refused Christ and his grace was "our own hardness of heart and ingratitude," not a predestination to damnation.

Predestination was still, in Burnet's phrase, "one of the longest, the subtlest, and indeed the most intricate of all the questions in divinity," the question on which, for his exposition of the *Thirty-Nine Articles*, he had "labored with more care" than on any other. It was, according to a leading Protestant devotional manual, "hidden to all carnal reason and yet filled with consolation," intended not "to disturb and terrify but to comfort." When Anglican critics of the Calvinistic doctrine of predestination sought patristic substantiation for their criticism, they were able to say that they "follow the doctrine of the Greek church, from which St. Austin departed and formed a new system," and that they therefore preferred the doctrine of those Western theologians, such as Cassian, whose views of grace, free will, and predestination, diverging from those of Augustine, carried "deep impressions of the doctrine of the Greek church."

Greek exponents of the doctrine of providence attacked "scholastic theologians" (and Augustine, their source) for identifying "providence" with "foreknowledge," at least partly because of the threat such an identification posed to the doctrine of free will. But to Western Augustinians the Greek doctrines of grace and free will were "Pelagian." The device, suggested by some Lutheran theologians and by others, of teaching that God had predestined the elect on the basis of their foreseen faith was rejected not only by Reformed but also by Roman Catholic teachers, who might have been expected to find it more congenial, considering their revulsion at the "horrendous, detest-

Bert.*Theol.disc.*6.17
(1792-I:285-88)

Wer.*Diss.*28 (Ryhinerus
1:481)

Strim.*Un.Ev.*1.28 (1711:36)

Mrck.*Comp.*7.13 (Velzen
18:136)

See vol.4:33-34

Nmnn.*Er.* (1701:84-86)
Nmnn.*St.Ver.*26
(1695:55);Nmnn.*Term.*
(1700:73)

Edw.*Fr.Wll.*pr. (Miller
1:129-32)

Mead (1942) 21

See vol.1:321;vol.4:237

1 Tim.2:4

Beb.*Gl.*4 (1685:47-50)

Mēn.*Did.*1.1 (Blantēs 3-4)

See vol.1:155-56

able, and altogether execrable dogma" of reprobation propounded by Calvin and his followers. Between Lutheran and Reformed teachers themselves, there was an effort to find common ground on the propositions that "to whomsoever the gospel is preached . . . efficacious grace is seriously offered" and that "it is man alone who excludes himself by stubbornly despising and rejecting this grace, which has been seriously offered." On the basis of Paul and Augustine, Lutherans did share with Calvinists the doctrine of a particular, even of an "immutable," election to salvation.

Yet a Pietism that had cut across traditional confessional boundaries seemed to be annulling such medieval and Reformation concepts as the fundamental distinction between the antecedent and the consequent wills of God and therefore to be blurring the difference between the universal offer of grace and particular election. And a Puritanism that began with a protest against what it took to be "Arminianism" in the doctrine of grace seemed by its adoption of the compromise of a "halfway covenant" to have "admitted to the churches a large number of persons who could not relate an experience of saving grace" and thus to have reintroduced human effort and human merit into the doctrines of grace to a degree that made the *Canons and Decrees of the Council of Trent,* not to mention the *Augustinus* of Cornelius Jansen, seem by comparison to be almost closer to the teachings of the original Protestant Reformers. Contemplating the complexity of the paradoxical relation between the universality of a gracious divine will for "all men to be saved and to come to the knowledge of the truth" and the particularity of a human free will that could frustrate this divine will and reject grace and salvation, a Greek Orthodox theologian was speaking for all Christians when he exclaimed that this was "an obscure and a sublime doctrine."

Since the ancient church, the doctrine of grace had been connected to the doctrine of the word of God and the sacraments as means of grace. Central to the Reformation apologia for the church, as formulated by Jewel, was the consideration of the "proper mark and badge" by which the church "may be known to be the

Jwl.*Apol*.4 (Booty 76)

See vol.4:174-82
See vol.4:215-16
Span.*Ev.vind*.1.17 (Marck
3:60-62)

Eccl.5:1

Lschr.*Hör.* (1734:4)

Deutsch.*Luth*.1.5.17
(1698:54-55)

Beng.*Gnom*.pr.5 (Steudel xix)

Lschr.*Hör.* (1734:26-28);
Frnck.*Id*.20 (Peschke 179)

Drnd.*Fid.vind*.2.40
(1709:306-9)

Conf.*Aug.*14 (*Bek*.69)

Mayr.*Red*.4 (1702:357-58)

Deutsch.*Luth*.1.3.3;1.5.4
(1698:21-24;115)

Mayr.*Red*.4 (1702:367)

Eug.Bulg.*Orth*.9 (Metaxas
35-38)

Mck.*Vor.* (1774:25-26)

Feld.*Hnd*.3 (1799:43)
Ath.Par.*Epit*.4.1.1
(1806:350-52)
Amrt.*Theol.eclec*.10.2.9-10
(1754-2-V:6);Amrt.*Theol.mor.*
11.2 (1757-II:102)
See vol.2:174-75
Cos.*Graec*.3.11.310-42
(1719-II:72-80);
Drnd.*Fid.vind*.4.35
(1709:628-31);
Bert.*Theol.disc*.32.7
(1792-VIII:35-47)

church of God"; for Reformation theology, this consisted in the preaching of the word of God and the administration of the sacraments (and, in some doctrines, the exercise of church discipline, which did not mean, however, absolute holiness of life). The words of the Old Testament, "To draw near to listen is better than to offer the sacrifice of fools," meant to Protestant orthodoxy that the church was primarily an "auditorium" rather than a "theater." When it lived up to this mandate, the church was "a custodian of the word of God": "the Scripture sustains the church, the church guards [custodit] the Scripture." Yet this was not to become an excuse for supposing that "one can edify oneself better" through reading the Bible, for "listening is enjoined upon us even more strictly than reading." A corollary of this rejection of conventicles was the insistence, in response to both Pietist anticlericalism and Roman Catholic clericalism, that, as the *Augsburg Confession* had enjoined, "nobody should publicly teach or preach or administer the sacraments in the church without a regular call." The ministry was a distinct "estate" in the church, not a special application of the doctrine of the universal priesthood of believers, for this doctrine "does not abolish the distinction among estates" in society and church.

The apologia for the sacraments in response to these various challenges was in some ways little more than a recitation of the historic positions of the several churches about them. Eastern Orthodoxy was concerned to protect the integrity and sanctity of the seven sacraments against the effort to depress them into "some sort of simple symbols of the commands of God." At a time when Baptists were contending for immersion as the only authentic form of baptism, which "has its origin from God," Eastern theologians also insisted on it, in opposition to the Latins, who were obliged to admit that immersion had been standard practice throughout most of the history of the church. The debate remained unresolved between the Western doctrine that only a bishop was the "ordinary minister" of confirmation and the Eastern view that it could be administered by a simple presbyter.

Hrn.*H.e.*2.1.11 (Leydecker 1:250-51)

Ath.Par.*Epit.*4.1.3 (1806:360-61)

Eug.Bulg.*Orth.*9 (Metaxas 37)
Drnd.*Diss.*4.9.3-11 (1703:400-403)
Coz.*Graec.*4.5.147 (1719-II:206);Bert.*Theol.disc.* 33.5 (1792-VII:96)
Amrt.*Theol.eclec.*13.2. 21.2-3 (1752-3-II:66)
Alph.Lig.*Theol.mor.*6.3.1. 202-3 (Gaudé 3:180)

Mrck.*Comp.*31.5 (Velzen 18:607)

Eug.Bulg.*Orth.*9 (Metaxas 39)
Bert.*Theol.disc.*33.7 (1792-VII:111-17);
Rndt.*Lit.Or.*int.1.2 (1716-I:xii)

Rndt.*Lit.Or.*pr. (1716-I:O3v)
See vol.4:122-25;
Brnt.*Art.*XXXIX.19 (1700:180)

Ang.Sil.*CTrid.*8 (1675:M3r-M9v)

Brnt.*Art.*XXXIX.25 (1700:267-68)

Brnt.*Art.*XXXIX.11 (1700:125)

See p. 64 below
See pp. 99-100 below
See vol.4:293
CTrid.7.*Decr.*1.1.1 (Alberigo-Jedin 684)

Over against Roman Catholicism the Greeks (and others) listed as doctrinal differences on the Eucharist: the Western use of "azymes [unleavened bread]," the Roman Catholic belief that the consecration and eucharistic miracle took place through the recitation of the words of institution rather than through the invocation of the Holy Spirit in the epiclesis, and the denial of the chalice to the laity. "Taking leavened bread" rather than unleavened was the norm for the East. According to the Latins, unleavened bread had been used in the original institution by Christ but leavened bread was also technically permissible; yet it was not "legally permitted for a licit consecration in a Latin church," and a Greek priest celebrating in a Latin church, or a Latin priest celebrating in a Greek church, was obliged to observe the local practice. But Protestants took both Greeks and Latins to task for making their form the necessary one.

The East taught that "by the power of the Spirit, who is the source of perfection, invoked through the epiclesis of the priests (and certainly not by the recitation of the words of the Lord [Christ])" the bread and wine were changed into the body and blood of the Lord. In response, the Latins cited various liturgies of the East in which the consecration was attributed to the words of institution, not to the epiclesis. Those liturgies, they argued, could not be understood properly except by being "explained in accordance with the Catholic doctrine of the Eucharist." And in reply both to Eastern Orthodoxy and to Protestantism, they cited patristic evidence in support of the practice of administering Holy Communion to the people under only one of the consecrated species. While Anglicanism also sought to avoid "sinking the sacraments so low as to be mere rites and ceremonies," it was at the same time set against the opposite "extreme" represented by the Roman Catholic doctrine, which threatened to turn the sacraments into "charms."

Replying not only to the objections of the Protestant Reformers but to the deepening skepticism about the credibility of postbiblical traditions (and sometimes also of biblical traditions), Roman Catholicism went on insisting, in accordance with the doctrine of the Council of Trent, that Christ himself had insti-

Amrt.*Theol.mor.*10.4
(1757-II:84);Bert.*Theol.disc.*
30.8 (1792-VI:153-55)
Ost.*Arg.ref.*Jer.31; John 4
(1720-I:522;1720-II:123);see
vol.4:362-73
Ost.*Cat.* (1747:179)
Ost.*Cat.* (1747:180-81)

See vol.4:194-95

Wer.*Diss.*10.1 (Ryhinerus
1:168)

tuted all seven sacraments of the church "immediately," not through the mediation of the apostles or of
later generations. Reformed theology made its distinctive concept of the covenant central to its definition of the sacraments, which it restricted to baptism
and the Lord's Supper; and against the Lutheran
charge of rationalism in the doctrine of the sacraments, it affirmed its faith in their "mystery," since it
was the Lutheran insistence on complete dogmatic
precision about them that was rationalistic. As Lutheranism strove to avoid the accusation that in the
sixteenth and seventeenth centuries it had distorted
the sacraments, intended by Christ to foster the unity

Frnck.*Pred.*Maund.Thu.
(1699:23-24)

of believers, into an occasion for controversy among
the learned, it emphasized the character of the sacraments as a gift, in which "our dear Savior wants to
give and grant himself to us, with all that he is and

Scriv.*Seel.*3.7 (Stier 5:16-17)

has, and to unite himself with us as intimately as
possible."

A Devout and Holy Life

Upon hearing the phrase "the crisis of orthodoxy,"
most members of most churches in the year 1700
would have thought immediately of the crisis of
Christian devotion and morality, which during that
very year was being lamented in many countries. A
book published in 1700 described how the czar of
Russia, who was "almost degenerating into savagery,"
had berated the patriarch of Moscow (whose office he
was about to abolish) for displaying the icon of the
Virgin Mary in a vain attempt to shield from "public

Krb.*Diar.*6-7.x.1698
(1700:83)
Fén.*Ep.*12.xii.1700
(Gosselin 8:625)

vengeance the crimes that tend to bring ruin to the
commonwealth." In that year one French Roman
Catholic warned against "ancient temptations," and
another published a tortured explanation of what was
meant by the morally disturbing thesis that "the

Qnl.*Clém.*IX.1.1 (1700:16)

commandments of God are impossible to keep," while
a French-speaking Reformed theologian in Neuchâtel
complained that "the breakdown of discipline is one
of the greatest imperfections to be noted in the
present state of the church and one of the most

Ost.*Corrupt.*2.2
(1700-II:36;81)

obvious and universal causes of corruption among
Christians."

Frnck.*Pred*.Ex. (1700:35;54)

A German Pietist, preaching on the Sunday after Ascension Day in 1700, described most church members as "wanting to have the kind of Christianity in which they can simultaneously please God and yet not displease the world," by contrast with someone to whom "his eternal salvation is a matter of dead earnest"; an orthodox Lutheran on Septuagesima Sunday of that year warned that through such movements

Mayr.*Red*.3 (1702:343)

as Pietism Satan was trying to undermine faith and confidence, "especially in these last times"; and a radical apocalypticist was denouncing both the Pietists and the orthodox as "semi-Christians, with their churchy piety, who cling to the teachings they heard

Pet.*Myst*.pr.17 (1700-I:C3r)

in their youth." Also in 1700, an Anglican bishop dedicated a book to his king with the admonition: "Your work is not yet done . . . till you have employed that power which God has put in your hands . . . above all things in the raising the power and efficacy

Brnt.*Art.XXXIX*.ep.ded. (1700:A3v-A4r)

of this religion by a suitable reformation of our lives and manners."

A few years later a book appeared in England whose content and very title articulated this aspect of the crisis of orthodoxy: *A Serious Call to a Devout and Holy*

Wsly.*Serm*.2.107 (Jackson 7:203)

Life, published in 1728 by William Law. Later generations were "greatly profited" by the book, and even its critics were impressed by its "equal severity

Gib.*Aut*.1 (Saunders 45)

and truth"—not because it was so original but because it was not, summarizing as it did a universal concern also voiced by a theologian mediating between Pietism and Rationalism, who preached, also in

Baum.*Pred*.2.5 (Kirchner 2:155-90)

1728, on the theme, "The Great Lack of Genuine Seriousness in Christianity." Christian life had to be, in the words of Law's title, both "devout" and "holy,"

Ost.*Arg*.Gal.5;Eph.4 (1720-II:241;247)

achieving, as a contemporary put it, "our advancement both in piety and in sanctity," to counteract those who, "with their damnable errors, are introduc-

Ost.*Arg.ref*.2Tim.3 (1720-II:277)

ing both a license in morals and an impiety." This aspect of the crisis of orthodoxy was closely connected

Lw.*Ser.Cl*.2 (Moreton 4:20)

with the crisis in the doctrine of grace; it was a consensus across the churches "that Christian practice, or a holy life, is a great and distinguishing sign of a

Edw.*Rel.Aff*.3.12 (Miller 2:406)

true and saving grace," and that "virtue and sanctity" characterized "the prophets, apostles, martyrs, virgins, ascetics, and whomsoever divine grace has

Mēn.*Did.*1.3 (Blantēs 33)
Edw.*Rel.Aff.*3.12 (Miller 2:398)
Ost.*Arg.ref.* Rom.6;Gal.2 (1720-II:192;237-38)

See vol.1:155-56

Lw.*Ser.Cl.*1 (Moreton 4:7)

Lw.*Ser.Cl.*1 (Moreton 4:8)

Lw.*Ser.Cl.*9;4 (Moreton 4:70;41)

Ang.Sil.*CTrid.*6 (1675:J10v-L2r);Arb.*Inst.*3.8 (1765:343);Bert.*Theol.disc.* 33.19 (1792-VII:190); Gtti.*Coll.* 3.7.2 (1727:544)

See vol.4:298-99
Amrt.*Theol.mor.*12.2 (1757-II:164)

Amrt.*Theol.eclec.*11.3.1 (1752-2-VI:67)

See vol.2:292

Eug.Bulg.*Orth.*9 (Metaxas 38);
Mēn.*Did.*1.6 (Blantēs 64)
Amrt.*Theol.mor.*12.1 (1757-II:162)

See vol.3:74-80

sanctified." Yet instead of being "active" in producing a "spiritual and divine life" that was devout and holy, "the doctrine of grace is being abused." As could have been expected from the ambiguous but reciprocal relation between the doctrine of grace and the doctrine of the means of grace, such an abuse of the former led to a grave abuse of the latter as well, once again at the expense of a truly "spiritual and divine life."

Therefore William Law opened his treatise with a definition: "Devotion is neither private nor public prayer. . . . Devotion signifies a life given, or devoted to God." Because so many church members "appear to have no other devotion but that of occasional prayers," they had earned "the jest and scorn of careless and worldly people." Yet a truly devout life was "as truly suitable to the gospel of Christ as to be baptized or receive the Sacrament." Such warnings against reliance on external adherence to the ritual of the sacraments came as the several systems of eucharistic doctrine and practice that had come out of the Reformation were once again facing reexamination. Notwithstanding the repetition of the sacrificial interpretation of the Mass and of the doctrinal legislation of the Council of Trent making transubstantiation binding "as a matter of faith [de fide]," it had to be conceded that the doctrine, including the puzzle of the continuing status of the "accidents" of bread and wine, was still "being explained in a variety of ways even by [Roman] Catholic writers." Following the formulas developed in its confrontations with Roman Catholicism and with Protestantism, Eastern Orthodox sacramentalism continued to affirm that Christ "truly and precisely changes and transubstantiates [μετουσιώσας]" the bread and wine into his own body and blood, although the centrality of the invocation of the Holy Spirit as the means by which the eucharistic miracle was performed brought together the doctrine of the presence and the doctrine of the church in a perspective that went beyond the Western distinctions between "real" and "symbolic" presence.

To a Reformed theologian, transubstantiation was the one "error" of Roman Catholicism that, above all others, he found simultaneously repellent and "im-

Wer.*Diss*.12 (Ryhinerus
1:205)
Gtti.*Coll*.3.6.9;3.6.19
(1727:530;542)
Neum.*Ev.Nach*.2
(1726-II:53-54)
Nss.*Dipp*.9
(1701:61);Spen.*Bed*.1.1.26
(Canstein 1:147)

Strim.*Un.Ev*.1.16
(1711:18);Wer.*Diss*.10.3
(Ryhinerus 1:180-81)

Brnt.*Art.XXXIX*.29
(1700:343-44)

Brnt.*Art.XXXIX*.pr.
(1700:vii)

Brnt.*Art.XXXIX*.28
(1700:308-9)

Zinz.*Zst*.50 (Beyreuther
3-II:386-89)

Lw.*Dem.Er.* (Moreton 5:15)
Lw.*Chr.Perf*.9 (Moreton
3:144)

Frnck.*Id*.20 (Peschke 179);
Mrck.*Scrip.exerc.* 6.28
(Velzen 10:426)

Leyd.*Jans*.2.3.9-10
(1695:490-97);Qnl.*Arn*.pr.21
(1699:xxxi-xxxii);Frnck.*Bcht*.
(Peschke 97)

Lw.*Ser.Cl*.1 (Moreton 4:7)

Arb.*Inst*.1.38 (1765:208-12);
Drnd.*Fid.vind*.3.49
(1709:495-98)

Amrt.*Ep*.1742 (Friedrich 62)

possible to believe." As their opponents recognized, the Lutherans, whether orthodox or Pietistic, while continuing to dissociate themselves from the theories of transubstantiation and sacrifice, repeated Luther's insistence on a presence so "real" that even the unworthy communicant received the true body and blood, an insistence that the Reformed still rejected. In his explanation of the *Thirty-Nine Articles* Burnet rejected it also, as yet another "mere point of speculation concerning the manner in which Christ is present," but he professed nevertheless to "assert a real presence of the body and blood of Christ," meaning by "real" a presence that was "true, in opposition both to fiction and imagination." What set all of this apart from earlier development was a greater sense that beyond any confession of the presence, eucharistic devotion was now finding its focus in a "right observation of the sacrament" where personal experience of "remembrance and acknowledgment" was seen as "a necessary part," over against an exclusive attention to "public occasions of divine service," so that it became necessary to urge people to attend "the shared public and solemn worship of God" even when they felt "that they could edify themselves better in private." Similarly, the admonition to receive communion more frequently seemed to be becoming, across confessional boundaries, more important than the definition of the presence. Although none of that explicitly threatened the doctrines of the sacraments set down in the confessional standards of the sixteenth and seventeenth centuries, it could tend to relegate them to a subordinate position.

Similarly, while few of his contemporaries, regardless of theological position, would have objected to Law's definition of "the devout man" as one "who makes all the parts of his common life parts of piety," such language could threaten to dissolve the specific duties of Christian "piety" into the universal content of the "common life," by elevating the extrasacramental experiences of piety to a normative status. Roman Catholics, while defending the use of indulgences against the Protestant Reformers, had to recognize, after studying its history (for the first time), that the externalization of the sacrament of penance in the later

Amrt.*Theol.mor*.13.14
(1757-II:304-62)

Amrt.*Theol.mor*.13.12
(1757-II:293);CTrid.25.*Decr*.6
(Alberigo-Jedin 796)
Reb.*Poen*.24-28
(1708:12-15);Span.*H.e*.16.5
(Marck 1:1906-10)

Frnck.*Bcht*. (Peschke 93)
Bert.*Theol.disc*.34.4
(1792-VII:238)

CFlor. (1438-45)*Decr.Arm*.
(Alberigo-Jedin 548)
See vol.4:296-97
CTrid.14.*Decr*.l.3;*Can*.4
(Alberigo-Jedin 703-4)

Amrt.*Theol.mor*.13.2-7
(1757-II:205-35)

Alph.Lig.*Theol.mor*.6.4.4.
506-30 (Gaudé 3:516-39)
Amrt.*Theol.eclec*.12.6.pr.
(1752-3-I:222);Drnd.*Diss*.4.22
(1703:475-79)

See vol.4:95-96;128-33

Amrt.*Theol.mor*.13.9;13.,18
(1757-II:257;380)

See vol.4:250

Schmdt.*Bcht*. (1662:18)
Wlch.*Pol*.4.1.83
(1752:1033-34)
Amrt.*Theol.eclec*.12.2.1
(1752-3-I:31)
Span.*Ev.vind*.3.13 (Marck
3:502-3);Wer.*Misc*.22
(Ryhinerus 2:321)

Reb.*Poen*.37 (1708:22)

Zinz.*Off.Red*.11 (Beyreuther
2-IV:100-104)

Frnck.*Bcht* (Peschke 94)
Frnck.*Meth*.1.6 (1723:19)
1 Tim.3:2;Tit.1:7

Middle Ages had contributed to the Reformation and hence to the shattering of the medieval sacramental system; and they quoted the Council of Trent on "moderation" in that use. Protestants, while rehearsing the Reformers' attacks on the scholastic doctrine of penance, were forced in turn to admit that by now an unthinking repetition of the formulas of confession substituted by the Reformers for the sacrament of penance had itself led to a new externalism. Even within Roman Catholicism, despite the assertion of a consensus on the definition by the Council of Florence, reaffirmed by the Council of Trent, that contrition, confession, and satisfaction were "so to speak, the matter" of the sacrament, it was obvious that problems about all three parts of penance remained unresolved in doctrine and in practice. Defending the objectivity of penitential "satisfaction" against various heretics, especially those who "having once forsaken the path of apostolic tradition, follow only reason as their guide," did not dispose of the late medieval—in fact, perennial—problem of how the objective sacrament was affected by the subjective state of the penitent who was "defective" in some aspect of the requisite "sorrow" over sin or by that of the father confessor who was himself "in a state of mortal sin."

Luther's followers praised his abolition of compulsory auricular confession and defended his retention of private confession, while Roman Catholics criticized the former and Calvinists the latter. Protestants approved of modifying the penitential "rigor" of earlier times, but "with many theologians and others we lament that almost all public repentance of grave transgressions has been dropped in the Evangelical churches." On the Protestant side no less than on the Roman Catholic, the subjective state of the penitent and that of the confessor demanded attention. There were many books about repentance, "but it is certain that most of those who have written them are themselves unconverted," and this despite "the repeated demand [of the New Testament] that they 'must be' " devout and holy. Lacking any personal "experience of what true repentance and conversion are," these authors had devised "formulas of confession

A Devout and Holy Life 53

that throw the entire act of conversion topsy-turvy, until it is impossible to know whether it pertains to the regenerate or the unregenerate." If the penitent did not bring "a heart filled with genuine repentance and true faith" to the confession of sins, it was "hypocrisy," because repentance was fundamental to faith. Without such a "living knowledge and experience of divine truth in the heart," a knowledge and experience of what it meant to be "born again [and] change our very natures," formal Protestant confession was no better than formal Roman Catholic confession. "Nothing less than this great change of heart and mind" was in a position to "give anyone any assurance that he is truly turned to God," and without such "good earnest in religion . . . we are nothing."

Although the summons and "serious call" to imitate the holiness of Christ was addressed to all believers, it carried special import for "the profession of a clergyman, [which] is a holy profession, because it is a ministration in holy things." The movement to reform the clergy in life and morals and to make them genuine "witnesses of Jesus" pervaded the churches at the beginning of the eighteenth century. Archbishop François Fénelon of Cambrai, in his opposition to Jansenism, strove to strengthen not only the professional and scholarly training of his priests, but above all their personal commitment and sanctity; and he analyzed in detail the requisite virtues of the office of bishop. The formula of ordination received "from the earliest times of the church," by which the bishop pronounced over the candidate the words of Christ to the apostles, "Receive the Holy Spirit!" conferred the grace of the priestly office, as the Council of Trent had confessed; but the "grace" was intended for the priest in his person, not only in his office, not only for the sacrifice of the Mass but for the sacrifice of his heart and life, and the personal wish to function as priest was necessary for ordination.

Spener directed much of his thought to the reformation of the Protestant clergy, who needed it "as much as any estate can ever need it." It was not enough for them to have a "literal knowledge" of the Bible, without "the grace and illumination of the Holy Spirit": they must be true Christians. Because

Frnck.Bcht. (Peschke 93-94)

Neum.Fünf.1 (1726-I:149)
Frnck.Pred.Trin.20 (1699:35);Reb.Poen. (1708:19-20)
Frnck.Bcht. (Peschke 99)

Lw.Chr.Perf.2 (Moreton 3:29)

Lw.Chr.Perf.2 (Moreton 3:35)
Edw.Rel.Aff.1 (Miller 2:99-100)

Lw.Ser.Cl.4 (Moreton 4:31)

Zinz.Soc.31 (Beyreuther 1-I:281)

Fén.Ep.30.xii.1704 (Gosselin 8:439-41)
Amrt.Theol.eclec.13.2.1.4 (1752-3-II:10)
John 20:22
Ambr.Spir.3.18.137 (CSEL 79:208)
CTrid.23.Can.4 (Alberigo-Jedin 744)
Bert.Theol.disc.36.8 (1792-VIII:76)

Alph.Lig.Theol.mor.4.2.1.113 (Gaudé 2:528-29)

Spen.Pi.Des. (Aland 16)

Spen.Gtts.4 (1680:138-40)
Spen.Pi.Des. (Aland 67)

Gtz.*Unt.*
(1693:M1v);Mayr.*Red.*4
(1702:357-58)

Spen.*Bed.*1.1.28 (Canstein
1:175-76)

1 Tim.3:2;Tit.1:7

Frnck.*Pred.*Mis. (1700:15)

Frnck.*Bcht.* (Peschke 101)

Frnck.*Id.*1 (Peschke 172)

Frnck.*Id.*29 (Peschke 189)
Spen.*Beant.*1.48 (1693:62)
Mayr.*Witt.*1 (1686:22-23)

Spen.*Pi.Des.* (Aland 68)

Span.*H.e.*8.3 (Marck
1:1270-72);Lmp.*Hist.*2.6
(1747:164)
Nss.*Dipp.*11 (1701:71)

Ess.Consist.24.viii.1709
(Neumeister 296)

Pnch.*Dict.* (1736:139-41)

Span.*Ev.vind.*2.21 (Marck
3:323-24)
Bert.*Aug.*6.3 (1747-II:496);
Pnch.*Dict.* (1736:186)
Beng.*Brüd.*2.42 (1751:311)

Lw.*Bngr.*2 (Moreton 1:39)

his opponents saw his campaign as an attack on the ministerial office itself, he made a point of insisting that he was not abolishing the distinction between clergy and laity or giving the laity the right to preach and administer the sacraments. His colleague Francke saw the requirement that a clergyman be "blameless" as "the presupposition for [all] the other attributes of a preacher," and he deplored, as a major source of the spiritual malaise of the church, the "unconverted" state of those who preached and heard confession; "what is to be looked for first of all and above all in a theological student," he said in the opening words of his treatise on the study of theology, "is that his heart be right with God." Theological erudition was not to be despised, but the personal faith of the theological student and future pastor was to be his "primary concern." For "the life of students, including students of theology, at the universities [was] so unchristian" that, as orthodox professors had to admit defensively, it sometimes erupted in scandal, because students were not "having it impressed upon them that holy life is not of less consequence than diligence and study."

History showed that the depravity of the clergy had been the source for the corruption of the church as a whole during the Middle Ages. But Pietism was in danger of "confusing the office and the person" and of supposing that the validity of word and sacrament depended "on the worthiness and the piety" of the minister, and of thus relapsing into the Donatist error, from which orthodox Protestantism sought to dissociate itself. This had been taken to be the error of the Hussites, and it was now being discerned also in their spiritual descendants, the Moravian Brethren. It was as well the error charged to Bishop Hoadly in the "Bangorian controversy"; for if he was right that "the natural weakness of men makes them incapable of being the instruments of conveying grace to their brethren," the conclusion was inescapable "that there can be no positive institutions in the Christian religion that can procure any spiritual advantage to the members of it." And "then the sacraments can no longer be any means of grace."

Sherl.*Def*.int. (1675:8)

Hcks.*Ltrs*.pr. (1705:C3r)

Pet.*Hchzt*.5.16 (1701:172-73)
Tol.*Milt*. (1699:139)

Tol.*Myst*.3.1 (1696:70)

Tin.*Chr*.9 (1730:109)

Lw.*Ser.Cl*.1 (Moreton 4:10)
Zinz.*Soc*.7 (Beyreuther
1-I:77-78)

Mos.*Vind.disc*.2.1
(1722:255-57);Lschr.*Hör*.
(1734:27)

Neum.*Fünf*.2 (1726-I:238)

Edw.*Rel.Aff*.3.4 (Miller
2:279)

Edw.*Rel.Aff*.3.44 (Miller
2.266-68)

Edw.*Rel.Aff*.3.5 (Miller
2:294)

See vol.1:2-3
Ath.Par.*Epit*.prol.2 (1806:6)

Ath.Par.*Epit*.4.prol.
(1806:343)

Gr.Naz.*Carm*.2.2.119.40
(*PG* 38:74)

Spen.*Pi.Des*. (Aland 68)

Mayr.*Red*.10 (1702:580-621)

But in the hands of anticlerical theologians—of whom their opponents said that they "reproach the loyal and conformable clergy" and "call the divine institution of priesthood by the spiteful name of 'priestcraft'"—these serious calls for a holy life among the ministers of the church became a denunciation of the entire "clerical estate" for its "somnolence" and negligence. "Whipping the Protestant clergy on the back of the heathen and popish priests" took the form of declaring that pagan priests had been "cunning" in manipulating "mysteries" for the superstitious rabble, and so by implication were the priests of all the churches, by whom "the Christian world was enslaved and religion forced to give way to destructive superstition."

The clergy had been led astray by the failure to realize that, as Law put it, "our blessed Savior and his apostles are wholly taken up in doctrines that relate to common life," not in theological doctrines as such. It was a recurring orthodox complaint that the moral content of Christianity was being preferred to its doctrinal content, which God had given to be received "without adulteration"; for while "a proposition concerning the will of God," through which "persons [were] to be informed of their duty," was "as properly a doctrine of religion as a proposition concerning the nature of God, or a work of God," a true sense of duty, together with "other truly spiritual and gracious affections," arose from "divine and spiritual doctrines," because "the truth of the gospel" was "the glorious doctrine the word of God contains concerning God, and Jesus Christ, and the way of salvation by him." Eastern Orthodox theology shared the common distinction between dogmatics and ethics, but it did so to emphasize "that the exposition of the divine dogmas should find its appropriate goal" in the doctrine of the sacraments and in ethics. The epigram of Gregory Nazianzus in his epitaph for Basil, that "his speech was like thunder because his life was like lightning," suited very well the Pietists' agitation for a recovery of the right relation between doctrine and life and for a change that their opponents also called "the improvement of the Christian way of life."

Frnck.*Meth*.3.29
(1723:185);Ost.*Corrupt*.1.7
(1700-II:272);
Reim.*Apol*.1.1.2.3
(Alexander 1: 86)

Spen.*Gtts*.6
(1680:319);Frnck.*Meth*.5.2
(1723:268)

Brnt.*Rom*. (1688:65)

Lang.*Antibarb*.
(1709-I:451);Gtz.*Unt*.
(1693:D3r)

Deutsch.*Luth*.1.3.17
(1698:33-34)

Epiph.*Haer*.55.3.8 (*GCS*
31:329)

Lschr.*Unfehl*.14 (1724:101)

See vol.1:69-71
Bert.*Theol.disc*.19.6 (1792-
IV:83)

Pnch.*Dict*. (1736:107)
Mrck.*Comp*.9.17 (Velzen
18:181-82)
Drnd.*Fid.vind*.1.29
(1709:97-98);
Bert.*Theol.disc*.10.19
(1792-II:169-71)

See vol.4:374-85

Brnt.*Art.XXXIX*.pr.
(1700:viii)

Budd.*Mod*.1 (1720:489)

From many sides there came criticisms of traditional catechisms and theological textbooks for their overemphasis on doctrine and their consequent neglect of morals; what was needed was "a theology that not only fills the intellect with knowledge but also completely changes the will." Admittedly it had been "the greatest defect of the Reformation that there are not in it such encouragements to a devout life," and simply quoting the sayings of the Reformation fathers about the need for a "living faith" did not annul that defect. Amid Pietist calls for "reformation of life," expounders of orthodoxy on the Continent also insisted that the only authentic reformation of the church must come, as it had in the sixteenth century, from the reformation of doctrine, since, "as Epiphanius says, the genuine [apostolic] succession [in the church] consists in the continuity of doctrine." Both in England and on the Continent, however, such insistence succeeded only in changing the venue of the litigation, not in adjudicating it.

The reconsideration of the relation between true and false doctrine had as its context the orthodox polemic against false doctrine, which previous generations had seen as a central duty of the church and its theologians. Responding to the "extremely fatuous" objections of the Reformers against the Catholic doctrine of merit, to the Calvinist doctrine of reprobation, and to the Reformed critique of the traditional doctrine of guardian angels, Roman Catholic polemical theology continued to affirm that duty and to carry it out. On the other hand, the willingness of Roman Catholic theology to live with a variety of theories about the gifts of grace also provided some Protestants with a basis for questioning the excessive "rigidity" of Lutherans and Calvinists in their mutual opposition. In its opening sentence, a treatise of 1720 entitled *On Moderation in the Controversies of Theologians* observed that it had been characteristic of "the teachers of heavenly truth" in all generations to indulge in hatred and rage against their opponents. But, as a nearly contemporaneous treatise noted, "one of the causes making controversies obscure is that the same principles which are favorable [to one's case] against some opponents" were damaging to the case

Byl.*Com.phil*.4.12
(1713-II:277)

Lmp.*Betr*.4.5 (1756-II:466)

Hcks.*Ltrs*.pr. (1705:A4r);
Wsly.*Serm*.22.3.18
(Baker1:508); Zinz.*Hom*.31
(Beyreuther 3-I:324)

See vol.4:267-68

Nmnn.*Spen*. (1695:7)

Lang.*Antibarb*.
(1709-II:486-87);
Ost.*Dz.serm*.4 (1722:139)
Span.*Praescript*.6 (Marck
3:1111)

Edw.*Rel.Aff*.3.8 (Miller
2:352-53)

Mck.*Vor*.pr. (1774:A6r)

Mayr.*Red*.15 (1702:835)

Wer.*Diss*.18 (Ryhinerus
1:327)

Wer.*Diss*.18 (Ryhinerus
1:332)

Wer.*Misc*.1.9 (Ryhinerus
2:104)

Neum.*Rch*.pr.
(1751:A3v-A4r);
Mayr.*Mis*.3.1 (1692:28);
Nss.*Dipp*.pr. (1701:6);
Spen.*Gtts*.6 (1680:150)

Spen.*Pi.Des*. (Aland 63)

Frnck.*Id*.28 (Peschke 187)

against others, leading to a relativism about such principles; "the doctrine of the Lord Jesus" was being "obscured even by its public confessors." The polemical zeal characterizing theological controversy during the two centuries since the period of the Reformation was itself turning into a polemical issue in the eighteenth century.

There were still versions of the "domino theory," which cautioned that indifference or the least concession on any point of doctrine could lead to a toleration of the most extreme excesses, but such an admonition that "fundamental truth cannot be ignored except at the cost of salvation" was often accompanied by the acknowledgment that this did not apply to "secondary elements of fundamental doctrine," nor to nonfundamental doctrines. Jonathan Edwards could speak of "zeal" expressed in "vigorous opposition" as "the fervor of this flame [of love]," but he cautioned that it was directed "against things, and not persons," a distinction that was not always easy to observe amid such "zeal." A theologian with "a contentious nature" could easily abuse doctrinal polemics for self-aggrandizement. Even those who urged the necessity of polemics added that the pulpit was no place for scholastic controversies about obscure theological points. It was, a professor of theology declared in his inaugural lecture of 1696, "the task of the theologian not only to confirm true doctrine, but to refute errors that are opposed to the truth, above all if they are dangerous and pernicious"; but he went on to urge that in polemics the theologian must strive to do justice to the opposing position, not to caricature it, because "nothing should be imputed to someone that he does not acknowledge in deed or in word."

The orthodox recognized the need for warning against excessive polemical zeal or unwarranted polemical generalization, which (as the Pietists warned) "often does more harm than good," as when the polemic was characterized by "invectives and personal insinuations" or when the theologian failed "to carry out the polemical assignment in a God-pleasing and practical manner" by relating errors of doctrine to the basic error of a wrong personal relation to God. No less important was the reminder that on some ques-

Wer.*Diss*.18 (Ryhinerus
1:334);Lang.*Antibarb*.
(1709-II:492);Sem.*Erkl*.2
(1777:247)

Sem.*Erud*. (1765-I:161-62)

Sem.*N.T.Int*.pr.5 (1767:12)

Casp.*Beyl*.1 (1724:29)

Sob.13.v.1666 (*DAI* 5:448)

Mayr.*Anti-Spen*.1 (1695:9-10)
See pp. 71-72 below
Casp.*Beyl*.19 (1724:87);
Albrt.*Vind*.1.16 (1695:23)

Spen.*Albrt*.41 (1696:45)

Lang.*Antibarb*. (1709-I:447)

ap.Spen.*Bed*.1.1.9 (Canstein
1:76-77)

Dipp.*Hrt*.3 (1706:48)

See pp. 308-9 below

tions "theologians can dissent and dispute among themselves without damage to the unity of faith." One of the means for "bringing theology back to its limitations" was to put polemical theology into a historical context, by providing a longer perspective on issues of current controversy: "the public dogmatic quarrels were often carried on only by bishops, in order to advance their own authority, without any benefit to Christian people."

On each of these four issues involved in "the crisis of orthodoxy"—church, doctrine, grace, and the Christian life—the advocates of renewal and of a "new Reformation" throughout the churches met with opposition from all directions. On the doctrine of the church, they were guilty of "sectarianism": Avvakum was charged with "leading simple folk astray and tearing them away from the one holy Eastern Orthodox Catholic Church [Vostočnaja Pravoslavno-Kafoličeskaja Cerkov]," Spener with "not believing that the Evangelical Lutheran religion is without error," and Quesnel with denying papal infallibility. On the norms of doctrine, Pietists did not "believe and speak with proper respect" about the creeds and confessions of the church, since they preferred to affirm them only relatively, "insofar as [quatenus]," not absolutely, "because [quia]," they agreed with Scripture. On the doctrine of grace they were, by their insistence on renewal, confusing grace with works, and "justification" with the "mystical union" between God and the believer that was its consequence. And their call for holiness represented a relapse from a "blasphemous [Roman Catholic] paganism" to "a Judaism of false zeal and hypocrisy."

At one level, such extravagant accusations served only to document the correctness of the widespread sense that theological education and ecclesiastical administration had been overemphasizing polemics at the cost of charity. Yet, often despite their intentions, the reform movements did succeed in relativizing the differences of doctrine between the churches by making the differences of doctrine and of life inside each of the churches more important; and by their call for the removal of unnecessarily offensive elements from Christian theology they helped to make the new

See p. 174 below

Hirsch (1960)
2:108-9;148;151

apologetic possible. Above all, the effort to salvage the objective and dogmatic content of the faith by transposing it into a subjective and ethical modality would help to make these movements, quite against their will and intention, a "transitional phenomenon," a "connecting link," and a "bridge" to the far more drastic reinterpretations of the Christian message that were to come.

2   The Objectivity of Transcendent Revelation

Hor.*Ep*.2.40
Knt.*Auf*. (Cassirer 4:169)

"Enlightenment," according to a celebrated definition at the end of the eighteenth century, "is man's exodus from his self-incurred tutelage." The definition went on to explain that a state of tutelage, "the inability to use one's understanding without the guidance of another person," could be characterized as self-incurred "if its cause lies not in any weakness of the understanding, but in indecision and lack of courage to use the mind without the guidance of another." Therefore the motto of the Enlightenment could be said to be: "Dare to know [sapere aude]! Have the courage to use your own understanding." The specifics of such use of the understanding varied significantly from the Enlightenment of one nation or period or school of thought to that of another, so that "no definition of the Enlightenment fits all the men usually assumed to belong to it," much less all the cultures in which it appeared on both sides of the Atlantic during the seventeenth and eighteenth centuries. Within those cultures, moreover, it affected different aspects of life and thought in quite different ways: education and politics, science and the arts, philosophy and religion.

May (1976) xiii

When applied to the Christian tradition and its doctrines, the Enlightenment represented what has been called "the revolution of man's autonomous potentialities over against the heteronomous powers which were no longer convincing," namely, the heteronomous authority of the church and of its dogma and ultimately the objective authority of Scripture and of transcendent revelation itself. When an

Tlch.*Prot.Theol*.2 (Braaten 1967:27)

eighteenth-century theologian defined it as "the first and foremost continuing purpose of the new religion" to bring about "the Enlightenment of each individual Christian, with the goal of an ever more voluntary and more purified worship of God," he was assigning it the task of conferring divine meaning upon the individual's quest for the full achievement of "man's autonomous potentialities." This implied not only that "all truth comes from God," regardless of whether it had come through the channels of nature or of revelation, but that an authentic revelation had to be self-validating, in accordance with "the criteria of a divine revelation." For Roman Catholic theology, this could be taken to mean that believers should not assent to alleged private "revelations that contradict tradition or the 'common sense of the faithful,' " while to Enlightenment rationalism the criteria of "divine wisdom and sound reason" were the only available means "to distinguish the oracles and will of God from the impostures and traditions of men," since "to imagine any external revelation not dependent on the reason of things is to make things give place to words." The program of applying these criteria to the received tradition of Christian creed and catechism raised several issues—all of them summarized in one question of an anonymously published critique of that tradition: "But where can one find a *Christian* catechism . . . that would separate what is *intelligible in religion* from unintelligible *mysteries* and merely *historical* reports?"

Miracle, Mystery, and Authority

Critics as well as defenders of the objectivity of transcendent revelation in the eighteenth century recognized that there were—in the words of a nineteenth-century Russian Orthodox writer who, while not a professional theologian, was simultaneously a critic and a defender—"three powers, three powers alone, able to conquer and to hold the conscience captive forever." These three powers, enumerated in the three questions of the tempter to Jesus, were "miracle, mystery, and authority [čudo, tajna, avtoritet]"; on them the edifice of the church's institution and teaching was founded, and the "greatness"

Sem.*Rel*.44 (Schütz 377-78)

Wlff.*Nat.Gott*.177
(1744-I:191)
Conc.*Rel.riv*.1.5
(1754-I:36-51);Bulg.*Kat*.57
(1940:119-20)

Wlff.*Nat.Gott*.522
(1744-II:183-85)

Amrt.*Rev*.1.1 (1750:3)

Tol.*Myst*.2.2 (1696:41)

Tin.*Chr*.12 (1730:188-89)

Reim.*Apol*.1.1.2.4 (Alexander 1:88)

Matt.4:1-11

Dost.*Br.Kar*.2.5.5 (Černecova 280)

Dost.*Br.Kar.*2.6.1 (Černecova 319)

Mēn.*Did.*1.6 (Blantēs 64)

Fén.*Ep.*11.viii.1689 (Masson 246-48);Gaz.*Prael.*1.1.2.7-8 (1831-I:62-78); Zinz.*Off.Red.* 1.8 (Beyreuther 2-III:125-62)

Mayr.*Red.*3 (1702:294-95)

See vol.4:332-33

Mayr.*Red.*1 (1702:41-45)

Tol.*Myst.*3.4 (1696:150)

Gtti.*Ver.eccl.*1.2 (1763:7-25)

Lw.*Reas.*3 (Moreton 2:107-13)
Pff.*Hist.theol.*2.10 (1724-I:379)
Mrck.*Text.exerc.*8.1 (Velzen 14:52); Swed.*Ver.Chr.*8.501 (1771:320)
Terst.*Abr.*1.5.21-22 (Becher 2:74)
Mēn.*Did.*2.2 (Blantēs 107)

Wlff.*Nat.Gott.*348 (1744-I:342-43)
Wer.*Diss.*5 (Ryhinerus 1:93);Mrck.*Scrip.exerc.*8.19 (Velzen 10:519)

Lw.*Reas.*3 (Moreton 2:108)

Tin.*Chr.*10 (1730:116)
Wer.*Diss.*4.1 (Ryhinerus 1:73)

Strz.*Enchir.*1.2 (1828:14)
Amrt.*Theol.eclec.*4.2.2.2 (1752-1-IV:87-90)
Gaz.*Prael.*1.1.2.8.205 (1831-I:70)

Tin.*Chr.*12 (1730:192)

Lmp.*Betr.*3.16 (1756-II:341)
Wlff.*Nat.Gott.*450 (1744-II:61-62)

of the authority of the Bible lay in its quality as mystery and as miracle. That triad, with some variations, was a familiar one in the Eastern Orthodox tradition of the eighteenth century, but it appeared among contemporary defenders and critics in the West also. Thus a defender of revelation, in a panegyric on "our blessed father Luther," described how the Reformer had adhered strictly to the authority of Scripture as the word of God, from which he had "proved the mysteries of the faith"; elsewhere, in considering whether Luther had a legitimate call from God, he connected the issue of authority with that of miracle. And a critic of the authority of traditional Christianity described how, "when all other shifts prove ineffectual, the partisans of mystery fly to miracles as their last refuge."

Last refuge or perhaps first refuge, miracle became throughout the eighteenth century a central topic for the "partisans" of the various positions and denominations, who sensed that "our age" differed from preceding ages by its incredulity toward miracles. Miracle could be defined as a "transgression of the common order of nature," as "a visible demonstration of divine power," as an event in which "created, subsisting things undergo changes that cannot be a consequence of their own power," or as an "extraordinary work of divine power, striking the senses and calling forth the astonishment of those who see it." Miracles bore an ambiguous relation to the doctrine of creation: it could be argued that they were simply a necessary corollary of belief in the creation and the Creator, or that it was wrong to suppose that the Creator "broke into the rule of his own conduct," something that, in any case, he did only rarely. Their relation to truth and falsehood was not ambiguous in the same way, for a miracle could not be the confirmation of a falsehood if it came from God. Yet that only compounded the ambiguity, for it could mean that "if miracles can be performed by evil as well as by good beings, the worst religion may have the most miracles, as needing them most." Denying their possibility altogether amounted to disobediently denying the existence of God, but they had to be related

Tol.*Myst*.3.4 (1696:152)
Wer.*Diss*.4.1 (Ryhinerus
1:72-73)
Hdly.*Flt.* (1702:3);
Mrck.*Comp*.20.11 (Velzen
18:392); Zinz.*Zst*.34
(Beyreuther 3-II:276-86);
Conc.*Rel.riv*.2.1.3
(1754-I:77-91)
Mrck.*Exeg.exerc*.6.4;6.8
(Velzen 9:95-98;108)

Mēn.*Did*.2.6 (Blantēs 154)
Gaz.*Prael*.1.1.3.3
(1831-I:106-25)
Spen.*Mess.* (1701:61-67)

Bert.*Theol.disc*.29.6
(1792-VI:90)

Arb.*Des.myst*.2.17 (1764:312)
Frnck.*Pass.Marc*.11
(1724:310);Lmp.*Betr*.1.18
(1756-I:407-8); Mmchi.
Orig.ant.2.14.4 (1749-I:285)
Wer.*Diss*.4.3 (Ryhinerus
1:88)

Wet.*N.T.* (1756:159)

Sem.*Frag*.47 (1780:344)
Reim.*Apol*.2.2.2.6 (Alexander
2:157);Sem.*Rel*.29 (Schütz
244)
1 Cor. 1:22

Gib.*Dec*.15 (Bury 2:70)
Gtti.*Ver.rel*.5.31.1
(1730-I:421-22)
Mēn.*Did*.1.2 (Blantēs 15)
Bec.*Lóp.Nuev.Ab.*
(1739:1);Edw.*Rel.Aff*.2
(Miller 2:148-49);
Frnck.*Pass.Marc*.10
(1724:289-91)
Beng.*Gnom*.John 2:11
(Steudel 330);Ost.*Arg.ref*.John
2 (1720-II:120-21)
Beng.*Gnom*.Matt.8:32
(Steudel 62-63); Ost.*Arg.ref.*
Matt.21:1-22 (1720-II:33)
Baum.*Pred*.3.8 (Kirchner
3:621)
Deutsch.*Luth*.2.3.2
(1698:92-93)
Mēn.*Did*.5.1 (Blantēs 226)
Bert.*Diss.hist.*
(1753-I:249-50);
Mos.*Vind.disc*.3.1.5
(1722:339-41)
Beng.*Gnom*.1 Cor. 15:12
(Steudel 675-76)
Baum.*Pred*.2.11;2.9
(Kirchner 2:370;309)
Baum.*Pred*.2.8 (Kirchner
2:278-79)

to their "special and important purpose," apart from which they were unbelievable.

Functionally, the most serviceable definition of "what the Scriptures and we call miracle" was: "the same works, or works of the same nature, with those done by Moses and Christ." That included such miracles as the crossing of the Red Sea by Moses, but in the most fundamental sense it meant that the incarnation of the Logos and the salvation wrought by him were the "two great and extraordinary miracles." Christ had performed wonders, which, as evidence that he was the promised Messiah, were "neither made up by the evangelists nor performed by natural or magical power"; the three hours of darkness on Good Friday, reported in all three synoptic Gospels, could not be explained away naturalistically as an eclipse. The events of New Testament history were harder to believe without the miracle stories than with them, but with the acceptance of the "total doctrine [of Christ] in all its parts" those stories also made sense.

In response to such defenses, critics saw miracles as a concession to the contemporaries of Jesus who, whether they believed the miracles to be genuine or not, sought a "sign"; the pagan writers of the time had been totally silent about the darkness on Good Friday (although orthodox apologists claimed to find evidence in them). Everyone recognized that the miracles had evoked "envy" among those contemporaries, and that many of those who had been following the miracle worker forsook him when he was crucified. The earliest miracles, such as the changing of water into wine, received particular attention, while the destructive miracles, such as the cursing of the fig tree, created particular difficulties. Above all, it was necessary to defend against critics the "truthfulness" of "the miracle of the supernatural conception" and birth of Christ, in which Mary was both Virgin and Mother of God, and of his resurrection, which, because of "the connection between the resurrection of Christ and the resurrection of the dead," had been, in the primitive church, a special component of the total "miracle of the redemption."

Span.*Ev.vind*.1.45 (Marck 3:182-87)

Lang.*Paul*.1.1.2 (1718:16)
Brnt.*Rom*. (1688:56-57)
Ost.*Arg.ref*.1 Cor.12 (1720-II:217-18)
Mid.*Mir*.4 (1749:119)
Baum.*Pred*.3.1 (Kirchner 3:16-17)
Brnt.*Art.XXXIX*.16 (1700:141)
Zinz.*Off.Red*.21 (Beyreuther 2-IV:225-32)
Mrck.*Scrip.exerc*.10.16 (Velzen10:620); Reim.*Apol*.1.5.1.3 (Alexander 1:688)
Mayr.*Red*.14 (1702:771);
Drnd.*Fid.vind*.3.53 (1709:508-11)

Amrt.*Rev*.1.22 (1750:134-35)
Grig.*Mont.Vr.dév*.19 (Gendrot 496-97);
Bert.*Theol.disc*.1.6;33.8 (1791-I:56;VII:125-26)
Gaz.*Prael*.1.2.3.7.3.321 (1831-I:116)
Sem.*Rel*.29 (Schütz 238-39)
Span.*H.e*.2.8 (Marck 1:661-62)
Edw.*Rel.Aff*.3.5 (Miller 2:309)
Mid.*Ltr.Rom*. (1729:62)
Tol.*Amyn*. (1699:42-43)
Mid.*Mir*.4 (1749:147);
Tin.*Chr*.8 (1730:90)
Socr.*H.e*.1.12 (Hussey 1:90-92)
Bulg.*Kat*.73 (1940:184)
See vol.1:137

Bert.*Diss.hist*. (1753-III:192)
Nss.*Dipp*.2 (1701:33)
Walt.*Mir*.3 (1756:157)

Walt.*Mir*.1 (1756:35)

Hdly.*Flt*. (1702:20)

Scriv.*Seel*.2.1 (Stier 3:317);
Frnck.*Pred*.Adv.2 (1699:14)
Hrn.*H.e*.3.1.1 (Leydecker 1:300)
Schpf.*Luth*.10.4-5 (1717:34-35);Lschr.*Dr.Pred*.1 (1738:18,27)
ap.Mid.*Mir*.int. (1749:xlii)
Gib.*Dec*.15 (Bury 2:29-30)
Mmchi.*Orig.ant*.2.17.3 (1749:409-13); Gaz.*Prael*.1.1.3.4.288;294 (1831-I:126-27); Gtti.*Ver.eccl*.1.2.4.27 (1763:15)

Yet the place of miracles in the primitive church provoked various difficulties of its own. If miracles like the conversion of Paul proved the inspiration of the apostolic writers by the Holy Spirit, did the cessation of miracles like speaking in tongues prove that such miracles were "no longer necessary" to guarantee the Spirit's presence, as well as that "no man is any more capable of [the] sin" against the Holy Spirit spoken of in the Gospels? Such questions reached over not only to the interpretation of the miracles reported in the Old Testament, but most of all to the status of alleged postbiblical miracles. While being careful not to maintain that miracles were an attestation for the validity of supposed private revelations, apologists argued that the histories of all centuries were filled with miracles, proving the superiority of Roman Catholic to Protestant doctrine. Depreciators dismissed such postbiblical miracles, even from the second century, as "clever deceptions" and "lying miracles of the papists," which had been "evidently forged or copied after the originals of paganism," perhaps "invented by heathens and Jews." They likewise dismissed as "trifling" or as "impudent forgeries" the miracles attributed by the orthodox tradition to such fourth-century figures as Spyridon or attributed by Athanasius, the premier defender of the Nicene doctrine of the Trinity, to the pioneer of monasticism in his *Life of Antony*. Supporters defended Athanasius not only for his loyalty to the see of Rome and for his integrity, but also for his *Life of Antony*; yet they distinguished between biblical miracles, which were "matters of faith," and these reports "by the primitive fathers and church historians," which had to be weighed carefully for their credibility and which did not, in any event, discredit the "long uninterrupted series of great miracles" in the Bible. Such distinctions, which did not easily comport with Protestant descriptions of "daily" miracles especially in the Reformation or in later vindications of the Protestant cause, could also have the opposite of their intended effect. Some Protestants were led to conclude that the same criteria which authenticated New Testament miracles also supported, as Roman Catholics contended, the "implicit belief that the gift of miraculous powers was continued in the church during the first four or five centuries of Christianity," and they came to accept, at least for a time, "most of the leading doctrines of popery."

Gib.*Aut*.3 (Saunders 82-83)

More often, the conclusion led in an opposite direction: the criteria used to discredit "the lying miracles of the papists" could not leave untouched "the history of our Savior's doctrine and miracles" as "the genuine ground on which Christianity rests" and "the clearest evidence that God could give." Examination of such evidence in the New Testament showed that the miracles were said to have produced faith and yet that Jesus did not perform them except in the presence of those who believed. "To what purpose served all those miracles," then, "if the doctrines of Christ were incomprehensible or [if] we were obliged to believe revealed nonsense?" asked those who, as their opponents said, refused to accept any miracle that was contrary to reason. Miracles had served as "letters of credit" intended to prove "that we ought to receive such doctrines both as true and good which we could not know to be true and good without such miracles," but in this new era it had become necessary to "demonstrate the truth of the miracles themselves against obstinate unbelievers." A treatise that began by arguing for the truth of Christian doctrine on the grounds that "there are greater and more miracles on one side than the other" went on to reverse the argument: "Since I believe Jesus Christ was the Son of God . . . because he taught so excellent a doctrine and because he was so perfectly good and holy himself, I cannot part with this belief only on the score of miracles." Negatively, this could also lead defenders of miracle to attack their opponents for preferring "a miraculous object to a saving object," and its satirical detractors to define "a right orthodox divine" as one to whom "nothing but the marvelous and the improbable" would appeal. Positively, it meant that since such miracles did not establish faith but rather were established by faith, traditional preachers described "the faith of Christians" as "more than all the miracles" and paraphrased Augustine's apologetic rejoinder, that "this one grand miracle suffices for us, that the whole world has believed without any mira-

Edw.*Rel.Aff*.3.5 (Miller 2:309)

Mid.*Mir*.int. (1749:xciv)
Brnt.*Art.XXXIX*.16 (1700:140-41)
Tol.*Myst*.2.3 (1696:47)
Ost.*Cat*. (1747:17,23);
Ost.*Arg.ref*.John 2;Matt.17 (1720-II:121;27)
Reim.*Apol*.2.2.1.5 (Alexander 2:133-35);Frnck.*Pred*.Trin.19 (1699:16)

Tol.*Myst*.2.3 (1696:49)

Mos.*Tol*.10 (1722:51-52)
Wer.*Diss*.4.1 (Ryhinerus 1:71)

Lw.*Reas*.3 (Moreton 2:107);
Stod.*Conv*.15 (1719:85)
Mrck.*Text.exerc*.8.1 (Velzen 14:52)
Bert.*Diss.hist*. (1753-I:227-28)

Hdly.*Flt*. (1702:6)

Hdly.*Flt*. (1702:20);
Zinz.*Sieb*.5 (Beyreuther 2-I:43)
Wer.*Diss*.10.3 (Ryhinerus1:179);Tor.*Car*.1.3 (1779-I:164)

Mid.*Wat*. (1731:15)
Zinz.*Lond.Pred*.2.6 (Beyreuther 5-I:200);
Zinz.*Rel*.5 (Beyreuther 6-I:78-79)
Neum.*Fünf*.1 (1726-I:172);
Wer.*Diss*.4.1 (Ryhinerus 1:74)
Mid.*Mir*.4 (1749:137)

Aug.*Civ*.22.5 (*CCSL* 48:812)

Gth.*Fst*.1.766 (Trunz 31)

Pff.*Hist.theol*.3.8
(1724-II:293-95)

Tol.*Myst*.3.2 (1696:75)

Tol.*Pan*.2.1 (1720:49)

Tin.*Chr*.11 (1730:170)
Tin.*Chr*.8 (1730:85);
Reim.*Apol*. 1.1.5.4
(Alexander 1:151-52)
Span.*H.e*.3.4 (Marck 1:721)

Conc.*Theol.chr*.1.3.2.11
(1772-III:57-61)
Alph.Lig.*Theol.mor*.3.1.1
(Gaudé 1:370);Mrkrd.*Off*.7
(1722:26-28)
Cmrda.*Const.ap*.2.13
(1732:147)
Amrt.*Theol.eclec*.12.9.51
(1752-3-I:433)
Poir.*Oec.div*.3.10
(1705-I:720);
Ost.*Arg.ref*.Matt.12:1-21
(1720-II:17); Krb.*Diar*.
(1700:199-200)
Jcksn.*Rem*. (1731:14-15);
Gaz.*Prael*.2.2.102
(1831-II:30);Aug.*Doctr.christ*.
2.20.30 (*CCSL* 32:54)
Span.*H.e*.7.3 (Marck
1:1181-82);Span.*Ev.vind*.1.42
(Marck 3:166-71)

Tin.*Chr*.11 (1730:168)

Mos.*Tol*.28 (1722:152)
Tin.*Chr*.8 (1730:99);
Gib.*Dec*.21 (Bury 2:350)

cles." Once again, it was a man of letters rather than a professional theologian who gave the most effective epigrammatic formulation to this insight that miracle came from faith, not faith from miracle: "The dearest child of faith is miracle."

Mystery did not have any easier a time of it than miracle. A century on whose eve Toland's book bearing the title *Christianity Not Mysterious* became an international and interdenominational cause célèbre would repeatedly turn to the definition and the resolution of mystery as it dealt with the bearing of Enlightenment on Christian faith and doctrine. "Mystery" was not merely a fancy name for ignorance: "Nothing can be said to be a mystery because we have not an adequate idea of it, or a distinctive view of all its properties at once; for then everything would be a mystery." Elsewhere its author made clear that he was opposing a use of mystery that led to "tyranny and superstition," since "mysteries to amuse the enthusiasts" and "ceremonies to bewitch the vulgar" were the "two ways which never fail to make superstition prevail." Such attacks on "superstition" were directed primarily against Roman Catholicism and Eastern Orthodoxy, often in the name of the "great simplicity" of early Christian ceremonies. Yet as far as they went, the Roman Catholic or Eastern Orthodox definitions of "superstitious magic" as "false religion or unsound worship, whether addressed to the true God or to a false god" even if this involved authentic Christian ceremonies or the use of the Bible, would have been acceptable, perhaps with the addition that it referred to "all ceremonies and all external actions that do not lead someone to internal actions," as these ceremonies had arisen in "all the very best systems of human laws among the Gentiles," such as the thought of Plato and Cicero, and among Christians most frequently in such areas as eucharistic practice and the cult of the saints. Every denomination recognized the danger of superstition by "affirming that superstition is crept into all other sects," although in "the celebrated controversy whether atheism is preferable to superstition" radicals regarded the latter as a greater danger whereas church theologians of varying positions

Strz.*Enchir.*2.1
(1828:48);Wer.*Misc.*14.2
(Ryhinerus 2:244);
Zinz.*Soc.*4;13 (Beyreuther
1-I:40;133)

Tol.*Myst.*3.3 (1696:91)

Tol.*Myst.*3.1 (1696:72-73)
Bulg.*Kat.*int. (1940:11);
Sth.*Animad.*1 (1693:6)
Mrck.*Exeg.exerc.*10 (Velzen
9:177-80)

Lw.*Reas.*3 (Moreton 2:103-4)

Mēn.*Did.*5.3 (Blantēs 241);
Bec.*Lóp.Sab.prod.*1 (1752:7)

Wer.*Diss.*18 (Ryhinerus
1:337)
Sth.*Animad.*1 (1693:2);
Zinz.*Lond.Pred.*5.5
(Beyreuther 5-II:177)

Reim.*Apol.*1.1.3.10
(Alexander1:115)

Lschr.*Pens.* (1724:16)

Mayr.*Red.*5 (1702:404)

Wer.*Diss.*10.3 (Ryhinerus
1:177)

Nss.*Dipp.*1 (1701:19-20)

Tin.*Chr.*12 (1730:222)
Wer.*Diss.*18 (Ryhinerus
1:337); Conc.*Rel.riv.*3.4-6
(1754-I:372-84)
Frnck.*Pass.Marc.*1 (1724:13)

perceived the former as the more serious threat, while rejecting both.

Although radical scholars cited New Testament usage to validate this understanding of mystery as "a thing intelligible of itself, but so veiled by others that it could not be known without special revelation," word study by less iconoclastic scholars continued to support the traditional distinction between "hidden" and "revealed" and the traditional definition of mystery as "that which is by the nature of things incomprehensible in creation and providence." By definition, a "work of the divine wisdom and power" was not only "perfect" but "transcendent." And if every such work was "to be judged by our ordinary notions and faculties," it was "useless" to try to persuade anyone to accept "the principal mysteries of the faith" as "a truth revealed by God, above the power of natural reason to find out or comprehend." Those who defended the new reliance on reason against the charge that it would dispel all mystery from religion were concerned to identify the "innumerable matters that cannot in any way be counted among the mysteries but that nevertheless make revelation seem offensive." In their consideration of which such matters should truly be counted as mysteries, eighteenth-century church theologians were responding to a proposed distinction between "internal, real religion," which concerned itself with morals, and "external" religion, which was said to be "without reality"—a distinction that seemed to them to be dismissing as unreal all "the mysterious truths and institutions of Christ."

For them, to be a theologian meant above all to "teach the mysteries in their transcendence." That implied the obligation to recognize that "this is a mystery," and then "to know it," which was not the same as trying to understand it in such a way as to dispel "the mystery of the Lord in his believers." In carrying out this obligation, they reviewed all the chief Christian doctrines, which, as their opponents were aware, were put forth by the church as "the principal mysteries of the faith." The problem of evil was to be regarded as a "mystery," the resurrection of

Strz.*Enchir*.2.4 (1828:67)

Scriv.*Seel*.3.8 (Stier 5:57)

Mēn.*Did*.5.3 (Blantēs 241); Zinz.*Off.Red*.1.2 (Beyreuther 2-III:34-55); Terst.*Abr*.2.1.17 (Becher 2:162-63) Lw.*Ser.Cl*.17 (Moreton 4:174); Terst.*Abr*.2.6.5 (Becher 2:207); Brnt.*Art.XXXIX*.2 (1700:55) Eph.5:32 See vol.3:212; vol.4:257,295,308 Ces.*V.Ges.Cr*.1 (1830:8); Hno.*Theol*.8.8.2.2 (1785-VIII:488)

Beng.*Gnom*.Eph.5:32 (Steudel 774); Mrck.*Comp*.29.35 (Velzen18:576) Zinz.*Zst*.26 (Beyreuther 3-II:207);Zinz.*Gem*.5 (Beyreuther 4-I:106); Zinz.*Aug.Conf*.18;20 (Beyreuther 6-II:195;353) Swed.*Cael*.40.366 (1890:229)

Hno.*Theol*.3.2.3.6 (1785-III:393-94) Nss.*Dipp*.2 (1701:24); Zinz.*Rel*.1 (Beyreuther 6-I:8-9); Ors.*Ist*.21.71 (1747-IX:332); Qnl.*Ex.piét*. 1.4 (1693:15) Sherl.*Vind*.pr. (1690:A2r) Pff.*Hist.theol*.2.10 (1724-I:305) See vol.4:187-88;323

Sem.*Rel*.26 (Schütz 220-22)

Bulg.*Kat*.72 (1940:182) Bert.*Theol.disc*.7.4 (1792-II:15-17) Mēn.*Did*.2.1 (Blantēs 93) John 1:49

Dipp.*Orth*.4 (1699:51); Nss. *Dipp*.2 (1701:24-25); Zinz. *Zst*.44 (Beyreuther 3-II:351)

ap.Naud.*Kouak*.7 (1699:28) Swed.*Ver.Chr*.3.177;11.634 (1771:134;386) Tin.*Chr*.12 (1730:206) Jeff.*Ep*.27.ii.1821 (Adams 402-3);Reim.*Apol*.int.6 (Alexander1:48) Brnt.*Art.XXXIX*.8 (1700:106) Zinz.*Sieb*.1 (Beyreuther 2-I:5-7);Zinz.*Gem*.3 (Beyreuther 4-I:71-75) Zinz.*Gem*.27 (Beyreuther 4-I:368-80);Zinz.*Zst*.13 (Beyreuther 3-II:90) Beng.*Brüd*.1.1.12 (1751:57-73); Mos.*Vind.disc*. 1.5.7 (1722:105-6)

the body as an "unfathomable mystery," and the doctrine of predestination as a "heavenly mystery." The "economy of the incarnation" of the Son of God was a great mystery, and there were other mysterious elements in the Gospels; but it was above all to "the mystery of Christ upon the cross" and to Christ's mysterious cry of dereliction that faith turned. Although the use of "mystery" in a New Testament passage about matrimony continued to provide exegetical warrant for including it among the seven sacraments of the church, more precise exegesis showed that "not human matrimony but the very union of Christ and the church is what is being called a mystery"; nevertheless there were some Protestants who now found in matrimony itself "a first principle" and "the greatest mystery," and in this sense a sacrament, and some who taught that it would continue in heaven.

Of all the mysteries of the faith, the dogma of "the Triunity in God" was, by ecumenical consent, the most fundamental and the most "sublime mystery of the Lord," but now, thanks to "atheists and heretics," it had become instead a "vast battlefield." Reversing the usual Reformation polarity, these critics charged that the dogma of the Trinity was established by tradition and could not be demonstrated from Scripture, while Roman Catholic and Eastern Orthodox theologians still sought to prove it from Scripture, sometimes from Scripture alone, beginning with "the first confession of orthodoxy," the words of Nathanael, "Rabbi, you are the Son of God!" Theologians who disagreed about almost everything else joined in warning against the attempt to make the Trinity acceptable to reason; this led some to reject it as "a mystery of metaphysics" that had "perverted the entire Christian church," one of those "orthodox paradoxes" that were in fact "incomprehensible," and others who still accepted it to criticize making "many explanations of a mystery hard to be understood . . . indispensably necessary to salvation." In an effort to give meaning to the "unfathomable" Trinity, Zinzendorf described the Holy Spirit as "Mother" alongside the Father and the Son, but this was rejected as a "presumptuous" revival of ancient heresy. An attempt

Sherl.*Vind*.4 (1690:49)

Sth.*Animad*.8 (1693:239)
Sth.*Animad*.3 (1693:68-89)

Tin.*Chr*.10 (1730:125)

Tol.*Myst*.3.2 (1696:81)

Lschr.*Pens*. (1724:29-30)

Lschr.*Dr.Pred*.1;3 (1733:6;61)

Sem.*Erkl*.2 (1777:209)

Sem.*Erkl*.2 (1777:191)
Sem.*Erkl*.1.3 (1777:73)

See vol.4:110;262
Bnrt.*Art.XXXIX*.int.
(1700:);Mrck.*Exeg.exerc*.44.1
(Velzen 9:703) Sherl.*Def*.2
(1675:150); Wer.*Diss*.15
(Ryhinerus1:259)
Hdly.*Flt*. (1702:11)
Brnt.*Art.XXXIX*.19
(1700:176-77)

Wer.*Diss*.4.1 (Ryhinerus
1:71)

Reim.*Apol*.2.1.2.3 (Alexander
2:43-44)

Ost.*Arg.ref*.pr. (1720:A3r)

by one Anglican divine to provide a "vindication" of the dogma by describing the "three divine persons" as so "mutually conscious to each other" that they were "truly and properly numerically one" led a champion of orthodox trinitarianism to level charges of tritheism against "this author's novel, heterodox notions about the Trinity," on the grounds that it was identity of essence that made the Trinity one. His position was in turn denounced by a far more radical opponent, who found it "shocking" to suppose "that the dictates of infinite wisdom do not carry their own evidence with them"; for, in the words of another contemporary, "neither God himself nor any of his attributes are so mysterious to us for want of an adequate idea." On the Continent, another champion of orthodox trinitarianism, rejecting the slander that the doctrine of the Trinity was "a frivolous question," devoted every Sunday sermon of the church year 1732 to a statement of the biblical case for that doctrine, while a historical scholar, citing the uncertain course that the development of the doctrine had taken in the patristic period, distinguished between a basic "faith in the Trinity shared by all Christians, even those who are not very sophisticated," and the questions that theological scholars were obliged to raise about it.

Both the problem of miracle and the question of mystery could be interpreted as functions or implications of the issue of authority, which could thus become, yet once more, "the fundamental article upon which . . . our church [and every other church] depends" and therefore the key to every other doctrine. Although some regarded miracles as a confirmation of authority, at least in biblical times if not in the present life of the church, a theologian who accepted both the inerrancy of the Bible and the credibility of miracles could call it "begging the question" to prove miracles by Scripture or Scripture by miracles. Theologians who sought to eliminate any unnecessary "mystery of faith" invoked the authority of the New Testament in doing so, and those who were concerned about the rise of superstition in the early church blamed it on a neglect of scriptural authority; to others, the authority of Scripture, of the fathers, and of papal bulls together proved the reality

1 Sam.28:7-25; Aug.*Civ.*
18.18 (*CCSL* 48:608);
Bnl.*Anim.cr.* 15;25;35
(1751:15;22;40)

Beng.*Gnom.*John 9:25
(Steudel 376)
Nmnn.*Spen.* (1695:55)

Frnck.*Mand.Scrip.*10
(1706:114)

See vol.4:290
Wlch.*Pol.*3.2.1.2
(1752:605);Gtti.*Coll.*3.9.1
(1727:589);Strz.*Enchir.*1
(1828:1-44)
CTrid.24.*Decr.*4
(Alberigo-Jedin 763)
Alph.Lig.*Theol.mor.*1.3.1.269
(Gaudé 1:548-49)
Grig.Mont.*Am.sag.*8.97
(Gendrot 144)
1 Cor.2:7

Tnnt.*Dang.* (1742)

Nss.*Dipp.*1 (1701:23)

Ost.*Arg.ref.*pr. (1720:A1r)

Ost.*Cat.* (1747:21-25)

Ost.*Cat.* (1747:27)

Byl.*Com.phil.*2.10
(1713-I:488)
Mrck.*Comp.*2.45 (Velzen
18:57)

Tol.*Myst.*int. (1696:5)

Tin.*Chr.*12 (1730:186)

Sem.*Erkl.*1.3 (1777:65)

See vol.4:209-10,
263-67,275-76
Drnd.*Fid.vind.*4.13
(1709:570-76);Sem.*Erud.*
(1765-I:6-7)

Strz.*Enchir.*1.pr. (1828:3-5)
Wlch.*Pol.*3.2.1.20
(1752:627-28)
Allat.*Purg.*41;47
(1655:268-70;294-99)
Span.*H.e.*int.2-3 (Marck
1:489-90); Mos.*Vind.disc.*
3.2.3;3.2.9 (1722:346;365)
Tol.*Amyn.* (1699:59-60)

of the supernatural order. The Pietist movement was seen as having made the rejection of all "false authority" and "the elimination of human authority" one of its principal goals, because it attacked as "miserable" those interpreters "who in determining the meaning of Scripture depend solely or even primarily on authority" rather than on experience.

Although Protestant theologians saw the authority of the church as a settled issue for Roman Catholics, the issue of authority had in fact become a burning one in every denomination. The decrees of the Council of Trent had declared the conscious neglect of the task of preaching to be a mortal sin, and there was desperate need for "preachers in this time who can say with Saint Paul: 'We are speaking the wisdom of God.' " The emphasis on experience within Protestantism raised again the perennial inquiry into "the dangers of an unconverted ministry" and into the capacity of an unbelieving preacher to speak a genuine word of God, and Protestant liturgical reform made the use and authority of Scripture so vital a matter that its reliability as the word of God was "the principle on which our faith is founded." According to some observers, acceptance of the authority of Scripture provided no basis for discriminating between orthodox and heretical teachers, since, despite appeals to "the analogy of faith," both conformed their interpretations of Scripture, "right or wrong, to the bulky systems and formularies of their several communions"; and the discussion of authority quickly led to an argument in a circle. Therefore questions of authority and biblical inspiration were "not to be counted among the fundamental articles of the Christian faith."

That applied above all to the questions about the relation of Scripture and church that had arisen during the Reformation debates over the canon. Eastern Orthodox theologians opened a catechism with a list of the canon; despite Protestant objections to it, Roman Catholics defended the list adopted at Trent. Since everyone had to rely principally on the testimony of such early Christian authors as Eusebius and Jerome, the continuing need "to have the canon of Scripture set in its due light" manifested itself in the

Brnt.*Art.XXXIX*.6 (1700:81)
Gaz.*Prael*.2.2.2.63
(1831-I:161)
See vol.4:263-64

Aug.*Ep.fund*.5 (*CSEL* 25:197)
See vol.1:303

See vol.4:126

Ang.Sil.*CTrid*.15
(1675:P10v-Q4v)
Pff.*Hist.theol*.2.10
(1724-I:290)

Mrck.*Comp*.2.7 (Velzen 18:24)

Bert.*Theol.disc*.20.19
(1792-IV:177)

Luke 22:32;Matt.16:18
Gtti.*Ver.eccl*.1.11.1.3
(1763:107)
Qnl.*Clém.IX*.pr. (1700:viii);
Qnl.*Déf.égl.Rom*.1.5
(1697:96); Budd.*Mod*.20
(1720:556-57)

Amrt.*Theol.eclec*.4.2.1.6
(1752-1-IV:55); Ors.*Ist*.11.4;
11.29 (1747-V:5;42)

Brnt.*Art.XXXIX*.19
(1700:176)

Amrt.*Theol.eclec*.4.2.1.4
(1752-1-IV:25-26)

Amrt.*Theol.eclec*.4.2.1.4
(1752-1-IV:39-42); Drnd.
Diss.1.7.10 (1703:50)

tension between a Protestant theologian's appeal to "an unquestioned and undisputed tradition" supporting the canon and his declaration that "the authority of those books is not derived from any judgment that the church made concerning them." One of the "most celebrated" themes of the Reformation debates, enunciated in Augustine's formula, "I should not believe the gospel except as moved by the authority of the catholic church," which had been taken to mean at least that the church had the authority to decide what belonged in the canon and what did not, now helped Roman Catholics to substantiate the thesis that "the Roman Catholic Church is the mother and teacher of other [churches]," while Protestants continued to argue that the formula did not speak of "authority to command" but only of an "objective authority of the church as it believes the Scriptures." It was also necessary for Roman Catholic theology to make clear that such a collection as Gratian's compilation of canon law "does not have any authority" beyond that of its sources.

The prayer and promise of Christ had guaranteed infallibility to Peter and his successors. But defenders of the authority of the Roman Catholic Church, responding to the charge that they were illegitimately extending it from matters of faith to matters of fact, devised a category of "questions of doctrinal fact" (e.g., whether Arius had taught the heresies attributed to him), on which the church and the pope could claim infallibility when speaking "ex cathedra." That term did not mean "an infallibility in general," as their Protestant critics called it, but contained the stipulation that "in defining articles pertaining to faith and morals" the pope was to speak only "after demonstrating a moral diligence in determining the sense of Scripture and of the uniform tradition of the churches" and hence that he could not, at his first dinner after being elected, take it upon himself "to settle at table all the theological controversies" that had been agitating scholars for years. Consequently a pope who would define a doctrine "in contradiction to the manifest tradition and evident sense of the church" would not be speaking "ex cathedra"; nor had Pope Honorius I been speaking with that authority.

Baum.*Pred*.1.12
(Kirchner 1:400;407)
Amrt.*Rev*.1.2 (1750:6);
Aug.*Cat.rud*.6.10 (*CCSL*
46:130-31)

Dör.*Pet*.3 (1718:13)

Bas.*Hex*.10 (*SC* 26:382)
Frnck.*Pred*.Epiph.2
(1699:23-24)
Beng.*Gnom*.John 10:35
(Steudel 381)
John 10:35
Ost.*Arg.ref*.pr. (1720:A3r)
Grig.Mont.*Am.sag*.12
(Gendrot 166-73)
1 Tim.1:15
Lmp.*Ghm*.14 (1719-II:967)
1 Cor.7:25
Neum.*Marp*.2.4 (1727:100)
Wlff.*Nat.Gott*.249
(1744-I:252)
Deutsch.*Luth*.1.4.2
(1698:35);Spen.*Bed*.1.1.57
(Canstein 1:303-4)
Mrck.*Comp*.2.23 (Velzen
18:38); Zinz.*Off.Red*.1.8
(Beyreuther 2-III:129)
Mrchn.*Sacr.Bib*.1.5 (1874:94)
Caj.*Mos*.Gen.2:21-22
(1539:xxiv)
Drnd.*Fid.vind*.2.3
(1709:212-14)

Sem.*Erkl*.3 (1777:317)
Sem.*V.T.Int*.1.4.50
(1773:188)
Sem.*Erkl*.1.3 (1777:42)

Nss.*Dipp*.1 (1701:19)

Sem.*Erkl*.1.5 (1777:97)
Nss.*Dipp*.1 (1701:11)

Deutsch.*Luth*.1.2.6 (1698:14)

Amrt.*Theol.eclec*.4.2.1.8
(1752-1-IV:67-68)

See vol.4:343-47

Opposing Roman Catholic ascription of authority to "meager" postbiblical traditions and the claims of new revelation among some Protestants and Roman Catholics, champions of scriptural authority went on affirming that the Holy Spirit had not kept the truth secret for centuries but had spoken decisively by inspiring Scripture.

To imply that there could be an idle word or syllable in Scripture was, as they quoted Basil of Caesarea, a blasphemy, for it was "the firmest of axioms" that not even the slightest part of Scripture could be broken: "revelation" implied "inspiration." The Gospels were "oracles of divine wisdom," and the doctrine of the apostles, being "divine and 'worthy of full acceptance,' " was inspired also when an apostle employed such a formula as "I have no command of the Lord, but I give my opinion." Not only the great "truths" of Scripture but its "figures of speech" or its historical notices had to be explained in such a way as to avoid the appearance that the Bible could ever contradict itself. The inerrancy that belonged to Christ by virtue of his person was communicated also to the sacred writers of the Bible, and a Franciscan could accuse the Dominican Cajetan of "heresy" for denying that Eve had literally been created from Adam's rib. Sometimes this assertion that the Bible was without contradiction meant only that "the primary sources of our religion have a divine origin insofar as they communicate the Christian truths to us," but not that all the parts of Scripture "have equal authority from the divine Source." Since "everyone knows" that Luther did not teach verbal inspiration despite his having been converted through reading Scripture, it was claimed that such "free criticism" was more in keeping with his spirit than was the orthodoxy of his epigones, who went on identifying "Scripture" and "word of God" and defending themselves against the charge of teaching "a mere theology of the letter." Some of their Roman Catholic opponents were careful to specify that the divine initiative in inspiration extended to the "content" but not to the "words and language," and hence they did not teach a verbal inspiration in the sense in which it was posited by Lutheran and Reformed orthodoxy, which declared that in inspiring a biblical writer "the Spirit of God may reveal . . . and dictate to him . . . . mysteries that otherwise would be above the reach of his reason." Orthodoxy of the Eastern variety also affirmed the inspiration (if not quite the verbal inspiration) of Scripture, but insisted that the several meanings of this inspired Scripture could be decided only by "the catholic church," not from the bare text. And the standard proof text for the doctrine of inspiration could even be read by radical Protestants as an exclusionary principle instead: "Does not St. Paul suppose no Scripture to be divinely inspired but what is profitable?"

The concrete interpretation of Scripture could therefore turn out to produce greater difficulty than the abstract doctrine of inspiration. A dogmatics that paid inadequate attention to the primacy of biblical exegesis "rests on a slippery foundation," Francke warned. The "undeniable" principle that not only a scholar but anyone could, also without the original languages, draw out of Scripture everything necessary for salvation had to be accompanied by the caution that unless such a reader practiced "discernment," the result could be "dangerous deception." It would soon become evident that various biblical interpretations clashed with one another, and such methodological rules as looking for "the intention of the author" or "not being guided by your prejudiced opinion, but reading in a nonpartisan way" flew in the face of the obvious fact that not a "nonpartisan" exegesis but the "systems and formularies of their several communions" determined how confessional exegetes interpreted Scripture. Such confessional interpretations often tore words or passages out of context. If more than one passage was usually needed "to raise a theory or found a doctrine," it seemed "axiomatic" that an obscure text should, through the use of "analogy, text, context, and parallelism," be explained on the basis of what the words of Scripture said in another passage that was not the subject of controversy. To others, a conflict in which texts could be taken in different senses implied that things were left to be determined by reason, by "natural light or the general principles of our knowledge." Yet that did not settle

Edw.*Rel.Aff*.3.6 (Miller 2:330)

Eug.Bulg.*Orth*.5 (Metaxas 22)
Bulg.*Kat*.61 (1940:132-34)
Eug.Bulg.*Orth*.5 (Metaxas 24)
2 Tim.3:16
See vol.4:343-47

Tin.*Chr*.13 (1730:328)

Frnck.*Mand.Scrip*.6 (1706:72); Frnck.*Meth*.1.9 (1723:26-27); Frnck.*Id*.28 (Peschke 185)

Wet.*N.T*. (1756:110); Ost.*Arg.ref*.pr. (1720:A2r)

Ost.*Arg.ref*.pr. (1720:C2v)

Wer.*Misc*.23.5 (Ryhinerus 2:344-45)

Lschr.*Unfehl*.12 (1724:85)

Tol.*Myst*.int. (1696:5)
Wet.*N.T*. (1756:116); Reim.*Apol*.int.5 (Alexander 1:46)
Brnt.*Art.XXXIX*.9 (1700:115)

Lang.*Paul*.2.2.1 (1718:331-32)
Wer.*Misc*.23.4 (Ryhinerus 2:341); Zinz.*Lond.Pred*.1.7 (Beyreuther 5-I:49)

Tin.*Chr*.4 (1730:37)
Byl.*Com.phil*.1.1 (1713-I:135)

Mid.*Wat.* (1731:21)

Sem.*V.T.Int.*pr. (1773:B1v)

Rndt.*Diss.*4 (Salaville 24);
Strz.*Enchir.*1 (1828:1-44)

the problem either, since to some interpreters allegory
and typology were necessary "for the satisfaction of
our reason," while to others they were just the
opposite. To Roman Catholic and Eastern Orthodox
teachers, meanwhile, all of this proved again the need
for an infallible church.

Ost.*Arg.ref.*pr. (1720:B3v)

The Old Testament provided, at least initially,
many of the most complex—and, supposedly, the
safest—exegetical puzzles. While it was said to have
"the same" content as the New, everyone, including
the most orthodox interpreters, objected to the practice of praying the imprecatory psalms against one's

Neum.*Rch.*18 (1751:580)

Thos.Aq.*S.T.*1.74.2
(*Ed.Leon.*5:190-91)
Nrs.*Vind.Aug.*4.9 (Berti
2:379-81)
Bert.*Theol.disc.*11.2
(1792-II:184-87)
Lmp.*Theol.elench.*4.6
(1729:23)
Sem.*Erkl.*3 (1777:285)
Aug.*Pecc.merit.*2.22.36 (*CSEL*
60:107-8)

personal enemies. Although Thomas Aquinas had
adopted a more literal exegesis of the creation accounts in Genesis, Augustine's nonliteral interpretation of the "days" had never been condemned by the
church; and in opposition to the standard view among
their confreres, some Protestants were urging such an
interpretation not only of the creation but of the fall
(which Augustine had interpreted literally). Some

Ost.*Arg.ref.*Ps.2;8;22
(1720-I:328;331;339)
Reim.*Apol.*1.5.2.2
(Alexander 1:727)

went so far as to call the christological interpretation
of the Old Testament, which most Christian exegetes
in all the churches were still practicing, nothing more
than "the playful activity of the imagination," not an
exegesis to be taken with intellectual seriousness,

Reim.*Apol.*1.5.1.1;1.5.4.16
(Alexander 1:685;813)

Ost.*Dz.serm.*4 (1722:126-27)
Ern.*Opusc.*10 (Fritsch
447-48); Sem.*V.T.Int.*1.3.38
(1773:105-8)

since the Old Testament contained at best "an imperfect grasp of some of the truths of natural religion."
Less drastic interpreters left open the question of
whether Old Testament passages quoted in the New
Testament actually referred to Jesus Christ, but they
did specify that to establish a teaching as distinctively
Christian doctrine it was necessary to prove it "directly from the sources of the New Covenant." With-

Sem.*Erkl.*pr. (1777:B4r)

out always arguing from the possible implications of
an opposing position, the defenders of the objectivity
of revelation in all the churches sounded the alarm
that such a methodology was threatening not only
miracle but mystery, not only mystery but
authority—and not only the authority of the church
but that of Scripture, and within Scripture not only
that of the Old Testament but that of the New, and

Tin.*Chr.*13 (1730:258-59);
Jcksn.*Rem.* (1731:40-41)

within the New Testament not only that of the
"grossly mistaken" apostles but that of Jesus Christ
himself.

The Contingent Truths of History

Strz.*Enchir*.7.3 (1828:304-21)

Mrck.*Scrip.exerc*.10.16 (Velzen 10:620)

Tol.*Myst*.3.3 (1696:118); Dipp.*Orth*.6 (1699:90-91)

Mid.*Mir*.5 (1749:231); Bl.*Unfehl*.28 (1791:562-98)

Brth.*Prot.Theol*. (1947:384)

Ern.*Opusc*.13 (Fritsch 513-34)

Zinz.*Zst*.17 (Beyreuther 3-II:105)

Amrt.*Thos.Kemp*.2.1.1-2 (1761:10)

Amrt.*Ep*.1742 (Friedrich 62)

Pff.*Hist.theol*.4.prol. (1724-III:1)

Pff.*Hist.theol*.4.4 (1724-III:185)

Budd.*Phil.Ebr*.pr. (1720:A6v)

Ost.*Cat*. (1747:1-11)
Brnt.*Art.XXXIX*.pr. (1700:iii-v)
Bnl.*Anim.cr*.ap. (1751:177-87)
Komn.*Prosk*.3 (Christophoros 27)
Gtti.*Ver.eccl*.2.2.13 (1763:224-30)

Bert.*Theol.disc*.23.2 (1792-V:3)

Miracle, mystery, and authority—whatever their scientific, philosophical, or theological status—were all questions of history as well. Orthodoxy was said to be the key to history, and the defender of a biblical miracle argued for its credibility from "the history of this miraculous event" and the history of subsequent belief in it; the critic of orthodox supernaturalism looked for historical anticipations of "the same notion of mystery that I have"; and the opponent of "submit[ting] our belief implicitly and indifferently to the mere force of authority" strove to prove that it "would certainly destroy the use of all history." In the development of Christian theology, the eighteenth (and then the nineteenth) century was the time of what a twentieth-century theologian called "the none too dignified sight of a general flight of the cleverest brains into the study of history," especially into the history of doctrine.

Many of those "cleverest brains" were conscious of their pioneering role. "I am going beyond other theologians," a Roman Catholic "critical" historian declared in investigating the doctrine of indulgences, by employing "a new way for treating the more momentous theological controversies with greater exactitude, in that I am expounding the history of this doctrine." A Protestant contemporary of his expressed his "joy to be living in an age when this branch of theology is beginning to flourish" by attracting "the most outstanding and the most learned" of scholars: "It is beyond words how noble, how outstanding, how necessary, how useful, and how vast this study of the history of dogma is!" It could illumine the study of the history of philosophy and be illumined by it in turn. History was used to introduce a catechism, to expound a Reformation confession, to examine the development of witchcraft, to review the conflict of Eastern Orthodoxy with Islam, to prove that Peter had been in Rome "personally," and to demonstrate that there had been a continuity of doctrine since apostolic days—except, of course, for some "contingent and accidental change."

Pus.*Hist.Eng.*1 (1828-I:51)

Kierk.*Afs.Uvid.Eft.*2.2.3
(Drachmann 7:74-85)

Less.*Bew.* (Rilla 8:12-14)
Reim.*Apol.*2.3.1.4 (Alexander 2:186)
Amrt.*Thos.Kemp.*2.1.25;
4.conc.223 (1761:13;251)
Rndt.*Diss.*2 (Salaville 9)

Sem.*Erkl.*pr. (1777:A6r)

Sem.*Rel.*21 (Schütz 182)

Sem.*Erkl.*pr. (1777:A6r-A6v)

Edw.*Rel.Aff.*3.5 (Miller 2:305)

Mos.*Tol.*6 (1722:20-21)

Sem.*Rel.*42 (Schütz 353-54)

Ern.*Opusc.*13 (Fritsch 514)

Tol.*Milt.*ded. (1699:7)

Ors.*Ist.*pr. (1747-I:viii)

One of the cleverest brains of all in the eighteenth century, Gotthold Ephraim Lessing, whom an orthodox Anglican in the next century would describe as "skeptical, but probably more Christian" than his orthodox opponents, recognized that the "contingent" and relative elements of the history of doctrine could not be dismissed quite so easily as that. In a formula that would continue to echo in the nineteenth century, he declared that "contingent historical truths can never serve as proof for necessary truths of reason"; "if I have no grounds historically on which I can object to the statement that Christ raised a man from the dead," he continued, "must I therefore consider it true that God has a Son in his own image?" It was a logical fallacy "to jump from that historical truth to an entirely different class of truths, and to ask me to alter my metaphysical and moral concepts accordingly." Arguing in the opposite direction was no less fallacious. History produced at best a "moral certainty," and its outcome was an ever deeper awareness of inexplicable "diversity." A scholar who had begun with the assumption of the "immutability of theology" learned from his research into "the history of public forms of doctrine" that there had been a "constant mutation" in theology no less than in other areas of human knowledge. As a result of such historical arguments, one theologian complained, "infidelity never prevailed so much in any age as in this, wherein these arguments are handled to the greatest advantage," as unorthodox pupils drew radical conclusions from the historical instruction of their orthodox teachers. This radical "new Christian religion arose through a new history"; but "since historical knowledge precedes universal knowledge," it was possible to claim that "the Christian religion, precisely because it has so much historical content," could serve as an avenue into universal religion.

Historical theology needed to set itself apart from other departments of theology. Because "historians are suspected rather to make their hero what they would have him to be than such as he really was," the distinction between writing a history and writing a panegyric was essential. The distinction between historical theology and polemical theology was an

Bl.*Unfehl.*26 (1791:533)

Anf.*Pan.serm.*3 (1817:29)

Sem.*Erkl.*2 (1777:236)

Span.*H.e.*3.9 (Marck 1:765)

Pnch.*Dict.*pr. (1736:C2v)

Gtti.*Ver.rel.*5.40.1
(1750-I:463-64)

Wlch.*Pol.*int. (1762:16-17)
Sem.*Frag.*1 (1780:9;1)
Ost.*Dz.serm.*2 (1722:44);
Sem.*Erud.* (1765-I:7-8)

Budd.*Phil.Ebr.*pr. (1720:A8v)

ap.Budd.*Mod.*8;20
(1720:507;554)
Zinz.*Aug.Conf.*19 (Beyreuther
6-II:308)

Mayr.*Mis.*5.2 (1692:47-48);
Canst.*Spen.*15 (1711:41)
Hrlss.*Enc.*2.5.13
(1837:232-33)

Spen.*Gtts.*ep.ded. (1680:A6v)

Bert.*Aug.*pr. (1747-I:lxi)

Bulg.*Kat.*62 (1940:139-40)
Wer.*Misc.*15.7 (Ryhinerus
2:270)
Mrck.*Pent.*Gen.49:10
(Velzen 1:124;127)
Lmp.*Hist.*prol. (1747:1-2)
Frnck.*Meth.*4.6 (1723:263)

Lw.*Bngr.*1 (Moreton 1:9)

Rndt.*Diss.*4 (Salaville 23)

Zinz.*Gem.*30 (Beyreuther
4-II:30-48)
Rndt.*Lit.Or.*int.1.8
(1716-I:lxxiii)

Tin.*Chr.*13 (1730:281);
Sem.*Rel.*32 (Schütz 261)
Reim.*Apol.*1.1.5.9
(Alexander 1:167)

important element in the changing situation between Roman Catholicism and Protestantism, perhaps also between Roman Catholicism and Eastern Orthodoxy. A critical Protestant theologian could write off the implacable fourth-century polemist Epiphanius as a "scribbler"; but even an orthodox Protestant historian criticized Epiphanius for slandering Origen, and one orthodox Roman Catholic found him not sufficiently historical in his treatment of heresy, while another rejected his interpretation of other historical questions. Of all the methods for dealing with polemical theology, the one that now commended itself most, in place of the older "heresy-hunting," was to begin with "a historical account of the origin, development, vicissitudes, distinctive doctrines, and writers of the principal sects." It was "so partisan, so unhistorical" to criticize the use of the historical approach to Old Testament doctrine; conversely, the refusal to use the history of doctrines to engage in partisan argument could bring upon the historian the charge of hiding behind his sources without committing himself personally. Although his chief protégé was deeply attracted to the field, one of the century's leading exponents of personal commitment in religion was, as critics and disciples agreed, at his weakest when it came to historical studies.

Nevertheless, even he and his associates were willing to look to history for precedent and to draw instruction from it, as was everyone else. Conservative theologians found in it a model for church-state relations, evidence of divine governance and providence, a source for resolving the enigmas of scriptural prophecy, a confirmation of the truth of the word of God, and a basis for Christian "prudence"; for some of them, it also confirmed "the uninterrupted succession" of ordaining bishops. There had been historical errors concerning the authorship of liturgies; and it was a lesson of history that despite their attacks on ritualism Protestants had not been successful in avoiding religious ceremonies, but also that "priestcraft and superstition" had been a chronic phenomenon of ecclesiastical history, along with "a maze of numberless, useless, loveless" squabbles over orthodoxy and the constant misrepresentation of adversaries' opin-

Tin.*Chr.*11 (1730:160-61)

Sem.*Erud.* (1765-II:125)

Sem.*N.T.Int.*2.1.68-69 (1767:173)

Bl.*Unfehl.*28 (1791:562-98)

Sem.*N.T.Int.*2.2.72 (1767:182)

Edw.*Rel.Aff.*3.5 (Miller 2:303);Lw.*Ser.Cl.*17 (Moreton 4:177)

Less.*Bew.* (Rilla 8:12)
Wlff.*Nat.Gott.*105 (1744-I:79)
See vol.4:29-32

Gib.*Dec.*15 (Bury 2:2)

Jcksn.*Rem.* (1731:31)

Byl.*Com.phil.*2.1 (1713-I:268)

Nrs.*Syn.quint.*9.2 (Berti 2:73)
Span.*H.e.*1.2 (Marck 1:522);
Mrck.*Syl.*1.1 (Velzen 15:1)

Qnl.*Clém.IX.*int. (1700:1)

Dipp.*Hrt.*pr. (1706:B1v)

Sem.*N.T.Int.*1.2.39 (1767:89)

Mos.*Vind.disc.*1.5.1 (1722:88)

ions. From the history of controversies among the learned it was possible to see that differences over "matters about which there is not firm and certain knowledge" did not affect the certainty of faith, and that even in matters that did affect it differences of belief were unavoidable. Under the title "results of this history," a revisionist Roman Catholic dogmatics made proposals for redefining proof and doctrinal authority. Yet amid all these efforts to "return to the condition of [past] times" in order to understand them, there were at least some who, though not historians themselves, grasped the inadequacy of "the force of arguments for the truth of Christianity drawn from history," as well as of "contingent" historical arguments against it. Attributing to God a "knowledge of all history," including its contingencies as well as its primary causes, did not vouchsafe a similar knowledge to the mortal historian. "The theologian," according to one historian, "may indulge the pleasing task of describing religion as she descended from heaven, arrayed in her native purity"; but the historian had the "more melancholy duty" of describing "the inevitable mixture of error and corruption which she contracted in a long residence upon earth."

Such recognition of the limitations inherent in historical methodology could also come out of the practice of historical research. The naive self-assurance that "common sense is always sufficient to determine about the greater or less probability of historical evidence" collided with the discovery that "evidence is a relative quality." That applied not only to the date of Justinian's death but also to the date of Christ's birth. If it was necessary to recognize in dealing with recent and contemporary developments that "a history of dogmatic facts is much more difficult than one that deals with ordinary events," this was true a fortiori of the dogmatic facts of the church's past; also because the "domestic history" of Christian doctrine and life had often been kept secret. One of the greatest difficulties of all arose in dealing with "the so-called histories of heresy," for the closer these came to Christian origins the more obscure they became. Although some theologians objected to the charges of

Allat.*Syn.Eph*.50
(1661:274-85);
Mmchi.*Orig.ant*.1.3.17
(1749:146)
Mid.*Ltr.Rom*. (1729:38);
Tol.*Milt*. (1699:91-92);
Tol.*Amyn*. (1699:14-15)
Pff.*Hist.theol*.prol.
(1724-I:7-8)

Frnck.*Pred*.Laet. (1700:12-18)
Bert.*Theol.disc*.29.6
(1792-VI:91-93); Eus.*H.e*.
1.13.6-10 (*GCS* 9:86-88)

See vol.1:344-49

See vol.4:90-91
Bert.*Diss.hist*.
(1753-III:149-52)
Mos.*Vind.disc*.1.6.10
(1722:146-49)

Sem.*Rel*.4 (Schütz 32)

Lmp.*Ew.Str*.2 (1729:248)

Sem.*Erud*. (1765-II:17-18)

Sem.*N.T.Int*.1.1.1 (1767:28)

Terst.*Abr*.1.11-14 (Becher
2:119-56)

Strz.*Enchir*.5.1 (1828:192-93)

See vol.3:301-3
Mrck.*Apoc*.pr.5-6 (Velzen
8:B2r-B3r)

Aug.*Civ*.22.30 (*CCSL*
48:865-66)

See vol.4:362-74

Bianch.*Pot*.2.1.2
(1745-III:116)

Ors.*Ist*.1.1 (1747-I:1)

wholesale forgery and tampering, it did appear necessary to admit that the sources had sometimes been corrupted by the intrusion of "the grossest forgeries." In the eighteenth century some were still prepared to attribute a great probability of genuineness to such apocryphal documents as the *Clementine Recognitions*, the correspondence between Christ and Abgar of Edessa, and the pseudonymous writings of Dionysius the Areopagite (although most were, by now, willing to surrender the *Donation of Constantine*, despite its noble defenders); but even so well-informed a scholar as Augustine had confused various ancient heresies. The rise of early Christianity was attested historically by the sources, beyond any reasonable doubt; but in handling those texts, "especially those that concern points of doctrine," historical context, including that supplied by secular history, was an essential component for determining the meaning of key words and concepts.

The periodization of church history was a methodological and a theological assignment. The Eastern Orthodox understanding of the church and its history led to this typical division: the age from Christ to Constantine as the first period; the era of the seven ecumenical councils ("in which the Western church participated as a genuine sister church") as the second; the time from the East-West schism to the fall of Constantinople as the third; and the present since 1453 as the fourth. In the West, the apocalyptic dispensationalism of the late Middle Ages had concerned itself with a schema of periods for which the concluding paragraphs of Augustine's *City of God* about the seven ages of world history had supplied the program; and Reformed covenant theology had reawakened interest in the successive stages—nature, law, and grace—in the history of God's dealing with his people. Because "the outward polity by which the church is governed" was not "a work of human invention" but the institution of Christ himself, it could be argued that the life of Christ was to be included as the opening of the history of the church; but theological and methodological considerations argued for beginning with the Book of Acts, not with the Gospels.

Ern.*Opusc.*13 (Fritsch 531)
Hrn.*H.e.*1.1.15 (Leydecker
1:119);Span.*H.e.*11.5 (Marck
1:1525-32)

Hrn.*H.e.*1.int. (Leydecker
1:99)

Lmp.*Ghm.*12 (1719-I:716)

Lmp.*Hist.*2.21 (1747:71-72)

Mrck.*Apoc.*pr.35-37 (Velzen
8:B3v-B4r)
See vol.3:302; vol.4:90,
321-22

Strz.*Enchir.*1.3 (1828:24-25)
Coz.*Graec.*4.16.484
(1719-II:283)
Ors.*Ist.*10.81
(1747-IV:329-80);
Bert.*Diss.hist.* (1753-III:46);
Span.*H.e.*4.3 (Marck 1:826);
Lmp.*Hist.*2.5 (1747:137)
Zinz.*Soc.*2 (Beyreuther
1-I:20-21);Byl.*Com.phil.*4.30
(1713-II:433);Bl.*Unfehl.*13
(1791:144-45)
See vol.4:154-55
Reim.*Apol.*1.1.5.5
(Alexander 1:153)

Bl.*Unfehl.*14 (1791:204-14)
See vol.1:333-39

Nrs.*Hist.pel.*2.11 (Berti
1:330); Bert.*Theol.disc.*15.3
(1792-III:170-72)
Vinc.*Ler.Comm.*2.3
(Moxon 10)
Mcks.*Ltrs.*1 (1705:30-31)

Brnt.*Art.XXXIX.*9
(1700:113-15)

Following the historiographic precedent of the Reformers, Protestant historians could be expected to see the rise of the papal Antichrist and the Reformation as marking major divisions. One system of historical theology identified three stages: from the time of Christ to the rise of Antichrist, from the rise of Antichrist to the Reformation, and from the Reformation to the present. A more elaborate periodization distinguished six eras (the apostolic age, the period until Constantine, from then until the beginnings of Antichrist, from then until the Reformation, from the Reformation to the Treaty of Passau in 1552, and from 1552 to the present), with a seventh still to come. Yet there remained a strong "prejudice against the system of periods" at work in such historical constructs. As it had been earlier, the conversion of Constantine was the clearest point of division not only between historical epochs but between historical theories across denominational lines: Eastern Orthodox hagiography continued to regard the emperor as a saint; conservative Roman Catholics insisted that he had not been the source of papal authority, and both they and Protestant historians hailed his genuine "if not total" conversion as the event that had brought about the peace of the church; Protestant and Roman Catholic critics attacked Constantine's use of political power to enforce doctrinal orthodoxy, and (echoing Luther's doctrine of justification) spoke of him as "believing and godless at the same time."

Those historiographic differences reflected differences in the theological understanding of Christian antiquity and its authority. The most "precise and careful" standard of that authority was enunciated in the *Commonitory* of Vincent of Lérins, which had appeared in dozens of editions and translations during the seventeenth century throughout Europe (although it was recognized that Vincent, as a Semi- Pelagian, had originally directed it against the Augustinian doctrine of grace): what had been believed "everywhere, always, by all [ubique, semper, ab omnibus]." Anglicans cited it as a principle and employed it to question the normative standing of the Augustinian doctrine, while acknowledging that Roman Catholic "writers make use of that prejudice in favor of

Mid.*Mir*.int. (1749:xli)
Gtti.*Coll*.3.1.4 (1727:433)

Mayr.*Red*.1 (1702:184-85)

Newm.*Proph.Off*.2.6 (*V.Med.* 1:55-56); Newm.*Dev*.int.8 (Harrold 11-12)

Amrt.*Theol.eclec*.3.2.4 (1752-1-III:121)

Nmnn.*Er.* (1701:187)

Ost.*Corrupt*.2.1 (1700-II:6); Terst.*Abr*.2.15;2.16.2 (Becher 2:309-19); Wsly.*Serm*. 4.1.10 (Baker 1:165)

Lmp.*Hist*.2.3 (1747:95)

Aug.*Civ*.20.7 (*CCSL* 48:708-12)
Bert.*Theol.disc*.3.8 (1792-I:138-39);
Amrt.*Theol.eclec*.1.4.5 (1752-1-I:76)
See vol.4:157-58;279-80
Poit.*Fid.rat*.3.2.6 (1708:34-35)
Bert.*Theol.disc*.2.2 (1792-I:75)

Sem.*Rel*.3 (Schütz 29-30)

Jwl.*Apol*.3 (Booty 41)

Lmp.*Hist*.2.5 (1747:137)

Chil.*Rel.Prot*.6.56 (1727:271);Tin.*Chr*.13 (1730:291-92);Tol.*Myst*.int. (1696:2)

Mid.*Mir*.pr. (1749:xxxi)

Tol.*Myst*.pr. (1696:xxiii)

Bert.*Diss.hist*. (1753-II:128)

Mid.*Mir*.3 (1749:44)

primitive antiquity which prevails even in this Protestant country, toward drawing weak people into their cause." Despite their defense, Roman Catholics were urged by their Protestant opponents to go beyond quoting it and to slough off such "new heretical doctrines" as purgatory and the denial both of the Bible and of the chalice to the laity.

Although it was obvious that, in the words of an early nineteenth-century writer, "the Rule of Vincent is not of a mathematical or demonstrative character, but moral, and requires practical judgment and good sense to apply it," it did posit the existence of a patristic consensus, which, if not quite "the unanimous sense of the ancient doctors," constituted, for orthodox Protestants as well, "a testimony of the church, though in no way a principle of faith." Therefore they spoke about the "purity" of the "Christianity of those first centuries," at least "in comparison with those that followed," praising them also for "correct belief about Holy Scripture, the Trinity, the deity of Christ, justification, and the Eucharist." Yet on some of these very doctrines, these centuries appeared to present something less than a unified orthodoxy. As Augustine's critique indicated, millenarianism had been widespread; but as Protestant scholarship admitted, attention to the doctrine of justification had not. In the second century anthropomorphic doctrines of God had circulated among orthodox teachers, and even "to the question, 'Who is Jesus Christ?' they used to give quite divergent answers."

Imitating Reformation apologias, Protestant polemics sought to pit a patristic consensus against modern Roman Catholic doctrine. But historical research had combined with theological change to make it clear that there were "some fathers against others, the same fathers against themselves, a consensus of fathers of one age against a consensus of fathers of another age, the church of one age against the church of another age." The ancient fathers had been "extremely credulous and superstitious"; their "labyrinths" were not needed in an age of reason. Justin Martyr had been guilty of "errors"; Irenaeus was a "diligent collector and assertor of apostolic traditions"

Sem.*Erkl.*2 (1777:234-35)
Sem.*Erud.* (1765-I:100);
Byl.*Com.phil.*2.3
(1713-I:312-13)

Bl.*Unfehl.*10 (1791:98);
Tol.*Myst.*3.3 (1696:118)
Ath.Par.*Epit.*3.2 (1806:288);
Thdt.*H.e.*5.34.11 (*GCS*
19:336)
Bert.*Theol.disc.*15.2
(1792-III:164-65)
Tin.*Chr.*13 (1730:286)
Sem.*N.T.Int.*2.1.59
(1767:141-42)
Dipp.*Hrt.*2 (1706:17)

Ptz.*Sed.inf.*2.9 (1763:128)

Ors.*Ist.*5.61 (1747-II:440-41)

Hrn.*H.e.*1.2.13 (Leydecker
1:153)

Pnch.*Dict.* (1736:334-48)

Nrs.*Syn.quint.*6 (Berti 2:49)

Ors.*Ist.*6.28 (1747-III:68)
Ors.*Ist.*6.15 (1747-III:35);
Zinz.*Zst.*29 (Beyreuther
3-II:225)

Bert.*Theol.disc.*8.6
(1792-II:80-83)

Drnd.*Fid.vind.*1.12 (1709:34)
Anf.*Pan.serm.*12-13
(1817:110-20)
Gtti.*Ver.eccl.*2.10.1.1
(1763:323);Allat.*Purg.*40
(1655:164-68)
See vol.1:151
Lmp.*Theol.elench.*28.7
(1729:108)
Pet.*Myst.*pr.3 (1700-I:A1v)

Nrs.*Syn.quint.*12 (Berti
2:131)

Nrs.*Syn.quint.*pr. (Berti 2:vii)

Ost.*Ist.*22.26 (1747-X:35-36)

See vol.1:337-38
Ors.*Ist.*41.70
(1747-XVIII:332-38)
Ors.*Ist.*7.33 (1747-III:200)

but the author of rather "miserable writings"; Tertullian was a learned scholar but a theological "dilemma"; Clement of Alexandria was "the first who tried to give Christianity a scientific form through philosophy" but now the alleged patron of Deists; and Chrysostom was "the teacher of the world" but probably a Semi-Pelagian. Patristic study revealed not consensus but "infinite divisions" and a "plurality of hypotheses"—the anomaly of a "pluralistic orthodoxy."

As he has been throughout the history of patristic scholarship Eastern and Western, the crucial test case for any such historical reconstruction was Origen of Alexandria. His "constancy" in persecution and martyrdom, his "supreme and incomparable erudition in every field of knowledge but above all in the Holy Scriptures," and his willingness to "submit all his writings to the church" had produced a "blind love for Origen." Yet the very "force of the imagination of Origen and his attachment to his Platonic and Pythagorean ideas" had also been responsible for "many errors" in his own and in his disciples' theology. Although his teacher Clement of Alexandria could be exonerated of the accusation of Arianism before Arius, Origen had to be seen as "the first Arian." While expounders of the Roman Catholic doctrine of purgatory against attacks from Eastern Orthodoxy and from Protestantism strove to disengage it from Origen's universalism, both the critics of purgatory and the latter-day advocates of universalism made the connection. Despite the efforts of "more recent" scholars "to defend the person of Origen against three ecumenical councils" which had condemned him and to hail "his doctrine of divine grace as not only 'Catholic' but 'most Catholic of all,' " he was in fact the father of Pelagianism. Still, this man whose books constituted "a storehouse of monstrous opinions and a corpus of theology with a medley of Platonic teachings that adulterated the entire system of Christian doctrine," for which he had been condemned at the Second Council of Constantinople in 553, had been "restored to communion and peace" with the church, in which he had also died. And in the atmosphere of the eighteenth century, with its

See pp. 116-17, 224-25 below

Lub.*Hist.esp*.2 (1950:47-91)

Lschr.*Dr.Pred*.1 (1733:16-17)

See vol.4:3-6

Brnt.*Art.XXXIX*.11 (1700:126)

Mayr.*Red*.3 (1702:305)

Deutsch.*Luth*.1.3.10 (1698:27);Zinz.*Hom*.25 (Beyreuther 3-I:254)

Beng.*Brüd*.1.3.28 (1751:230)

See p. 169 below

Swed.*Ver.Chr*.14.796 (1771:480-81)

Wsly.*Serm*.1.3.9 (Baker 1:129)

Schpf.*Luth*.7.3 (1717:24-25)
Mayr.*Red*.3 (1702:261-62)
Schpf.*Luth*.2.1 (1717:4)

Mayr.*Red*.3 (1702:218-346)

growing recognition and acceptance of a pluralism rather than a simplistic patristic consensus, there developed that reinterpretation of Origen whose outcome was to be, if not an official canonization, then an eventual rehabilitation not only of his piety and spirituality as "a man of the church," but of his doctrine on some of the very points that had rendered him suspect.

Alongside the patristic era, the age of the Reformation occupied a special place in the history of the church and of its doctrine; the relation between the two periods became a topos of Protestant historiography. One reason was the Reformation origin of the doctrinal standards by which most of the churches continued to define themselves. In that sense it was possible to claim that the Reformation was "a great blessing to the world" and that it had "proved so even to the church of Rome," which had to admit that because of its "love for the word of God" Luther's Reformation was immortal. Above all, it occupied this position among those who regarded themselves as the heirs of the "work of the Reformation, abounding in grace," such as the biblical scholar who felt able to declare, "and without sectarian fanaticism: the Reformation is and remains the most important epoch of the Christian church in the West." Even Emanuel Swedenborg had to claim, in support of his novel vision of life everlasting, that Luther after his death, having been "a very bitter propagator and defender of his own dogmas" upon first coming to heaven, eventually "underwent a change of state" and learned the true nature of the church.

In a particular way, Luther's doctrine—as well as the person of "that special champion of the Lord of hosts"—had in its own right become a chapter of historical theology and of dogmatics, generating a library of apologias, biographies, and systematic summaries of his thought. Stressing that it was not the same as Roman Catholic saint worship, devotees of the commemoration of "Martin Luther, the prophet of Germany, the restorer and defender of true religion" went beyond the ranks of orthodox Lutherans; their panegyrics on "the immortal Luther" and defenses of his doctrine and life against Roman Catholic distor-

Lschr.*Unfehl.*13 (1724:94-96)

Acts 9:15
Neum.*Rch.*18 (1751:576)
Bgn.*Luth.* (1546:A4r)
Neum.*Fünf.*2
(1726-I:398-99);Mayr.*Red.*1
(1702:16-132);Rev. 14:6

ap.Frnck.*Ber.Obs.*1
(Peschke 57)
Canst.*Spen.*18 (1711:51);
Zinz.*Soc.*25 (Beyreuther
1-I:254)
Maj.*Mayr.* (1705:12)
Frnck.*Ber.Obs.*1 (Peschke
255); Zinz.*Aug.Conf.*19
(Beyreuther 6-II:325)

Baum.*Pred.*1.12 (Kirchner
1:407-8)

Sem.*Erud.* (1765-II:A3r)
Lmp.*Hist.*2.12 (1747:370);
Span.*Ev.vind.*1.12 (Marck
3:45)

Wlch.*Rel.aus.*4.1.6
(1733-I:400-401)
Lmp.*Hist.*2.12 (1747:371);
Terst.*Abr.*2.16.8 (Becher
2:325)
Hrn.*H.e.*3.1.29 (Leydecker
1:327-28)
Pnch.*Dict.* (1736:253-66);
Ptz.*Sed.inf.*3.5 (1763:161-66)

Drnd.*Fid.vind.*4.36
(1709:632)

Gib.*Dec.*54 (Bury 6:125)

Gtti.*Ver.eccl.*2.7.4.14
(1763:279)

See vol.4:221-27
Amrt.*Indulg.*pr.2 (1735-I:3);
Gtti.*Ver.eccl.*1.4.2
(1763:36-38)
See vol.4:134-36
Amrt.*Indulg.*2.1.23
(1735-II:16-19)

See vol.4:136-38;250-51

Allat.*Purg.*35 (1655:252)
Remp.*Cour.*6 (1698:B3v)

tions celebrated him as (in a biblical title originally given to Paul) "the chosen instrument of Christ," and followed the sermon at his funeral by seeing him as "undoubtedly" the angel with the eternal gospel foretold in the Book of Revelation. Pietists, whom the orthodox accused of despising and blaspheming Luther, affirmed their continuity with the "heroic faith" of this "great man" and his "solid theological doctrine," declaring that no other reformation of the church (not even their own) could claim to come from God if it ran contrary to his. Those who mediated between Pietism and Rationalism joined in recognizing him as the one who had rescued the Bible from medieval obscurity, but dissociated themselves from his "prudent imitators" who followed him according to the letter but not according to the spirit. Reformed historians, for whom Calvin was a "special instrument of God for propagating the truth," nevertheless saluted Luther (in a way that very few Lutheran historians ever saluted Calvin) as "a great man" and "an intrepid defender of the truth," who had dared things that the whole world had to admire. While not surrendering the polemical initiative, Roman Catholic theologians were obliged by more recent research to revise earlier polemics and "with many historians to excuse him from the error" of denying the real presence, though it was still true that he denied transubstantiation. "After a fair discussion," a critical historian summarized, "we shall rather be surprised by the timidity than scandalized by the freedom of our first reformers."

All such continuity notwithstanding, it was the discontinuity between the Reformation and previous history that now drew most attention: it was a "monstrosity," a Roman Catholic theologian charged, to "conflate the doctrine of Calvin and Saint Augustine," as Reformed teachers since Calvin had been doing. One Roman Catholic scholar bent on "proving that indulgences have existed at all times in the church of God" reprinted the full text of the *Ninety-Five Theses* to demonstrate Luther's break with the doctrinal tradition. The evolution of Luther's attitude toward purgatory was a documentation of such discontinuity, as was his idiosyncratic biblical exegesis.

Sem.*N.T.Int.*2.2.70
(1767:175)

Edw.*Rel.Aff.*pr. (Miller
2:86-87)

Jeff.*Ep.*26.vii.1818 (Adams
385)

Felb.*Hnd.*3 (1799:73)
Dipp.*Orth.*8 (1699:106-18)

Felb.*Hnd.*3 (1799:73)
Byl.*Com.phil.*4.31
(1713-II:450-51)
Dipp.*Hrt.*2 (1706:23-24)
Reim.*Apol.*1.1.3.9
(Alexander 1:114)
Lang.*Nach.*9.1 (1707-IX:8-9)
Han.Consist.27.x.1709
(Neumeister 115)

Terst.*Abr.*2.16.9 (Becher
2:325)

See vol.4:175

Spen.*Pi.Des.* (Aland 60)

Spen.*Pi.Des.* (Aland 42)

Wsly.*Serm.*39.10 (Baker 2:86)

Wer.*Diss.*24 (Ryhinerus
1:414)

Mid.*Mir.*int. (1749:ci)

Sem.*Erkl.*3 (1777:272)

On the Protestant side, this very novelty of the Reformation's exegesis made it a turning point in history. Its discontinuity proved, to two Americans with drastically contrasting theologies, that there had been "a stop to [the Reformation's] progress," so that what the Reformers had left undone, "the half reformation of Luther and Calvin," made it incumbent on their heirs to "complete what they began and place us where the evangelists left us." Although it had, according to the radicals, made substantial progress, "coming much closer to the true faith than the darkness of the papacy had been," the Reformation had not penetrated to the roots of "the real heresy" and had been unable to cast off such vestigial remnants as infant baptism, the use of constraint to enforce doctrinal conformity, the authority of the dead letter of Scripture, and the appeal to "blind faith." Evangelical Pietists, too, were—unjustly, in their judgment—attacked for preferring the writings of the young Luther to his later and more dogmatic ones, because they charged that the Reformation itself had "fallen" and that the doctrine of the universal priesthood of all believers had "hardly been pursued very much since the time of Luther."

The slogan of "continuing the Reformation" and "correcting the defects that still remain" expressed a widely held conviction: it was "the right of private judgment on which the whole Reformation stands." The "unique foundation" of the Reformation or "the Protestant principle" was defined by a Swiss theologian to mean that "all Christians not only have the right but are in conscience obliged to examine with their own judgment all dogmas of religion, regardless of the source from which these have been proposed." But did that mean "all dogmas," not only the distinctive Roman Catholic or Eastern Orthodox ones but trinitarian orthodoxy itself and the "many rites and doctrines" that the Reformers had kept? "I and others," wrote one scholar, "want to come to a different judgment" from that of the confessional generation, according to whom "Luther had accomplished the Reformation perfectly." As one Anglican writer saw it, "our first and principal Reformers, in the reign of Henry VIII, had not the power to carry

Mid.*Mir*.int. (1749:ci);
Wsly.*Serm*.61.29 (Baker
2:464-65)

the Reformation as far as they desired." Yet the
Reformers' rejection of "the human laws of the
church" should not be taken to imply, another
Anglican argued, "that we broke through that authority [which] is not founded in any human laws, but is

Lw.*Bngr*.3 (Moreton 1:196)

the authority of Christ." A fear that all the churches

Lschr.*Hör*. (1734:14);
Lschr.*Dr.Pred*.1 (1733:21)

which had come out of the Reformation might suffer
apostasy from the faith of Christendom tempered
Protestant celebration of Reformation doctrine as a
treasure that would "abide unimpaired for all time, to

Schpf.*Luth*.1.4 (1717:3)

the end of the world," as well as Roman Catholic
celebration of "the papacy and the true Catholic
Church, for which [it is premature] to sing the

Remp.*Luth*.4 (1699:16-17)

requiem."

So it was that tradition itself—the supposedly
shared tradition of the ancient fathers and councils, as
well as the specific traditions of the Reformation
(including its traditional denial of the authority of
tradition)—came to be classified among the "contingent truths of history," from which it was illegit-

Less.*Bew*. (Rilla 8:12-14)
Ath.Par.*Epit*.4.29
(1806:400-401);
Ang.Sil.*CTrid*.17
(1675:R6r-R6v)
See vol.4:103
Amrt.*Brd*. (Friedrich 36-37)

imate to argue for "necessary truths." Eastern
Orthodoxy and Roman Catholicism still put the
councils of the church with Scripture as authority and
discussed the question of whether a majority at a
council was necessary to establish that authority, but
one Roman Catholic who had accepted the principles
of the Enlightenment stated the methodology to
which much of the future belonged: "From now on
the councils cannot have any function in dogmatics
except a historical one. They are merely a part of the

Bl.*Unfehl*.28 (1791:577)
Bl.*Unfehl*.13 (1791:179)
Bl.*Unfehl*.28 (1791:564)

history of dogma." This applied to the ecumenically
accepted general councils of Nicea and Chalcedon,
still more to the Council of Trent. It was characteristic of the "Hebrew philosophy" contained in the Old

Budd.*Phil.Ebr*.pr.
(1720:B1r-B1v)
See vol.1:109-15

Testament that it was derived from tradition rather
than, as Greek philosophy had been, from reason. But
the testimony of church fathers such as Origen to the
existence of a tradition that had been present "undoubtedly since the time of primitive Christianity"
could no longer be referred to an allegedly uniform
"dogmatic tradition," since there had in fact been
great "variety in its application" in various places;

Sem.*V.T.Int*.prol.1-2
(1773:2-3)

tradition had to be read critically if it was to be
employed for "genuine history and interpretation."

Tin.*Chr*.1 (1730:11)

Bert.*Theol.disc*.18.8
(1792-IV:38-43);Marc.*Inst*.27
(Tomassini 5:5-95)

Hno.*Theol*.7.4.pr.1.3
(1785-VII:367-69)
Deutsch.*Luth*.1.3.9
(1698:26); Lw.*Bngr*.2
(Moreton 1:34)

Hdly.*Def*.6 (1707:69-79)

Mmchi.*Orig.ant*.4.1.3.1
(1749-IV:271)
Cmrda.*Const.ap*.2.5
(1732:113-16)

Bianch.*Pot*.1.6.6
(1745-II:477-502)

See pp. 250-52 below

Brnt.*Art.XXXIX*.19
(1700:187)

Zinz.*Zst*.20 (Beyreuther
3-II:152;155-56)

Lschr.*Unfehl*.11 (1724:78)

See vol.2:146-98; vol.4:
176-77,224-25,263-68,324

See vol.2:279-80;4:250-51

When it was read that way, tradition could often illumine, but could sometimes also relativize, the history of church doctrines. In the debates over the relation of sufficient grace to efficacious grace, the history of doctrine showed that otherwise orthodox doctors of the church had sometimes denied the former in the interest of affirming the latter. The continuity of the doctrine of the real presence could be historically substantiated. Historical research demonstrated that there had always been a distinct ministerial office in the life and teaching of the church (although the title "bishop" had not always meant the same thing), but also that beyond its authority there had been extra-ecclesiastical associations; history substantiated the primitive "institution of bishops or presbyters," but not of cardinals. Papal authority or papal infallibility was an obvious candidate for historical treatment, since its defenders were compelled to explain any abuse of authority (for example, by Boniface VIII) or any irrefutable exception to infallibility (usually Honorius I); but in practice this relativizing method applied "not only against the infallibility of popes, but against that of general councils likewise, and also against the authority of oral tradition. For here in a succession of many ages, the tradition was wholly changed from the doctrine of former times."

The historical discovery that "no period of church history is completely good," not even the apostolic era, and that there had undeniably been a development of doctrine created problems for the doctrinal positions of all the churches. As an orthodox Lutheran summarized that discovery, "the Catholics are even less able than the Lutherans to point to a single church father who agreed with them on all points and did not write anything that was contrary to them"; when he went on to add that this was "not necessary, for it does not do any damage to the truth if one cannot point to such a church father," that could not conceal the disappearance, through historical research, of the orthodox patristic consensus over which, in the East-West schism and again in the Reformation, all sides had contended. The arguments of Eastern and Protestant scholars pointing to the lack of historical

Eug.Bulg.*Orth*.12 (Metaxas
50); Wlch.*Pol*.3.2.13.10
(1752:789-90)
Coz.*Graec*.6.15.882-83
(1719-IV:255-56)
Bas.*Spir*.27.66 (*SC*
17b:478-82);see vol.4:121
Gaz.*Prael*.1.2.1.1.15
(1831-I:137)

Allat.*Purg*.35 (1655:251-56)
Eug.Bulg.*Orth*.6 (Metaxas
25);Komn.*Prosk*.5
(Christophoros 43)
Span.*H.e*.5.5;8.7 (Marck
1:971-72;1303-8); Hrn.*H.e*.
1.3.24 (Leydecker 1:201)

Rndt.*Lit.Or*.int.1.1
(1716-I:iii-vi)

Rndt.*Diss*.4 (Sallaville 27)

Rndt.*Lit.Or*.pr. (1716-I:E4v)

Span.*H.e*.4.5 (Marck
1:849-51)

See vol.3:75-80;184-204
Hrn.*H.e*.2.2.10;2.2.14
(Leydecker 1:265;269);
Span.*H.e*.9.10 (Marck
1:1375-79)

See vol.2:183-98

Wlch.*Spir*.pr. (1751:A4r)

Ath.Par.*Epit*.1.2.4
(1806:156-57)

Pnch.*Dict*. (1736:53-74)

Sherl.*Soc*.3 (1698:124-49)

Bert.*Theol.disc*.26.15-18
(1792-V:235-59)

See vol.1:275-77

evidence for the doctrine of purgatory compelled its defenders to appeal not only to patristic testimony but particularly to the familiar words of Basil of Caesarea about unwritten tradition, an unwritten tradition whose existence had to be posited a posteriori from later Roman Catholic dogma. Eastern appeals to the same authorities as proof for the antiquity of the cult of images clashed with historical research into when and how that cult had arisen. Even Protestants had to concede that in the eucharistic liturgy the consecration through the words "This is my body" had originally been transmitted by oral tradition and was therefore older than the New Testament; but the effort to use such evidence to support a liturgical "apostolic tradition" or a uniform belief "across all the languages" about "a single ancient faith concerning the Eucharist, which the Reformers have vainly charged with being a novelty," was difficult to square with the results of patristic scholarship—chiefly, to be sure, as carried out by Protestant patristic scholars. In turn, the attempt to brand the doctrine of the real presence taught by Radbertus against Ratramnus as a "novel error" and Berengar's denial of the real presence as "a light in the midst of darkness" was a reflection more of Calvinist theology than of critical historiography as such.

Orthodox Calvinism, Anglicanism, and Lutheranism were no less offended than Eastern Orthodoxy and Roman Catholicism, however, when the same critical historiography was applied to the doctrines that they all held in common, above all to the doctrines of the Trinity and the person of Christ. The Filioque, the drawn out conflict between East and West over the procession of the Holy Spirit, for which neither exegesis nor speculation nor church politics had succeeded in proving a resolution, was now being subjected to resolution by historical examination. A historical catalogue of trinitarian heresies as recounted by Epiphanius; a full-length history of Arius and Arianism; "a brief account of the Sabellian heresy, and by what arguments the Catholic fathers opposed it"; an extensive history of the development of christology in the fifth century; a chronological review of the controversy over the "three chapters" in the sixth

Nrs.*Syn.quint.*3 (Berti
2:15-20)

Mos.*Vind.disc.*1.8.6
(1722:225)
Ors.*Ist.*14.105
(1747-VI:266-68);Zinz.*Gem.*3
(Beyreuther 4-I:51-52)

Sem.*Frag.*24 (1780:155)

Matt.28:19-20

Sem.*Frag.*24 (1780:155)

Sem.*Erud.* (1765-I:158)

Sem.*Erkl.*1.2 (1777:28)

Sem.*Erkl.*2 (1777:197)

Lmp.*Hist.*2.2 (1747:74)

Ost.*Dz.serm.*2 (1722:49)

Ost.*Dz.serm.*8 (1722:290)
Ost.*Arg.ref.*pr. (1720:B4v)
Frnck.*Meth.*3.19 (1723:98);
Frnck.*Pred.*Epiph.3 (1699:6)

Bert.*Theol.disc.*12.2
(1792-III:7-8)

century—any of these forms of historical excursus could still be, within all those churches, a method for introducing an essay in dogmatic theology. But historians also had to deal with the early worship of the Son of God as divine and with the vexing question of why the orthodox doctrine of the Holy Spirit had taken such an inordinately long time to develop if it had been taught "everywhere, always, by all," and therefore with the question of "whether or not the early church, that is, its teachers, looked for a creed" at all in the baptismal formula, "the name of the Father and of the Son and of the Holy Spirit."

When the historian who raised the latter question went on to stipulate, "Nor do we grant that everything not known or done by the first centuries is automatically incorrect," such a recognition of the variety in the modes of doctrine—as documented in the history of the first five centuries, as well as in the later development of doctrine after the confessions of the Reformation era—could not, despite his efforts, stop short of the privileged sanctuary of the first century. The attempt to use chronology as a basis for drawing the distinction in authority between the "canonical" writings of the New Testament and the "ecclesiastical" writings of later centuries had been frustrated historically and hence was embattled theologically. If orthodox theology had to admit that there had been progressive revelation through the history of the Old Testament, did it not have to recognize a similar progression through the history of the church since the New Testament, and therefore a clarification of the obscure teachings of Christ as given to the first disciples? Despite warnings to employ "moderation" in applying the historical method to the study of Scripture, the teachings of Christ and the person of Christ could no longer be exempt from the use of such a method.

Christological Dogma and the Historical Jesus

For history was history: insisting that sacred history was history in the sense that it had really happened necessarily implied agreeing that it was history also in the sense that it was subject to change. "In a higher world it is otherwise," a leading nineteenth-century

Newm.*Dev*.1.1 (Harrold 38)

Eug.Bulg.*Orth*.4 (Metaxas 20)
Conc.*Rel.riv*.2.1.7
(1754-I:121-22);
Mmchi.*Orig.ant*.2.1.4.5
(1749-I:288-92)
Beng.*Gnom*.Luke 2:2 (Steudel 225)
Lmp.*Hist*.2.10 (1747:295)

Ost.*Arg.ref*.Matt.28;1 Cor.15
(1720-II:46;220)

Wer.*Diss*.4.3 (Ryhinerus 1:90-91)
Reim.*Apol*.2.3.1.3
(Alexander 2:183)

Spen.*Mess*.pr. (1701:v)

Spen.*Bed*.2.1.2 (Canstein 1:329)
Dipp.*Hrt*.1 (1706:10-11)
Sem.*Erud*. (1765-I:25-27;49)

Sem.*N.T.Int*.pr.8 (1767:19)

See vol.4:306-11

Nrs.*Hist.pel*.1.2 (Berti 1:13-14);Sem.*Erud*. (1765-I:21)
Bec.Lóp.*Nuev.Ab*. (1739:14)

Ors.*Ist*.20.32 (1747-IX:80)

Bert.*Diss.hist*. (1753-I:177)

Neum.*Rch*.23 (1751:749);
Lang.*Paul*.1.2.2 (1718:59);
Sem.*V.T.Int*.2.2.123
(1773:352)
Frnck.*Ber.Obs*.1-3 (Peschke 257-63)

Tin.*Chr*.6 (1730:66)

defender of orthodoxy would say, "but here below to live is to change, and to be [mature] is to have changed often." By the incarnation, the God beyond time had voluntarily become subject to the sequence of time, and so it was possible—and permissible—to subject the history of that life within time to the study of historical evidence. If evidence showed that Quirinius had truly been governor of Syria when Jesus was born but that the accounts of the stigmata of Francis of Assisi were "impudent lies," the method for weighing such evidence needed to be consistent. And if, in the Gospel accounts of the resurrection, the very absence of evidence from many witnesses demonstrated to some "the character of a completely honest historian," the contradictions between those accounts looked to others like proof of "manipulation." A historically conscious age, in which believers were admonished by a fellow believer "not to accept the Christian religion uncritically and blindly" and to make "exegetical study the foundation of all other parts of theology," saw a special opportunity for "diligent scholarly research" into the historical books of the Bible.

Standing as they did in the succession of Erasmian humanism, biblical scholars continued to make sacred philology—biblical languages and textual criticism—the foundation of such research. Among the biblical scholars of Western Christian history, the most influential had been the two translators, Jerome and Luther. Because of his orthodoxy and because of his scholarship, Jerome, "the greatest of the fathers," had been uniquely qualified, perhaps even "destined by Providence," to undertake the task of turning the Bible into Latin; yet everyone had to admit that biblical philology had made progress since the Septuagint and the Vulgate. Among Protestants, scholars of all parties had similar praise for Luther's German translation as embodying the best biblical knowledge of its time, but they also agreed that it now needed to be corrected in the light of more recent research. The call for critical scholarship came with the greatest urgency from those who wanted the received orthodoxy to be revised or rejected, while the caution that theological scholarship was legitimate only if it was

Lw.*Chr.Perf.*14 (Moreton 3:237)

Zinz.*Gespr.*1 (Beyreuther 1-III:5)

Gtz.*Unt.* (1693:G4r)

Frnck.*Meth.*3.15 (1723:88)
Frnck.*Mand.Scrip.*1 (1706:2);Frnck.*Id.*26-27 (Peschke 182-83)
Sem.*N.T.Int.*pr.10 (1767:25);Krks.*Theol.diat.*8 (1898:131);Ub.*Int.*1.3.prol. (1886-II:503);Rtl.*Recht.*1.11.73 (1882-I:606-8)

Beng.*Gnom.*pr.8 (Steudel xx)

Sem.*N.T.Int.*1.1.14 (1767:35)

See vol.4:346
Mrck.*Text.exerc.*46.1 (Velzen 14:441)
Pff.*Hist.theol.*2.10 (1724-I:295)
ap.Zinz.*Gespr.*9 (Beyreuther 1-III:84)

Tnnt.*Serm.*22 (1744:424)

Reim.*Apol.?*5.1.7 (Alexander 2:436);Milt.*Doct.*1.5 (Patterson 14:214-16)

Dipp.*Orth.*5 (1699:65)
Bert.*Theol.disc.*7.3 (1792-II:11-14)
Strz.*Enchir.*5.2 (1828:197-98);Wsly.*Serm.*55 (Baker 2:374-86); Mrck.*Comp.* 5.18 (Velzen 18:110-11)
Neum.*Rch.*24 (1751:782-83);
Terst.*Abr.*1.3.1;1.3.12 (Becher 2:49;54)
Sherl.*Soc.*1.2 (1698:4);
Sherl.*Vind.*6 (1690:209-10);
Zinz.*Lond.Pred.*1.8;5.12 (Beyreuther 5-I:62-63; 5-II:195)
Brnt.*Art.XXXIX.*1 (1700:38); see vol.1:216-18; vol.4:327
Beb.*Gl.*2 (1685:33);
Strz.*Enchir.*5.2 (1828:197-98)

"serviceable to the one thing needful" issued from those who saw a continuity of rationalism betweeen a certain kind of orthodoxy and a certain kind of antiorthodoxy. Yet the frequently heard charge that Pietism was endemically hostile to philological scholarship was refuted by the work of such scholars as August Hermann Francke, who as professor of Greek and Oriental (Semitic) languages at the University of Halle urged study of the biblical languages and at the same time pointed out the limitations of a superficially historicist understanding of Scripture, and Johann Albrecht Bengel, whose technical achievements scholars of every party and every denomination had to praise.

A leader in New Testament textual criticism and yet a firm believer in the inspiration of the Bible, Bengel agreed with his opponents that the same principles and methods of textual criticism were to be applied to Scripture as to any other text. As it had been for the humanists, the "Johannine comma," 1 John 5:7, was "the most vexatious" problem in textual criticism, not only among scholars and theologians but among laymen as well. It was "not found in diverse ancient manuscripts and versions drawn from them," one preacher observed, adding: "On the other hand, it is found in many others." Enemies of the doctrine of the Trinity cited this "later interpolation" as evidence of orthodox tampering with the biblical text, maintaining (though without historical evidence) that it had been used or invented by the defenders of the "homoousios" at the Council of Nicea. Some defenders of the orthodox doctrine disallowed explanations that it had come into the text by inadvertence or guile, and quoted it as authentic. One of them had "not the slightest doubt that Saint John really wrote it" and expressed indignation that "among Protestants there are some that claim to be theological scholars who question or deny" it. Nevertheless, the "first and chief" biblical proof for the dogma remained the passage to which "the Catholic fathers have always appealed," the trinitarian baptismal formula in the "charge and commission" of Christ in Matthew 28:19, which those who took the Johannine comma as genuine as well as the most extreme

Reim.*Apol*.2.1.3.6 (Alexander 2:89-90)
Reim.*Apol*.2.5.1.2 (Alexander 2:427)
Strz.*Enchir*.2.5 (1828:69-70); Drnd.*Fid.vind*.1.11 (1709:32);Mrck.*Comp*.1.17 (Velzen 18:109-10);Zinz.*Gem*.3 (Beyreuther 4-I:46-76)

Zinz.*Hom*.33 (Beyreuther 3-I:363)

See vol.4:155-67
Zinz.*Red*.1 (Beyreuther 1-II:12)
Zinz.*Red*.1 (Beyreuther 1-II:12)
Zinz.*Off.Red*.21 (Beyreuther 2-IV:218-19)

See vol.1:175-90
Frnck.*Pred*.Epiph.2 (1699:40-42);Zinz.*Lond.Pred*. 1.4 (Beyreuther 5-I:23-28)
Ath.Par.*Epit*.3.13 (1806:340-43); Strz.*Enchir*. 2.4 (1828:58)
Calv.*Inst*. (1559)2.15 (Barth-Niesel 3:471-81); Eus.*H.e*.1.3.7-9 (*GCS* 9:32)
Ern.*Opusc*.6 (Fritsch 384-91)
Stod.*Sfty*.3 (1687:41-43); Drnd.*Diss*.2.26.2 (1703:193); Baum.*Pred*.2.2 (Kirchner 2:62-69); Nss.*Dipp*.3 (1701:34); Frnck.*Pred*. Epiph.2 (1699:48-49)
Wlch.*Pol*.2.4.50 (1752:239)
Edw.*Rel.Aff*.3.1 (Miller 2:236)
Baum.*Pred*.2.3 (Kirchner 2:93); Zinz.*Lond.Pred*.3.6 (Beyreuther 5-I:361-62)
Sem.*Rel*.3 (Schütz 27)
Mrck.*Cant*.pr. (Velzen 2:B1r); Mrck.*Apoc*.pr.91 (Velzen 8:J4r)
Zinz.*Hom*.24 (Beyreuther 3-I:237)

Pet.*Hchzt*.6.8 (1701:198-99)

among those who rejected it linked with it; but despite the aspersions of the latter on its authenticity, the attestation of the text in the Gospel of Matthew was virtually unanimous, and church theologians of all confessions could expound it with impunity.

Beyond any authentication of the text of the New Testament, the interpretation of the text depended on the hermeneutical presuppositions of the interpreter. "Someone who has never learned any Greek and Hebrew," Zinzendorf promised, "can become an exegete by means of a hermeneutic based upon the wounds of Christ," a Christocentrism for which he claimed Luther's theology of the cross as a precedent: it was a "disaster" in theology to begin with the doctrine of God rather than the doctrine of Christ, or to define sin as doing something evil rather than as refusing to believe in Jesus. A convenient index to alternative hermeneutical systems for the Gospels continued to be provided by various titles for Jesus Christ. Eastern Orthodoxy spoke of him as "king, lawgiver, and judge," a variant on the triad of titles familiar from Calvin's *Institutes* but present already in the *Ecclesiastical History* of Eusebius, "prophet, priest, and king"; despite criticism, the formula, as a unit or in one or more of its parts, enjoyed wide support, even from Socinians (although they were accused of using it "in a totally distorted sense"). Like that triad, "Redeemer" as the one who was "the purchaser and the price" and "Mediator" as a more appropriate object of faith than the term "Son of God" had the advantage of coordinating his person and his work. Rationalist opponents of dogmatic christology tended to speak of him as the "founder of a new religion." The Song of Solomon and the Revelation of John, both of which were difficult to interpret by the methods of critical-historical hermeneutics, were a particularly fecund source of titles for Christ; beyond king, priest, shepherd, and brother, "the word 'bridegroom' is the sweetest name that is applied to our Savior in Holy Scripture." "Savior [Heiland]" became so common in the usage of Pietists and especially of Moravians, for whom it was "a complete theology of God, a systematic theology" (though in organic relation with "the theology of God the

Zinz.*Gem*.35 (Beyreuther
4-II:110-11); Zinz.*Lond.Pred.*
3.4;6.2 (Beyreuther 5-I:309;
5-II:331-32)

Beng.*Brüd.*1.1.14 (1751:12

See vol.1:200-211;256-66

Zinz.*Gem*.3 (Beyreuther
4-I:67)

Zinz.*Hom*.14 (Beyreuther
3-I:136)

Dipp.*Orth*.4 (1699:52)

Lmp.*Hist*.2.6 (1747:176)

Phil.2:5-6
Mrck.*Exeg.exerc.*41-42 (Velzen
9:661-89)

Phil.2:7

Eug.Bulg.*Orth*.4 (Metaxas19);
Fil.*Sl*.124 (*Soč.Fil*.3:65-70)

John 1:1;1:14

Beng.*Gnom*.John 1:14
(Steudel 322)

Fusc.*Sac.cr.* (1756:21-22);
Neum.*Fünf*.2 (1726-I:216)

Spen.*Mess.* (1701:43-47)

Nmnn.*St.Ver*.29 (1696:69)
Deutsch.*Luth*.2.3.11
(1698:98-99)
See vol.4:194

Gtz.*Bek.* (1696:24-25)
Arb.*Des.myst*.5.6.50
(1764:617); Bert.*Theol.disc.*
27.1 (1792-V:270-73)
Hrn.*H.e*.3.1.45 (Leydecker
1:352); Mrck.*Comp*.19.25
(Velzen 18:383); Span.
Ev.vind.3.6 (Marck 3:460)
Lmp.*Theol.nat*.236-37
(1734:68-69)
See vol.4:350-62

Father"), that other Pietists themselves objected to it as a cliché.

Carrying as it did the traditional authority of a millennium and a half of orthodox dogmatic development, the christology articulated above all by the Councils of Nicea and Chalcedon represented the "consensus" of all the mainline churches and theologians—Anglican and Eastern Orthodox, as well as "Dr. Luther, with whom the Reformed and Catholic churches agree." Critics, evangelical or rationalistic, might see its technical terminology about "hypostatic union" and "communication of properties," or "person" and "natures," as a Hellenization of the gospel and "an academic quarrel of pagan philosophy" that obscured the message of the historical Jesus; but quoting the Chalcedonian decree as such a consensus provided the basis for doctrinal examination of other christological questions—including the question of the historical Jesus. The language of Paul about "Christ Jesus, being in the form of God" was not merely symbolic but helped to explain his term in the next verse, "he emptied himself," since the paradoxical meaning of that verse was that "he emptied himself in a nonemptying way"; the first and the last verse of the prologue of the Gospel of John were the supreme example in all Greek, whether pagan or Christian, of "the difference between 'being' and 'becoming.' "

The technical language of christological dogma was not confined to dogmatics but permeated orthodox devotion as well, and it was defended by Pietists such as Spener, despite the accusation that they had "abolished" it. They were also accused of holding to a christology that was "practically no different from that of the Reformed," which Lutherans still charged with being fundamentally rationalistic; but Reformed theologians were joined by Roman Catholic theologians in denouncing the doctrine of the Lutheran "Ubiquitists" as "mad" and "monstrous," for teaching that "incommunicable" attributes of the divine nature such as ubiquity had been communicated to the human nature of Christ. By the eighteenth century there was on this issue, as on most of christology, a special sensitivity to those aspects of the orthodox

Ath.Par.*Epit*.3.4-5
(1806:300-307)

See vol.2:57

See vol.1:263-64
Ath.Par.*Epit*.3.7
(1806:313-17)

See vol.1:228;248
Pnch.*Dict*. (1736:49-51);
Drnd.*Fid.vind*.1.35
(1709:118-21); Bulg.*Kat*.73
(1940:185-86)
Amrt.*Theol.eclec*.8.1.6
(1752-2-III:22)
Amrt.*Theol.eclec*.8.4.1
(1752-2-III:62-63)
See vol.2:62-75
Bert.*Theol.disc*.26.10
(1792-V:211-12)
Sem.*Rel*.3 (Schütz 26-27)

Tin.*Chr*.1 (1730:9)

Bnyn.*Lw.Gr*.2 (Sharrock
2:100)
Lschr.*Del*. (1707:11)
Eug.Bulg.*Orth*.4 (Metaxas
19-20)
See vol.2:227-42

Mynst.*Betr*.25 (1846-I:302)

Sherl.*Def*.3 (1675:295-96)
Fil.*Sl*.50 (*Soč.Fil*. 2:51)

Jeff.*Ep*.31.x.1819 (Adams
388)

Ost.*Arg.ref*.pr.
(1720:B4v-C1r);Lw.*Dem.Er*.
(Moreton 5:25)

Tin.*Chr*.5 (1730:48)

Sem.*Frag*.5 (1780:37)
Reim.*Apol*.1.1.5.9;2.1.2.3
(Alexander 1:165;2:45)

tradition in which the integrity of the human nature of Jesus had been affirmed and stressed. Both textual variants of the decree of Chalcedon were theologically correct: the divine-human person of Jesus Christ was "from two natures" but also "in two natures." Orthodox christology required the condemnation of the Apollinarist heresy that the divine Logos had taken the place of the soul in the human nature of Jesus: he was fully human and fully historical, possessing a fully human soul as well as whatever else was necessary for genuine humanity, including a distinct human will and a distinct human "action," though without the possibility of sin.

"Then who is, or who was, this Jesus?": that was "a question partly of historical, partly of moral content." Even a thinker who reduced "external revelation" to natural religion had to address both the historical content and the moral content of the question, the "sufficient [historical] evidence of a person being sent from God" and the "noble [moral] example" of "this divine person." Whatever else Jesus was and whatever else he had done, he was "the messenger of God touching His mind and the tenor of the covenant unto the poor world"—more than a prophet, as those who confronted Islam had special reason to go on insisting, but certainly not less than a prophet. He preached the love of God and the kingdom of God, but he also provided "a holy example" to be followed. "Setting up the person of Christ in opposition to his Gospel," therefore, as though obedience to the message of the Gospels were not part of reverence for his person, simply would not do, because what Jesus taught and what Jesus did were inseparable: "the two are one." In the effort to recover "the character of Jesus Christ" and "the outlines of a system of the most sublime morality which has ever fallen from the lips of man," there were some who found that the literary structure of the Gospels made the task of "abstracting what is really his from the rubbish in which it is buried" more complex and ambiguous than such rationalistic reductionism supposed. How much of what he actually taught was new and how much was the reaffirmation of Jewish morality remained moot. And that, in turn, raised the question stated in the title of the most

Less.*Frag*.epil. (Rilla
7:812-52)

Less.*Zw*.int. (Rilla 8:254-58)

See vol.3:144

See vol.1:243-56

Brnt.*Art.XXXIX*.2 (1700:53)

Zinz.*Hom*.5 (Beyreuther
3-I:57)

Nss.*Dipp*.3 (1701:35-36)

See vol.4:145-53

Aug.*Praed.sanct*.15.30
(*PL* 44:981-82)

sensational book on the subject written in the eighteenth century, by Hermann Samuel Reimarus, as posthumously—and anonymously—published by Lessing: *The Intention of Jesus and of His Disciples*.

Although the term "christological dogma," strictly speaking, referred only to the person of Christ, there being no ecumenically accepted dogma of his work, both East and West contended as they did for orthodox christology not merely to protect a system of sacred metaphysics but to affirm a way of salvation. Regardless of specific content, all were agreed that Christ was what he was in order to do what he did; among the alternative theologies of the incarnation set up by the dogma of Nicea and Chalcedon about the person of the God-man, particular traditions and individual theologians selected one or another in relation to the alternative metaphors they had for his redemptive work. It was consistent with that correlation between person and work within the orthodox tradition when the critics of christological dogma made the received theories of redemption an object of their criticisms as well. There is much to be said for the historical hypothesis that the rejection of Chalcedonian christology and the quest of the historical Jesus were primarily intent on a redefinition of the doctrine of the atonement.

As eighteenth-century criticism of christological dogma coexisted with its continued hold on the official belief, teaching, and confession of the churches, so traditional theories of the atonement still provided the public definition of the work of Christ even as various revisions of them were being proposed. The atonement was a topic that "must be treated of strictly, and with a just exactness of expression," because so much was at stake. "A book or special treatise in opposition to 'the merit of Christ' is one of the most evil wiles of the wicked foe," warned one preacher and church leader, who was joined by a variety of defenders of that concept of "merit." Protestants had been attacking the Roman Catholic doctrines of merit and grace since the Reformation, but they would have joined their opponents in affirming the teaching of their common ancestor, Augustine, that Christ had not merited his own

Amrt.*Theol.eclec*.8.3.2
(1752-2-III:55)
Aug.*Pecc.merit*.1.33.62
(*CSEL* 60:63)

Albrt.*Vind*.1.13 (1695:21-22)

Spen.*Bed*.1.1.62 (Canstein
1:315);Mayr.*Red*.13
(1702:747)
Mēn.*Did*.5.17;1.7
(Blantēs 344;73)

Ost.*Dz.serm*.5 (1722:184-85)

John 10:18
Drnd.*Fid.vind*.1.58
(1709:186)
Mēn.*Did*.1.6 (Blantēs 65)

ap.Lw.*Reas*.1 (Moreton
2:75-80)

Gen.22:1-19

ap.Jcksn.*Rem*. (1731:22)

Reim.*Apol*.2.5.3.16
(Alexander 2:516)
Reim.*Apol*.1.5.2.7-8
(Alexander 1:742-49)
Strz.*Enchir*.1.2 (1828:18-19)
See vol.1:18-19

See vol.3:150-51
Mēn.*Did*.1.3 (Blantēs 31);
Bnyn.*Lw.Gr*.2 (Sharrock
2:106-9)

Ost.*Arg.ref*.John 19:17-42
(1720-II:148)

Poir.*Oec.div*.3.17
(1705-II:820)
Mrck.*Comp*.20.17 (Velzen
18:397); see vol.4:163-64
Frnck.*Pass.Joh*.4;9;1
(1733:73-74;148;18)

Zinz.*Soc*.14 (Beyreuther
1-I:147)

incarnation, but had by his incarnation and redemption merited grace for mankind. Orthodox Protestants had been attacking Pietists for their alleged retreat from the Reformation doctrines of merit and grace, but both were using much the same language to affirm that "without the merit of Christ as this has become our own" it was impossible to attain salvation. The cross was a royal throne and the foundation of the church, "the foundation of our justification" as well as "the principle of our sanctification." It had to be defended against the charge that since Christ said that he was laying down his life of his own accord, his death was a suicide; the paradox was that "the impassible one suffers, the immortal God dies."

Two of the most fundamental objections against "the atonement for sins made by the Son of God" were that "it is a human sacrifice, which nature itself abhors" and that it "represents God as punishing the innocent and acquitting the guilty." The first of these was sometimes elaborated by the charge, in an allusion to the binding of Isaac, that such a view of atonement was nothing more than "a confirmation of the Jewish law admitting human sacrifices." The repudiation of "the system of salvation, concept by concept, sentence by sentence, as false and full of contradictions" also required a retranslation and reinterpretation of the fifty-third chapter of Isaiah, which, as in the ancient church, was seen as stating, more amply than any New Testament passage, that the substitutionary character of the death of Christ had come, in the medieval phrase, "not only to us, but for our sakes." But the description of the death of Christ as "a sacrifice on Mount Golgotha," which "he offered to God to expiate our sins, to deliver us from death, and to enable us to acquire a right to eternal life," meant that the "necessity" of such a sacrifice came neither from God the Father nor from Christ himself, but from sinful humanity, in whose stead Christ had rendered both active and passive obedience. That definition of "Christ in our place" was to be "preserved more than all other doctrines." Yet paradoxically, just when the emphasis on the wounds of Christ was becoming more explicit, the easy assumption of

Zinz.*Hom.*5 (Beyreuther 3-I:51)

Mayr.*Red.*13 (1702:731)

Jeff.*Ep.*21.v.1803 (Adams 331)

Edw.*Rel.Aff.*1 (Miller 2:123-24)

Lmp.*Betr.*1.14 (1756-I:318)

Lw.*Ser.Cl.*17 (Moreton 4:175)

Scriv.*Seel.*1.3 (Stier 3:74)

Lmp.*Betr.*1.15 (1756-I:343)

See vol.4:149-50;152; 154-55;283-85;323-24 Nss.*Dipp.*3;4 (1701:36;37); Bnyn.*Lw.Gr.*2 (Sharrock 2:86) Mayr.*Witt.*1 (1686:17)

Mayr.*Red.*13 (1702.739)

Mēn.*Did.*1.7 (Blantēs 75-76)

Edw.*Rel.Aff.*3.4 (Miller 2:273-74)

Swed.*Ver.Chr.*11.640 (1771:389)

See vol.3:129-44

See vol.4:156-57; 161-63;238;359-61

Mēn.*Did.*1.7 (Blantēs 74); Grig.Mont.*Am.sag.*4.42 (Gendrot 113)

universal Christian agreement on the sacrificial atonement was itself coming into question.

In part, this question also involved the second criticism, the whole idea of "the terrible blood judgment which God pronounced upon his only-begotten Son on Good Friday." The very point on which the most radical critics agreed with the christological dogma, the supreme moral force and utter innocence of the man Jesus as the embodiment of "every human excellence," seemed to be violated by depicting Christ in his death as the revelation of the punitive justice of God through "an exemplary punishment of God upon sin." Some defenders of orthodoxy sought to mitigate the harshness of this picture by suggesting that "to have a true idea of Christianity, we must not consider our blessed Lord as suffering in our stead, but as our representative, acting in our name," or by reminding the believing soul of the infinite value that Christ had placed upon it by suffering for it, or by describing Christ in his passion as "the true guarantee for all the elect." But the corollary of the Reformation doctrine of justification by faith, which was the reciprocal imputation of human sins to Christ and of his righteousness to sinners, only seemed to exacerbate the image of "the righteous God, the angered God," and "the embittered God," who had been appeased by "the blood of Jesus," which, as the blood of the incarnate Logos, possessed infinite worth. Not everyone found it convincing any longer to speak as though "the sufficiency of Christ as a mediator" were a confirmation of this "sense of the moral beauty of divine things," and some even found "the imputation of Christ's merit and righteousness impossible."

The two themes of the death of Christ as a sacrifice and as a vindication of divine justice had been ingeniously brought together in Anselm's doctrine of the atonement as satisfaction, which, together with its corollary in the christological dogma, had survived the Reformation and was, if anything, even more entrenched now than it had been in medieval teaching. Although it was anthropopathism to speak of a "conflict" between "the justice of God and his mercy, [which] embraced together, and fulfilled the great

Wsly.*Hom*.1.3 (*LPT* 125);
Bert.*Theol.disc*.2.3
(1792-I:80-81)

Dör.*Pet*.12-13 (1718:35-36)

Lw.*Reas*.2 (Moreton 2:98)
Tin.*Chr*.4 (1730:40);
Tnnt.*Disc*.1 (1745:29-30);
Wsly.*Hom*.1.1 (*LPT* 124)

Bnyn.*Lw.Gr*.2 (Sharrock
2:108);Stod.*Sfty*.11
(1687:322)
Poir.*Théol.cr*.1.1.2
(1690-I:15); Brnt.*Art.
XXXIX*.13 (1700:131);
Nss.*Dipp*.5 (1701:43);
Terst.*Abr*.2.7.2 (Becher
2:214-15)

Strim.*Un.Ev*.1.2 (1711:4)

See vol.3:143; vol.4:250
Fusc.*Sac.cr*. (1756:11);
Amrt.*Theol.eclec*.8.2.4-5
(1752-2-III:39-44)
Bert.*Theol.disc*.28.4
(1792-VI:18-20);
Amrt.*Theol.mor*.13.12-13
(1757-II:290-304)

Dipp.*Hrt*.1 (1706:14);
Tin.*Chr*.13 (1730:289)
Sem.*Rel*.22;23 (Schütz
184;196)

Brnt.*Rom*. (1688:25)

Bnyn.*Lw.Gr*. (Sharrock
2:119)

Frnck.*Id*.45 (Peschke 197)
See vol.4:18-19;147;
364-65;381
Rom.9:16
Zinz.*Red*.1;2 (Beyreuther
1-II:21;34);Wsly.*Serm*.5.4.7
(Baker 1:197);Wer.*Diss*.29
(Ryhinerus 1:484)

Poir.*Oec.div*.14.3 (1705-II:85)
Neum.*Fünf*.1 (1726-I:125);
Lmp.*Ew.Str*.1 (1729:127-28);
Poir.*Oec.div*.3.5
(1705-II:660-61)
See vol.4:260-61
Lmp.*Theol.elench*.15.23-25
(1729:66-67)
Mrck.*Comp*.20.27 (Velzen
18:408-9);Tnnt.*Disc*.1
(1745:24)

mystery of our redemption," both attributes were described with equal explicitness in Scripture and neither was to be elevated above the other: "there is neither justice in God without mercy nor mercy without justice." To the objection that "justice and mercy can't at the same time be exercised in one and the same instance on the same subject," orthodoxy set forth the doctrine of satisfaction through the "voluntary substitution" of the death of Christ, "standing in the room of sinners," as both the outcome of the justice of God against sin and the method by which "the goodness and mercy of God" achieved its desired end in human salvation.

This doctrine of the work of Christ represented, at least in the West though also partly in the East, almost as much of a common ground as did the dogma of Chalcedon on the person of Christ. Nevertheless, its Roman Catholic expositors had the advantage, which its systematizer Anselm had also had, of being able to connect the "condign satisfaction of outraged justice by Christ" with the idea of satisfaction in the sacrament of penance, as "a Catholic dogma confirmed by the perpetual tradition of the fathers." Radical Protestants had a corresponding advantage in being able to attack both kinds of satisfaction as "deception." But evangelical Protestants could only follow the precedent of the Reformers in charging that the practice of penitential satisfaction had "derogated from the value of this satisfaction" rendered by Christ. Their insistence that salvation came through grace alone, without works, had its corollary in the doctrine of satisfaction through Christ, as "the chief foundation of apostolic doctrine"; and the locus classicus for the Augustinian doctrine of grace, "It is not of him that wills, nor of him that runs, but of God who shows mercy," proved that everyone needed the "satisfaction and sacrifice of Christ on the cross." The death of a saint or martyr could have provided an example, but the death of Christ conferred eternal merit, to match the eternal punishment merited by sin.

Against the usual Arminian objections, orthodox Calvinism defended "satisfaction" as preferable to the theory of "acceptilation"; and against the standard

ap.Sherl.*Def*.6 (1695:512)
See vol.4:324-31

Wlch.*Pol*.2.4.61;2.4.63
(1752:253-54;256)
Wet.*N.T.* (1756:133)

Dipp.*Orth*.8 (1699:111-12)

Tin.*Chr*.4 (1730:38)
Reim.*Apol*.2.5.3.6
(Alexander 2:488)

Lw.*Reas*.1 (Moreton 2:80)
Poir.*Oec.div*.4.3 (1705-II:88)

Sherl.*Def*.1;4
(1675:34;391-92)
Ern.*Opusc*.16 (Fritsch 562);
Mayr.*Red*.14 (1702:761-62)

ap.Zinz.*Red*.8 (Beyreuther
1-II:104)

Reim.*Apol*.2.1.2.11
(Alexander 2:66)

Reim.*Apol*.2.6.2.2;2.5.1.6
(Alexander 2:546;435)
Edw.*Rel.Aff*.1 (Miller 2:109)

Ors.*Ist*.2.5 (1747-I:208);
Drnd.*Diss*.1.6.9-10
(1703:18-19)

Socinian objections, which had gone further than Arminianism by attacking orthodoxy on the person as well as on the work of Christ, theologians of various confessions urged that "satisfaction" was genuinely scriptural despite the absence of the term from Scripture. But now, in addition to these left-wing churches of the Reformation, critics were arising within the confessional churches to challenge the assumptions of the doctrine of satisfaction. It was, they asserted, "opposed to Holy Scripture." It "dishonored" God by misrepresenting him as "an injured party who wants satisfaction or reparation of honor"; but "God, as he can never be injured, so he can never want reparation and . . . can gain no addition of satisfaction." Therefore the very idea of satisfaction was unnecessary. "All these objections," one defender found, "proceed upon this supposition, that atonement, or satisfaction, when attributed to Jesus Christ, signify neither more nor less, nor operate in any other manner, than when they are used as terms in human laws, or in civil life." And hence it was a "childish" quibble to object to the word "satisfaction," and a false alternative to demand a choice between denial of satisfaction and acceptance of "a furious and merciless Deity." Though the term was absent, the concept itself was present throughout Scripture. The real ground of the objection to "satisfaction" was not its absence from Scripture, but a revulsion at terms that Scripture did employ frequently, such as "redemption," and therefore at the orthodox understanding of "the intention of Jesus" as Savior and Redeemer.

To this the critics objected that even if that understanding of the intention of Jesus, together with the christological dogma, could legitimately claim to be scriptural, it did not represent "the system of Jesus, but rather that of his disciple John," or that of "the principal originator and founder of Christianity" as a system, the apostle Paul. Though still identified as "the most eminent servant of Christ that ever lived" and as the writer of all the Epistles attributed to him (including sometimes, on the basis of what was said to be "the common tradition of the church," the Epistle to the Hebrews), Paul was now being singled out by

Jeff.*Ep.*13.iv.1820 (Adams 392)

a few critics as the "first corrupter of the doctrines of Jesus." That pertained not only to the doctrine of grace, of which he was regarded as the principal expositor theologically and the principal exemplar

Lang.*Paul.*1.1.2 (1718:23)

personally, but to the doctrine of redemption. Orthodox theologians conceded that the disciples of Jesus had not understood from his life and teachings either the doctrine of his divine nature or "the doctrines concerning Christ's death, the nature, necessity, and merits of his sacrifice and atonement for the sins of the

Lw.*Dem.Er.* (Moreton 5:27)
Beng.*Gnom.*Rom.1:4 (Steudel 538)

world," but that all of this had become clear to them only after Easter and Pentecost. But now the explanation for their failure to understand was said to be that he had neither taught these doctrines nor intended to teach them. "Then who is, or who was, this Jesus?" truly was "a question partly of historical,

Sem.*Rel.*3 (Schütz 26-27)

partly of moral content."

Also for those who were still trying to answer that question with a degree of fidelity to the tradition of christological dogma, therefore, the fundamental issue, whether moral or historical, was, in Reimarus's formula, the relation between "the system and intention of Jesus" as it could be historically discerned and

Reim.*Apol.*2.2.2.con. (Alexander 2:173)

Wer.*Diss.*4.2 (Ryhinerus 1:83)
Baum.*Pred.*3.10 (Kirchner 3:310-11)
Luke 3:41-51
Zinz.*Zst.*9 (Beyreuther 3-II:65)

"the system and intention that the disciples [attributed to him] after his death." According to the picture in the New Testament, his intention had been, also in his miracles, to establish a kingdom that was not of this world, and finally to do so by his death. His visit to the temple at the age of twelve did not mean that he was some sort of "child prodigy," but that in his dealings with his Jewish countrymen he had accommodated himself to their religious traditions and

Zinz.*Off.Red.*13 (Beyreuther 2-IV:26)
Budd.*Phil.Ebr.*23 (1720:112-13)

Baum.*Pred.*1.2 (Kirchner 1:48-49)

Lmp.*Betr.*2.7 (1756-I:581-85)

forms, acting as the restorer of Hebrew wisdom. So also in his dealings with the disciples he had accommodated himself to their human weakness and had disclosed the full truth to them only "gradually." Despite such a "frank confession" about himself as his words "I am" in response to the high priest's question, "Are you the Christ, the Son of the Blessed?" he

Mark 14:61-62

Phil.2:7
Baum.*Pred.*3.10 (Kirchner 3:311)
Pet.*Hchzt.*13.8; Matt.24:36;
See vol. 1:205
Matt.16:28;John 21:22

had "emptied himself" in his state of humiliation and had admitted his ignorance about "the day and hour" of the Last Judgment. Passages in the Gospels that seemed to predict that this would take place before the death of some of the disciples had to be explained

Mrck.*Exeg.exerc*.26.7;35.7
(Velzen 9:534;617);
Sem.*Frag*.38 (1780:308)
Zinz.*Red*.5 (Beyreuther
1-II:65)

Matt.21:1-11

Mēn.*Did*.1.6 (Blantēs 63-70)

Reim.*Apol*.2.3.1.2
(Alexander 2:180)

Mmchi.*Orig.ant*.2.14.4
(1749-I:277-78)
Matt.26:39
Mark 10:38-39
Fil.*Sl*.51 (*Soč.Fil*.2:60)
Frnck.*Pass.Marc*.2;3;7
(1724:38;71-72;192-93)
Zinz.*Hom*.21 (Beyreuther
3-I:210);Zinz.*Rel*.1
(Beyreuther 6-I:12-13)
Reim.*Apol*.2.2.2.3 (Alexander
2:150)

Matt.27:46;Ps.22:1
Frnck.*Pass.Marc*.11
(1724:319-20);Lmp.*Betr*.4.14
(1756-II:643);Mrck.*Syl*.10.3
(Velzen 15:310-11);
Hno.*Theol*.6.2.16.5
(1785-II:479)
Reim.*Apol*.2.3.1.1 (Alexander
2:179)

See p. 240 below

Jeff.*LJ* (Adams 297)

Reim.*Apol*.2.5.3.3 (Alexander
2:481)

Sem.*Rel*.3 (Schütz 26-27)

away: it was not fair to tear out of context statements that had come from the state of humiliation.

Reimarus and others had begun to argue that such explanations of his life and teaching, and particularly of his suffering and death, were now to be judged not by the christological dogma, with its language about states of humiliation and exaltation, but by "the quest of the historical Jesus." The triumphal entry into Jerusalem on Palm Sunday, which adherents of the dogma interpreted as acknowledgment of his divine nature and preparation for his death and resurrection, was read by radical critics as his abortive attempt to establish a theocratic kingdom of God on earth. Orthodoxy interpreted the words of agony in Gethsemane, "Let this cup pass from me," in the light of the earlier question to the disciples, "Are you able to drink the cup that I drink?" Now this acceptance of suffering and death, which he "had always had before his eyes since assuming his teaching office and coming out of the desert," was reversed completely into an effort "if at all possible to escape his death." The cry of dereliction on the cross, "My God, my God, why hast thou forsaken me?" which "was meant to express the burden of sin of the entire human race that he was bearing," the evil and the shame of it all, became an exclamation of his heartbreak at the ultimate disappointment of all his messianic hopes and dreams for the restoration of the kingdom to Israel. And the belief in his resurrection either was seen as an event in the history of the ancient church rather than in the history of Jesus himself or, if possible, was simply eliminated from the history altogether.

The Essence of True Religion

Revising the history of Jesus from triumph into tragedy, and then from tragedy into pathos, was a complete break with the entire tradition of Christian doctrine; but both as a "historical" and as a "moral" question, it also opened in a new manner the inquiry into the essence of religion and the essence of the gospel. Having described how the theocratic dream of Jesus came to naught, Reimarus immediately went on to speak about "the reasonable, simple, exalted, holy, and practical religion" of Jesus, intended for all

Reim.*Apol.*2.1.1.7 (Alexander 2:27); Sem.*Frag.*20 (1780:108-9)

Zinz.*Gem.*17 (Beyreuther 4-I:265)

Sem.*Erud.* (1765-I:56)

Reim.*Apol.*2.1.1.6 (Alexander 2:25)

Brnt.*Rom.* (1688:8-9); Reim. *Apol.*2.1.1.9 (Alexander 2:35)

Jab.*Sal.*18 (Basler 212)
Tnnt.*Disc.*6 (1745:312)

Fil.*Sl.*116 (*Soč.Fil.* 3:33)
See pp. 66-67 above
Sem.*Rel.*25 (Schütz 209)
Tin.*Chr.*7 (1730:76)
Wsly.*Serm.*39.1.9 (Baker 2:85)

Sem.*Frag.*pr. (1780:A3r);
Bl.*Unfehl.*10 (1791:80)

Brnt.*Art.XXXIX.*19 (1700:180)

Ost.*Arg.ref.*Rom.3 (1720-II:188)
Calv.*Inst.* (1559)2.2.11 (Barth-Niesel 3:253-54)
Edw.*Rel.Aff.*3.6 (Miller 2:315);Lw.*Ser.Cl.*16 (Moreton 4:163)

John 13:35
Edw.*Rel.Aff.*1 (Miller 2:107)

humanity. The eighteenth century found in the Jesus of the Gospels the problem as well as the solution of its quest for a "universal religion." He had not left behind a summa of teachings, and therefore it was necessary to distinguish historically and morally between that element of the teaching attributed to him which represented him as "the teacher of the entire human race" who had appealed to reason and universal experience, and that which made him little more than the reformer of a corrupt Judaism, who had cited and confirmed the authority of the Old Testament. The first of these was characterized by "genuine simplicity and perspicuity," and "all its doctrines and rules are clearly and distinctly held out to us, not like the heathen divinity."

The quest for a universal religion became a quest for the "sum total" or "very essence" of religion, as well as for what a Russian Orthodox theologian called "the spirit of true Christianity," the essence of the gospel midway between the extremes of atheism and superstition, enthusiasm and bigotry. If history was a documentation of the kaleidoscopic variety of doctrine, it was not possible to equate the essence, in a reductio ad absurdum of the Vincentian canon, with everything that had ever been taught anywhere by anyone; rather it was the historian's assignment, together with other theological scholars, to discriminate "what is essential in Christian religion and doctrine" from "what can be called truly accidental and constantly changing," which had only "temporary value." One definition of a true church, consequently, could be "a society that [has] preserved the essentials and fundamentals of Christianity." Such a definition could lead to no more than a recitation of confessional (or anticonfessional) positions. It could be predicted that an heir of the Protestant Reformation would define justification by faith as the essence of the Christian religion; another could quote Calvin as proof that genuine humility was "one of the most essential things pertaining to true Christianity." From such sayings of Jesus as "By this all men will know that you are my disciples, if you have love for one another" it was evident that "the essence of all true religion lies in holy love"; but radicals found in these

Dipp.*Hrt*.1 (1706:5-6);
Tin.*Chr*.5 (1730:53-54)

Nss.*Dipp*.pr. (1701:9)
Swed.*Ver.Chr*.6.357
(1771:231)

Nss.*Dipp*.14 (1701:83-84)

John 3:30
Scriv.*Seel*.3.24 (Stier 5:803)

Bl.*Unfehl*.26 (1791:537)
Ost.*Arg.ref*.Heb.1
(1720-II:286)
Frnck.*Id*.4 (Peschke 173)

Zinz.*Soc*.21 (Beyreuther
1-I:212-13)
Poir.*Oec.div*.4.4 (1705-II:98)

Lw.*Chr.Perf*.2 (Moreton 3:25)

Lw.*Chr.Perf*.1 (Moreton
3:12-13)

Lw.*Chr.Perf*.2 (Moreton
3:23;25)

Conc.*Rel.riv*.2.2.6.2
(1754-I:319-20)

Byl.*Com.phil*.1.2 (1713-I:153)

Spen.*Pi.Des*. (Aland 79)

Ost.*Dz.serm*.4 (1722:149)

Edw.*Rel.Aff*.3.12 (Miller
2:413)

Sem.*Rel*.23 (Schütz 198)
Strim.*Un.Ev*.1.24
(1711:31-32)
See vol.4:156
Mel.*Loc*. (1521)
(Plitt-Kolde 63)

same words a basis for excluding "word, sacraments, and sound orthodoxy" from the essence altogether and for making this "love" a universal quality. For this they were attacked as subverters of "the heart and core of our Christian faith": they were right in defining the essence as union with Christ, but word and sacraments were an indispensable part of that. The essence of union with Christ and of true Christianity was contained in the words of John the Baptist about Christ, "He must increase, but I must decrease."

The irreducible minimum of the "essence" could come down, alternately, to an acceptance of Jesus as no more than a teacher sent from God, or in addition as divine, or in addition as "one's personal Savior and Lord" through his suffering, death, and resurrection. In any case, everyone agreed that the essence was more than an "opinion," but that it had to include the dimension of practice. One writer defined "new birth" and the "principle of a new life," but not "articles of faith," as "the very essence and soul of Christianity." Yet in the same work he affirmed that "the whole frame of Christianity" was built on the "great doctrines" of "the deplorable corruption of human nature and its new birth in Jesus Christ," and he rejected the idea that Christianity was "a school for the teaching of moral virtue, the polishing [of] our manners, or forming us to live a life of this world with decency and gentility." The essence of religion could be defined by one author—whom the orthodox called "pestiferous" and "detestable"—as consisting of "the judgments that our spirit forms concerning God, and the feelings of respect, fear, and love that our will has for him"; or it could be "the inner man or the new man, whose soul is faith and whose expressions are the fruit of life."

For some, this essence specifically implied referring to "the merit of Jesus Christ" or professing "either explicitly or implicitly that Jesus satisfied for our sins"; but for others, the notion of satisfaction could be eliminated "without doing any harm to the essence of the Christian religion," and the same was true of the doctrine of predestination. Paraphrasing the axiom of Philip Melanchthon that "to know Christ is to know the benefits that come from him," one definition of the essence directed attention away from the confession that Father, Son, and Holy Spirit "are three persons" to the affirmation of the "benefits" associated with them; the dogmatic "forms and religious definitions of the church" did not belong to "the essence of the Christian religion," which consisted, according to the teachings of Jesus, in the two great commandments of love for God and love for neighbor (described also by the orthodox as "the mother of all virtues"). Those who advanced such redefinitions were accused of limiting the essence to the natural elements of Christianity at the cost of the supernatural elements.

What they were actually doing was proceeding in the serene confidence that in its content this essence of the gospel would turn out to be identical with the best of "natural religion." Historical research in the usual sense would not discover the essence, nor could the quest for the essence in turn "disprove or invalidate that historical evidence on which Christianity is founded"; for "the records of all history" made it clear that "natural religion" in this sense had never existed concretely in any nation but had to be abstracted from the revelations, ceremonies, and traditions of the historical religions. Nevertheless, if, as a Greek Orthodox theologian affirmed, "the knowledge that God exists is naturally implanted in us," the defenders of supernatural knowledge, too, had to find some congruence between the two, at the very least acknowledging that the Golden Rule was "a natural and at the same time a divine law" and that "the Ten Commandments (Ex. 20) contain the substance of natural religion"; therefore some sins prohibited by revealed law were forbidden also by natural law, and vice versa. Beyond that, such ideas as virtue, perfection, and beauty were, at one level, "purely natural and human," but in Christ they all became "completely divine and supernatural." Even beyond that, many orthodox theologians had taught that there was a natural appetite for the vision of God, and had in other ways made the concept of what was "natural" an essential part of Christian theology. There was, then, a continuity between natural and revealed knowledge, which made it possible (despite the charge that

Sem.*Frag.*10 (1780:57)

Dipp.*Orth.*5 (1699:72-73)
Matt.22:37-40;Luke10:27
Swed.*Cael.*3.15;27.238
(1890:18;135); Reim.*Apol.*
2.1.1.8 (Alexander 2:30)
Strz.*Enchir.*3.4 (1828:116)

Lschr.*Pens.* (1724:15)

Wlff.*Nat.Gott.*40 (1744-I:28)
Sem.*Rel.*15 (Schütz 108)

Lw.*Reas.*int. (Moreton 2:57)

Sem.*Rel.*16 (Schütz 115)

Mid.*Wat.* (1731:50)

Ath.Par.*Epit.*1.1.1 (1806:49)

Ern.*Opusc.*23 (Fritsch 617-40)
Matt.7:12
Mrkrd.*Off.*14 (1722:100)

Jcksn.*Rem.* (1731:13); Drnd.
*Diss.*2.2.7 (1703:119)
Alph.Lig.*Theol.mor.*3.5.7.759
(Gaudé 2:203-4)

Poir.*Théol.cr.*1.1.3
(1690-I:27)
Bert.*Aug.*2.1
(1747-I:197-206);
see vol.3:303-7

Bert.*Aug.*2.3 (1747-I:272-73)
Ost.*Cat.* (1747:15)

Reim.*Apol.*1.1.2.2 (Alexander 1:84)

Ost.*Dz.serm.*1-2 (1722:1-78)

Tin.*Chr.*6 (1730:60)

Phil.4:8
Tin.*Chr.*12 (1730:205)

Lw.*Reas.*1 (Moreton 2:66)

Spen.*Gtts.*2 (1680:17)
Zinz.*Soc.*4 (Beyreuther 1-I:39-40);Prstly.*Soc.*2 (1803:6)
Span.*Ev.vind.*2.16 (Marck 3:298-99)
Tin.*Chr.*12 (1730:199-200)
Lw.*Reas.*1 (Moreton 2:60-61;70)
See vol.1:43-44,349-50; vol.2:35-36; vol.3:95-105, 255-67,284-93;vol.4:61-63, 66-67,166,194,347-50

Cochrane (1961) 103-4
Grig.Mont.*Am.sag.*1.12 (Gendrot 99)
Rom.11:33

Brnt.*Art.XXXIX.*1 (1700:17)

Swed.*Ver.Chr.*13.699-700 (1771:430-31)

Fén.*Ep.*28.v.1687 (Gosselin 7:200)

Neum.*Fünf.*1;2;3 (1726-I:78;363;456)

orthodox textbooks never did so) to proceed from the case for religion in general to the case for the Christian religion in particular.

The radical theologians of the eighteenth century were prepared to go much further, insisting that "there's a religion of nature and reason written in the hearts of every one of us from the first creation, by which all mankind must judge of the truth of any instituted religion whatever" (especially the institutions of traditional Christianity), and quoting in substantiation the words of the apostle about "whatever is true." But defenders of orthodoxy reminded their radical colleagues that many of the arguments being employed against traditional revealed religion would just as easily strike natural religion, and that in biblical usage "natural men" referred to those who had neither grace nor the Holy Spirit. Socrates may have been a defender of some of the truths of natural religion, but there was no salvation on the basis of natural religion.

Whether it was seen as no more than a republication of the religion of nature or as a completion of it that would have been necessary even if mankind had continued in a state of perfect innocence, revelation needed, as it had throughout Christian history, to locate itself in relation to reason. The need was by no means uniform across cultures and across churches. One scholar has noted "the absence, among Tuscans, of any of the open hostility between science and orthodoxy that raged beyond the Alps," because in Florentine thought "every branch of learning was, to some extent, a part of theology"; similarly, a Roman Catholic in France could speak of "Jesus Christ as the depth of all knowledge." Yet the use of reason was as fundamental to the absence of hostility there as it was to the hostility elsewhere, because it was fundamental to the theological enterprise itself. No doctrine of theology, except perhaps for the Trinity, was as completely bound up with the notion of mystery and the claims of revelation as the Eucharist; "mystery [μυστήριον]" had been the Greek term for "sacrament" since patristic times. While defenders of the real presence could demand that "reason must be held captive here," the disputes over the presence, which

Zinz.Zst.25 (Beyreuther
3-II:196)

Sem.N.T.Int.1.3.5.7
(1767:129)
Wer.Diss.11 (Ryhinerus
1:200)
Blrt.S.T.Grat.3.2 (Lequette
3:77-80)

Lw.Reas.4 (Moreton 2:116)
See vol.3:255;259

Pnch.Dict. (1736:1)

Mos.Tol.10 (1722:50)

Amrt.Theol.eclec.4.2.1.2
(1752-1-IV:14)

See vol.4:232-39

Poir.Fid.rat.1.11;1.16
(1708:12-13;23)

See vol.1:42-44,349-50;
vol.3:265

Zinz.Gem.8 (Beyreuther
4-I:148)

Frnck.Bcht. (Peschke 99)

Ost.Eth.prol.2 (1727:5)

Budd.Phil.Ebr.18 (1720:70);
Frnck.Meth.3.20 (1723:108)
Deutsch.Luth.1.2.4
(1698:12-13);Mayr.Mis.4.6
(1692:45-46)
Spen.Bed.1.1.13 (Canstein
1:95);Spen.Beant.4.13
(1693:107)
Wlff.Nat.Gott.295
(1744-I:294);Sem.Erkl.1.4;2
(1777:82;147-50)

Poir.Théol.cr.pr.
(1690-I:A3r-A3v);
Poir.Chr.ed.35 (1694:46)

Mid.Wat. (1731:56)

Poir.Fid.rat.1.16 (1708:23)

Stod.Gd.Chr. (1714:36-38)

could be seen as providential despite the havoc they had wrought, had proved how indispensable reason was, through the use of such concepts of logic as analysis, definition, and contradiction, in interpreting revelation or, for that matter, in defending it against reason.

"The true state of the question," then, was "not whether reason is to be followed, but when it is best followed." The proposition attributed to Abelard, that "faith is subject to reason," was heretical, also in its eighteenth-century version. It was likewise misguided to treat as an article of faith a theological conclusion whose major premise came from revelation but whose minor premise came from reason. The Remonstrants, who had begun with a protest against the Calvinist doctrines of sin and predestination, appeared to their opponents to have fallen into rationalism, with devastating consequences for all of Christian doctrine. Boethius's *Consolation of Philosophy*, celebrated though it had been as a masterpiece of Christian philosophy, could now be attacked as a book "in which the Savior and his redemption are totally forgotten." At the universities logic and metaphysics were being preferred to the catechism, philosophical ethics to Christian ethics, and the Hellenization of Christianity to a faithful exposition of "the doctrine of the Hebrews" contained in Scripture. Although partisans of Lutheran orthodoxy attacked him as a rationalist and as a patron of extreme mysticism, Spener dissociated himself from both; similarly, though perhaps less successfully, other Protestant theologians sought to dissociate themselves from various rationalistic philosophies. Despite its boast of being "a century of enlightenment [un siècle éclairé]," the eighteenth century was a time of "blindness of the spirit"; despite its exaltation of reason, rationalism was itself "irrational"; and despite its rejection of authority, it had to admit that "natural knowledge, or the light of nature, is a knowledge and light that is made natural to us by the same authority which makes a certain language, certain customs and modes of behavior natural to us."

Church orthodoxy, in its own way, had as much of a stake as rationalism did in the quest for what Kant

Knt.*Rel.* (Cassirer 6:139-353)
Mid.*Mir.*int. (1749:xcii);
Reim.*Apol.*int.13 (Alexander
1:62)
Ath.Par.*Epit.*1.1.1
(1806:49-51)

Wlff.*Nat.Gott.*413
(1744-II:4)
Brnt.*Art.XXXIX.*1
(1700:21);Bert.*Theol.disc.*
prol.2 (1792-I:5)
Conc.*Rel.riv.*5.1.2
(1754-II:155-62)
See vol.4:347-50
Spen.*Pi.Des.* (Aland 22);
Frnck.*Meth.*3.20 (1723:106)

Tin.*Chr.*11 (1730:151)
Reim.*Apol.*int.13 (Alexander
1:63-64)

Jcksn.*Rem.* (1731:9)

Sem.*Rel.*35 (Schütz 279)

Dipp.*Orth.*9 (1699:118-24)

Lw.*Reas.*2 (Moreton 2:92-93)

Brnt.*Art.XXXIX.*17
(1700:147)
Amrt.*Theol.eclec.*2.1.1
(1752-1-II:1)

See vol.1:51-55

Conc.*Rel.riv.*5.1.1.8
(1754-II:316); Mmchi.
*Orig.ant.*3.2.1 (1749-III:272);
Tnnt.*Serm.*4 (1744:87-106)

See vol.3:285-93

Heb.11:6

called "religion within the boundaries of reason alone." Whatever its status in the apologetics of the earliest centuries may have been, the method described by an Eastern Orthodox theologian as "the syllogistic demonstration" of the existence of God had now become, since John of Damascus and Thomas Aquinas, "the great and solid argument on which religion rests." Roman Catholicism traditionally made more of the rational proof for its doctrine than confessional Protestantism had, even at the height of the orthodox era; Pietism was more suspicious still of a "pure doctrine" in which "the world's wisdom has been introduced gradually into theology." But now there were Protestants who took it to be "the chief business of preachers to show the reasonableness of the doctrines they teach" and who saw such preachers as the authentic Christians. According to orthodoxy, natural religion could become perfect only "by the addition of revelation," but the converse was also true: the consideration of natural religion had been good for orthodox Christianity, whose doctrine was built on reason as well as on the revelation of Christ; and there were questions in traditional theology such as predestination that some (though not all) theologians interpreted as belonging to reason rather than to revelation, as well as other questions such as the doctrine of angels that belonged to both.

In its content, the essence of true religion often turned out to be coextensive with the two a prioris that Christian doctrine had been taking for granted since the ancient church: the definition of the nature of God as absolute and the definition of the human soul as immortal. Applying the principle, formulated by Thomas Aquinas but affirmed by his predecessors in East and West for centuries, that "grace does not abolish nature, but completes it," orthodox theology had, on the authority of revelation, built its dogma of the Trinity on the basis of the first of these a prioris and its doctrine of resurrection and eternal life on the basis of the second. Biblical warrant for identifying these as the essence seemed to be provided by the verse, "Whoever would draw near to God must believe that he exists and that he rewards those who seek him" (not only in this life but especially in the

Drnd.*Diss*.1.8.2
(1703:21);Arb.*Inst*.1.20.4
(1765:99)

Zinz.*Soc*.29 (Beyreuther
1-I:271-72)

Brnt.*Art.XXXIX*.7
(1700:101-2)

Amrt.*Theol.eclec*.4.2.3.16-17
(1752-1-IV:99)

Zinz.*Gespr*.6 (Beyreuther
1-III:50-51)

Ost.*Dz.serm*.12 (1722:415);
Neum.*Hnd*. (1700:A3v)
Mrck.*Comp*.1.17
(Velzen 18:8);Wlch.*Pol*.2.1
(1752:87-101)
Wlff.*Nat.Gott*.427
(1744-II:26)
Mos.*Vind.disc*.1.6.2
(1722:123)
Byl.*Com.phil*.pr. (1713-I:124);
Gib.*Dec*.2 (Bury 1:28-33)

Mid.*Wat*. (1731:54-55)

Pnch.*Dict*. (1736:79)
Lmp.*Theol.nat*.119-31
(1734:36-42)
Drnd.*Fid.vind*.1.1 (1709:1-5);
See vol.1:17
Acts 17:22-31
Amrt.*Theol.eclec*.1.1.pr.
(1752-1-I:1);Ost.*Arg.ref*.Acts
17 (1720-II:172); Tnnt.*Serm*.
15;21 (1744:305-6;405);
Lang.*Paul*.1.2.3 (1718:87)

Acts 17:28 (AV)

Tol.*Pan*.2.2 (1720:54-55)

See pp. 183-84 below

life to come). The two requirements of that verse served a variety of interpreters in this period as a key. To Zinzendorf they provided the starting point for considering the "fundamental truths" of true religion, to Burnet "the foundation of religion," and to Eusebius Amort the proof that "for the heathens implicit faith in these mysteries is sufficient" even without such doctrines as the Trinity, incarnation, and resurrection.

Defenders of church doctrine in this period perceived that for the first time in its history it was facing a challenge to these fundamental truths of all religion as well as to its own specific dogmas. It was evident to all that since the Reformation the sense of reverence had been lost and that in its place had come "irreligion and unbelief, these detestable sentiments which attack religion itself and lead to atheism." Atheism had become an item on the theological agenda. There might be a difference between agnosticism and atheism, but there was none between open mockery and subtle subversion. When their opponents idealized the religious toleration in classical antiquity, orthodox theologians argued that it was "not the believers of religion, but infidels and atheists who in every country have always been the severest persecutors and cruelest oppressors of all civil as well as religious liberty." It was difficult or impossible to trust the adherents of atheism, because it was not only anti-Christian but unreasonable, rejecting as it did the evidence which, according to Romans 1:20, was "clearly seen from the creation." The sermon of the apostle Paul on the Areopagus also continued to be a convenient précis of natural theology and a summary of doctrines and obligations; but its quasi-creedal formula (perhaps derived from the Greek thinker Epimenides), "In him we live and move and have our being," became a congregational response in the secular worship ritual that some Deists were proposing as a substitute for orthodox liturgies.

From such biblical passages it was clear that natural theology was an article of faith: as the First Vatican Council was to decree in the next century, it was the teaching of revelation that the existence of God as an "independent and eternal Being, upon whom all

Wer.*Misc*.15.1 (Ryhinerus
2:252-55)
Lmp.*Theol.nat*.40-41
(1734:15-16)
Wlff.*Nat.Gott*.486;381
(1744-II:116-17;I:375-77)
Ost.*Arg.ref*.Gen.1 (1720-I:1)
Neum.*Rch*.2 (1751:59)
Hno.*Theol*.1.1.8 (1785-I:
247-74);Wsly.*Serm*.67 (Baker
2:535-50); Gaz.*Prael*.
1.1.1.6.176 (1831-I:32);
Fén.*Inst*.4 (Gosselin 6:78)
Ern.*Opusc*.14 (Fritsch
537-56);Terst.*Ep*.1.82-83
(Becher 5:181-85); Terst.*Abr*.
1.5.18 (Becher 2:72);
Zinz.*Aug.Conf*.20
(Beyreuther 6-II:343)
Lmp.*Theol.nat*.221-25
(1734:55-68); Amrt.
Theol.eclec.1.3.1 (1752-1-I:33)
Fén.*Tr.ex*. (Gosselin 1.76);
Wlff.*Nat.Gott*.35
(1744-I:24-25)
Tnnt.*Serm*.6 (1744:136);
Wlff.*Nat.Gott*.35 (1744-I:15)
Wlff.*Nat.Gott*.75;224;276
(1744-I:48-50;231;271)

Brnt.*Art.XXXIX*.1 (1700:17)

Wlff.*Nat.Gott*.166
(1744-I:173-75)
Lmp.*Theol.nat*.360-64
(1734:108-9)

Reim.*Apol*.1.5.2.1;1.5.4.1
(Alexander 1:721;769)

Wlch.*Pol*.2.1.18 (1752:101)

Mēn.*Did*.2.3 (Blantēs 117)
Swed.*Cael*.1 (1890:11);
Pff.*Hist.theol*.2.10;3.8
(1724-I:323-24;II:269-74)
Drnd.*Fid.vind*.2.10
(1709:231-35)
Mrck.*Comp*.16.11-12 (Velzen
18:330-31);Lmp.*Ew.Str*.1
(1729:149-50)
Reim.*Apol*.1.5.4.4 (Alexander
1:775)
Ath.Par.*Epit*.2.2.8 (1806:262)
Scriv.*Seel*.1.2 (Stier 3:46)
Strz.*Enchir*.2.1;2.5
(1828:49;76)
Mynst.*Betr*.58
(1846-II:312-22)

beings that are in the world are dependent" was established not only by revelation but by reason. The doctrine of God as Creator, without whom the reality of the world was unthinkable, was "the premier truth," together with its corollary doctrine (seen also in the widespread tendency of the time to speak of Providence rather than of God) of "a providence that extends itself to all things both natural and free," accomplishing its will even through war. Reason and nature confirmed monotheism by contrast with the irrational belief in many gods, as well as the doctrine of the "simplicity" of God by contrast with the compound nature of creatures. From "simplicity" it was a logical step, still by natural theology, to the immutability of God as "the most perfect Being," and thence to divine impassibility, in the light of which biblical language about divine sorrow and wrath was to be explained. Except for the Trinity, "which peculiarly belongs to the Christian religion," every tenet of the Christian doctrine of God was "founded on the principles of natural religion" and was therefore exposed to threat when those principles themselves came into question.

It was likewise orthodox doctrine that without the aid of revelation reason was able to prove that God possessed a perfect knowledge of the past and was the judge of the quick and the dead. Accordingly, the proponents of "a purely rational religion" insisted that the immortality of the soul was an essential component of it. The close connection between the doctrines of God and the soul meant that those who denied immortality were "on the way to atheism." There had long been differences of opinion among philosophers about the nature of the soul; now there was controversy about its immortality among theologians as well. This needed to be defended against its deniers past and present, who took refuge in the notion of "annihilation." Despite the effort to deny that there was any mention of it in the Hebrew Scriptures before the Babylonian captivity, "the hypothesis of the immortality of the human soul" was identified as biblical doctrine, indeed as the foundation and the essential content of the Christian doctrine of resurrection. The imperative to "reach for eternal life" was

Scriv.*Seel*.5.1 (Stier7:29);
Conc.*Rel.riv*.5.1.18.1
(1754-II:320-28)
Spen.*Bed*.1.1.19 (Canstein
1:109)
Mos.*Tol*.26 (1722:143-44)

Zinz.*Gespr*.9 (Beyreuther
1-III:80)

See vol.4:312-13
Lmp.*Theol.elench*.2.6
(1729:17-18)

Ost.*Dz.serm*.2 (1722:64)
Mrkrd.*Off*.16 (1722:132);
Wsly.*Serm*.63.1-4 (Baker
2:485-87); Wlff.*Nat.Gott*.429
(1744-II:31-32); Brnt.*Art.
XXXIX*.1 (1700:18);
Wilb.*Pr.Vw*.2 (1798:26)
Manuel (1959) 15-53

See vol.1:17-41; vol.4:284-93

Tnnt.*Serm*.4 (1744:101)
Ost.*Arg.ref*.Gen.5
(1720-I:5-6)
Pal.*Evid*.1.2.1 (Wayland
3:171); Ost.*Arg.ref*.Gen.5
(1720-I:5-6)
Tol.*Pan*.1.2 (1720:4);
Tnnt.*Serm*.20 (1744:389);
Prstly.*Soc*. (1803:48)
Ath.*Par.Epit*.3.2
(1806:293-95); Reim.*Apol*.
1.5.2.6 (Alexander1:738-39)
Dipp.*Orth*.6 (1699:89-91)
Zinz.*Rel*.5;6 (Beyreuther
6-I:89;112)

Tin.*Chr*.13 (1730:342)

Mid.*Ltr.Rom*. (1729:31)

Lw.*Reas*.3 (Moreton 2:112)

Ost.*Cat*. (1747:15-16)

universal, and immortality was "a truth acknowledged throughout the world." Yet that did not prove that it arose from pure reason or from heathen funeral practices, since it had originally come from divine revelation before the systems of the pagan philosophers, who, whatever their theories, had continued to regard the prospect of death with terror.

The doctrines of God and immortality were a documentation of the ambiguous relation between this essence of true religion and the specific historical religions. Earlier efforts to posit an affirmative kinship between them came in for criticism, but the attempt to find "a unity of design" within and behind the "great variety" of the religions persisted, complicated though it had been in modern times by the voyages of discovery. As these voyages contributed to "new views of pagan religion," a natural theology that had been based primarily on the philosophical theology of classical antiquity, with only occasional attention to the pre-Christian religions of the peoples who now belonged to the church, had to confront new data about nations in which there appeared to be "no worship" of a deity at all. At the same time, the discovery of accounts of a flood "among all the peoples and most ancient authors" helped to confirm the Genesis account; and the continuing appeal to the standard parallels between Socrates and Jesus, between the *Fourth Eclogue* of Vergil or the Sibylline books and the Gospels, and between the Hermetic writings of late antiquity and the Christian Scriptures was enriched by a deeper awareness of other sages, especially Confucius, whose "plain and simple maxims" could be used "to illustrate the more obscure ones" of Christ. Negatively, the parallels between non-Christian religions and Christian practices supplied arguments for polemics against the cult of the saints. Deists such as Toland were accused of putting "all traditional religions on a level," including Christianity itself, but church theologians sought to classify them. A taxonomy that listed four groups—all of paganism lumped together, and then the three book-monotheisms of Judaism, Christianity, and Islam —was representative of this effort.

Mēn.*Did*.1.4 (Blantēs
44-47);Coz.*Graec*.5.23.1294
(1719-III:315)

Strz.*Enchir*.5.1 (1828:193-94)

Fil.*Sl*.136 (*Soč.Fil*.3:132-38)

Pal.*Evid*.2.9.3 (Wayland
3:331-45);Conc.*Rel.riv*.2.2.4
(1754-I:298)

Wsly.*Serm*.63.21 (Baker
2:495-96)

Tnnt.*Serm*.1 (1744:24)

Less.*Nath*.3.7 (Rılla 2:403-8)

See vol.1:12-27;2:200-216

See pp. 334-35 below

Ex.3:14

Tnnt.*Serm*.5 (1744:110)

Brnt.*Art.XXXIX*.1 (1700:24)
Zinz.*Aug.Conf*.20 (Beyreuther
6-II:335);Zinz.*Soc*.25
(Beyreuther 1-I:250)

Zinz.*Zst*.39 (Beyreuther
3-II:316-17)

Sem.*Frag*.39 (1780:309)

Of these, Islam continued to evoke a variety of responses from Christians. Among those for whom the fall of Constantinople in 1453 was still a powerful memory, some articulated an eschatology in which the impending "fall of Mohammedanism" would be a sign that the Last Judgment was at hand. Military and political détente between Eastern Orthodoxy and Islam was an occasion for thanksgiving to God, but also for expressions of Christian caution. Some Christian polemists pointed to the Muslim method of propagation through conquest as palpable demonstration of its falsity, while others hoped that with genuine Christian reform, "the grand stumbling block being thus happily removed out of the way, namely the lives of the Christians, the Mahometans will look upon them with other eyes." Still others equated "the chief things that I find inculcated in the Alcoran" with "some main branches of natural religion," an equation that enabled one of the most eloquent pleas for religious toleration in the eighteenth (or any other) century, Lessing's *Nathan the Wise*, to urge Jews, Christians, and Muslims to acknowledge their common origin and to treat one another with the awareness that each had some kind of legitimate claim upon their common legacy.

In a class by itself as a persistent and fundamental question for the very definition of the essence of Christianity, despite this existential awareness of Islam, was still—as it had been, whether consciously or not, throughout Christian history since its very beginnings, and would become even more in the twentieth century—the positive and negative connection between Christianity and Judaism. There was an acknowledgment that "I am who I am," as revealed to Moses, was "the only proper and incommunicable name of God," and that monotheism had been "the chief design of the whole Old Testament," without which there would not have been a Christian doctrine of God. Jesus was "an observant Jew, a patriot," and when he spoke of God as "my Father," he was referring to "none other than the God of the Jews, the same God whom the Jews of that time worshiped." Therefore there were some Christian thinkers who defended Judaism and the Jews against Christian hostility, or

Wer.*Diss*.4.3 (Ryhinerus 1:90)

Frnck.*Pass.Joh*.3 (1733:45-46)

See vol.1:23

Spen.*Pi.Des*. (Aland 43-44)

Rom.11:26
Hfkntz.*Jüd*. (1706:7-8);
Terst.*Ep*.2.122 (Becher 6:269-71)

Dör.*Pet*.20 (1718:53)

Nmnn.*Spen*. (1695:43-55)

Byl.*Com.phil*.2.4 (1713-I:327)

Frnck.*Pred*.Trin.2 (1699:30)

Strz.*Enchir*.7.3 (1828:308)

Arb.*Des.myst*.2.17 (1764:312)
Bec.*Lóp.Sab.prod*.1 (1752:11);
Ost.*Arg.ref*.Matt.27:1-26
(1720-II:44); McGl.*Ess*.1.8
(1786:143)
Bnl.*Diss.apol*.1.23;2.84
(1747:17;72)
Lschr.*Dr.Pred*.1 (1733:4)

ap.Hfkntz.*Jüd*. (1706:14)
See vol.2:203-4
Drnd.*Fid.vind*.1.11
(1709:31-32)
See vol.1:20
Span.*H.e*.1.5 (Marck 1:533-34)

Gen.49:10
Ost.*Arg.ref*.Gen.49
(1720-I:33);Strz.*Enchir*.1.2
(1828:15);Ath.Par.*Epit*.3.3
(1806:196-97); Wsly.*Serm*.
66.1.2 (Baker 2:523)

Reim.*Apol*.1.5.2.4 (Alexander 1:732-34)

Spen.*Mess*. (1701:18-25)

who maintained that it ill behooved Gentile Christians to cast the blame for Christ's death upon the Jews, since not all of them had been involved and the Gentiles had been equally implicated in it. One of the by-products of Pietist eschatology was a heightened expectation, based on the ninth, tenth, and eleventh chapters of Romans, that, contrary to Luther's interpretation, truly "all Israel will be saved," as promised there. To many Pietists, such a total conversion of Jews to Christianity was "beyond doubt," but their orthodox critics took it as something "more to be wished than hoped" and went on defending Luther's restrictive exegesis. Although the Jewish people had in fact not managed to preach their religion throughout the world, the message of the Old Testament had never been limited to that one people but was intended to be universal: the history of the people of Israel was the history of all peoples.

Such affirmations must, however, be seen in relation to the majority doctrine about the meaning of Jewish history, expressed even in manuals of mystical devotion: that God was wreaking vengeance on the Jewish people for the death of his Son, and that Jews continued to be guilty of atrocities against Christians. Attacking both "the obdurate Jews and the vain secular scholars, who unfortunately take their side," orthodox Christian exegesis defended the direct application of the Old Testament not to Israel and Judaism but to Christ and the church. A convert from Judaism proved this from the point-by-point correspondence between the life of Christ and the writings of the prophets. The use of Hebrew plurals for God was still proof for the doctrine of the Trinity, and despite the objections that had been raised against it the testimony of Josephus to Jesus was authentic. As "an oracle that fixes the time of the coming of the Messiah," the prophecy of Jacob about Judah continued to serve as a chief focus for the Christian argument that the place of Judaism in the history of salvation was, though providential, only provisional. Reimarus sought to explain away use of the prophecy as a reference to Jesus Christ, and the Jewish exegesis of it as a reference merely to the history of Israel required a Christian response. One Reformed scholar devoted

Mrck.*Pent*.Gen.49:10 (Velzen
1:119-84)
See vol.1:55-56;
vol.2:35,205-6; vol.3:251-52

Baum.*Pred*.3.6 (Kirchner
3:179-210)

Budd.*Phil.Ebr*.31 (1720:154)

Lw.*Dem.Er*. (Moreton 5:18)

Bnl.*Diss.apol*.6.9
(1747:290-91);Zinz.*Gespr*.13
(Beyreuther 1-III:110-20)

Jeff.*Syl*.2 (Adams 332)

Aug.*Spir.et litt*.8.13-14
(*CSEL* 60:164-66)
Wlch.*Pol*.2.3.6 (1752:133)

Reim.*Apol*.1.5.1.6-7
(Alexander 1:698-705)

Reim.*Apol*.1.5.1.4 (Alexander
1:690-94)
Reim.*Apol*.1.5.2.1 (Alexander
1:721)

Reim.*Apol*.int.8 (Alexander
1:51);Mid.*Wat*. (1731:29)

Schtz.*Haer*.2.11 (1724:48)

Tin.*Chr*.1 (1730:2)

an extended and erudite philological and theological commentary to each of the key Hebrew terms in the verse, vindicating its Christocentric interpretation. It meant what it always had: that the covenant of God, which had "previously been enclosed within the narrow confines of Judaism, was now to be . . . extended over all peoples, languages, and kingdoms."

Despite an admiration for Maimonides as "the greatest ornament of his people," Christians disparaged most of postbiblical Judaism as a set of corrupt traditions based on a "poor, literal exactness" and largely preoccupied with the trivia of ritual behavior, and they attacked the Talmud as a distortion of the biblical message. "Their system was Deism," one radical interpreter declared, "that is, the belief of only one God. But their ideas of him, and of his attributes, were degrading and injurious." Repeating the long-standing charge that Judaism was "Pelagian" in its doctrine of sin and grace, another Christian thinker took this to be the source of other Jewish errors. As it had been before, Judaism became the target for philosophical-theological attacks that were aimed, additionally or even primarily, at the particularity of Christianity itself. At the hands of Reimarus, the picture of God in the Old Testament was one of a petty tyrant, whose revealed "law," with such ridiculous commandments as the Sabbath, contained very little of the essence of true religion, and who had never promised a Savior as Christianity claimed. "I find it difficult to comprehend," Reimarus concluded, "that out of so many wiser and more tractable nations God would choose such a stubborn and perverted people as his possession and his beloved."

For an increasing number, as defenders of orthodoxy were forced to recognize, the outcome of this quest for the essence of true religion was a sense of detachment from the competing truth claims of the various Christian sects and even of the various world religions. "Complaint was general," one critic of orthodoxy noted, "of the coldness and indifference with which people received the speculative points of Christianity, and all its holy rites"; church leaders blamed this on the preoccupation with natural religion. There was widespread recognition that religious

Reim.*Apol.*1.1.5.13
(Alexander 1:177)

Jeff.*Vir.*17 (Peterson 287)

Tol.*Milt.* (1699:79)

Zinz.*Zst.*24 (Beyreuther
3-II:186-92)

See pp. 307-8 below

and doctrinal unanimity was impossible except on a very few "general first principles." Therefore, as Thomas Jefferson observed, "religion is well supported; of various kinds, indeed, but all good enough; all sufficient to preserve peace and order." Anything more than this was not to be forced on anyone's conscience. It is ironic that the eighteenth century was also a time of rapid expansion for the Christian missionary enterprise, especially in Pietist Protestantism after a period of relative inactivity in the aftermath of the Reformation. Many of the doctrinal implications of this expansion were to make themselves felt only later.

Reim.*Apol.*int.7 (Alexander 1:50)

Even now, however, these concerns raised with new force and poignancy the status of the rest of the human race: "My own salvation," Reimarus exclaimed, "gets lost amid the piteous cries of millions of souls condemned to unending torture!" Or, in Tindal's formulation, could Christ "be said to be sent as a Savior of mankind if he comes to shut heaven's gates against those to whom before they were open, provided they followed the dictates of their reason?"

Tin.*Chr.*13 (1730:250)

During this period, a small number of Christian radicals in England and on the Continent made explicit and definite what a far greater number seem to have been pondering as at least a possibility and a hypothesis—the universality of salvation. If "all nations of the world are agreed on the essential article of Christianity," the love of God and of neighbor, it seemed to follow that all would finally be brought together into one. That was "the eternal gospel, the joyous message of 'the restoration of all things,' " whatever that biblical phrase may originally have meant. Such a revival of universalism evoked widespread attack from the orthodox. "For the universality of all men," a Calvinist declared, "we substitute the universality of the elect." Universalism was, a Lutheran court preacher insisted, an unwarranted extension of the love of God and a circumvention of those means of grace to which the church was bound, even though, as had to be conceded to the universalists, God was not bound to those means.

Swed.*Cael.*36.318 (1890:191)
Dipp.*Orth.*6 (1699:86-87)
Swed.*Cael.*3.15;27.238
(1890:18;135)

Pet.*Myst.*pr.11 (1700-I:B4r)

Acts 3:21

Ern.*Opusc.*9 (Fritsch 437-41)
Conc.*Rel.riv.*2.2.8.1
(1754-I:330);Naud.*Myst.*
2.3.82 (1713:203-4);
Wrns.*Myst.* 17.14 (1729:190)
Mrck.*Comp.*20.25 (Velzen
18:408)
Engsch.*Pet.* (1720:89;110)

Dipp.*Orth.*6 (1699:92)
Stod.*Conv.*3 (1719:13);
Tnnt.*Nec.*1 (1743:8)

The two chief fountainheads for the development of speculative theology, Origen in the East and Augustine in the West, were also key figures in the development of the Christian answer to the question of particularity and universality. For each of them, moreover, one passage from the Pauline Epistles had been the crux: for Augustine, the declaration of 1 Timothy 2 that "God our Savior . . . desires all men to be saved and to come to the knowledge of the truth"; for Origen, the promise of 1 Corinthians 15 that at the end of history, "when all things are subjected to [Christ], then the Son himself will also be subjected to him who put all things under him, that God may be all in all."

1 Tim.2:4
1 Cor.15:28

Augustine's maneuvers to harmonize this universality of the will of God for the salvation of "all men" with his doctrine of absolute predestination, according to which the particularity of the will of God for the salvation only of certain individuals always achieved its end, had led him to propose a variety of exegetical solutions, which continued to claim serious attention from the Middle Ages to the eighteenth century. Especially attractive seemed his suggestion that "all" referred to all classes of human beings, not to all individuals. The predestinarian doctrines of Calvinism in the sixteenth century and of Jansenism in the seventeenth, both of which had aggressively laid claim to the Augustinian legacy and were asserting that there were "but a few that go to heaven," made it imperative to affirm the doctrine of the universal salvific will of God while asserting that this did not require that all punishment in fact be remedial. There were some who found help in the medieval distinction between the universalistic "antecedent" and the particularistic "consequent" will of God. As the Council of Trent had put it, "though [Christ] died for all, yet all do not receive the benefit of his death, but only those to whom the merit of his passion is communicated."

Gaz.*Prael*.2.5.3.178 (1831-II:155-56)
See vol.1:321
See vol.1:325-27; vol.3: 90-91,277; vol.4:34-35,237
Amrt.*Theol.eclec*.1.6.3 (1752-1-I:125-27);
Bert.*Aug*.4.1 (1747-II:127)
Bert.*Theol.disc*.17.4 (1792-III:224-25)
See vol.4:224-25;375-85
Bnyn.*Lw.Gr*.2 (Sharrock 2:143)
Baum.*Pred*.1.10 (Kirchner 1:309-11)
Aug.*Civ*.21.13 (*CCSL* 48: 778-80);Conc.*Rel.riv*.5.2.13 (1754-II:444-55)
See vol.4:34
Bert.*Theol.disc*.5.1 (1792-I:215-16)
CTrid.6.*Dec*.3 (Alberigo-Jedin 672)
Bert.*Aug*.4.1 (1747-II:201);
Hno.*Theol*.6.1.16.3 (1785-VI:379-83)

Such resolutions of the paradox continued to claim the loyalty of those throughout the churches who were defending the traditional teaching about divine justice, whether this included double predestination or not. Against "Reformed universalists," radicals who were threatening to change hell into purgatory, they contended that universalism was not a necessary

Dör.*Pet*.8 (1718:23-24)
Mrck.*Comp*.20.24 (Velzen 18:405-8);Engsch.*Pet*. (1720:119)
Strim.*Un.Ev*.1.22 (1711:29-31);Tnnt.*Nec*.1 (1743:23;11)

Dör.*Pet.*12 (1718:34);
Stod.*Sfty.*10 (1687:275)

Brnt.*Art.XXXIX.*18
(1700:172-73); Poir.*Oec.div.*
3.13 (1705-I:749-62)

Tin.*Chr.*12 (1730:196)

Pet.*Myst.*pr.2 (1700-I:A1r)

See vol.1:151-52

Engsch.*Pet.* (1720:95)

Lmp.*Ew.Str.*2 (1729:196-206)
Neum.*Wied.*5 (n.d.:83)

Allat.*Purg.*23 (1655:166-77);
Lmp.*Ew.Str.*1 (1729:173)
Brnt.*Art.XXXIX.*9
(1700:110)
Tnnt.*Nec.*1 (1743:23);
Lmp.*Ew.Str.*2 (1729:206;307)

Engsch.*Pet.* (1720:15)
Ern.*Opusc.*10 (Fritsch
448-49;460-61);Sem.*Erud.*
(1759-I:39)

Zinz.*Aug.Conf.*4 (Beyreuther
6-II:96-97)

Spen.*Bed.*1.1.55 (Canstein
1:298-300)

implication of divine mercy. Yet many were increasingly inclined to "stretch the mercy of God" further than his justice and therefore to look with fresh attention at those passages of the New Testament that "seem to import that those who make the best use they can of the small measure of light that is given them shall be judged according to it." For a small but growing number, that was still not enough. "Is it not incumbent," they asked, "on those who make any external revelation so necessary to the happiness of all mankind to show how it is consistent with the notion of God's being universally benevolent not to have revealed it to all his children, when all had equal need of it?" In the light of such a question, the words of Paul in 1 Timothy 2 seemed to be "sheer universalism," and Origen's speculation about universal salvation seemed more attractive than ever.

While the condemnation of that speculation by the ancient church applied as well to the modern advocates of universal salvation, they seemed in some respects to be worse than Origen, for he had set it forth as only a possibility and had not been unaware of the dangers in such a doctrine. The orthodox spurned the efforts by some of Origen's latter-day devotees to attribute his universalistic doctrine of "restoration" to Gregory of Nyssa, whose standing as a church father of unquestioned orthodoxy would have given it unearned respectability. Origen was led astray by a theory of the preexistence of souls and a related version of the doctrine of free will, and he had pressed his universalism to the eventual salvation not only of the entire human race but of the devil, a theory that had been condemned then and needed to be rejected now.

Nevertheless, his formidable standing as perhaps the most brilliant exegete of early Christianity made it impossible to evade the responsibility of coming to terms with the apparent universalism of the prophecy in 1 Corinthians 15 that Christ would eventually surrender his particular kingdom to the universal rule of God, who would then be "all in all." These words were not inconsistent with the orthodox doctrine of the Trinity, for they pertained "only to the end of the economic kingdom of Christ, which he has been

Lmp.*Ew.Str.*1;2 (1729:53;66)

Zinz.*Red.*4 (Beyreuther 1-II:57)
Symb.Nic.-CP (Schaff 2:57);
*Conf.Aug.*3.4 (*Bek.*54)

Zinz.*Hom.*30 (Beyreuther 3-I:307)

administering in the church militant on earth until the Last Judgment" and therefore to his reign through word and sacrament, which would be superseded in the church triumphant; they could not be used to support universal salvation. As the creeds and confessions of the church had unanimously affirmed, "of his kingdom there will be no end." Still there was a deepening sense, in the face of the universalistic "speculations" of Origen as well as of the predestinarian "speculations" of Augustine, that one could not unequivocally assert the doctrine of the eventual redemption of the devil and yet that one must entertain it as "the wish of a devout heart."

As the fundamental content of the essence of true religion, the notions of the existence of God and the immortality of the soul not only corresponded to the unquestioned—and hitherto all but unquestionable—natural presuppositions of supernatural revelation. They were also what Immanuel Kant identified as "the two cardinal propositions of pure reason"; for neither of them, he contended, would it ever be possible to provide "sufficient demonstrations" from pure reason, and they would be, "for the speculative reason, always transcendent." Neither those who defended them on the grounds of reason alone nor those who rejected them on those grounds could lay claim to objective and rational verifiability. Although this "negative aspect" of Kant's philosophical enterprise did not consist in "an attempt to dispute or even only cast doubt upon the metaphysical reality or unreality" of these cardinal propositions, it certainly did consist in a "criticism of the means by which they are known" and of the way by which they were to be established. Quoting the apostolic formula, "I will show you a still more excellent way," namely, the way of love, champions of the received doctrine now found themselves obliged to turn elsewhere for proof.

Knt.*Krit.rn.Vern.*2.1.2 (Cassirer 3:500-12)

Brth.*Prot.Theol.* (1947:245)

1 Cor.12:31
Zinz.*Lond.Pred.*4.14 (Beyreuther 5-II:116);
Beng.*Gnom.*1 Cor.12:31 (Steudel 667); Wsly.*Serm.* 24.3.2-3 (Baker 1:542-4?)

3   The Theology of the Heart

See p. 60 above

See p. 117 above

Knt.*Krit.pr.Vern*.2.con.
(Cassirer 5:174)

Wsly.*Pl.Acct*.3.4-5 (*LPT*192)
Wsly.*Serm*.1.3.8 (Baker
1:128)

When Immanuel Kant, author of an all but canonical definition of the Enlightenment and of a *Critique of Pure Reason* in which the fundamental principles of the "essence of true religion" were identified as antinomies that could be neither proved nor disproved by reason alone, concluded his *Critique of Practical Reason* of 1788 with the confession that "two things fill the mind with ever new and increasing wonder and awe," namely, "the starry heaven above me and the moral law within me," many defenders of the faith in the eighteenth century saw this as a philosophical confirmation of the belief, already widespread among theologians during that century, that God was opening one door for faith after having closed another. "The moral law within" and the entire range of affections, obligations, and experiences that accompanied it in the inner life could stand even when the supposedly transcendent grounds of faith demonstrated by "the starry heaven above" were being subjected to persistent attack. "I have sometimes been almost inclined to believe," one especially acute observer commented, "that the wisdom of God has, in most later ages, permitted the external evidence of Christianity to be more or less clogged and encumbered for this very end, that men (of reflection especially) might not altogether rest there, but be constrained to look into themselves also and attend to the light shining in their hearts."

Nothing, it seemed, could be more "seasonable"; for because the "modern Pharisees" who had "learned to prate a little more orthodoxly about the new birth"

118

Tnnt.*Dang.* (1742:11-12)

Terst.*Bros.*3.3 (Becher 5:127)

Arb.*Des.myst.*pr. (1764:A3r);
Arb.*Inst.*pr. (1765:iiir)

Spen.*Gtts.*5 (1680:185-86)
See p. 60 above
Wsly.*Serm.*21.1.12 (Baker
1:482)
Wsly.*Serm.*2.1 (Baker 1:131)
Terst.*Bros.*2.2 (Becher 4:47)
Tnnt.*Serm.*2 (1744:29)
Wsly.*Serm.*pr.6 (Baker 1:106)
Zinz.*Lond.Pred.*2.1
(Beyreuther 5-I:154)
Mrkrd.*Off.*3 (1722:11)

Wlff.*Nat.Gott.*366
(1744-I:360)

See vol.3:284-93;
vol.4:347-50
Zinz.*Lond.Pred.*3.1
(Beyreuther 5-I:157-58);
Wsly.*Serm.*int.1 (Baker
2:155-56)

Jam.*Serm.*32 (1789-II:136)

Poir.*Théol.cr.* (1690:i)

meanwhile remained "as great strangers to the feeling experience of it" as ever, the authentic answer to the crisis of orthodoxy brought on by "the calamitous times in which we live" was a more intense "experience" of the "holy seclusion with the heavenly Bridegroom." When the promoters of this inner life spoke of "theology," they did not mean human "enlightenment [Aufklärung]" but "divine illumination [göttliche Erleuchtung]." To the motto of the Enlightenment, "Dare to know!" they opposed the motto of the gospel, "Dare to believe!" "The almost Christian," believer in name but not in fact, needed to progress to "the main spring of practical religion," "from mere outside religion" to "heart religion," which was beyond rational argument. "God seeks the whole heart, the complete soul," and so the argument from morality to religion and from the subjective experience of the soul to the reality of God was no less legitimate than the traditional cosmological arguments for the existence of God. To document this new and simple theology, which was comprehensible to every sincere heart, John Jamieson preached a series of fifty sermons each of which treated some aspect of the superiority of the religion of the heart over that of the understanding, and Pierre Poiret published a collection of treatises in French on these and related themes by those whom its subtitle identified as "simple and pure souls" past and present, under the general title *The Theology of the Heart.* Each of the doctrinal themes involved in the defense of the objectivity of transcendent revelation was susceptible of treatment, and of defense, in quite another modality.

The Affectional Transposition of Doctrine

See pp. 61-74 above

Frnck.*Pred.*Epiph.2 (1699:55)

Terst.*Bros.*1.2 (Becher 3:63)
Wsly.*Serm.*6.7.22 (Baker
2:546)
Fén.*Inst.*32 (Gosselin 6:141)

Miracle, mystery, and authority, whose validity as objective realities seemed to have reached a dead end, took on new life when they became, instead, ways of speaking about the subjective validity of inward experience. Miracle was seen in relation to its "utility to the soul of the individual Christian believer," as that by which "we become children in our devotion and simplicity of heart"; in this sense, "every answer to prayer is properly a miracle," when God moved the heart. Even the defenders of supernatural mystery

Nss.*Dipp*.1 (1701:19-20)

Poir.*Oec.div*.3.10 (1705-I:720)

Conc.*Rel.riv*.3.1
(1754:355-56)

Tin.*Chr*.8 (1730:92)

Tol.*Myst*.3.5 (1696:160)

Tin.*Chr*.13 (1730:282)
Matt.7:29

Zinz.*Rel*.5 (Beyreuther
6-I:82);Tnnt.*Dang*. (1742:6)
Beb.*Gl*.1 (1685:24-25);
Conc.*Rel.riv*.4.15
(1754-II:132)

See pp. 75-89 above

Ern.*Opusc*.10 (Fritsch 477)
Matt.20:1-16

Frnck.*Pred*.Sept. (1700:12-13)

Zinz.*Aug.Conf*.19 (Beyreuther
6-II:305-7)

Fusc.*Sac.cr*. (1756:9)

Zinz.*Aug.Conf*.19 (Beyreuther
6-II:307-10)

resorted to the argument that it "refers to the mystery of the Lord within his believers" and distinguished mysteries from superstitions precisely on the grounds that the latter "do not lead a man to the inner life, to the intimate recesses of his heart"; mystery was incomprehensible, while virtue and morality were visible. Meanwhile, their radical opponents distinguished original, authentic Christianity, an "inward natural religion" that was "easy first, and plain," from the later "mysteries" that arose when "Christianity was put on an equal level with the mysteries of Ceres or the orgies of Bacchus," which "the priests . . . imposed on the credulity of the people." The special "authority [ἐξουσία]," which the New Testament attributed to the teaching of Christ as the quality that distinguished him from his contemporaries, referred to the experience of the heart, the internal feeling by which the external word authenticated itself.

Nor was it necessary to accept as valid all of the negative conclusions to which historical research seemed to be leading. Thus a historical review critical of the Christian exegesis of so-called messianic prophecies in the Old Testament concluded that a Christian who could nevertheless "see Christ in the Old Testament where someone else did not see him at all" should above all be sure "that you receive him also into your heart, with his meekness and gentleness, lest you see him in vain." The "brief history of the church" set forth in the parable of the laborers in the vineyard could, and should, be applied also to the several ages of the individual. But what was needed was a new historiography, "which would deal with something other than the heresy-hunting and the various miscellaneous matters that have been carried on in the world in the name of religion." Such a history, by concentrating on figures like Bernard of Clairvaux, Bonaventure, the Hussites, and Luther, would identify the succession through the centuries of those who showed "that the bride [the church] has always been in love with her Bridegroom" and would thus discover genuine continuity rather than the zigzag movement of church history from "hiatus" to "lacuna" that now dominated the historical accounts.

See pp. 89-101 above

See vol.1:263-66

Fusc.*Sac.cr.* (1756:21-22)

See vol.2:68-75
Fusc.*Sac.cr.* (1756:9-10)

See vol.2:261;266

Fl.*Sl.*186 (*Soč.Fil.*3:374)

Fil.*Sl.*12 (*Soč.Fil.*1:101)

Frnck.*Pred.*Epiph.6 (1699:37)

See vol.3:136-44
Frnck.*Pred.*Adv.3
(1699:74-75)

Mrck.*Syl.*8.1 (Velzen 15:253)
Zinz.*Red.*7 (Beyreuther
1-II:91)

Frnck.*Pass.Marc.*pr.
(1724:A4v-A5v)

See pp. 101-17 above
Lmp.*Theol.nat.*66 (1734:21)
Frnck.*Pred.*Adv.1 (1699:63)
Arb.*Inst.*1.20.1 (1765:98);
Wsly.*Serm.*3.2.1-2
(Baker1:147)

As part of the history of the church, the controversies past and present over the person and work of Christ required a similar shift of perspective. One Franciscan treatise, which confessed in the technical terminology of the Council of Chalcedon of 451 the ancient orthodox dogma of the "hypostatic union" between "the impassible and glorious divinity" of the second person of the Trinity and "the mortal weakness" of the human nature of Jesus Christ, and which repeated the anti-Monotheletist dogmatic formulas of the Third Council of Constantinople of 681 about his "most holy twofold will," invoked all of this creedal language in order to promote a devotion to the cult of the Sacred Heart of Jesus. The emphasis on the transfiguration of Christ as the event by which Christ was made manifest after having "concealed the power of his kingdom" continued to be a distinguishing mark of Eastern Orthodox dogma and devotion in opposition to "the philosophy of this generation," but to others it could also mean that "the foretaste of eternal life consists of the transfiguration of Christ within us." Similarly, the interpretation of the death of Christ as the satisfaction rendered to divine justice for human sin, which was an equally distinguishing mark of Western dogma and devotion, became a means for the illumination of the Holy Spirit in the individual heart, through the consideration of Christ's "sorrows of soul," which were the content and the price of the satisfaction. "What he suffered for us" was still "the main object" of a God-pleasing contemplation of the cross and passion; but a theology would not be "genuinely apostolic" if it neglected "to build on this foundation also the divine doctrines of how Christ exists, lives, dwells, and works within us through faith."

To many defenders as well as to most critics of traditional belief, the search for the essence of true religion as an objective "presence of things outside myself" appeared to have bankrupted itself. In place of "this rotten and cold essence of Christianity," it was necessary, precisely in an "exposition of Christian doctrine," to "ponder seriously" and to "awaken" to the discovery that the essence did not consist in "knowing, averring, and chattering, nor in high

Frnck.*Id*.4 (Peschke173);
Wsly.*Pl.Acct*.2.7 (*LPT*189)

Sem.*Rel*.11 (Schütz 61)

Edw.*Rel.Aff*.1 (Miller 2:122)

Lw.*Chr.Perf*.9 (Moreton
3:150)

Mynst.*Betr*.3 (1846-I:20-31)
Fén.*Man.piét*.1 (Gosselin
6:7-8)
Wlff.*Nat.Gott*.70
(1744-I:43-4)

Jam.*Serm*.40 (1789-II:277)

Edw.*Rel.Aff*.1 (Miller 2:120)

Lschr.*Pens*.pr. (1724:7)

See vol.4:12

Sem.*Rel*.1 (Schütz 4-5)

Sem.*Rel*.11 (Schütz 64-65)

Lschr.*Del*. (1707:9)

Terst.*Ep*.2.76 (Becher
6:172-77)
Wrns.*Myst*.9.3 (1729:92)

Mrkrd.*Off*.4 (1722:15)

See vol.1:1-6;vol.4:3-6

speculations," nor yet "in all kinds of strange opinions"; but "true Christianity consists in this, that one acknowledge the Lord Jesus as personal Savior and Lord." To the plaintive question raised by relativism, "Where can the true Christian religion be, amid so many forms of religion?" the answer was: "It is completely in the souls of all true Christians regardless of party," which was indeed where it had always been. Human affections had been given by God "that they might be subservient to man's chief end, and the great business for which God has created him, that is, the business of religion." Although the Holy Spirit did not contradict reason, it did transcend reason and was "the Deity that dwelleth in" the human heart, so that "the feeling that naturally lies in the human heart" as it moved beyond "reasonings" to "affective sentiments" was a proof for the existence of God and a way of discovering the attributes of God; for "till once Christ himself speak to the heart, the strongest evidence will have no force." The essence of true religion was more than subjective affection, but it was not less; it could not be equated with morality, but it could not be separated from it either.

The dichotomy between the authenticity of this private "theology of the heart" and the artificiality of the public and political confessional theology of the churches, between "private" and "public" religion, which applied to all the churches "in all sorts of ways," was an epitome of the crisis of orthodoxy. It was beginning to sound anachronistic when a newly elected professor of theology affirmed a continuity between his university chair and his pastoral office. The indifference of a theology of the heart to the particulars of doctrinal distinction among the several confessions seemed to substitute experience for Scripture, implying a rejection of the orthodox obligation "to confess both privately and publicly the necessary dogmas of the catholic church" as these had been defined in "the unblemished orthodox faith and in the traditions of the church, avoiding all innovation"; and it represented nothing short of a reversal of the relation between "teaching" and "confessing" (not to mention "believing") in the very definition of doctrine. For a mixture of political and theological

Sem.*Erud.* (1765-II:147)

Sem.*Rel.*18 (Schütz 138-40)

Sem.*Rel.*38 (Schütz 310-12)

Sem.*Rel.*19 (Schütz 145)

Sem.*Erkl.*1.2 (1777:39-40)

Sem.*Erkl.*2 (1777:158-61)

Sem.*Rel.*28 (Schütz 234-35)
Ern.*Opusc.*11 (Fritsch 484)

Casp.*Beyl.*1 (1724:20)

Zinz.*Gem.*1 (Beyreuther 4-I:6)

Zinz.*Aug.Conf.*pr. (Beyreuther
6-II:iv);Syn.Br.*Auf.* (1748)
(Beyreuther 6-II:4)

Zinz.*Lond.Pred.*1.12
(Beyreuther 5-I:109)

See vol.2:254-70; vol.3:303-7

reasons, the churches of the Reformation had, in their public stance, issued confessional statements, and in confusing variety. But these had been intended only to be declarations of independence from a despotic church, and consequently they now possessed "merely an external, political authority" and were not properly the kind of doctrinal norm they had become in some churches.

Thus "theology, as a calling and profession of academics, has an altogether different purpose from that of the Christian religion as a public and political allegiance of the people." From this it followed that "the preparation for theological scholarship in our century is and must be completely different" from what it had been in previous centuries. The individual theologian, functioning "privately" as an academic scholar and teacher of Christianity, had "no dogmas": he was accountable not to the "public doctrine" of any church but only to the forum of conscience, and his work had a technical autonomy. On balance, it was not too severe a judgment when a critic of this position declared that, consistently carried out, it amounted to the "burial" of confession, creed, and church doctrine. It was possible nevertheless to affirm that "this our confession, this religion of the heart, transforms all those symbolical books whose truth it accepts into sheer creeds of the heart," which was how the confessions had wanted to be understood. If all the symbolical books were to be destroyed, they could be reconstructed from what lay in the hearts of true believers.

Each in its own way, therefore, the major creeds and confessions of the historic churches all lent themselves to transposition in the light of the theology of the heart: "We believe" had to become "I believe." This was happening not only within British and Continental Protestantism, where it could in some sense have been expected, but within Eastern Orthodoxy and Roman Catholicism as well, where it was also able to attach itself to earlier developments in spirituality and theology. Against Western theology, whether Roman Catholic or Protestant, the Christian East contended that all the dogmas of the church were already contained in the historic creeds, especially

Strz.*Enchir.*1.3;1.4
(1828:22;40-41)

Strz.*Enchir.*2.3 (1828:54)
Fil.*Sl.*279 (*Soč.Fil.*4:401-6)

See vol.4:260-61

CTrid.25.*Decr.*1
(Alberigo-Jedin 775)

Arb.*Des.myst.*3.12 (1764:471)

Tnnt.*Nec.*3 (1743:60)
Tnnt.*Disc.*pr.;1
(1745:iv;45-46);Tnnt.*Serm.*1
(1744:10-11)

Tnnt.*Dang.* (1742:9)

Wsly.*Pl.Acct.*3.5-6
(*LPT*192-93)

Wsly.*Pl.Acct.*2.5 (*LPT*189)

Wsly.*Serm.*7.1.5-6 (Baker
1:220)

1 Peter 3:4

Wsly.*Serm.*13.1.3 (Baker
1:317-18)

those from the councils of Nicea and Constantinople; but it seemed appropriate to add the explanation that these dogmas were meant to be accepted and followed personally by the individual believer, since "dogma" had to become "commandment." Against the Protestant Reformation, the Council of Trent had defined "the legitimate use of images" as one that accorded them "due honor and veneration" but without any notion of a "divinity or virtue" in the images as such; but it was necessary to explain that the purpose of this doctrinal legislation was "to spiritualize our affections" and to awaken them to "an authentic devotion."

The doctrine of the Protestant confessions underwent a similar transposition. Against Zinzendorf and the Moravians, Gilbert Tennent defended the *Westminster Confession of Faith* as a "precious system of truths," part of "the harmonious suffrage of the Reformed churches" of all lands in their confessions; but it was, he asserted in a discourse entitled *The Danger of an Unconverted Ministry*, the clear implication of the "points of Calvinism" affirmed in these standards that "the ministry of natural men is dangerous" and that the personal conversion of the minister was requisite to an effective ministry. Against the intellectualism into which he sometimes accused confessional dogmatics of having fallen, John Wesley charged that "a man may assent to three or three-and-twenty creeds . . . and yet have no Christian faith at all," since the real nature of true religion did not consist in "orthodoxy or right opinions," but "deeper still, even in 'the hidden man of the heart' "; yet he was sure that, in this insistence as in his theology generally, he was in accord with the *Thirty-Nine Articles* of the Church of England, in which "our own [Anglican] church (as indeed in most points) exactly comports after the primitive."

One of the most ambitious attempts in the eighteenth century to transpose a symbolical book into a "creed of the heart"—an attempt that may therefore serve as the basis for reviewing the phenomenon across all the confessions—was the reinterpretation of the *Augsburg Confession* in Nikolaus Ludwig Graf von Zinzendorf's *Twenty-One Discourses on the Augsburg*

Conf.Aug.conc. (Bek.83c)

Zinz.Aug.Conf.21 (Beyreuther 6-II:360)

Zinz.Rel.2 (Beyreuther 6-I:17)

Beng.Brüd.2.43 (1751:322-23);Tnnt.Nec.3 (1743:60)

Zinz.Off.Red.12 (Beyreuther 2-IV:112)

Zinz.Aug.Conf.21 (Beyreuther 6-II:363-64)

Zinz.Zst.44 (Beyreuther 3-II:351-52)

Zinz.Aug.Conf.13 (Beyreuther 6-II:232-33)

Zinz.Aug.Conf.21 (Beyreuther 6-II:366)

Conf.Aug.1 (Bek.50-51)

Zinz.Aug.Conf.1 (Beyreuther 6-II.41)

Symb.Apost. (Schaff 2:45)
Luth.Kl.Kat.2.2 (Bek.510)
Zinz.Aug.Conf.4 (Beyreuther 6-II:93)

Arb.Inst.1.20.9 (1765:105)
Arb.Des.myst.3.4 (1764:374)
Arb.Inst.1.20.26 (1765:137)

Pnch.Dict.pr. (1716:B3v)

Fén.Ep.10.iii.1696 (Gosselin 8:453)

Chrys.Matt.64.4 (PG 58:614)

Conc.Rel.riv.3.7 (1754-I:385)

Confession of 1747/48. The twenty-one discourses did not correspond to the "summary of doctrines" in the first twenty-one articles of the confession, but recast both the sequence and the content of those articles. Zinzendorf's criticism that outward confession without inner conviction was a travesty seemed to his critics to replace the confessional criterion of pure doctrine and correct understanding with "sheer feeling, untrammeled by understanding." But he felt able to claim the authority of the *Book of Concord* for his principle that faith was "not in thoughts nor in the head, but in the heart, a light illumined in the heart." He would not, he explained, have any part in the "contempt for the *Augsburg Confession*" that had become fashionable among certain theologians. He cherished it because, in support of his own polemics against "demonstration and disputation," it consistently refused to resort to "demonstrating" the articles of faith a priori, but contented itself with "affirming" them on the basis of Scripture; and he gave the *Augsburg Confession* credit for having rescued his own fellow believers from the doctrinal chaos into which their theological naiveté could have led them.

As a creed of the heart, the *Discourses* did not open in its first article with the doctrine of God as Trinity, as the *Augsburg Confession* had, but with an examination of the "vast difference" between doctrine and faith, between "being a believer" and merely "acknowledging a truth": Luther's *Small Catechism* had transposed the opening words of the Apostles' Creed, "I believe in God . . . the Creator," into "I believe that God has created me." An author who demanded that one "believe everything that our holy mother, the Church of Rome" holds concerning the articles of faith could define "Christian doctrine" as the contemplation of virtue, intended to be grasped by the affections. "New heretics," French Roman Catholics were told, were those who strove to "establish the dogmas of doctrine on their own"; yet "questions of doctrine" were a matter not primarily of knowledge, but of the heart. As Chrysostom had pointed out, "Christ discoursed only rarely about dogmas" and the mysteries of the faith, but almost exclusively about "sincerity of life"; and the same could have been said

Bert.*Theol.disc*.15.2
(1792-III:164-65)

about Chrysostom himself. While "real, genuine Christianity" was both "a principle in the soul" and "a scheme or system of doctrine," it was, also as the latter, "that system of doctrine which describes the [Christian] character . . . and promises that it shall be mine"; any other system was no more than a "skeleton for the body of teaching."

Wsly.*Pl.Acct*.2.1 (*LPT*188)
Zinz.*Aug.Conf*.21 (Beyreuther 6-II:364)

Rom. 16:17

The warning of the New Testament against those who "cause divisions . . . contrary to the doctrine" did refer to "the main doctrines of religion," which were the foundation of true piety, but it was directed specifically against those who "alienate the affections of good men from each other." The term "doctrine" referred to much more than the creeds, confessions, and dogmas that were the stuff of dogmatic theology: there was a "doctrine" of the monastic life, a "doctrine" about the cure of souls and about the exercise of compassion toward others, a "doctrine" of the proper way to conduct a papal election, a "doctrine" about moral purity and perfection. As one theologian put it, "The proposition or doctrine that I would raise . . . is this: True religion, in great part, consists in holy affections"; or, in the formula of another, "What Christianity (considered as a doctrine) promised, is accomplished in my soul." It was not only a description but in some sense a criterion when a Danish theologian declared: "The doctrine in which my soul can find repose is a divine truth."

Tnnt.*Serm*.pr. (1744:i)

Tnnt.*Nec*.3 (1743:51)

Arb.*Inst*.8.14 (1765:649)
Bec.Lóp.*Nuev.Ab*. (1739:3)
Bec.Lóp.*Sab.prod*.int.
(1752:5)
Cmrda.*Const.ap*.pr. (1732:vi)
Arb.*Des.myst*.1.2;1.4
(1764:21;38)

Edw.*Rel.Aff*.1 (Miller 2:95)

Wsly.*Pl.Acct*.2.12 (*LPT*191)

Mynst.*Praed*.60 (1845-II:347)

Every doctrine, including the doctrine of the Trinity itself, had to measure up to that criterion. Zinzendorf was convinced that because "no system . . . may legitimately take its beginning from the mystery of the Holy Trinity," the first article of the *Augsburg Confession* was "an item detached from the rest." Academic theologians "who do not love their Savior" could nevertheless go on "chattering about the mystery of the Trinity." The decisive issue in the doctrine of the Trinity was not, as such theologians supposed, what Father, Son, and Holy Spirit were to one another, but "what they are to us." Put into so absolutely disjunctive a formula as that—and Zinzendorf himself did not always speak that way—his polemic was certainly extreme even in its own time, but it was an extreme instance of a more general tendency to salvage the doctrine of the Trinity by trans-

Zinz.*Aug.Conf*.2 (Beyreuther 6-II:60-61)

Zinz.*Rel*.1 (Beyreuther 6-I:8-9)

Zinz.*Lond.Pred*.5.12
(Beyreuther 5-II:294)

Sherl.*Vind*.5 (1690:126)

See vol.3:20-22

Arb.*Inst*.1.20.3-5
(1765:98-101)

Poir.*Oec.div*.1.14
(1705-I:199-200)

Wsly.*Serm*.55.17 (Baker
2:385)
Arb.*Inst*.1.20.11
(1765:111-14)

Strz.*Enchir*.7.2 (1828:303)

Zinz.*Aug.Conf*.9 (Beyreuther
6-II:186)

Terst.*Bros*.2.3 (Becher
4:88-89)

Lang.*Nach*.1.11 (1707-I:85)

See p. 92 above

Terst.*Abr*.2.3.10-22 (Becher
2:178-84)

Frnck.*Pred*.Laet. (1700:52)
Zinz.*Aug.Conf*.4 (Beyreuther
6-II:102)

Fusc.*Sac.cr*. (1756:9)

posing it. "St. Austin . . . explains this Trinity in Unity by examples of mutual consciousness," and Augustine's pioneering exploration of the human "trinities within" that reflected the divine Trinity was both a model and a justification for a continuation and expansion of such speculations. To the compiler of a manual for novices in the religious life, the Trinity served primarily as a means to explain the significance of making the sign of the cross in private and public worship. The editor of *The Theology of the Heart* found it possible to resolve the historic conflicts of East and West over the Filioque by transposing Father, Son, and Holy Spirit into "properties of the soul," each of which proceeded from both of the others. "The knowledge of the Three-One God," Wesley took genuine orthodoxy to mean, "is interwoven with all true Christian faith, with all vital religion."

"Articles of faith" that they were, the dogmas of the Trinity and of the two natures in Christ could therefore be epitomized in the exclamation that Christ was "king of my heart." Hence it was possible to summarize the "entire content" of Christian doctrine as: "that we belong to the Savior and become one heart and one soul with him, so that his death and suffering . . . constantly repose in our heart." It was a vain and groundless hope to trust in "a historical knowledge of Christ, if in the process Christ remains alien and distant from us," though this was not to be taken "in the least" to imply that the historicity of such Gospel events as the ascension of Christ was unimportant. But it was also possible that under the cover of an orthodox defense of historicity and true doctrine, "under the pretext that they want to preach 'Jesus for us,' they have the audacity to steal Jesus from our hearts—the very one who wants to be 'Jesus in us.' " Each of the three offices of Christ as prophet, priest, and king was to be understood not only "outwardly and universally" but above all "inwardly and individually." To "come to Jesus" as prophet, therefore, certainly meant finding him in the word of Scripture, but that was in vain unless "the Holy Spirit works faith within us and through its power brings us to the grace of Christ," one person at a time. The doctrine of Christ was the doctrine of new birth. Roman Catholic devotion to the Sacred Heart of Jesus found its

Terst.*Bros*.4.6 (Becher 6:241)

counterpart in such Protestant admonitions as Gerhard Tersteegen's: "Our entire heart should become the heart of Jesus, so that he can impress his seal upon it and say: 'This is my heart.'"

The affectional transposition of Christian doctrine involved every article of faith in the tradition and every issue over which the churches and the theologians had been in conflict, to each of which it would have been possible to apply the principle that "we do not want to go into the controversies; . . . only let us inquire into our own heart, our own conscience." The seven sacraments, as affirmed by the Eastern Orthodox Church (as well as by Roman Catholicism), described the pilgrimage of the individual soul from birth to death. The "real presence" of Christ in the sacrament of the Eucharist was a presence "in body and soul," uniting itself with the soul of the believer. The difference between the doctrine of the real presence and the teaching that "we see nothing else in [the elements] than that the bread is the symbol and seal of the crucified body of Christ, which is truly set forth [exhibitum] in the Holy Supper" could, then, be reinterpreted to mean that the Eucharist would be of benefit to all regardless of their theories about the presence—provided only that they truly believed what they confessed, whatever it might be. And when a child at its first communion declared, "I do not understand all of this, but it does give me a good feeling," that was "not so bad," since "Scripture calls that a feeling which is often as good as if the person understood the words themselves."

Terst.*Bros*.2.3 (Becher 4:87)

See vol.2:291;vol.3:209-10

Strz.*Enchir*.6.1 (1828:233-34)
Arb.*Inst*.20.14 (1765:ll9);
Zinz.*Aug.Conf*.18 (Beyreuther 6-II:294)

Wer.*Diss*.10.1 (Ryhinerus 1:165)

Poir.*Oec.div*.4.7 (1705-II:169-70)

Zinz.*Gespr*.3 (Beyreuther 1-III:24)

As that appeal to scriptural precedent suggests, there was a strong case to be made—a strong exegetical and hermeneutical case, as well as a theological and a psychological one—for a method of studying the Bible that emphasized not only its authority but above all its personal application, "Scripture interpreted not by lexicons and dictionaries, but by doctrines revealed by God and by an inward teaching and unction of the Holy Ghost." Also where there might not be explicit reference to it, the affectional element had to be drawn out of the text of Scripture. The word of God in the Bible was indeed a light, but a light that was intended to shine "not only before our

Frnck.*Pass.Joh*.6 (1733:98)

Lw.*Dem.Er*. (Moreton 5:20)

Frnck.*Mand.Scrip*.10 (1706:107)

Frnck.*Pred.*Epiph.2
(1700:11-12)

Frnck.*Pass.Joh.* (1733:126)

2 Tim.3:16

See vol.4:343-47

Stod.*Sfty.*11 (1687:336-37)

Stod.*Conv.*10 (1719:47)

Deutsch.*Luth.*1.4.13
(1698:43-44)

Wer.*Diss.*19 (Ryhinerus
1:352-53)

Wer.*Misc.*23.1 (Ryhinerus
2:331)

Beng.*Gnom.*pr.6 (Steudel xix)

Erb (1983) xiii
Syn.Br.*Auf.* (1748)
(Beyreuther 6-II:12)
Zinz.*Aug.Conf.*14 (Beyreuther
6-II:264)

Spen.*Gtts.*5 (1680:212-13)

eyes but in our heart." Even the minute and "external" details of biblical history were intended for the benefit of "our soul" and were to be read that way. The point of the chief proof text supporting the inspiration of Scripture was to stress how "useful" Scripture was in its "majesty and commanding authority," in order to reassure the individual believer. Orthodox warnings that "the external word of God is also the internal voice of God," so that the two must not be separated, attacked what was deemed to have become an overemphasis on the subjective element in exegesis. Yet the same theologian who cautioned against "excessive reliance on personal feeling in the interpretation of Scripture" could nevertheless speak about "the subjective certainty" that must accompany "the objective certainty" of the exegete. "Whoever wishes to move ahead in the interpretation of Scripture," Bengel warned, "ought to explore to see where the personal motivation for this is coming from."

A campaign of this kind to recover the centrality of "practice" in the definition of Christianity was, by its very nature, preoccupied with lay piety and the exercise of the Christian life, as well as with the concrete structures and institutions of the church. It called for "a renewed emphasis on biblical preaching and on the experience of repentance and the new birth, the establishment of conventicles for the mutual edification and admonition of 'reborn' believers, and a reform of pastoral training that would place less emphasis on scholastic polemical theology and more on the development of a sensitized ministry concerned with the practical devotional and moral life of parishioners." Yet such a resolve to "avoid all abstractions when it comes to matters of the heart" and to concentrate above all on "purely inward matters" could not avoid the inseparable connection (in both directions) between Christian life and Christian theology.

Warning against an exclusive reliance either on an intellectual understanding of doctrine or on "the emotion of heart and conscience," one Pietist leader in Protestant Germany urged that all of this must lead to "a continuous and persistent penitential struggle, to the work of faith and of love, and to [the experience

Frnck.*Pred*.pr. (1700:B5v)

Arb.*Des.myst*.int. (1764:1-2)

Fén.*Ep*.11.v.1689 (Masson 136-37)

Wlff.*Nat.Gott*.78 (1744-I:52-53)

See vol.1:256-66

Phil.2:6-11 (AV)
See vol.1:148-49

Matt.20:26-28
See vol.1:51

Aug.*Soliloq*.1.2.7 (PL 32:872)

of} patience and hope." An almost exact contemporary in Roman Catholic Spain opened his treatise on the difficulties that souls encountered in their devotional life with an analogous catalogue of the three components of the theology of the heart: "It cannot be doubted that the blessed *souls* are very few and scarce who climb to the summit of *perfection* in this mortal life"; this was, he continued what "*experience* teaches us" and what "*the Holy Spirit* says." And Archbishop Fénelon described the state of grace in similar terms: "In this state, righteousness is not only imputed, but is in reality granted to the *soul*. This does not imply that the soul has a spirit of selfishness, which is the very opposite of *perfection*; rather, this state becomes real in the soul through the *infusion of the Holy Spirit* and through the total surrender of the soul and its activity."

God and the Soul

It was not an invention of eighteenth-century Pietist theology—rather, it had been one of the standard methods of Christian piety and theology in all centuries—to draw a correlation between the objectivity of God and the subjectivity of the self. The celebrated christological formula of "preexistence, kenosis, and exaltation" in the Pauline Epistles was introduced with the words, "Let this mind be in you"; and the most explicit statement of the doctrine of redemption anywhere in the synoptic Gospels, "the Son of man came . . . to give his life as a ransom for many," took the form of a subordinate clause supporting the admonition of Jesus to his disciples, "Whoever would be great among you must be your servant." Augustine had given the correlation its classic expression in one of his earliest writings: "What do you wish to know? I desire to know God and the soul, that is all." At the hands of an Augustine, and presumably of the apostle Paul and the writers of the Gospels as well, such a device presupposed the teaching of the church as an objective given and then proceeded to base subjective experience and exhortation upon it. But now that the objectivity was itself coming into question, the subjectivity could be called upon to assume the burden of verifying what it had hitherto been able to take for granted.

Some combination of the two methodologies was at work in the declaration that "an attentive reflection on what we perceive in ourselves will carry us further than any other thing whatsoever to form just and true thoughts of God," so that "the liveliest way of framing an idea of God is to consider our own souls." Such qualities of the soul as the consciousness of self were therefore, with appropriate adjustments to eliminate any unworthy conceptions, to be predicated also of God, just as attributes of God like omnipresence were "mirrored in [the believer's] heart." Traditional theology had used the word from the burning bush to Moses, "I am who I am," as the basis for "a metaphysics of Exodus," which legitimated the language of ontology as part of Christian doctrine; what the passage meant now was "that God wishes always to be recognized and known according to his presence in the soul." The *Summa Theologica* of Thomas Aquinas had taken up the exposition of the divine attributes after demonstrating the objective existence of God through the cosmological arguments from causality, motion, and the like; now it seemed more convincing to begin a summary of theology by making personal knowledge and personal illumination the topic of a chapter entitled "On the Means of the Knowledge of God" and then taking up, in turn, the doctrines of divine attributes and of the Trinity. It was a "mistake" to interpret even "natural religion" as "the work or effect of natural reason" rather than of the heart; it was as true of natural religion as it was of revealed religion that "reason is not the power or strength of our religion, because what our heart is, that is our religion" and "much of true religion lies in the affections."

According to patristic exegesis, the biblical question, "What person knows a man's thoughts except the spirit of the man which is in him?" had been intended, in its context, to express a human psychological analogy for the knowledge of God that was uniquely possessed and then revealed by the Holy Spirit of God; now that question became the "indu-

Brnt.*Art.XXXIX*.1 (1700:41)

Wlff.*Nat.Gott*.86;134;213 (1744-I:60;117;222)
Frnck.*Gl*.1 (1691:C3r)

Ex.3:14
See vol.1:54

Zinz.*Soc*.6 (Beyreuther 1-I:59)

See vol.3:284-93

Terst.*Abr*.1.1 (Becher 2.11-25)
Terst.*Abr*.1.2 (Becher 2:25-49)
Terst.*Abr*.1.3 (Becher 2:49-58)

Lw.*Dem.Er*. (Moreton 5:93-95)
Edw.*Rel.Aff*.1 (Miller 2:106)

1 Cor.2:10-11

Bas.*Spir*.16.40 (*SC* 17b:183); Hil.*Trin*.9.69 (*CCSL* 62A:449-50)

Fén.*Inst*.22 (Gosselin 6:122);
Strz.*Enchir*.2.5 (1828:72)

Terst.*Abr*.1.8.5 (Becher 2:93)
Poir.*Chr.ed*.7 (1694:12)

Fén.*Inst*.36 (Gosselin 6:149)
Terst.*Bros*.3.8 (Becher
5:334-80)
Fén.*Man.piét*.1 (Gosselin 6:7)

Strz.*Enchir*.5.2 (1828:197-98)

Terst.*Bros*.2.4 (Becher 4:139)
Strz.*Enchir*.1.pr. (1828:2)

Terst.*Bros*.3.1 (Becher 5:23)

Fén.*Inst*.40 (Gosselin 6:154)

Terst.*Bros*.3.8 (Becher
5:334-80)

Edw.*Rel.Aff*.1 (Miller 2:97)

Stod.*Conv*.13 (1719:57-58)

Wsly.*Serm*.31.4 (Baker
1:672-73)

Mmchi.*Orig.ant*.3.2.pr.
(1749-III:271)

Elrt.*Morph*.1.13
(1931-I:151-53)
Luth.*Post*.Chr. (*WA*
10-I-1:74)

Zinz.*Zst*.39 (Beyreuther
3-II:321)

Frnck.*Pass.Marc*.5 (1724:148)

Zinz.*Red*.7 (Beyreuther
1-II:96)
Fén.*Inst*.18 (Gosselin 6:103)

Gib.*Dec*.50 (Bury 5:337)
Terst.*Ep*.1.94 (Becher 5:212)

bitable" biblical proof text for the direct activity of God in the human soul. The soul could be defined as "the life and the ground of [a person's] senses and sense perceptions—of love, affections, wrath, and desire"; and it was through "the desire of the soul," sometimes called the "heart" or the "will," that the grace of God entered the person. Paradoxically, while grace came through the self, "the operation of grace detaches us from ourselves," and "the eternal rest of our souls" was achieved through a meditation, "ever more profound and intimate," by which the truth of divine grace "enters into the very substance of our soul." Jesus, "the Bridegroom of the soul," was "a man who suffered for your soul, battled for your soul, prayed for your soul." When, by "the beautiful and passionate free choice of the soul," a person "hurried to Jesus," that was the path of "the progress of the soul" through the abandonment of the external world and then even of the self, to find that "eternal rest of our souls." Yet throughout the process, "will" and "affections," as well as "will" and "understanding," all remained parts of "one and the same soul."

"One and the same soul," in turn, was another way of speaking about one and the same individual and "singular" person. "You must," John Wesley warned, "be singular or be damned. The way to hell has nothing singular in it, but the way to heaven is singularity all over." The early Christians had made it their primary concern "that each one should equip his mind with the highest thoughts and teachings," so as to moderate the individual will and tame its evil desires. Luther had (though primarily in the printed versions of his sermons, as edited by his disciples) spoken about the individual as having been united with God or Christ into "one loaf [ein kuchen]"; now it was necessary "for each of us to apply this to ourselves, each of us for himself." Each had to be able to say, personally and individually: "I, a lost human being, have been found. I, a condemned human being, have received grace." The depths of the individual soul were "impenetrable," save to God alone; not only was solitude, therefore, "the school of genius," but "love of solitude and of inward prayer" was the indispensable point of encounter between God

Arb.*Des.myst.*4.1;3.26
(1764:565;551-52)

Zinz.*Lond.Pred.*2.2
(Beyreuther 5-I:163)

Wsly.*Serm.*7.1.3 (Baker
1:218-19)

Terst.*Bros.*1.1 (Becher 3:33)
Spen.*Gtts.*8 (1680:375)

Tnnt.*Disc.*4 (1745:196)

Frnck.*Pass.Joh.*3 (1733:49-50)

Frnck.*Pred.*Epiph.1 (1700:27)

Fil.*Sl.*18;27
(So.*Fil.*1:142;198-99)
Cyr.H.*Catech.*23.4
(Reischl-Rupp 2:382)

Lmp.*Brt.*13 (1737:207-8)
Alph.Lig.*Theol.mor.*1.3.1.313
(Gaudé 1:576-78)
Arb.*Des.myst.*2.6 (1764:202)
Drnd.*Diss.*2.26.6;4.17
(1703:194;369)

CFlor. (1438-45)*Decr.Arm.*5
(Alberigo-Jedin 540-41)

ap.Alph.Lig.*Theol.mor.*6.2.1.13
(Gaudé 3:13)

and the individual soul. There was no mistaking the cruciality of the individual decision for all of Christian life and doctrine: "We must become acquainted with the Savior personally; otherwise all theology is for naught."

At the basis of such individualism lay a fundamental distinction between "inner" and "outer," especially as this applied to worship and devotion. Sometimes the distinction could take the hyperbolic form of declaring flatly that "true religion does not consist . . . in any outward thing whatever, in anything exterior to the heart." It was characteristic of most people that "they serve God merely in an external way," contenting themselves with "ceremonies," while "their heart remains far distant from God"; such external observance, to the neglect of inner illumination, caused "inexpressible damage." Not only had most Israelites remained "unacquainted with the spiritual internal part of religion and rested upon externals," but this continued to be "so now, under the gospel dispensation." The "hypocrisy" of scrupulously avoiding external "pollution" in the very act of betraying "the pure, innocent, and immaculate Jesus" was not unique to the enemies of Christ, but was reenacted whenever Christians "attend to external worship but neglect the internal" by acting more from custom than from truth.

To be "full and complete," a festival such as Easter had to be celebrated both publicly and "in the interior of the soul." For the ancient liturgical summons "Lift up your hearts! [Sursum corda!]" called for just that, the elevation of the heart, not only of the hands, to the Lord. "Attending" Mass meant not merely "attendance" but "attention," an attention of both soul and body, just as "confecting" a valid sacrament required the "intention" of the celebrant. For a sacrament to be valid, according to the decree of the Council of Florence in 1439, "the person of the minister conferring the sacrament" had to have "the intention of doing what the church does." But quoting that formula in the atmosphere of the eighteenth century tended to leave the concept of "intention" open to the interpretation that what was required was "the faith or probity of the minister," in spite of what

Amrt.*Theol.eclec*.9.5.4
(1752-2-IV:108)

Cmrda.*Const.ap*.2.35
(1732:236)

Aug.*Ev.Joh*.46.6
(*CCSL* 36:402);Aug.*Bapt.*
4.11.17 (*CSEL* 51:241)
See vol.4:96;273

Matt.23:2-3

Spen.*Gtts*.7 (1680:366-74)
ap.Mrck.*Exeg.exerc*.27 (Velzen
9:537-46)
Tnnt.*Dang*. (1742:15)

Cypr.*Ep*.67.3 (*CSEL* 3:737)

Mck.*Vor*. (1747:24)

Terst.*Bros*.1.3 (Becher 3:99)

Wsly.*Serm*.16.1.5 (Baker
1:380)

Conc.*Rel.riv*.4.15
(1754-II:124);Fén.*Ep*.6.iv.
1689 (Masson 104)

Aug.*Ev.Joh*.15.25
(*CCSL* 36:161)

John 4:23

Hdly.*Kngdm*. (1717:6)

Fén.*Man.piét*.5.10
(Gosselin 6:62);Fén.*Inst*.22
(Gosselin 6:124)

Fén.*Inst*.2 (Gosselin 6:74)

Thos.Aq.*S.T*.2.2.84.2 ad 1
(*Ed.Leon*.9:213)

Gaz.*Prael*.1.1.2.2.13-14
(1831-I:42-43)

had been "repeatedly defined by the church," which did not judge "purely mental" sins or heresies in determining fitness for ministry. Even the repetition of the principal proof text used by Augustine to establish the objectivity of sacramental grace—"The scribes and the Pharisees sit on Moses' seat; so practice and observe whatever they tell you"—could not dissipate that interpretation. Some were urging that the passage spoke only of obedience to "the civil magistrate," not to an unconverted minister; and historical research showed that predecessors of Augustine such as Cyprian had required for the minister of a sacrament not only that "the congregation have selected him" but that he personally have "a true and sound faith in Christ."

Although "the inward feelings, convictions, and impressions" were "more important" than the outward participation in "the means of grace," that was not to be understood "as if outward religion were absolutely nothing." Because so much of the origin of opposition to church and revelation lay in "the internal struggle" of the individual, of which "the external harassment" was an expression, the distinction between "inner" and "outer" could easily become an absolute dichotomy, which was how some critics of the church were construing it. They seemed to find corroboration in one of the best-known sayings from the Gospels, by which, as Augustine had put it, "we are sent back inward after having gone out of doors": the words of Jesus to the Samaritan woman, "The hour is coming, and now is, when the true worshipers will worship the Father in spirit and truth." Both in England and on the Continent, the charge that the interpretation of this verse had "become quite another thing . . . in many Christian countries" was turning it into a fatal attack on churchly piety. Yet the patrons and reformers of churchly piety were also making effective use of it. Fénelon quoted it repeatedly, adding that "all the rest is nothing but a religion consisting of ceremonies." Citing the comments of his Dominican master, Thomas Aquinas, on "spirit and truth," Pietro-Maria Gazzaniga protested against the misappropriation of these words of Christ by the enemies of his church and of its public worship.

Wsly.*Serm*.27.int.1
(Baker1:592);Frnck.*Pred*.pr.
(1700:B4v)

Gaz.*Prael*.1.1.2.2.11
(1831-I:42)

Schl.*Chr.Gl*.24 (Redeker
1:137)
Schl.*Chr.St*.2.1 (Reimer
12:516-25)

Fén.*Aut.égl*. (Gosselin1:203)

Zinz.*Lond.Pred*.4.2
(Beyreuther 5-II:14)

Luke 17:21 (AV)

Luke 17:21 (RSV)

Fén.*Let.div*.
(Gosselin1:102;144)

Protestant churchmen, too, attacked "the endeavor of Satan from the beginning of the world to put asunder what God has joined together, to separate inward from outward religion." God demanded both internal and external worship, and neither of them without the other.

The dichotomy between internal and external worship corresponded in many ways (though by no means in all) to a dichotomy between the individual and the church. When a theological descendant of Moravian Pietism early in the nineteenth century defined the difference between Protestantism and Roman Catholicism (as well as Eastern Orthodoxy) as consisting in this, that "the former makes the individual's relation to the church dependent on his relation to Christ, while the latter contrariwise makes the individual's relation to Christ dependent on his relation to the church"—a difference that he himself sought to transcend—he was reflecting a polarity that had in fact appeared within Protestantism, Roman Catholicism, and Eastern Orthodoxy during the preceding century. Exhorting his readers that "God is knocking at the door of your heart," a Roman Catholic churchman drew the contrast in almost completely the opposite direction: "If you want a serious reformation, do not begin from the outside, as the Protestants do. . . . Rather turn to yourselves. What a blessed and solid reformation that would be! The more you reform yourselves that way, the less you will need to reform the church." The purpose of preaching was "not to create congregations or to found or preserve a religious denomination, but to direct individuals to their own heart," according to one who was himself the founder of a new religious denomination and who created many congregations in various lands.

If, as most translators and interpreters regardless of denomination understood a well-known saying in the Gospels, Jesus had said "the kingdom of God is within you" (rather than "the kingdom of God is in the midst of you," as later exegetes were to take it), this could be combined with the other saying from John 4:23 to produce the admonition: "This is the kingdom of God that is within us, this is the worship in spirit and truth"; and, in combination with yet

Matt.6:33 (AV)
Wsly.*Serm*.29.23 (Baker
1:644)

Terst.*Bros*.4.3 (Becher 6:125)

Wsly.*Serm*.52.int.2 (Baker
2:302)

Strz.*Enchir*.2.5 (1828:80)

Strz.*Enchir*.3.5 (1828:133);
Fén.*Inst*.22 (Gosselin 6:124)

Matt.28:18-20

Strz.*Enchir*.5.3 (1828:204)

Strz.*Enchir*.5.5 (1828:219-20)
1 Tim.3:15;Strz.*Enchir*.5.3
(1828:209)
See vol.4:173-74

See vol.4:75-76

Strz.*Enchir*.5.1 (1828:187)

Terst.*Abr*.2.1 (Becher
2:261-77)

See vol.1:137-40

See vol.1:339

Alph.Lig.*Gl.Mar*.1.4.1 (Prato
97)

another saying of Jesus, "Seek ye first this kingdom of God in your hearts." But individual and church were "not mutually exclusive," since efficacious prayer was possible either in private or in community. By one definition of the church, therefore, it was "a body of men compacted together in order, first, to save each his own soul, then to assist each other in working out their salvation" and in carrying out the tasks of evangelism and service. The sequence of "first" and "then" in that Protestant definition was significant. An Eastern Orthodox *Enchiridion* addressed Christ in its second book as "Bridegroom of the church," and then in its third book as "Bridegroom of our souls"; for, it continued in its fifth book, the purpose of "the authority of the church" was "to teach, or rather to set straight, or rather to enlighten, human souls," because (blending the two elements) Christ was "the soul of the church." The church, therefore, was "the pillar of truth"; and while, for most of Protestantism and also for the Augustinianism within Roman Catholicism, the church in the strict sense of the word consisted only of the truly elect individuals, this textbook called it "the congregation of both the called and the elect . . . both the sinners and the righteous, [all] those who have the same confession of faith."

In the context of a deepened emphasis on the inwardness of authentic worship "in spirit and truth," both the practice and the theology of the time turned with renewed interest to the doctrinal significance of personal prayer. This had been initially formulated in patristic theology, but the "doctrine of prayer" was not a dogma of the church in the precise sense of the term that the doctrines of the Trinity and the person of Christ were. Rather, together with the commandments governing the Christian life, prayer both personal and corporate was seen as the unmistakable expression and the inevitable outcome of the church's teaching, and at the same time—particularly in the formula, "the rule of prayer should lay down the rule of faith," which referred primarily to corporate, liturgical prayer, not to private, individual devotion—as its authoritative presupposition, during this period, for example, on the doctrine of Mary.

Fén.*Inst*.1 (Gosselin 6:73)
Aug.*Serm.mont*.2.3.11
(*CCSL* 35:101-2)

Arb.*Des.myst*.2.1 (1764:168)

Fén.*Inst*.26 (Gosselin 6:129)

Terst.*Ep*.2.67 (Becher 6:149)

Mmchi.*Orig.ant*.3.2.2
(1749-III:276)
Fén.*Aut.égl*. (Gosselin 1:202)

Strz.*Enchir*.4.2 (1828:146-58)

See vol.2:268-70
Tnnt.*Serm*.6 (1744:145)

John 15:15
Frnck.*Pred*.Rog. (1700:45)

Gtti.*Ver.eccl*.1.15.3.8
(1763:154)
See p. 46 above

Lw.*Sr.Cl*.3 (Moreton 4:29)

Lw.*Chr.Perf*.13 (Moreton
3:231-32)

Spen.*Beant*.2.20
(1693:120);Frnck.*Id*.19
(Peschke 178)

Grig.*Mont.Am.sag*.15.184
(Gendrot 193)

But now it was the personal prayer of the individual, "the most secret and most intimate communication with God, prayer the necessary source of all good," that called for fresh attention. Augustine had recommended "the prayer of the heart" as essential; and beyond all the "sweet sensations" and "imagination aflame" that might accompany it as "external" results, this "inner prayer of the heart and secret communication with the God whom one believes to be inwardly present is the best, indeed the only, means for overcoming all enemies." The early success of the gospel in overcoming its pagan enemies had been the result "not of doctrine or of a good example alone, but also of prayer." It was still true that "it is prayer that puts an end to all disputes." Prayer was a "saving action" and one of the "essential gifts of the Holy Spirit" ("action [ἐνέργεια]" and "essential [οὐσιώδης]" both being technical terms from the distinctively Eastern Orthodox version of the doctrine of God as Trinity). Because "the design of prayer is not to move God, but our selves," the promise of Christ that prayer to the Father in his name would always be answered was an epitome of the entire mystery of redemption.

As Roman Catholic defenses against the accusation of prohibiting it made clear, one of the principal means for cultivating personal devotion was the private reading of the Bible, from which would come "the piety of the Gospel," because "nothing is so likely a means to fill us with [Christ's] spirit and temper as to be frequent in reading the Gospels." But one had to "read them . . . not to know what they contain, but to fill our hearts with the spirit of them," which required above all that one read them by and for oneself. More and more, the most appropriate setting for such edification seemed to be not public worship but private devotion. With no disparagement intended toward the church's liturgy and sacraments, a Roman Catholic devotional writer (joined by Protestant writers) could exhort that "prayer is the ordinary channel through which God communicates his graces, particularly his wisdom." Similarly, with no disparagement intended toward public preaching or the biblical admonition against "neglecting to meet

Heb. 10:25

Lschr.*Hör.* (1734:26-27)
Beb.*Gl.*1 (1685:23);
Terst.*Abr.*1.1.14
(Becher 2:18-20)
Frnck.*Unt.*2 (Peschke 217);
Frnck.*Id.*5 (Peschke 174);
Zinz.*Hom.*15 (Beyreuther
3-I:143)

Ost.*Arg.ref.*pr.
(1720:A4r);Ost.*Eth.*3.3.5
(1727:283-90)

Frnck.*Gl.*1 (1691:B2v)
Frnck.*Meth.*3.10
(1723:73-76)
Frnck.*Mand.Scrip.*8;10
(1706:95;105);Frnck.*Meth.*3.23
(1723:132);Ost.*Eth.*3.3.5
(1727:285)
Lang.*Paul.*2.2.2
(1718:334-35)
Frnck.*Mand.Scrip.*10
(1706:112)

Terst.*Abr.*1.1.16 (Becher
2:22)
Baum.*Pred.*2.9 (Kirchner
2:320)

Deutsch.*Luth.*1.5.17
(1698:54-55);Beng.*Gnom.*pr.5
(Steudel xix)

Frnck.*Bcht.* (Peschke 102)

Neum.*Fünf.*1 (1726-I:4);
Mayr.*Ger.* (1708:25);
Lw.*Sr.Cl.*3 (Moreton 4:25)

Luke 17:21
Lw.*Chr.Perf.*9 (Moreton
3:142)

together, as is the habit of some," which meant that "hearing is enjoined upon us even more strictly than reading," Protestant devotional writers could nevertheless exhort that it was through personal study of the Bible, incumbent upon "all adults" but also upon children, that one became a "believing and devout Christian," because this brought the individual believer certain "advantages that the public reading does not," for "nourishing and maintaining piety and devotion." "The Holy Spirit does indeed come through preaching about faith," according to Francke, but this implied that "one begin searching in Holy Scripture" oneself.

Scripture was the basis of meditation; conversely, the formation of the affections by meditation was the basis of sound exegesis, also because to understand a text it was often necessary to understand the affections of the biblical writers themselves, who had not been purely passive instruments in the writing. Far from taking away the authority of Scripture, such a method of interpretation enabled the modern reader to understand it "as though God in this very hour were speaking about and to me, or about and to the present day." Yet contempt for the word of God had grown "unbelievably greater than one can imagine" even among those who attended church. Ideally perhaps, public worship and private devotion were to be mutually supportive, as church and Scripture were. But it was too easy to suppose that a sermon was meant for someone else, as it was to dismiss the Last Judgment as a far-off prospect; therefore the word of God struck the individual most effectively in private or in small groups, and the prospect of divine judgment had its greatest impact with the individualistic realization that "even if Judgment Day were a long time off, I shall still have to die." A piety that was churchly and yet individualistic could affirm: "We are true members of the kingdom of God when the kingdom of God is within us, when the spirit of religion is the spirit of our lives." In such a climate, a more radical individualism that found church doctrine irrelevant if not antiquated could dismiss churchly piety as quaint if not superstitious, and turn to private devotion and Bible study as a substitute rather than merely a supplement.

The connecting link between the individual soul and God was faith, which was "the beginning and the effect of Wisdom in our soul"—not just any faith, however, but a genuine personal faith. Such a faith was "not a barely notional or speculative faith," not the same as the "common illumination" available to unbelievers as well. Nor, on the other hand, could it be the kind of irrational and anti-intellectual faith which laid itself open to the charge of the detractors that "nothing . . . makes people believe faster than being frightened." It was undeniable that much of what passed for faith among most conventional Christians was nothing more than "historical faith," believing in a general sense that something had happened but not believing "in a more particular sense . . . not only that 'God was in Christ, reconciling the world unto himself,' but also that 'Christ loved *me* and gave himself for *me*.' " This was a "living faith," because the believer's "heart lives in such a faith and through it finds itself powerfully drawn to Christ, yearning with an inner and passionate desire to be ever more closely united with him"; genuine faith, then, was "not a train of ideas in the head, but also a disposition of the heart," which had to be "not a hypocritical heart, but a heart that is sincere." Therefore it was "built on no precarious foundation," but was "a relying upon God through Jesus Christ for salvation, as offered in the gospel." Only such an "actual" faith could be said to bring the "justification by faith alone, without works" for which the Reformers had contended; not works, moreover, but only an actual faith could achieve the "sanctification" that was its necessary outcome and accompaniment.

Although faith was, according to Reformation doctrine, the only condition of justification, yet "both repentance and fruits meet for repentance are, in some sense, necessary to justification. But they are not necessary in the same sense with faith, nor in the same degree." While the sovereign grace of God was, according to the decrees of the Synod of Dort, "irresistible" in those whom God had predestined, the

---

Grig.Mont.*Am.sag.*15.187 (Gendrot 195)
Wsly.*Serm.*18.1.2 (Baker 1:418)

Stod.*Sfty.*1 (1687:5)
Poir.*Fid.rat.*2.21 (1708:29-32)

Reim.*Apol.*1.1.2.5 (Alexander 1:91)

Stod.*Gd.Chr.* (1714:26);
Frnck.*Pass.Marc.*7 (1724:194)
See vol.4:153-54
Wsly.*Serm.*43.2.2;5.4.2 (Baker 2:161;1:194)

2 Cor.5:19
Gal.2:20

Frnck.*Pass.Marc.*7 (1724:196)

Wsly.*Serm.*1.1.4 (Baker 1:120)

Frnck.*Pred.*Epiph.3 (1699:15)

Stod.*Sfty.*5 (1687:95-96)

Stod.*Conv.*3 (1719:12);
Wsly.*Serm.*5.4.6 (Baker 1:196)

Wsly.*Serm.*43.3.3 (Baker 2:163)

See vol.4:138-55

Wsly.*Serm.*43.3.2 (Baker 2:162-63)

See vol.4:235-42

THE THEOLOGY OF THE HEART

Terst.*Bros*.3.2 (Becher 5:58);
Baum.*Pred*.1.5 (Kirchner
1:147)

Tnnt.*Disc*.6 (1745:341)

Stod.*Conv*.5 (1719:20)
Wsly.*Serm*.7.2.1;14.1.1
(Baker 1:225;336)

Frnck.*Pred*.Jub. (1699:24)
Grig.Mont.*Am.sag*.15.181
(Gendrot 190-91)
Scriv.*Seel*.2.5 (Stier 1:575)

Stod.*Conv*.1 (1719:3)

Mynst.*Pr*.51 (1845-II:235)

Frnck.*Pred*.Oc. (1700:30)

Stod.*Conv*.4 (1719:15)

See vol.4:349-50

See vol.4:165

Edw.*Rel.Aff*.3.7 (Miller
2:340)
Frnck.*Pass.Marc*.12
(1724:358)
Luke 19:41-42
Frnck.*Pred*.Adv.3
(1699:94;99)
Terst.*Bros*.2.6 (Becher 4:223)

Stod.*Conv*.1 (1719:1-2)

Pff.*Hist.theol*.2.10
(1724-I:280-84)

Frnck.*Meth*.2.4 (1723:37)

Lw.*Dem.Er*. (Moreton 5:12)

new emphasis on conversion and repentance led even descendants of the Reformation to stress its "voluntary" character and therefore its resistibility. Repentance in this sense, which had been "one of the principal subjects of Paul's ministry," was a radical change of mind and a coming to self-knowledge, the outcome of "a true and earnest penitential struggle that has first taken place in the heart." In that penitential struggle, the yearning of the soul for God, though not always verbally articulated, was the "antecedent to conversion, but no part of conversion" itself. Through the proclamation of both the law and the gospel, the neutrality of the heart between God and Satan was replaced by faith in Christ, which was, strictly speaking, "the first act of conversion." Blaise Pascal's "argument of the wager [argument du pari]," with its echoes of Luther's definition of faith as wager, was well suited to this renewed insistence that the "transforming" power of a conversion "attended with a change of nature" and affections was diametrically opposed to a mere "Christianity of the reason." The tears of Christ over Jerusalem were a sign that repentance must not be postponed any longer, but that "we must be converted in our very heart," by a genuine "saving conversion" and a divine "work of regeneration."

For the development of Christian doctrine, as distinguished from the life of the Christian church or of the Christian individual, no theological controversy of the time so accurately reflected the implications of this almost universal demand for conversion and change in all the churches as the "long conflict" provoked by Pietism over the question of "the theology of the unregenerate [theologia irregenitorum]": "Is it essential, or is it not, that in the very first place someone who studies theology have the knowledge and the experience of having been truly converted to God"—essential, that is, not only for eternal salvation (as was generally agreed), but for a correct understanding of Scripture and of Christian doctrine? Or could "a heathen, ignorant of all divine revelation, if he found such a paper" with the words of institution of the Eucharist written on it, "know what it related to?" Not only Pietists but orthodox theologians in

Lschr.*Dr.Pred*.1 (1733:8);
Wer.*Misc*.16 (Ryhinerus 2:293)
Nrs.*Hist.pel*.2.3 (Berti
1:243-44)

Edw.*Rel.Aff*.2 (Miller 2:183)
Edw.*Rel.Aff*.3.4 (Miller
2:278)

Edw.*Rel.Aff*.3.4 (Miller
2:270-71)

Frnck.*Pred*.ep.ded.
(1700:A7r-A7v)

Spen.*Gtts*.1 (1680:9);
Spen.*Bed*.1.1.39 (Canstein
1:224);Lang.*Paul*.2.2
(1718:315);Edw.*Rel.Aff*.3.4
(Miller 2:280)
Frnck.*Mand.Scrip*.11
(1706:116-19)

Spen.*Gtts*.3 (1680:75)

Lang.*Antibarb*. (1709-I:186)

Lang.*Nach*.5.9 (1707-V:70)

Lang.*Antibarb*. (1709-I:21;31)

Casp.*Beyl*.8-14 (1724:56)

Dipp.*Orth*.4 (1699:47)

Nss.*Dipp*.pr. (1701:8)

Nss.*Dipp*.1 (1701:19)

Neum.*Marp*.2.1 (1727:51-52)

every church taught that "doctrine" and "life," or "doctrine" and "discipline," were to be coordinated. But as Jonathan Edwards noted, "the delusions of Satan and the wicked and deceitful heart . . . may be attended with a good doctrinal knowledge of religion," since spiritual understanding did "not consist in any new doctrinal knowledge" but was a "supernatural understanding of divine things that is peculiar to the saints, and which those who are not saints have nothing of." Therefore it was essential to identify as "false teachers" not only those who taught false doctrine but those who were false in their hearts even if they taught orthodox doctrine.

Everyone conceded that the technical philological understanding of the Hebrew or Greek text of Scripture was possible without conversion or spiritual understanding, but "sound interpretation" of Scripture had to engage not only the intellect or the scholarship but the person of the interpreter. The apostle Paul attributed "true divine knowledge only to divine illumination," not to an external philological grasp of the biblical text. "What I am denying," the Pietist theologian Joachim Lange announced, was "that a teacher who is wicked and unregenerate can teach the word of God . . . soundly and without corruption." Such a view would be, he said elsewhere, "a deification of the letter of Scripture" at the cost of its spirit. Not every kind of "literal knowledge," even if it was "in conformity with the letter of Scripture and therefore true," could be called "spiritual, divine, living, and supernatural." For this definition of doctrine and biblical exegesis Lange and other Pietists were denounced. When some took the Pietist argument further and attacked the notion of a theology of the unregenerate as "the first deception of reason," their orthodox adversaries had to grant that they had made some valid points; but they had gone too far, since Scripture was intended also for readers who were still "unconverted." Such an emphasis on the "illumination" of the biblical interpreter was "a species of Donatism": it confused the theologian's subjective personal status with his objective ecclesiastical task.

The reconsideration of the relation between God and the soul and the claim that "men may have the

Stod.*Conv.*15 (1719:78)

Bnyn.*Lw.Gr.*2 (Sharrock 2:215)
Span.*Ev.vind.*1.36 (Marck 3:145-46)

See vol.4:149-50

Tnnt.*Serm.*17 (1744:328)
Calv.*Inst.* (1559)3.2.7
(Barth-Niesel 4:15-16)
See vol.4:288-89

Gaz.*Prael.*2.6.6.218
(1831-II:202)

Fén.*Ep.*11.viii.1689
(Masson 249)

Pet.*Hchzt.*4.15 (1701:130)

See vol.4:145-53

See vol.4:154

Deutsch.*Luth.*1 (1698:3)

Scriv.*Seel.*2.7 (Stier 4:65)

Canst.*Spen.*26 (1711:64)

Spen.*Bed.*1.1.13 (Canstein 1:93-94)

knowledge of their own conversion" raised with new insistence the question of the assurance of grace and election. "Before thou canst know whether thou art elected," Bunyan had counseled, "thou must believe in Jesus Christ"; faith was the key to certainty. The Reformation doctrine of justification by grace through faith was based on the specification that grace was not something subjective in man, but "a property of the Deity, whereby he is inclined to dispense undeserved kindnesses upon his creatures freely and in a sovereign way." Grace was the foundation of faith, as Calvin had maintained. But in opposition to Calvin and Luther the Council of Trent had warned that, except by a special revelation, no one could possess the certainty of salvation; that warning was being repeated now. "It is not at all necessary," Fénelon contended, "that one should always be certain of salvation"; rather, "the state of the soul that God wishes to make perfect" ultimately required it to be ready to abandon any such certainty. When radical Protestants now launched a polemic against Trent on the question of certainty, that could be read as substantiation of the perennial Roman Catholic criticism that for the subjective scholastic definition of grace as a "habitude" within the human soul the Reformers had been in danger of substituting a subjective definition of faith as "assurance," which would become the ground of personal certainty about justification.

Pietism, whether radical or conservative, was perceived as a threat to Reformation orthodoxy in the doctrine of justification because by its subjectivism it appeared to have made that danger a reality. A seventeenth-century handbook of piety had affirmed the orthodox position that justification was "undoubtedly the chief article of the Christian religion," in relation to which "all other points of doctrine are auxiliary." The authorized biography of Spener took pains to include the assurance that he had "stood fast" on the doctrine of justification by faith, and he himself spoke of being "troubled as well as frightened" by what he took to be contemporary weakness and confusion about that doctrine. Yet it was of weakness and of a fundamental confusion between justification and sanctification that Spener himself

Deutsch.*Luth*.2.4.1
(1698:101)

Nmnn.*Er.* (1701:176-85)
Nmnn.*Term.* (1700:8)

See p. 101 above

Reim.*Apol*.2.3.1.1
(Alexander 2:179)

Nürn.Sen.20.x.1707
(Neumeister 284)

Lmp.*Betr*.2.2 (1756-I:499)

Fén.*Inst*.15 (Gosselin 6:98)
Matt.26:38
Lmp.*Betr*.3.1 (1756-II:14)

Mark 15:34;Ps.22:1

Fusc.*Sac.cr.* (1756:19-20)

Phil.2:8

Song Sol.4:9
Fusc.*Sac.cr.* (1756:7)

Terst.*Bros*.2.4 (Becher 4:139)

Pff.*Hist.theol*.2.10
(1724-I:346- 47);
Amrt.*Theol.eclec*.7.2.4
(1752-2-II:36-51)
Nrs.*Vind.Aug*.5.11 (Berti
2:423-24)
Lmp.*Theol.elench*.12.20
(1729:55);Baum.*Pred*.3.9
(Kirchner 3:282)
Fil.*Sl*.19 (*Soč.Fil*.1:150)

stood accused. For in answer to the question of whether God continued to keep the door of grace open to all, even to the fallen, he and his associates, it was charged, "have no compunction in answering No."

Not a subjectivism that undercut doctrinal orthodoxy, but a Christocentrism that rescued it from the intellectualism that had threatened to distort it, was what Spener and his contemporaries in all the churches claimed to have recovered. At a time when the objective biblical ground for christological orthodoxy was increasingly coming into question and such New Testament passages as the cry of dereliction on the cross were being employed as a contradiction of such orthodoxy, there was a powerful attraction in the thesis, "crude" though its formulation might seem, that "unless we first have 'Christ in us,' we do not have 'Christ for us.' " The concept "Christ in us" meant that to establish and preserve a healthy relation between God and the human soul, it was necessary to contemplate the relation between God and the "truly human soul" of Christ. One of the "remedies for sadness" available to "an enfeebled and humiliated soul" in its troubled state was a study of the subjective "sorrow even unto death" of Jesus in the garden of Gethsemane and on the cross, where, "pressed to the point of death, he cried, in a voice that truly came from the heart: 'My God, my God, why hast thou forsaken me?' " The cry of dereliction and the language of the New Testament about his "obedience unto death, even the death of the cross," when conflated with the language of the Song of Songs in the cry, "You have wounded my heart, my sister, my bride," led to the contemplation of the Sacred Heart of Jesus, broken on the cross. Jesus was "a man who suffered for your soul, battled for your soul, prayed for your soul."

This was also a time when the entire tradition of the church about Mary was under attack. Debate continued over the Roman Catholic doctrine of her immaculate conception, with its checkered medieval history; Protestantism went on rejecting it, while Eastern Orthodoxy did not need it, celebrating her nativity and dedicating churches in its honor without being obliged to posit an explicit definition of how and why she had been exempt from the universal rule of original sin. Another topic of debate was the mariological orthodoxy of the Reformers, all of whom had retained the doctrine of the virgin birth and many of whom had retained the title "Mother of God" as well. Some of the descendants of the Reformation deplored the tendency "to derogate as much from the Blessed Virgin on the one hand as she has been overexalted on the other," and, without relapsing into what they took to be a superstitious Mariolatry, sought to rehabilitate an evangelical picture of her as one who gave birth to Christ not only physically but also spiritually.

In Roman Catholic devotion, subjective visions could be used to corroborate such mariological doctrines as the immaculate conception; conversely, a contemplation of the subjectivity of Mary similar to the contemplation of the inner life of Christ could be presented as a path to self-knowledge. Her response to Gabriel at the annunciation was the example, apart from the humility of Christ himself, of the content of submission to the will of God: "What would have become of us," asked one Orthodox preacher, if "in boundless devotion she had not replied to the heavenly messenger, 'Let it be to me according to your word'?" That response made her "Mother of God [Θεοτόκος, Bogorodica}," a title whose legitimacy, as established by the ancient church, needed to be defended again. The "mariological maximalism" of Duns Scotus was paraphrased during this period in one of the most influential books ever written about Mary, *The Glories of Mary* by Alphonsus Maria de Liguori, which assigned presumptive authority to "an opinion when it tends in any way to honor the Most Blessed Virgin, when it has some foundation, and when it is not contrary to faith or to the canons of the church or to truth."

Mary was, for such a view, "the living image of God" and "the chief work of his hands." She was also "advocate of sinners," set apart from humanity and even from all the other saints because she alone had received the glory of God completely, not only in measure. Even the seemingly harsh language that Christ sometimes used to her was in fact meant to

See vol.4:261

Brnt.*Art.XXXIX*.2 (1700:51)
Mayr.*Red*.1
(1702:151-52;169)

Lschr.*Hör*. (1734:34)

Gtti.*Ver.eccl*.1.7.3.15
(1763:65-66)

Grig.Mont.*Vr.dév*.213
(Gendrot 629-30)
Luke 1:38

Fén.*Inst*.18 (Gosselin 6:104)

Fil.*Sl*.28 (*Soč.Fil*.1:205)

Mēn.*Did*.5.1 (Blantēs 228-29)
Bert.*Diss.hist*.
(1753-III:386-88)
Drnd.*Fid.vind*.1.38
(1709:129-32)
See vol.4:47-50

Alph.Lig.*Gl.Mar*.1.5.1 (Prato 123)

Grig.Mont.*Vr.dév*.50
(Gendrot 515)
Alph.Lig.*Gl.Mar*.1.6 (Prato 144-77)

Mēn.*Did*.5.19 (Blantēs 358)
John 2:4;Mark 3:33

Alph.Lig.*Gl.Mar.*1.6.1 (Prato 148-49);Fil.*Sl.*131 (*Soč.Fil.*3:109-14)
Luke 2:35

Mēn.*Did.*1.7 (Blantēs 84)
Alph.Lig.*Gl.Mar.*2.9 (Prato 394-411)
Alph.Lig.*Gl.Mar.*2.7 (Prato 362-78)

Mēn.*Did.*5.19 (Blantēs 356)
Lmp.*Theol.elench.*29.2 (1729:109)
Fil.*Sl.*362 (*Soč.Fil.*5:163-66)

See vol.3:160-74

Alph.Lig.*Gl.Mar.*1.5 (Prato 118-19)

Grig.Mont.*Vr.dév.*61-62 (Gendrot 523-24)
Luke 17:21

Grig.Mont.*Vr.dév.*38 (Gendrot 508)

Arb.*Des.myst.*3.20 (1764:510-18)

Grig.Mont.*Am.sag.*17.203 (Gendrot 204)
Neum.*Fünf.*1 (1726-I:112)

Wsly.*Serm.*9.1.3 (Baker 1:252)
Lang.*Nach.*6.3 (1707-VI·16)

Lw.*Chr.Perf.*1 (Moreton 3:14)
Terst.*Bros.*4.1 (Becher 6:33);
Terst.*Abr.*1.1.1-2 (Becher 2:11)

Tnnt.*Disc.*1 (1745:48)

Wsly.*Pl.Acct.*1.15 (*LPT*187)

honor her. The prophecy that a sword would pierce through her soul was fulfilled when she shared in the crucifixion of Christ, sorrowfully offering the life of her Son to the Father for human salvation. Thus also the death (or "dormition") of the "queen of heaven" proved that she was a truly human participant in the common lot of all mankind; but her resurrection (which Protestants, of course, denied as nonbiblical) set her apart also at the end of her life. All those experiences of her own inner life made her uniquely accessible to the prayers of sinners as "mediatrix"— not indeed mediatrix of the justifying grace of God, which came through the merit of Christ alone, but of other graces and blessings, so that devotion to her was inseparable from devotion to him as "the final goal of all our devotions." Like the kingdom of God itself, therefore, "the kingdom of the most holy Virgin" was principally " 'within,' that is, in the soul."

Such a "picturing in the heart" of Christ or of Mary, whether or not it was described in the traditional language of the threefold way of mystical theology (purgation, illumination, and union), was a path to complete self-knowledge, which, though indispensable, was unattainable by any other means. Natural man apart from grace was "secure, because he is utterly ignorant of himself." Turning in on oneself, consequently, was a necessary step toward faith, because a "knowledge of ourselves makes human life a state of infinite importance, placed upon so dreadful a point betwixt two such eternities." The earnest and sincere observance of the state of one's soul was a continuing duty. While there could be "various degrees of our persuasion of this matter respecting ourselves," the real question was not "what [theological] opinion you are of," but whether or not "you are conscious to yourself that you are the man I have been . . . describing."

Those who were using such methods of "describing" and encouraging the introspection and contemplation that fostered an intimate association between God and the soul were nevertheless conscious of its potential dangers. They recognized that it could all too easily degenerate into an attitude that was "not sufficiently concerned about understanding, but sat-

Zinz.*Lond.Pred.*1.3
(Beyreuther 5-I:19)

Edw.*Rel.Aff.*3.pr. (Miller 2:196)

Stod.*Sfty.*9 (1687:247)

Frnck.*Pred.*pr. (1700:B5v);
Arb.*Des.myst.*int. (1764:1-2);
Fén.*Ep.*11.v.1689 (Masson 136-37)

Bert.*Aug.*3.1 (1747-I:339)

Aug.*Doct.christ.*1.3.3-1.5.5
(*CCSL* 32:8-9);Aug.*Civ.*11.25
(*CCSL* 48:344-45)

Edw.*Rel.Aff.*3.2 (Miller 2:240)

Frnck.*Pred.*Inv. (1699:43)

Zinz.*Beth.*2 (Beyreuther 6-IV:23)

Fén.*Ep.*26.vii.1689 (Masson 224-25)

Jer.31:31
Zinz.*Lond.Pred.*4.7
(Beyreuther 5-II:57)

Wsly.*Pl.Acct.*3.5 (*LPT*192)

isfied with merely 'having' and 'experiencing.' " No amount of egocentric introspection or "strictness of examination" could bring "assurance" if it were cut off from moral effort: the apostle Paul "obtained assurance of winning the prize, more by running than by considering." Hence the most effective way to prove "the truth of your faith" was "by that holiness that does accompany and flow from faith in Jesus Christ." That was why the doctors of the inner life in this period like Francke, Arbiol, and Fénelon consistently linked "soul" with "perfection" (and both of these with "the Holy Spirit").

Evangelical Perfection

It could be dangerous for the theology of the heart to describe the relation between God and the soul as though the inner life of the soul were an end in itself. The Augustinians of the eighteenth century recalled that Augustine had distinguished between those things that were intended to be "used [uti]" and those that were intended to be "enjoyed [frui]" and that he had put God into the latter category. But such "enjoyment of God [fruitio Dei]" did not imply at all that the sovereign Lord of heaven and earth would become a means by which the creature attained a solipsistic self-fulfillment. On the contrary, when a heart was finally grounded in grace and "as soon as the Savior takes possession of the heart, . . . he immediately tells it about the difference between right and wrong." The inner life could be no less an obstacle to the will of God for perfection than were the outer circumstances of society: as the prophet Jeremiah had promised, authentic morality was to be implanted as a law written upon the heart.

In the effort to replace "the external evidence of Christianity," which had become "more or less clogged and encumbered," with an appeal to "men (of reflection especially) . . . to look into themselves also and attend to the light shining in their hearts," the moral dimension of conversion, transformation, and inner renewal seemed to provide an indispensable component of the new apologetics. "When the clergy are without religion and the people abound in superstition," a satirist had observed, "the church, you may

Tin.*Chr*.11 (1730:169)

Gib.*Dec*.49 (Bury 5:299)

Conc.*Rel.riv*.3.1 (1754-I:355)

Tnnt.*Serm*.13 (1744:259)

Edw.*Rel.Aff*.3.1 (Miller 2:208)

Fén.*Inst*.19 (Gosselin 6:113)

Wsly.*Serm*.21.1.9 (Baker 1:480)

Tnnt.*Disc*.6 (1745:312)

Mēn.*Did*.1.5 (Blantēs 52); Conc.*Rel.riv*.3.15 (1754-I:455);Fén.*Ep*.11.viii. 1689 (Masson 247); Lw.*Ser.Cl*.3 (Moreton 4:22)

Blach.*Log*.7 (1882:82-92)

Reim.*Apol*.2.1.1.8 (Alexander 2:30-33)

Matt.5:48

Mrkrd.*Off*.14 (1722:116)

Wsly.*Serm*.43.1.9 (Baker 2:160)
Brnt.*Art.XXXIX*.16 (1700:140)
Gtti.*Coll*.3.3.5 (1727:480-81)

See vol.1:308-13
Deutsch.*Luth*.2.2.10 (1698:89-90)
Spen.*Albrt*.12 (1696:10)

be sure, is in a flourishing condition." But the church was, he added, "in great danger when men place their religion in morality," since, as another critic suggested, "to a philosophic eye the vices of the clergy are far less dangerous than their virtues." To meet that danger on its own ground, the church needed to recognize that its presentation and defense of the Christian message as "revealed religion" had to make "holiness" its theme: whatever the philosophical status of other theological claims for metaphysical transcendence might be, it was undeniable that Christian life and ethics were characterized by "transcendent holiness"; and whatever the analogies might be between supernatural or "spiritual affections" and other, more "natural" affections, the pagan notion of friendship was transcended by the Christian idea of love, so that "Christianity begins just where heathen morality ends." Among the Christian "doctrines to be known, promises and threatenings to be believed, and precepts to be obeyed," the doctrinal form of the precepts was what, within a few years of one another, a Greek Orthodox bishop, an Italian Dominican, a French archbishop, and an Anglican Nonjuror joined in identifying as "evangelical perfection" or "the perfection of the gospel." "The perfection of the evangelical law" was a theme of Greek Orthodox preaching later in the century, too.

The imperative of perfection seemed unambiguous in the Sermon on the Mount: "You, therefore, must be perfect, as your heavenly Father is perfect." The difference between the law of Moses and the gospel could be identified as lying precisely in the "more perfect life" open to New Testament believers. Nevertheless, the very term "perfection," even with the qualification "perfection of the gospel" or "evangelical perfection," had a singularly unevangelical and heretical sound to many ears, since "the word has various senses." The Novatians in the third century and the Donatists in the fourth were remembered for having asserted the possibility, perhaps the necessity, of a perfect church here on earth, and for having claimed that it had appeared in the form of their own sect. In this period Spener was accused of teaching a false perfectionism; but he denied the charge and strove to

Spen.*Bed.*1.1.20 (Canstein 1:110-12)

Spen.*Pi.Des.* (Aland 47)

Zinz.*Lond.Pred.*5.8 (Beyreuther 5-II:234); Zinz.*Gespr.*1 (Beyreuther 1-III:7-8)

Beng.*Brüd.*1.1.15 (1751:135)
Tnnt.*Nec.*app. (1743:78)

Wsly.*Serm.*48.3.2 (Baker 2:249)
Wsly.*Serm.*13.1.5 (Baker 1:318-19)

Wsly.*Serm.*40.2.20;40.2.28 (Baker 2:116;120)

Wsly.*Serm.*43.1.5-6;43.3.11 (Baker 2:158-59;166)

1 John 3:9

Lw.*Chr.Perf.*2 (Moreton 3:27)
Edw.*Orig.Sn.*1.1.4 (Miller 3:135)
1 John 1:8

See vol.4:154-55

Rom.7:23

Stod.*Conv.*16 (1719:88)

Wsly.*Serm.*13.5.2 (Baker 1:333)

explain how the imperative of perfection was to be understood, even as he reminded his readers that "we are not forbidden to seek perfection, but we are urged on toward it." Regarding themselves as Spener's theological heirs, the Moravians, under Zinzendorf's leadership, often spoke as though total moral perfection were attainable this side of heaven. For this perfectionism of theirs they were in turn attacked by theologians in Europe as well as in America.

Among those who attacked the Moravians for this, despite his debt to them and affinity with them, was John Wesley, who called Zinzendorf "that great, bad man" and equated their perfectionism with antinomianism. Yet Wesley was at the same time the most effective spokesman in the eighteenth century for the definition of "evangelical perfection." On the one hand, he could assert that "a Christian is so far perfect as not to commit sin" and that "Christians are saved in this world from all sin"; on the other hand, he warned against "the extreme mischievousness of that seemingly innocent opinion that there is no sin in a believer" and against "that inference: 'I feel no sin; therefore I have none.' " Such a paradoxical treatment of perfection had its roots within the New Testament itself. One passage had promised that "no one born of God commits sin, for God's nature abides in him and he cannot sin because he is born of God"; this was, however, "not to be understood as if he that was born of God was therefore in an absolute state of perfection, and incapable afterwards of falling into anything that was sinful," since "John wrote his first Epistle to the Christians that then were" and warned that "if we say that we have no sin, we deceive ourselves." Another passage of the New Testament—at least as it was being interpreted, in keeping with the exegesis of it by the Reformers—had described the believer as afflicted by "another law . . . making me captive to the law of sin," which meant that "grace given in conversion is imperfect."

Thus, as Wesley noted, "perfection" could mean various things. Although, one scholar has suggested, "Wesley's doctrine of justification . . . must not be read as a considered, balanced piece of doctrinal instruction . . . [but] is much more in the order of a

Deschner (1960) 180

Wsly.*Serm*.40 (Baker
2:99-124)

Wsly.*Pl.Acct*.1.12 (*LPT*186)

Beng.*Gnom*.Matt.19:21
(Steudel 118)

Wsly.*Serm*.13.5.2 (Baker
1:333)

Wsly.*Jour*.14.v.1765
(Jackson 3:212)

Nss.*Dipp*.7 (1701:46);
Ost.*Eth*.1.4.4 (1727:116-17)

Wsly.*Serm*.17.x.1787
(*LPT*106-8)

Lw.*Chr.Perf*.int. (Moreton 3:9)

See vol.4:157

Zinz.*Lond.Pred*.4.7
(Beyreuther 5-II:55)

Mrkrd.*Off*.19 (1722:192-97)

Fén.*Gr.préd*.1.5
(Gosselin 2:173)

Wsly.*Serm*.13.3.9 (Baker
1:324)

Stod.*Apl*.1 (1709:34)

journal of his theological pilgrimage," his basic understanding of perfection would appear to lie in the distinction between "perfecting perfection" and "perfected perfection." "Perfected" perfection was an essential attribute of God, who was an "immense ocean of all perfections," but for the believer it remained a goal, ultimately reserved for the life everlasting. "Perfecting" perfection, by contrast, was a gift and a process here in this life; it began with the divine act of justification by grace through faith, in which the believer was "renewed, cleansed, purified, sanctified" but "not . . . altogether," and by which the believer progressed toward the goal and would continue progressing until the end. "I think in justification," Wesley wrote in his *Journal*, "just as Mr. Calvin does. In this respect, I do not differ from him an hair's breadth." Perfection was growth toward Christian maturity. William Law's *Christian Perfection*, which Wesley endorsed and continued to read despite his criticisms of the author, had confessed in its introduction: "Did not God pardon frailties and infirmities, the best of men could not be rewarded."

Like the corollary doctrine of justification, the doctrine of regeneration and perfection had had a surprisingly uneven career in Christian history, often having been taken for granted rather than explicitly worked out in a full theological exposition. At least in part, this was attributable to a certain reluctance to speak about sanctification, for fear of falling into hypocrisy, or at any rate of giving the appearance of hypocrisy. To be sure, the classical ideal of "goodness combined with beauty [καλοκαγαθία]" could claim a continuity of support from Christian as well as pagan authors. Yet while it was accurate simultaneously to appeal to a consensus about the demand for perfection among "all the fathers, all the ascetic authors, and all the contemplatives approved by the church" and yet to conclude that there had not been "the least intimation of [the notion of absolute sinless perfection] either in any ancient or modern writer," it likewise remained true that "many divines both ancient and modern" were strangely silent about the doctrine of regeneration.

See vol.4:117-18

See p. 15 above

Mmchi.*Orig.ant*.3.pr.
(1749-III:2)

Clem.*Q.d.s.* (*GCS* 3:159-91)
Mrkrd.*Off*.19 (1722:202-6)

See vol.1:307-18

Gtti.*Coll*.3.3.5 (1727:480-81)

Ambr.*Off*.1.7.24 (*PL*16:30)

See vol.2:20
Mrkrd.*Off*.1 (1722:5)

Mrkrd.*Off*.12
(1722:69-70;71-72;78-79;83)

Blrt.*S.T.Jur.just*.5.1-2
(Lequette 4:81-86)

Scriv.*Seel*.4.12 (Stier 6:621)
See vol.4:131-33

Tnnt.*Nec*.1 (1743:20-21);
Tnnt.*Disc*.3 (1745:178)

As in earlier periods, reformers within various denominations who were calling for improvement and change appealed to an idealized picture of the morality of the ancient church, where there had been "only a very few" who did not take the moral imperatives of the gospel seriously. A précis of one of the relatively few positive treatments of wealth in the early church, *Who Is the Rich Man that Is Saved?* by Clement of Alexandria, served as a way of inculcating an ethically responsible attitude toward property. Again, the Augustinian interpretation of perfection as an attribute that was not possible under the conditions of historical existence and that applied to Christians and the church only in an eschatological sense acted to temper the unrealistic expectations about a sinless life and a community of saints to which a superficial reading of the Bible might lead. Augustine's mentor, Ambrose, had written a book, *On Duties {De officiis}*, frankly patterned after Cicero's famous work of the same name; when a Greek Orthodox manual of ethics in the early eighteenth century also took that title, Ambrose's treatise, despite its Western and Latin provenance, was singled out as a model.

Nevertheless, the churches all tended, in ethics no less than in doctrine, to appeal specifically to their own traditions. For example, John Chrysostom dominated the discussion of "temperance [σωφροσύνη]" in the teaching of an Eastern Orthodox moral theologian. The position of doctrinal authority occupied by Thomas Aquinas gave his discussions of ethics, whether philosophical or theological, a special place in eighteenth-century Roman Catholicism, as was evident, for example, in the several definitions of "justice" in Charles-René Billuart's *The Summa of Saint Thomas Accommodated to Present-Day Academic Procedures*. The misinterpretations to which the Reformation doctrine of justification by faith without works had been subject already in the sixteenth century made the moral earnestness of the Reformers, as this had been expressed in Luther's experience of "trial [Anfechtung]," and the Reformer's resistance to antinomianism seem especially relevant to a new situation. At the same time, an ironic shift had taken place: the Reformers had accused medieval Catholicism of exalting works at the expense of grace and

See vol.4:146-47

Zinz.*Aug.Conf.*14 (Beyreuther 6-II:252-54)

faith, but now Protestants were obliged to admit that moralism had a stronger hold in many Protestant lands than it did in Roman Catholicism.

Consequently, one of the differences between these traditions of ethical doctrine and the ethical transposition of doctrine that was becoming audible now was the consideration of the very question of how the moral imperative was related to Christian doctrine. "Christian doctrine," one writer could warn, "is the only solid and firm foundation for the highest perfec- Arb.*Inst.*1.19 (1765:91) tion." A theology that remained in the intellect without forming the will was dead, but the converse was also true: the soul had to be shaped and animated by a living theology if it was to undergo genuine Frnck.*Meth.*1.2 (1723:4) change. The works of creation and providence taught Stod.*Conv.*4 (1719:18)
Lw.*Ser.Cl.*2 (Moreton 4:20)
Frnck.*Pass.Marc.*10
(1724:301)
Wsly.*Serm.*5.2.1 (Baker
1:187)
Baum.*Pred.*1.4 (Kirchner
1:109-10)
Wsly.*Serm.*5.3.2 (Baker
1:191)
Stod.*Conv.*7 (1719:32)
Terst.*Bros.*2.4 (Becher 4:155) holiness, but they did not accomplish it in the individual; for that, divine grace was needed, and the danger of losing grace was the Christian's "only concern." In justification love was distinct from faith, but in regeneration they were inseparable. It was mistaken to "affirm that universal holiness or obedience must precede justification," but no less mistaken to forget that "the knowledge of God is inseparable from holiness." In the "striking expression" of Phil.3:14 (Luth.) Luther's translation of the New Testament, the believer was to "pursue [jagen] sanctification."

Edw.*Rel.Aff.*3.12 (Miller
2.444)

Spen.*Pi.Des.* (Aland 61)

It was necessary to recognize that "Christian practice is the sign of signs" and that "Christianity consists of practice," because "the design of knowledge in religion . . . is practice, and without the latter the former will only serve to increase our present guilt Tnnt.*Disc.*5 (1745:249) and future punishment." A "conviction about the truth of doctrine" by itself was not enough, since "the pure life of Christians is the only recommendation of Sem.*Erkl.*pr. (1777:B8v-C1r)

Tnnt.*Disc.*5 (1745:275)
Lang.*Mttl.*2.2 (1712:115-18);
Zeis.*Unver.Gew.* (1696:23);
Span.*Cont.* (Marck 3:894)

Lschr.*Dr.Pred.*1 (1733:19) pure doctrine," and those who desired the comfort of grace had to be diligent in its exercise. When even quite moderate critics accused the Protestant churches of indiscriminate "heresy-hunting," defenders of orthodoxy could not disagree, since they had to acknowledge that there had sometimes been a misplaced "zeal for orthodoxy" and that theologians had misused the term "faith" to refer only to doctrine at the cost of Nss.*Dipp.*5 (1701:44) holiness of life. But they urged that practice by itself was not sufficient for salvation and that both doctrine

Wer.*Misc.*16 (Ryhinerus
2:293);Ost.*Dz.serm.*5
(1722:190-91);Lschr.*Hör.*
(1734:27);Lschr.*Dr.Pred.*1
(1733:8)

Luth.*Kl.Kat.*3.4 (*Bek.*512)

Casp.*Beyl.*2 (1724:35-36);
Zinz.*Red.*5 (Beyreuther
1-II:66); Zinz.*Sieb.*6
(Beyreuther 2-I:55)

John 7:17

Zinz.*Soc.*21 (Beyreuther
1-I:211);Zinz.*Off.Red.*26
(Beyreuther 2-IV:298)
Dipp.*Orth.* (1699)
Dipp.*Hrt.*1 (1706:9)
Matt.25:41

Dipp.*Hrt.*2 (1706:33)

See vol.4:128-55;279-89

Lw.*Ser.Cl.*10 (Moreton 4:90)

Lw.*Sr.Cl.*4 (Moreton 4:37)

Matt.9:22
James 2:19
Gal.5:6

Fil.*Sl.*58 (*Soč.Fil.*2:105)
See vol.4:286
Wsly.*Serm.*2.2.6 (Baker
1:139)

Lang.*Antibarb.* (1709-I:454)

Tnnt.*Disc.*1 (1745:17)

and morality were necessary; as Luther's *Small Catechism* had taught, the name of God was hallowed "when the word of God is taught clearly and purely and we, as children of God, lead holy lives in accordance with it." Yet in their copies of the Gospels, too, Jesus had said to the "orthodox" scribes and Pharisees of his time: "If any man's will is to do [God's] will, he shall know whether [my teaching] is from God." Making this the epigraph of one book and the theme of another, a critic of Protestant orthodoxy could paraphrase another saying of Jesus, at the Last Judgment: "Depart from me, you well-meaning orthodox evildoers. . . . I never commanded you to have the right opinions, but to do the right deeds, for that is the basis of all truth and of its confession." This implied that in life and in "right deeds" there had to be conformity, but that the doctrine and the confession of the church had now become little more than "opinions."

Since the Reformation debates, or perhaps since the Epistles of Paul and of James, the relation of life and doctrine had been rooted above all in the distinction and yet inseparable connection between the doctrines of justification and sanctification. William Law, in his *Serious Call to a Devout and Holy Life*, stated it as a fundamental that "this and this alone is Christianity, an universal holiness in every part of life." But he did not intend to reduce the gospel to moralism by ignoring redemption, because this fundamental was a corollary of the fundamental he had enunciated earlier: "The Son of God has redeemed us for this only end, that we should, by a life of reason and piety, live to the glory of God; this is the only rule and measure for every order and state of life." When Christ said, "Your faith has saved you," he was referring not to the faith that demons could also have, but to what Paul had described as "faith working by love": Eastern Orthodox theologians, the fathers of the Council of Trent, and John Wesley all made that a favorite text for the corollary relation between justification by faith and holy living. It was indeed "the universal consensus of everyone who is orthodox" (at least according to Reformation definitions) that while "the word 'justify' is not to be taken in a moral sense," a justifying faith nonetheless had to be a living faith, which brought about not only the forgiveness of sins but a renewal of life, and it was a gross "abuse of the doctrine" of justification to conclude from it "that one can be saved without good works."

In seeking to rescue justification from that abuse, the Pietists interpreted it as "a continuous action" and state, as a line rather than a point. But then they had to defend themselves against the charge, despite New Testament usage, that defining faith as "obedience" was a confusion of "justification" with "renewal." There was an almost universal conviction that the recovery of the discipline of the early church was "of the greatest importance" now, because "Jesus Christ has established the authority and the discipline of the church" and the church had to maintain and defend its freedom to exercise such authority and discipline. The Holy Spirit who had dwelt in the early church would not confer true wisdom except on those who no longer lived for themselves. That called for "a real as well as a relative change." The goal of "complete holiness" remained an ideal even when it appeared unattainable, and yet it was "evident on every hand that none of the precepts of Christ is openly observed." If, in such an atmosphere, it had become increasingly difficult to credit the claims of an ortho-dox "theology of the heart" that it was needed to effect the "real" as well as the "relative" transforma-tion for which everyone was calling inside as well as outside the churches, the alternative was to "place religion in the practice of morality in obedience to the will of God," that is, "the practice of those duties that result from the relation we stand in to God and man," or, in the more familiar formula of Immanuel Kant, to define religion itself as "the recognition of all our duties as divine commands."

One authority for evangelical perfection, an author-ity that was at one and the same time both moral and doctrinal, still stood impregnable, verified by the internal testimony of the heart and untouched either by the attacks of rationalistic "speculation" or by the breakdown of an external orthodoxy that consisted of "rote recitation": the call to "action" in imitation of Christ, as this was taught in the New Testament, "an

Lang.*Antibarb.* (1709-I:455)

Ost.*Corrupt.* 1.4 (1700-I:128-29)

Frnck.*Bcht.* (Peschke 94)

Rom. 1:5;16:26
Nss.*Dipp.* 5 (1701:42)

Spen.*Pi.Des.* (Aland 49-51); Frnck.*Bcht.* (Peschke 103)

Ost.*Arg.ref.*Matt. 18;1 Cor. 5 (1720-II:28;209);Ost.*Cat.* (1747:59-60)
Dtr.*Lmp.* 51 (1717:94);
Lmp.*Dtr.* (1717:13)

Grig.Mont.*Am.sag.* 16.194 (Gendrot 199)
Wsly.*Serm.* 40.1.4 (Baker 2:158)
Mēn.*Did.* 1.2 (Blantēs 102)
Lw.*Chr.Perf.* 14 (Moreton 3:235)

Spen.*Pi.Des.* (Aland 28)

Tin.*Chr.* 13 (1730:298)

Tin.*Chr.* 2 (1730:20)

Knt.*Rel.* 2.con. (Cassirer 6:227)

See vol.3:119-20;128-30;150

Terst.*Bros.* 3.5 (Becher 5:208)

example of virtue, which, were it not for a dreadful depravity of nature, would have influence on them that live under the gospel, far beyond all other examples." For his exposition of evangelical perfection, William Law drew consciously on the tradition of Catholic and Protestant devotional literature, above all on *The Imitation of Christ* of Thomas à Kempis. Nor was he alone in doing so during this era, for despite an occasional demurrer the recognition of the value of the *Imitation* cut across the boundaries between the churches. Within Protestant Germany the Lutheran Johann Olearius had translated it into German in 1671; the Reformed Gerhard Tersteegen did so again in 1727; and it received the commendation of Spener, Francke, and Zinzendorf. Within Roman Catholic Germany the Augustinian Eusebius Amort composed a scholarly dissertation in 1728, as part of a critical edition, defending the authorship of Thomas à Kempis; the Benedictine Thomas Aquinas Erhard in the following year sought to prove that the *Imitation* had been in use as early as the thirteenth century and must have been written by a medieval Benedictine monk; and Johann Michael Sailer, future bishop of Regensburg, for whom the *Imitation* and the writings of Fénelon were second only to Scripture in religious value, published his own German translation in 1794, which he recommended to those who were "inward [innig] Christians"; Sailer's translation continued to be reprinted into the twentieth century.

In agreement with these German Protestants and Roman Catholics, *The Theology of the Heart* by the French Protestant Pierre Poiret admonished, "Imitate Jesus Christ, for he is the supreme guide of souls," while orthodox Lutherans and other Lutherans taught that "the imitation of Jesus also in his cross and suffering is a necessary part of true Christianity." According to Roman Catholics in France and Italy, *The Imitation of Christ* was an authority for the priority of practice over theological definition, but also for the centrality of the Virgin Mary to the Christian life. Eastern Orthodoxy and Methodism joined in quoting the early church fathers in support of "the imitation of the God whom you worship" as central to Christian worship and life. Therefore Gilbert Tennent could

Edw.*Orig.Sn.*1.1.9 (Miller 3:199)

Lw.*Chr.Perf.*13 (Moreton 3:215-32)

See vol.4:36-37

Naud.*Myst.*1.1.2 (1713:3)

Poir.*Oec.div.*5.10 (1705-II:617)

Spen.*Pi.Des.* (Aland 75); Frnck.*Id.*46 (Peschke 198); Zinz.*Off.Red.*1.1 (Beyreuther 2-III:9)

Amrt.*Thos.Kemp.* (1761)

Erhrd.*Kemp.*13 (1729:72-75)
Erhrd.*Kemp.*24 (1729:122-25)

Sail.*Ep.*18.ii.1800 (Schiel 195)

Sail.*Ep.*29.ix.1797 (Schiel 157)

Poir.*Théol.cr.*1.1.4 (1690-I:51); Ost.*Arg.ref.* Matt.10 (1720-II:15)

Baum.*Pred.*3.10 (Kirchner 3:336);Nss.*Dipp.*4 (1701:39) Fén.*Inst.*40 (Gosselin 6:153); Fén.*Gr.préd.*1.5 (Gosselin 2:174) Thos.Kemp.*Im.Chr.*1.3 (Pohl 1:8-11) Alph.Lig.*Gl.Mar.*1.10 (Prato 235-36) See vol.4:40

Mrkrd.*Off.*16 (1722:125); Strz.*Enchir.*5.4 1828:218); Wsly.*Serm.*29.6 (Baker 1:635)

have been speaking for all of the churches when he
defined "the imitation of Christ" as consisting in
"those moral virtues of which the law is a rule, under
which Christ as man was made and to which he
perfectly conformed." William Law interpreted the
theme of the imitation of Christ as the principal
innovation that Christ had introduced in his moral
precepts, and he was willing to identify the imitation
of Christ as "the sole end of all the counsels, commands, and doctrines of Christ."

Such a subordination of "all the doctrines"—
which, it would seem, must include the orthodox
doctrine about the person and work of Christ
himself—to the "chief ground of religion," the imitation of Christ in his cross and suffering, was a
weapon that could easily be turned against orthodox
doctrine. Johann Konrad Dippel, under the pen name
"Christian Democritus," also pledged allegiance to
Christ's "example for imitation," since "the doctrine
and the words of Christ are simple and clear, without
any contradiction." Just what that amounted to became even more "simple and clear" a little later in the
same treatise, however, when he identified the so-
called heretics of the past, who had opposed orthodox
doctrine, as "those innocent people who have often
been excommunicated by the 'true church' " even
though it had been they, not the orthodox, "who in
their way of life came close to the words and example
of Christ." William Law showed his awareness of this
very danger when he reminded his readers: "Could we
do and suffer all that Christ himself did or suffered,
yet if it was not all done in the same spirit and temper
of Christ, we should have none of his merit."

Yet the "spirit and temper of Christ" in the Gospels
included, often in bewildering mixture, both elements in what the Reformation, on the basis of the
Pauline Epistles, had set forth as the distinction
between the law and the gospel. A striking illustration of the difficulty with the distinction was the most
beloved statement of the teachings of Christ in the
New Testament, the Sermon on the Mount in the
fifth, sixth, and seventh chapters of the Gospel of
Matthew. A Reformed theologian called it "the law of
the gospel," Wesley made it the basis of a series of

Tnnt.*Disc*.4 (1745:199)

Lw.*Ser.Cl*.20 (Moreton 4:215)

Lw.*Chr.Perf*.13 (Moreton
3:216)

Lmp.*Ghm*.5
(1719-I:171-259);
Frnck.*Id*.42 (Peschke 193)
Zinz.*Soc*.28 (Beyreuther
1-I:266)

Dipp.*Orth*.4 (1699:34-35)

Dipp.*Orth*.7 (1699:102)

Lw.*Chr.Perf*.2 (Moreton 3:33)

See vol.4:168-72;212-15

Ost.*Arg.ref*.Matt.5
(1720-II:7)

Wsly.*Serm*.21-33 (Baker
1:469-698)

Conc.*Rel.riv*.3.11
(1754-I:417-24)

Strz.*Enchir*.3.3
(1828:100-102)
Wsly.*Serm*.21.1.1 (Baker
1:475)

Matt.7:12

Mmchi.*Orig.ant*.3.3.2.1
(1749-III:420)

See pp. 225-26 below

See vol.2:255-56

Thos.Aq.*S.T*.2.1.108.4
(*Ed.Leon*.7:287-88)
Span.*Ev.vind*.3.4 (Marck
3:440-41)

Wsly.*Serm*.21.int.5 (Baker
1:472)

Lw.*Chr.Perf*.int. (Moreton 3:5)

Trlsch.*Soz*.3.1 (Baron 1:507)

Wsly.*Serm*.17.x.1787
(Jackson 7:202-13)

Zinz.*Lond.Pred*.1.10
(Beyreuther 5-I:77)

Bnyn.*Lw.Gr*.pr. (Sharrock
2:11)

Edw.*Rel.Aff*.2 (Miller 2:154)

thirteen sermons, and a Roman Catholic defender of the primacy of revelation reprinted the text of all three chapters in full. To the Russian Orthodox lay theologian Aleksandr Sturza, the Beatitudes, with which the Sermon on the Mount opened, were an epitome of "the new law," while John Wesley spoke of them as "the sum of all true religion." The Golden Rule laid down in the Sermon on the Mount, "Whatever you wish that men would do to you, do so to them," contained, at least in principle, all the kinds of duties involved in human relations. Amid all this agreement, however, there was denominational controversy on one aspect of the Sermon on the Mount. Its absolute demands (whose significance was to become a grave theological and exegetical issue again in twentieth-century debates over "consistent eschatology") had been construed in the medieval thought of both East and West as not binding on ordinary believers in the way that the universal demands of the law were, but as incumbent only on the ascetic adherents of "the religious life," who lived up to them as evangelical counsels of perfection, especially the "perfection" of total poverty and complete celibacy. But the Protestant Reformers had rejected this distinction, making the moral imperative of evangelical perfection applicable to all. At the same time, they had reinterpreted those commandments not to mean a complete renunciation of marriage and property; "instead, the spirit of world-renunciation is to be carried into the natural course of daily life within the world itself."

Because it seemed to some of the heirs of the Reformation that no one had been "more ignorant on the doctrine of sanctification, or more confused in his conceptions of it" than Luther, his distinction between law and gospel was a device with which many were growing restive. The very title of Bunyan's *The Doctrine of the Law and Grace Unfolded* had made that evident, as did his requirement that "these two be . . . held forth, . . . together with the nature of the one and the nature of the other." Edwards referred to the relation as an "analogy," but also referred to the "distinction to be made between a legal and [an] evangelical" method of teaching and experiencing the will

Edw.*Rel.Aff*.3.6;2 (Miller
2:311;151-52)
Wsly.*Serm*.25.2.3 (Baker
1:554)
Tnnt.*Disc*.2 (1745:99)

Tin.*Chr*.1 (1730:8)

Dipp.*Orth*.4 (1699:37-38)

Mos.*Vind.disc*.2.1.5
(1722:264-65)

See vol.4:212-17

Ost.*Eth*.1.2.2 (1727:57)

Ost.*Eth*.1.2.2 (1727:56);
Ost.*Arg.ref*.Ex.20 (1720-I:48)

Ost.*Dz.serm*.2 (1722:56)

Mrkrd.*Off*.1 (1722:3)

Aug.*Civ*.19.25 (*CCSL* 48:696)

Nrs.*Vind.Aug*.3.4 (Berti
2:306-13)

Amrt.*Theol.eclec*.7.3.8
(1752-2-II:104)
Bert.*Theol.disc*.18.4
(1792-IV:14)

Bert.*Aug*.3.2 (1747-I:403)

Drnd.*Fid.vind*.1.25
(1709:81-87)

of God; Wesley called for "the closest connection that can be conceived" between them; and Tennent spoke of their "harmony." Tindal went far beyond mere analogy, connection, and harmony to assert that "the design of the gospel was not to add to, or take away from this law [of nature or of reason], but to free men from that load of superstition which had been mixed with it." Any such view of the identity between law and gospel had to reject as "absurd heresy" the "gloss on the words and commands of Christ" that appeared to be implied by the disjunction between the two in Luther's thought, as though "Christ as the interpreter of the law wanted only to show what is demanded of man by a perfect obedience to the law, so that he could reveal to man how depraved he was," not how man could in fact obey the law.

The view of "Jesus Christ as the supreme lawgiver of all" and the use of the law as a norm for the Christian life, which Calvin and his followers had formulated with greater consistency than had Lutheran theologians, also implied, according to a Reformed ethicist, that "the laws [of God] were given in order to be observed, for otherwise they would have been useless." The gospel of Christ had not added to the law or annulled it, but had "explained the true meaning of the law," so that "the perfect knowledge [of the commandments] is to be sought in the gospel." In another context, however, the same theologian could speak also about "the difference, or rather the opposition, between the law and the gospel." The doctrine of "virtues and duties" was the essential content of moral theology. Therefore Augustine's aspersions on all "virtues" without God and grace as in fact "vices" were prompting even some within Roman Catholicism to suggest that he had perhaps gone "too far," or at least to explain that good works performed outside a state of grace were not in fact "sins." Without grace it was impossible to love God above all creatures, but good works done in that state could nevertheless be called good "with respect to their object and their proximate goal, though not with respect to their ultimate goal."

Claiming to be closer to Augustine than was this official Roman Catholic position, orthodox Lutherans

Neum.*Marp.*2.5 (1727:150);
Qnl.*Clém.*IX.1.1 (1700:16)

Schmdt.*Bcht.* (1662:5)

Deutsch.*Gnad.* (1701:4r)

Schmdt.*Bcht.* (1662:7)

Mayr.*Anti-Spen.*5 (1695:32)

Spen.*Beant.*4.14 (1693:208-9)

Rom. 10:4

Frnck.*Pred.*Trin. 18 (1699:4);
Zeis.*Unver.Gew.* (1696:19)

Stngr.*Ges.* (1693:9)

John 8:9 (var.)
Beng.*Gnom.*John 8 (Steudel 364-65)

Strz.*Enchir.*1.2 (1828:13)

Beng.*Gnom.*1Tim.1:5 (Steudel 829)

Aug.*Conf.*10.27.38
(*CCSL* 27:175)

Fén.*Let.div.* (Gosselin 1:144)

Frnck.*Pred.*Epiph.5
(1700:24-25); Frnck.
*Pred.*Sexag. (1699:47)
Mrck.*Comp.*13.13 (Velzen 18:272)

Pff.*Hist.theol.*5.3
(1724-III:353-57)
Zinz.*Hom.*27 (Beyreuther 3-I:279)
Drnd.*Diss.*2.9 (1703:134-38)
Alph.Lig.*Theol.mor.*1 (Gaudé 1:3-70)

Wsly.*Serm.*12.3 (Baker 1:301)
Baum.*Pred.*1.12;1.1
(Kirchner1:427;27)

Wer.*Misc.*15.6 (Ryhinerus 2:269);Ost.*Cat.* (1747:14)

Knt.*Krit.pr.Vern.*2.con.
(Cassirer 5:174)

(as well as Jansenists) continued to stress "the impossibility of fulfilling the law" and the absolute need for preserving the proper "order and distinction" between the law and the gospel: "The law is not the gospel, and the gospel is not the law." This principle applied in ethics and in preaching, "but above all and especially in penitential practice." Although the attacks by such orthodox Lutherans compelled Pietism to defend itself against the charge of confusing the law and the gospel, it voiced its protest against "the abuse of the proof text, 'Christ is the end of the law,' " as though there were no imperative in the doctrine of grace to live a life in accordance with the law of God. It was not at all "a paradox" to speak of "the law of the gospel."

Despite its absence from the Gospels, except for one variant reading within a pericope that was itself textually suspect, the New Testament concept of "conscience [συνείδησις]," or, as one Eastern Orthodox thinker called it, "the conscience of the individual," proved to be a useful device for internalizing the ethical imperative as an integral element of the "theology of the heart." In the technical psychological vocabulary of the day, the seat of the conscience was said to be in the intellect, while that of love was in the heart; as Augustine's example showed, conscience was subject to examination on the basis of love. Nonetheless, by contrast with the "hypocrisy" of external conformity, the authentic summons to conversion and moral change was addressed to both "your heart and your conscience." The term had been used in diverse ways, also by biblical writers. In earlier theological literature "conscience" had seemed to refer chiefly to questions of casuistry, as in the frequent book title, *On Cases of Conscience* [*De casibus conscientiae*], and despite criticisms of the usage it was still being employed that way, forming the opening chapter of a *Moral Theology*; but now it had become a "word that is in everyone's mouth" through the widespread use of the "appeal to conscience," and it was, for many thinkers, replacing the cosmological argument and the other Thomistic proofs for the existence of God: "the moral law within" was more decisive evidence than "the starry heaven above."

For some, in fact, the internal voice of conscience was in danger of superseding all external moral authorities; "the only tribunal God has erected here on earth," according to Matthew Tindal, "is every man's own conscience." If it was incumbent upon "everyone to investigate the book of his own conscience," what was to be the relation of this book of conscience to other books and other authorities, especially to church and law? Although "there is an authority, both in the civil and ecclesiastical powers, of enjoining things indifferent, . . . no authority besides Christ's can reach the conscience," an Anglican theologian asserted. The "freedom of conscience" was an inviolable right of the individual in the church, a court of appeal against the claims of an infallible papacy, an inextinguishable "light" in the face of persecution by church or state. Yet when the content of conscience was equated with that of natural law and its function was defined as one of "dictating, on the basis of reason, concerning the conformity or opposition of one's actions to the law of God," that implied that conscience was in some sense subordinate to the authority of divine law, or even of human law, and that therefore an erring conscience stood in need of instruction. "It would be ridiculous," one theologian observed, "if an atheist were to allege as his authority a conscience that obliges him to teach an atheism that he regards as true. For what conscience can there be where God is not acknowledged?"

Conscience, then, had a twofold function: as a "rule" for life but also as a "judgment" upon sin. Although it may have been an "incontestable principle" that "whatever is done contrary to the dictate of the conscience is a sin," experience showed that, deprived and gravely impaired though it was through the fall, conscience, when instructed on the basis of divine revelation, did testify to the sin and sickness of the soul. "The tarnished conscience" could not be regarded as "perfect," but "the primary concern of all souls that aspire to perfection" was to acknowledge and confess their sins. To such souls, as the church in its teaching function and pastoral ministry dealt with them, "conscience is as a thousand witnesses" accusing them. The ground for "the quieting of our

Tin.*Chr*.9 (1730:106)

Frnck.*Pred*.Trin.2 (1699:53)

Brnt.*Rom*. (1688:33)

Zinz.*Gem*.13 (Beyreuther 4-I:219)

Span.*Cont*. (Marck 3:744)

Byl.*Com.phil*.2.1 (1713-I:255)

Strz.*Enchir*.3.1 (1828:84)

Amrt.*Theol.eclec*.3.2.prol. (1752-I-III:75)

Ost.*Eth*.1.2.2 (1727:52); Drnd.*Diss*.2.1.3 (1703:116)

Alph.Lig.*Theol.mor*.1.1.4 (Gaudé 1:4)

Wer.*Misc*.14.1 (Ryhinerus 2:242)

Ost.*Eth*.1.2.1 (1727:43-44)

Byl.*Com.phil*.2.8 (1713-I:391)

Terst.*Abr*.1.9.15 (Becher 2:106)

Baum.*Pred*.1.10 (Kirchner 1:303-4)

Arb.*Des.myst*.1.16 (1764:113-14)

Alph.Lig.*Theol.mor*.1.1.11-19 (Gaudé 1:6-10)

Tnnt.*Disc*.1 (1745:22)

Terst.*Bros*.2.1 (Becher 4:12)

Stod.*Sfty*.4 (1687:89)

Wsly.*Serm*.40.1.2 (Baker 2:156)

Strz.*Enchir*.6.4 (1828:244-54)

Mrkrd.*Off*.15 (1722:119)

Arb.*Des.myst*.2.11 (1764:236-39)

Luke 15:21

Strz.*Enchir*.1.1 (1828:8)

Edw.*Orig.Sn*.2.2.2 (Miller 3:270-71)

Ps.51:5

Ps.51:4

1 Cor.11:28

Mynst.*Betr*.56 (1846-II:297)

Lmp.*Brt*.4 (1737:50-60)

Fén.*Inst*.13 (Gosselin 6:92)

Luke 23:43

Terst.*Bros*.1.4 (Becher 3:138)

Frnck.*Pass.Joh*.2 (1733:38)

Matt.26:69-75;
Mark 14:66-72;Luke
22:54-62;John 18:15-27

Lmp.*Betr*.2.8 (1756-I:610)

Frnck.*Pass.Marc*.6 (1724:159-60)

Frnck.*Pass.Joh*.2 (1733:25)

Frnck.*Pass.Marc*.6 (1724:164)

Frnck.*Pass.Marc*.6 (1724:184-85)

Lmp.*Betr*.3.6 (1756-II:120)

conscience before God, through the forgiveness of our sins" was to be sought in "the resurrection of Christ [and] the satisfactoriness of his sufferings." In this way, all that was "wrought in the soul by what is frequently termed 'natural conscience,' but more properly 'preventing [prevenient] grace,' " helped to bring about "the work of salvation."

For the "Orthodox Christian" in the East, but as well for all Christians Eastern or Western who claimed to be "orthodox," this awareness of their sins, accompanied by repentance and confession, was a religious and moral duty and a means of grace. Christ died on the cross "so that by approaching God through repentance we might attain salvation," and the knowledge of sin was a "remedy" for the soul. The repentance and confession of the prodigal son, "Father, I have sinned against heaven and before you," was a theme that pervaded all of Scripture. Psalm 51, the "Miserere," ascribed to David in its superscription, summarized the doctrine of sin and the practice of Christian repentance, also because it included both original sin and actual sin in its confession: "In sin did my mother conceive me," and yet "against thee, thee only, have I sinned." The apostle's admonition, "Let a man examine himself," pertained not only to preparation for the worthy reception of the Lord's Supper, but to the continuing process of self-examination, in which "the publican deplores his faults, while the Pharisee recites his virtues." Although the last-minute repentance of the thief on the cross had often been abused by those who made excuses for their delay, he was, when he finally got around to it, the model of how a sinner ought to behave: he recognized his sin, he felt it, and he confessed it. Also subject to frequent abuse, the prime example of repentance in Scripture was nevertheless the fall of Peter. His denial was one of the relatively few events to appear in all four Gospels and was "one of the chief parts of the suffering" of Christ; it had not come by a deterministic "necessity" but by "an inward fall," which then expressed itself in his outward sin. Therefore his tears were not an "outward work" but expressed "the deepest bitterness of his soul." Like any genuine repentance, his was motivated by the consciousness of

Stod.*Conv*.2 (1719:8)

Fén.*Ep*.8.vi.1708 (Gosselin 7:265-66)

ap.Gtti.*Ver.rel*.2.3.3 (1750-I:76)

2 Pet.1:4

Terst.*Abr*.2.1.19 (Becher 2:165)

ap.Deutsch.*Luth*.2.1.3 (1698:80)

Conf.Aug.1.1 (*Bek*.50)
Zinz.Aug.Conf.2 (Beyreuther 6-II:70);*Zinz.Sieb*.5 (Beyreuther 2-I:51);
Zinz.Gespr.3 (Beyreuther 1-III:26)
See vol.1:344-46;
vol.2:10-16; vol.4:66-68
Zinz.Lond.Pred.1.7 (Beyreuther 5-I:55)
Spen.Bed.1.1.9 (Canstein 1:76-77)

Sim.Thess.*Lit*. (*PG* 155:253)

Mēn.*Did*.1.6;5.18 (Blantēs 69;353)

See vol.4:27-28
Neum.*Adv*. (1737:17-18);
Wsly.*Serm*.59.1.1 (Baker 2:425)

Edw.*Rel.Aff*.2 (Miller 2:158)

having done "a wrong to a God of infinite glory," and it led to a firm resolve to shake off the dominion of sin.

Peter was likewise, despite doubts ancient and modern, taken by common consent to be the writer of the New Testament Epistle in which there appeared the grandest of all biblical terms for evangelical perfection, "partakers of the divine nature," which promised that "we can become participants in [Christ's] divine nature as he has become a participant in our human nature." Yet Spener was suspect in the eyes of confessional Lutherans because he had spoken as though "the new man . . . *is* a divine nature" through the Holy Spirit, when it was said to be the orthodox doctrine, as expressed in the first article of the *Augsburg Confession*, that there was only "one single divine being," that of God himself. In fact, Spener and other Pietists, especially Zinzendorf, were only repeating here the widely held definition of salvation as "deification [ϑέωσις]," while they continued to draw a fundamental distinction between Creator and creature as well as between the "mystical union" and justification.

The definition of salvation as deification was not confined during this period—any more than it had been in earlier periods—to Eastern Orthodox theologians, who quoted earlier Greek versions of it to declare that the purpose of the incarnation, crucifixion, and resurrection of Christ had been "in order to make the human divine." For example, a strictly confessional Lutheran and an implacable foe of Pietism, echoing Eastern language about deification as well as that of Duns Scotus and medieval Franciscan theology, found it possible to celebrate the boon that through the advent of Christ "we attain to the glory that was lost in Adam, yes, to an even greater glory." Jonathan Edwards repeatedly quoted 2 Peter 1:4 to prove that "the grace which is in the hearts of the saints is of the same nature with the divine holiness," adding the proviso that this would be only "as much as 'tis possible for that holiness to be, which is infinitely less in degree"; such language was not to be taken to mean "that the saints are made partakers of the essence of God, and so are 'Godded' with God, and 'Christed' with Christ, according to the abominable and blasphemous language and notions of some heretics." Whether he was one of the "heretics" Edwards had in mind or not, the Deist John Tindal did also quote 2 Peter 1:4 in propounding a rationalistic version of the doctrine, holding out the possibility that a life "according to the rules of right reason" could "so implant in us the moral perfection of God" that "we then, if I may say so, live the life of God."

As the "theology of the heart" needed to find a way for the consideration of "God and the soul" to be delivered from solipsism, so "evangelical perfection" had to be rescued from perfectionism, and "deification" from pantheism. The means for such deliverance in each case was the recognition that the divine principle of immanence, also the principle for the immanence of subjective experience, was the Holy Spirit. Therefore the correlation of what "experience teaches us" with what "the Holy Spirit says" was a necessary counterpart of the new preoccupation with the soul of the individual and with the morality of evangelical perfection.

The Experience of the Holy Spirit

The crucial question for any understanding of "perfection" was "the gift of the Holy Spirit": this judgment by a New Testament exegete expressed the recognition that when the language of the church spoke about "evangelical perfection," it was referring primarily to a divine gift, not merely to a human achievement, and that the specific divine source of that gift was God the Holy Spirit. Christian perfection and the imperative of the Christian ethic could be summarized in the Pauline formula of "walking according to the Spirit." Taking "Wisdom" in a divine and personal sense as "referring to the Holy Spirit," Louis Marie Grignion de Montfort interpreted the words of Job, "But where shall Wisdom be found? It is not found in the land of those who live pleasantly [suaviter viventium]," to mean that the Holy Spirit did not take up an abode among those who were "at ease." And that sanctifying Holy Spirit was not confined to some golden age at the beginning of the history of the church, but was still alive and active

---

Marginal references:

Edw.*Rel.Aff.*3.1 (Miller 2:201-3)

Tin.*Chr.*3 (1730:23-24)

Arb.*Des.myst.*int. (1764:1-2)

Beng.*Gnom.*Heb.6:1 (Steudel 896)

Rom.8:4
Wsly.*Serm.*8.1.1-6 (Baker 1:235-37)

Job 28:12-13 (Vulg.)

Grig.Mont.*Am.sag.*16.194 (Gendrot 199)

Spen.*Pi.Des.* (Aland 52)

Edw.*Dist.Mrks*.2.2 (Miller 4:250-53)

Baum.*Pred*.2.3 (Kirchner 2:99)

Tnnt.*Disc*.4 (1745:217)

See vol.1:301; vol.4:252

Rom.5:5

Zinz.*Beth*.3 (Beyreuther 6-IV:33);Zinz.*Rel*.5 (Beyreuther 6-I:94); Wsly.*Serm*.4.1.4;7.2.12 (Baker 1:162;231)

See pp. 134-35 above

John 4:23-24

Blrt.*S.T.Reg.fid*.2.3 (Lequette 3:303)

Edw.*Brnrd*.7 (Miller 7:333)

Strz.*Enchir*.7.1 (1828:297)

Cmrda.*Const.ap*.2.13 (1732:147)

Fén.*Man.piét*.5.2 (Gosselin 6:54)

Anal.Hymn.50:193-94

Poir.*Théol.cr*.pr. (1690-I:B5v)

Zinz.*Lond.Pred*.1.1-15 (Beyreuther 5-I:3-146)

Rufin.*Symb*.2 (*CCSL* 20:134-35)

now. The awakening of conscience as the "candle of the Lord" and the "viceregent of God in the soul" was a positive mark of the presence of the Holy Spirit; therefore the appeal to conscience was at the same time an appeal to experience.

Because "the Holy Spirit who consecrates us as the temples of his residence has not only the office of a comforter but [that of a] sanctifier," the theme of "God and the soul," like the theme of "evangelical perfection," was a way of speaking about the experience of the Holy Spirit. Augustine's favorite New Testament passage, "God's love has been poured into our hearts through the Holy Spirit which has been given to us," commended itself to the exponents of the theology of the heart as a way of speaking that could emphasize the subjectivity of the relation between God and the soul without falling into the subjectivist trap of confusing the two. Therefore the orthodox response to the antithesis between formal liturgy and authentic worship "in spirit and truth" was not only to equate the "truth" in that New Testament passage with the teaching of the church and the "worship" with the worship of the church, but to identify "spirit" as in fact the "Holy Spirit" present in the church. This presence in the church, which could, under unusual circumstances, even take the form of an "inspiration of the Holy Spirit" at the election of a pope, ordinarily manifested itself in far humbler ways. Thus a spirituality that interpreted the purpose of the relation between God and the soul as the annihilation of the self could break out in a petition to the "Destroyer Spirit" (as a counterpart to the "Creator Spirit," still being invoked in the language of medieval hymnody).

In any "affectional transposition of Christian doctrine," therefore, the doctrine of the Holy Spirit was bound to occupy the pivotal position. While in London during the year 1752, the author of two extensive transpositions of the *Augsburg Confession* in that style delivered a series of fifteen sermons based on the exposition of the "third article" of the Apostles' Creed in Luther's *Small Catechism* (the creed having been divided there not into twelve articles, one for each apostle, as in the ancient church, but into three,

Luth.*Kl.Kat.*2.5-6
(*Bek.*511-12)

Zinz.*Zst.*36 (Beyreuther
3-II:292-93)

Fén.*Man.piét.*5.15
(Gosselin 6:67)

Matt.12:31;Mark 3:29

Tin.*Chr.*7 (1730:73)
Stod.*Gd.Chr.* (1714:14-15)

Fén.*Inst.*1 (Gosselin 6:72)

Tnnt.*Disc.*1 (1745:7)

Tnnt.*Serm.*23 (1744:449-65)

Zinz.*Lond.Pred.*5.11
(Beyreuther 5-II:275)

See vol.1:211-25
See vol.2:183-98

Terst.*Abr.*2.8.4 (Becher
2:229-30)

one for each person of the Trinity). It was, he insisted elsewhere, an error for anyone to "regard what happened on Pentecost . . . as more important than what every child of God always experiences as a secure possession in the bosom of the Holy Spirit." The possession of the Holy Spirit by such a child of God could be said to be a greater gift "than the possession of the Son of God himself." Loss of the Holy Spirit and the sin against the Holy Spirit—which, according to the Gospels, was the only sin that could never be forgiven—had not been drained of their historic meaning, but remained as grave a threat as ever. A "continual dependence on the Spirit of God, receiving from moment to moment what it pleases him to grant us," was the key to the salutary human employment of time.

It was the divine employment of time that underlay the human employment of it. "As God the Father has from eternity proposed to confer saving benefits upon the elect in time, so the Son of God in consequence hereof has made a purchase of them by his blood and obedience; and these very benefits does the Holy Spirit apply in time to the heirs of salvation." It is evident from that trinitarian schema, with which Gilbert Tennent opened his *Discourses on Several Important Subjects*—as well as from other contemporary treatments of the doctrine of the Trinity, including his own expositions of the controverted "Johannine comma"—that in this period the primary focus of the doctrine of the Holy Spirit, as indeed of the doctrine of the Trinity altogether, would be on the "economic" activity of the Holy Spirit within time and history, rather than, as it had been in the trinitarian controversies of the fourth century and again in the conflict between East and West over the Filioque, chiefly on the eternal, ontological bond between Father, Son, and Holy Spirit.

This new awareness of the activity of the Holy Spirit did imply the criticism that, as a consequence of an excessive rationalism and traditionalism in the discussions of Christian doctrine, "this great evangelical truth [about the witness of the Holy Spirit] . . . had been for many years well-nigh forgotten," until now at last it had been "recovered" and "confirmed by

Wsly.*Serm.*11.1.4 (Baker 1:285-86)

Wsly.*Serm.*30.16 (Baker 1:657)

Arb.*Des.myst.*3.8 (1764:447)

Edw.*Rel.Aff.*3.1 (Miller 2:198-99)

Poir.*Oec.div.*5.1 (1705-II:331)
Lw.*Chr.Perf.*9 (Moreton 3:138)

Edw.*Rel.Aff.*3.1 (Miller 2:200)

Rom.8:16
Wsly.*Serm.*10.1.7-8;11.2.2 (Baker 1:274;287)

Scriv.*Seel.*2.12 (Stier 4:350)

Stod.*Sfty.*8 (1687:217-18)
Wisd.of Sol.10:10
Grig.Mont.*Am.sag.*8.92-93 (Gendrot 141)

the experience" of this generation. Nevertheless, such criticism was still being voiced in an orthodox trinitarian framework, one that was concerned to locate the doctrine of the Holy Spirit within "the holy, the peculiar doctrines of the gospel." Therefore this method of emphasizing the experience of the Holy Spirit—for which, within Roman Catholicism, Teresa of Avila, "Saint Teresa of Jesus," could serve as "that celebrated Doctor of the truth of the Spirit"—still included, also beyond Roman Catholicism, the insistence that the epithet "spiritual" in biblical usage did not refer to the relation of persons or things with the human spirit but to their relation with God the Holy Spirit.

The polemical edge of that insistence clearly manifested the recognition that a totally immanent definition of "spirit" and therefore an anthropocentric understanding of "experience" and ultimately of "Holy Spirit" could threaten to engulf the experience of the Holy Spirit in an undifferentiated subjectivity. As a result, even with the reminder that the communication of the Holy Spirit was "internal" to human experience and the admonition that the human mind and spirit had to be prepared for such communication, the priority of the "divine supernatural spring of life and action" had to be acknowledged, since "this 'testimony of the Spirit of God' must needs . . . be antecedent to the 'testimony of our own spirit.' "

The relation between the Holy Spirit and the human spirit, therefore, together with the significance of both for the understanding of "experience," required careful attention in any "theology of the heart," whether it called itself that or not. The theology of the heart was concerned to emphasize that "the Holy Spirit is received by believers in such a way that he unites himself with their spirit, that is, with their soul and its powers, in the closest and most intimate possible manner." As a consequence, the soul, though filled with doubts and questions, could be assured of the truth of the gospel by the Spirit of God, who, as the personal Wisdom of God, communicated to the soul "the great knowledge of the saints." This called for not just "any relation . . . to the spirit or soul of man," but the specific "relation to

Edw.*Rel.Aff.*3.1 (Miller 2:198)

the Holy Ghost, or Spirit of God." For, Jonathan Edwards warned those who were having "spiritual" experiences, "it does not thence follow that it was from the Spirit of God. There are other spirits who have influence on the minds of men besides the Holy

Edw.*Rel.Aff.*2 (Miller 2:141)

Ghost," including above all the devil as the evil spirit.

As in the chronological sequence of the church year, so in the logical sequence of both doctrine and experience, it was fitting to move on from the life and

Baum.*Pred.*1.3 (Kirchner 1:70;77)
Terst.*Bros.*3.7 (Becher 5:285)

teaching of Christ to the life and teaching of the Holy Spirit and to invoke its presence and blessing. Hence

Frnck.*Pred.*Ex. (1700:71)

"the support of the Holy Spirit" was primary, and a *Summary of Fundamental Christian Truths* could not be regarded as complete without a full chapter on the

Terst.*Abr.*2.8 (Becher 2:228-40)

subject, since the "application of redemption to the soul, by the Holy Spirit's influence, is as necessary in its place in order to salvation [sic] as the purchase of it by Christ's blood and obedience." It was the Holy

Tnnt.*Disc.*1 (1745:8)
Terst.*Bros.*3.6 (Becher 5:253)
Phil.2:5
Wsly.*Serm.*4.int.4 (Baker 1:160)
Frnck.*Pass.Joh.*pr. (1733:x)
Frnck.*Pred.*Epiph.6 (1699:14)

Spirit that worked "contrition of the heart" and repentance over sin, granted believers "the mind which was in Christ," brought illumination to the human spirit, and restored the image of God lost through sin. Otherwise, as in those churches that neglected the doctrine of the Holy Spirit, faith was

Wsly.*Serm.*46.2.2 (Baker 2:212)
Bnyn.*Lw.Gr.*2 (Sharrock 2:156)

"naked," that is, "stripped both of love and peace and joy in the Holy Ghost." All of this reinforced the appeal to "my own experience" and to "the experience of all real Christians" that there was in every believer

Wsly.*Serm.*10.1.1 (Baker 1:271)

both the testimony of the divine Spirit and the testimony of the human spirit. Yet that very appeal to experience was accompanied by this paradoxical realization: "Experience plainly shows that God's Spirit is unsearchable and untraceable in some of the best of Christians in the method of his operations in their

Edw.*Rel.Aff.*2 (Miller 2:161)

conversion."

By a corresponding paradox, the conventional au-

Terst.*Abr.*1.1.2-5 (Becher 2:11-13)

thorities and proofs for the truths of the gospel pointed beyond themselves to the experience of the Holy Spirit, by which alone their probative force could substantiate itself: first came the experience of

1 Cor.1:24
Beng.*Gnom.*1 Cor.1:24 (Steudel 625)

"the power of God," and only then the experience of "the wisdom of God." Among all the arguments for "the divinity of the Christian religion" and the credibility of miracles, the one that "has the greatest

Wer.*Diss*.4.2 (Ryhinerus 1:82)

Terst.*Abr*.1.1.6;1.1.12 (Becher 2:13-14;17)

Edw.*Rel.Aff*.2 (Miller 2:176) Zinz.*Red*.6 (Beyreuther 1-II:81);Spen.*Gtts*.6 (1680:287);Beng.*Gnom*.2 Cor.1:4 (Steudel 690) Baum.*Pred*.1.9 (Kirchner 1:266-67) Baum.*Pred*.1.9;1.2 (Kirchner 1:274;49)

Edw.*Rel.Aff*.2 (Miller 2:162)

Edw.*Fthfl.Narr*. (Miller 4:207-9)

Anal.Hymn.50:193-94

Terst *Abr*.2.8.7 (Becher 2:232)

Baum.*Pred*.1.3 (Kirchner 1:87)

See vol.4:153-54;286

Edw.*Rel.Aff*.2 (Miller 2:127)

Edw.*Dist.Mrks*.2.int. (Miller 4:248)

possible effect on the heart of a devout person" was the personal experience of "being so affected by all the sayings of Jesus that it would clearly be impossible for Jesus to be speaking this way if the Christian religion were false." The promise of the Holy Spirit to the apostles who wrote the New Testament had as its necessary counterpart the inner testimony of the selfsame Spirit in the heart of the reader of that New Testament now. Without inner "sensible Christian experience" of that kind, there could be neither faith nor understanding nor "a strong or lively trust in God." The experiences had to be "sensible" and perceptible in some manner or other, although, as was evident from Christ's own pedagogical method with his disciples, this often happened very gradually; and the Holy Spirit did not "proceed discernibly in the steps of a particular scheme." The religious revivals manifested a similar ambiguity between the palpable experience of being born again and the less conspicuous program of Christian nurture that had preceded—and had to follow up on—such intense experiences.

In keeping with the traditional medieval designation of the Spirit in the "Veni Creator Spiritus" of Rabanus Maurus as "sevenfold in gift [septiformis munere]," one catalogue of such experiences of the Holy Spirit listed seven of them: conviction; repentance; faith in Jesus; regeneration, or being born again; progress in daily sanctification; earnest conflict and constant prayer; and perseverance to the end. Yet both the theology of the orthodox churches and the evidence of religious experience demonstrated that except for "faith in Jesus," all of these "experiences" were entirely possible quite apart from authentic Christian conversion; and even the "faith in Jesus" could be reduced to "a merely literal and historical knowledge about Christ," which, everyone had to agree, was not what the New Testament meant by saving faith. The subjective intensity of the experience, moreover, was no valid criterion, one way or the other, of its genuineness. Therefore it was necessary "to show positively what are the sure, distinguishing, Scripture evidences and marks of a work of the Spirit of God."

Stod.*Gd.Chr.* (1714:4);
Stod.*Sfty.*8 (1687:179-80)

Edw.*Rel.Aff.*3.4 (Miller
2:277)

Frnck.*Meth.*3.7 (1723:61-62);
Baum.*Pred.*1.4 (Kirchner
1:97-126)
Frnck.*Pred.*Epiph.6 (1699:60)
Frnck.*Pred.*Oc. (1700:37)

Frnck.*Pass.Marc.*11
(1724:348)

Wsly.*Serm.*11.3.8 (Baker
1:292)
Baum.*Pred.*3.7 (Kirchner
3:232)
Edw.*Rel.Aff.*3.1 (Miller
2:205)
Edw.*Rel.Aff.*2 (Miller 2:160)

See vol.4:63-68

Poir.*Théol.cr.*pr. (1690-I:A5v)

Amrt.*Rev.*1.4 (1750:42-52)

Aug.*Civ.*22.29 (*CCSL*
48:857-62)
See vol.3:303-7

Scriv.*Seel.*5.9 (Stier 7:604-48)

Wsly.*Serm.*11.1.2 (Baker
1:285)
Wsly.*Serm.*37 (Baker 2:46-60)

Poir.*Fid.rat.*1.18 (1708:25)
Baum.*Pred.*1.9 (Kirchner
1:260-62)

Once again, the crucial problem of specificity needed to be faced, since "there is not one in a thousand but does [not] experience such religious affections long before he is converted." Because there was a "natural good" that was metaphysically and religiously distinct from the supernatural good and from the "spiritual" good ("spiritual" in the sense of "relation to the Spirit of God"), the regeneration and conversion that was the specific work of the Holy Spirit had to be accompanied by "the transfiguration of Jesus Christ in our souls," the experience of one's sinful state, the religious and moral commitment to "discipleship [Nachfolge]," and an inward testimony that was based not on a generalized religious feeling but on the particularized consciousness of having been justified and transformed by divine grace through recognizing Jesus as personal Savior. All of that was "above nature," different both in degree and in kind from natural affections, including the affections of natural religion. Jean Gerson and other masters of the "ambidextrous" spiritual life, which was simultaneously active and contemplative, had known what was meant by such a "union of the soul with God in experience and grace."

Gerson was at the same time a leading traditional authority on a phenomenon that was sure to acquire a new prominence in such an atmosphere: the problem of visions and new revelations. The "vision of God" was not a doctrine of the church in the strict sense, but it had always played a part in the exposition of Christian doctrine, especially when, as for example during the Franciscan revival of the Middle Ages, the experience of the Holy Spirit moved to the center of attention; therefore the question of the vision (and visions) of God was becoming an issue once again now. If the theology of the heart was directed against the externalization of religion through "formalism," it had to be careful not to fall into the opposite extreme of "enthusiasm" by claiming immediate revelation, also because its critics were always ready to dismiss any subjective illumination as "enthusiasm" or "fanaticism"; in this area, "too much" was as dangerous as "too little." It was "the danger of fanaticism" that, having "neither any authority nor any external law to check or counterbalance the imagination," a self-centered experience would come to regard "its own private preferences as the leadings of grace." As the title of one of his best-known works, *Heaven and Its Wonders, and Hell, from Things Heard and Seen*, suggests, one of the most celebrated exponents of visions and revelations in the eighteenth century was the scientist and seer, Emanuel Swedenborg. Although "the ancients frequently did so," he said, speaking with spirits was now regarded as "dangerous." He had, nevertheless, "spoken with angels," and it had been given to him to converse with them "as one man does with another." Despite the church's rejection of his visions, he could charge that this simply proved a lack of faith in "the man of the church" and that "immediate revelation" could claim great antiquity.

Thus Constantine's vision of the cross on the eve of his conversion proved both to the Greek and to the Latin tradition that private revelations and visions had never been absent from the life and experience of the church; in a similar vein, the appeal of the *Apology of the Augsburg Confession* to the visions of a late medieval apocalypticist, the German Franciscan Johannes Hilten, was authoritative evidence for Protestantism that if God in his freedom chose to do so, he could grant such visions now. The real question was whether there was any reason to suppose that he would do so, as Swedenborg or the Quakers (and the prophet Muhammed) claimed, or whether "such extraordinary things as immediate revelations" were usually a temptation of Satan. "Immediate revelations" were being claimed as a "key" to the hidden meaning of the Book of Revelation, but it was important to remember that even these were not "immediate" in the sense of having come outside the medium of the external word of God. The words of the Gospel of John, that Jesus had done many things "which are not written in this book"—whether they applied only to the period after the resurrection or to the entire life of Jesus—were being invoked again in support of the legitimacy of supplementary revelations, as they had frequently been invoked in support of the claim that there was an unwritten tradition in the church alongside the tradition written in Scripture. Yet the words of the very

Fén.*Aut.égl.* (Gosselin 1:213)

Swed.*Cael.*28.249 (1890:141)
Swed.*Cael.*3.16 (1890:18)

Swed.*Cael.*19.174 (1890:102)

Swed.*Cael.*33.302 (1890:177)
Swed.*Cael.*34.306 (1890:181)

Eus.*V.C.*1.28 (*GCS* 7:21);
Amrt.*Rev.*1.3 (1750:16-17)

See vol.1:105-8

*Apol.Conf.Aug.*27.1 (*Bek.*377)

Spen.*Bed.*1.1.11 (Canstein 1:80)

Naud.*Konuk.*1 (1699.6)

Frnck.*Id.*47 (Peschke 200)

Dör.*Pet.*3 (1718:12)

Baum.*Pred.*1.4 (Kirchner 1:115-16)

John 20:30
Schl.*Leb.Jes.*3.68 (Reimer 6:486-87)

Mor.*Luth.*1.14 (Sylvester 5:242); Grh.*Loc.*1.18 (Cotta 2:290-92)

John 20:31

Mayr.*Red*.4 (1702:361-62)

Amrt.*Rev*.1.2 (1750:7-10)

Aug.*Conf*.7.17.23
(*CCSL* 27:107)
Aug.*Conf*.9.10.24
(*CCSL* 27:147-48)

Aug.*Civ*.14.24 (*CCSL*
48:447-48)

Aug.*Gen.ad litt*.12.7 (*CSEL*
28:387-88)

Amrt.*Rev*.1.22 (1750:134)
Amrt.*Theol.eclec*.4.2.1.1
(1752-1-IV:11)

Mayr.*Red*.14 (1702:769);
Amrt.*Rev*.2.pr. (1750:149)

Edw.*Rel.Aff*.3.2 (Miller
2:251)

Zinz.*Soc*.14 (Beyreuther
1-I:147)

Tnnt.*Nec*.3 (1743:61)

Frnck.*Pred*.Inv. (1699:35);
Beng.*Gnom*.pr.4 (Steudel xix)

Frnck.*Pred*.pr. (1700:B4v)

next verse, "But these are written that you may believe," stood against the notion that such new revelations were needed (though not, of course, against the belief that they were possible).

From Augustine—whose *Confessions* contained two accounts of ecstatic visions, the first couched in general Neoplatonic terms, the second in specific Christian terms—there came not only the reminder that being transported into an ecstatic state lay within the natural capacity of some people and did not necessarily have anything directly to do with supernatural intervention, but also a distinction among the various kinds of visions, only some of which could qualify as having come from God alone, and that very rarely. Above all, just as a private revelation was not authenticated by the orthodoxy of the person who received it, so it in turn could not become an object of faith. Protestantism denied to the church and its tradition any binding authority to interpret Scripture, while Roman Catholicism and Eastern Orthodoxy claimed precisely that authority for the tradition; nevertheless everyone agreed that any purported new revelation was to be measured against the authority of the revealed word of God, which it dared not contradict. Thus the normative question was unavoidable in the evaluation not only of alleged private revelations, but even of the experience of the Holy Spirit in less dramatic and less controversial forms.

The unavoidable normative question was: Did the devotees of the theology of the heart "put their experiences in the place of Christ"? When Zinzendorf exclaimed, "Whether the teaching of Jesus is true or not, there is no need to discuss, for it has given me peace and I do not ask for anything else!" did that prove that he and his followers had elevated "experience, affection, and piety" over "principles"? The knowledge of Scripture by itself was not enough "if the Spirit of God does not dwell in you." It was the preacher's task to proclaim "the truth of God in all faithfulness and clarity," but to do so only "as I myself have come to recognize it from the word of God through the grace and illumination of the Holy Spirit and as I have experienced it to be useful and blessed in my own soul." The internal testimony of the Holy

Tnnt.*Serm*.3 (1744:61-85)

Beng.*Gnom*.Rom.9:1 (Steudel 586)

Baum.*Pred*.1.3 (Kirchner 1:83);Terst.*Bros*.2.5 (Becher 4:181)

1 John 2:20;27

Fén.*Aut.égl*. (Gosselin 1:213)

Lw.*Dem.Er*. (Moreton 5:20)

Arb.*Des.myst*.1.7 (1764:53)
Aug.*Spir.et litt*.17.30-26.46 (*CSEL* 60:183-201)

2 Cor.3:3

Wsly.*Serm*.11.3.6 (Baker 1:290)

Wsly.*Pl.Acct*.3.1 (*LPT* 191)

Spirit was said to be a necessary prerequisite for an acceptance of the "divine authority" of Scripture, since such testimony would illumine and confirm the conscience and the heart. In this way, the internal testimony would itself become "the criterion of truth." The Holy Spirit still worked outwardly, "through the proclamation of the word of God," but "chiefly it happens through the inner movements of the heart." The New Testament spoke about "an unction from the Holy One" and "the anointing which you have received"; but to some that implied "an unreserved docility and an absolute submission with regard to the visible church," while for others it referred primarily to "an inward teaching and unction of the Holy Ghost."

The phrase "the theology of the heart" could be nothing more than a particularly vivid figure of speech for the demand of the orthodox "saints of experience" and the doctors of the church in every age that a theology which could remain a dead letter locked in tomes on library shelves must instead be "written not with ink, but with the Spirit of the living God; not in tables of stone, but in fleshy tables of the heart." Once invoked, however, the concept could go on to acquire a life and an identity of its own, leading to theological conclusions that went beyond—or eventually went against—received ecclesiastical doctrine. John Wesley described how "the experience of the children of God—the experience not of two or three, not of a few, but of a great multitude which no man can number" served "to confirm this scriptural doctrine"; but when he went on to add that "it is confirmed by your experience and mine," he was making it clear that although he did not undervalue the evidence of tradition, such evidence was "weakened by length of time," by contrast with the "internal evidence" of personal experience, which was "equally strong, equally new, through the course of seventeen hundred years," because "it passes now, even as it has done from the beginning, directly from God into the believing soul."

One eighteenth-century treatise, therefore, could open with the definition, "The study of theology is the cultivation of the soul, under the gracious guid-

Frnck.*Meth*.1.1 (1723:1)

Edw.*Rel.Aff*.3.12 (Miller 2:461)

Zinz.*Soc*.9 (Beyreuther 1-I:98-100)

Stod.*Gd.Chr*.pr. (1714:ix)

Wsly.*Serm*.pr.6 (Baker 1:106)

Tnnt.*Dang*. (1742:11)

Schl.*Herm*.2.1 (Reimer 7:143-44)

ance of the Holy Spirit," while another could close with a description of the conflict between the allurement of "infidelity and atheism" and the power of an "experimental [experiential] and powerful religion." The current "experimental philosophy" was to find its counterpart in a genuinely experimental theology; for "whatever books men have read, there is great need of experimental knowledge in a minister." That alone was "the true, the scriptural, experimental religion." To a growing number, the books were not the place to look, nor was academic theology the resource, for the authentic understanding of the Christian message. Speaking for that growing number, one reformer of church, education, and theology declared that it was time for a change: "The most likely method to stock the church with a faithful ministry, in the present situation of things, the public academies being so much corrupted and abused generally, is to encourage private schools, or seminaries of learning, which are under the care of skillful and experienced Christians; in which those only should be admitted who, upon strict examination, have, in the judgment of a reasonable charity, the plain evidences of experimental religion."

From such a call it was still a considerable distance—but, in the judgment of many, a straight line—to a more drastic redefinition of the very nature of Christian doctrine that would move from "grammatical" to "psychological" hermeneutics and make the "experimental" character of doctrine constitutive. Such a redefinition would not have to exclude other and older ways of defining doctrine on the basis of the authority of Scripture and tradition in conjunction with the testimony of reason. But it could seek to put experimental theology on an equal footing with biblical theology or confessional theology, and then to transpose both of these into the new key. If it could be shown, exegetically and historically, that "all propositions which the system of Christian doctrine has to establish can be regarded either as descriptions of human states, or as conceptions of divine attributes and modes of action, or as utterances regarding the constitution of the world," and, moreover, that "all three forms have always subsisted alongside of each

Schl.*Chr.Gl.*30 (Redeker
1:163-65)

other" both in Scripture and in the tradition of the church, the way was open for a method of examining and expounding Christian doctrine in which, with due respect to the second and third of those ways of speaking about it, the first of them, "the direct description of the religious affections themselves," would become determinative. And then "the theology of the heart" would truly have come into its own, by carrying out a thoroughly "affectional transposition of Christian doctrine."

4

Foundations
of the Christian
World View

Clrdge.Ess.3.i.1800 (Coburn
3-I:72);Grnvg.Snd.Chr.
(Begtrup 4:444-45)

Nvn.Schf. (Merc.1:33;44)

Mich.Od.Ev.1.2 (1865:38)

Blms.Escép.1 (Casanovas
5:245;253)

Schl.Rel. (1806) 1 (Pünjer 24)

Schl.Rel. (1799) 3 (Pünjer
173)

See vol.3:146
Brd.Clr.Cant.22.1.3
(Leclercq-Rochais 1:131)

Schl.Rel. (1799) 1 (Pünjer 4)

The nineteenth century opened with a deep and widespread sense that "the disbelief of revealed religion" had become well-nigh universal, at least "among the people of education" in Christian lands. A German Protestant pastor, "the gifted, noble" Friedrich Daniel Ernst Schleiermacher—soon to become, through his systematic theology, *The Christian Faith*, the most influential and revered Protestant theologian since the Reformation—had just issued (anonymously) *On Religion: Addresses to the Cultured among Its Despisers*. Sharing the conviction of many of his contemporaries that skepticism was "the problem of the age" and "one of the characteristic plagues of the epoch," he called upon his skeptical contemporaries to look beyond the superficialities of conventional piety and official dogma, to "turn from everything usually reckoned religion, and fix your regard on the inward emotions and dispositions," and to find deep within themselves the wellsprings of an authentic religion, which were still there, above all in their aesthetic aspirations, despite all their denials of the church and its orthodox piety. Carrying "the affectional transposition of doctrine" to new heights, he spoke lyrically of the mystery of the self that he would communicate to them. In the twelfth century Bernard of Clairvaux had declared: "As a man I speak of Him [Christ] as a Man to men." But now Schleiermacher's version of that declaration was: "As a man I speak to you of the sacred mysteries of humanity . . . , of the innermost springs of my own being."

174

At almost exactly the same time, the lay leader both of the Evangelical movement in the Church of England and of the crusade against slavery, William Wilberforce, had opened "a new era in the history of Anglicanism" (as a Roman Catholic historian was to call it) by publishing his *Practical View of the Prevailing Religious System of Professed Christians*. Unlike Schleiermacher's *Addresses*, this book was not intended "to convince the skeptic," but was rather "addressed to those who acknowledge the authority of the Holy Scriptures." In it he complained that despite all the public commitment to sincerity and to the moral system of Christianity, doctrine and theology were being neglected, so that "the grand radical defect in the practical system of these nominal Christians is their forgetfulness of all the peculiar doctrines of the religion which they profess." Both the "professed Christians" and the "cultured among the despisers of religion" apparently needed such exhortation. Two-thirds of the way through the century, Pope Pius IX issued his so-called *Syllabus of Errors* of 8 December 1864, denouncing an entire catalogue of modern errors, from pantheism to various species of rationalism to latitudinarianism to the separation of church and state, and concluding with the rejection, often quoted and attacked, of the thesis: "The Roman pontiff can and should reconcile himself and come to terms with progress, with liberalism, and with modern civilization."

Each of the major churches faced special forms of the problem and (so it believed) had special resources in its own history for overcoming it. Yet all of them were pervaded by the sense that while a patristic saying quoted by a future pope in 1799 might still be true—that it would be easier to extinguish the sun than to destroy the church—nevertheless the church was "sick and languishing." Eastern Christendom, both Russian and Greek, continued to celebrate the Sunday of Orthodoxy, but with a growing sense, as one Russian theologian said in 1814, that "the voice of God has been resounding in the church like a voice in the wilderness for a long time," and, as another put it, that "our century has seen the most extreme development of the principle of abstract philosophy

Mntl.*Ang*.14 (Lecoffre 5:372)

Wilb.*Pr.Vw*.int. (1798:7)

Wilb.*Pr.Vw*.2 (1798:44)

Wilb.*Pr.Vw*.4 (1798:226-27)

Döll.*Ppst.Conc*.1 (Janus 22-23)

Pi.IX.*Syl* 10.80 (*ASS* 3:176)

Bau.*Vers*.3.4 (1838:743)

Gr.XVI.*Tr*.pr. (Battaggia viii)
Lam.*Mx.égl*.2 (Forgues 12:207)
Fil.*Sl*.420 (*Soč.Fil*.5:393-98);Blach.*Log*.31 (1882:374-83);Hrth.*Log*.16 (1882:668-77)

Fil.*Sl*.28 (*Soč.Fil*.1:205)

Slv.*Krit*.46 (Radlov 2:330)

Blach.*Log*.25 (1882:290)
Lacrd.*Cons*.pr. (Poussielque
7:5);Blms.*Prot*.11 (Casanovas
4:105)

Sail.*Ep*.17.vi.1800 (Schiel
199-200)

Art.*Pi.VII*.5 (1837-I:95)

Mntl.*Int.cath*.1 (Lecoffre 5:4)
And.*Pan.serm*.19
(1817:165-66)
See vol.4:72-85
Lacrd.*Conf*.4 (Poussielque
2:87)

Mynst.*Praed*.29 (1845-I:363)

Söd.*Tl*.1 (Stolpe 24)

Chan.*Evid.Chr*.1 (AUA
189;192)

Kbl.*Nat.Ap*. (1833:14)
Wlb.*Inc*.15 (1849:410)
Lam.*Indiff*.17 (Forgues 2:128)

Newm.*Apol*.1 (Svaglic 43)

Kbl.*Nat.Ap*.pr. (1833:3)

and of the principle of abstract science," far removed from the truth of the church fathers; it was time to summon "the Orthodox Zion" to repentance. The churches, all of them, presented the spectacle of "a vast ruin." As one theologian and priest wrote in 1800, amid the Napoleonic Wars, "the future lies in the hand of God." "On 1 January 1800," another Roman Catholic apologist would recall later in the century, Pope Pius VI had recently died, "an exile and the prisoner of an atheist republic," and the College of Cardinals charged with electing his successor "remained in seclusion for 104 days, preoccupied with what one contemporary called 'the state of the flagrant betrayal of Catholic Europe,' " before finally electing Pius VII; it was a crisis for the papacy unsurpassed even by the "Babylonian Captivity" and Great Schism of the late Middle Ages. In Lutheran Scandinavia, one critic noted that "in most people the Christian faith undoubtedly remains confined to a poor knowledge," having been changed "from a living and firm conviction [Overbeviisning] to a doubting supposition [Formodning]," and at the very end of the century another Scandinavian churchman identified as the theme of the century "emancipation" from external authority, "from all a priori dogmas of ancient or recent date regarding the manner and the limits of existence." Even someone who refused to "join in the common cry against infidelity as the sure mark of a corrupt mind" did identify it as "a gross and perilous error."

All of these expressions of concern throughout Christendom East and West were "omens and tokens of an apostate mind," of a "chilling apathy" and self-isolation. Thus the words of the "Assize Sermon" delivered at Oxford on 14 July 1833 by an Anglican priest, John Keble, which came to be regarded by John Henry Newman and others as "the start of the religious movement [the Oxford Movement] of 1833," could as well have been spoken anywhere else in Christendom, whether within Eastern Orthodoxy or Roman Catholicism or the various branches of Protestantism, howsoever they might have defined the word "church": "It is a moment, surely, full of deep solicitude to all those members of the church who still believe her authority divine." The pathos of the

Luke 18:8

question in the Gospel, "When the Son of man comes, will he find faith on earth?" had now found its dismaying answer in "this funereal and discouraged epoch, where the faith is completely dead or dying,"

Mntl.*Av*.3.viii.1831 (Lecoffre 4:202;205)

as the shrinking company of its surviving devotees huddled together in mourning beside its "sacred grave."

Such jeremiads had often been heard in every period throughout Christian history. Thus in the high Mid-

Crnly.*Int*.1.3.2.14.248 (1885-I:657)

dle Ages, to which during the nineteenth century not only Roman Catholics but even Protestants often looked back nostalgically as a period when the Chris-

Schf.*Prin.Prot*.2.5 (*Merc*.1:175)

tian faith had been "the all-moving, all-ruling force," a Latin Christian poet had opened his masterpiece with a denunciation of "the latest of hours, the worst

Brd.Cln.*Cont.mnd*.1 (Hoskier 1)

of times [hora novissima, tempora pessima]." But now, while echoing these words that "the times are

Newm.*Min.Com*. (*Tr.Tms*.1:1)

very evil, yet no one speaks against them," the interpreters of the faith were taken with a sense that fundamental and far-reaching historic changes had taken place, even in comparison with the Enlightenment battles of the past century or two over "the

Bau.*Neun*.2 (Scholder 4:176)
Slv.*Bogočlv*.1 (Radlov 3:9)
Hrlss.*Enc*.2.5.11 (1837:201)

dogmatics of Rationalism" in its conflict with "traditional theology." Though often without an adequate basis in scholarship on either side, "for the last hundred and fifty years" it had been "the approved line of opinion in the world" that although the institutional church and its orthodox dogmas were expendable, the gospel and the Bible would nevertheless abide; but "the view henceforth is to be that

Newm.*Scr.Perf*.7 (*Tr.Tms*.85:99)

Christianity does not exist in documents, any more than in institutions" and thus that it did not (or would not) exist at all in any recognizable form.

"Since the beginning of the eighteenth century there has been, more and more, a complete revolution

Bau.*DG*.113 (1858:343)

of Protestant consciousness," one historian asserted, namely, as another historian described it, the feeling that "the historic dogma has lost its power"; it was "a time that is characterized by negation" of dogma,

Klfth.*DG*.65 (1839:205)

tradition, and authority. "In times of much leisure and unbounded curiosity" such as the present, therefore, "a sober standard of feeling in matters of practical religion" as represented in the historic norms

Kbl.*Chr.Yr*.pr. (1827-I:v-vi)

of church teaching was no longer fashionable. Tradi-

Jer.Niž.*Uč*.B (1864:13-14)
Thom.*Chr*.86
(1856-IV:435-36)

Lam.*Déf*.pr. (Forgues 5:v)
Wms.*Res*.6.10
(*Tr.Tms*.87:119)
Lam.*Ep*.12.x.1825 (Forgues
13:137);Lam.*Par.cr*.13
(Forgues 11:49)

Wms.*Res*.6.1 (*Tr.Tms*.87:85)

Rtl.*Fid.imp*.1.7 (1890:37)

Slv.*Bogočlv*.1 (Radlov 3:1-2)
Blms.*Rel*.10 (Casanovas
5:13-15)
Lam.*Indiff*.4 (Forgues 1:75)

Hfmnn.*Enc*.2.2.1.2
(Bestmann 270-71)
Camp.*Ev*.7 (Owen 99)

Camp.*Syst*.23.1 (1956:54)

Ces.*Ep*.12.vi.1795
(Manuzzi 2:295)

Lam.*Indiff*.7 (Forgues 1:160)
Ub.*Int*.1.1.21.int.
(1886-I:375)

Clrdge.*Ref*.7.7 (Shedd 1:229)

Thom.*Chr*.65 (1865-III:395)

Ces.*St.eccl*.1.3;1.8
(1881:28;101)

Matt.16:18-19
Newm.*Dev*.1.1.1.3 (Harrold
33-34)
Clrdge.*Ess*.9.xii.1815
(Coburn 3-II:422);Feod.*Prav*.7
(1860:196)
Lam.*Mx.égl*.2 (Forgues
12:222)
ap.Krth.*Cons.Ref*.5
(1871:181)

tional proofs for such Christian beliefs as human immortality, though still being employed, had been deprived of their validity, and the unbelief that had been generally characteristic of the preceding century had given way to the next stage, which was radical doubt. Without being "considered or calculated upon," a spirit of "want of reverence in religion" had achieved a grand alliance of "all the efforts against religion" into a single campaign.

"In one point of view," many contemporary observers felt, "our case indeed differs from that of former ages, in that the great and essential truths of our religion . . . are now generally known" but no longer accepted, whereas, in some previous ages of "implicit faith," they had been generally accepted without always being very well known. Whether generally known or not, however, these "great and essential truths" became the focus of attention. The "absence of principles" and the attacks on the faith from the "lamentable blindness" of an "indifference" that was "more dangerous than atheism" were compelling all Christian groups to give such attention to "the first truths of Christianity," to "fundamental principles," to "the fundamental conceptions of all the revelations and developments of the Divinity," and to "the Christian religion as a more reasonable and better foundation for everything that is known." It was essential to concentrate "on the system of fundamental points" and "the foundations of revealed religion," which had been revealed already in the Old Testament and were "the groundwork of Christianity, and essentials in the Christian faith, but not its characteristic and peculiar doctrines." Within and beneath one or another of these doctrines, consequently, was "the firm anchor ground of the faith," which was (wherever one might locate the historical continuity of its authority) "the rock of foundation and truth" on which Christ, in his declaration to Peter, had promised to build his church, the "leading idea" or "fixed principles" that set it apart from the "foundations of the system" of indifference and unbelief. Far from having been "an idea unknown to our church in her purer days," as some suspected, such an interest in locating a "foundation" beneath and beyond the

*Apol.Conf.Aug.*7.20 (*Bek.*238)

Hrmnn.*Nt.* (1913:21)

See p. 326 below

Slv.*Bogočlv.*1 (Radlov 3:1)

Schf.*Prin.Prot.*1.2;2.3
(*Merc.*1:120;135)

Mhlr.*Ath.*3 (1827-I:242-51)

Mhlr.*Pat.*1 (Reithmayr 137)

Rtl.*Rechr.*3.1.7 (1882-III:33);
Rtl.*Unt.*3.60 (Ruhbach 52);
Dry.*Apol.*1.1.2 (1838 I:2)

Thom.*DG.*1.2.1 (1874-I:178)
Lacrd.*Dom.*2 (Poussielque
1:31)
Lacrd.*Conf.*26 (Poussielque
3:124)

Wilb.*Pr.Vw.*1 (1798:15)
Hrth.*Herm.*epil. (1882:247)

particular dogmas had ample precedent in the Christian tradition. "We know," it was said at the end of this period, "that not everyone can see the foundation of our faith"; nevertheless, "no one can destroy it, either." Just how equivocal the consideration of this issue could be was shown by the appearance within the English-speaking Christian world, also at the end of this period and at almost the same time, of two publications with strikingly similar titles but with radically divergent tendencies, *The Fundamentals* of 1909 in the United States and *Foundations* of 1912 in England.

At stake in the conflict of Christian doctrine with modern culture in the nineteenth century was nothing less than (in the opening words of the most important work of one Russian Orthodox thinker) "the truths of positive religion, matters that are distant and alien to the modern consciousness and to the interests of modern civilization." A German expositor of the patristic tradition, called also by his Protestant critics "the most important Roman Catholic theologian of the present age," spoke of "the foundations of the Christian world view [die Grundanschauungen des Christentums]," which he found to be the "fundamental truth" on which the church fathers had based their teaching; such an interest in "the comprehensive Christian world view" was common to many other nineteenth-century theologians of widely differing perspectives. In opposition to the errors confronted by the church during the patristic era as well as to those it was confronting in his own era, another student of the fathers saw in their teaching "the correct world view, in the combination of divine transcendence with divine immanence." Those foundations formed, on the one hand, "the soul of Christianity," and, on the other hand, "the primary passion of humanity." For traditional Christians, whether Evangelical or Catholic or Orthodox, consequently, they implied the particular imperative "to believe the doctrines, and imbibe the principles, and practice the precepts of Christ," or else to suffer "moral shipwreck." At the same time, for those whose Christian concerns went beyond the Christian tradition to the belief that theology included "those fundamental truths which

are the common groundwork of our civil and our
religious duties," these foundations were "not less
indispensable to a right view of our temporal concerns
than to a rational faith respecting our immortal
well-being."

Clrdge.*Const.*1.5 (Coburn
10:47-48)

The Reality of God

"Against the background of this debris of all the
doctrines of religion," the defenders of the faith
concentrated on "the existence of God" as "this grand
and sublime truth" on which all else depended, as
"the foundation of natural religion," but as "the same
foundation" for faith as well; for "the [Eastern]
Orthodox Church begins all of its teaching about God
in the [Nicene] Creed with the word: 'I believe.' "
Religion could be defined as "an intimate and constant persuasion of the existence of a God, creator of
the universe, lawgiver and supreme judge of humanity"; and again, as "the knowledge of God, of his will,
and of our duties towards him." At the beginning of
the Protestant theological development of the nineteenth century, a leading apologetic treatise, rejecting
the canard that the religious believer knew nothing
except a semblance of reality, defined the believer
instead as "reality which knows reality." A century
later, two of the summations of the outcome of that
development, one by a liberal Protestant and another
by a liberal Roman Catholic, were devoted to "the
Reality of God, to the presence within our lives, as in
the great world of realities around us, of God, a
Reality, *the* Reality." The question was: "Does Faith in
God Still Make Sense?" A Roman Catholic apologetic
made "The Existence of God" the title of one of its
most important chapters. "We contemplate in [God]
pure, perfect, and proper reality": the infinite for
which the human spirit was longing and striving
could have its reality only in the reality of God, the
point of departure and the point of arrival for all
human endeavor, "the very foundation of all religion,"
namely, "suitable reverence for the Divine Majesty."
An authentic "sense of religion in man" could not be
"a mere sentiment," for "devotion without the fact of
a Supreme Being" was nothing but "a dream and a
mockery," and the universe itself no more than "a

Lam.*Indiff.*5 (Forgues 1:102)
Hdge.*Darw.* (1874:3)
Jam.*Sac.Hist.*3.1 (1802-II:2)

Mak.*Prav.bog.*9 (Tichon 1:66)

Tor.*Car.*1.1 (1779-I:11)
Newm.*Gram.*2.10.1
(Ker 1985:251)

Schl.*Rel.* (1806) 2 (Pünjer 49)

Hrmnn.*Wirk.* (1914)

Hüg.*Real.*int. (Gardner 14)
Söd.*Tl.*3 (Stolpe 146)

Lam.*Indiff.*14 (Forgues
2:35-70)
Clrdge.*Log.*2.1.25 (Coburn
13:129)
Khns.*Dogm.*2.9.2
(1861-I:138)

Lacrd.*Conf.*14 (Poussielque
2:264)
Wilb.*Pr.Vw.*4 (1798:207)
Tor.*Car.*2.1 (1779-II:21-32)

Newm.*Apol.*2 (Svaglic 54)

Lam.*Indiff*.15 (Forgues 2:76)

Blms.*Escép*.25 (Casanovas 5:448)

Wilb.*Pr.Vw*.6 (1798:265)

Tor.*Car*.1.10 (1779-I:324)

Chan.*Evid.Chr*.1 (AUA 193)
Lacrd.*Conf*.27 (Possielque 3:143-44)

See pp. 66-67 above

Kol.*Káz*.5 (1844:67);
Chan.*Evid.Chr*.2 (AUA 210;215)

Pal.*Nat.Theol*.23 (Wayland 4:280)

Wilb.*Pr.Vw*.4 (1798:200)

Kbl.*Oc*.5 (Pusey 166)

Lam.*Indiff*.2 (Forgues 1:36-37)

John 4:23-24;
ap.Newm.*Scr.Perf*.1
(*Tr.Tms*.85:7);Mak.*Prav.bog*.17
(Tichon 1:97-98)
Kierk.*Fr.bv*.2.2 (Drachmann 3:118);Rtl.*Ges.
Auf*.3 (1893:76)

ap.Nvn.*Schf*. (*Merc*.1:36)

Wilb.*Pr.Vw*.1 (1798:17)
Dry.*Apol*.1.2.1.6
(1838-I:115-16)

Schl.*Chr.Gl*.4 (Redeker 1:23-30)

grand illusion." That "reality, grand and mysterious," was fundamental in any apologetic addressed to the modern skeptic.

Yet it was the very reality of God that was now itself becoming problematical, also among professing Christians. "God is forgotten, his providence is exploded," William Wilberforce lamented. Perhaps it remained true that "the name of 'atheist' still sounds horrible to the greater part of humanity," so that the enemies of religion sought to cover "the insanity of atheism" by pretending to accept a version of Christian theism. In that sense a "positive and effective" Christian theism represented the third possibility in the conventional Enlightenment dispute over the choice between atheism and superstition, especially because of the remnants of superstition that were still evident within traditional Christian piety itself. But "the old system of atheism and the new agree" in rejecting the reality of "a particular, personal intelligence" as God, and often in rejecting with it the sense of "the reality of unseen things" altogether. In the name of an "unhallowed, because self-sufficient enquiry," the "missionaries of evil [were] preaching atheism" and skepticism. The principle of "religious indifferentism" had originally been directed against the superstition and fanaticism thought to be prevailing in all the churches. In their stead, "behold, what it has managed to preserve is the fanaticism of impiety [et voilà ce qui la preserve du fanatisme de l'impiété]!"

Not least was the problem manifesting itself in some of the very defenses of religion themselves, which continued to employ the biblical formula of "worship in spirit and truth," as well as the corollary distinctions between "inwardness" and "outwardness" in religion or between "a religion of forms" and "a religion of the spirit." Such principles as "sincerity is all in all" seemed to be leading to utter subjectivism, as did the definition of religion itself as "the feeling of absolute dependence [schlechthinnige Abhängigkeit]." In his earlier apologetic work, the author of that definition had left himself open to the charge that he was demonstrating only the subjective reality of piety, not the objective reality of God. "The contemplation of the pious," he had said, "is the immediate consciousness of all finite things, in and through the Infinite," and therefore religion meant "to have life and to know life in immediate feeling, only as such an existence in the Infinite and Eternal." He described "religion"—changing this in the second edition to "piety"—as the spiritual womb in which his life had been nourished, and he spoke out against an equation of religion with the "doctrines and systems" of theology, with a "mixture of opinions about God and the world" or "a mess of metaphysical and ethical crumbs."

Calling the Reformation's exaltation of faith as trust "a revolution of the spirit from the objective to the subjective" could, critics warned, eventuate in the substitution of subjective religiosity for the objectivity "of a real Other" as the content of "religion." While human reason operated with the "hypothesis of a One as the ground and cause of the universe," it was the task of "the idea which is the basis of religion" to elevate this hypothesis "into the idea of the Living God." To speak of God as "Being," therefore, was "opposed to what is merely thought, and to a mere force or power"; it "meant that which has a real, substantive existence." This was what the church and its teachers had meant when they called God "substance [suščestvo]." Since patristic times, Christian theologians had found biblical support for this ontological conception above all in the self-revelation of God to Moses: "I am who I am." Those words could be rendered: "I am the One who is ['Εγώ εἰμι ὁ ὤν]." The passage continued to be a mainstay, as denoting the "living God" who was a "person," an "existing and self-subsisting reality, a real and personal Being"; it taught Christians, no less than Jews, "the eternal, necessary, immutable, and incomprehensible existence of God." That self-revelation meant that God was "knowable" but at the same time remained "incomprehensible" (though "not therefore unintelligible," some wanted to add): " 'Verily, Thou art a hidden God, the God of Israel, the Savior' is the very law of his dealings with us."

One source of the difficulties of Christians in the face of the denials of the reality of God was the largely

Schl.*Rel.* (1799) 1 (Pünjer 11-12)
Schl.*Rel.* (1806) 1 (Pünjer 11-12)

Schl.*Rel.* (1806) 2 (Pünjer 41)

Luth.*Dtsch.Kat.*1.1.1-3 (*Bek.*560)
Bau.*Vers.*2.1.1 (1838:287); Rtl.*Recht.*1.5.31 (1882-I:219-20); Rtl.*Fid.imp.*2.11 (1890:60)
Drnr.*Syst.*47 (1879-I:551); Söd.*Tl.*3 (Stolpe 200)

Clrdge.*Ref.*7.2 (Shedd 1:210-11)

Hdge.*Syst.Theol.*1.5.5 (1981-I:367)

Mak.*Prav.bog.*16 (Tichon 1:92-95)

See vol.1:54

Ex.3:14
Hrth.*Thrsk.*2.2 (1895:56)
Marc.*Inst.*9.5.4 (Tomassini 2:40);
Camp.*Syst.*3.1 (1956:6)

Slv.*Bogočlv.*5 (Radlov 3:65-67)

Clrdge.*Ref.*7.2 (Shedd 1:217-18)

Jam.*Vind.*2.8 (1794-I:250)
Hdge.*Syst.Theol.*1.4.1 (1981-I:337)
Grnvg.*Pr.*25.v.1823 (Thodberg 1:285);Döll.*Heid. Jud.*10.3.2 (1857:821)
Chan.*Calv.* (AUA 463)
Isa.45:15
Newm.*Gram.*2.9.1 (Ker 1985:227)

Thom.*Chr*.7 (1856-I:15)

Thom.*DG*.1.2.1
(1874-I:155;263-66)

Bau.*DG*.80 (1858:245-50);
Rtl.*Theol.Met*.5 (1887:40)

Geiselmann (1960) 446-47

Clrdge.*Log*.2.1.6 ((Coburn
13:111)

Clrdge.*Rev.Rel*.1 (Coburn
1:93)
Blms.*Escép*.3 (Casanovas
5:265)
Clrdge.*Rev.Rel*.1 (Coburn
1:93)

Gffrd.*Trst*. (Jaki 72-73)

implicit role that the doctrine of God as such had played in much of the history of Christian dogma. "The church did not draw up a dogma about the concept of God," one historical theologian observed, "although [the history of] ecclesiastical theology does manifest a series of attempts to achieve one." As he noted elsewhere, therefore, Christian dogma had not proceeded "on the basis of a presupposed speculative concept of God"—or, at any rate, not of an explicit a priori concept—when it went about formulating its teachings about the person of Christ and the Trinity. It had remained for medieval scholasticism to advance "the philosophical and dogmatic development of the doctrine of God." The result of that history became evident in the evolution of the very theologian who spoke about "foundations of the Christian world view," Johann Adam Möhler: in his early work, *The Unity of the Church* of 1825, "God is the starting point from which Möhler's theology takes its beginning," as he proceeded to argue for "the divine element in Christianity" on the basis of such an a priori concept of God; but when his grasp of patristic theology deepened through further research in preparation for his study *Athanasius the Great and His Time*, published two years later, he began to argue in the opposite direction, as had the church fathers, "starting from man and his freedom to point to God as the One beyond and above the world." In dogma as well as in logic, then, "the idea of God is presupposed."

And therefore "the belief of a Deity" was "almost an axiom," for which there was "no need of nice or subtle reasonings" or "scientific apparatus" and against which "artful reasonings . . . may puzzle us, but never convince." Nevertheless, there continued to be "artful reasonings" aplenty on the side of the opponents, matched by no smaller a quantity of "nice or subtle reasonings" on the side of the defenders. It was in the nineteenth century that the Gifford Lectures were established in Protestant Scotland, "for 'promoting, advancing, teaching, and diffusing the study of natural theology,' in the widest sense of that term, in other words, the knowledge of God, the Infinite, the All." Likewise in the nineteenth century, but within Roman Catholicism, the rational validity

Rom. 1:19-20

Grh.*Loc*.2.4 (Cotta 3:54)

CVat. (1869-70).3.2;3.4
(Alberigo-Jedin 806;808)

See p. 117 above

Prn.*Prael*.2.3.1
(1877-III:228-45)

Krth.*Cons.Ref*.pr. (1871:vii)

Chan.*Evid.Rev*. (AUA 226)

Wilb.*Pr.Vw*.3 (1798:76-88)

Wilb.*Pr.Vw*.3 (1798:83)

Hrmnn.*Wirk*. (1914:13)

Rtl.*Theol.Met*.1 (1887:7-8)

of natural theology in demonstration of the existence of God itself became, for the first time, the explicit subject of dogmatic definition at a church council (although it, too, had been "presupposed" in earlier definitions), when, quoting what orthodox Protestantism had called the "locus classicus" of natural theology, the First Vatican Council declared, before going on to specify the content of divine revelation: "Holy Mother Church holds and teaches that God, the beginning and the end of all things, can be certainly recognized [cognosci] by the natural light of human reason from the things created." Authoritative revelation, in other words, affirmed that revelation was not the only way to know the reality of God. This was directed both against philosophers who, without denying the existence of God as such, did deny that reason could prove it, and against theologians who, sometimes on the basis of such philosophers, ascribed to divine revelation alone the capacity to lead to a valid knowledge of God. In this setting the Thomistic proofs for the existence of God on the basis of motion and cause enjoyed a new birth of interest and elaboration as the presupposition of doctrinal theology within Roman Catholicism.

In Protestant theology, too, there was a continuing effort to argue for doctrine from "purely natural evidence" as well as from revelation, to ascribe faith to "a divine original because no adequate cause for it can be found" elsewhere, and to assert the "reasonableness" of human "affections toward an invisible Being," but often with the addition of the stipulation that "here, no less than in other particulars, the Christian's hope is founded, not on the speculations or the strength of man, but on the declaration of Him who cannot lie, on the power of Omnipotence." More representative was the approach formulated by Wilhelm Herrmann in *The Reality of God*: "Even though it is impossible to prove the reality of God, it still remains possible for everyone to find the reality of God." Among many Christians in all the confessions, the traditional cosmological demonstrations of the existence of God, as "the nest in which a metaphysical knowledge of God has always been nourished," were being seen as merely hypothetical at best and as

Lacrd.*Conf*.45 (Poussielque 4:265);Clrdge. *Log*.2.9.6 (Coburn 13:207); Slv.*Bogočlv*.3 (Radlov 3:31-32)

Kierk.*Syg.Dd*.2.1.app. (Drachmann 11:213)

Trtn.*Inst*.3.1.16-17 (1688-I:191-93)

Lam.*Indiff*.14 (Forgues 2:47)

Lam.*Indiff*.14 (Forgues 2:42-44)

Camp.*Ev*.10 (Owen 138)

Lam.*Indiff*.22 (Forgues 3:20)

See pp. 256-57 below

Hdge.*Syst.Theol*.1.1 (1981-I:191)

Tor.*Car*.1.1 (1779-I:55-61)

Hrth.*Log*.16 (1882:673)

irrelevant whether or not they were impossible, since they strove to prove something that "passes all understanding." They were receding behind two other arguments, which seemed to be more in keeping with the nature of revelation itself as well as with the intellectual spirit of the time: the historical and the moral.

The arguments for the existence of God from reason had always shared their place with the argument "on the basis of the consensus of the nations [a populorum consensu]," even after the voyages of discovery and the beginnings of scientific anthropology had begun to shake the assumption of some about the very existence of any such "consensus." This continuing assumption expressed itself in the declaration that there was evident, all the way from Africa to the Arctic, a "belief in a First Being, the Father of all beings": even the atheists had to acknowledge that "there is no tradition that is more universal or more continuous." The reality of God was "a truth that is universally held and unanimously attested among all men and in all centuries—a truth of fact, of feeling, and of the evidence of reason." Where there was less reliance on the last of these, "the evidence of reason," the contention that "all nations have derived their ideas of Deity . . . from tradition and not from the light of reason" was called upon to carry more of the apologetic burden, with the awareness of the danger that, paradoxically, such a reliance on the evidence of "universal tradition" could in turn lead back to a species of rationalism and could as well create problems for the definition of the specifically Christian tradition. That danger was in part offset by a definition of the universal tradition among "all men" as a "conviction that there is a Being on whom they are dependent, and to whom they are responsible."

More and more, nineteenth-century Christians came to rely on that conviction of responsibility and on what their immediate predecessors had identified as the relation of "religion" to "virtue" as their primary argument for the reality of God. There were two ways of knowing, the "logical" and the "ethical," and the second no less than the first had an apologetic role to play. "No truth has found a clearer expression

Söd.*Upp*.3 (1930:152)

Dost.*Br.Kar*.4.11.8
(Černecova 683)

Hno.*Theol*.1.1.1.3
(1785-I:33-34)

Slv.*Krit*.26 (Radlov 2:183);
Slv.*Duch.osn*.1.2 (Radlov
3:306)

Chan.*Hon.* (AUA 69)

Wrds.*Dty.* (Hayden 1:605)

Clrdge.*Conf.Fid.*1 (Shedd
5:15)

Newm.*Dev.*1.1.2.7 (Harrold
45)

Newm.*Gram.*1.5.1 (Ker
1985:72)

Chan.*Lke.* (AUA 293)
Kierk.*Kjer.gjer.*1.2A
(Drachmann 9:21-27)

Söd.*Upp*.1.1 (1930:19)

Camp.*Ev.*17 (Owen 212)

Döll.*Heid.Jud.*8.1 (1857:571)

Hrmnn.*Wirk.* (1914:39-40);
Slv.*Rus.égl.*3.9 (Rouleau 279)

in modern times," one theologian observed, "than the truth that moral independence belongs to the essence of Christianity." For "if there is no everlasting God, there is no such thing as virtue [dobrodetel], and there is no need for it," a character in a Christian novel avowed, echoing earlier arguments; the converse of his position was the claim, which intitially seemed to be only pragmatic but was in fact ultimately metaphysical, that if there was such a thing as virtue and a need for it, there had to be an everlasting God, since "duty [dolžnoe]" ultimately depended on "being." "The sense of duty is the greatest gift of God," the American Unitarian William Ellery Channing affirmed; "duty," a poet said, was the "stern daughter of the voice of God." From the acknowledgment "I believe that I am a free agent" it followed, according to another poet and philosophical theologian, that "it becomes my absolute duty to believe, and I do believe, that there is a God, that is, a Being in whom supreme reason and a most holy will are one with an infinite power." Conscience was a reality "the existence of which we cannot deny." As such it was "a proof of the doctrine of a Moral Governor, which alone gives it a scope"; not "any sensible phenomena," but the "mental phenomena" that were "found in the sense of moral obligation" identified "the intimations of conscience" with "an external admonition" and thus led the inquirer necessarily to "the notion of a Supreme Ruler or Judge." Only "through our own moral nature" was the moral perfection of God comprehended. Religion was, then, "unconditional obedience to God." Yet that was not to be taken to mean that the roots of morality went deeper in human life than did the roots of religion itself.

Thus it had been the peculiar quality of the monotheistic faith of Israel—by a remarkable contrast with "a polished nation like the Greeks, embracing a system full of theological absurdities," or with the philosophy of Cicero—that in Israel, rather than in Greece or Rome, "the idea of the one almighty God grows solely out of the human experiences that pertain to the moral imperative [der sittliche Verkehr mit Menschen]." The moral law was a key to the history of Israel, and several of its prohibitions as well as many

Jam.*Sac.Hist*.3.1 (1802-II:5)

Iv.*Thsm*.8 (1899:247-48)

Gen.22:2

Kierk.*Fr.Bv*.2.1 (Drachmann 3:109)

Camp.*Syst*.2.1 (1956:2)

Clrdge.*Const*.2 (Coburn 10:123)

Chan.*Calv*. (AUA 461)

Knt.*Krit.pr.Vern*. (Cassirer 5:174)

Pal.*Nat.Theol*.25 (Wayland 4:295 98)

Döll.*Gnos*.2 (1890:16)

Jam.*Sac.Hist*.3.1 (1802:4)

Tert.*Marc*.1.3.1 (*CCSL* 1:443)
Marc.Inst.9.7 (Tomassini 2:49)

Chan.*Evid.Chr*.2 (AUA 212)

Thom.*Chr*.52;57 (1856-III:37;114-15)

Bush.*Nat*.1 (1858:31)

of its positive injunctions were intended to teach or to safeguard the doctrine of the unity of God. The history of Israel was said to be unique in another respect as well. "Only once in history," one philosophical theologian asserted, "do I find that a progressive development of morals was also a progressive revelation of the character of God"; otherwise, the practice of religion and the precepts of morality had often come into conflict. At the same time, the ultimacy of the monotheistic faith of Israel implied that there could not be a simple equation between the moral imperative and the mystery of the divine will: in the command from God that Abraham was to sacrifice his son Isaac, Søren Kierkegaard found what he defined as "the teleological suspension of the ethical," when Abraham "by his act overstepped the ethical entirely and possessed a higher telos outside of it, in relation to which he suspended the former."

"One God, one moral system": morality and monotheism were historically inseparable and mutually supportive, and taken together they could even be used to attack various forms of Christian orthodoxy. "The moral law within" may originally have been intended by apologists to supplement, but now it often supplanted, "the starry heaven above" as a philosophical and theological proof for divine unity and reality. A rationalistic orthodoxy was hard put, on purely cosmological grounds, to demonstrate "the unity of the Deity" on the basis of "the uniformity of plan observable in the universe," particularly as such a uniformity of plan was becoming less and less evident to those who had begun observing the universe, whether biological or physical, in more careful scientific detail. Yet orthodox rejection of various species of dualism demonstrated that a denial of the unity of the Supreme Being was, for the biblical world view, tantamount to atheism: as Tertullian had asserted against Marcion, "God is not if he is not one." Nature held out the doctrine of one God, though it did not compel acceptance of it. Christian spirituality itself had long sensed a "difficulty, and not merely a subjective one" in bringing together the idea of the love of God with the idea of the holiness of God, as well as in bringing together "the rigid unity of the

Bush.*Nat*.4 (1858:98)

Pal.*Nat.Theol*.27 (Wayland 4:298-351)
Makr.*Log.kat*.4 (1871:56-57);
Blach.*Log*.13 (1882:142-43);
Jer.Niž.*Uč.Z* (1864:174-76);
Clrdge.*Rev.Rel*.1 (Coburn 1:103-11)

Rtl.*Unt*.2.41-42 (Ruhbach 38-39)

Mhlr.*Ath*.2 (1827-I:148-49);
Bau.*DG*.18 (1858:94)

Acts 17:28
Pal.*Hor.Paul*.13.1 (Wayland 3:307-8)
Döll.*Heid.Jud*.2.1 (1857:55)

Wilb.*Pr.Vw*.4 (1798:117)

Mnkn.*Bl*.20 (1828:246)

Lid.*Div*.7 (1867:634)

See vol.1:191-200

Mhlr.*Ges.Schr*.1.7.2 (1839-I:371)

Bau.*DG*.21 (1858:99);
Rtl.*Recht*.3.4.30 (1882-III:213)

Iv.*Gd.Kn*.2 (1887:12-37);
Iv.*Thsm*.7 (1899:195-226)

Aug.*Trin*.5.8-9.10 (*CCSL* 50:215-17)

system of God" with "the admission or fact" of evil, which "annihilates the unity of God's empire, leaving it in a fragmentary, cloven state." "Of the origin of evil," it had to be conceded in an apologetic understatement, "no universal solution has been discovered," and squaring it with the notions of God as first cause and of God as good remained a standard problem in many statements of Christian doctrine; but in any case it was mistaken to see some sort of correlation between degrees of evil and degrees of "punishment" in human experience.

But the arguments against polytheism, which had formed so prominent an element in the patristic case against paganism—often, beginning already with the sermon of the apostle Paul on the Areopagus, supported by testimony from pagan sources—were not only a critique of nature worship and a polemic against idolatry as "the crime against which God's highest resentment is expressed," but an affirmation of "one eternal and omnipresent power and Godhead." Sometimes, to be sure, this "utmost possible stress upon the unity of the Supreme Being" in ante-Nicene thought as "the primal truth which [the church] had to assert most emphatically in the face of polytheism" had led the church fathers to employ subordinationist language about the relation between the Father and the Son, which had then needed to be clarified in the fourth-century controversies over the doctrine of the Trinity. Christianity was set apart not only from these polytheistic religions, but from other forms of monotheism as well (specifically, it was thought, from Islam), by the intimate connection between this doctrine of one personal God and the concept of a single humanity and of a single universal religion destined to be the religion of all humanity.

From Judaism Christianity had inherited this "personal and concrete" formulation of "the concept of God." The conception of personality itself was an "unexplored enigma," but it was the key to the knowability of God. The very usage of the term "person [persona]" by Western theologians to render the Greek trinitarian term "ὑπόστασις," a rendering that the most prominent and influential of those Western theologians had himself found confusing, accounted for a certain ambiguity in its use as part of

Slv.*Bogočlv*. 5 (Radlov 3:67)

Newm.*Gram*. 1.5.2
(Ker 1985:85)

Newm.*Gram*.2.10.2.3
(Ker 1985:273-74)
Pal.*Nat.Theol*.23 (Wayland
4:268)

Newm.*Gram*. 1.5.2
(Ker 1985:86)

Lacrd.*Conf*.45 (Poussielque
4:265)
Hfmnn.*Enc*.1,1
(Bestmann 58)
Thom.*Chr*.7 (1856-I:12)

Clrdge.*Inq.Sp*.1 (Hart 40)

Camp.*Syst*.3.2 (1956:7);
Blms.*Rel*.2 (Casanovas 5:7-8)

the argument for the reality of God as "a personal God," which meant that God, as "self-existent [samosuščij]," was a person but "more than a person." Also among those who would have dissented from many of the presuppositions and implications attached to it, there would have been general acceptance of John Henry Newman's insistence that, quite apart from specifically Christian doctrine, "no one is to be called a theist who does not believe in a personal God, whatever difficulty there may be in defining the word 'personal.' " William Paley, whom Newman described as "this clear-headed and almost mathematical reasoner," had felt able to reason that "contrivance" in the universe "proves the personality of the Deity." Newman's statement of such personality as a tenet of natural religion led him to go on to the declaration of "the belief of Catholics about the Supreme Being that this essential characteristic of his nature is reiterated in three distinct ways or modes, so that the Almighty God, instead of being one person only, which is the teaching of natural religion, has three personalities," each of whom was to be identified with "the one personal God of natural religion." Whatever its intent, such a trinitarian statement could be construed as saying that to "prove the personal Divinity" natural theology was insufficient and it was necessary to appeal to "the divine authority" of "Jesus Christ" and of his church: while the "personality of God" would always remain a problem for philosophy, it had to become the primary axiom for Christian theology.

Other aspects and "attributes" in the doctrine of God—representative affirmations included "the Absolute, the innominable Self-caused [Αὐτοπάτωρ et Causa Sui], in whose transcendent 'I Am,' as the ground, is whatever verily is," and the repetition, several times, of the attributes "infinite, immutable, eternal"—were beset with a similar ambiguity. Paley's confidence led him to posit, "even in natural religion," a set of divine attributes that included the following: "omnipotence, omniscience, omnipresence, eternity, self-existence, necessary existence, spirituality." All of these were, he maintained, evident from the structure of the cosmos alone. Nevertheless, even on that basis he strove to avoid claiming

Pal.*Nat.Theol.*24 (Wayland
4:291)

See vol.4:23-24

Marc.*Inst.*10.3 (Tomassini
2:75)

See vol.2:261-70

Marc.*Inst.*10.3 (Tomassini
2:74)

See pp. 95-100 above

Jam.*McGl.*3 (1787:64);
Jam.*Sac.Hist.*3.4 (1802-II:71)

Hrth.*Log.*10 (1882:610);
Hrth.*Es.*45:21 (1883:420)

Chan.*Un.Chr.*3 (AUA 376)

Rtl.*Recht.*1.1.4;1.6.39
(1882-I:33-36;264-70)

Drnr.*Syst.*15 (1879-I:183)

Chan.*Lke.* (AUA 293)

Rtl.*Unt.*1.15 (Ruhbach 21);
Slv.*Rus.égl.*3.2 (Rouleau 245)

Drnr.*Syst.*15 (1879-I:183)

"more precision in our ideas than the subject allows of"; this he did by "confining our explanations to what concerns ourselves." It was necessary to defend the orthodoxy of theologians like Gregory of Rimini, who had rejected any "intrinsic" distinction between these various attributes of God; on the other hand, Latin theologians also rejected the teaching of Gregory Palamas, who, in order to defend the Eastern definition of salvation as participation in the divine nature, had distinguished between the essence of God and the attributes of God. The various doctrines of the atonement—and especially the theory of vicarious satisfaction—with their concepts of contradiction between divine mercy and "vindictive justice as essential to God" provoked debate over the doctrine of attributes; from opposite ends of the theological spectrum, a Greek Orthodox theologian and a Unitarian theologian both insisted on "harmony" between divine justice and divine mercy. Considered in themselves, it was being argued, these "attributes" of God did not have some sort of reality of their own, as though they were distinct and "habitual" parts of the divine being (which was how Anselmic orthodoxy was accused of treating them); they were "nothing but subjective human conceptions," since it was "from our own souls" that "we derive our knowledge of the attributes and perfections which constitute the Supreme Being." When this insight into their ontological status was combined with a definition of "omnipotence" as "first cause" and an emphasis on "the absolute transcendence" of God, however, the outcome could be "damaging to piety in a way that is foreign to Holy Scripture." The resolution of the dilemma between the objective and the subjective elements of the doctrine of God lay in "the doctrine of the image of God."

Maker of Heaven and Earth

Symb.*Apost.* (Schaff 2:45)

Jam.*Sac.Hist.*1.1 (1802-I:149)

When the Christian world view affirmed the reality of God, it did so by confessing, in the words of the Apostles' Creed: "I believe in God the Father Almighty, Maker of heaven and earth," and going on to affirm the doctrine of the Trinity; nothing could provide a more exalted idea of divine power than the history of the creation. This was, then, not only the

Lam.*Indiff*.26 (Forgues 3:178)
Makr.*Herm*.Acts 17:24
(1891:1483)

Döll.*Heid.Jud*.5.1 (1857:222)

Makr.*Log.kat*.2 (1871:22)

Mnkn.*Bl*.22 (1828:268)

Newm.*Gram*.1.5.2 (Ker 1985:86)

Jam.*Sac.Hist*.3.2
(1802-II:45-46)
Tor.*Car*.1.6 (1779-I:235-38);
Slv.*Bogočlv*.6 (Radlov 3:76)

Jam.*Sac.Hist*.3.2 (1802-II:40)
Pol.*Ep*.sal. (Bihlmeyer 114)
Jam.*Vind*.5.1 (1794-II:9)

Slv.*Rus.egl*.3.2 (Rouleau 245-48)

See vol.2:199-251

Clrdge.*Rev.Rel*.2 (Coburn 1:137);Slv.*Id.rus*.2 (Rouleau 85)
Pal.*Hor.Paul*.5.1 (Wayland 2:195)
Bau.*Röm*. (Scholder 1:202-3)

Dry.*Apol*.2.3.52
(1838-II:195-98)

first article of the Apostles' Creed, but "the first article of the creed of all the nations." God was known first as the Creator. The Christian doctrine of God as Maker of heaven and earth was the divine answer to the questions of cosmogony that had been raised in the world religions and in the speculations of thinkers like Hesiod, because according to the Christian faith the knowledge of the world, and not only the knowledge of God, came from revelation. All "language and teaching about God," according to one nineteenth-century review of New Testament doctrine, "begins with that with which originally all revelation on God's side and all knowledge of God on the side of rational beings began, with the creation of the world." Whatever its status among "all the nations," however, for orthodox believers of all the churches in all the centuries the doctrine of the "Maker of heaven and earth" as Trinity was "the normal faith which every Christian has," at least implicitly, and it was inseparable from the doctrine of redemption. In much of biblical history—and perhaps also in pre-Christian Greek speculation—the doctrines of unity of essence and plurality of persons were as closely interrelated as they were in biblical doctrine. When an ancient Christian writer spoke of "God Almighty" and meant by that title "God essentially considered," therefore, it did not necessarily follow that this referred only to the Father and not to the Son as well. The names Father, Son, and Holy Spirit in the Trinity were not mere metaphors, but referred to the mystery of divine being.

In this "vindication of trinitarian monotheism," Christianity was at the same time continuing to differentiate itself from the monotheism of the Jewish tradition. It had been God's purpose, through that monotheistic revelation to Israel, to preserve one nation from idolatry, in order to make it "a safe receptacle for the precursive evidences of Christianity." Therefore the Jewishness of primitive Christianity, as this was being uncovered by the historical-biblical research of the nineteenth century, had carried out a providential function. But now this function had been completed, and Judaism itself therefore had fulfilled its historic purpose; the Christian church, not

See vol.1:12-27
Döll.*Heid.Jud.*10.3.4
(1857:832-33);Lam.*Indiff.*23
(Forgues 3:42)

Gen.49:10;see vol.1:55-67
Newm.*Gram.*2.10.2.7 (Ker
1985:184-85)

Marc.*Inst.*22.1 (Tomassini
4:6-8)
Slv.*Bogočlv.*5 (Radlov 3:71);
Jam.*Sac.Hist.*3.5
(1802-II:148)
Schl.*Rel.* (1799) 5 (Pünjer
275)

Mak.*Prav.bog.*24 (Tichon
1:156)

Grnvg.*Pr.*17.vi.1832
(Thodberg 5:232)

Ex.3:14
Lam.*Par.cr.*42 (Forgues
11:158)

See vol.4:155-57;322-23

Grnvg.*Snd.Chr.* (Begtrup
4:459)

Mhlr.*Ath.*2 (1827-I:135)

Bush.*Nat.*12 (1858:39)

See vol.4:322-31

Clrdge.*Rev.Rel.*5 (Coburn
1:212);Clrdge.*Ref.*int.1
(Shedd 1:104-5)

See pp. 24-35, 91-92 above

See vol.4:322-31

the Jewish people, had the right to the title "the true Israel." Once again, the words of the prophecy of Jacob to Judah were read as an expression of that view of history: "A leader shall not fail from Judah, nor a ruler from his thighs, until that which has been laid up for him shall come; and he shall be the expectation of the nations." Although the Hebrew text could be translated in various ways, a word-by-word explication of the prophecy confirmed the traditional Christian exegesis of it, as well as of the related prophecy of Jeremiah 31:31-34 that there would be a new law and a new covenant. For most Christians, then, Judaism was "long since dead." Confessing no more than its monotheistic faith did not give one the right to be called a Christian, unless the specifically orthodox form of Christian monotheistic faith, the confession of "the great threefold name of God" as Trinity, was included. The primitive revelation given to Moses, "I am who I am," referred not merely to the oneness of God, but to "Father, Son, and Spirit."

Yet for a variety of reasons, most of them going back to the eighteenth century and earlier, the doctrine of the Trinity, though confessed by the Protestant Reformers no less than by the church fathers of East and West, had now become "a pestilence for rationalistic theologians"; and the assumption that it was a "revealed doctrine," an assumption that had characterized the thought of such theologians as Athanasius and had represented, as even its critics acknowledged, "a new, or modified conception of God, to accommodate the new fact of a gospel," could no longer be taken for granted in the professedly Christian theology of the nineteenth century. Ever since the Reformation era, Socinianism had been criticizing the received dogma on both biblical and rational grounds, but during the eighteenth and nineteenth centuries that criticism of "the idolatrous doctrine of the Trinity and the more pernicious doctrine of redemption" appeared with growing frequency and insistence also within churches that were professedly trinitarian in their confessed doctrine. At the same time Unitarianism, having begun in the period of the Reformation as a distinct form of Christian belief, was gradually beginning to take its

Schl.*Gesch*.4 (Reimer
11:599-600)

Chan.*Evid.Rev*. (AUA 221)

Chan.*Un.Chr*.1 (AUA 371)

Emer.*Div*. (Ferguson 1:90)
Emer.*Ep*.28.vii.1838 (Rusk
2:146-50)

Schl.*Krit*.1 (Reimer 7:293-94)
Marc.*Inst*.16.3 (Tomassino
3:22-28);
Grnvg.*Pr*.26.xii.1837
(Thodberg 11:98);
Makr.*Herm*.1 John 5:7
(1891:2446)

Schl.*Krit*.2 (Reimer 7:359)

Hdge.*Rom*.9:5 (1886:472)

Rom.9:5 (AV)

Schltz.*Röm*.9.5 (JDT
30:462-506)

Schl.*Ein.N.T*.2.1.50 (Reimer
8:169-70)

place alongside the trinitarian churches. As articulated by its most influential interpreter, William Ellery Channing, this Unitarianism saw itself as unequivocally Christian, defending the credibility of the miracles of Jesus and the reality of the supernatural revelation, but obliged to "object to the doctrine of the Trinity, that, whilst acknowledging in words, it subverts in effect, the unity of God." But when, in 1838, its most celebrated interpreter, Ralph Waldo Emerson, attacked traditional Christianity (including much of Unitarianism) for being excessively preoccupied with objective revelation from without and called on the preacher, as "a newborn bard of the Holy Ghost," to "acquaint men at first hand with Deity" without relying on external revelation, the resulting "dissent" over "the substantial truth of the doctrine" appeared to confirm the warnings long voiced by orthodox polemics that loss of the orthodox doctrine of the Trinity would eventually lead to loss of the reality of God.

One group of reasons for the jeopardy into which the orthodox doctrine of the Trinity had come was basically literary and textual. The most pertinacious and conservative in various communions were still holding out for the authenticity of the "Johannine comma" in 1 John 5:7, despite all the textual and patristic evidence against it, but there was an all but unanimous consensus among textual critics that it represented a later interpolation. In opposition to the standard way of parsing Romans 9:5, which orthodoxy had regarded as the "one interpretation of this important passage which can . . . be maintained" grammatically, there was debate over the possibility of punctuating it in such a way as to change the relative clause and apposition, "Christ, who is over all, God blessed for ever" (which identified Christ with God in a way that seemed to support the trinitarian dogma), into a separate exclamation, reading the verse to say: "Christ. God who is over all be blessed for ever." Although some philologists and orthodox theologians still read the abbreviation in 1 Timothy 3:16 (an Epistle whose Pauline authorship critics, beginning with Schleiermacher, were questioning in any case) to read "θεός [God] was

Hrth.*Herm.*1 Tim.3:16
(1882:103)

Lid.*Div.*5 (1867:311-12);
Mich.Od.*Ev.*4 (1865:173-75)

Jer.Niž.*Uč.*E (1864:152)
John 13:23

Hnbrg.*Vers.*8.3
(1852:670-80);
Marc.*Inst.*2.6 (Tomassini
1:122-23)

Ces.*St.eccl.*2 (1881:147)

Lam.*Déf.*12 (Forgues 5:122)

See pp. 265-81 below

manifest in the flesh," there was growing support for the theologically less explicit reading "ὅς [who] was manifest in the flesh."

Above all, "St. John's Gospel," it was observed, had become "the battlefield of the New [Testament]," because it was "the most conspicuous written attestation to the Godhead of Him whose claims upon mankind can hardly be surveyed without passion." Yet if, as an increasing number of New Testament critics maintained, the Fourth Gospel was not, as tradition had taught and as loyalists continued to teach, the work of "the disciple whom Jesus loved" but of some unknown (and considerably later) pseudonymous writer—who was, in turn, not necessarily the same one who had composed the three "catholic" Epistles of John or the Book of Revelation bearing the name of "John the Theologian," as traditional views of authorship still held—then its anticipation of "all the errors that ever have arisen or will arise against the divinity of Christ" and its attestation of the unique relation of Jesus to the Father were significantly diminished. One Roman Catholic noted that although Protestants still claimed to "believe with reason" that the Trinity and related doctrines "are clearly taught in Scripture," they had been unable, since the Reformation, to convince various antitrinitarians of this and were therefore compelled, at least in practice if not yet in theory, to "abandon their fundamental principle" of the sole authority of Scripture if they wanted to retain their affirmation of the orthodox doctrine of the Trinity.

Such textual, isagogical, and exegetical disputes connected with the biblical proofs for the dogma would continue to rage, but the special contribution of the nineteenth century to the discussion of the doctrine of the Trinity was its minute attention to research into the history of that doctrine, as the major part of its absorption in the history of dogma. The conclusions reached by such historical research did not in any simple way correspond to the theological orthodoxy or unorthodoxy of the various historical theologians pursuing it. Thus a scholar whose commitment to the orthodox doctrine of the Trinity as well as to the sole authority of Scripture permitted

Jam.*Vind*.pr. (1794-I:v)
Tert.*Praescrip*.13 (*CCSL*
1:197-98)
Jam.*Vind*.6.1
(1794-II:256-59)

Newm.*Scr.Prf*.5
(*Tr.Tms*. 85:68)

Newm.*Dev*.1.int.10
(Harrold 13)

Hrth.*Herm*.1 Tim.4:1
(1882:107)

Grnvg.*Ref*.3 (Begtrup 5:321)

Clrdge.*Ly.Serm*. (Coburn
6:181)

Mhlr.*Ath*.2 (1827-I:209-14)

Newm.*Ar*.2.5 (1890:219-21)
See vol.1:175;191-200

Bau.*Chr*.4 (Scholder
3:356-57)

Vnzi.*Rec*.2.9 (1864-II:112)

Marc.*Inst*.17.8.1 (Tomassini
3:92-96)

him to allow that even if "the majority of Christian writers, in the age immediately succeeding that of the apostles, had held a doctrine contrary to the obvious meaning of Scripture, they would not have merited our regard," nevertheless went on to assert that "the current of antiquity" did not in fact "oppose the trinitarian doctrine" but supported it, as the evidence of Tertullian's *Prescription of Heretics* from around the end of the second century demonstrated. On the other hand, one who warmly espoused the authority of that "current of antiquity" was compelled to admit that "there is on the whole a great secrecy observed in it concerning such doctrines (e.g.) as the Trinity and the Eucharist"; eventually he felt obliged to acknowledge concerning "the Catholic doctrine of the Trinity": "I do not see in what sense it can be said that there is a consensus of primitive divines in its favor" that would not support other and more doubtful doctrines as well or better.

When history supplanted polemics as a way of understanding the orthodox doctrine of the Trinity, the "supreme heresy" of the early centuries, subordinationism and Arianism, which had been the principal ancient opponent of that doctrine and which was now the one that was once again coming into favor among "its secret adherents, outwardly of other denominations," inevitably came in for new attention. Möhler's *Athanasius*, while written from the standpoint of its orthodox hero, nevertheless sought to grasp the biblical exegesis underlying what was eventually condemned as the Arian heresy. At about the same time, Newman's first book, *The Arians of the Fourth Century*, likewise an apologia for Athanasius, also strove to recognize how it could have been possible for the Arians to read Scripture in such a way. The "passages of distinction" in Scripture, which drew some difference between the Father and the Son, had provided exegetical support for the Arian position; the preservation of that distinction was the special program of Arianism. It was also the valid religious and theological concern underlying some of the "subordinationist" language of Origen, by which ancient and modern students of his works had often been offended.

Döll.*Gnos*.4 (1890:37)

See vol.1:176-80

Schl.*Chr.Gl*.172.3 (Redeker 2:471-73)
Slv.*Rus.égl*.3.10 (Rouleau 281)

See vol.1:201

Schl.*Chr.Gl*.171.3 (Redeker 2:465-66)

Thom.*Chr*.13 (1856-I:82)

Marc.*Inst*.17.9 (Tomassini 3:102-5)

Krks.*Dok*.2.2 (1874:116-17)

Ath.*Syn*.43 (Opitz 2:268-69)

Ath.*Ep.Afr*.2 (PG 26:1032)
Gen.14:14
Camp.*Prcl*.14.i.1837 (1875:45)

Rtl.*Theol.Met*.3 (1887:29)

The Sabellian alternative to Arianism, which had been revived in other systems, was likewise a heresy by ancient definition. Because it placed its emphasis on "passages of identity" that posited a simple identification of Christ with God, it could meanwhile be proposed by some as a preferable device for preserving the authentic concern at work in the early Christian experience of God. The doctrine of the Trinity safeguarded the doctrine of the unity of God; before saying anything at all about the Trinity of divine persons, the Council of Nicea had opened its creed with a declaration of faith in the divine unity: "We believe in one God." That declaration was compromised, however, whenever interpreters of the creed made "the Trinity superordinate, in which case the unity, as being abstract, falls into the background," which could lead to the consequent "danger of falling into tritheism." Thus it was evident historically as well as theologically that the primitive faith of the church had included "both elements, the unity and the differentiation, the deity and the distinct personality of Christ," and therefore that "these two elements constitute the dialectic of the entire historical movement of the dogma [of the Trinity]."

In form as well as in content, the climax of that historical movement, and therefore also of the historical and theological interest in the dogma of the Trinity now, was the formula of "homoousios" adopted by the Council of Nicea, which was directed against both extremes, the Arian and the Sabellian. It could be seen as the most flagrant historical instance of the Hellenization of the gospel, since, of the 318 bishops attending (a number that did not reflect the documents immediately surrounding the council, which usually speak of roughly 300, but the typological application, beginning already with Athanasius himself, of the number of servants who fought for Abraham), "315 were Greek and 3 Roman." Responding to such critics, who were alleging that through the homoousios and the dogma of the Trinity the Christian message had been corrupted by the introduction of an alien "layer of metaphysical concepts" derived from the natural philosophy of the Greeks, even its champions had to grant that the homoousios was "the one instance of a scientific word having been introduced into the Creed from that day to this," virtually all the rest of the creedal language being biblical in origin. In relation to "the dialectic of the entire historical movement of the dogma" between passages of distinction and passages of identity, the homoousios came out clearly on the side of the latter; in this formula, therefore, "the pattern of the development of the dogma of the deity of Christ reached the high point of the direction toward which it had been tending from the beginning and beyond which it was impossible to go, namely, the tendency to identify the Son with the Father as completely as possible."

Newm.*Gram.*1.5.3 (Ker 1985:97)
Thom.*Chr.*13 (1856-I:82)
Bau.*Chr.*4 (Scholder 3:361)

Eastern Orthodox supporters of the unalloyed dogmatic and creedal tradition of the Council of Nicea presented the dogma of the Trinity as the fundamental speculative principle of Christianity, and they attacked the West for tampering with the text of the Nicene Creed, particularly by inserting the doctrine of the Filioque. As Western theologians also had to acknowledge, patristic testimony on the Filioque was at best equivocal, though they continued to defend it against the East; Eastern theologians sometimes sought to argue, even from the strong language of the fifteenth book of *On the Trinity*, that Augustine's view of the procession of the Spirit was also ambiguous. "The Holy Spirit," Eastern theology insisted, "proceeds only from the Father" ontologically and in eternity, although the "economic" or historical "sending" of the Spirit was indeed also from the Son. Antitraditional Protestants, meanwhile, saw the Nicene Creed as "the first document of the kind embalmed on the pages of ancient history"; with it had "commenced the reign of creeds." Protestants whose confessional tradition included an explicit acceptance of the authority of the Nicene Creed and of its dogma of the Trinity defended this dogma against the charge that it was a "remnant of popery," and they urged that it belonged to the doctrines that were at one and the same time "confessedly Catholic" and "distinctive of Evangelical Christianity." Rejection of trinitarianism had once been confined to the Socinians and other radical groups of the Reformation period, but now the various species of rationalism within the mainline

Slv.*Bogočlv.*6 (Radlov 3:76)
Mak.*Prav.bog.*43 (Tichon 1:284-88)
Vnzi.*Rec.*2.12 (1864-II:167)
Marc.*Inst.*17.16 (Tomassini 3:142-49)
Aug.*Trin.*15.27.48 (*CCSL* 50:529-30)
Fil.*Ent.* (Sondakoff 32-34)
Jer.Niž.*Uč.*D (1864:146)
Chom.*Crk.*7 (Karsavin 28-29);Fil.*Ent.* (Sondakoff 27-28)
Camp.*Rce.*6 (Gould 796)
See vol.4:156-58
Krth.*Cons.Ref.*6 (1871:207); Grnvg.*Snd.Chr.* (Begtrup 4:459)
Krth.*Cons.Ref.*6 (1871:254-55)

Jam.*McGl*.1 (1787:8)
See vol.4:322-23

Drnr.*Syst*.30 (1879-I:379)

Schl.*Chr.Gl*.172 (Redeker
2:469)

Drnr.*Pers.Chr*.3.1.3
(1845-II:1192-97)

Newm.*Gram*.1.5.2 (Ker
1985:84)
Slv.*Duch.osn*.2.1.2 (Radlov
3:323)

See pp. 119-30 above

Thom.*Chr*.13 (1856-I:67-68)

Protestant churches were "just erect[ing] a platform for Socinians." The occasional comments critical of trinitarian terminology by various of the Reformers aside, it was clear to Protestant historians and theologians that, without denying the Trinity, the Reformers had relegated it to a secondary position in relation to their "immediate moral-religious interest, which sought and found its satisfaction in justifying faith" rather than in the Trinity, where the patristic tradition, especially in the East, had found it. From this reduction of emphasis on the trinitarian dogma within Reformation doctrine it appeared to follow that "we have the less reason to regard this doctrine as finally settled, since it did not receive any fresh treatment when the Evangelical [Protestant] Church was set up."

That observation was voiced in support of a version of the doctrine of the Trinity that many of its critics regarded as a recrudescence of Sabellianism. In its received form, as it was still being set forth by Eastern Orthodox, Roman Catholic, and confessional Protestant theology, the doctrine of the eternal being of an ontologically "immanent" Trinity, which "belongs to theology" but also to "the faith and devotion of the individual," was the presupposition for the doctrine of creation through the Logos, for the doctrine of the incarnation of the Logos, and for the "economic" relation within history between Father, Son, and Holy Spirit, as this was experienced by the church and by the individual believer. Part of the continuation of the eighteenth century's effort to interpret all Christian doctrines in the light of Christian experience was a reversal of roles between the "immanent" and the "economic" doctrines of the Trinity: the former was now said to be based on the latter, rather than the other way around, although the immanent metaphysical Trinity was still defended as an "objective reality," since "the objective standing of the trinitarian relationship is the necessary presupposition of our relation to God, of our personal fellowship with him, and we cannot retain this without that." When it appeared that a "doctrine of a historical Trinity, a threefold revelation of one God" was jeopardizing that objective reality, such a theory was rejected by traditional

Hdge.*Ess.Rev.*13
(1857:434-35)

Protestants as a "cheating mirage of a Trinity" and a betrayal of the doctrine taught by church and Scripture alike.

Although the nineteenth-century versions of the Arian and the Sabellian heresies appeared to be the immediate provocation for a vigorous reassertion of the orthodox doctrine of the Trinity, there was perceived to be, within and behind them, another and an even more basic error at work, "the subtle pantheism of the present hour": the teaching, with whose condemnation the *Syllabus of Errors* began, "that there is no supreme, all-wise, all-provident Divine Power [Numen divinum] that is distinct from this universe of things." The threat of pantheism to "identify the Creator with the creation, or else represent the Supreme Being as a mere impersonal law . . . differing from the law of gravitation only by its universality" had to be countered by the doctrine of the Trinity. Protestant and Orthodox theologians joined with Roman Catholics in recognizing that where that threat had prevailed, "the idea of personality" in God, in which "the theistic interest expresses itself the most decisively," yielded to "equivocation" and therefore to a position in which the ecclesiastical doctrine of the Trinity lost its "objective meaning" and became nothing more than a "formally binding proposition." Advocates of pantheism were presenting it as "of all the religious solutions, the most in accordance with scientific discoveries" and at the same time "not the least in accordance with the religious instinct that pervades the heart of every earnest man." Although defenders of orthodoxy acknowledged that "the strength of pantheistic systems lies in that craving both of the intellect and of the heart for union with the Absolute Being, which is the most legitimate and the noblest instinct of our nature," pantheism was not a proper account of the divine in Christ, which had to be based on "a restriction in favor of a single personality," not on an identification of the divine with the all, in which the particularity of Jesus Christ, together with every other kind of particularity, would be altogether submerged. The true religion was one in which both unity and distinctness, both

Iv.*Gd.Kn.*10 (1887:212);
Blms.*Escép.*9 (Casanovas
5:39-46)

Pi.IX.*Syll.*1.1 (*ASS* 3:168)

Clrdge.*Ref.*7.2 (Shedd 1:216)

Hüg.*Real.*6 (Gardner 65-68)

Bau.*Neun.*2 (Scholder
4:202-4);Slv.*Bogočlv.*5;7
(Radlov 3:68;106);Lid.*Div.*1
(1867:42-43);Mhlr.*Ath.*3
(1827-I:305-25)

Plmp.*Pan.*3.14 (1883-II:277)

Lid.*Div.*8 (1867:673-74)

Lid.*Div.*1 (1867:42-46)

Slv.*Soph*.int.1 (Rouleau 11)
Slv.*Bogočlv*.3 (Radlov 3:34)

Hdge.*Darw.* (1874:7;9)

Dry.*Apol*.2.1.11 (1838-II:39)
Slv.*Bogočlv*.5 (Radlov 3:68)
Döll.*Heid.Jud*.5.1
(1857:229;271)
Hdge.*Syst.Theol*.1.3.5
(1981-I:299-334)
Plmp.*Pan*.3.1
(1883-I:280-81)
See vol.3:95-105
Bau.*DG*.61 (1858:208-9)

Mhlr.*Lehr*.75 (1835:44-45)

Mntl.*Int.cath*.1 (Lecoffre 5:14)
Emer.*Nat*.7 (Ferguson
1:36-39)
Hdge.*Ess.Rev*.3 (1857:87)

Gffrd.*Lect*.1 (Jaki 105)

Clrdge.*Ref*.7.2 (Shedd
1:220-21)

Wlb.*Inc*.1 (1849:26)

Kol.*Káz*.7 (1844:86)

Kierk.*Syg.Dd*.2.B.B
(Drachmann 11:227)

Newm.*Scr.Prf*.7
(*Tr.Tms.* 85:99)
Lacrd.*Conf*.45 (Poussielque
4:255-79);Drnr.*Syst*.34
(1879-I:459);Pal.*Nat.Theol*.23
(Wayland 4:271)

"the one and the all," came together, without either being subordinated to the other.

Pantheism had been "one of the most widely diffused and persistent forms of thought" throughout human history, being present in various forms of primitive folk religion and in Western thought at least since the Greeks, as for example in the notion of God as the world soul. It had since passed through a long history, but not a continuous one, having appeared in at least one complete theological system, that of John Scotus Erigena, during the early Middle Ages. Not only the orthodox doctrine of the Trinity and the doctrine of creation, but such specifically Roman Catholic teachings as transubstantiation had been directed against it. Under the influence of recent trends in philosophy and in reaction to recent developments within the natural sciences, pantheism seemed now to pose a special danger to Protestant theology, especially in Germany but also in America, where Emerson's first work, *Nature*, was called by his critics a "rhapsodical oration in favor of pantheism" and was recognized as "the higher or subjective pantheism" even by his admirers. Pantheism had a natural affinity with rationalism and, as the outcome to which "the so-called demonstrations of a God" led, was "the natural resource of reflective minds." When a Christian preacher could assert that nothing in the doctrines of the church "teaches us more fervent prayer or higher thoughts and aspirations than the temple of the stars, with its flaming letters," it was evident that within the conventional belief of "Christendom," too, "the qualitative difference between God and man is pantheistically abolished, first in a highbrow way through speculation, then in a lowbrow way in the highways and byways." In the form of "the religion that is of beauty, imagination, and philosophy, without constraint moral or intellectual, a religion speculative and self-indulgent," the pantheistic spirit was spreading and would, so it was feared, become "the great deceit which awaits the age to come." Against that deceit, Christian theology affirmed a doctrine of God according to which the created world was distinct from its Creator and "the perpetual acting of God upon the lines of causes in

Bush.*Nat*.9 (1858:254)

Holb.*Evol.Scr*.8 (1892:239)

Mhlr.*Ath*.2 (1827-I:150-51)
Slv.*Bogočlv*.11/12 (Radlov
3:152);Slv.*Duch.osn*.2.1.5
(Radlov 3:334)

Lacrd.*Conf*.41 (Poussielque
4:140-41)

See p. 74 above

Marc.*Inst*.20.1 (Tomassino
3:279-83)

Clrdge.*Const*.1.1 (Coburn
10:20)

Hdge.*Syst.Theol*.3.19.8
(1981-III:322)

Jam.*McGl*.2 (1787:39)

See vol.1:35-37

Döll.*Gnos*.10 (1890:132-57)
Camp.*Ev*.3 (Owen 50);
Bau.*Chr*.3 (Scholder
3:185-88)

Lacrd.*Conf*.47 (Poussielque
4:314)

Tol.*Pan*.1.15 (1720:40)

nature" was distinct from the activity of nature as such, a doctrine that distinguished "clearly between a God omnipotent in nature and a God identical with it." Upon that distinctness depended such fundamentals of the Christian world view as the distinction between soul and body, the doctrine of the incarnation (which would have been impossible as well as unnecessary if pantheism were correct), and ultimately the very dogma of creation itself.

This "dogma of creation" was "an idea that separates [Christian believers] totally from idolaters." Despite Thomistic objections, Augustine's effort to affirm the freedom of God by positing a simultaneous creation of all things in a single instant rather than in six days of twenty-four hours each continued to find support, perhaps all the more so because during the nineteenth century science was replacing the six days of the Genesis account with eons; both those who had taught an instantaneous creation and those who now taught a gradual evolution were, in effect, reading the six days allegorically. In the biblical world view, "the idea of the Creator" was a presupposition fundamental "to the existence, yea, to the very conception of the existence, of matter itself." Although the doctrine of creation necessarily implied the doctrine of God and the two doctrines were inseparable corollaries, they were not identical doctrines, as though creation were attributed not "to absolute sovereignty," but "to a necessity of nature in the display of divine goodness." That insistence on the sovereignty and freedom of God the Creator had, in the history of Christian doctrine already during the patristic period, acquired the form of the definition of creation as "creation out of nothing [creatio ex nihilo]," a free divine action that had taken place without archetype, without demiurge, and without "cooperation between God and a certain inferior substance that is coeternal with God."

John Toland, who seems to have coined the word "pantheist," had, in his *Pantheisticon* of 1720, come out against "creation out of nothing" as a theory that neither Jewish cabbalists nor Greek philosophers acknowledged, but he maintained that he was "not contradicting the Mosaic cosmogony" when he called

Tol.*Pan*.1.4 (1720:8-9)

See pp. 243-44 below

Mak.*Prav.bog*.72 (Tichon
1:417);Ub.*Int*.1.1.38.int.
(1886-I:672-73);
Hdge.*Syst.Theol*.2.7
(1981-II:123-24)
Mak.*Prav.bog*.52 (Tichon
1:351)
Ub.*Int*.1.1.38 (1886-I:696)
Mynst.*Praed*.34 (1845-II:7)

Gen.1:1

Trtn.*Inst*.6.1.1 (1688-I:539)
Blms.*Rel*.2 (Casanovas 5:7-8)

Bas.*Spir*.8.19 (*SC* 17b:139)

Mak.*Prav.bog*.96 (Tichon
1:515)
Hrth.*Thrsk*.2.1 (1895:27-28)

Schl.*Chr.Gl*.38 (Redeker
1:190-93)

Symb.*Apost*. (Schaff 2:45)

Luth.*Kl.Kat*.2.2 (*Bek*.510)

Bush.*Nat*.13 (1858:406-7)

God "the eternal cause of the eternal world." Along with the other biblical narratives, however, that "Mosaic cosmogony," describing as it did the creation of heaven and earth and their continuing structure, was now being characterized as a myth rather than a scientifically credible account of the origins of the world and of the human race. Eastern Orthodox, Roman Catholic, and Protestant exegetes joined in defending the historicity of the creation narrative (or narratives) in the first chapters of Genesis; without it, Christian doctrines ranging from the angels and original sin to the ascension of Christ and his return to judgment seemed to be in jeopardy.

Another device for coping with that threat was to abolish, or at least to blur, the conventional theological distinction between creation and preservation. Traditionally, "creation" had been the term for the original establishment of the universe out of nothing "in the beginning," while "preservation" or "providence" was the term for the continuing activity of the Creator in maintaining it ever since: God was "Creator, Preserver and Orderer of all things." According to Basil of Caesarea as quoted by modern Eastern theologians, "all created nature, both this visible world and all that is conceived of in the mind, cannot hold together without the care and providence of God"; as "the perfect Creator" of the world, God was at the same time its "perfect Healer." Now it was being suggested that the authentic "content of the original expression" of faith could "be evolved out of either of the two doctrines," whether creation or preservation, since either of them, when pressed to its full meaning, tended to make the other "superfluous." In his *Small Catechism* Luther had explained the first article of the Apostles' Creed, "I believe in God the Father Almighty, Maker of heaven and earth," to mean "I believe that God has made me and all creatures"—not out of nothing, nor at the beginning, but by a "continuing creation" that church dogmatics preferred to call "preservation." Nevertheless, while it might be helpful to distinguish between "special" and "general" providence, and while it was certainly the case that "the Orthodox Church ascribes not only the work of creation, but the work of providence as well,

Mak.*Prav.bog.*100 (Tichon
1:529-30)

Drnr.*Syst.*34 (1879-I:478-80)
Hdge.*Syst.Theol.*1.11.1
(1981-I:578)

Mak.*Prav.bog.*120 (Tichon
1:597)
Hrth.*Es.*45:18 (1883:418);
Mak.*Prav.bog.*82 (Tichon
1:453-58)

Ath.*Inc.*13 (Cross 19-21)

Mak.*Prav.bog.*126 (Tichon
2:22)

Ath.*Ar.*3.10 (*PG* 26:344)

Wlb.*Inc.*3 (1849:73)

Joh.D.*Exp.fid.*26 (Kotter
2:75-77)

Jer.Niž.*Uč.*T (1864:411);
Hrth.*Thrsk.*1.3 (1895:15)

Blach.*Log.*1 (1882:15)

Feod.*Prav.*3 (1860:72-73)

Slv.*Bogočlv.*9 (Radlov 3:129)

Slv.*Bogočlv.*10 (Radlov 3:138)
Epiph.*Haer.*70.2.3-4 (*GCS*
37:234)

to all the persons of the Holy Trinity," that did not abolish the distinction between them, since "to identify them leads not only to confusion but to error."

The Divine Image

Both creation and providence were expressions of the divine "economy" and "order," Eastern Orthodox theologians affirmed, but this was expressed above all through "the divine image and likeness in man." According to the Athanasian treatise, *On the Incarnation of the Logos*, therefore, the Logos in the Trinity was identified "as the divine image according to which man was created. 'What then was God to do?' asks Saint Athanasius, 'or what was to be done except the renewing of that which was in God's image, so that by it men might once more be able to know Him? But how could this have come to pass except by the presence of the very image of God, our Savior Jesus Christ?" Athanasius had stated elsewhere that "although we were made after God's image and are called God's image and glory," the true meaning and content of this title could be learned only through a consideration of the Logos as "the true image and glory of God, which afterwards for our sakes became flesh, that we might have the gift of this appellation." Nineteenth-century theologians were quoting such statements of Athanasius to show the intimate connection between the doctrine of man as created in the divine image and the doctrine of the Logos as the divine image after which man was created. John of Damascus had emphasized "intelligence [τὸ νοερόν]," "free will [αὐτεξούσιον]," and "virtue [ἀρετή]" as the components of the image, and his definitions of these three continued to be quoted as orthodox doctrine; the image consisted of the human reason and spirit. But all of these qualities found their fullest expression in the Logos as "the substantial image of God," through whom "the image of archetypical humanity [pervoobraznoe čelovečestvo]" could be said to have its reality.

That connection was increasingly important for another reason as well: " 'Church doctrine,' according to Saint Epiphanius, 'believes that man is, in general, created according to the [divine] image; but it does not define, when it comes to the image, precisely in

Mak.*Prav.bog*.82 (Tichon
1:454)

Bau.*DG*.46 (1858:178-79)
Döll.*Heid.Jud*.5.1 (1857:287)

Gen. 1:26-27

Gen.9:6
1 Cor. 11:7;James 3:9

2 Cor.4:4;Col.1:15;Heb.1:3

Makr.*Herm*.Col.1:15
(1891:2028-29)

See vol.3:20-21
Makr.*Anth*.9 (1882:134)

Kierk.*Begr.Ang*.1.1
(Drachmann 4:298-99)

Andrts.*Dok.symb*.2.5.1
(1901:136-41)

Mhlr.*Symb*.2.5 (Geiselmann
57-63)

Mar.*Inst.symb*.21 (1825:34)

See pp. 243-44 below

which part [of man] this is to be found.' " Hence the
doctrine of the divine image was not, in the strictly
technical sense of the word, a dogma defined by the
church. There had been anticipations of the doctrine
of the image of God in Greek thought. But the
creation story in the Book of Genesis had left the
content of the divine image unspecified, and so it had
remained throughout the Old Testament, being employed, if at all, in substantiation of ethical commands and prohibitions rather than in clarification of
the doctrine of man. In the New Testament, likewise,
that ethical usage of the concept was prominent, but
the identification of the Logos in Jesus Christ as "the
divine image" in the original and eternal sense of the
word, the image that had existed before creation and
before time, eventually provided church doctrine with
a content for the assertion that man was created after
the divine image. The Augustinian theory that the
image in which man was created was the image of the
entire Trinity and that therefore there were "foot-
prints of the Trinity [vestigia Trinitatis]" in the
human soul found an echo also in Eastern Orthodox
anthropology. Yet as a "review of the different confessions" on original sin disclosed a "gradation" in
their teachings, so conversely it was possible to
discern a confessional difference also here on the
continuity of the image, a difference that had developed in the absence of an explicit dogma of the
universal church about the divine image: Roman
Catholic (and, to some degree, also Eastern Orthodox)
theologians invoked a distinction between the divine
image, which was retained even after sin, and "the
state of pure nature [pura naturalia]" before the fall,
which was lost, while Protestant theologians tended
to "teach that the divine image, [which consisted in]
holiness and righteousness, was intimately connected
with human nature before the fall" but that it had
been lost through the sin of Adam and Eve.

All of that took on critical importance in the
nineteenth century, since the doctrine of the special
creation of man carried theological consequences
graver still than those of the doctrine of creation as
such, being closely connected not only with the
doctrine of the inspiration of Scripture, as creation

Ub.*Int*.1.1.38 (1886-I:696)

Blach.*Log*.9 (1882:102-3)

See vol.2:75-90

See vol.2:85

Mak.*Prav.bog*.76 (Tichon 1:427)

Hfmnn.*Enc*.2.1.2 (Bestmann 194)

Clrk.*Darw*. (1873:10)

Tor.*Car*.2.2 (1779-II:67)

Clrk.*Darw*. (1873:2-4)

Bush.*Nat*.3 (1858:80)

Wilb.*Pr.Vw*.5;4 (1798:252;152)

Amrt.*Theol.eclec*.7.16 (1752-2-II:10);
Terst.*Abr*.1.8.8-10 (Becher 2:94-95); Wsly.*Serm*.1.int.1 (Baker 1:117)

Felb.*Hnd*.1 (1799:3)
Marc.*Inst*.21.2.3 (Tomassini 3:315);Drnd.*Fid.vind*.2.14 (1709:243-45)
Brnt.*Art.XXXIX*.9 (1700:110)
Bec.Lóp.*Sab.prod*.1 (1752:8);Mén.*Did*.2.3 (Blantès 119)
Wsly.*Serm*.5.1.1 (Baker 1:184)

Kol.*Káz*.2.15 (1844:199)

Hdge.*Syst.Theol*.2.5.2 (1981-II:96-99);
Spen.*Bed*.1.1.30 (Canstein 1:193-95);Slv.*Duch.osn*.1.int. (Radlov 3:274)

See vol.4:140-45

also was, but with the doctrines of original sin and of grace, as well as with the divine institution of marriage in the Garden of Eden—and, of course, with the doctrine of the incarnation of the Logos as "universal man." Man was, as Christian theologians had long taught, a "microcosm," because according to the Old Testament account all of the work of divine creation had reached its culmination with the creation of man in the divine image on the sixth and final day. But now "this account of the origin of man" in the divine image and likeness was facing an alternative to the Christian world view, in various "bizarre beliefs about the origin of man." "By the word 'image,' " one Christian response affirmed, "is understood the natural attributes of God, in which man resembled his Creator. By the word 'likeness' is understood the resemblance to God's moral attributes, in conformity to the divine nature." Because of the doctrine of creation in the divine image, "there neither is nor can be any middle position between humanity and no humanity"; there could not be a missing link.

When William Wilberforce, at the end of the eighteenth century, summarized the doctrine of the creation of man as a creation in which we were "made at first in the likeness of God and still bearing about us some faint traces of our high original," he was continuing that century's concern with the meaning of the divine image. The image consisted in dominion over the rest of creation, in the human body but in more than the human body, since it implied the uniqueness of the human soul among all earthly creatures and its reflection of the very Trinity of persons in the Godhead, "an incorruptible picture of the God of glory" and an image of divine love. In continuity with such eighteenth-century ideas, a representative nineteenth-century statement of the divine image described it as that by which God had "adorned man with the most capable body of any creature, endowed him with reason, free will, conscience, and an immortal soul." The image did not consist exclusively in human rationality or in moral responsibility, but in both. The denial of the freedom of the human will, which Roman Catholic theology continued to denounce as one of the "capital errors" of

Blms.*Prot.*11;23 (Casanovas
4:103;234-36)

Blms.*Rel.*11 (Casanovas 5:16)

Fil.*Sl.*52 (*Soč.Fil.*2:69)
Ath.Par.*Epit.*2.2.6
(1806:253-54)
Slv.*Rus.égl.*3.7 (Rouleau 263)

Döll.*Heid.Jud.*10.3.3
(1857:827)

Mnkn.*Bl.*23 (1828:281)

Acts 17:26

Mak.*Prav.bog.*87 (Tichon
1:478)

Fil.*Sl.*24 (*Soč.Fil.*1:177)

Gen.2:7 (AV)

Clrdge.*Ref.*1.9 (Shedd
1:119-20)

See vol.1:278-331
Lacrd.*Conf.*60 (Poussielque
5:222)

Kierk.*Begr.Ang.*1.3
(Drachmann 4:307)

Hdge.*Syst.Theol.*2.7
(1981-II:123-24)

Wilb.*Pr.Vw.*2 (1798:21)

Krth.*Cons.Ref.*9
(1871:365-66)

Luther and Calvin, amounted to a denial of creation in the image of God. While God had rule over man as He did over all creatures, He had, in the case of man, "individually made him His own, impressing upon him His seal, His image," which made man the king of creation and endowed him with sovereignty and freedom. Because the Maker of heaven and earth, the Creator in whose image humanity was formed, was, according to biblical teaching, a personal God, the divine image had to be reflected in human personality as well.

From the biblical version of "the descent of man," which consisted in the creation of Adam and Eve after the divine image as the common ancestors of all humanity and therefore in the descent of the entire human race from them, it followed that humanity did not have a multiple origin but was one race, since, as the apostle Paul declared, God "made from one every nation of men to live on all the face of the earth." In that primitive state, "Adam and Eve were perfect in both soul and body." Human nature, as the "temple of God," was "pure . . . and blessed, because the image of God was implanted in it." The words of the creation account, "And man became a living soul," made clear that man "did not merely possess it, he became it. It was his proper being, his truest self, the man in the man." As the Augustinian doctrine of nature and grace taught, Adam and Eve had possessed divine grace in "conjunction [concours]" with nature. Yet the more extravagantly the interpreters of the creation story portrayed the glory with which Adam was arrayed in receiving the image of God, "the more inexplicable became the fact that he could sin" at all, and therefore the more unbelievable became the entire biblical account, whether of the creation or of the fall.

To the spokesmen for orthodox doctrine, however, it was obvious and necessary "that the account of the probation and fall of man is neither an allegory nor a myth, but a true history." They saw the assertion of human corruption through the fall as "eminently the basis and groundwork of Christianity," for it located man, whether in nature or in history or in grace, between God the Creator and Christ the Redeemer. Although they felt able to present this view of the fall

Mak.*Prav.bog*.93 (Tichon 1:507-12)

Newm.*Dev*.1.int.16 (Harrold 20)

See vol.1:320

Rtl.*Unt*.2.35 (Ruhbach 35)

Krks.*Ekkl.Hist*.95 (1897-I:300)

Thom.*Chr*.30 (1856-I:375)

Döll.*Gnos*.11 (1890:163-64)

Döll.*Ref*.3 (1846-III:31)

Ps.51:5

Döll.*Ref*.3 (1846-III:490)

See vol.4:142-45

Rtl.*Theol.Met*.6 (1887;55-65); Pus.*Hist*.1 (1828-I;10-11;35)

Holb.*Evol.Scr*.8 (1892:253-54)

Acts 17:26

Rom.5:12

See vol.1:299-300

and original sin (or "hereditary sin," as many languages called it), as far as it went, as the common property of the Christian doctrinal tradition, Eastern and Western, the historical scholarship of the period was disclosing that on this very doctrine there seemed to be less agreement in the ancient doctrinal tradition than on some that were now at issue between the heirs of that tradition. As Augustine's opponents had contended, his explanation of original sin had been a theological innovation; thus, as one Greek Orthodox historian put it, both Augustine and Pelagius had been driven by their controversy over sin and grace into "total antithesis and extreme exaggeration." By contrast with Augustine, the Greek church fathers, contending as they were "against the fatalism of the pagan world view" and against the dualistic understanding of original sin in Gnosticism, had made the defense of human free will a necessary and primary corollary of the divine image. When the disciples of the Reformers pressed Augustine's (and Luther's) exegesis of the words of the psalm, "Behold, I was brought forth in iniquity, and in sin did my mother conceive me," to the extreme of debating whether, as a consequence of the fall, original sin had become part of the "essence" of human nature or was an "accident," they were no longer debating a point of biblical doctrine but had moved over into the realm of Greek metaphysics.

In many ways, the implications of the evolutionary hypothesis represented a still more profound danger to the doctrine of original sin than they did to the doctrine of creation in the divine image. Even those who did not accept the literal historicity of the account in the first chapters of Genesis wanted to hold to the common origin of the human race. Although the statement of Paul to the Athenians that God had "made from one [that is, from Adam] every nation of men" had been taken to prove that the entire human race was descended from a single set of parents, it was another passage, the statement of Paul to the Romans that "in [Adam] all have sinned," that had become, especially through the speculations of Augustine, the locus classicus for the transmission of human sin from a single set of parents. Therefore the nineteenth-century Christian responses to evolutionism, which sometimes tended to make the authority and inspiration of Scripture the primary question when the origin of species and even the descent of man were at issue, finally located the fundamental threat here in the doctrine of the fall and of original sin. The authoritative twentieth-century summary of those nineteenth-century responses, the encyclical of Pius XII, *Humani generis* of 1950, rejected "polygenism," the suggestion that " 'Adam' signifies some sort of multitude of first parents," basing that rejection almost solely on the specific grounds that "it is impossible to see how such a statement can be squared with those that the sources of revealed truth and the acts of the magisterium of the church set forth about original sin, which proceeds from a sin that was truly committed by a single Adam."

For the "magisterium" of the Roman Catholic Church, one of the major corollary dangers in any view that seemed to negate the Augustinian doctrine of original sin was the threat that thereby the entire structure of the church's doctrine of Mary would be undercut. Although Eastern Orthodoxy and Protestantism continued in their opposition to the immaculate conception of the Virgin Mary on the grounds that the biblical statement "all have sinned" knew no exception except Christ himself, it finally became an official dogma in 1854, by the action of Pope Pius IX: "From the beginning and before the ages" God had elected the Virgin Mary to be the mother of Christ, and therefore "the most blessed Virgin Mary in the first instant of her conception was, by the singular grace and privilege of Almighty God and in view of the merits of Christ Jesus the Savior of the human race, preserved immune from all the stain of original guilt." The doctrine of the immaculate conception, as it had been developed in the later Middle Ages above all through the theology of Duns Scotus and as it had now "become common since the time of Scotus," strove to hold together two Augustinian teachings: the universality of original sin through the fall of Adam and Eve, and the exceptional privilege of Mary. Its promulgation by the Council of Basel-Ferrara-Florence had been disqualified not on the substantive

See pp. 242-45 below

Pi.XII.*Hum.gen.* (*AAS* 42:576)

Chom.*Crk*.9 (Karsavin 38); Andrts.*Symb*.2.6 (Regopoulos 201-2); Grnvg.*Pr*.12.iii.1837 (Thodberg 10:151-56)

Rom.3:23

Krks.*Antipap*.2 (1893:43-44)

Pi.IX.*Ineff.* (*Pii IX Acta* 1:616)
See vol.3:71-72;171; vol.4:38-50;302-3

Hno.*Theol*.5.pr.;6.2.2.1 (1785-V:A2r;VI:408)

See vol.1:314

See vol.4:44-45

See pp. 248-52 below

Dmls.*Arch*.2.3 (1865:80-85)

Kbl.*Oc*.3 (Pusey 137)

Wilb.*Pr.Vw*.7 (1798:310)
Jam.*Sac.Hist*.3.4
(1802-II:102)
Or.*Cels*.6.63 (*GCS* 3:133-34)

Thom.*Chr*.24 (1856-1:225)
Schl.*Chr.Gl*.93 (Redeker
2.34-43);Bau.*Vers*.3.2
(1838:619-27)
Grnvg.*Pr*.26.xii.1825;
8.v.1823;11.iv.1823
(Thodberg 4:49;1:259;2:167)

Lid.*Div*.6 (1867:475-76)

Ces.*V.Ges.Cr*.14 (1830:282)

Ces.*V.Ges.Cr*.2 (1830:38)
Ces.*V.Ges.Cr*.2 (1830:27);
Lacrd.*Conf*.6.3 (Poussielque
6:232)

Blach.*Log*.15 (1882:189)

See vol.4:27-28

grounds of the doctrine itself, but on the procedural grounds of the schismatic status of the council by the time it legislated this doctrine. The doctrine had continued to hold the loyalty and devotion of believers; and now it seemed necessary to make it unquestionably official, both for the sake of vindicating, against ecclesiastical and political enemies, the authority of the pope to define doctrine and on account of the contemporary attacks upon the entire Augustinian system of sin and grace.

For a growing number, and not only within Roman Catholicism, it was becoming evident that both the doctrine of the divine image in man and the doctrine of the fall of man had developed historically—and now had to be formulated theologically—not a priori from the doctrine of creation, but a posteriori from the doctrines of the incarnation and the redemption: the image consisted in "supernatural goodness, like to that which our Lord restores to us by his grace"; and the "guilt of sin" could be fairly estimated only "by the costly satisfaction which was required to atone for it," which was "the most striking display" of divine holiness and justice in the entire history of the world. As Origen had already argued against Celsus, it was essential to distinguish "between what is 'in the image of God' and His image. . . . The image of God is the firstborn of all creation, the very Logos and truth." Man was created in the "divine image [Ebenbild Gottes]," but the Logos as divine image was the "primal image [Urbild]" and, as such, the "ideal image" as well as "the eternal image of God." Man was "the highest point in the visible universe," but Christ as the Logos was "the adequate image of God, God's self-reflection in His own thought, eternally present with Himself." The image of God had become incarnate through the Virgin Mary. Salvation, therefore, achieved far more than the simple restoration of the "original righteousness" that had been given in creation: salvation conferred a participation in the divine nature itself. "The resurrection of our Lord Jesus Christ from the dead," one Eastern Orthodox preacher asserted, had disclosed the mystery of the will of God "for the salvation and the deification of man." As it had in previous periods, such discussion

Thom.*Chr*.26;34
(1856-I:261-69;II:2-3);
Marc.*Inst*.22.12.1 (Tomassini
4:81-83)

Grnvg.*Chr.Brnlr*.11 (Begtrup
9:433)

Mak.*Prav.bog*.132 (Tichon
2:42-43)

Schl.*Chr.Gl*.22 (Redeker
1:129-34)

Fil.*Star*.4 (1855:67-84);
Mak.*Rask*.1.4 (1858:84-88)

Aug.*Vera relig*.44.82 (*CCSL*
32:241-42);Wlb.*Inc*.6
(1849:169)

Thom.*Chr*.37 (1856-II:57)
Bush.*Vic.Sac*.1.2 (1866:73);
Iv.*Gd.Kn*.9 (1887:187)
Slv.*Bogočlv*.11/12 (Radlov
3:151)

Kbl.*Spir*.89 (Wilson 163)

Matt.22:42

Kierk.*Syg.Dd*.2.2.3
(Drachmann 11:240)

Str.*Chr*.3 (Geischer 99-100)

of salvation as "deification" once again managed to raise, but once again failed to settle, speculation about whether or not there would have been an incarnation of the Son of God if there had not been a fall.

Less controversial was the insistence that although the fall of man had made the incarnation necessary, it was the divine image in man that had made it possible. Therefore the "natural heresies" in the doctrine of Christ could be described not only in the conventional way as those (such as Arianism) that denied his complete divinity and those (such as Apollinarism) that denied his humanity, but also as those (including Pelagianism) that seemed to make Christ unnecessary and those (including Manicheism and pantheism) that seemed to make Christ impossible. Even behind the apparently trivial disputes between Russian Orthodoxy and the Raskol over the right way to pronounce the name "Jesus" lay the concern with identifying the right relation of the individual and the church to him. Augustine, who formulated the doctrine of original sin, also saw the divine image as the indispensable presupposition of redemption and revelation. In assuming human nature through the incarnation, the Logos did not come to an alien element, but to one that he had, already by the original act of creation in the divine image, prepared as his habitation. As the divine image in person, he was the guide to the nature of God. The God-man was the Second Adam.

While Christian worship did not distinguish between his divine and his human nature, it was the doctrine of his divine nature that now seemed to be in jeopardy. The familiar question in the Gospels, "What do you think of Christ?" was still, as it had been then, "actually the most crucial of all questions." Going far beyond the tentative suggestions of his predecessors, David Friedrich Strauss criticized them, especially Schleiermacher, for failing to come to terms with the elements of "myth" that appeared not at the periphery but at the center of the picture of Jesus in the Gospels. The writers of the New Testament, Strauss said, "narrate about him chiefly things that are supernatural, but we can accept, also about him, only what is natural." Since such

See pp. 225-26 below

Bau.*Chrpart.* (Scholder 1:37)

2 Cor.5:16

Jam.*McGl.*3 (1787:80)

Kierk.*Syg.Dd.*2.2.3
(Drachmann 11:237)

See vol.1:256-66

Lid.*Div.*6 (1867:472-75);
Jam.*McGl.*4 (1787:115-19)

Slv.*Bogočlv.*11/12 (Radlov
3:156)

Thom.*Chr.*40 (1856-II:141)

Drnr.*Pers.Chr.*3.2.C
(1845-II:1261-66)

See vol.1:52-54

Slv.*Bogočlv.*11/12 (Radlov
3:151)

Mēn.*Did.*1.7 (Blantēs 71)

Kierk.*Begr.Ang.*1.2
(Drachmann 4:305)

Thom.*Chr.*20 (1856-I:186);
Vnzi.*Rec.*1.6 (1864-I:45)

"supernatural" passages were the very ones that had served church dogma as the foundation for orthodox christology, the concentration of nineteenth-century New Testament scholars on the historical and literary issues in the study of the Gospels inevitably raised theological and doctrinal issues also, well before the special problem of the "eschatological error" in the teachings of Jesus compelled attention. Whatever its original polemical intent may have been, the stricture of the apostle Paul on "knowing Christ according to the flesh" applied to anyone who now "sets aside both the deity of Christ and the truth of his atonement at one stroke."

At the same time, Christ was to be seen as the revelation not alone of God to man, but of man to man: "He says, 'Here you see what it is to be a human being.'" The orthodox doctrine of preexistence, kenosis, and exaltation continued to be the normative way of reading the christology of the New Testament in most of the churches, and the reality of kenosis required the reaffirmation of the conciliar doctrine that in Christ there had been not only a divine will but a distinct and free human will. But in some theologians "kenosis" as a concept of "the self-limitation of the divine" was being carried to a point that seemed to be attributing the suffering and death of Christ to his divine as well as to his human nature and thus to be endangering long held dogmatic presuppositions about the absoluteness and impassibility of God. In the Pauline concept of Christ as the second Adam there appeared to be a parallelism that made it possible to do justice to the "double image" of God in man, as represented by Paradise and by the cross; but interpretations of that parallelism in the form of a "doctrine that they correspond to each other" led to a warning against a theory that "explains nothing at all but confuses everything." Rather, it was necessary to begin with Christ the Logos as the "primal image of man" and then to proceed, as Irenaeus and other church fathers such as Gregory of Nyssa had done, to the interpretation of "redemption as the renewal [of man] to this image." In an unfallen state revelation would have been needed to impart the knowledge of God, but in a fallen state it had a new

Dry.*Apol*.1.2.3.18
(1838-I:170-71)

Clrdge.*Ref*.1.20 (Shedd
1:125)

Mhlr.*Ges.Schr*.1.3
(1839-I:138)

Thom.*Chr*.53 (1856-III:52)
See vol.3:129-44

Wilb.*Pr.Vw*.2 (1798:46)
Wilb.*Pr.Vw*.5 (1798:247)

Thom.*Chr*.51 (1856-III:22)
Blach.*Log*.14 (1882:162)

Döll.*Heid.Jud*.7.4 (1857:532)

Jam.*McGl*.1 (1787:13)

Ces.*V.Ges.Cr*.12 (1830:246)

Camp.*Prcl*.19.i.1837
(1875:267);Camp.*Syst*.10
(1859:21-30)

See vol.4:149-50;254-55

Döll.*Ref*.3 (1846-III:80)
Dmls.*Arch*.3.2.1.1
(1865:126-41)

purpose in addition: to counteract sin and to grant redemption.

As an intervention by God in human life and history, and then as an "undertaking of man," this "intention to form the human mind anew after the divine image" was central to Christian doctrine and life, as Anselm's enterprise of "faith in search of understanding" had shown. Although it was possible to say, in one sense, "that the incarnation itself is already the establishment [Herstellung] of fellowship with God," the incarnation was not the "reestablishment [Wiederherstellung]" of that fellowship, which came only through redemption and reconciliation, as, once again, Anselm's speculations in *Why God Became Man* had shown. Exponents of the Anselmic "scheme of redemption by the atonement of Christ" followed him in positing a correlation between sin and redemption. Consequently, as Anselm had insisted, a simple "amnesty" was not an adequate way for a just God to forgive sin, because God could not contradict his own justice, which was his very nature; paganism had already recognized the need for sacrifices of atonement. It was "necessary to the whole of our faith and hope" to distinguish between the relation that Christ as Son of God had with the Father, according to which "he was always the object of the Father's delight," and the relation that he had "in so far as he bare our sins," according to which "he was, on our account, the object of His anger."

Thus God had commanded the death of his beloved Son. Even (or perhaps especially) those theologians who did not want to be identified as upholders of the medieval and Anselmic tradition, or of any other postbiblical tradition, could assert: "That the death or sacrifice of Christ is the great sin offering, and the only sin offering, is a cardinal doctrine of Protestantism." Roman Catholic theologians did criticize the Reformation doctrine of justification as imputation on the grounds that it had fundamentally altered the doctrine of redemption as satisfaction; in their expositions of "the righteousness of faith," Eastern Orthodox theologians criticized it on the grounds that it failed to distinguish between "first justification," which came solely by faith in the

Makr.*Herm.*James 2:14
(1891:2339);Blach.*Log.*2
(1882:22-46)

See vol.4:324-25

Marc.*Inst.*25.2 (Tomassini
4:276);Fil.*Ent.* (Sondakoff 8)

Bush.*Vic.Sac.*int. (1866:30)
Chan.*Calv.* (AUA 459)

Chan.*Un.Chr.*2 (AUA 375)

Klfth.*DG.*37 (1839:87)

Jam.*Sac.Hist.*3.13
(1802-II:349)

Slv.*Bogočlv.*11/12 (Radlov
3:150-51)

Bau.*Vers.*1.2.1 (1838:169)

Bau.*Christpart.* (Scholder
1:71)

merit of Christ, and the "justification" on Judgment Day, which would be based on works as well as on faith, since faith without works would be useless there. Yet in opposition to the Socinian rejection of the doctrine of vicarious satisfaction through the death of Christ, Roman Catholic and Eastern Orthodox theologians could still declare it to be an ecumenical consensus that "all the rest of Christendom," whether Roman Catholic or Eastern Orthodox or Protestant, refused to be content with the idea that "redemption" through the death of Christ was merely "metaphorical, not true or real."

Nevertheless, the most striking feature of discussions about redemption through the cross of Christ in the nineteenth century was the widely held feeling that "if Christ has simply died to even up a score of penalty . . . , there is much to revolt the soul, at least in God's attitude, and even to raise a chill of revulsion" and of "abhorrence." Some went so far as to charge that the orthodox doctrine of the atonement through the death of Christ "robs his death of interest, weakens our sympathy with his sufferings, and is, of all others, most unfavorable to a love of Christ." It was felt that the concentration of the fathers and church councils on the Trinity and the person of Christ had caused the doctrines of soteriology—except for such an essay as Anselm's—to be largely neglected throughout the development of Christian doctrine and that they were coming into their own only now. Despite the conventional definition of sacrifice as "the substitution and punishment of the innocent instead of the guilty," Anselm's explanation of the transaction involved in redemption came in for criticism on the grounds of its total and excessively "juridical" preoccupation with the satisfaction of divine justice: divine love did not enter into the Anselmic calculations until at the very end. Such a theory of redemption likewise ignored the polemical context of the Pauline emphasis on the death of Christ. Earlier attempts to formulate a doctrine of the atonement, such as that of Origen, against which Anselm's critique had been directed, proved, upon closer inspection, to have exhibited the message of the

Thom.*Chr.*59
(1856-III:189-98)

Wms.*Res.*4.13 (*Tr.Tms.*87:38)

Rtl.*Recht.*1.4.21
(1882-I:141-45)

Rtl.*Recht.*1.6
(1882-I:256-346)

Rtl.*Recht.*2.3.29
(1882-II:246)

Gal.1:4;Eph.5:2
Rtl.*Recht.*2.3.27
(1882-II:228)
See vol.3:137
Rtl.*Unt.*2.50 (Ruhbach
43-44)

Rtl.*Recht.*3.6.50
(1882-III:438)

gospel more faithfully than had been supposed. Although Anselm presupposed the orthodox dogma of the two natures of Christ in his construction of the meaning of the atonement, the church fathers had proceeded in the opposite direction: "Christ crucified is the first doctrine taught; the knowledge of our Lord's divinity, the last men come to learn."

There was perhaps no review of this doctrine more thorough in its historical examination and exegetical grounding, nor more influential in its proposal of an alternative to the Anselmic theory, than that of Albrecht Ritschl, whose three-volume work, *The Christian Doctrine of Justification and Reconciliation*—the first volume on the history, the second on the biblical exegesis, and the third on the systematic theology— amounted to a dogmatics written from the point of view of justification and reconciliation. The order of the two doctrines in the title was significant: Ritschl believed himself to be recovering the centrality of the Reformation doctrine of justification by faith as the ground also for any doctrine of reconciliation and atonement; relating the two the other way around, as classical Protestant dogmatics had done, made the teaching of the Reformers about justification an adjunct to the medieval Anselmic theory about reconciliation. That theory itself should not have been accepted as uncritically as the successors of the Reformers (though not the Reformers themselves) had accepted it. Not only were there, "alongside the statements about the saving value of the death of Christ that are arranged according to the scheme of the concept of sacrifice, several others in the apostolic letters that are unrelated to this manner of viewing it"; but the use of the idea of sacrifice itself in the Pauline Epistles did not need to be interpreted as though "Paul intended to promulgate a dogma." Rather, as the church had long been teaching, Christ was to be seen as both sacrifice and priest. Hence the Anselmic "supposition of an antithesis between the grace or love of God and his justice, which in relation to sinful humanity would lead to a contradiction that must be resolved through the work of Christ, is unbiblical."

The Progress of the Kingdom

See vol.4:138-55;279-89
Rtl.*Recht*.2.1.5
(1882-II:26-34);Söd.*Und*.1
(1933:4)

Rtl.*Recht*.2.4.33
(1882-II:296)

Lam.*Par.cr*.37 (Forgues
11:142)

Clrdge.*Ref*.4.1 (Shedd 1:146)

Mnschr.*DG*.1.2.1
(Coelln-Neudecker 1:41-76)

See p. 321 below

Rtl.*Unt*.1.8 (Ruhbach 17)
Lam.*Déf*.16 (Forgues
5:166-67)
Matt.11:12

Lam.*Par.cr*.22 (Forgues 11:84)

What Albrecht Ritschl proposed to substitute for the Anselmic schema of reconciliation and justification, as these doctrines were taught—and in that order, with objective reconciliation being followed by subjective justification—alike by orthodox Protestants and by Roman Catholics (in spite of the differences between them on the doctrines of justification by faith and justification by faith and works), was the recovery of the central meaning of the original "proclamation of the kingdom of God," which was "the dominant idea of Jesus" in the synoptic Gospels, despite its absence from the Epistles of the New Testament: the proclamation neither of justification nor of reconciliation nor ultimately even of redemption (as all three of these had been traditionally understood by all the churches), but of the rule of God. In his concentration on the kingdom of God and in his effort to recover it as a doctrinal theme, Ritschl was reflecting a concern that had become general among his contemporaries, as a central part of their attention to "the foundation of faith in God and faith in Christ" on which the kingdom of God, as the rule of justice in the human spirit and the rule of love in the human heart, was grounded. Like the original apostles, therefore, "all teachers of moral truth" could without presumption consider themselves to be "ambassadors for the greatest of kings." Although the doctrine of the kingdom of God was not a dogma of the church in the precise sense of the word, its history was the topic in one of the first chapters of the first "history of dogma." It would also become a fundamental presupposition for the theology of the social gospel in the late nineteenth and early twentieth centuries.

The kingdom of God was, in Ritschl's words, both "supernatural" and "supramundane"; it nevertheless existed "for the sake of preserving the truth on earth," being obliged, as the Gospel said, to "suffer violence" within human history and society. The concern for the kingdom of God in the nineteenth century was expressed perhaps most succinctly in the slogan

Lacrd.*Conf.*40 (Poussielque 4:95-123)

Matt.6:10
Lam.*Ep.*8.vi. 1834 (Forgues 14:371)

Klfth.*DG*.28 (1839:57)

Ub.*Int*.2.prol. (1886-III:8)

Bush.*Vic.Sac.*1.2 (1866:62)

Bush.*Nat*.8 (1858:221)

Jam.*Sac.Hist.*1.1
(1802-I:147-48);Clrk.*Darw.*
(1873:22)

Hdge.*Darw.* (1874:52;168)

Iv.*Chr.Evol.*4 (1894:50-68)

Hdge.*Syst.Theol.*2.1.2
(1981-II:23)

Bush.*Nat*.9 (1858:264)

coined by a French Roman Catholic: "The perpetuity and the progress of the kingdom of Jesus Christ"; as another French Roman Catholic put it, commenting on the second petition of the Lord's Prayer, "his kingdom comes progressively." A sense of "progress" as the pattern of Christian faith and teaching was manifesting itself across confessional boundaries: a Protestant historian of doctrine could describe the "change" that had taken place in his own field since the eighteenth century as "progress," and a Roman Catholic Scripture scholar could use the same term to characterize what was happening to biblical hermeneutics, at any rate within his own church. While "there is and can be no such thing as internal progress in God, that is, in his character," it was nevertheless true that in the history of "the ways of God"—for example, in the contrast between the Old Testament and the New, or for that matter between earlier stages of Christian history and the present—there could be genuine progress.

The theme of progress in the nineteenth century was not confined to the interpretation of the kingdom of God and the Christian message, but was manifesting itself throughout the literature, philosophy, history, and natural science of the time. "The world is just now taken, as never before," one theologian observed, "with ideas of progress." The most perceptive theological critics of the evolutionary philosophy recognized that, for all its threat to the Christian doctrine of the origins of the world and of humanity, its most devastating consequences lay rather in its implications for Christian eschatology and teleology and for the biblical picture of human destiny. It was "neither evolution, nor natural selection, which gives Darwinism its peculiar character and importance," one theological critic observed; "it is that Darwin rejects all teleology, or the doctrine of final causes" in his "exclusion of design in the origin of species." If this "strife against purpose" was successful, "teleology, and therefore mind, or God, is expressly banished from the world." Without teleology it was impossible to understand "what is meant by the fact that the supernatural works of God are dispensed by fixed laws." It was important to remember that

Slv.*Soph*.2.1 (Rouleau 54)

Slv.*Rus.égl*.int. (Rouleau 146-47)

Lam.*Indiff*.25 (Forgues 3:141)

Lam.*Indiff*.37 (Forgues 4:390)

Iv.*Chr.Evol*.11 (1894:207)

Iv.*Thsm*.10 (1899:318-19)

See vol.3:42-43

Lam.*Indiff*.17 (Forgues 2:121)

Gers *Aufer*.2 (Gloricux 3.298)

Lam.*Rel*.6.1 (Forgues 7:126-27)

Gr.XVI.*Tr*.disc.pr.25 (Battaggia 42-44)

Ces.*St.eccl*.1.1 (1881:13)

Slv.*Bogočlv*.2 (Radlov 3:14-15)

Slv.*Krit*.22 (Radlov 2:155-59)

Matt.18:18

Fil.*Sl*.77 (*Soč.Fil*.2:213)

Hrth.*Es*.9:6 (1883:130)

"progress" could be highly ambiguous: there had likewise been a "progress of atheism," of anarchy, and of secularism.

Therefore a belief in "the progress of the kingdom" and an awareness that "the true religion develops in accordance with the progress of the times," as it had done at the beginnings of the gospel, constituted an important part of the theological response to evolution as well. While they still strove to make Christ an exception to the evolutionary process, philosophical theologians like James Iverach at Aberdeen, who were intent on harmonizing evolution and theology, likewise had recourse to that belief in the kingdom, arguing that the acceptance of evolution as a method of divine working meant that revelation itself was "of a piece with that process of evolution which has for end and purpose the establishment of the kingdom of God." The climax and conclusion of a series of apologetic lectures that Iverach delivered just before the end of the century under the title *Theism* was a statement of the faith that "this God is represented as working and toiling through the ages in order to make man, and to raise man to that divine ideal for each man and for all men in the kingdom of God."

Since the patristic and medieval periods, the term "kingdom of God" had often been equated with "church," and it still was. The universe was a monarchy in which the Almighty was king; but as Gerson had said, "the church was founded by Christ upon one monarch over all," namely, upon Peter and his successors, when he gave them the keys of the kingdom of heaven and all the "privileges and promises" that went with these. The Eastern Orthodox agreement with this identification of the church as the kingdom of God on earth was accompanied by a warning against "false theocracy" and "abstract clericalism," as well as by the reminder that the keys of the kingdom had subsequently been given to all the apostles, not solely to Peter; the power and the greatness of the kingdom of Christ were to be found, moreover, not in the worldly authority of the church, but in the cross. When it was asked, "Does the kingdom of heaven exist on earth?" the immediate response, and not only

Lid.*Div*.3 (1867:178)

Hrsn.*Kngdm*. (*Tr.Tms*.49)

Wms.*Res*.6.4
(*Tr.Tms*.87:93-98)

See vol.4:71;81-82;
106;174-75

See p. 194 above

Schl.*Ein.N.T*.2.1.51 (Reimer
7:172-76)

Bau.*Chr*.2 (Scholder 3:121)
Jer.Niž.*Uč*.C (1864:448)
Thom.*Chr*.81
(1856-IV:363-64)

Rtl.*Ges.Auf*.5 (1893:158)

Slv.*Bogočlv*.2 (Radlov 3:14)

Drnr.*Syst*.146;127
(1879-II:878-79;686)

Bau.*Episk*. (Scholder 1:417)

Grnvg.*Pr*.25.iii.1838
(Thodberg 11:158)

the Roman Catholic and Eastern Orthodox response, was: "The church of Christ is the living answer to that question." In 1834 one of the *Tracts for the Times*, published by the Oxford Movement for the renewal of the Church of England, bore the title *The Kingdom of Heaven*; according to another of the *Tracts*, issued four years later, "the church realizes the kingdom," albeit "in secret."

Earlier forms of uneasiness with such a facile identification of kingdom and church, going back to the Reformation and to late medieval reform movements, were intensified as a result of the historical, exegetical, and theological thought of the nineteenth century. As the reconsideration of the historical authenticity of the Gospel of John was casting doubt on the orthodox doctrine of the Trinity, so the questions being raised about the traditional ascription of the pastoral Epistles to the apostle Paul were removing some of the biblical support for the institutions of the church. Such biblical terms as "house of God" and, most of all, "body of Christ" were more appropriate metaphors for the church than "kingdom." The Augustinian equation of church and kingdom had, among its other effects, sometimes tended to relegate eschatology to a minor place at the end of systematic theology, with great damage to the understanding of what the New Testament and the early centuries of Christianity had meant by church or kingdom. On this exegetical and historical basis Eastern Orthodox and Protestant theologians attacked Roman Catholicism for using the kingdom of this world to defend the truth of God, for making "the church a continuation of the kingly activity of Christ," and for claiming that he had abdicated and delegated his kingly authority to the hierarchy of the church. The attack was also addressed to those fellow Protestants who, by taking over Roman Catholic views of the church and its unity, were blurring the distinction between the two traditions.

Simultaneously opposing "papist" and Protestant "error [Vildfarelse]" in the interpretation of "the real kingdom" of Christ, Nikolai F. S. Grundtvig summarized much of contemporary thought when he took what a Greek Orthodox theologian also called "the

Hrth.*Thrsk*.2.2 (1895:279)

Grnvg.*Pr*.17.iii.1833
(Thodberg 6:145)
Grnvg.*Pr*.21.xi.1824
(Thodberg 2:397);
Blach.*Log*.31 (1882:374-75)

Grnvg.*Pr*.31.v.1832
(Thodberg 5:206)

John 18:36
Grnvg.*Pr*.25.iii.1832
(Thodberg 5:106)
Grnvg.*Chr.Snd*. (Begtrup
4:578)
Grnvg.*Pr*.1.i.1823 (Thodberg
1:98);Hrth.*Es*.52:7
(1883:461)

See p. 290 below

Bush.*Chr.Nurt*.1.4 (Weigle
74-75)

Hrth.*Thrsk*.2.2
(1895:250-51)
Luke 17:21

Mynst.*Pr*.37 (1845-II:39-50)

Mynst.*Pr*.60 (1845-II:336-50)

Kbl.*Spir*.33 (Wilson 62)

Clrdge.*Ref*.4.23 (Shedd
1:173)

Mntl.*Lib.égl*. (Lecoffre 1:397)

See vol.1:158-59
Mhlr.*Pat*.3 (Reithmayr 850)

See pp. 302-13 below

Lam.*Av*.18.x.1830 (Forgues
10:151)

idea of the kingdom" as one of the themes of his own preaching and writing. It was not enough to see Christ as a prophet, as so many Protestant contemporaries were inclined to do, for it was "the genuine kingly power and sovereignty of Jesus Christ" that had set him apart from the other prophets of Israel. He bore a royal title, and the day of his ascension into heaven had been "the coronation festival of King Jesus Christ." That meant, however, as Christ's answer to Pilate made clear, that his kingdom was heavenly and "not of this world." It was not a political structure, but a "kingdom of truth," of divine righteousness and of eternal peace. In his preaching and teaching about the kingdom of God, Grundtvig was also giving voice to the widespread sense that the age of extreme individualism was yielding to a new and deeper awareness of the corporate nature of all human life, hence also of the Christian life. The "coming of the kingdom" was to be perceived not only "individually," but "universally," as Christ exercised his rule over nations as well as over persons: the kingdom of God was both "in your midst" and "among you." Sermons with such titles as "How Is the Church of Christ Defined?" and "How Should We Work for the Improvement of the Church?" expressed both a resolve and a hope, "a very [encouraging] and growing hope that a better generation is coming on" in the church.

This "better generation" was by no means to be taken as meaning an easier time for the church. It was "the sum of church history" that "in times of peace the church may dilate more and build as it were into breadth, but in times of trouble it arises more in height" and in depth; that was what it was doing now. The "power of schism," manifest for example in Russia, had been spent; and now there was a readiness to discover the resources in church fathers such as Cyprian for new life and new unity in the church, as well as a "firm belief"—which was to become a dominant and universal belief in the following century—that a "successive progress" toward authentic and catholic unity was at work in the Christian world. Protestants continued to speak of this as a "unity known in its essence to God only, knit by

Krth.*Rel.* (1877:29)

Thom.*Chr*.82
(1856-IV:370-404)

Rtl.*Ges.Auf*.5 (1893:158)

Rtl.*Unt*.1 (Ruhbach 5-33)

Rtl.*Unt*.1.5 (Ruhbach 15)

Lam.*Indiff*.36 (Forgues 4:358)

Lam.*Indiff*.36 (Forgues 4:376)

See p. 110 above

Hfmnn.*Enc*.2.2.1.1
(Bestmann 264-65)

Lam.*Av*.7.iv.1831 (Forgues
10:283)

Blms.*Prot*.45 (Casanovas
4:470-73)

Edw.*Sm.Thts*.4 (Miller 4:410)

invisible bonds," and to distinguish between the visible and the invisible elements in "the empirical form of the church." But also in the Protestant churches, liturgical renewal and a new attention to the apostolic and catholic tradition gave many a sense of having gone beyond the ecclesiological impasse of the Reformation. Even Ritschl, having attacked the way "kingdom" and "church" had been related in the catholic tradition, could nevertheless define the kingdom of God, in the chapter entitled "The Doctrine of the Kingdom of God" that opened his own summary of Christian doctrine, as "the universal goal of the community [Gemeinde] that has been founded through the revelation of God in Christ, as well as its communal product, in that its members bind themselves together through a prescribed mutual way of dealing with one another."

One source of encouragement about the "progress of the kingdom" was the "astonishing sight of the triumph of the Christian religion" through the growing number of conversions at home and abroad. The "indefatigable zeal" of the missionaries had penetrated into distant places and peoples, abolishing their barbaric customs, correcting their vices, and achieving "a marked progress toward a higher state." Although the discovery of the lands beyond the seas had raised problems for the Christian understanding of the natural knowledge of God and natural law, it had also become the occasion for an unprecedented expansion in the missionary enterprise, which, according to one comparison, Roman Catholics interpreted as the task of bringing to non-Christians a saving institution into which they would be incorporated, but Protestants took as the task of proclaiming the word of Jesus that would convert them. By no means all Roman Catholics saw the missionary task that way; they urged, rather, that when "Jesus sent his apostles for the conquest of the world, he did so with the cross," not with political and military might, and they reminded Protestants how long it had taken for the heirs of the Protestant Reformation to rediscover the missionary imperative. Reacting against the acknowledged "excesses and extravagances" of the revival movement, some Protestants, too, warned that

Bush.*Chr.Nurt*.1.2 (Weigle 46-47)

Bush.*Chr.Nurt*.1.1 (Weigle 4)

Rtl.*Recht*.3.1.6 (1882-III:29)
Rtl.*Unt*.1.26-33 (Ruhbach 29-33)

Rtl.*Piet*.42 (1880-II:548-49)

See pp. 313-25 below

CVat. (1869-70).4
(Alberigo-Jedin 811-16)
Dup.*Souv.pont*.9
(1860:167-82)

the church had been relying too much on "conquest" rather than on "growth": it was the aim of the church and of its nurture "that the child is to grow up a Christian, and never know himself as being otherwise."

"The kingdom of God," Ritschl was at pains to explain, "is through and through a religious concept," not the importation into religion of an essentially moral concept. It expressed an activity of God directed toward humanity, but as such the kingdom was at the same time a human task, since the rule of God established itself on earth only through human obedience. That made it not only a religious concept, but "the fundamental idea of ethics" as well. But because the very term "kingdom" was antithetical to the individualism for which Ritschl so severely criticized Pietist versions of Reformation faith, an ethic of the kingdom had to address itself to the corporate dimension of human existence, especially as this was embodied in the state and nation. While the theological articulation of the Christian responsibility for the redemption of society was not to achieve its definitive formulations until later, with the social gospel in Protestantism and the social encyclicals in Roman Catholicism, the nineteenth-century attention to the foundations of the Christian world view did have to address these concerns as well.

It did so in a variety of ways, which were shaped not only by the doctrinal presuppositions being examined here, but by political structures in the various nations of Christendom. Thus the Dogmatic Constitution on the Church at the First Vatican Council in 1869/70 was formulated in the context of the church's struggle against an "Italy without the papacy" and against a militantly anticlerical secularism throughout Christendom. In the "Assize Sermon" of 1833, Keble articulated, in an Anglican context but in terms whose implications were far broader, the fundamental religious concerns underlying both the doctrinal and the political crisis. He did so, as he explained in its opening sentence, on the basis of "that portion of Holy Scripture which exhibits to us the will of the Sovereign of the world in more immediate relation to the civil and national conduct of mankind"; as he

Kbl.*Nat.Ap.* (1833:7)

Kbl.*Nat.Ap.* (1833:10-12)

Slv.*Rus.égl.*3.11 (Rouleau 289)

Mak.*Prav.bog.*117 (Tichon 1:583-89)

Matt.22:21

Slv.*Krit.*22 (Radlov 2:158); Slv.*Bogočlv.*2 (Radlov 3:14)

Fil.*Sl.*44 (*Soč.Fil.*2:13)

John 18:36

Fil.*Sl.*4 (*Soč.Fil.*1:24)

McGl.*Ess.*1.6 (1786:105)

Lam.*Av.*10.x.1831 (Forgues 10:382)

Lam.*Par.cr.*38 (Forgues 11:147)

Prov.8:15

Lam.*Rel.*10 (Forgues 7:300)

Lam.*Av.*7.xii.1830 (Forgues 10:197;199)

Gr.XVI.*Mir.* (*ASS* 4:341-42)

Clrdge.*Const.*1.9;2 (Coburn 10:81;118)

Mark 1:14-15

explained, "we naturally turn to the Old Testament when public doctrine, public errors, and public dangers are in question." Both individuals and nations, "having accepted God for their king," were now in grave danger of "throwing off the restraint" of that kingship.

In a drastically different political context, Russian Orthodoxy was also pondering the meaning of the kingship of Christ for the church, together with the witness of the biblical and patristic traditions to the special providence of God not for individuals alone but for "kingdoms and nations," especially because the command of Christ to render to Caesar what was Caesar's had been stated at a time when Caesar stood outside the kingdom of God, whereas now Caesar had entered into the kingdom. This providence implied that there was a specific "anointing from God" for the Czar, but also that the words of Christ to Pilate, "My kingdom is not of this world," still pertained to the church in all ages. To a radical Scotch Presbyterian as well, those words "spoke of a kingdom which [Pilate] had never heard of before." Striving to disengage the church as an immortal kingdom from the rise and fall of earthly kingdoms and institutions, one French Roman Catholic theologian and man of letters, Félicité Robert de Lamennais, affirmed that by His resurrection the conquering Christ had vanquished "the ministers of the prince of this world," and as the personified Wisdom described in the Book of Proverbs He had declared: "By me kings reign." Therefore the pope was indeed "the sovereign pontiff, the vicar of Jesus Christ on earth," but this implied "the total separation of the church and the state." Even that, however, would not have been enough to satisfy either the papacy that condemned Lamennais or the critics of Roman Catholicism who regarded "the acknowledgment of any other visible head of the church but our sovereign lord the [English] king" as disqualifying anyone from holding political office.

Whatever its applicability to political or ecclesiological questions, however, the metaphor "kingdom of God" in the New Testament was fundamentally eschatological in its import. When "Jesus came into Galilee, preaching the gospel of God, and saying,

Jam.*Sac.Hist.*2.2
(1802-I:308-9)

Rtl.*Unt.*1.7 (Ruhbach 16)

Dry.*Apol.*2.3.52
(1838-II:195-96)

Blach.*Log.*45 (1882:513)
Mak.*Prav.bog.*267 (Tichon
2:641);Jer.Niž.*Uč.*C
(1864:442)
Joan.Kv.*Jub.Sbor.*7
(1899:513-20)
Matt.25:34;Ces.*V.Ges.Cr.*10
(1830:190)

Drnr.*Syst.*154 (1879-II:960)

Lid.*Div.*2 (1867:109)

Kbl.*Nat.Ap.* (1833-26)

1 Cor.15:50

1 Cor.15:25-28

'The kingdom of God is at hand,' " this gospel of the kingdom was a concept derived from Israel, but one that had shaken off the political and ceremonial accents it had possessed there and had replaced them with an eschatological summons to repentance, faith, and obedience. As anticipated in the transfiguration of Christ, therefore, Christian eschatology awaited "the end of Christ's kingdom of grace and the beginning of the kingdom of glory," the "terrifying judgment [strašnij sud]" in which Christ would say to the righteous: "Come to me, for my kingdom is yours." The teleology that belonged to the essence of Christian faith required that the temporary and uncertain judgments of world history, to which secular thought looked as though they were the final judgment, should finally yield to a judgment that would be certain and eternal. Without such a teleology there was no hope, no "looking forward to something," which was "the soul of moral vitality" and an essential foundation of the Christian world view.

In the nineteenth century, this rehearsal of Christian teleology and eschatology raised at least two fundamental questions about the kingdom of God, one of them almost as old as the church itself and the other (at least in this form) a recent discovery, though in fact older than the Gospels. When John Keble spoke of the Christian as being "calmly, soberly, demonstrably sure that, sooner or later, his will be the winning side," but went on immediately to add "that the victory will be complete, universal, eternal," he could not help but raise thereby the troubling question of how any such victory of the kingdom of God could truly be "complete, universal, eternal" if it still excluded any of God's creatures, and particularly any member of the human race, from participation in the kingdom of his love. The text, "Flesh and blood cannot inherit the kingdom of God," came in the same chapter of 1 Corinthians as the prophecy that Christ "must reign until he has put all his enemies under his feet," but that "when all things are subjected to him, then the Son himself will also be subjected to him who put all things under him, that God may be all in all." In addition to the apparent subordinationism in the words about the subjection of

See vol. 1:208
See pp. 116-17 above

See vol. 1:151-52

Slv.*Duch.osn*. 1. 1 (Radlov
3:287)

Matt. 6: 10;Slv.*Bogočlv*.2
(Radlov 3:15)
Wms.*Res*.4. 11
(*Tr.Tms*.87:32);
Mak.*Prav.bog*.66 (Tichon
1:397)

Mhlr.*Pat*.3 (Reithmayr 568)

Grnvg.*Ref*.3 (Begtrup 5:321)

Mhlr.*Ath*.1 (1827-I:92)
See vol. 1:109-15

Or.*Princ*.pr.2 (*GCS* 22:8)

Pal.*Evid*.1.1.9.6 (Wayland
3:136)

Vnzi.*Rec*.2.pr. (1864-II:vi)

Vnzi.*Rec*.1.6 (1864-I:42)

Vnzi.*Rec*.1.13
(1864-I:113-22)

Lam.*Par.cr*.27 (Forgues
11:102)
Thom.*Chr*.56
(1856-III:98-99)

Thom.*Chr*.67 (1856-III:457)

the Son to the Father, the tentative expressions by Origen and other church fathers, notably Gregory of Nyssa, of the hope that "all in all" might refer to the establishment of a "complete, universal, eternal" kingdom of God returned to the theological debate. "We must desire," one Russian Orthodox thinker announced, "that the kingdom of God should not only be 'over' all (for it is that already), but also 'in' all, that God should be 'all in all' and that 'all should be one in him.' " The kingdom of God, he urged, was to be a universal kingdom, one in which not only humanity, but the cosmos, would attain to that unity; "it is for this manifest and universal kingdom that we pray" in the Lord's Prayer.

For such "errors," as well as for other "rash" eschatological "speculations," Origenism had been condemned, and more than once, in the early centuries of the church. As a towering figure of saintliness and of scholarship, Origen was "the first one who ever brought Christian doctrines together into some kind of system." He was, as he affirmed in his book *On First Principles*, committed to "the preservation of the preaching of the church handed down by tradition [tradita] through the order of succession from the apostles, and preserved until the present in the churches." Nevertheless, he recognized that in this tradition there were many points that had been left "obscure" and that "needed explanation," and he set his talents as a biblical scholar and as a speculative thinker to the task of explanation. Did he or Gregory of Nyssa mean by "the restoration of all things" nothing more than "the restitution of corrupt man to incorruptibility" through the resurrection of all, or did he, as most scholars contended, foresee an eventual end to punishment for all, even for the devil? Origen's dilemma continued to face the expositors of the "apostolic tradition." According to one element of that tradition, the mercy of God in Christ was all- inclusive, promising a kingdom in which everyone would be saved, a "universal relation to all of mankind." Yet this salvific will of God was "not unconditionally universal," since it made salvation conditional on its acceptance through faith. Even those who harbored thoughts and hopes of universalism, moreover, had to contend with the unequivocal "declarations of eternal punishment" in the Gospels, in which Christ "never betrays one system of doubt or delicacy, as if there might be some injustice or over-severity in them."

In addition to such declarations, the message of the Gospels about the coming of the kingdom contained another set of prophecies and promises that "needed explanation" now. A reading of the sayings of Jesus in the Gospels without the presuppositions of orthodox doctrine led to the conclusion that "the direct and immediate end of his mission was to preach the gospel of the kingdom," not "to die on a cross." Even with those orthodox presuppositions, moreover, the exeget-ical conclusion seemed unavoidable that the "im-pression which would be left on an unbiased reader by the New Testament would be that the world was soon to come to an end. Yet it has not." Eastern Orthodox exegesis might still read the words of Jesus about the disciple John, "It is my will that he remain until I come," as proof that John did not die but was, like Enoch and Elijah, assumed alive into heaven. Earlier controversies about the meaning of the words of Jesus that "of that day and hour no one knows, not even the angels of heaven, nor the Son, but the Father only" had recently taken on new meaning. Reversing the argument by citing these very passages as proof that no impostor would "have given this expectation . . . after experience had proved it to be erroneous" seemed to many to be an artificial contrivance, once the principle was established that the Bible was to be read historically. Apologists could still find that since there were two "comings" of Christ, all of Christ's predic-tions had been fulfilled in the first coming or were still to be fulfilled in the second, and that "the eschato-logical discourses in the synoptists do but tally with the prologue of St. John's Gospel" in portraying Christ as presiding over the world as the legitimate occupant of "the throne of its Creator," since other-wise he would have been "the most extravagant and even wildest of all human enthusiasts."

Yet such extravagance now seemed more and more to be confirmed by the "impression which would be left on an unbiased reader by the New Testament." Reimarus had foreseen this more than a century

Bush.*Vic.Sac.*3.5 (1866:344)

Or.*Princ.*pr.2 (*GCS* 22:8)

See p. 101 above

McGl.*Es.*2.1.1 (1786:244-45)

Newm.*Scr.Prf.*5
(*Tr.Tms.*85:59)

John 21:22
Gen.5:24;2 Kings 2:11
Makr.*Herm.*John.int.
(1891-I:980)
Matt.24:36;see
vol.1:205;2:86-87;
p. 100 above
Hno.*Theol.*6.1.7.2.1
(1785-VI:153)

Pal.*Hor.Paul.*9.1 (Wayland 2:273)

Hrth.*Log.*6 (1882:571);see
vol.1:19

Dry.*Apol.*2.4.2.78
(1838-II:311-16)

Lid.*Div.*5 (1867:379-80)

Bush.*Nat.*10 (1858:298)

Newm.*Scr.Prf.*5
(*Tr.Tms.*85:59)

See pp. 94-101 above

Pal.*Evid*.3.2 (Wayland
3:351-52)

Wss.*Ur*.3.15 (Knopf 342)

Wss.*Ur*.1.4 (Knopf 97)

See p. 326 below

Lacrd.*Cons*.3 (Poussielque
7:73;59)

Marc.*Inst*.30.7.1 (Tomassini
6:48-49)

earlier, but it was only at the end of the nineteenth century, with the exegetical scholarship of Johannes Weiss, that "consistent eschatology" became a way of reading the Gospels. No longer would it be sufficient to consider the "eschatological error" of the apostles as an "objection" to which apologetics had to reply, because the source of the "error" did not lie with the apostles and their misreading of the message of Jesus but with the message and the expectations of none other than Jesus himself. "Through all of primitive Christianity," including the teaching of the apostle Paul, Weiss concluded, there ran "a combination of joy in the present with a bold belief in the future," in the imminent end of all things and the coming of the reign of God through a radical apocalyptic intervention. For it was "on the basis of sayings of the Lord," which were not of its own making, that the early church expected "its own generation, or at least some of the immediate disciples of the Lord, to live to see the end."

In response to all of these challenges to "the foundations of the Christian world view" at the end of the nineteenth and the beginning of the twentieth century, the authors of *The Fundamentals* within Evangelical Protestantism, the authors of *Foundations* within Liberal Protestantism, the spokesmen for the Eastern Orthodox alternative to both Protestantism and Roman Catholicism, and the expositors of Roman Catholicism—all of whom differed so widely on almost every question of Christian doctrine—all joined in identifying the perennial question of doctrinal authority as a (or the) decisive question. "The defense of Christianity," a member of the last group declared, "is always borne by three fundamental points: the inability of reasoning to unite men in the truth; the necessity of divine teaching as an authority to arrive at this goal; and the existence of this authority of infallible teaching solely in the Catholic Church." About the locus of such "authority of infallible teaching" there would be much controversy among those who, by various definitions, identified themselves as "orthodox" in doctrine; but about the need for this authority to establish the definition of orthodox doctrine they were all agreed: "The formal object of faith is the authority of the revealing God."

5

The Definition
of Doctrine

Clrdge.*Ref*.7.7 (Shedd 1:229)

Although everyone had to recognize that the "foundations of the Christian world view" with which the nineteenth century was concerning itself were not simply identical with the doctrines of Scripture or with the dogmas of the church, but were rather presuppositions or implications for both of these, the debate over foundations could not long avoid giving attention to the specific questions connected with the definition of doctrine. William Wilberforce had commented on "the amazing disproportion" between "the sentiments and views of the bulk of the Christian world" and the doctrines or "articles still retained in their creed," singling out as "the main distinction between real Christianity and the system of the bulk of nominal Christians" above all "the different place which is assigned in the two schemes to the peculiar doctrines of the gospel." Johann Adam Möhler, whose influence extended far beyond the borders of his own country and his own church, identified it as "the fundamental error" of his Protestant colleague Ferdinand Christian Baur that instead of accepting as "doctrine that which has already been given and acknowledged as such by authority," he supposed Christian doctrine to be the outcome of the clash between theological antitheses, philosophically understood. It was a distinctive characteristic of Christianity to "possess a theology," and moreover to have a "doctrine or dogma" that had been held and required by "the churches collectively, since the Council of Nice at latest," by contrast with "the opinions which individual divines have advanced in

Wilb.*Pr.Vw*.3 (1798:51)

Wilb.*Pr.Vw*.4 (1798:244);
Hrth.*Homn*.Tit.1:9,
Tit.2:1 (1882:222–23;230)
Schf.*Prin.Prot* 1.2;2.3
(*Merc*.1:120;135);
Newm.*Dev*.1.int.21
(Harrold 28)

Mhlr.*Lehr*.4.78 (1835:492);
Blms.*Prot*.11 (Casanovas
4:102-3)
Lacrd.*Thos.Aq*. (Poussielque
8:299)

Clrdge.*Inq.Sp*.1 (Hart 42-43)

Blach.*Log*.1 (1882:13);
Blms.*Prot*.14 (Casanovas
4:137);Gr.XVI.*Tr*.
disc.pr.34 (Battaggia 56)

Kol.*Káz*.pr. (1844:iv);
Emer.*Div*. (Ferguson 1:85)

Kierk.*Begr.Ang*.4.2.2
(Drachmann 4:406)

Bau.*Neun*.int. (Scholder 4:5)

Mntl.*Int.cath*.1 (Lecoffre
5:10;24-25)
Pus.*Hist*.2.6 (1828-II:88-90)

Bush.*Chr.Nurt*.1.5 (Weigel
113);Hrth.*Herm*.Tit.1.1
(1882:214)
Dry.*Apol*.1.2.3.15
(1838-I:158-62);Slv.*Krit*.46
(Radlov 2:331-32)

Heb.13:8-9
Strz.*Enchir*.1.3;5.4
(1828:29;179);Makr.*Herm*.
Heb. 13:8 (1891:2312)

Feod.*Prav*.9 (1860:222);
Joan.Kv.*Jub.Sbor*.2 (1899:34)

Grnvg.*Ref*.1 (Begtrup 5:289)

Mynst.*Pr*.29 (1845-I:358-69)

lieu of this doctrine." Each of the churches individually, and the church as a whole, confessed public
doctrines.

While there were some who complained that "few
if any" sermons took account of "the spirit of the
time," it was, Søren Kierkegaard suggested, paradoxically characteristic of this time that "in one direction
truth is increasing in scope and in quantity, and partly
also in abstract clarity, while in the opposite direction
certainty is constantly declining." Hence Baur himself
pointed out that the very nineteenth century in which
the champions of the faith so often felt embattled by
the forces of unbelief and skepticism also merited the
label "restoration period" as to "its ecclesiastical and
theological character." In the words of one Roman
Catholic observer, "everything is transformed": from
being "completely forgotten or annihilated," the
Christian message was now being taken seriously
again. It was truly a "new era in theology." In
considerable measure, the transformation was due to
changes in the position of the institutional church
within state and society, but those changes were
simultaneously both the cause and the effect of a
deepened awareness, on all sides, of the centrality of
doctrine. Divine revelation had to be more than
doctrine, but it could not be less.

The use of such terms as "restoration," "restitution," or even "repristination" of doctrine notwithstanding, there could, in some fundamental ways, be
no going back behind either the emphasis on experience or the critical and historical study of doctrine
that had become standard parts of the theological
enterprise also within the life of the churches. The
biblical formula, "Jesus Christ is the same yesterday
and today and for ever," followed as it was by a
warning against being "carried about with diverse and
strange doctrines," could perhaps still be applied not
only to the person of Christ himself but to the
church's doctrine about Christ, serving as the epigraph for an exposition of "the revelation of Christ to
the world." The Christian faith, the faith of the
church, as distinct from the philosophical theology
supposedly based on it, was the same for all. Until
modern times theology had been able to confine itself

Bau.*Neun*.2 (Scholder
4:218-19)

to a received body of doctrine, on the assumption
(mistaken though it may have been even then) that
this body of doctrine had remained unchanged
through time; but it could afford to do so no longer.

Hfmnn.*Enc*.1 (Bestmann 37)

Everyone had to learn to deal with what happened to
"a great doctrine . . . as it floats along the stream of

Lid.*Div*.7 (1867:528-30)

time." Even to the most devoted, consequently, "the
facts of revealed religion, though in their substance
unaltered, present a less compact and orderly front to
the attacks of its enemies now than formerly." The
reason for the change was "the introduction of new
inquiries and theories concerning its sources and its

Newm.*Dev*.1.int.21 (Harrold
29)

use," the historicizing of all truth and of all doctrine,
including the very definition of Christian doctrine.

The plethora of such definitions, as uncovered by
the historical research of the eighteenth and nineteenth centuries, imparted an urgency to the continuing quest for an "essence of Christianity" beneath,

Jer.Niž.*Uč*.Ch. (1864:436)

behind, or beyond the varieties of historic Christian
experience: "Does its essence consist only in a few
speculative opinions," one inquirer asked, "and a few

Wlbr.*Pr*.*Vw*.4 (1798:107)

useless and unprofitable tenets?" Channing rejected
the effort of some "sincere Christians who incline to
rest their religion wholly on its internal evidence,"
because this was no way out of the inherent difficulty
that "Christianity is not only confirmed by miracles,
but is in itself, in its very essence, a miraculous

Chan.*Evid*.*Rev*. (AUA 221)

religion." Others found "the very essence of Christi-

Camp.,*Syst*.10.17 (1956:26)
See p. 104 above
Amvr.Nov.*Sobr*.1.34
(1810-I:337)

anity" in its "doctrine of the cross," or, as earlier
thinkers had, in the two "great commandments" of
love for God and love for neighbor, or—according to
one Orthodox theologian, this was the peculiar error
of contemporary Protestantism—in the substitution

Slv.*Bogočlv*.7 (Radlov 3:103-4)

of the teachings of Jesus for the person of Christ. As
the nineteenth century came to an end, in one of the
most widely acclaimed— and most widely attacked—
attempts of all to find this essence, the historian Adolf
Harnack set out, just one hundred years after the
apologetics of Schleiermacher, *On Religion*, to answer
the question, "What is Christianity?" by proceeding
to ask the question of essence "purely in the historical
sense [lediglich im historischen Sinn]" rather than in

Harn.*Wes*.1 (1901:4)

a philosophical or speculative sense. To Adolf Harnack
as to his polar opposite, John Henry Newman, the

Newm.*Dev*.int. 1-5 (Harrold 3-7)

essence of Christianity would be found in its history or it would not be found at all. Only it was necessary to abstract the "idea" of Christianity from the ambiguities of its history, to find its principles, the abiding "kernel" after the shell had been discarded.

The Principle of Historical Mediation

Distinguishing between "the facts of revelation and its principles," Newman identified the doctrine of the incarnation as a fact of revelation, unique to Christianity; but "the doctrine of mediation" was a principle, and one for which there were many analogies also apart from revelation. Within revelation, however, the principle of mediation was subject to a further distinction: between divine mediation through the incarnation of the Son of God in the person of Christ; and "created mediation" through the lives of the saints, above all that of the Virgin Mary, and through the history of the church. This statement of the principle of created and historical mediation expressed, albeit in the interest of establishing and vindicating the doctrines of orthodox Catholic trinitarianism, a widely held confidence, also among the critics of trinitarian orthodoxy, that because "the past may be known as truly as the present," it followed that "we know enough of the earliest times of Christianity to place the question of its truth within our reach."

Christianity was a "positive religion" in that it posited a divine revelation; but it was at the same time a "historical religion," and "in the first instance Christianity is recognizable only historically." History was "the workshop of God" and "the world's memory of itself," and therefore it was alive within the present. "Religion begins and ends with history," Schleiermacher urged, and to be "religious" meant to be "historical throughout"; but he added that scientific historiography was not capable of communicating the finest and tenderest content of history. Because the history of all "historical" nations was in some sense a part of the history of revelation, and in that sense of the history of the Christian gospel, Christianity had to define itself as "spiritual, yet so as to be historical," paying attention both to its own history of itself and

Newm.*Dev*.1.2.2.10 (Harrold 78)

Newm.*Dev*.1.2.3.2;1.4.2.5 (Harrold 86;128)

Gr.XVI.*Tr*.disc.pr.39 (Battaggia 64)

Chan.*Evid.Chr*.1 (AUA 197)

Dry.*Apol*.1.1.1;1.1.3 (1838-I:1;3)
Söd.*Upp*.3 (1930:145);
Lacrd.*Conf*.42 (Poussielque 4:163);Hrmnn.*Wirk*. (1914:14)
Schl.*Rel*. (1806) 2 (Pünjer 102)
Schl.*Rel*. (1799) 5 (Pünjer 273)
Schl.*Rel*. (1806) 2 (Pünjer 103)

Krks.*Ekkl.Hist*.3 (1897-I:11-12)

Clrdge.*Inq.Sp*.1 (Hart 40-41)

Jer.Niž.*Uč*.S (1864:361-62)

Makr.*Log.kat*.2 (1871:34)
Jam.*Sac.Hist*.1.3 (1802-I:226)

Clrdge.*Ref*.7.7 (Shedd
1:234-35)

Newm.*Dev*.int.5 (Harrold 7);
Newm.*Gram*.2.9.3;
2.10.2.9 (Ker 1985:
240;297); Chan.*Fén*.
(AUA 561)
Krks.*Theol.diat*.8 (1898:131)
Pus.*Hist*.2.8 (1828-II:127-28)

Krks.*Ekkl.Hist*.6 (1897-I:17);
Grnvg.*Snd.Chr*. (Begtrup
4:447)

Sail.*Past*.1.2.4.88
(1835-I:191)

See vol.4:137;209-10;
263-64;266-67;275-76

Hfmnn.*Enc*.2.3.2 (Bestmann
246)

Ub.*Int*.2.prol. (1886-III:8-17)

Rtl.*Fid.imp*.2.11 (1890:57)

Pus.*Hist*.1 (1828-I:39)

to the broader history in which it participated. For this reason there was no contradiction, but a complementarity, between the sense of history and an understanding of religious faith as self-awareness; "self- awareness [samopoznanie]" could be part of the theological method of a strict orthodoxy. The gospel had been set down as history before it had become doctrine; among the several ways of knowing, "the advantages arising from the historical mode of writing," as well as the disadvantages, had permanently fixed the boundaries for determining its "most important doctrinal truths." All the more regrettable was it, as two theologians of widely divergent viewpoints noted, that "the only English writer who has any claim to be considered an ecclesiastical historian is the unbeliever Gibbon." Although the Enlightenment had employed historical criticism as a weapon, it had in fact neglected history, and so had its orthodox opponents.

Even while they echoed formulations of the principle of historical mediation that had come down to them through tradition from earlier periods of the history of the church, these interpreters of the Christian message were acutely conscious of their own special position in that history, and specifically in the history of the understanding of that history. At least since the Reformation, there had been continuous theological discussion about the biblical canon, but there had not been until now a solid historical critique of the canon. Closely connected to it was the critical study of the "history of biblical hermeneutics among Christians" as a prolegomenon to exegesis. To the extent that definitions of orthodox belief in all the several denominations had equated faith with the knowledge of revealed truth and assent to it, they had left little room for history and its ambiguities. It seemed that in constructing its theological systems, "a scholastic age has but little feeling for historical inquiry"; as a result, when, in the modern age, a radical historical criticism undertook to examine the origins and development of cherished institutions, persons, and ideas, "the system began to give way, with a dazzling and perplexing, because unaccustomed, light." When, conversely, the defense of received doctrine responded to the attacks of these radical historical theologians on the tradition, it was frequently necessary to detach the "many native and excellent observations" they made as historians from the doctrinal "errors" associated with such observations and supposedly derived from them.

Jam.*McGl*.1 (1787:5)

"Modern histories," based as they were on that method of employing historical criticism to prepare the ground for the enunciation of a new theological or philosophical position by first clearing away traditional views, were described by one astute critic as "not so much histories as recapitulations of the most prominent facts, with philosophical comments on them." Although the era of medieval scholasticism, by contrast with the modern era, may have overemphasized reason and therefore have been deficient in the theory and the practice of critical history, it had recognized that history, dogma, and morality should be mutually supportive; consequently its conception of the inseparable relation between "the three elements that form our understanding"—knowledge, reason, and faith— pertained to critical history no less than it did to the natural sciences. Augustine had pointed out that "reason is not entirely absent from authority" but was a preparation for it, and Anselm had accepted the authority of the church and of its rule of faith as the foundation for reasoning; so it was that critical reason and truth, including historical truth, continued to need each other. The Old Testament passage that had served both Augustine and Anselm as the justification for the principle of faith in search of understanding, "Unless you believe, you will not understand," was still applicable to the necessity for critical reflection. The faithful successor of Augustine and Anselm, Thomas Aquinas, who remained without a rival after six centuries, had demonstrated that in relation to faith the twofold task of reason consisted of "preparation" and "confirmation."

Thomas and the scholastics had been obliged to prove that it was possible, while affirming the authority of the church and its doctrines, to make use of reason and philosophy in theology. For this they had brought upon themselves the criticism of the Protestant Reformers on the grounds of alleged rationalism.

Clrdge.*Ess*.7.xii.1809
(Coburn 3-II:41);Blms.*Prot*.13
(Casanovas 4:128-29)

Pus.*Hist*.1 (1828-I:39)

Lacrd.*Dom*.9 (Poussielque 1:161)

Lacrd.*Thos.Aq.* (Poussielque 8:294)
Aug.*Vera relig*.24.45 (*CCSL* 32:215-16);Lacrd.*Cons*.10 (Poussielque 7:125-26)

See vol.3:255-67
Mntl.*Ans*.1 (Lecoffre 8:350)

Mnkn.*Bl*.25 (1828:309)
Aug.*Trin*.7.6.12 (*CCSL* 50:267);Ans.*Pros*.1 (Schmitt 1:100)

Isa.7:9

Clrdge.*Ref*.4.6 (Shedd 1:158)

Lacrd.*Thos.Aq.* (Poussielque 8:304;314)

Lacrd.*Cons*.8 (Poussielque 7:111)

See vol.3:284-93
Thos.Aq.*Gent*.2.3.9
(*Ed.Leon*.13:277-78)

Lacrd.*Cons*.8;7 (Poussielque 7:108;104)

See vol.4:165-66;347-50

Amvr.Nov.*Sobr*.1.24
(1810-I:217)

Jam.*McGl*.2 (1787:37)

Schf.*Prin.Prot*.2.3
(*Merc*.1:130)

Hdge.*Ess.Rev*.11 (1857:389)
Nvn.*Myst.Pres*.1
(*Merc*.4:38-39)

Bau.*Neun*.2 (Scholder 4:175)

Jam.*McGl*.2 (1787:34)
Dry.*Apol*.1.2.5.32
(1838-I:262-74)

Mntl.*Int.cath*.3 (Lecoffre 5:52)

Mhlr.*Lehr*.1.28 (1835:145)

Clrdge.*Ref*.4.6 (Shedd 1:152)

Rtl.*Fid.imp*.1.4 (1890:13)
Acts 17:22-31

The present obligation moved in the opposite direction: to declare "the inadequacy of reason" and to reject the claim that revelation must contain no mystery that was not consonant with the products of right reason. By an ironic twist, as the leading Protestant church historian in the English-speaking world during the nineteenth century acknowledged, such rationalism had now become an endemic Protestant disease, especially in German Lutheranism, even though that historian's own closest associate was himself to be criticized by another Reformed theologian for manifesting "a specious form of rationalism" in his doctrine of the Eucharist. Although rationalism had experienced its heyday during the eighteenth century, "the first methodologically developed statement of the rationalistic view and conception of Christianity" did not appear until 1813, in the *Letters on Rationalism* published (anonymously) by Johann Friedrich Röhr. On the other hand, rationalism itself had appeared earlier, in the period of the Reformation, as "the foundation of the whole Socinian scheme." Roman Catholic theologians criticized "the mistakes and failings of rationalism"; some of them sought to establish the connections of rationalism backwards to the Reformation of the sixteenth century and forwards to the democratic ideology of the eighteenth and nineteenth centuries, while others took the opposite tack of using the rise of rationalistic history within Protestant theology as an occasion to point to the contrast between the Reformation tradition and the new Protestantism. The main body of Roman Catholic, Eastern Orthodox, and Protestant thinkers would all have been able to affirm, though certainly on differing grounds, that "the spiritual doctrines of the Christian religion are not at war with the reasoning faculty."

In the nineteenth century, the complex interrelation between faith and reason, or between faith and knowledge, which had been a component of the articulation of church doctrine since the apostolic era, took the special form of a deepening concern with the relation between faith and history. Everyone had to admit that in some sense the Christian religion, like the Judaism out of which it had come, was founded on

Camp.*Ev.*14 (Owen 173)

Camp.*Ev.*15 (Owen 190)

Less.*Bew.* (Rilla 8:12-14)

Schl.*Chr.Gl.*129 (Redeker 2:288-91)

Hrlss.*Enc.*1.2.9 (1837:29)

Rtl.*Unt.*1.25 (Ruhbach 28-29)

See pp. 225-26 above

Hrmnn.*Nt.* (1913:34)

Newm.*Dev.*1.int.2-3 (Harrold 4-5)

Newm.*Gram.*2.10.2.10 (Ker 1985:313)

Rtl.*Fid.imp.*2.12 (1890:68)

certain events—the Exodus from Egypt for Judaism, the life, death, and resurrection of Christ for Christianity—that purported to be matters of historical fact: if these were true as history, so the argument ran despite important demurrers, the whole Christian system was true; but if they were not historically factual as measured by the appropriate rules of evidence (whatever those might be), the truth claims of Christianity would lose their credibility. The history of Christ, together with the history of the apostles and of the early church, occupied a special place. It was, at one level, the first chapter in a series that constituted the entire history of Christianity; but at another level it enjoyed a normative status as the standard by which the entire subsequent historical development of the church was to be judged.

Sometimes, however, that simple distinction proved to be extremely complicated. The historical-critical study of the Gospels and the church's doctrinal understanding of the person and work of Christ were supposed to coincide, but it was obvious from the state of theology and of the church during most of the nineteenth century that they often did not. For example, the message of the churches went on preaching and teaching about the kingdom of God as though the historical study of the New Testament were not raising at this very time the question of the "consistent eschatology" of the message of Jesus in the synoptic Gospels. Defenders of such critical study might argue that it could only enrich authentic faith by its uninhibited historical investigation of every issue, howsoever sacred. But even some who themselves practiced and inculcated the historical method of understanding Christianity and who attacked "the hypothesis . . . that Christianity does not fall within the province of history" resisted any suggestion "that it is a mere historical religion"; on the contrary, they urged, "our communion with it is in the unseen, not in the obsolete." Or, as another historian with an altogether different set of theological presuppositions insisted, authentic Christian faith was not ultimately concerned with judgments of historical facticity, which were always subject to revision on the basis of further research, but with "judgments of value."

So it was that the judgments of historical reason came to occupy much of the high ground in the apologetic position of the churches, in opposition to a historical skepticism "which makes the present moment the measure of the past and future." "If they can criticize history," it would be said in counterattack, "the facts of history certainly can retort upon them." The historical argumentation could take the form of maintaining that the unflattering description of the Jewish nation in the Old Testament proved that it was not the work of an impostor and, similarly, that the "undesigned coincidence" evident in the relation among various books of the New Testament, which appeared to manifest such carelessness, was in fact evidence for their authenticity. Such argumentation could, alternately, defend the use of allegory as a method for affirming, not denying, the historicity of Scripture. Once the genuineness of the biblical books was accepted, the divine origin of the Christian faith was established. Conversely, "historical authority" and authenticity depended on the genuineness of a text, its historical credibility, and its author; such "authority" did not establish the certitude of faith, which depended on supernatural verification, but would at best confirm its "probability." What it could do, according to some, was to show that the definition of Christianity characteristic of the church in subsequent centuries stood in continuity with the teachings of Christ and the apostles. The Holy Spirit had founded the church in continuity with the historical career of Jesus Christ as the Lord of the church.

Such a continuity of the gospel and the faith throughout the centuries of church history was part of a divine plan and a law of history— not "a dead spectacle," but "a living being" that advanced from the past into the future. At the same time, close scrutiny of that history in comparison with the present disclosed a discontinuity so drastic and fundamental "that we are tempted to think that to base our conduct now on the principles acknowledged then is but theoretical and idle." Clearly, then, the affirmation of continuity did not depend on an empirically verifiable series of phenomena, but on some accepted definition of what truly belonged to the history of the

Chan.*Evid.Chr*.2 (AUA 214)

Newm.*Dev*.1.int.5 (Harrold 7)

Kbl.*Oc*.13 (Pusey 437)

Pal.*Hor.Paul*.1 (Wayland 120;115)

Vnzi.*Rec*.2.28 (1864-II:395)

Clrdge.*Rev.Rel*.4 (Coburn 1:178-79)

Ub.*Int*.1.1.int. (1886-I:16-17)

Marc.*Inst*.7.2.2 (Tomassini 1:381)

Newm.*Dev*.1.int.3 (Harrold 5)

Thom.*Chr*.64 (1856-III:388)

Lacrd.*Loi hist*. (Poussielque 7:268)

Newm.*Prim.Prac*. (*Tr.Tms*.6:1)

church and what did not: only those who genuinely qualified as the "holy fathers" of the church were also "an eternal mine" of wisdom and knowledge about divine truth. To those who had such a definition, history could serve as "God's commentary on God's word," which could be ignored only at great peril, and theologians who lacked the knowledge of secular and ecclesiastical history for reading that commentary were liable to fall into all sorts of absurd errors.

In the concrete execution of the historian's task, these speculations about the theology of history (corresponding to, and not infrequently depending upon, the many contemporary speculations about the philosophy of history) often yielded to a definition of historical theology shaped by the methods and limitations inherent to all historiography. Both the nature of the assignment and the apologetic stance of the ecclesiastical historian required that the methodology employed by the history of church and doctrine be defined in a manner that would be recognized as valid by any other historian, regardless of field or presupposition. There was finally no exemption from "the rules of historiography in general, when applied to the distinctive content of the history of dogma." Although Eastern Orthodox historians had a special regard for the life and career of Constantine as the "goal" of early church history and for the Byzantine church in the period of Photius, Roman Catholics for the thirteenth century as a "golden age," and Protestants for the sixteenth century, especially for the life and teaching of Luther—and all of them for the uniqueness of the first century—they would all have affirmed the axiom: "The true church historian leaves to every age its own peculiar advantages, with no concern." Like any good historian, the historian of the church and of Christian doctrine in any period had the responsibility to begin with the sources and to lead the reader back to the sources.

In the course of doing so, the historians of all the churches learned how questions that seemed to be purely historical could become doctrinally explosive and profoundly divisive. "The assembly in Moscow of ancient manuscripts from various places of Russia" in the seventeenth century might have seemed to an

Ces.*Ep*.2.v.1825 (Manuzzi 2:402)

Krth.*Rel*. (1877:5)

Marc.*Inst*.7.2.1 (Tomassini 1:380-81)

Klfth.*DG*.92 (1839:303)

Krks.*Ekkl.Hist*.75 (1897-I:236)
Dmtr.*Orth*. (1872:1-2);
Krks.*Antipap*.3 (1893:52)
Crnly.*Int*.1.3.2.14.248 (1885-I:657)

See pp. 83-86 above

See pp. 63-66 above

Schf.*Prin.Prot*.2.5 (*Merc*.1:176)

Klfth.*DG*.106 (1839:363)

Oik.*Gr.Nyss.* (1850:xi)

Mak.*Rask*.2.1 (1858:161-65)

Hrth.*Thrsk*.1.2 (1895:10-12)

Newm.*Insp*.1.1
(Holmes-Murray 101)

Mhlr.*Lehr*.3.71 (1835:432)

See pp. 248-52 below

Döll.*Vat.Dekr*.1 (Reusch 4)

Hrmnn.*Nt.* (1913:44)

Mntl.*Int.cath*.2 (Lecoffre 5:40)

Newm.*Dev*.1.int.5 (Harrold 7)

Marc.*Inst*.4.6.1 (Tomassini
1:175-77)

Fil.*Ent.* (Soudakoff 53)

Mhlr.*Ein*.2.4.71 (1843:247)

outside observer to be a harmless exercise in antiquarianism and what Orthodoxy called "ecclesiastical philology," but a nineteenth-century historian showed how it had become the occasion for the Russian schism or "Raskol"; the history of the liturgy was an indispensable part of the history of the church. Even while one Roman Catholic historical theologian was seeking to reject as a slander the charge that the Catholic faith required "an assent to views and interpretations of Scripture which modern science and historical research have utterly discredited" and another was declaring the rejection of the sacrificial interpretation of the Mass by the Protestant Reformers to be a "stubborn denial" of the clear results of honest historical investigation, the debate over the doctrine of papal infallibility was about to involve yet another in researches whose conclusion it was that "to the adherents of the theory of infallibility the history of the ancient church for the first millennium must appear to be an insoluble riddle." Such contradictions were taken by Protestants as proof that honest historiography would necessarily clash with the authoritarian teachings of "the Roman church." For their part, Roman Catholics strove to rescue and rehabilitate history from its domination by "Germans and Protestants" and, because Protestants denied both the authority of tradition and the validity of doctrinal development, to insist that "to be deep in history is to cease to be a Protestant."

The treatment of various periods of church history during the nineteenth century manifested an inescapable combination of Tendenz and objectivity. Debates over papal infallibility and related issues obliged Roman Catholics not only to reexamine such mooted historical questions as the condemnation of Pope Honorius I, but to explain in what sense it could be said that "only the Roman pontiff has the ordinary authority to preside over a general council" and that the pope of Rome was the head of the church, which the Eastern Orthodox denied, or to explain why the evidence for the primacy of the pope was so equivocal in the first three centuries of the church. Similarly, the recognition that "Reformation" was not confined to the sixteenth century but was an impulse

Schl.*Chr.St.*1.1.B (Reimer
12:178-82)

See p. 294 below

See pp. 62-66 above

Söd.*Bid.*3 (1911:26);
Söd.*Upp.*3 (1930:157);
Thos.Aq.*S.T.*1.110.4
(*Ed.Leon.*5:514)

Dry.*Apol.*1.2.6.46
(1838-I:354)

Holb.*Evol.Scr.*3 (1892:51)

ap.Chan.*Evid.Rev.* (AUA 222)

Chan.*Evid.Chr.*2 (AUA
210-18); Dry.*Apol.*2.2.3
(1838-II:316-63)

Chan.*Evid.Rev.* (AAU 221)

See pp. 65-66 above

Aug.*Civ.*22.8 (*CCSL* 48:815)

Ces.*St.eccl.*1.7 (1881:80)

running throughout church history would eventually help to stimulate the "Luther renaissance" in the first half of the twentieth century and through it would contribute to the theological revival within European and American Protestantism (and, to some extent, within Roman Catholicism as well).

Still, the prime case study for the relation between the principles of reason and the principle of historical mediation, and therefore for the application of the methods of a critical historiography to the data of revelation, remained the perennial dilemma of how to handle the miracles of the Bible. A miracle constituted an instance not merely of historical mediation, but of historical intervention: by a fairly standard definition, echoing that of Thomas Aquinas, it was "a phenomenon in which the familiar causal nexus is interrupted and the effect is utterly inexplicable on the basis of purely natural forces." Those who strove for a compromise between Christian faith and the theory of evolution argued for "the fact that God works naturally, and not by miracle, in all departments of which man has any knowledge" and hence for the methodological premise that Scripture was to be read accordingly. A one-dimensional understanding of the "uniformity of nature" was no less objectionable to an American Unitarian than to a German Roman Catholic, both of whom continued to invoke the miracles recorded in the Gospels as proof for the divine origin of Christianity. The former acknowledged that the only objection to Christianity "which has much influence at the present day" was based on the inherent incredibility of miracles and the self-evident falsehood of "the supernatural character of an alleged fact," but that did not prevent him from invoking such supernatural facts as evidence for the truth of the Christian message.

Being a historical problem, miracle simultaneously presupposed faith and yet was set forth as evidence in support of faith; it was helpful, though not perhaps ultimately convincing, to invoke once again the Augustinian argument that, however great other miracles may have been, the conversion of the world and the belief in miracles had to be regarded as itself the greatest of all miracles. Even without applying "a

Döll.*Heid.Jud*.8.5 (1857:647)

Matt. 12:27

Schl.*Leb.Jes*.2.30 (Reimer 6:210)

Clrdge.*Rev.Rel*.1 (Coburn 1:112-13)

Hno.*Theol*.6.2.13 (1785-VI: 457)

Ub.*Int*.1.1.15 (1886-I:284)

Luke 19:2-5
Lacid.*Cons*.3 (Poussielque 7:65-66)

See vol.4:306-9

Schl.*Herm*.1.2 (Reimer 7:54-69)

Bau.*Neun*.3 (Scholder 4:359)
See pp. 210-11 above

Ub.*Int*.3.2.19;1.1.37 (1886-III:333;I:656)

later, Christian standard of measurement," the historical investigation of miracle was compelled to come to terms with the analogies between biblical miracles and those that were allegedly taking place in the pagan and Jewish milieu surrounding the early church— analogies that, according to the New Testament, Jesus had acknowledged. Therefore it was inappropriate to apply to his miracles "the contrast between natural and supernatural as sharply as the term 'miracle' connotes to us." If the credibility of a historical fact depended on the three criteria "that the testimony be numerous and manifestly disinterested, that the agent be sufficiently powerful, and the final cause sufficiently great," biblical miracles were seen as passing all three tests, at any rate for someone "who previously believes the existence of a God and his attributes," one of which was the attribute of going beyond the laws of nature that God himself had set down. Because the message of Christ contained much that contradicted ordinary knowledge, he had needed and employed miracles to authenticate it.

That, ultimately, was the decisive issue: Did "the authors of the books of the New Testament merit our complete confidence, whether in their narrative of facts or in their presentation of the doctrine of Christ"? Was it justifiable, for example, to speak of such an event in the Gospels as the confrontation between Jesus and Zacchaeus as "a miracle of historical certitude"? Under the continuing influence of the "sacred philology" of the Renaissance humanists, the "special hermeneutics" of the New Testament presented itself, at the grammatical level, as an undertaking in objective and scientific literary criticism, dealing with such questions as authorship, text, and transmission, and in this sense as not differing from other historical-critical enterprises being applied to other materials. Finally, however, it could not avoid the question to which all of these questions led, "the credibility and historical truth of the Gospel history as such." That question supplied the basis for David Friedrich Strauss to raise the specter of myth in the Gospels; the church and its theologians found it unacceptable even to treat the histories of Moses that way, and a fortiori the Gospels. Nor was it necessary to resort to a distinction according to which "the moral ideas and spiritual truths only of the Scriptures are infallibly given, and their historic matter left to be disposed of as it may," since critical investigation would show that "the great, commanding, principal facts are shown to be historically true."

Bush.*Nat.*15 (1858:495)

The greatest and the most commanding of all these "principal facts" was the resurrection of Jesus Christ, as witnessed to by all four Gospels. His "miraculous conception," together with the wonder of his virgin birth, was important enough to be listed first among the five "fundamentals" in the Evangelical tracts bearing the title *Fundamentals* and to be defended elsewhere as "the great mystery on which the church stands or falls." Yet the "silence" about the miracle of the virgin birth in the Gospels of Mark and John and in all the Epistles of Paul, for whom by contrast the resurrection of Christ was obviously an event of nothing less than cosmic significance, did make it necessary to draw some distinction between the miracles at the beginning of Christ's life and those at the end, and therefore to give a unique place to the miracle of the Easter story. "When Christ was raised from the dead," a Russian preacher exclaimed in speaking about the resurrection, "how the earth gave evidence!" Once again, however, such "evidence" was circular. The resurrection of Christ was both the validation for the general resurrection of all humanity and a specific instance of a general immortality and resurrection that were already presupposed.

Jam.*Sac.Hist.*3.12 (1802-II:337-46)

Amvr.Nov.*Sobr.*2.54 (1810-II:198)

*Fund.*1.1 (1910-I:7-20)
Grnvg.*Pr.*17.iii.1839 (Thodberg 12:162);Ub.*Int.*1. 1.16 (1886-I:311-12)

Schl.*Leb.Jes.*1.9 (Reimer 6:59)

Mich.Od.*Ev.*4.5 (1865:353-62);
Grnvg.*Pr.*30.iii.1823 (Thodberg 1:202-7)

Fil.*Sl.*24 (*Soč.Fil.*2:71);
Jer.Niž.*Uč.*V (1864:87-88)

See p. 63 above

Amvr.Nov.*Sobr.*2.46 (1810-II:82)

The history of Christ and of his resurrection, therefore, could be said to have been established by the proofs for the general veracity of the New Testament narratives as a whole, and yet the faith of the apostles and early Christians in the resurrection of Christ made it in turn a proof for that veracity. When historical criticism concluded that as a phenomenon this faith of the apostles in the resurrection was a proper object for historical study but that "what the resurrection itself is, lies outside the circle of historical investigation," that could be seen as an effort to locate the uniqueness of the biblical message, specifically of the life, teaching, and resurrection of Christ, in a privileged position to which the ordinary canons

Ub.*Int.*1.1.20 (1886-I:350)
Grnvg.*Pr.*7.iv.1833 (Thodberg 6:167);
Pal.*Evid.*2.8 (Wayland 3:301)

Bau.*Chr.*1 (Scholder 3:39)

Jam.*Sac.Hist.*1.2 (1802-I:208)

Dry.*Apol*.2.4.2.69 (1838-II: 259-64)

of historical investigation did not apply one way or the other. But that raised with new urgency the doctrines of inspiration and inerrancy regarding the Scriptures, and thus also of indefectibility and infallibility regarding the church.

Inspiration and Infallibility

Camp.*Prcl*.17.i.1837 (1875:168)

In asserting, during a debate with a Roman Catholic in 1837, "We both agree that the true reason of infallibility is inspiration," Alexander Campbell, founder of the Disciples of Christ, was not only accurately describing the common ground between himself and his opponent (which was the basis for their fundamental differences), but voicing what had been an almost universal conviction about the relation between inspiration and infallibility, at least as it pertained to the Scriptures themselves. "The Scriptures," another nineteenth-century Protestant

Hdge.*Syst.Theol*.int.6.2 (1981-I:153)

theologian declared, "are infallible, i.e., given by inspiration of God." To some observers there seemed to be a structural analogy between Protestant doctrines of "infallible dictation" as applied to the text of the Bible and "the Romish tenet of

Clrdge.*Inq.Sp*.4 (Hart 61)

infallibility": not the character of the infallibility, only its locus, was in dispute.

That sense of analogy involved the recognition that Eastern Orthodox and Roman Catholic descriptions of the linkage between inspiration and infallibility, while sharing the beliefs of Protestants about the historicity of the Scriptures as such, took on a decidely

Sail.*Pust*.1.3.1.100 (1835-I:233)
Mak.*Prav.bog*.3 (Tichon 1:20);Ub.*Int*.3.2.10.int. (1886-III: 240)
Newm.*Insp*.1.8 (Holmes-Murray 106-7)

different cast because of the relation they posited between the Scriptures and the church. In this sense inspiration and infallibility were "two dogmas," not one: one of them pertained to the authority of Scripture as inspired, the other to its interpretation by an infallible church. It was necessary, but it was not sufficient, to declare that Scripture was "divinely inspired throughout," for the extreme application of the principle of private judgment throughout the history of Protestantism had compelled the recogni-

Newm.*Insp*.1.15 (Holmes-Murray 111)

tion that the church was "the one infallible expounder of that inspired text"; infallibility, but not inspiration, was the proper term for this. Consistent Protestants rejected altogether the designation of an

Hdge.*Ess.Rev.*5 (1857:196)

Clrdge.*Inq.Sp.*2 (Hart 45-46)

See vol.4:262;
pp. 69-74 above
Hrth.*Thrsk.*2.3 (1895:337)
Krks.*Theol.diat.*11 (1898:164)

Rtl.*Ges.Auf.*8 (1893:234-47)

Kbl.*Oc.*6 (Pusey 213-14)

Lacrd.*Conf.*35 (Poussielque
3:349)

Lam.*Indiff.*20 (Forgues
2:186-204)

Clrdge.*Inq.Sp.*7 (Hart 77)

Döll.*Heid.Jud.*4.1 (1857:184)

Bau.*Chrpart.* (Scholder 1:53)

Lacrd.*Conf.*3 (Poussielque
2:51)

Piep.*Chr.Dogm.* (1917-I:
172-228)

Innok.*Bog.oblič.* 5 (1859-I:15)

See vol.4:336-50

infallible church as the guarantee for an inspired Scripture. In that form at least, both theories were absolute: there could not be "degrees" either of infallibility or of inspired inerrancy.

The fundamental issue, as it had been in the Reformation and in the Enlightenment, was authority. Although the terminology was employed also by Greek Orthodox theology, the effort of Continental Protestants to define a "material principle" (justification by faith alone) and a "formal principle" (the authority of the Bible alone) promised more than it delivered in attempting to clarify that fundamental issue. "We are," Keble lamented, "practically without a court of final appeal in doctrinal causes." If authority was defined as "a superiority that produces submission and veneration," it had to follow that the true religion would be the one that rested on the greatest possible visible authority. Inspiration and revelation were closely related, but they were not identical. For the nature-religions, everything could be a revelation, and yet it was above all the unusual occurrence that was thought to carry special prophetic authority. In the New Testament likewise, apostolic authority was identifiable by its "immediacy" and directness. An authority authenticated itself by such criteria as the superiority of knowledge, of virtue, and of the numbers that it could claim.

The question of where to locate the doctrine of Scripture and its inspiration within the systematic sequence of Christian doctrines, while seemingly a matter only of the systematic theologian's own methodology and principle of organization, frequently became a way of addressing the entire issue of authority, particularly when "systematic theology" meant "polemical theology." Some theologians in the age of Protestant Orthodoxy had opened their systems with the doctrine of Scripture as the word of God, while their Roman Catholic opponents had tied the discussion of Scripture to the discussion of the church. By the nineteenth century, that confessional distinction, too, had been blurred. A Roman Catholic systematician asserted that since theology dealt with sublime and divine matters, the first question to be considered had to be authority, and he then proceeded

Marc.*Inst*.1 (Tomassini 1:7)

Thom.*Chr*.66
(1856-III:446-53)
Grnvg.*Snd.Chr*. (Begtrup
4:447)

Grnvg.*Pr*.19.iv.1832
(Thodberg 5:141)

Grnvg.*Chr.Brnlr*.7 (Begtrup
9:386)

Pus.*Hist*.2.5 (1828-II: 58-59)

Clrdge.*Inq.Sp*.6 (Hart 67-68)

Grnvg.*Pr*.23.v.1836
(Thodberg 9:228)

Ub.*Int*.1.2.45 (1886-II:101)
Grnvg.*Snd.Chr*. (Begtrup
4:473)

Fil.*Knig.Bit*.1 (1867-I:4)
Jer.Niž.*Uč*.R (1864:340-42)
Grnvg.*Snd.Chr*. (Begtrup
4:447)
Holb.*Evol.Scr*.8 (1892:247)
Pont.Com.Bib.30.vi.1909
(*Ench.Bib*.109-11)

directly to the doctrine of Scripture and its inspiration. In an alternate method, Scripture as the word of God was grouped with the church and other "means of grace," and a Protestant theologian could make the case for not including it under the "prolegomena" of dogmatics but in the later ecclesiological chapters. Despite his high estimate of biblical inspiration, Grundtvig went even further by insisting that it was "the oral word of the Lord" as pronounced in the baptismal confession that had to be the starting point: "New Testament" was in the first instance the name of a covenant, not of a book.

Whatever its location, the doctrine of the authority and inspiration of Scripture was seen to be sometimes a premise, but sometimes a conclusion, of the theological argument. At an earlier time, when the facts reported in the Bible had enjoyed almost universal acceptance on their own merits, it had been easy to suppose that their credibility depended on an equally universal acceptance of the doctrine of inspiration; increasingly, the question of inspiration was being deferred until after the issues of content and credibility had been adjudicated. Was the Bible, then, to be accepted a priori as the word of God, and on that basis to be regarded as true and holy, or was the experience of its truth and holiness to be the basis for an a posteriori acceptance of it as the word of God? The case for its a priori authority rested on an understanding of inspiration as a supernatural operation of the Holy Spirit, "the schoolmaster of Christendom," by which the biblical writers not only were preserved from error but were moved to "write all the things, and only the things, that God willed"; it rested on the authority of Christ himself. In the apologetic situation of the eighteenth and nineteenth centuries, that necessitated a defense of biblical history, including the accounts of creation and of the fashioning of Eve out of Adam's rib, as "literally true," against modern hypotheses that these accounts were "an allegory altogether." The first three chapters of Genesis were "history," not "mythology." History was at least as threatening to inspiration as science was. The "difficulties" in harmonizing the contradictions between various historical accounts in the Bible "should not be dissembled," one of the most widely read harmonists admitted, but he then proceeded to resolve them nevertheless.

Instead of the distinction between "a priori" and "a posteriori," the distinction between "objective" and "subjective" was probably the one invoked most often in the discussion of these problems. In the nineteenth century Swedenborg continued to elicit admiration for his "miracles of enthusiasm" and "moral insight," which, in the judgment of some, took him "out of comparison with any other modern writer." But most church theologians regardless of denomination continued to regard alleged private inspiration even of a church council as an inadequate ground for verifying "the true religion" (which had been the title of Swedenborg's systematic theology) and hence to explain "visions" in a way that did not contradict objective authority. That did not prevent a Roman Catholic theologian from citing such subjective criteria as "immediate consciousness, that is, a feeling, as well as mediated consciousness or reflection" to authenticate inspiration; the "consciousness of the faithful [sensus fidelium]" could be relied upon to tell the difference between Scripture and all other books, including the infallible decrees of the church and the pope. A staunch Protestant defender of "the Scriptures as infallible, i.e., given by inspiration of God" could nevertheless invoke as "the highest possible evidence" for the authority and inspiration of those Scriptures not some objective criterion (especially, of course, church authority), but "the testimony of God himself with and by the truth to [one's] own heart." In Russian Orthodoxy, too, there was an appeal to the Orthodox heart as the guide to the word of God in Scripture.

But subjective appeals to the testimony of the heart and to feeling could—and often did— lead as well to precisely the opposite conclusions about inspiration; and once a dictation theory of inspiration had been surrendered, there arose a need to give due recognition to the place of the human component in the divine action of inspiration. That need was not confined to those who maintained that the classic text "All Scripture is given by inspiration of God" did not

Pal.*Hor.Paul*.5.10 (Wayland 2:219)

Clrdge.*Inq.Sp*.7 (Hart 79)
See p. 169 above
Emer.*Nat*.8 (Ferguson 1:43)

Emer.*Rep.Mn*. (Ferguson 4:70)

Lam.*Indiff*.18 (Forgues 2:136-37); Döll.*Vat.Dekr*.3 (Reusch 49-50)

Jer.Niž.*Uč*.V (1864:73-74)

Dry.*Apol*.1.2.5.37 (1838-I:309-17)

Ub.*Int*.1.2.44 (1886-II:80)
Hdge.*Syst.Theol*.int.6.2 (1981-I:153)

Hdge.*Ess.Rev*.5 (1857:191)

Amvr.Nov.*Sobr*.1.7 (1810-I:54-60)

2 Tim.3:16

Holb.*Evol.Scr.*5 (1892:141)

Chan.*Un.Chr.*int. (AUA
367-68)

Newm.*Scr.Prf.*3
(*Tr.Tms.*85:30)

Ces.*Ep.*vi.1821;10.iv.1821
(Manuzzi 1:207;280)

CTrid.4.*Decr.*
(Alberigo-Jedin 663);CVat.
(1869-70).3.2 (Alberigo-Jedin
806)

Newm.*Insp.*1.13
(Holmes-Murray 109-10)

Ub.*Int.*1.1.14 (1886-I:265)

See vol.4:309-10
Marc.*Inst.*1.9.2 (Tomassini
1·53-54)

Crnly.*Int.*1.2.5.18 (1885-I·
440-60)

Fil.*Nač.*9 (1819:594-95)

See vol.4:344-45

Grnvg.*Pr.*30.x.1836
(Thodberg 9:338-39)

say anything about the manner in which the writers of
Scripture were enabled to perform their task, or to
those whose leading principle in interpreting Scripture was "that the Bible is a book written for men, in
the language of men" and who therefore used it to
repudiate the trinitarian doctrine of the orthodox
churches. The chief defenders of orthodox trinitarian
doctrine were no less compelled to admit an inability
to explain in what way inspiration was compatible
with that personal agency on the part of its writers
which the composition of the Bible so unmistakably
evidenced. For example, to understand the "elo-
quence" of the Pauline Epistles, it was necessary to see
them as part of the entire history of pagan classical
rhetoric in which the apostle had been schooled,
rather than to attribute his use of rhetorical language
to the immediate operation of the inspiring Holy
Spirit. Yet the "remarkable" language of the Council
of Trent and of the First Vatican Council regarding
"the inspiration of Scripture in respect to 'faith and
morals,' " with no corresponding statement about
"inspiration in matters of fact," was not to be taken to
mean that the "facts" recorded in Scripture did not
participate in its inspiration.

Another declaration of the Council of Trent about
Scripture, the elevation of the Latin Vulgate to
normative status, was becoming more difficult to
defend against the accusation that it derogated from
the authority of the Hebrew and Greek texts and
therefore rejected sound biblical scholarship; the normative standing of the Greek Septuagint in the East,
buttressed though it was by the ancient legend that all
seventy translators had produced identical versions,
was in similar trouble. Because of the commitment of
the Reformers to the authority of the original Hebrew
and Greek texts of the Bible, Protestants could not
put any translations on the same level; but that did
not keep them from celebrating vernacular versions as
faithful renderings of the word of God and as monu-
ments in the history of the language. The detailed
history of biblical criticism, especially in the nineteenth and twentieth centuries, is a subject for
research in its own right and cannot occupy us here,
except as it affected, and was affected by, the formu-

lation of various Christian doctrines. Whatever solutions a theologian might find for the trinitarian implications of biblical criticism, its most direct implications were those that affected the doctrine of inspiration.

To mention only one instance out of many, interpreters of the Book of Isaiah had long been aware of a decided break between its first thirty-nine and its final twenty-seven chapters, but they had attributed both sections to the same author and had equated that author with the historical figure of the prophet, "Isaiah the son of Amoz . . . in the days of Uzziah, Jotham, Ahaz, and Hezekiah, kings of Judah." Through the application to the Book of Isaiah of the same methods of literary analysis being employed by eighteenth- and nineteenth-century classical scholars in the study of the *Iliad* and the *Odyssey*, the hypothesis of multiple authorship commended itself to nineteenth-century biblical scholars as a more plausible explanation of the break. Protestant champions of verbal inspiration rejected the hypothesis throughout the nineteenth century and beyond, as did the Pontifical Biblical Commission in 1908. But nineteenth-century theologians who dismissed the literary question as not a doctrinal question, "both Isaiahs being inspired," anticipated what was to become for most of the churches the eventual resolution of the issue.

Underlying such an approach was a gradual shift in the doctrine of inspiration itself, not merely by the acceptance of a concept of "accommodation" according to which divine inspiration had adjusted itself both to the language of the biblical writers and to their imperfect world views or scientific and historical "limitations," but by a critique of the received doctrine itself. Older theories of inspiration had been "rather mechanical," but such a view was now "altogether untenable." It was one of "the current errors of Protestants without learning, and of bigots in spite of it," that they confused "the inspiring Spirit with the informing word, and both with the dictation of sentences and formal propositions," thus petrifying the Bible and the Holy Spirit. By treating inspiration as "entirely passive" and therefore overlooking the

See pp. 193-94 above

Crnly.*Int*.2.3.2.252
(1885-III:319)
Hnbrg.*Vers*.5.3.22
(1852:270-71)
Mrchn.*Sacr.Bib*.
(1874:275-79)

Isa.1:1

Fund.7.5 (1910-VII:70-87)
Pont.Com.Bib.29.vi.1908
(*Ench.Bib*.100-101)

Newm.*Insp*.1.24
(Holmes-Murray 123)

Clrdge.*Inq.Sp*.6 (Hart 71)
Clrdge.*Ref*.4.14 (Shedd
1:164-65)

Newm.*Insp*.2.32
(Holmes-Murray 135)

Dry.*Apol*.1.2.4.28
(1838-I:223;225)

Clrdge.*Const*.1.3 (Coburn
10:33)

Clrdge.*Inq.Sp*.3 (Hart 51-52)

Pus.*Hist*.2.5 (1828-II:54-57)

Hrth.*Herm*.2 Tim.3:16
(1882:200)

Gen.30:37-42
Fil.*Knig.Bit*.30
(1867-III:45-50)
Fil.*Nač*.5 (1819:240-58)

Josh.10:12-14

differences among the biblical writers as well as the differences between the Old Testament and the New, the doctrine shared by all the churches that "the Holy Scripture was written by the suggestion and inspiration of the Holy Spirit" had led to a method of biblical interpretation according to which even the slightest imprecision in genetics (as in Jacob's use of prenatal influence to affect the color of Laban's sheep) or in astronomy (as in the history of Joshua, including the "long day" when he made the sun stand still) that appeared in the Bible would have to be attributed to God himself and would therefore have to be accepted as historically and scientifically accurate.

Conservative Protestantism, Eastern Orthodoxy, and Roman Catholicism stood largely together in defense of the traditional doctrine of biblical inspiration during the nineteenth century. Where they parted company and all went their separate ways was over the question of whether or not "the gift of inspiration requires as its complement the gift of infallibility"— referring not to the "infallibility of Christ" as "an original and necessary endowment of his higher nature," which was a necessary implication of the orthodox trinitarianism that they all had in common, but to the infallibility of the church. Stated in an extreme form that many would not have accepted without significant qualification, the Protestant view was that because the New Testament was "the gift of Christ and was written by his guidance and inspiration," it came to stand "to us now in the stead of the personal presence of the Lord and his apostles." The Catholic doctrine, by contrast, was that instead of having "left Christianity as a sort of sacred literature, as contained in the Bible," God had "actually set up a society," which was his church. Eastern Orthodox teachers went on affirming the patristic doctrine that the Holy Spirit and the church as the kingdom of God were inseparable.

As the people of God, the church was charged with the mission of proclaiming the word of God, and therefore there was no salvation outside it: on this patristic teaching as such there was no disagreement between Roman Catholic, Eastern Orthodox, and Protestant doctrines. The disagreement came over the

Newm.*Insp*.1.15
(Holmes-Murray 111)

Lid.*Div*.8 (1867:680)

Camp.*Syst*.12.2 (1956:34-35)

Newm.*Vis.Ch*.1
(*Tr.Tms*.11:4-5)

Flrn.*Stlp.ist*.6 (1929:136-39)

Mynst.*Pr*.37 (1845-II:47)

Cypr.*Ep*.73.21 (*CSEL* 3:795)

Hrbn.*Crk*.8 (1861:310)

Newm.*Min.Com.* (*Tr.Tms.*1:2)

Hno.*Theol*.3.2.3.3
(1785-III:316)

Luke 22:32 (Vulg.)

See vol.2:148-57

Ces.*St.eccl*.1.8 (1881:101-2)
Hef.*Conz*.29.548
(1855-IV:728-31)
Slv.*Rus.égl*.2.14 (Rouleau
235-39)

See vol.2:148
Gr.XVI.*Tr*.9.7 (Battaggia
341);Marc.*Inst*.5.14
(Tomassini 1:301)
Lacrd.*Cons*.11 (Poussielque
7:149)
Lacrd.*Cons*.pr. (Poussielque
7:8)
Newm.*Gram*.1.5.3 (Ker
1985:102)

Amvr.Nov.*Sobr*.1.17
(1810-I:145)

John 17:11

Matt.16:18-19
See vol.1:352-53
vol.2:158-70
Fil.*Ent.* (Soudakoff 93)
Aug.*Retract*.1.20.2 (*CSEL*
36:97-98)

identification of the "credentials" of "apostolical descent" with which the church had been sent into the world to proclaim the word, and over the correlative promise that "the visible church of Christ is indefectible." Christ had said to Peter: "I have prayed for you that your faith be indefectible [ut non deficiat fides tua]; and you, when you have been converted, confirm your brethren." According to Roman Catholic teaching, that prayer was fulfilled not only in the life of Peter as an individual but in the see of Peter, whose faith had always been indefectible and whose mission it had been throughout the history of the church to "confirm" and restore others who had fallen from the apostolic faith—including the see of Constantinople and the Protestant Reformers. As a Russian Orthodox theologian, more sympathetic to Rome than many of his colleagues, reminded his readers, "Peter spoke through the mouth of Leo" at the Council of Chalcedon in 451. But "indefectibility" necessarily implied "infallibility" in faith and morals, as the supreme form of authority in the life of the church, because error was incapable of establishing a faith or a church. It was axiomatic: "That the church is the infallible oracle of truth is the fundamental dogma of the Catholic religion," whether Roman Catholic or Eastern Orthodox.

The disagreement between those two forms of Catholicity—and, during much of the nineteenth century, between the several forms of Roman Catholicism itself—was over the agency or agencies through which the church, as the infallible oracle of truth, exercised and articulated that infallibility. Eastern Orthodox ecclesiology likewise saw the church as having been "confirmed" in its faith, through the prayer of Christ to the Father to "keep them in my name"; but that confirming did not take place through subordination to Rome, which was only one of the sees of Christendom, though the one with a certain kind of primacy. The promise of Christ to Peter that He would build His church on the rock—"rock" being a reference not to Peter's person but to his confession, as Eastern theologians sought to prove also on the basis of the Latin fathers—was the same as the promise to all the apostles at the ascension: "And

Matt.28:20
Joan.Kv.*Jub.Sbor.*4
(1899:122)
Feod.*Prav.*11 (1860:254-55)
Hrth.*Herm.*1 Tim.2:5
(1882:72-73)

Dry.*Apol.*3.6.62
(1838-III:311-12)

See vol.4:115

Acts 15:28

Jer.Niž.*Uč.*S (1864:387)
Innok.*Bog.oblič.*67
(1859-I:241)
Jer.Niž.*Uč.*S (1864: 386-87)

Döll.*Ppst.Conc.*3 (Janus 207)

Döll.*Ref.*3 (1846-III:194)

Kbl.*Oc.*6 (Pusey 213-14)

Camp.*Prcl.*18.i.1837
(1875:202-3)

Döll.*Vat.Dekr.*3 (Reusch
45-46)

Marc.*Inst.*4.0.4 (Tomassini
1:188-89)

Hef.*Conz.*int. (1855-I:49-58)

Lacrd.*Conf.*3 (Poussielque
2:63-66)

Lam.*Rel.*6.1 (Forgues 7:131)
Schl.*Gesch.*1 (Reimer
11:69-70);Bau.*Chrpart.*
(Scholder 1:76);
Innok.*Bog.oblič.*
87 (1859-I:369-81)
Ces.*St.eccl.*1.8 (1881:98)

lo, I am with you always, to the close of the age." Christ himself was the head of the church; it was in him, not in the pope, that the unity of the church was to be sought. As some Roman Catholic thinkers also acknowledged, when Christ promised infallibility to the church, he intended that the church as a whole, as represented by an ecumenical council, should be the arbiter of doctrine; only to such a council, not to any individual bishop, belonged the prerogative of saying, as the first "apostolic" council had, "It has seemed good to the Holy Spirit and to us." When the East, in its opposition to "Latinism," spoke about councils, therefore, it was referring to the first seven, all of which, as Roman Catholic theologians sometimes reminded their own church, had been held in the East and not under any direct papal authorization.

Luther had spoken for the Protestant principle in his hostility to the authority of church councils, but some Protestants were now expressing regret that through its divisions the church had been deprived of this court of final appeal. Contrary to Protestant charges that a bare majority at an ecumenical council had been able to legislate doctrine for the entire church, there was no instance in church history when a simple majority at a council had promulgated a dogma in opposition to the views of a significant minority of those attending. Infallibility, according to Roman Catholic teaching, did pertain to the ecumenical council, though only when it spoke about questions of faith and morals. Roman Catholic teaching warned, against Eastern Orthodoxy as well as against Protestantism, that the church could not afford to fall back on the first seven councils (the last of which had been held more than a thousand years earlier, in 787), as though it were bereft of any continuing locus of infallible authority. It was impossible for the church to be certain of its mission unless it could also be assured of its own infallible authority, and so it was "absurd" to affirm the infallibility of the church but to deny that of the pope. Despite all the questions that Protestant and Eastern Orthodox historians might raise about the tradition of Peter's having been in Rome and having died in Rome, Rome had been predestined to be Peter's church.

Döll.*Ppst.Conc*.3 (Janus 40)

CVat. (1869-70).4.4
(Alberigo-Jedin 816)

CVat. (1869-70).4.4
(Alberigo-Jedin 816)

Chom.*Crk*.3 (Karsavin 23)
Döll.*Ppst.Conc*.3 (Janus
54-68)
See vol.2:150-53
Gr.XVI.*Tr*.16.4 (Battaggia
416)

Thus the polemical accusation that the church was being identified and equated with the pope, to the neglect not only of the council but of all the other patriarchs of the church, seemed in the nineteenth century to be in the process of becoming a self-fulfilling prophecy. In promulgating as "a divinely revealed dogma" the infallibility not only of the church in general or of the ecumenical council, but specifically of the pope, the First Vatican Council explicitly claimed for the pope "that infallibility by which the divine Redeemer wished his church to be instructed when it defines doctrine concerning faith or morals." It therefore represented itself as affirming the infallibility of the church when it defined, as the teaching of "the tradition that has been received from the inception of the Christian faith," the infallibility of "the Roman pontiff when he speaks ex cathedra, that is, when, functioning in his office as the pastor and teacher of all Christians, he defines, in accordance with his supreme apostolic authority, the doctrine concerning faith or morals that is to be held by the universal church." His definitions of that doctrine concerning faith and morals, moreover, were "not subject to reform, not merely by the consent of the church but in their own right [ex sese, non autem ex consensu ecclesiae, irreformabiles]."

In many ways the most important substantive objection to this definition of the dogma of papal infallibility was historically grounded: the various historical instances of papal fallibility, and above all the case of Pope Honorius I, as the champions of infallibility themselves acknowledged. The most scholarly history of church councils written during the nineteenth century, that of Karl Josef von Hefele, published while he was still a professor in the Roman Catholic faculty at Tübingen, had carefully examined the Greek and Latin texts of the *Acts* of the Third Council of Constantinople in 681, concluding, against the theories advanced by apologists for the papacy, that the transmitted texts were accurate and that the council had indeed condemned the pope as a heretic. "As for the bearing of the history of Honorius upon the infallibility of the pope," Hefele ended his

Hef.*Conz*.16.324
(1855-III:264-84)

Krks.*Ekkl.Hist*.101
(1897-I:321-23)

Hef.*Hon*.2.3 (1870:19)

Hef.*Hon*.2.4 (1870:22-23)

Hon.I.*Ep*.4 (*PL* 80:472)

Hef.*Hon*.2.5 (1870:25)
Zin.*Infall*. (1870:5)

See vol.2:150-53
Pnnch.*Hon*.15 (1870:252-85)
Pnnch.*Hon*.7 (1870:165-68)

See vol.2:148-49
Gyar.*Infall*.2 (1870·13)
Gyar.*Infall*.1 (1870:11)

Cstrpln.*Infall*. (1870:65)

Iren.*Haer*.3.3.1 (Harvey
2:8-9)

Stec.*Un.cons*.4 (1870:28)
Zin.*Un.suf*.4 (1870:38-41);
see vol.1:333-39;p. 259
below

Gyar.*Infall*.2 (1870:14-15)
Frpl.*Prim*.int. (1870:4)

See vol.4:103

Zin.*Un.suf*.1 (1870:18-19);
Stec.*Un.cons*.8 (1870:61)

Card.*Infall*.6 (1870:173)
Cstrpln.*Infall*. (1870:66-68)

narrative of the sixth ecumenical council, published in 1858, "it is not our task to discuss this in detail." Having meanwhile been made bishop of Rottenburg just before the opening of the Vatican Council, Hefele did go on to discuss the question in detail, in a tract read also in the East, entitled *The Case of Pope Honorius*, published in 1870, the year of the council. The claim that the *Acts* were inauthentic was "an excessively audacious hypothesis, totally devoid of any solid basis"; but since any dogma of papal infallibility must necessarily be retroactive in its implications, it would be historically dishonest, as well as fatally injurious to the credibility of the church, to fly in the face of the historical evidence that a pope who, speaking in his official capacity, had declared, "We confess a single will of our Lord Jesus Christ," was in fact subsequently condemned as a Monotheletist heretic by a legitimate ecumenical council of the church.

Hefele's monograph evoked many responses. One dissertation prepared for the First Vatican Council sought to show, by a comparative chart, that the doctrine of Pope Honorius agreed with that of Pope Leo I and that when the council condemned him, it was not a legitimate ecumenical council. The saying of the fathers at Chalcedon, "Peter has spoken through the mouth of Leo," applied to each of Leo's successors—not, of course, "as a private person and a mortal man," but when speaking "ex cathedra." The "fallibilists" did not, it was argued, have any adequate grounds for opposing the doctrine of papal infallibility. The historical arguments in favor of it were formidable: the testimony to Roman authority by Irenaeus, who had uniquely spoken for both the East and the West; the witness of Vincent of Lérins on tradition; the affirmation of "the authority of the See of Saint Peter" by the church of Hungary in the sixteenth century, together with similar declarations by provincial synods of the church of France. Although there remained the old question of whether a council had to be speaking unanimously when it laid down such a doctrinal definition, the doctrine of papal infallibility, its advocates insisted, was eminently "definable" and "most opportune," provided that the

Vatican Council and the pope found it to be so, as they went on to do.

The ecumenical case against the doctrine was stated by the leading figure among those who never submitted to that decision, Johann Joseph Ignaz von Döllinger, whom Eastern Orthodox scholars also cited. "If the doctrinal opinion about papal infallibility were truly to become a dogma of the church," he warned in 1869, "that would open up an immense chasm [between the Roman Catholic Church and] the separated churches, the Greek and Russian [Orthodox] and the Protestant." Under the pseudonym "Janus," he published a theological and historical study of the relation between the pope and the ecumenical council as authorities in the church, seeking to prove that in the doctrinal disputes of the past the church had relied on the corporate decision of all the bishops assembled in an ecumenical council, not on the individual decision of the bishop of Rome. But when the Vatican Council in its Dogmatic Constitution on the Church seemed to be formally abdicating that authority by declaring the pope to be infallible also when he spoke without a council, Döllinger felt obliged to reject its authority as "simultaneously destroying the dignity of the episcopate and the magisterium of the church—something unprecedented in 1800 years." And he continued to ponder the problem of "subjection to authority." Eastern Orthodox theologians denied to the Vatican Council—or for that matter to any of the so-called councils held by the separated Latin church since the schism between East and West—the title of "ecumenical council" and consequently the right to speak on matters of faith and doctrine in the name of the universal church. They denied as well the claim of the pope to speak infallibly in the absence of a proper council, for Christ and the Holy Spirit were the only two "infallible witnesses of the truth" to the church. Protestants responded to the promulgation of papal infallibility by reaffirming the Reformation doctrine that neither a council nor a pope, but only the word of God in the Bible, could claim infallibility: that, and that alone, was the meaning of the promise of Christ to Peter to build his church "on this rock."

Krks.*Antipap*.9 (1893:145-50)

Döll.*Vat.Dekr*.1 (Reusch 26-27)

Döll.*Ppst.Conc*.3 (Janus 207)

Döll.*Ep*.16.v.1870 (Conzemius 2:357)

Döll.*Ep*.2.vi.1882 (Conzemius 3:275)

See pp. 269, 287 below

Chom.*Crk*.9 (Karsavin 36)

Makr.*Herm*.John 16:13 (1891:1233)

Piep.*Chr.Dogm*. (1917-I:248-50)
Matt. 16:18
Camp.*Prcl*.14.i.1837 (1875:83-85)

The Consensus of Christian Tradition

Those who found themselves no longer able to accept either the inerrancy of an inspired Scripture or the infallibility of the church and the pope saw a theological and historical connection between the two positions. By pitting the inspired word of God in the Bible against the human words of the church fathers and councils, the dogmatic doctrine of verbal inspiration had come into being within Protestantism as an antithesis to the Roman Catholic and Eastern Orthodox belief in the authority of an alleged oral tradition traceable back to the apostles. Such a theory of opposition found its counterpoise in the argument that while the passages of the New Testament usually quoted for inspiration and infallibility pertained to the Old Testament alone (there having been no "New Testament" as such when these passages were written), the primary support for the doctrine of the divine inspiration of the New Testament in turn, and thus for the inspiration of Scripture as a whole, was derived from the continuing tradition of the church. A point-by-point summation of the case for divine revelation and for the doctrine of inspiration led to the assertion that "information and knowledge about all genuine revelations is mediated to us only through tradition," whether written down in sagas and scriptures or transmitted orally as "living tradition." Similarly, the supporters of the doctrine of papal infallibility had to defend themselves against charges of denying tradition; for it was widely held that "it is the primary duty of the highest official in the church to watch, to pray, and to fight, lest the 'light burden' of Christ become, through the imposition of new and unnecessary weights, a heavy yoke."

Like the doctrine of inspiration, the principle of historical mediation likewise led to the question of the continuity of tradition, to what could be identified as (synonymously) "the historical or the traditional" element of Christian dogma. It was standard dogmatic teaching in both Eastern Orthodoxy and Roman Catholicism that God had preserved traditions through the continuity of church usage, through the acts of the councils and the writings of the church

Rtl.*Recht*.2.int.3
(1882-II:11-12)

Fund.4.2 (1910-IV:59)

Ub.*Int*.1.2.45 (1886-II:71)

Dry.*Apol*.1.2.7.49
(1838-I:381)

Gr.XVI.*Tr*.pr. (Battaggia xii)

Matt.11:30

Sail.*Mor*.5.2.252
(1817-III:135)

Klfth.*DG*.22 (1839:44);
Slv.*Krit*.2 (Radlov 2:17)

Marc.*Inst*.3.4.2 (Tomassini
1:146-47);Chom.*Crk*.5
(Karsavin 24)

Lacrd.*Cons*.1 (Poussielque
7:41)

Lam.*Indiff*.6 (Forgues
1:147-49)

Schf.*Prin.Prot*.1.2
(*Merc*.1:110)

Grnvg.*Chr.Snd*. (Begtrup
4:534-35);Grnvg.*Ref*.3
(Begtrup 5:347)

Schf.*Prin.Prot*.1.2
(*Merc*.1:115-16)

Mhlr.*Ein*.1.2.10 (1843:29)

Lam.*Indiff*.37 (Forgues
4:385-86)

fathers, and through his own providence. The criteria for the "distinctive character" of truth, therefore, could be found in the two qualities of "universality and perpetuity." After having rehearsed the traditional marks of the church as one, catholic, and apostolic, Lamennais formulated his case for these marks by itemizing most of the standard arguments: "on the basis of good sense and of the formal texts of Scripture, as confirmed once more by a unanimous tradition, by the authority of the councils, of the fathers, and of the ecclesiastical writers of all ages, by the liturgies, and by the entire history of the church since its origin."

Working from a similar taxonomy of traditions, a Protestant scholar distinguished between ritual, historical, and dogmatic traditions; in the case of all three, he averred, Protestantism "affirms their historical necessity," but it "places them under" the Scriptures. The third of the three, the notion of a "formal dogmatic tradition," was the most problematical for Protestants; yet it was simultaneously contained in Scripture and affirmed in the creeds, and therefore the dogmatic tradition was "not a part of the divine word separately from that which is written, but the content of scripture itself as apprehended and settled by the church against heresies past and always new appearing." That tradition, consequently, was "the one fountain of the written word, only rolling itself forward in the stream of church consciousness." From a similar understanding of church consciousness, a Roman Catholic theologian argued that since, at least at one level, the question "What is Christ's teaching?" was a "completely historical" one, it could be paraphrased to read, "What has always been taught in the church by the apostles?" which was in turn tantamount to asking, "What is the content of the universal and perpetual tradition?"

Invoking that same criterion of "the universal and perpetual tradition," another Roman Catholic theologian rejected the Protestant contention that Christianity in its origins had been opposed to such a tradition, for on the contrary it had laid claim to an identity with it; Protestantism was seen as the beginning, within Western culture, of the emancipation of

Slv.*Bogočlv*.2 (Radlov3:16)

Oik.*Gr.Nyss*.pr. (1850:iii)

Schf.*Prin.Prot*.2.6.83
(*Merc*.1:230);Krth.*Cons.Ref*.pr.
(1871:viii)

Schf.*Prin.Prot*.2.4
(*Merc*.1:157-64)

Nvn.*Schf.* (*Merc*.1:35)

Pus.*Hist*.1 (1828-I:8)

Bau.*Neun*.3 (Scholder
4:528-31)

Bau.*Chrpart.* (Scholder 1:102)
Bush.*Vic.Sac*.4.3
(1866:546-47)

Chan.*Evid.Chr*.1 (AUA 189)

Mhlr.*Ein*.app.3
(1843:260-64)

Mark 7:8

2 Thess.3:6

the human personality from the authority of tradition. That Protestant contention, which, as Orthodox and Roman Catholic critics noted, could claim a tradition of its own going back to the Reformers themselves, was asserting itself with new vigor just as the argument from the consensus of tradition was also being formulated with new force not alone in the Eastern Orthodox or Roman Catholic systems that were its familiar setting, but in the call that emanated from various Protestants for a "Protestant Catholicism" as "the true standpoint, all necessary for the wants of the time." Yet the writer of those very words sought at the same time to dissociate himself from the Oxford Movement in the Church of England (what he called "Puseyism"), which he saw as a symptom, though not a remedy, of the diseases of Protestantism, including its indifference to tradition; "with all its errors," however, it did embody the moving force of a truth whose rights needed to be asserted. E. B. Pusey himself had, in his first book, published in 1828, expressed his admiration for Luther's "intuitive insight into the nature of Christianity," which had "raised him not only above the assumed authority of the church" but "above the might of tradition." But as Pusey's appreciation of Catholic tradition deepened, more radical Continental Protestants expressed their amazement and shock at Puseyism, finding in its neo-Catholic sacramentalism a "crassness" verging on superstition. Such long held traditions as the claim that Peter was the first pope were no more than a "deceptive illusion." Indeed, some were ready to dismiss most tradition as "accumulated rubbish," and its acceptance as "blindly walking in the path of tradition" or yielding passively to a "hereditary faith."

Bandied about though it was in the nineteenth century and earlier, "tradition" was far from being an unequivocal term: the Greek noun "tradition [παράδοσις]" and its equivalents in other languages covered a wide variety of concepts already in the usage of the New Testament, which identified errors as "the traditions of men" in opposition to "the commandments of God," but authentic Christian teachings as "the tradition that you received from us [apostles]." God had chosen to employ two voices for the instruc-

Lacrd.*Conf.*5 (Poussielque 2:94)

Lacrd.*Conf.*9 (Poussielque 2:175)

Dry.*Apol.*3.2.12 (1838-III:66)

Clrdge.*Rev.Rel.*4 (Coburn 1:174)

Dry.*Apol.*3.1.2.4 (1838-III:17-22)

Dry.*Apol.*1.2.7.50 (1838-I:383-86)

Blms.*Escép.*18;21 (Casanovas 5:403;422)

ap.Lam.*Indiff.*4 (Forgues 1:65)

Blms.*Rel.*6 (Casanovas 5:10); Camp.*Ev.*10 (Owen 138)

Döll.*Heid.Jud.*5.1 (1857:270)
See pp. 206-8 above
Krth.*Cons.Ref.*9 (1871:367)

Ub.*Int.*1.1.37 (1886-I:665)

Clrdge.*Rev.Rel.*1 (Coburn 1:118)

Lam.*Indiff.*29 (Forgues 4:12)

tion of the human race, the voice of tradition and the voice of conscience. The former could be defined as "the link of the present with the past and of the past with the future," and thereby as "the principle of identity and of continuity"; yet it was this not primarily from one individual to another, but through the history of the church. Thanks to its transmission through that history "from father to son in unbroken tradition," the continuity of faith and teaching did not finally depend on literacy or learning, or on the ability to "give any minute account of the doctrines of Christianity," but on "the general account which had been handed down." The "ordinary means" by which the Christian tradition had been handed down were "oral language, written language, and symbol."

Those three were the same "ordinary means" by which any tradition anywhere in human history would have been handed down. It was an attractive method of argumentation, therefore, to appeal to the notion of "universal tradition" as a general principle in support of the specifically Christian and Catholic tradition. Even an opponent of the latter could be taken to be speaking as "the organ of the universal tradition." The doctrine of immortality was not peculiar to Christianity, but came from primitive human tradition, as did "ideas of Deity." Thus the history of philosophical speculation among the ancient Greeks manifested the complex relation between "primitive tradition" and "higher knowledge." In the dispute over polygenism, "the traditions of the races" could be cited as evidence for the single and common origin of all humanity, and more generally for the accuracy of the historical accounts in the Pentateuch. The very propensity of the people of Israel to be "superstitiously jealous of their traditions and ceremonies" made the accusations of tampering with the Old Testament "morally impossible." From this argumentation it was only a short step to a case for Christianity as "the universal religion or the true religion," on the grounds that it alone embodied "this infallible rule of truth" and therefore was "the same religion," based on "the same authority" of universal tradition as religion in general. In the hands of rationalistic critics, however, that same method could lead to a far-reaching relativism, particularly when the history of tradition in general was seen to contain corruptions and gross forgeries; then it was necessary to insist that the biblical and Christian tradition was unique among traditions because all of the others were "traditions of men" while it alone was "divine tradition."

Ub.*Int*.3.2.19 (1886-III:336)

Although the concept of "divine tradition" was by no means confined to Eastern Orthodox theology, it was seen to have a special place there, chiefly in its positive function as the content and the theme of Christian doctrine, but also as a polemical instrument against doctrinal or liturgical novelties whether Eastern or Western. Ecclesiastical tradition had been the authority by which the church had defeated the Gnostic heresy of secret tradition, and its "unanimous consensus" was still the basis for a proper understanding both of Scripture and of church doctrine. Thus one Protestant historian of dogma, who had defined "traditionalism" as "the isolation of the historical element in dogma" and its consequent ossification into a sterile orthodoxy and who had criticized the excessive preoccupation of scholars with the early Greek fathers at the expense of the Latin, went on to characterize "the later history of the Greek church" as "the most glaring example of a church life that has become extinct in tradition," also "in the area of doctrine." Because, as Schleiermacher admitted, "the Eastern church appears to us as almost an unknown quantity, about which only now and again a more precise bit of information comes to us," that caricature of Eastern Orthodoxy, both Greek and Slavic, became virtually canonical in the historiography of nineteenth-century Protestantism, according to which "through [Dionysius] the Areopagite and [John of] Damascus the Eastern church drops out of the movement of the history of dogma" altogether. Such a caricature seemed to find substantiation when Eastern Orthodoxy became involved in disputes over such questions as whether two fingers or three were to be used in making the sign of the cross, or whether even the Church Slavonic translation of the Nicene Creed was sacrosanct.

Krks.*Dok*.1.2 (1874:57)
Mtz.*Theoph.* (1788:2v)
Fil.*Ent.* (Soudakoff 43)

Klfth.*DG*.59 (1839:170)

Klfth.*DG*.34 (1839:79)

Klfth.*DG*.85 (1839:283)

Schl.*Gesch*.int. (Reimer 11:33)

Rtl.*Ges.Auf*.5 (1893:156)

See p. 33 above

Mak.*Rask*.1.2;1.3;1.4 (1858:23-25;77;105-7)

Nevertheless, there were some in the West who had to recognize that the Eastern Orthodox understanding

Mak.*Prav.bog.*181 (Tichon
2:245)

Camp.*Rce.*1 (Gould 262-63)
See vol.2:279-80

Mak.*Prav.bog.*259 (Tichon
2:611)

Innok.*Bog.oblič.*112-17
(1859-II:79-118)
See p. 197 above

Papad.*Symb.*3 (1924:26-34)

Mak.*Prav.bog.*44 (Tichon
1:292)

Newm.*Univ.Serm.*14
(1843:324)

Chadwick (1957) 235

of "apostolic tradition [apostolskoe predanie]" ran far deeper than that. Thus Baptist and other critics of baptismal doctrine and practice in Roman Catholicism and magisterial Protestantism found support in the custom of baptism by immersion within the Eastern church (despite its practice of baptizing infants). As it had done at the Council of Florence in the fifteenth century, Eastern theology criticized the Latin doctrine of purgatory for its misuse of the authority of patristic tradition. To Eastern polemics, the most flagrant instance of such "corruption of the symbol of faith," in many respects forming a class unto itself, continued to be the Western Filioque. Western patristic scholars were forced to conclude that the evidence for it among individual Greek church fathers was largely inconclusive. But even if it were not, what counted as authoritative on such an issue as the doctrine of the Trinity and thus the Filioque was not the "private opinions [θεολογούμενα]" of individual teachers, but the official voice of the church speaking through an ecumenical council. One by one, the seven universally acknowledged ecumenical councils were reviewed on this issue, and none could be cited in support.

Acknowledging in his own treatment of the Filioque that "the doctrine of the double procession was no Catholic dogma in the first ages," John Henry Newman, while still an Anglican, maintained nevertheless that "if it is now to be received, as surely it must be, as part of the [Nicene] Creed, it was really held everywhere from the beginning, and therefore, in a measure, held as a mere religious impression, and perhaps an unconscious one." Here, as has been observed, "the historian in Newman concedes that the 'doctrine' was not a 'Catholic dogma' in the first ages," but "the theologian . . . must contend that the church has always 'held' the doctrine." In the nineteenth century, that tension between "tradition" as the object of the historian's research and "tradition" as the authority for the theologian's doctrine (and for the church's doctrine) came to a head in the disputes surrounding the definition of the doctrine of papal infallibility by the First Vatican Council. For historical research demonstrated not only that individual popes had been condemned for false teaching, notably Honorius I, but also that the claim of a consensus in tradition for the doctrine itself "rests . . . upon a total misunderstanding of the tradition of the church in the first millennium of the church and upon a distortion of its history."

Döll.*Vat.Dekr.*10 (Reusch 75)

Vinc.Ler.*Comm.*2.3 (Moxon 10)

See vol.1:333-39

Therefore the canon of Vincent of Lérins, "what has been believed everywhere, always, by all," which had originally been formulated in opposition to Augustine and which had then been invoked against the innovations of the Protestant Reformers such as justification by faith alone, was now being used in opposition to other doctrinal innovations, even when such an innovation was about to take the form of official church dogma at the First Vatican Council. Protestants and Roman Catholics alike felt able to cite it without even identifying it; Eastern Orthodox theologians likewise invoked it. But closer study of the Vincentian canon disclosed a "defect in its serviceableness." It had become a Gordian knot that the church "is not able to unloose, but only to cut in a violent way." The Vincentian canon seemed to be raising again the chimera of "unanimous consensus" in the Christian tradition; otherwise it had to be taken to mean no more than "what has been believed in most places, at most times, and by most [authoritative] teachers." On the question of the disputed books of the New Testament, for example, the principle of consensus could be stated to read: "Not indeed that there has never been any disagreement about certain books, but in the sense that by far the largest part of the churches and theologians has always agreed on the integrity of the [biblical] canon."

See vol.4:281

See pp. 80-81 above

Clrdge.*Inq.Sp.*4 (Hart 64); Döll.*Vat.Dekr.*1 (Reusch 1) Andrts.*Dok.sym.*2.3.1 (1901:97)

Newm.*Dev.*1.int.8 (Harrold 11)

Schf.*Prin.Prot.*2 (Merc.1:102)

See pp. 26-33 above

Ub.*Int.*1.2.46 (1886-II:372)

See vol.4:266-67

As it had in the disputes of the Reformation period, the question of the biblical canon brought into focus the larger questions of the relation between the authority of Scripture and the authority of church tradition. Thus one of the first declarations of a multi-volume Roman Catholic dogmatics had stated that the ascription of the books of the New Testament to the authors and dates assigned to them was based on an argument derived from tradition. If this tradition was to be the subject of free historical investigation, which would reveal that the roster of canonical

See p. 89 above

Marc.*Inst.*1.1.2 (Tomassini 1:10)

Khns.*Dogm.*3.17.4
(1861-I:659-60)

Camp.*Prcl.*19.i.1837
(1875:257)

Nvn.*Schf.* (*Merc.*1:37-38)

Makr.*Herm.*1 Cor.11:23
(1891:1778)

Mhlr.*Ein.*1.2.16 (1843:53)

Döll.*Heid.Jud.*10.3.1
(1857:818-21)

Ub.*Int.*2.1.3 (1886-III:73-74)

books could not claim to have been established by divine right but only by historical evolution, the result of such historical investigation had direct implications for the Protestant doctrine of the priority of Scripture over church and tradition. One formulation of the Protestant doctrine identified it as "the first and characteristic difference between the Protestant and the Roman Catholic": "the former believes the Scriptures first, and the church afterwards, whereas the latter believes the church first and the Scriptures afterwards." Other Protestants, working with a less simpleminded disjunction, strove to avoid the "abominable usurpation" by which the church placed its own tradition alongside the word of God in the Bible, as well as the "presumption equally abominable" by which a single individual felt qualified to cast off all authority and all tradition on the basis of a private reading of the Bible alone, even though in fact no one could read the Bible as if it had never been read before.

On the Eastern Orthodox and Roman Catholic sides, too, there was an effort to rule false disjunctions out of order. Spokesmen for Eastern Orthodoxy saw the two positions on the relation of Scripture and tradition coming out of the Reformation, the Protestant and the Roman Catholic, as equally rationalistic and subjective, since both of them seemed to overlook the profoundly scriptural content of authentic tradition together with the corollary necessity for a traditional exegesis bound to the biblical text. It was, one Roman Catholic insisted, a wrong question—and therefore a question to which any answer would likewise be wrong—to ask whether tradition should be coordinated with Scripture or subordinated to it; for this assumed that they were distinct though parallel lines, when in fact history demonstrated that they constantly "crossed each other and lived in each other." Early Christianity had inherited from Judaism the concept of a tradition "that constantly leaned upon the text of the Torah," and the earliest Christian tradition had been attached to the same text, whose allegorical interpretation was attested by tradition. If it was true in the first century that the apostolic writings needed an oral tradition to validate their

Dry.*Apol*.3.2.8-9
(1838-III:41-51)

Gtti.*Ver.eccl*.2.4.4.22
(1750:246)

See vol.4:276-77

Marc.*Inst*.3.2.3 (Tomassini
1:139-40)

CVat. (1869-70) 3.2
(Alberigo-Jedin 806)

Mhlr.*Ein*.1.2.15 (1843:46-47)

See p. 328 below

Mar.*Inst.symb*.17 (1825:28)

Clrdge.*Inq.Sp*.5 (Hart 65-66)

historical trustworthiness, it seemed to follow that they continued to need it also for their proper interpretation.

Defenders of the doctrine of papal infallibility had long been contending for a "two-source doctrine of revelation," by which Scripture and unwritten tradition were to be seen as separate channels through both of which the revelation to the apostles continued to be communicated. It was possible to read the language of the Council of Trent as support for such a theory, if its phrasing that "this truth of the gospel is contained in written books and unwritten traditions" were taken as equivalent to the formula of an earlier (and discarded) draft, "partly [partim] in written books, partly [partim] in unwritten traditions"; Trent had retained from that earlier draft the declaration that both Scripture and tradition were to be treated "with an equal feeling of piety and reverence [pari pietatis affectu]," and this latter formula continued to be employed in defense of the authority of tradition. The First Vatican Council did not, however, go beyond the Council of Trent on this question, contenting itself with the recitation of the earlier decree, which it labeled "the faith of the universal church declared by the Council of Trent." Therefore those who opposed a two-source theory were neither condemned nor vindicated by the First Vatican Council, which postponed the adjudication of the question.

Whatever their dogmatic presuppositions for "repudiating dogmas constructed without the authority of holy Scripture as merely human traditions" may have been, the researches of Protestant historical theology could only confirm the conclusion that in the life and teaching of the primitive church the oral word had preceded the written word. Nor had the appearance of the written word, in the Epistles of the New Testament and the Gospels, together with their collection into a distinct sacred book (eventually called "New Testament") alongside the sacred book inherited from Judaism (eventually called "Old Testament"), obviated the need for an oral tradition, which continued to exist alongside Scripture; thus the word of God had a "double form, in which it could and would move through all the subsequent periods of

Thos.*Chr*.66 (1856-III:418)

Hrlss.*Enc*.2.1.2 (1837:62)

Bas.*Spir*.27.66 (*SC* 17b:478-82); see vol.4:121

Krth.*Cons.Ref*.pr. (1871:viii)

Camp.*Mcla*.16.x.1823;18.x. 1823 (1824:112;253)

Piep.*Chr.Dogm*. (1917-III:325-27)

See vol.4:347 Lam.*Indiff*.6 (Forgues 1:141-42)

See pp. 230-41 above

Dry.*Apol*.1.2.7.49 (1838-I:382-83)

See vol.1:27-41

Bau.*Chr*.3 (Scholder 3:256); Krks.*Dok*.1.2 (1874:57)

Mhlr.*Pat*.2 (Reithmayr 344)

church history." Protestant scholars did seek to argue that in the first five centuries of church history the oral had been subordinated to the written, and that only gradually had the two been placed on the same level; the appeal to an "unwritten" tradition in Basil's *On the Holy Spirit* to prove the deity of the Holy Spirit was one of the first instances of that change. All of that, however, was seen as profoundly different from the Roman Catholic appeal to "perishing human traditions" in place of the inspired word of God in Scripture. Some Protestants maintained "that infant sprinkling is a human tradition," as Jewish proselyte baptism had been, while others argued for it as "presupposed" on the basis of "a combination of passages from Scripture" alone, without reference to tradition; but most would still have taken it as accurate when a French Roman Catholic critic quoted the familiar formula of William Chillingworth, "the Bible only is the religion of Protestants."

Because it was the period in which historical theology came into its own, especially among Protestants but also among Roman Catholic and (particularly toward the end of the period) among Eastern Orthodox scholars, the nineteenth century confronted the idea of the consensus of Christian tradition, and specifically of patristic tradition, in a new way. It did seem remarkable that the apologists of the first three centuries in their defenses of the Christian message against pagans and Jews had "totally ignored the living tradition in their theory and criticism of revelation," which they sometimes seemed to reduce to the rational notions of God, creation, and immortality. A growing interest in the historical significance of Gnosticism for the emergence of orthodox Catholic doctrine led to the judgment that since Catholics and Gnostics alike had appealed to the authority of Scripture, the authority of tradition as "a principle standing above Scripture" became a way for Catholic orthodoxy to defeat Gnostic heresy. Irenaeus deserved recognition for being the first who "penetrated to the full value of the Catholic principle of tradition and developed its probative force." Having supported the authenticity of the books of the New Testament from the tradition of the universal church, he had, more-

Ub.*Int*.1.1.1 (1886-I:28)

Iren.*Haer*.3.3.1 (Harvey 2:9)
Mhlr.*Pat*.2 (Reithmayr 352)

Fil.*Ent*. (Soudakoff 78-81)

Clrdge.*Inq.Sp*.6 (Hart73);
Grnvg.*Chr.Snd*. (Begtrup
4:694)

Mhlr.*Ath*.2 (1827-I:125-26)

Ath.*Syn*.47;43 (Opitz
2:271-72;268-69)

Newm.*Ar*.1.2 (1890:35)

Newm.*Ar*.2.5 (1890:220)

Mhlr.*Ath*.2 (1827-I:122)

See pp. 114-16, 157-58
above

See vol.4:138-41;221-25

Döll.*Ref*.3 (1846-III:363-72)

over, helped to preserve the very Scripture that Protestants now sought to dissociate from tradition; and he had proved his thesis concerning the unity and apostolicity of the Catholic Church and its tradition by reference to the church of Rome, whose authority Protestants denied; Eastern theologians had to make a special point of explaining his statements about Roman primacy.

Irenaeus had come originally from the East, presumably from Smyrna, but had become bishop of Lyons in the West, where, however, he had still written in Greek; he united the traditions of East and West. As one of the few church fathers after Irenaeus to have been active both in the East (in Alexandria, as bishop) and in the West (in Rome, as exile), Athanasius constituted another important source from which to derive a patristic consensus about Christian tradition. In his treatise on church councils, he insisted that when the fathers at any council spoke, they had in turn "fallen back upon fathers," so that those who had "received the traditions from them" were obliged to acknowledge the continuity of those traditions. From Athanasius Newman professed to have learned of a precreedal "traditionary system, received from the first age of the church," which then gradually became explicit, for example in the Nicene Creed and in the writings of Athanasius, as the challenge of heresy made that necessary. He went on in the same book to speak of it as "a traditional system of theology, consistent with, but independent of, Scripture, [a tradition which] had existed in the church from the apostolic age." Möhler, too, saw Athanasius as standing with all his roots in the church, in its communion and in its tradition.

Augustine, the one church father whose special authority was acknowledged by all parties in the West, if not always in the East, held a special place in the discussions about tradition. The Protestant use of his writings in support of Reformation positions about sin and grace made it necessary for Roman Catholics to attempt to explain away statements in which he did seem to favor positions espoused by the Reformers. Conversely, his familiar words about not believing the gospel except for the authority of the

Aug.*Ep.fund*.5 (*CSEL* 25:197)

Ces.*St.eccl*.1.1 (1881:15)

Lacrd.*Cons*.3 (Poussielque 7:53-59)

Marc.*Inst*.21.3.1 (Tomassini 3:377)

Krks.*Ekkl.Hist*.88 (1892-I:277-78); Mhlr.*Pat.* int. (Reithmayr 45-48)

Marc.*Inst*.14.8.3 (Tomassini 2:312-13)

Lam.*Indiff*.6 (Forgues 1:147-49)

Mntl.*Int.cath*.2 (Lecoffre 5:37)

Mntl.*Lib.égl*. (Lecoffre 1:369)

Lid.*Div*.7 (1867:537)

Newm.*Scr.Prf*.2 (*Tr.Tms*.85:21)

Harn.*DG*. (1931-I:806-8)

Catholic Church continued to serve Roman Catholics as proof that Christ had constituted the Catholic Church as the authoritative interpreter of Scripture and teacher of the truth. His arguments against the Manicheans for the authority of Catholic orthodoxy, of which that quotation was the most familiar part, could still be quoted in extenso to support Catholic doctrine. Yet any use of Augustine as part of the tradition needed to come to terms with the ambivalence in his own relation to tradition. That necessitated explaining the language of early church fathers about original sin in such a way as to prove that Augustine had not been innovating in his own version of that doctrine, but had in fact been reflecting the consensus of the Christian tradition. Greek Orthodox and Roman Catholic scholars both recognized that the Greek fathers had been more abstract and theoretical than the Latin, but according to Roman Catholic scholars they could be harmonized with Augustine even on the doctrines of sin and grace if they were read properly.

The last of the voices of "unanimous tradition" enumerated by Lamennais was "the liturgies." His sometime colleague Montalembert elaborated on it, describing liturgy as "this sacred deposit of the faith, of piety, and of Catholic poetry"; in the church's liturgical practice there resided "the formal doctrine of the church, its continuous practice from age to age." To qualify as a doctrine of the church, a teaching did not have to be stated theologically, in a formal creed; it could be confessed liturgically as well, "by acting in a manner which necessarily implies that you hold it." Yet by contrast with this thesis that "from the earliest times" there had existed "one definite system" of both faith and worship in the church, it was the surprising conclusion of the most important history of Christian doctrine written during this period that "the exceptional nature of Christianity" had manifested itself in an absence of ritual, so that "the history of dogma during the first three centuries is not reflected in the liturgy."

Nevertheless, at a time when the doctrinal content of the pulpit had fallen into desuetude, the "grand truths" of the Christian confession continued to be

Wilb.*Pr.Vw*.3 (1798:53)

Wilb.*Ep*.1786
(Robert-Samuel 1:16-17)

See vol.3:172-73

Hno.*Theol*.6.2.2.8
(1785-VI:431)

Newm.*Art.XXXIX*.8
(*Tr.Tms*.90:52)
Newm.*Dev*.1.int.19 (Harrold 25)

See vol.3:208-10

Marc.*Inst*.34.5.2 (Tomassini 6:356)

Gr.XVI.*Tr*.3.2 (Battaggia 186)

Newm.*Proph.Off*.2.6
(*V.Med*.1:55-56);
Newm.*Dev*.int.8
(Harrold 11)

Congar (1967) 211

Gr.XVI.*Tr*.disc.pr.5
(Battaggia 6-7)

Lam.*Indiff*.22 (Forgues 3:24)

"forced upon our notice in their just bearings and connections, as often as we attend the service of the church": the "public liturgy and ritual" and the "scriptural formulary or confession of faith" supported each other. As the example of Bernard of Clairvaux had already shown, the doctrine of the assumption of Mary received its validation from "ecclesiastical tradition," primarily from liturgical tradition and only later from doctrinal tradition. Only from the chronological priority of liturgy over formal dogma was it possible to argue for the existence of the doctrine of the real presence—though not of the doctrine of transubstantiation—in the early centuries of the church. And it was by reasoning backward from liturgical practice to doctrine that it was possible to deal with the still unresolved medieval question of the silence of Scripture about the institution of most of the seven sacraments by Christ.

The presence of a few historical exceptions could not negate the consensus of "the entire tradition." Yet if the tradition about the consensus of Christian tradition in any form was to withstand the scrutiny of the historical consciousness of the nineteenth century, a simple notion about the "unanimous consensus" across the centuries would have to yield to a redefinition of the consensus of tradition in which its temporal dimension became a decisive component. It would have to be recognized that, for all its language about what had been believed everywhere at all times by everyone, "the rule of Vincent is not of a mathematical or demonstrative character, but moral"—and historical as well. Thus it was that in the nineteenth century there came "a decisive contribution to the problem of the relationship between magisterium and history in tradition," in the form of "the idea of development" of doctrine, which thus "became an inner dimension to that of tradition."

Dogma and Its Development

Because of the standard equation of orthodoxy with "immutable" truth, it was by no means obvious to everyone that the recent notion of "development of doctrine" was making such a positive contribution to the concept of the authority of "primordial tradition."

Accusing Newman and other converts from Anglicanism to Roman Catholicism of "substituting development for tradition," Keble saw the interest in development as evidence of "a growing disdain of the authority of the fathers, and a substitution of the later

Kbl.*Spir.*113 (Wilson 201-2)

church for them." Roman Catholic and German Protestant theories of development were both attacked by an American Protestant theologian for confusing "the modern doctrine of development" either with "the Romish doctrine of tradition" or with the doctrines of contemporary philosophies about time

Hdge.*Syst.Theol.*int.5.6 (1981-I:116-20)

Krks.*Ekkl.Hist.*2;88 (1897-I:11;277)

and history. Yet he conceded, as did a Greek Orthodox church historian in his discussion of the issue of "development [ἀνάπτυξις]," that "that there has been, in one sense, an uninterrupted development of theology in the church."

The real issue, however, was not simply a "development of theology in the church," but a "development of doctrine" and a "development of dogma," and with it the very status of "dogmatic divinity." While Eastern Orthodoxy defined "the true faith" as

Jer.Niž.*Uč.*D (1864:130);Hrth.*Log.*19 (1882:695)

"correctly holding to and confessing the true dogmas," the conviction was widespread, also among those who still strove to retain as much as possible of the miraculous and supernatural element of the gos-

See p. 238 above

pel, that with the eighteenth and nineteenth centuries "the dogmatical age of Christianity"—represented by Catholicism East and West, but still shared by classical Protestantism—had drawn to a close; for "we

Chan.*Cath.* (AUA 471);Clrdge.*Const.*2 (Coburn10:119)

have now come to learn that Christianity is not a dogma, but a spirit." It was simply impossible for any dogmatic formula to express adequately what the gospel meant by the person and work of Christ, which was not "a theorem or form of thought, but a process," and the New Testament had shown its difference from later systematic theologies by refusing to "make up any formula of three or four lines" that

Bush.*Vic.Sac.*2.4 (1866:211-12)

would attempt to encapsulate that process: "When," the cry went up, "will theological dogmatism understand the language of passion?"

Bush.*Vic.Sac.*2.4 (1866:229)

Although eighteenth-century historical critics had demonstrated that neither in the New Testament nor in subsequent church usage could the term "dogma" be taken unequivocally in the sense of the officially

See p. 27 above

See p. 182 above

Schl.*Rel.* (1806) 1 (Pünjer
11-12)

Newm.*Apol.*2 (Svaglic 54-55)

Newm.*Scr.Prf.*1
(*Tr.Tms.*85:23)
Newm.*Insp.*1.3
(Holmes-Murray 102)

Newm.*Gram.*1.5 (Ker
1985:69-102)

Newm.*Gram.*1.5 (Ker
1985:69)

Newm.*Insp.*1.17
(Holmes-Murray 113)

Harn.*DG.* (1931-I:33-34)

See vol.1:2
Cyr.H.*Catech.*4.2
(Reischl-Rupp 1:90)

Bas.*Spir.*27.66 (*SC*
17b:232-33)

Mnschr.*DG.*int.1
(Coelln-Neudecker 1:1-2)

Bret.*Dogm.*7 (1826:65-66);
Hag.*DG.*1 (Benrath 1-2)

legislated and enforceable confession of the church, it was that sense of the term that was the object both of theological and of historical interest in the nineteenth century. By contrast with Schleiermacher, for whom "piety" but not "doctrine" had been his spiritual "womb," Newman admitted that "from the age of fifteen, dogma has been the fundamental principle of my religion: I know no other religion; I cannot enter into the idea of any other sort of religion"; and he declared that he had never had any serious "temptation to be less zealous for the great dogmas of the faith." He maintained, moreover, that this was not a personal idiosyncracy, for "men want a dogmatic system" and had found it in Christianity "from the beginning to this day." In formulating a dogma, the church "more than insists, she obliges," so that "belief in dogmatic theology" came as the third item, right after "belief in God" and "belief in the Holy Trinity," in his list of obligations of Christian faith and assent. As he put it in a summary definition, "a dogma is a proposition; it stands for a notion or for a thing; and to believe it is to give the assent of the mind to it, as it stands for the one or for the other." Therefore "to give a real assent to it is an act of religion; to give a notional [assent] is a theological act," by which the "real assent" of religious faith took intellectual form. Nor could the term be confined to "formal judgment" about a question of doctrine, for there could also be in patristic tradition "a certain interpretation of a doctrinal text" that was "so continuous and universal" as to qualify it for "virtually or practically" dogmatic status.

In the work acknowledged by successors in the history of dogma as "the first complete presentation of our discipline," Wilhelm Münscher began by citing such distinctions as that of Cyril of Jerusalem between "dogmas [δόγματα]" and "practices [πράξεις]," or that of Basil of Caesarea between "dogma [δόγμα]" and "proclamation [κήρυγμα]," in order to define "dogma" as "synonymous with the teachings of faith," and "church dogmas" as "those that are recognized by an entire Christian communion as normative"; Cyril's and Basil's distinctions proved useful for other such definitions as well. The most influential of these

successors of Münscher in the discipline opened his
own history of dogma with a related definition:
"The dogmas of the church are those Christian
doctrines of faith, formulated in concepts and set
down for a scientific-apologetic treatment, that
comprehend the knowledge of God and the world
and present the objective content of religion"; but
immediately he went on to stipulate that "they have
standing in the Christian churches as truths which
are contained in the Holy Scriptures (or perhaps also
in the tradition), which circumscribe the deposit
of faith, and acceptance of which is a precondition
for obtaining the salvation that is promised by re-

Harn.*DG*. (1931-I:3)

ligion."

So juridical a definition of "dogma" as the
legislated doctrine of the church (or of the churches)
presupposed that alongside those teachings that had
attained the status of dogmas, there stood other
teachings that did not (or at least did not yet) have a
position in the official body of legislation by church

Blms.*Escép*.15 (Casanovas
5:388-89)

and state that would entitle them to such a
designation. When the official dogma of the ancient
church was viewed from the later perspective of the
Western Middle Ages and especially of the Reforma-

See vol.3:108

tion, one such teaching was especially prominent.
"The doctrine of redemption and reconciliation lay
outside that activity of the ancient church by which
dogma was formed. . . . Yet this must not be taken
to mean that the subject matter itself was absent

Thom.*Chr*.59 (1856-III:169)

from the faith of the church." Rather, the doctrine of
the atonement through the work of Christ, even
more explicitly than the doctrine of the incarnation
of the person of the Logos, was seen as preeminently
a liturgical doctrine, belonging more appropriately
to the "rule of prayer" articulated in the ritual than
to the "rule of faith" articulated in dogmatic

See vol.1:339

theology. Although it was true of all dogmas and
creeds that they "have a place in the ritual, they are
devotional acts, and of the nature of prayer, addressed

Newm.*Gram*.1.5.2 (Ker
1985:90-91)

to God," the several root metaphors employed for the
doctrine of reconciliation—among them, sacrifice,
satisfaction, and deification—all spoke in the accents

See vol.3:129-44

of worship. That had not, however, prevented them
from becoming the objects of attack in a period when

See pp. 95-101 above

Krth.*Rel.* (1877:2)
Hrth.*Herm.*Tit.3:10
(1882:243-44);Lam.*Indiff.* 12
(Forgues 1:425)

Camp.*Syst.*28.9 (1956:79)
Acts 24:5

Döll.*Gnos.*9 (1890:127)

See p. 287 below
Jer.Niž.*Uč.*E (1864:161-62)

Mak.*Prav.bog.*109 (Tichon
1:560-61)

Ces.*St.eccl.*1.9 (1881:108-14)
Tor.*Car.*1.int. (1779-I:9)

Jam.*Vind.*6.2 (1794-II:339)
See vol.3:18;p. 34 above

1 Cor. 11:19 (Vulg.)

Mhlr.*Ein.*app. 10
(1843:295-98)

Newm.*Gram.*1.5.3 (Ker
1985:99)

both dogma and ritual were receiving critical scrutiny.

Because of such scrutiny, it was probably accurate to suggest that "there is no problem more delicate, none more difficult, yet none more important or urgent, at this hour, than the mode in which the Christian Church in her purity should treat schism, sect, heresy, and error." It was widely recognized that the Greek word "heresy [αἵρεσις]" had meant simply "choice," whether good or bad, and that originally "in its scriptural application . . . it never relates to doctrine, tenet, opinion, or faith"; enemies had called the early church "the sect [αἵρεσις] of the Nazarenes." "Ketzer," the German word for "heretic," came from the name of the medieval dualists called "Cathars." The question of the doctrinal procedure by which a divided church should and could treat a heresy that had arisen in the millennium since the seven ecumenical councils created particular difficulties for Eastern Orthodoxy, because of its special definition of authority; but that did not preclude the compilation of itemized lists of those condemned by the councils, and then the condemnation of various modern teachings about such questions as the doctrine of angels. In the West, too, there were ways of coping with the challenge of heresy without incurring the accusation of lack of charity. That accusation had been raised concerning ancient heresiologists such as Epiphanius, even by those who were concerned about modern heresy. Also from ancient heresiologists came the standard observation, based on the New Testament's declaration that "there must be heresies [oportet haereses esse]," that heretics had contributed to the development of orthodoxy by forcing a clarification of the church's teachings. For in many ways "the disavowal of error" had been more productive than "the enforcement of truth."

Both the enforcement of truth and the disavowal of error had been expressed primarily through creeds and confessions. Conversely, the opposition to dogma took the form of resistance to the authority of such ecclesiastical statements of faith and teaching. Statements of faith like the Apostles' Creed and the Nicene Creed were seen as "religious impositions practiced upon the credulity of less favored ages than the present," since they went beyond "the only apostolic and divine confession of faith" that enjoyed biblical sanction, the confession of Peter to Christ; they were therefore "both the cause and the effect of partyism, and the main perpetuating causes of schism." Defenders of the creed, on the other hand, saw it as an "homage to the Bible, not an offense to it." The "faith" that, according to the New Testament, "overcomes the world" was the Nicene Creed, "the full and complete confession of the church," which, with the Ten Commandments, was the essential content of Christianity. Even the Athanasian Creed could be defended if, like the young Newman, one "drew up a series of texts in support of each verse of the Athanasian Creed." In addition, the proper method of interpreting a creed was to see it "as expressing the sense of the primitive church" as contained in the writings of the church fathers. The long experience of the history of the church had shown that "mere subscription to Holy Scripture" without any creed was "absolutely nugatory" and that therefore some sort of statement of faith was "absolutely necessary . . . to the well-being of a church," as the christological confessions of the early councils showed.

One critic who founded a denomination on the rejection of all creeds was sometimes willing to acknowledge that "a Grecian symbol [such as the Apostles' Creed] had some truth and some philosophy on its side," because it was "a compound of Christian truths, a summary or synopsis of prominent facts." The "Roman creeds" merited no such concession. By "Roman creeds," moreover, he meant not only the *Decrees and Canons of the Council of Trent*, but the *Augsburg Confession* and the *Westminster Confession of Faith*, as well as (though he did not happen to include it here) the *Thirty-Nine Articles* of the Church of England; these were "not portraitures of ancient truths or facts, so much as records of modern opinions and inferences concerning them." They were, of course, not uniform either in their doctrinal content or in their standing as norms of Christian doctrine in their communions. Thus one Lutheran felt able not only to claim for the *Augsburg Confession* of 1530 the title of "the oldest

Camp.*Rce*.6 (Gould 759)

Camp.*Syst*.17.1 (1956:42)
Matt.16:16

Camp.*Rce*.6 (Gould 784)

Mrce.*Sub*.5.2 (1835:84)
1 John 5:4
Makr.*Log.kat*.1 (1871:3-17)
Chom.*Crk*.7 (Karsavin 27)

Fil.*Ent*. (Soudakoff 6)

Newm.*Apol*.1 (Svaglic 18)

Jam.*Vind*.6.1 (1794-II:259)

Pus.*Hist.Eng*.2.3 (1828-II:33)
Slv.*Bogočlv*.11/12,n. (Radlov 3:154-55)

Camp.*Rce*.6 (Gould 760)

Krth.*Cons.Ref*.6 (1871:216)

Krth.*Cons.Ref*.pr. (1871:x)

Grnvg.*Snd.Chr.* (Begtrup 4:458-59)
Grnvg.*Chr.Snd.* (Begtrup 4:575)
Grnvg.*Chr.Brnlr*.4 (Begtrup 9:357-66)

ap.Krth.*Cons.Ref*.6 (1871:228-29)

Pus.*Hist.*1 (1828-I:21)

Joan.Kv.*Jub.Sbor*.3 (1899:73-76);Pi.X.*Sacr.ant.* (*AAS* 2:669)

Slv.*Bogočlv*.6 (Radlov 3:90-91)

Bau.*Neun*.3 (Scholder 4:506)

Hrbn.*Crk*.6 (1861:165)

*Conf.Aug.*1.1 (*Bek*.50)

Krth.*Cons.Ref*.6 (1871:265)

Mar.*Inst.symb*.pr. (1825:xii)

distinctive creed now in use in any large division of Christendom" (the *Decrees and Canons of the Council of Trent* not having been finally promulgated until 1563) but also to identify the Lutheran *Book of Concord* as "the most explicit confession ever made in Christendom" and the Anglican *Thirty-Nine Articles* as "the least explicit among the official utterances of the churches of the Reformation." When another nineteenth-century Lutheran, while citing the *Augsburg Confession* as authoritative in its doctrine of the person of Christ, spoke of "the confession of the Christian faith," he was referring above all to the Apostles' Creed.

One reason for the differences between Lutheranism and Anglicanism in the degree of their "scrupulous adherence" to their confessions—and this despite the efforts of latter-day critics of the Lutheran confessions to drive a wedge between Luther and the *Augsburg Confession*—was Luther's authorship of several of the creedal statements in the *Book of Concord*, for which there was no counterpart in the Reformed confessions, including the *Thirty-Nine Articles*. Eastern Orthodox and Roman Catholic prelates took it for granted that professors in the theological academies of the church were to teach nothing but the doctrines of the church, which had their own validity quite apart from the speculative constructs of the intellectuals; but university professors of Protestant theology found it almost incredible that confessionalists among the clergy should have had the audacity "to bind clergy, doctors, and teachers of theology with an oath to teach its public profession faithfully." To these confessionalists, the opening words of the Latin text of the first article of the *Augsburg Confession*, "Our churches teach with great unanimity," meant that "it is not simply great princes, nor great theologians," but "the churches which teach these doctrines"; for "the private opinions of the greatest of men are here nothing." Extrapolating from that definition of the function of confessions as statements of the public doctrine of the churches for which they spoke, the study of "comparative symbolics" as a distinct branch of theology prescribed that the interpretation of what any particular church taught as doctrine or dogma be based on its confessions (if it had any).

Whether or nor they deserved to be branded "the least explicit among the official utterances of the churches of the Reformation," the *Thirty-Nine Articles* became a focus of controversy during the nineteenth century. F. D. Maurice defended subscription to them on the ground that they did not compete with the Bible, for the Bible and the creed were fundamentally different in genre. The widespread belief that the Bible was made up of "propository articles" constituted a "monstrous insult to the divine word." The *Thirty-Nine Articles*, then, described "conditions of thought" and did not impose a yoke on thought and scholarship. The most provocative—and, in the event, the last—of the *Tracts for the Times* through which the Oxford Movement in the Church of England sounded its call for Catholic renewal within the framework of Anglicanism was *Tract 90*, which bore the seemingly innocuous title, *Remarks on Certain Passages in the Thirty-Nine Articles*, issued in 1841 by John Henry Newman. Quoting the most authoritative among the expositions of the *Thirty-Nine Articles*, that of Gilbert Burnet, Newman argued that despite their vigorous polemics, "the *Articles* are not written against the creed of the Roman Church, but against actual existing errors in it, whether taken into its system or not." Although they were "the offspring of an uncatholic age," they were, "to say the least, not uncatholic"; it was therefore a "duty which we owe both to the Catholic Church and to our own" to read the confessions "in the most Catholic sense they will admit." Thus, although the twenty-fifth article had flatly declared, "There are two sacraments ordained of Christ our Lord in the Gospel, that is to say, baptism and the Supper of the Lord," it seemed possible to say that the other five sacraments of the Catholic Church also "may be sacraments," though not sacraments "ordained by God or Christ."

Such a treatment of the confessional documents of the Christian past raised with special force the question of change, that is, of the development of doctrine. Responding to the charge that "we have thoroughly changed and disfigured our faith," and echoing earlier discussions of "new" creeds, representative treatments insisted that "the change, if indeed

Mrce.*Sub*.5.2 (1835:84-85)

Mrce.*Sub*.1 (1835:13)

Brnt.*Art.XXXIX*.31 (1700:482)

Newm.*Art.XXXIX*.9 (*Tr.Tms*.90:59)

Newm.*Art.XXXIX*.int. (*Tr.Tms*.90:4)

Newm.*Art.XXXIX*.con. (*Tr.Tms*.90:80)

Art.XXXIX.25 (Schaff 3:502)

Newm.*Art.XXXIX*.7 (*Tr.Tms*.90:43)

Thos.Aq.*S.T*.2.2.1.10 (*Ed.Leon*.8:23-24)

it can be called a change at all, is merely accidental, not essential"; for the "new" dogmatic definitions of faith were nothing more than "new explanations of the articles of faith that were originally handed down by tradition [traditi] from the Holy Spirit to the apostles, and from the apostles to the first believers of the church." The paradigm for such "development" was the progressive revelation from the Old Testament to the New, and then within the New Testament itself, from the naive conceptions attributed to the disciples in the Gospels to the formulations in the Book of Acts and in the Epistles, which were inspired by the presence of the Holy Spirit in the apostolic community.

A comparison of the early Epistles of Paul with his later ones, or of the Epistles of John with his Gospel at the end of his life, had already shown Zinzendorf "how even the faith of the apostles has evolved." That impression had taught him to "read the Bible according to its epochs, according to the patterns in the course of time, according to the stages by which the preaching of the gospel has grown from one time to the next." Thanks to such growth, the crisis faced by the first apostolic council, which could have led to a schism in the early church, did not turn out that way, but helped to produce a genuinely catholic church, made up of both Jews and Gentiles. So profound a grasp of what the gospel implied did not break upon the church all at once, but "it was only by gradual steps that the Christian mind gained such practical mastery over its spiritual inheritance." Coping with the historical actuality of those "gradual steps," and therefore with the relation between the supposedly changeless truth of the Christian message at one stage and then again at the next, called for a fundamental reconsideration of the theological significance of "universal-historical development," which was "the fundamental idea in our civilization."

Although the Roman Catholic theologian Johann Sebastian Drey in Tübingen was perhaps the first to recognize this need, the reconsideration can most graphically be traced in the very development of "development" within the thought of its most celebrated exponent, John Henry Newman. As late as

---

Marginal references:

Marc.*Inst*.30.3.1 (Tomassini 6:19-20); Gr.XVI.*Tr*.5.10 (Battaggia 249-52)

Slv.*Soph*.2.2 (Rouleau 72)

See p. 77 above

Zinz.*Rel*.4 (Beyreuther 6-I:70-71)

Acts 15:6-29

Mnkn.*Bl*.8 (1828:89-90)

Wlb.*Inc*.5 (1849:104)

Grnvg.*Nrd.Myth*.1 (Begtrup 5:397)

Söd.*Upp*.3 (1930:149); Söd.*Kat.prot*.2.17 (1910:415-19)

Newm.*Art.XXXIX*.int.
(*Tr.Tms*.90:3)

See p. 263 above

Luke 2:19

Newm.*Univ.Serm.*14
(1843:311-54)

Löl.*Symb*.2 (1958:17-18)

Söd.*Kat.prot*.1.2 (1910:35)

Schf.*Prin.Prot*.2.6.83
(*Merc*.1:230)

Tract 90, published early in 1841, Newman was still speaking about "a change in theological teaching" as involving "either the commission or the confession of sin," since it was "either the profession or renunciation of erroneous doctrine"; thus "if it does not succeed in proving the fact of past guilt, it ipso facto implies present [guilt]." Meanwhile, however, he had been examining the role of tradition in the controversies between Arianism and the Nicene orthodoxy espoused by Athanasius, and had begun to see that on some troubling points the Arians appeared to have the argument from antiquity on their side; application of the Vincentian canon would not have led automatically to the orthodoxy of the Council of Nicea. By early in 1843, in a sermon on the text, "But Mary kept all these things, and pondered them in her heart," he was prepared to announce what he was to call in the title of the published version of that sermon "the theory of developments in religious doctrine." And in 1845 he published the first edition (revised in 1878) of "the prototype of the idea of the development of Christian dogmas," his *Essay on the Development of Christian Doctrine*, which "constitutes the theologically most important production of England's outstanding theologian and Catholicism's—at least besides Leo XIII—most significant personality in the last [nineteenth] century." In the same year Philip Schaff published an essay delivered as an inaugural lecture in German the year before, bearing the title *The Principle of Protestantism as Related to the Present State of the Church* and devoted to the principle of "development"; his colleague John Williamson Nevin had translated it into English and supplied an introduction that was itself a further exposition of what "development" meant.

Although these four versions of the principle of development of doctrine drew diametrically opposite ecclesiological conclusions from it—Drey and Newman finding in it the imperative to accept Roman Catholicism, Schaff and Nevin employing it to justify a "Protestant Catholicism" in the heritage of the Reformation as "genuine historical progress"— they all shared considerable common ground. Drey saw "the law of the temporal," which pertained also to historical revelation, in "the process of becoming, by means of the progressive disclosure of itself in time, and the unfolding into the open of the embryo that has been concealed." Applying this principle specifically to the development of Christian doctrine, Schaff cited "the doctrine of the Trinity before the time of Athanasius" as a particular historical instance of the general rule that "it is possible for the church to be in possession of a truth and to live upon it, before it has come to be discerned in her consciousness." For Nevin, the "organic" character of Christianity implied, "in the nature of the case, development, evolution, progress." In keeping with that "inward history" of Christianity, "all its leading doctrines have a history, too, and cannot be understood . . . apart from their history"; yet "the idea of such a development" implied "just the contrary" of the suggestion that there had been "any change in the nature of Christianity itself."

Proceeding on the basis of the premise that "from the nature of the human mind, time is necessary for the full comprehension and perfection of great ideas," Newman argued that "the highest and most wonderful truths, though communicated to the world once for all by inspired teachers, could not be comprehended all at once by the recipients," but had "required only the longer time and deeper thought for their full elucidation"; to that observation he gave the label "the theory of development of doctrine." He professed to be able to discern this rule of "development" at work throughout the history of human thought, and in that sense to see the development of Christian doctrine as a specific illustration of an overall pattern. In relation to previous views of change, including his own, however, the most revolutionary implication of his theory was that orthodox Christian doctrine was not exempt from the general rule of development but was its most profound and brilliant instance. Although he was not, therefore, either the first one or the only one to hold it or to state it, Newman came to be identified with it, and for this and for his other insights into the nature of Catholic faith and doctrine he was at one and the same time a puzzle to the age of the First Vatican Council and an "eternal honor to the Catholic Church."

Dry.*Apol*.1.2.3.19
(1838-I:173)

Schf.*Prin*.*Prot*.2.6.16
(*Merc*.1:221)

Nvn.*Schf*. (*Merc*.1:45)

Newm.*Dev*.1.int.21 (Harrold 28)

Döll.*Vat*.*Dekr*.17 (Reusch 109)

Mntl.*Ang*.12 (Lecoffre 5:352)

One distinctive feature of Newman's presentation of development was his concern with the normative aspects of the question even more than with the descriptive ones. That set him apart from most of the historians of dogma among his contemporaries, especially those of Protestant Germany, who, while giving the normative issue some explicit attention—in addition to a great deal of implicit consideration—claimed to be taking the descriptive task as primary. Already in the scholastic thought of the Middle Ages, the obvious contradictions in the dogmatic tradition had demanded clarification, which usually took the form of a dialectical juxtaposition but also, though subordinately, involved attention to the historical relations between different aspects of the tradition. Enlightenment historiography had made such relations central, and thus it had founded the history of dogma as a scholarly and theological discipline. The irresistible drive of the faith of the church to take the form of dogma made the need for historical understanding of that dogma no less irresistible. This could lead to a relativistic historicism that defined any dogma or system of dogmatics as a temporary pause of the ever-flowing stream of the history of dogma, soon to be swept away by that stream again.

Recognizing as he did that in most areas of life most thoughtful minds "neither can possess, nor need certitude, nor do they look out for it," Newman strove not only to identify, as a historian, the patterns of development, but, as a theologian, to define "certain characteristics of faithful developments, which none but faithful developments have, and the presence of which serves as a test to discriminate between them and corruption." The seven notes of authentic development were, in his final formulation: preservation of type; continuity of principles; power of assimilation; logical sequence; anticipation of the future of the development; conservative action upon its past; and chronic vigor. As both Newman and his contemporaries recognized, "preservation" and "continuity" were fundamental to all the others. A review of the treatment of the doctrine of the Trinity by the church fathers of the first three centuries could lead to equivocal conclusions, from which it was not clear

See pp. 230-41 above

See vol.3:223-29

Rtl.*Ges.Auf*.5 (1893:147)

See pp. 75-101 above

Klfth.*DG*.90 (1839:299)

Bau.*DG*.2 (1858:2-3)

Newm.*Gram*.2.7.2.4 (Ker 1985:155)

Newm.*Dev*.2.5.int.2 (Harrold 158)

Newm.*Dev*.2.5 (Harrold 157-91)

Newm.*Dev*.1.int.10-14 (Harrold 13-19)

Mhlr.*Ath*.1 (1827-I:110)

Mynst.*Betr*.53 (1846-II:253)

Lam.*Mx.égl*.1 (Forgues
12:188)

Krth.*Cons.Ref*.7 (1871:270)
Matt. 16:18

Matt. 13:31-32
Slv.*Rus.égl*.2.9 (Rouleau 215)

Slv.*Bogočlv*.11/12 (Radlov
3:159)

Grnvg.*Pr*.13.i.1839
(Thodberg 12:121)
Luke 2:52

Chan.*Calv*. (AUA 467-68)

Eus.*H.e*.1.1.1 (*GCS* 9:6)

Lid.*Div*.7 (1867:641-42)

whether the declaration that nevertheless "the faith of
the church was constantly like unto itself, even
though a development took place" expressed a historical judgment or a dogmatic principle—or both.

For if there had been a "development and ordering"
of the church through the "many times" of its history,
what was there that still remained? In what sense was
it accurate to say that God not only "develops" the
church, but at the same time "conserves" it? Organic
metaphors seemed to many a helpful way to answer
that question: the continuity was "not the sameness of
a rock, but rather the living identity of a man." The
inorganic biblical metaphor of the "rock" could be
replaced by the organic and no less biblical metaphor
of the "tree" as a way of speaking about the history of
the church. There were some who were prepared to
argue that among such organic terms for the church,
the title "body of Christ" was meant "not in the sense
of a metaphor, but of a metaphysical formula," for—
heretical though it might seem in both cases to say
so—the church, like Christ himself, had "increased in
wisdom." Yet the organic metaphor for development
seemed to have as its unavoidable converse the recognition that creeds could not only be born but die, and
that once-cherished beliefs could become peripheral or
meaningless, while through habit they were still
being defended as articles of faith.

The concepts of identity and continuity were a way
of protecting the idea of development of doctrine
against the charge of innovation. Because "novelty-
mongering" had, since the early centuries of the
church, been seen as the mark of heresy, this recent
discovery of development needed to confront the issue
of whether a doctrinal development was to be defined
as "the positive substantial growth" of a doctrine, be
it "through an enlargement from within" or "through
an accretion from without of new intellectual matter,"
or whether it was nothing more than the process of
making the implicit explicit, "an explanation of an
already existing idea or belief, presumably giving to
that belief greater precision and exactness in our own
or other minds, but adding nothing whatever to its
real area." That way of putting the question made it
evident that in addition to all the other objections

See pp. 196-97 above

now being raised against it, the Nicene dogma of the Trinity, with its designation of the Son of God as "homoousios with the Father," stood as the prime instance, at any rate in orthodox history, of "development of doctrine," thus perhaps also of doctrinal innovation. For Protestant theology, it was as well the most prominent illustration of the tension, inherited from the Reformers and from the Reformation confessions, between the theoretical principle of the authority of Scripture over tradition and the practice of demanding acceptance for a dogma not stated in the ipsissima verba of Scripture but received from the tradition of the church. Roman Catholic critics, therefore, characterized Unitarians as "the most consistent in applying the principles of Protestant theology" against the claim that the dogmas of the ancient church were infallible.

Bau.*DG*.103 (1858:306)

Lam.*Indiff*.6 (Forgues 1:140)

The obverse side of that problem in Protestant theology was the doctrine of justification by faith. In Reformation teaching this was not simply one doctrine in a series, but the key to all other doctrines, and hence was the central point in the total transformation of theology achieved by the Reformers. And yet, as its defenders during the Reformation era had been forced to acknowledge, finding patristic authentication for it was difficult or impossible, even in the writings of an Augustine, whom it seemed possible to cite in support of other Reformation positions on the sacraments or on grace and predestination. Picking up on that acknowledgment, nineteenth-century Roman Catholic critics of Protestantism pointed out that not a single church council could be cited in evidence for the definition—championed by Luther and his followers, as well as by Calvin, against the doctrines of Andreas Osiander—of justification as the imputation to the sinner of the righteousness achieved by the obedience of Christ. Such admissions of discontinuity with the tradition, they argued, put that doctrine outside the pattern of authentic development.

Hrlss.*Enc*.2.3.6 (1837:123)

See vol.4:157-58

See vol.4:196; 224-25

See vol.4:150-52

Döll.*Ref*.3 (1846-III:195)

During the nineteenth and twentieth centuries, however, the most flagrant "novelty-mongering" seemed to Protestant and Eastern Orthodox critics to be taking place within Roman Catholicism itself, the bastion of traditionalism at any rate in the West,

Pi.IX.*Ineffab.* (*Pii IX Acta*
1-I:597-619)
Pi.XII.*Mun.* (*AAS*
42:767-70)

Bau.*Neun.*3 (Scholder
4:318-20)

Lid.*Div.*7 (1867:649-50)

Newm.*Dev.*1.3.1.8 (Harrold
100)

Newm.*Dev.*2.5.4.4 (Harrold
388-91)

Andrts.*Symb.*con. (Regopoulos
409)
Hrth.*Herm.*1 Tim.3:2
(1882:88-89)

Innok.*Bog.oblič.*22-27
(1859-I:77-90)

Joh.D.*Hom.*9 (*PG* 96:721)

through the promulgation by Pope Pius IX in 1854 of the "new" dogma of the immaculate conception of Mary, and then by Pope Pius XII in 1950 of her bodily assumption. The past history of the immaculate conception helped to make its eventual dogmatization intelligible, perhaps even inevitable, especially with the addition of a theory of papal sovereignty according to which the pope even had the power to create "new" dogmas. As for the supposed "correspondence," alleged by defenders of the papal dogma, between the dogma of the immaculate conception and the Nicene homoousion, the two dogmas were, according to critics of the Marian dogma, to be seen as in fact fundamentally different. Not only did the immaculate conception represent a teaching accepted by only one section of a divided Christendom, while the homoousion was a matter of ecumenical consensus; but the homoousion was a way of affirming "a truth which was held to be of primary and vital import from the first." Thus the fathers at the Council of Nicea "were explaining old truth, they were not revealing truth unrevealed before," while by contrast the immaculate conception was an unwarranted addition to the creed. In his explanation of "anticipation of its future" as a criterion of faithful development of doctrine, Newman freely admitted that the "special prerogatives" being attributed to Mary, including her immaculate conception, "were not fully recognized in the Catholic ritual till a late date," but he insisted nevertheless that "they were not a new thing in the church, or strange to her earlier teachers." Therefore they had, in his sense of the word, "developed."

As its responses to the promulgation of the immaculate conception in 1854 demonstrated, Eastern Orthodoxy, with its definition of its essence as "authenticity with freedom," including the freedom to go beyond the rules and practices of the apostolic era, stood in a peculiar position in relation to the entire issue of development of doctrine. Unlike Protestantism, it took no umbrage at the high position being assigned to the Virgin by the dogma: she had been celebrated as "the all-holy [πανάγια] Theotokos and Ever-Virgin Mary" more consistently and more anciently by the East than by the West, and she

Amvr.*Sobr*.3.5 (1810-JII:48)

See p. 36 above

Innok.*Bog.oblič*.123
(1859-II:137)

Mntl.*Ans*.8 (Lecoffre 8:401)

See vol.2:117-33
Hrth.*Thrsk*.2.2 (1895:57-58);
Jer.Niž.*Uč*.P (1864:301-3)

Marc.*Inst*.25.12.1 (Tomassini
4:346)

Dyob.*Joh.Dam*.1 (1903:3)

Bau.*Vers*.int. (1838:15-16)

was still being hailed there as "glorified and all-blessed." Not having committed itself so unequivocally to the distinctively Augustinian doctrine of original sin, the East did not have the same obligation to define why Mary was an "exception" to that universal rule. Above all, it objected to the immaculate conception on the grounds that it was not in the tradition but had developed later, as had the Western notion of Filioque, which Roman Catholic theologians continued to praise for its insight.

Ironically, one of the most impressive cases of development of doctrine in all of church history had been the Byzantine apologia for images in response to the attacks of iconoclasm. Eastern theologians in Greece and Russia went on repeating that apologia, and Western scholars continued to echo its argumentation, explaining that because the converts to Christianity in the early centuries of the church had to come either from Judaism (which prohibited images) or from paganism (which made images into idols), it would have been imprudent for the church to create icons for the veneration of the faithful. That had to await the further development of the Christian cultus, as well as the deeper development of the Christian dogma of the incarnation, which provided the doctrinal justification for image-worship. On the other hand, a Greek study of John of Damascus at the end of this period had the obligation to consider in what sense, if any, he had been responsible for "an innovation."

Consideration of various doctrines and of the varying patterns they had taken in their development led to discussion of the problem of how to divide the history of Christian doctrine into periods. An extreme instance was one German Lutheran periodization of the history of the doctrine of the atonement, published in 1838, which felt able to discern three principal stages: from the New Testament to the Reformation (fifteen centuries); from the Reformation to the beginning of the nineteenth century (three centuries); and from the beginning of the nineteenth century to the present (three decades). There was a widespread sense that "every period of the church and of theology has its particular problem to solve, and every doctrine . . . has its classic age in which it first

Schf.*Prin.Prot.*2.6
(*Merc.*1:219-20)

Schf.*Prin.Prot.*1.2 (*Merc.*1:78)

Hrbn.*Crk.*5 (1861:84-85)

Klfth.*DG.*37 (1839:98-99)

comes to be fully understood and appropriated by the consciousness of the Christian world": in the first three centuries, the Trinity; in the age of Augustine, sin and grace; in the Middle Ages, the sacraments; in the Reformation, "the full exposition of the Christian soteriology, as standing in the subjective appropriation of the work of redemption"; in the period of Protestant orthodoxy, the inspiration of Scripture. And now the turn had come for ecclesiology, which had long been the principal point of division. It was the conviction of various Protestant theologians "that the period of dogmatic development that is beginning anew in our own time will have its special assignment in the doctrine of the church." Within all the denominations, many heirs of the nineteenth century would come to believe that it had bequeathed this "special assignment" to the twentieth century, which some of them therefore came to call "the age of the church."

6   The Sobornost of the Body of Christ

Schf.*Prin.Prot.*1.2 (*Merc.*1:79)

James 1:27;Matt.5:13

Doc.*Chr.Un.*1 (Bell 1:3)

As the twentieth century began, each of the major churches of a divided Christendom was obliged, for reasons of its own, to address anew the doctrine of the church—its place in the mind of Christ, its essential message, its nature and identity, its marks of continuity, its authority and structure, its response to its twofold mission of keeping itself "unspotted from the world" and yet of being "the salt of the earth," and above all its authentic unity despite and beyond its historic divisions. By the beginning of the final third of the twentieth century, not only each of the churches individually, but all of them together (or at least in some sense together) were engaged in probing with unprecedented vigor the "vision . . . of a church genuinely catholic, loyal to all truth, and gathering into its fellowship all 'who profess and call themselves Christians,' " yet with "a rich diversity of life and devotion."

Ecumenicity was the great new fact in the history of the church, and hence also in the history of Christian doctrine; and the doctrine of the church became, as it had never quite been before, the bearer of the whole of the Christian message for the twentieth century, as well as the recapitulation of the entire doctrinal tradition from preceding centuries. In a special way, therefore, twentieth-century ecclesiology was based on constant cross-reference to the Christian past, and it needs to be understood chiefly on that basis; yet it was a doctrine that looked to the present and to the future no less than to the past.

See vol.1:108-20

Delmp.*Oik*.2.3 (1972:89)

See vol.4:203-17

See vol.4:262-74

See vol.4:156-58

See vol.4:175-76;313

See vol.4:274-303

See vol.4:275-76

See pp. 208-9 above

See pp. 248-52 above

See vol.2:16-22

See vol.2:22-30

For the mainstream churches in the East and in the West at the beginning of the twentieth century, some version of the "criteria of apostolic continuity"— formulated most succinctly by Irenaeus, but by the nature of the case believed, taught, and confessed as the common doctrine of the church catholic—still stood as the presupposition for the definition of authority in faith and order: the apostolic Scriptures, the apostolic tradition, and the apostolic office. With considerable accuracy, though not without some over-simplification, each of the three components in that definition had been described as having become constitutive for one or another of the branches of Christendom. Thus, as it was understood by friend and foe, the Protestant Reformation had elevated the authority of Scripture over that of the creedal tradition (while keeping much of the latter), and over the identification of "apostolic office" with the historic episcopate (by insisting that only a polity that could be established by Scripture should be binding on the church, though not agreeing on precisely which system of polity, if any, met that criterion). As it had defined itself at the Council of Trent, Roman Catholicism also professed to retain all three criteria of apostolic continuity; but even some in its own midst had charged that it was attaching the authority of Scripture (whose canon a council of the Roman Catholic Church had, for the first time in Christian history, taken it upon itself to fix for all of Christendom) and the authority of the creedal tradition (to which the pope had, also in a sense for the first time, asserted his prerogative to "add" doctrines by proclaiming the dogma of the immaculate conception of Mary, a prerogative that was codified by the First Vatican Council in laying down the dogma of papal infallibility) to the growing centralization of authority in the pope. Meanwhile, it could be said that historic Eastern Orthodoxy had fixed the authority of tradition, represented (but by no means exhausted) by the actions of the first seven ecumenical councils, as the norm for the orthodox interpretation of Scripture, and had denied to any member of the episcopate, even to the one who was "first among equals," the right to

See vol.2:157-70

See vol.4:313-31

Doc.Chr.Un.1 (Bell 1:3)

See vol.1:167

See vol.2:174-79;
vol.4:291-303;pp. 45-48
above

Brgs.Theol.Symb.3 (1914:274)

See p. 272 above

exercise authority apart from that tradition. And the Radical Reformation could be seen as having undercut, one by one, all three of these criteria.

On the basis of that threefold standard of apostolicity formulated by Irenaeus, there was set forth, at the end of the nineteenth and the beginning of the twentieth century, one of the most widely discussed of modern proposals for the renewal and the reunification of the church: the Anglican *Lambeth Quadrilateral*, first affirmed in 1886, made official by the Lambeth Conference of Anglican bishops in 1888, and then incorporated as the central doctrinal affirmation of the "Appeal to All Christian People" issued by the Lambeth Conference in 1920. In addition to the three criteria of Irenaeus, a fourth, which had of course been implicit in Irenaeus as well, was made explicit, when acceptance of the two sacraments of baptism and the Eucharist was stipulated as a condition for church unity. That addition was warranted by the role the sacraments had played in the history of division and schism. Doctrinal and ecclesiastical cartography recognized that "the primary and fundamental differences between the Reformers, Roman Catholic and Protestant, were with reference to Christian institutions, especially the sacraments." The addition of the sacraments to the list of requirements for unity was warranted in a positive sense as well, by the place that the sacraments came to occupy in the twentieth century as a unifying force. Yet the Bible, the creed, and church structure, together with the relations between them, were still the key to understanding the positions of the several church traditions on faith and order, including their very doctrines of the sacraments.

In originally issuing the *Lambeth Quadrilateral*, the bishops of the Anglican communion had, in a way, only been summarizing the historic ecclesiology of their own tradition as this had been clarified through the response to the debates brought on by the Oxford Movement. In the strict sense, the *Lambeth Quadrilateral* may be said to contain nothing that had not already been articulated in the *Thirty-Nine Articles*, and to have made no overt concessions to Anglo-Catholic emphases, keeping, for example, the restriction of the concept "sacrament" to "the two

Art.XXXIX.25 (Schaff
3:502-3)

sacraments ordained by Christ himself—baptism and
the Supper of the Lord—ministered with unfailing
use of Christ's words of institution, and of the
elements ordained by him." Yet the role of the
Lambeth Quadrilateral as a basis for the discussions of
church unity throughout the twentieth century on all
sides—Protestant, Roman Catholic, and Orthodox—
is a reflection of its roots not only in Irenaeus but in
the entire patristic tradition, as well as of the new
urgency about the imperative of reunification stimulated by the ecumenical experience. This helped, in
turn, to raise many of the other theological questions
with which Christian thinkers and churches were to
concern themselves during the twentieth century, and
it provides us here with a touchstone by which to
select, through a rather random sampling of both
theologians and doctrines, from among the mass of
such questions in the voluminous literature.

Art.XXXIX.6 (Schaff 3:489)

Quoting verbatim from the *Thirty-Nine Articles*, the
first article of the *Lambeth Quadrilateral* specified, as
prerequisite to the reunion of the church, acceptance
of "the Holy Scriptures of the Old and New Testaments, as 'containing all things necessary to salvation,' and as being the rule and ultimate standard of
faith." In its second article, it identified the creedal
basis for the reunion of the church: "the Apostles'
Creed, as the baptismal symbol; and the Nicene
Creed, as the sufficient statement of the Christian
faith." Practically as well as doctrinally, however, the
most controversial of the conditions laid down in the
Lambeth Quadrilateral was its final one: "the historic
episcopate, locally adapted in the methods of its
administration to the varying needs of the nations and
peoples called of God into the unity of his church." In
the British context, this was directed to the ecclesiology of the several congregational "free churches"
that had broken with Anglican doctrine at least in
part over the question of the form and power of the

Doct.Chr.Un.32 (Bell 1:106)
Doc.Chr.Un.51 (Bell
1:182-83)

historic episcopate, and to the Reformed ecclesiology
of the Presbyterian Church of Scotland. But its
severest test, once again practically as well as doctrinally, came in 1947, with the creation of the Church
of South India, which explicitly took the *Lambeth
Quadrilateral* as its doctrinal basis: "all the other

ministers of the uniting churches [whether congregational or presbyterian or episcopal in polity] shall be acknowledged as ministers of the word and the sacraments in the united church," and the "historic episcopate" was made the norm for its continuing ministry thereafter. At the same time, by specifying "the historic episcopate" and by explaining that in view of "varying needs" throughout the church and its history this was to be "locally adapted," the *Lambeth Quadrilateral* was intended to reject the claim that any one particular and local form of "the historic episcopate" was to be accorded normative status.

A short time after the initial discussions of the *Lambeth Quadrilateral*, a group of Protestant churches in the United States met to form the Federal Council of the Churches of Christ in America, whose purpose it would be "to manifest the essential oneness of the Christian churches of America in Jesus Christ as their divine Lord and Savior." In expressing that oneness concretely, the churches joined together in the Federal Council "for the prosecution of work that can be better done in union than in separation." That work included, within the Christian family, the cultivation of "devotional fellowship and mutual counsel concerning the spiritual life and religious activities of the churches." Despite the great divergences among the churches of the Reformation regarding the application of the law of Christ to human life and society, the Council had the aim, within the context of the growing ecumenical concern for the redemption of society, "to secure a larger combined influence for the churches of Christ in all matters affecting the moral and social conditions of the people, so as to promote the application of the law of Christ in every relation of human life." And though they did not agree about the forms of unity necessary for the expression of various degrees of Christian fellowship, all the churches were coming to "the belief that the beginnings of unity are to be found in the clear statement and full consideration of those things in which we differ, as well as of those things in which we are at one." As the Christian doctrine of the church had recognized in other times of separation and schism, unity was both a gift and a task.

*Doc.Chr.Un.*139 (Bell 2:147-48)

See pp. 248-52 above

FCC.*Const.*pr. (Sanford 512)

FCC.*Const.*1 (Sanford 512)

FCC.*Const.*3.3 (Sanford 513)

See vol.4:217

See pp. 312-25 below

FCC.*Const.*3.4 (Sanford 513)

Zēz.*Hen.*int. (1965:1-26)

*Doc.Chr.Un.*4 (Bell 1:16)

See vol.4:72

The theological rediscovery of the doctrine of the church was thus closely tied to the existential rediscovery of the reality of the church itself, and the experience of millions of twentieth-century Christians in all denominations either with the pain of separation or with the joy of reunion contributed to their concern with the doctrinal issues, as well as to their impatience with the way these doctrinal issues had sometimes functioned in the life and teaching of the churches. As the attention of the eighteenth and nineteenth centuries to the experiential foundation and "experimental" implication of Christian doctrines had shown, every doctrine in the corpus of theology was susceptible of such "affectional transposition" and existential reappropriation. Yet the doctrine of the church, as the supreme expression of the social character of Christianity, was uniquely sensitive to corporate and individual experience, just as it was in turn immediately applicable to the concrete need of empirical Christendom for reformation and renewal, revival and reunion.

Already in the nineteenth century, Eastern Orthodoxy had been seen, by Western as well as by Eastern thinkers, as having been providentially prepared for just such a time. A sign of its increasing influence was the adoption, as almost a technical term, of the Russian word "sobornost" by Western theologians of many linguistic and denominational traditions. The term "sobornaja" had been—if not, as Aleksej Chomjakov claimed, already in the usage of Cyril and Methodius, "the apostles to the Slavs," then at least as early as the eleventh century—the Old Church Slavonic rendering of "catholic" in the Nicene Creed; use of the word "sobor" for the church councils to which Eastern Orthodoxy assigned authority in the church helped to make the term a way of distinguishing Eastern ecclesiology from both the "papal monarchy" of Roman Catholicism and the "sola Scriptura" of Protestantism. "Sobornost" in this sense entered the vocabulary and the thought world of the West just as, for reasons that lay in the political and cultural upheavals of the modern era, Western Christianity, whether Roman Catholic or Anglican or Protestant, was, throughout the twentieth century, rediscovering

See pp. 119-46 above

Plmr.*Russ.Ch.*1 (1882:1-6); see p. 310 below

Chom.*Égl.lat.Prot.*6 (1872:389-400)
See vol.2·158

See vol.2:22-30
Krtšv.*Sob.*3 (1932:41-71);Lōl.*Symb.*2 (1958:13)

Doc.Chr.Un.1.17-23 (Bell
1:9-10)

the Christian East, whether Slavic or Greek or Near
Eastern, within much of which the nineteenth century
had been a period of such intense ecclesiological
renewal.

The Renewal of Ecclesiology

See vol. 1:156-58
Symb.Apost. (Schaff 2:45)

Rufin.Symb.37 (CCSL
20:171-72)

See vol. 1:201

Symb.Nic.-CP (Schaff 2:58-59)

See vol.4:69-126

See vol. 1:226-77;
vol.2:37-90;vol.3:106-57;
vol.4:158-61,350-62;
pp. 89-101, 190-99 above

See vol. 1:158-60

See vol. 1:308-13

Phds.Pent.epil. (1969-II:256)

See vol.2:157-70
See vol.4:69-126

See vol.4:262-74

See vol.4:70-71
See vol.4:180-81;
218;290-303;313-22
See vol.4:336-50

The doctrine of the church had been a part of the
Christian confession from earliest times. The Apostles' Creed contained the clause, "the holy church,"
later expanded to "the holy catholic church," and the
earliest exposition of that creed explained that believing in the existence of "one holy church" and faith in
God as Trinity were essential components of what the
faithful were obliged to affirm. Although the phrase
was not part of the creed adopted at the Council of
Nicea itself, the liturgical and creedal text that came
to be known as the Nicene Creed, in its eventual
formulations both in Greek and in Latin, included
"one holy catholic and apostolic church" directly after
the confession of the doctrine of the Holy Spirit; in
that sense there had always been an ecclesiology, and
those four marks of the church were to serve repeatedly as a way of giving systematic organization to the
church's doctrine about itself.

Christology, however, had engaged the central
attention of the church and of its theologians in every
century, but ecclesiology had gone through a history
best described as episodic. The questions of baptism
by heretics and the authority of bishops had made it
an issue between Rome and Carthage in the third
century, and a related but quite distinct set of
ecclesiological problems had focused attention on it
again in the fifth—both of these primarily in the Latin
West. Ecclesiology, this time in the form of relative
patriarchal authority, can be said to have been a
fundamental point of division in the schism between
the Latin West and the Greek East. Yet it was not
until the schisms within the Western church, in the
later Middle Ages and above all in the Protestant
Reformation, that the church as a doctrine became the
subject of explicit theological concern and then of
confessional formulation. Except for the rehearsal of
the problematics of the Reformation, the seventeenth
century had once more permitted it to become rela-

tively peripheral, and even the vigorous discussions of the nature of the church and its holiness occasioned in various but related ways by Jansenism, Puritanism, and Pietism had not succeeded in bringing about a fundamental reconsideration of ecclesiology throughout Christendom.

See pp. 12-24 above

That reconsideration had begun to come into its own only in the nineteenth century. The Slavophils and Soloviev in Russian Orthodoxy, Möhler and the Tübingen school in German Roman Catholicism, Wilhelm Loehe and the liturgical renewal in German Lutheranism, Grundtvig and the church movement in Danish Lutheranism, Newman and the Oxford Movement in the Church of England, Schaff and the Mercersburg theology in the Reformed Church of America—these and other theologians and theological movements of the nineteenth century, many though not all of them influenced by one another as well as by common sources in the literary and philosophical Zeitgeist (still identifiable, despite criticism of the term, as "Romantic") reawakened interest in ecclesiology within most or all of the churches and moved many of the participants in these various movements to predict that as previous periods of church history had found their distinctive theological vocation in the doctrine of the Trinity or in the doctrine of justification, so now it was to be the doctrine of the church that would become the leitmotiv of this age. Yet it fell to the twentieth century, far more than to the nineteenth, to carry out that prediction, as developments of doctrine that began in the nineteenth century—including the very concept of development of doctrine itself—now finally attained ecclesiological maturity.

Wellek (1963) 128-221

Lovejoy (1948) 228-53

See pp. 280-81 above

See pp. 273-78 above

As it had always been, the doctrine of the church was especially sensitive to the fundamental interpretation of the relation between the individual and the corporate dimensions of human life. The individualism of the eighteenth and nineteenth centuries had shaped—and had, in turn, been shaped by—the understanding of Christian faith and experience as a phenomenon based on the relation between "God and the soul, the soul and God." So now, the deepening awareness throughout modern culture that individuals

Plot.Rask.2 (1902:47-50)

See pp. 130-46 above

Aug.Soliloq.1.2.7 (PL 32:872)

See pp. 219, 221 above

Nieb.*Chr.Min*.1.3
(1956:17-27)

were never isolated from one another but always participated in various communities had its counterpart in a growing recognition of the specifically social character of Christian teaching and life. The first—and still the most influential—history of Christian social teachings, that of Ernst Troeltsch, originally published in 1912, articulated that recognition in its study of "the intrinsic sociological idea of Christianity, and its structure and organization," which, it continued, had always contained "an ideal of a universal fundamental theory of human relationships in general, which will extend far beyond the borders of

Trlsch.*Soz*.int.4 (Baron 1:14)

the actual religious community or church." As part of the renewal of ecclesiology, this task of applying, to the church and to its history, the insights and

Found.7 (1913:348-50)

methods of the social sciences sought to do for the doctrine of the church what philosophy and philology

See vol.3:95-105;284-93; vol.4:306-13;pp. 90-92 above

had long been called upon to do for other doctrinal concerns. When applied, for example, to research into the complex historical problem of the origins of confessional and denominational division, these insights and methods illumined the pathology of schism in ways that significantly affected the theological interpretation both of the nature of the church and of

See pp. 302-3 below

the meaning of its unity.

Doc.Chr.Un.284.18 (Bell 4:237)

External threats to the church and the Christian confession during the twentieth century evoked responses in which ecclesiology necessarily took a central place. In Germany, the *Düsseldorf Theses* of 1933 opened with the preamble: "The providence of God has led us to an hour in which we are obliged to ask ourselves the question anew: 'What is the Evangelical

Düss.Th.pr. (Niesel 327)

Church [Was heisst evangelische Kirche]?'" And the first thesis declared: "The holy Christian church, whose only head is Christ, is born from the word of

Düss.Th.1 (Niesel 327)

God; in this it abides, and it does not hearken to any alien voice." Early in the following year that commitment to the independence of the church from "any alien voice" and to its sole dependence on the word of God became the message of the first of two German Protestant theological synods held at Barmen. Under five headings—"The Church in the Present Day," "The Church under Holy Scripture," "The Church in the World," "The Message of the Church," and "The

Structure [Gestalt] of the Church"—a Reformed synod, in the (First) *Barmen Declaration*, affirmed its opposition to "a devastating, centuries-old error in the Evangelical Church," which had now become "mature and visible": the notion "that alongside the revelation of God, the grace of God, and the glory of God, a legitimate autonomy of man should decide about the message and the form of the church, that is, about the temporal way to eternal salvation." Capitulation to this error would represent the destruction of the Evangelical Church. For in the light of the Reformation heritage the church was to be defined as "the visibly and temporally structured reality of the community that has been called, gathered, sustained, comforted, and governed by the Lord himself through the ministry of proclamation, as well as the no less visibly and temporally structured reality of the unity of such communities." As such a community, the church was universal, transcending all differences of race, state, and culture.

In the (Second) *Barmen Declaration*, those accents became even more prominent. Its third thesis defined the church as "the community of brethren, in which Jesus Christ acts by the Holy Spirit in the present, through word and sacrament," without any dependence of the church on other powers or authorities, be they "spiritual" or "secular." In defining the church this way, the *Barmen Declaration* was carrying out the necessary implications of its opening words, which were to be echoed in the following years: "Jesus Christ, as he is witnessed to us in Holy Scripture, is the one Word of God, to whom we hearken and to whom, in life and in death, we are to bear trust and obedience." In addition to its explicit polemic against the politicization of the church's preaching and teaching under the Nazi regime, this first thesis of the *Barmen Declaration* was also a protest against the tendency, dominant in much of the interpretation of the Gospels since the nineteenth century, to distinguish radically between Jesus and the church and even to maintain that "the historical Jesus" had not intended to found a church but had proclaimed and expected an apocalyptic kingdom of God. "More and more, after the death of Jesus, did the preaching of

*Erkl.Bek.*1.1 (Niesel 329)

See vol.4:180-81; 218;290-303;313-22

*Erkl.Bek.*5.1 (Niesel 332)

*Erkl.Bek.*5.3 (Niesel 332)

*Theol.Erkl.*3 (Niesel 335-36)

Brth.*Krch.*4 (*TheolEx* 27:20)

*Theol.Erkl.*1 (Niesel 335)

See pp. 225-26 above
See p. 321 below

See p. 299 below

Hüg.*Ess.*1.5 (1949-I:127)

the kingdom, indeed all direct thought of the kingdom, wane," one Roman Catholic Modernist had said,
"and did the church take the place of the kingdom."
In the ecclesiological crisis of the 1930s, such a
dichotomy became unacceptable.

See pp. 89-101 above

The very methods of literary analysis and historical
research that had been inspired by "the quest of the
historical Jesus" had led instead to the recognition
that the Gospels, in fact all of the books of the New
Testament, must be read as church documents, not
only written for the church but in a real sense written
by the church. The church had written the New
Testament and had existed before there ever was a
New Testament. In eliciting a "theology" from any
passage, therefore, a sound understanding of the text

Bltmn.*Th.N.T.*epil.
(1953:577-81)

required that the life and situation of the primitive
Christian community serve as the context. The historic disputes of the Reformation era over the relation

See vol.4:262-74

between Scripture and tradition underwent a change
of polarity when the focus became the tradition that
had preceded the New Testament: chronologically,
perhaps then also logically, tradition did have an

Bltmn.*Th.N.T.*3.2.54
(1953:464-73)

undeniable priority. An exegesis that sought to pit the
individual's private religious experience against the

See pp. 162-73 above

collective reality of the church—which was taken by
some exponents and by many critics to be what the
Reformation principle of the right of private interpretation of Scripture and then the Pietist emphasis on
personal experience meant—collided with that priority. Even the apostle Paul had acknowledged the
authority of the "primitive community [Urge-

Smdt.*TWNT* (Kittel 3:538)

meinde]" at Jerusalem.

Although this necessarily implied that the Christian church was older than the New Testament, it did
not mean that the Christian church was older than the
Bible. When the New Testament employed the singular or the plural of the Greek word "γραφή
[Scripture]," also and especially in the passages regu-

John 5:39;John 10:35;
2 Tim.3:16
Schrnk.*TWNT* (Kittel
1:750-54)

larly cited in support of the doctrine of biblical
inspiration, it was referring to the Scripture of Israel,
which Christians called the "Old Testament." During
the twentieth century—despite the judgment of one
influential scholar that "to go on conserving the Old
Testament within Protestantism as a canonical author-

Harn.*Marc*. 10 (1924:217)

Doc.*Chr.Un*.279 (Bell 4:211)

Ẅsz.*TWNT* (Kittel 9:37)

Stffr.*Th.N.T*. 1 (1947:5)

See pp. 225-26 above

Söd.*Chr.Fell*.4 (1923:141)

Prksch.*TWNT* (Kittel
4:89-100);Mrr.*TWNT* (Kittel
7:906-12)

Tlch.*Syst.Theol*.5.1
(1967-III:308-13);
Nbr.*Ch.Lt*.2 (1944:42-85)

See vol.1:23

Rom.11:26

ity after the nineteenth century is the consequence of a paralysis of religion and the church"—the Christian understanding of the Christian view of the relation between church and Scripture had special reason to become aware once more of the profound continuities "between the old and the new Israel." Research into the history of the Pharisees by Jewish and then by Christian scholarship demonstrated that the tendentious treatment of the Pharisees in the Gospels "presented an understanding of the relation between Jesus and the Judaism of his time that undoubtedly does not correspond to the historical facts." As the historical study of Judaism "presse[d] deeper into the world of apocalyptic" and found ever more frequent "contacts" between the New Testament and the faith and experience of Judaism in the very period during which Christianity arose, the troubling question of the apocalyptic elements in the preaching of Jesus about the kingdom became, if not less troubling to Christian believers, then at least more intelligible, especially when they came to believe that they themselves were living in apocalyptic times. The unprecedented attention of twentieth-century biblical study to the vocabulary of the Greek New Testament drew the lines of development backward from the New Testament not only to the classical and Hellenistic Greek usage of such crucial terms as "word [λόγος]" and "conscience [συνείδησις]," to mention only two prominent examples among many, but to the roots of these very concepts also in the Jewish community. Above all, Christian theological reflection on the implications of Jewish history for the Christian message included the recognition that for both Judaism and Christianity the object of the saving and judging action of God was not merely the individual but primarily the community, and that therefore the vision of the relation between Israel and the church in the most profound discussion of the question within the New Testament had concluded with an affirmation of the hope that "all Israel will be saved."

Of special interest, particularly to the advocates of revisions in the ecclesiology of Roman Catholicism, were those Eastern churches that had preserved a considerable measure of Eastern liturgy and theology

Slp.*Taj*.7 (Choma 6:302-9);
see vol.2:277-78
Slp.*Ep*.28.v.1963 (Choma 12:68-70)

See vol.1:339

Blgkv.*Prav*. (1985:277-387);
Flrv.*Bib.Ch*.5 (Nordland 1:83-85)

Flrv.*Bib.Ch*.6 (Nordland 1:93-103)

Plmr.*Russ.Ch*.84 (1882:395-96)

Hll.*Luth*.4 (*Ges.Auf.KG*. 1:289)

McNeill (1954) 214-15

Calv.*Inst*. (1551) 4.1.4 (Barth-Niesel 5:7)

Trlsch.*Soz*.3.4 (Baron 1:811-12)

even on such a question as the epiclesis in the Eucharist, while keeping (or establishing) ties with the See of Rome. Although the wording of the principle that "the rule of prayer should lay down the rule of faith" had been Latin rather than Greek, historians, theologians, and churchmen joined in the view that it was above all the liturgy and the icons of the Eastern churches that embodied this principle. For as a third way beyond the antitheses that had been set up during the Reformation era, Eastern Orthodox ecclesiology seemed to present a view of the church that hallowed its traditions as even Roman Catholicism did not and that nevertheless did not identify those traditions with an authoritarian and juridical institution. When challenged by such an ecclesiology, the interpreters of Western doctrine had been obliged to probe their own historic formulations and to reexamine the deeper sense of the church at work there.

Such reexamination led many twentieth-century interpreters of the Reformation to lay new emphasis on its churchly character. Karl Holl, who took issue with many of Ernst Troeltsch's conclusions, argued that "the concept of the church with which Luther comes out in opposition to the Roman hierarchy . . . . did not grow out of any sort of opposition, but simply in consequence of his fundamental religious ideas." A leading interpreter of Calvin described him as having "no tolerance for any solitary piety that detaches itself from this active interchange of spiritual values" in the church, since, in Calvin's own words, "there is no way of entrance into life unless [the church] conceive us in her womb and give us birth." And the *Social Teachings* of Troeltsch stimulated new attention to the "enormous number of small groups" of the Reformation era "whose main ideal was the formation of religious communities of truly 'converted' persons, on a basis of voluntary membership," thus to the centrality of ecclesiology also in the doctrines of the Radical Reformation.

The historic principle that "the rule of prayer should lay down the rule of faith" went far beyond the relations between East and West in its influence upon the renewal of ecclesiology during the twentieth

Hll.*Wst*.10 (*Ges.Auf.KG.* 3:220-33)

century. Throughout Christendom this was a time of new attention to the centrality of worship in both life and doctrine, leading not alone to the exploitation of "ways of worship" as an interpretive ecumenical tool, in addition to or even in place of doctrine, for understanding the distinctiveness of the individual churches and for discovering paths of convergence between them, but also to the fundamental redefinition of the church as, in its essence, the worshiping community. Within twentieth-century Roman Catholicism the pioneers of ecclesiology drew upon the precedent of the early church to document "the harmony of spirit between liturgy and chant" and therefore "the common sacrificial action of priest and people," and they protested against an excessively external definition of the church. The Second Vatican Council joined itself to that new and yet ancient emphasis when it affirmed concerning the liturgy of the church that "no other action of the church can match its claim to efficacy, nor equal the degree of it [cuius efficacitatem eodem titulo eodemque gradu nulla alia actio ecclesiae adaequat]"; therefore the council identified the liturgy as uniquely "the summit toward which the activity of the church is directed and at the same time the fountain from which all her power flows."

WCC.*Wys.Worsh*.2 (Edwall 20)

Mchl.*Lit*.16 (1938:329-30)
Adm.*Kath*.10 (1949:206-8)

CVat. (1962-65).3.
Sacr.Conc.1.7;1.10
(Alberigo-Jedin 822;823)

Although this exalted status for worship in the definition of ecclesiology was not in any sense intended to derogate from the place of the papacy within Roman Catholicism, nor from that of preaching and evangelism within Protestantism, as ways of identifying the nature and purpose of the church, it did serve notice that the polemical ecclesiologies in the textbooks of comparative symbolics issued by the various denominations had been found wanting. It was to "be a primary object of the liturgical renewal of our own day to recover the objective expression of corporate faith and worship in the service whose name means 'the Thanksgiving,' " the Eucharist. From such liturgical renewal and from doctrinal reflection upon it, all the churches developed "a growing sense that worship is not to be thought of as a gathering of individual pious Christians, but as a corporate act in direct relation to the Lord of the church."

Brlth.*Euch*.con. (1930:278)

WCC.*Wys.Worsh*.2 (Edwall 20)

See vol.1:155-71

Symb.Apost. (Schaff 2:45)

See vol.3:174-84

See vol.3:211-12;
vol.4:257,295,308
Eph.5:31-32 (Vulg.)

Pi.XI.Cast.con. (AAS
22:552-54)

Hll.Ost.7 (Ges.Auf.KG.2:
121-22)

Symb.Apost. (Schaff 2:45)

Brth.Tf.4 (1943:36)

See vol.4:317-19

Trlsch.Soz.3.4 (Baron
1:797-848)

Brth.Tf.4 (1943:39)
See vol.4:172-82;262-74

Schl.Chr.Gl.138 (Redeker
2:335-40)

Another index to the change was the reinterpretation, within and between the several denominations
and confessions, of the doctrine of the sacraments,
whose relation to the doctrine of the church had from
the beginning been close but complex. The conjunction of the two phrases of the Apostles' Creed, "the
holy catholic church, the communion of saints," had
frequently provided the occasion for consideration of
that relation. During the twentieth century almost
every reconsideration of sacramental doctrine involved
some new perspective on its locus within the doctrine
of the church. For example, in view of its history and
of the principal (and sometimes only) proof text used
to support it, it was to be expected that the chief
ground for defending the traditional inclusion of
matrimony as one of the seven sacraments would be its
ecclesiological significance as a typological represen-
tation of the relation between Christ and the church.
Similarly, "if anything at all is historically sure" from
the early church, one scholar concluded, it was the
centrality of baptism to the words of the Apostles'
Creed about "the forgiveness of sins."

While the far-reaching controversy, set off by Karl
Barth's searching critique, over the legitimacy of
infant baptism as a practice that was "impossible to
rescue without exegetical and factual artificiality and
sophistry," necessarily dealt with the issues that had
been a part of the discussion since the Anabaptist
disputes of the sixteenth century, the context of the
twentieth-century reexamination—and, significantly,
of the twentieth-century reinterpretation of those
sixteenth-century disputes—was primarily the doctrine of the church. Opposition to the traditional
practice proceeded from the argument that it rested
upon a defense of "the existence of the Evangelical
Church within Constantinian Christendom [corpus
Christianum]," with which, at least in principle, all
the Protestant Reformers had broken. Protestant
theologians had long been criticizing any understanding of infant baptism as a quasi-magical action
dispensed by the institutional church, through which,
without accepting the responsibility of membership
in the church, both parents and infants were supposed
to share in the church's means of grace. Replies to

Jrms.*Kndtf.* (1958:26)

See vol.3:184-204
Brlth.*Euch.* (1930)

See vol.2:176-79;p. 47 above

See vol.1:146-47
See vol.1:166-69

See vol.3:184-204

See vol.4:179;192;200-201

See vol.4:158-61

See vol.4:298-99

Luth.*Serm.sacr.*4 (WA 2:743)

Brlth.*Euch.*4.3 (1930:143-44)

Barth, too, recognized that "if we want to understand biblical texts aright, we must make a radical break with modern individualistic thinking." The church was the matrix within which baptized infants were to grow into mature responsibility; the opponents of infant baptism were charged with making that responsibility a prerequisite rather than a consequence of the church's action.

Yet it was once again what one important study called "eucharistic faith and practice" that not only carried most of the weight of sacramental doctrine for all the other sacraments (howsoever many they were said to be), but illumined the discussion of the nature of the church. In addition to the controversies between Rome and Byzantium over the use of unleavened bread (or "azymes"), much of the history of doctrinal discussion about the Eucharist had dealt with the dual, though related, questions of its sacrificial significance and of the real presence, with the doctrine of the latter having at least in part come out of reflection on the former during the Western Middle Ages. Both questions had figured prominently in the conflicts of the Reformation era. The Protestant Reformers unanimously attacked the interpretation of the Mass as in any sense a propitiatory sacrifice, but they differed from one another in their continued acceptance of the Catholic doctrine of the real presence (which was to be distinguished from transubstantiation). In part because of this dispute with other Reformers, Luther had moved from an early emphasis on "the significance or effect of this sacrament as fellowship" in his *Sermon on the Sacrament* of 1519 to an almost exclusive concentration on the reality of the "real" presence, with a consequent reduction of emphasis on the aspect of fellowship, in his polemics against the Swiss Reformers, although the theme of fellowship continued to play a significant role in his devotional, exegetical, and homiletical works.

The development of the doctrine of the Eucharist and of the eucharistic liturgies (sometimes in that order, but often the other way around) in the various churches during the twentieth century can be seen as, in effect, a reversal of that change of emphasis. In part through a deeper appreciation of the Eastern patristic

Dyob.*Myst*.1 (1912:7-36)

Nvn.*Myst.Pr*.1 (*Merc*.4:38-39)

Doc.Chr.Un.283 (Bell 4:230-31)

See p. 286 above

1 Cor. 10:17

Brlth.*Euch*.1 (1930:17)

See pp. 66-69 above

See p. 277 above, pp. 301-2 below

1 Cor. 11:29

Schwzr.*TWNT* (Kittel 7:1065)

See pp. 325-26 below

heritage, it had become evident to Western theology and liturgics that the common medieval distinction between "spiritual" and "real" in the doctrine of the Eucharist could represent a false antithesis, and that the two were inseparably tied together through the doctrine of the church. The official doctrine and practice of many denominations insisted that agreement was a necessary prerequisite to "intercommunion," whether agreement on the proper nature and structure of the church or on the proper doctrine of the presence or on both. From the further study of the New Testament and of the liturgical tradition it became evident to many that although some measure of unity did indeed have to precede a sharing in the Eucharist, there was also a unity that could be achieved only through such sharing. "We who are many are one body," the apostle Paul declared, "for we all partake of the one bread."

At about the same time, theologians of all traditions were likewise discovering that, among the terms for the Eucharist, the concept of "mystery . . . embraces and unites all the others," despite all the problems that the concept had been creating for the church and its theologians since the Enlightenment. No theological theory of the eucharistic presence could adequately express this mystery, which was best apprehended by and through the worship of the church. Both the Eucharist and the church were called "body of Christ," and in the New Testament the two meanings of the term were often so blended that in as crucial a passage as the Pauline warning to "any one who eats and drinks without discerning the body" it was not at all clear which of the two was intended, if indeed it was valid to suppose at all that only one of them was.

On other grounds as well, it was evident that doctrinal theology had to be church theology. Although the actions of Pope Pius X against Modernism in *Lamentabili* and *Pascendi dominici gregis* and in the anti-Modernist oath were concerned ex professo with drawing the line between the Christian message and modern culture, the opening item in the indictment of the "errors of the Modernists," as enumerated by *Lamentabili*, was the teaching that "the law of the

Pi.IX.*Lam.*1 (*ASS* 40:470)

Pi.IX.*Pa*ʃ. (*ASS* 40:613-14)

Pi.IX.*Lam.*52 (*ASS* 40:476)

Pi.X.*Sacr.ant.* (*AAS* 2:669)

See p. 174 above

Brth.*Röm.*pr. (1940:vi)

Brth.*Prol.*24.3 (1927:444-46)

church does not extend" to the practice of scholarly exegesis. *Pascendi* anathematized any naturalistic explanation of the origin of the church, be it individualistic or collectivistic, and it attributed this error to a false antithesis between "the church of history and the church of faith," from which had come the contention that "it was foreign to the mind of Christ to establish a church as a society that was to endure on earth through a long series of centuries." The anti-Modernist oath opened with the asseveration: "I firmly embrace and accept anything and everything [omnia et singula] defined, asserted, and declared by the inerrant magisterium of the church, especially those articles of doctrine that are directly opposed to the errors of this present time." Underlying all these other issues, therefore, were the definition of the church as divinely founded and the specification of the doctrinal authority of the church's magisterium as infallible.

In quite another sector of Christendom and from quite another definition both of Christian doctrine and of the church, this thesis that doctrinal theology had to be church theology received massive substantiation through the developments of the twentieth century. Karl Barth's *The Epistle to the Romans*, first issued in 1919 and drastically revised in 1922, was, like Schleiermacher's *On Religion*, a summons—not, however, a summons to acknowledge the underlying affinities between the spirit of the time and the Christian gospel, but to recognize the authority of the gospel. "Paul," its opening sentence read, "spoke as a child of his time to his contemporaries"; therefore a historical exegesis, as this had been urged by the theological scholarship of the eighteenth and nineteenth centuries, was valid. But by itself such an exegesis was inadequate, for "it is far more important that as a prophet and apostle of the kingdom of God he speaks to all men of all times." Although Barth began to give systematic formulation to this "churchly character [Kirchlichkeit]" of dogmatics in his *Prolegomena to Christian Dogmatics*, that title soon yielded to *Church Dogmatics [Kirchliche Dogmatik]*, becoming in the process the most monumental Protestant systematic theology since Calvin's *Institutes of*

Brth.*K.D.*int.1 (1932-I-1:1)

Brth.*K.D.*1.2.8
(1932-I-1:312)

See pp. 192-94 above

Schl.*Chr.Gl.*170-72 (Redeker
2:458-73)

Lnrgn.*D.Tr.*1.1
(1964-I:17-28)

Brth.*Prot.Theol.*2.1
(1947:395)

Schl.*Chr.Gl.*2 (Redeker 1:10)

See vol.3:129-44

Brth.*K.D.*13.58.4
(1932-IV-1:140-70)

Blrd.*Brth.*1.3.3
(1957-I:148-51)

the Christian Religion. On its very first page he explained the change, not only in title but in approach, as an expression of his recognition that Christian theology was not a personal statement by the theologian speaking in his own name, but a ministry to the church and a voice from the church. This stress on the churchly character of dogmatics required that "the doctrine of revelation begin with the doctrine of the Triune God," after a century or more of comparative neglect (symbolized by Schleiermacher's having relegated it to an appendix in his own systematic theology). At about the same time, by incorporating "the evolution of dogma" into his method, the Roman Catholic systematician Bernard Lonergan was also contributing to this revival of trinitarian dogmatics.

As Barth himself was the first to admit, his movement from the lonely prophetic voice of his *Romans* to the witness on behalf of a past and present community in his *Church Dogmatics* had its most striking precedent, for all the fundamental differences of both methodology and theology, in Schleiermacher's transition from *On Religion* as a "virtuoso" performance to *The Christian Faith*, whose definition of the task of systematic theology at the very beginning of the work had asserted: "Since dogmatics is a theological discipline, and thus pertains solely to the Christian church, we can only explain what it is when we have become clear as to the conception of the Christian church." But while Schleiermacher had gone on from that definition to a highly idiosyncratic exposition of Christian doctrine in which the point of reference in the tradition and dogma of the church was often little more than an allusion or a starting point, Barth's *Church Dogmatics* (for example, in its presentation of Anselmic and other doctrines of the atonement) located its propositions in a review of tradition and dogma whose plenitude enabled those who agreed as well as those who disagreed to consider the theological alternatives. That plenitude was also an expression of the churchly character of the work as a whole and was at least partly reponsible for the unwonted seriousness with which Roman Catholic theologians treated this work of Reformed Protestant "church dogmatics."

Brth.*K.D.*15.62.2
(1932-IV-1:726-809)

Stffr.*Th.N.T.* 38
(1947:132-36)

See pp. 334-35 below

See vol.3:122-23

Rtl.*Piet.*28 (1880-II:42)

Sail.*Mor.*5.2.230
(1817-III:66-75)

Gbts.*Ekkl.* (1967:123)

See vol.3:74-80;186-202

See vol.3:45-46

The chapter on "the being of the church" in Barth's *Church Dogmatics* took the form of a thoroughgoing review of the principal terms and ways of speaking about the church in the Old and New Testaments, together with a repeated warning against permitting any one of these ways of speaking to carry ecclesiological speculation in directions not compatible with the other terms. During the twentieth century the increasing cultivation of "biblical theology" as a distinct field of study and the application to it of an intertextual method of word study that once again connected the two Testaments to each other, not only historically but theologically, led to several such reviews of biblical language about the church, in which each of the metaphors was examined for its distinctive contribution to the total biblical picture of the Christian community as (among others) people of God, bride of Christ, and body of Christ. The first of these emphasized, at a time when there were momentous historic reasons to be reminded of it, the continuity of the New Testament people with Judaism. The second caught up many of the ecclesiological themes that had come out of the history of the Christian exposition of the Song of Songs; although the Song had sometimes, especially in the Pietist period, been read as an allegory of "the spiritual marriage of the individual believer with Christ," the vast majority of exegetes throughout the history of exegesis had interpreted the bride as the church rather than the soul.

The last of these figures for the church, "body of Christ," had often been seen as combining many of the most important features of the others, and thus as belonging to a class by itself as the title that "completes the whole of ecclesiology." During those periods of history that had not made ecclesiology a central focus of doctrinal attention, "body of Christ" had, also because of its eucharistic associations, figured prominently in the theological vocabulary nevertheless. Its linguistic and conceptual affinities with the legal concept of "corporation" had helped to give it, even in medieval canon law, a standing not matched by other terms. On the other hand, for some of the most ambitious ecclesiological speculations of the

Slv.*Bogočlv.*11/12 (Radlov 3:159)

nineteenth century, it had assumed an existence of its own as "not a metaphor, but a metaphysical formula." The concept of "the mystical body of Christ [corpus Christi mysticum]," despite criticism from those to whom anything "mystical" seemed to carry dangerous connotations, acquired new prominence with the promulgation of the papal encyclical *Mystici corporis*, in which the term "mystical" became a means both for associating and for distinguishing the church as "body of Christ" in relation to his "physical" or "natural" or "eucharistic" body.

Brth.*K.D.*15.62.2 (1932-IV-1:736)

Pi.XII.*Myst.corp.* (*AAS* 35:221-22)

The ambiguity of "body of Christ" as connoting either "mystical body" or "corporation" (or both) suggests the fundamental antithesis with which the ecclesiology of the twentieth century, like that of preceding centuries, had to come to terms: the contrast, or even the contradiction, between the church as an article of faith in the Apostles' and Nicene Creeds and the "wounds in the body of the mystical Christ" as an empirical, historical, political institution caught in the compromises of its history— the relation, yet again, between spirit and structure in the church, as well as between its unity in the one Christ and its empirical divisions.

Adm.*Kath.*13 (1949:256)

See vol.4:313-22

Theological Resources for Unity

The blurring of confessional distinctions during the twentieth century was accompanied by the growing historical recognition that those distinctions had not been purely (perhaps, in some cases, not primarily) theological in origin at all, and that the churches "often allow themselves to be separated from each other by secular forces and influences." The sack of Constantinople by soldiers from the Latin church during the Fourth Crusade in 1204 had been at least as powerful a wedge driving Eastern Orthodoxy and Western Catholicism apart as the doctrine of Filioque or the use of the epiclesis and of azymes in the Eucharist, perhaps as powerful as the authority of the pope (of which it was taken by some Eastern polemists and historians to be the inevitable result). One historical monograph examined the relation of "secular political interests" to "the question of faith" in the backgrounds of the *Augsburg Confession*, and a

Doc.*Chr.Un.*281 (Bell 4:224)

See vol.2:271

Krks.*Ekkl.hist.*175a (1897-II:131-32); Krks.*Antipap.*1 (1893:4)

Schbrt.*Bek.*8 (1910:238)

Nieb.*Soc.Srcs.* (1929)

See pp. 313-25 below

Doc.*Chr.Un*.app.3 (Bell
1:377-79)

Delmp.*Oik*.3.2 (1972:159)

Adm.*Un*.2 (1948:37-39)

Goodall (1961) 58

Doc.*Chr.Un*.app.3 (Bell
1:378)
Gr.Naz.*Or*.4.113 (*PG*
35:649-52)

Söd.*Chr.Fell*.4 (1923:123)

pioneering American study was devoted to the decisive role played by such questions as slavery and class structure in the history of how the churches of the United States (and, by extrapolation, all churches throughout Christian history) had divided from one another, regardless of the doctrinal justifications that may have been provided, after the fact, for their divisions. Coming as it did at the same time as the fundamental reconsideration of the social mission of the church in relation to the secular order, this recognition of the "nontheological factors" in the separation of the churches seemed to have as its corollary the cultivation of other, more positive nontheological factors, such as a sharing in social action, as a means of overcoming the separation.

But it would be a oversimplification of the history —an oversimplification of which ecumenical leaders were repeatedly accused by those who regarded any ecumenical cooperation as doctrinal compromise—to forget that there were theological resources for church unity just as there had been theological issues in the disunity of the churches, and thus to overlook what could be called the theological significance of nontheological factors both as a cause in bringing about the original separation and as a historical force in beginning to recover a lost unity. Alongside the consideration of church and doctrine embodied in "Faith and Order," therefore, the "Universal Christian Council for Life and Work," with its explicitly practical assignment "to assert the supra-national role of the Church and to voice its call to reconciliation," sometimes shaped the doctrinal discussion no less decisively. Its leader, doctrinally as well as practically, was Nathan Söderblom, who believed that since "doctrine divides but service unites," practice could be the basis of theory (as the patristic epigram had put it), and that the moral imperative of a common participation in the ministry of Christian relief after the First World War was at the same time a theological resource for understanding the deeper meaning of the doctrines of the church held as articles of faith by the several churches. Thus it would be possible for them "finally to become of one mind, not only in love, but also in the doctrinal expressions for the revealed truth."

The churches were also driven to such an understanding by the theological assessment of their common predicament as a consequence of what had been happening to the Christian tradition within each of them during the crises of the eighteenth and nineteenth centuries. Much of the initial response to that predicament had been mutual recrimination. Spokesmen for Roman Catholicism claimed to find a natural affinity between classic Protestantism, which rejected the authority of the pope, and modern unbelief,

Mntl.*Int.cath.*3 (Lecoffre 5:52)

which rejected all authority; Protestant polemics, for which "the official Catholic doctrine of original sin

Nbr.*Nat.Dest.*1.9 (1943-I:247)

. . . does not greatly vary the emphasis of Pelagianism," drew a historical line between the optimism about human nature and human reason at work in the "Semi-Pelagianism" and rationalism of scholastic theology, also after the Council of Trent, and the extreme forms of such optimism in the Enlightenment; and Eastern Orthodox analysts saw little to choose between a Protestant "spiritualistic rationalism" and a

Chom.*Égl.lat.Prot.*1 (1872:67-68)

Roman Catholic "materialistic rationalism," finding in both of them a false objectivism and its antithesis—which was in fact its corollary—a rationalistic subjectivism, all of which would be corrected

Makr.*Herm.*1 Cor. 11:23 (1891:1778)

only by an acceptance of the illumination that could come from the Christian East.

Amid such mutual recrimination, the theology of each of these churches was compelled to recognize as well the imperative of "catholicity" as "taking into

Hlr.*Alt.*2.7 (1941:384)

account the totality of the life of the church," and therefore the need to acknowledge the doctrinal and religious debts of its history to other traditions than its own, together with its possible need to be taught by them still further. Eastern Orthodox theologians, for example, discovered that they could not draw upon the resources of their own Greek church fathers except through critical editions and scholarly monographs produced largely by Western historians and theologians such as Adolf Harnack, who, despite his per-

See p. 257 above

Harn.*Wes.*12 (1901:135-41)

petuation of the stock image of Eastern Orthodox

Harn.*Wrk.Voll.*4.8 (1930:240-48)

doctrine as a petrified traditionalism, carried out in his lifetime the most ambitious critical edition ever undertaken of the sources of Eastern Christianity. The same Eastern Orthodox scholar who was able to say

Krks.*Antipap*.8 (1893:122-23)
Krks.*Ekkl.Hist*.4
(1897-I:12-15)
Krks.*Ench.Pat*.5-6
(1898:11-13)

Mak.*Prav.bog*. (1895)

CTrid. (1545-63).4.*Decr*.2
(Alberigo-Jedin 664)

See vol.4:309-10

Pi.XII.*Div.affl.Spir*. (*AAS*
35:309)

Pi.XII.*Div.affl.Spir*. (*AAS*
35:314-16)

See pp. 75-89, 230-41 above

(correctly) that in the first three centuries the Western fathers had usually followed the theology of the Eastern fathers was also obliged, in listing the critical editions of those same Eastern fathers, to rely almost exclusively on the work of modern Western scholars. The systematization of Eastern doctrine during the nineteenth century had been decisively shaped by Protestant and Roman Catholic scholasticism, being organized on the principles of Protestant and Roman Catholic catechisms.

A similar dependence on sources of doctrinal inspiration beyond the borders of the denomination was manifesting itself within Roman Catholicism and Protestantism. After centuries of functioning as often little more than an adjunct to church dogma, to which its results were expected to conform at all costs, the study of the Bible within Roman Catholicism achieved a new maturity of its own. Journals of Old and New Testament study became the organs for this biblical revival, which received its charter in *Divino afflante Spiritu*, the encyclical of Pope Pius XII issued in 1943. The encyclical interpreted the decree of the Council of Trent about the status of the Vulgate to mean that "doctrine is also to be proved and confirmed on the basis of the original texts." Study of the Hebrew and Greek texts, moreover, was to draw illumination from the best available archeological and historical scholarship, and it was to proceed with a sensitivity to the special literary forms at use in the Bible, as these reflected the general patterns of ancient Near Eastern literature and thought. For all of these enterprises in which Roman Catholic biblical scholarship was now to be engaged, the methodological presuppositions had evolved during the eighteenth and nineteenth centuries largely under Protestant auspices, so that before scientific biblical research within the Roman Catholic Church could take the independent strides it did at the middle of the twentieth century, it devoted the earlier decades of the century to catching up with Protestant scholarship. In the process there developed a mutuality also of doctrinal influence between Protestants and Roman Catholics, and it was often difficult to discern any explicit confessional orientation in works of biblical theology.

Hlr.*Alt*.int. (1941:1)

See vol.4:373-74

See pp. 86-89 above

Marit.*Thos.Aq*. (1958:87)
Carlson (1948) 28

See vol.4:313-331

See vol.4:290

Söd.*Chr.Fell*.4 (1923:138)

See p. 313 below

The historical method of treating theology played a decisive role in that redefinition. From having been, in Reformation and post-Reformation polemics, a tool for proving that the doctrines of one's opponents were conditioned by history (while one's own were supposed to have been derived directly from Scripture and/or tradition without any such conditioning), church history became a universal solvent, to whose workings one's own denomination was no less subject than were any others. The history of each denomination or region of the church understandably elicited special attention from its own constituency. Thus much of Neo-Thomism was a Roman Catholic phenomenon, intent on showing "that Saint Thomas Aquinas is our predestined guide in the reconstruction of Christian culture," while "the history of theology in Sweden is a history of Luther research." On the other hand, some of the most momentous discoveries of twentieth-century historical theology came as a result of the crossing of confessional, national, and linguistic boundaries. The twentieth-century recognition of the "Radical Reformation" as a legitimate subdivision of Reformation history alongside the "magisterial Reformations" would not have been possible except for work both by scholars and theologians standing in the "magisterial" traditions and by Anabaptist and Unitarian historians. While the shift from "Counter-Reformation" to the broader term "Catholic Reformation" resulted from the efforts of Roman Catholic scholars, they were joined by others, whose reinterpretation of the several Reformations now included the Catholic Reformation and the Radical Reformation as full partners in the total enterprise of the Reformation and therefore as its joint heirs.

Behind these changes lay the dawning recognition that "the same problems occupy the church in all its sections," regardless of how profound might be the doctrinal differences still separating the churches from one another. Measured by these problems, what the churches continued to have in common was vastly greater than what differentiated any of them from any other. The historical relativism that had come out of the eighteenth and nineteenth centuries led to a recognition that even such fundamental theological

Hll.*Luth*.2
(*Ges.Auf.KG*.1:111-54)

Trlsch.*Chr.Rel.* (Baron
2:328-63)
Nieb.*Chr.Cult*.7.2
(1951:234-41)

See p. 114 above

WMC.*Co-Op*.5 (1910:83)

WMC.*Co-Op*.7 (1910:142-43)

See p. 220 above

antitheses as that over the doctrine of justification had been historically conditioned by the events of church history and of individual psychology during the period of the Reformation. At the same time, theologians whose perspective on doctrine had been fundamentally shaped by such relativism recognized the need for Christian doctrine to find some place to stand beyond the relativities of history, and in this their versions of historicism strove to set themselves apart from their secular counterparts by articulating "the relativism of faith." Because the scholarship and the thought of theologians and church leaders in all the denominations were vulnerable to these influences, the relation between the denominations could not avoid a gradual but fundamental redefinition.

A special instance of this recognition of common convictions in the face of alien philosophical and religious systems was the experience of all the churches in the mission field, which led in 1910 to the convoking of the World Missionary Conference at Edinburgh. Participants had agreed to come on the proviso that no expression of opinion was to be sought from the conference on any matter involving any ecclesiastical or doctrinal questions on which those taking part in the conference differed among themselves. Such questions proved nevertheless to be unavoidable. Whatever rationalizations there might still have been for the perpetuation of the historic divisions among the churches within the boundaries of traditional Christendom, the exportation of those divisions into the mission field had become increasingly difficult to justify—certainly on strategic grounds, but also on doctrinal grounds. In that sense it was possible to claim at Edinburgh that it was "the aim of all missionary work to plant in each non-Christian nation one undivided church of Christ," and that this was "the ideal which is present to the minds of the great majority of missionaries." Representatives of the missionary societies through which, during the eighteenth and nineteenth centuries, many of the churches had carried out their task of evangelization in seeking to further "the progress of the kingdom" joined at Edinburgh with spokesmen for many of the churches themselves to consider the historic obstacles to unity, as these were now manifesting themselves in the younger churches that had not participated in the original debates over doctrine and polity.

Both the theological coming-of-age of the younger churches and the almost universal adoption of the historical method of doing theology uncovered a deep-seated doctrinal pluralism within the confessional churches. In the words of a leading historian both of Christian missions and of ecumenism, "the ecumenical movement was in large part the outgrowth of the missionary movement." The efforts of any younger church in a non-Christian nation to define a Christian identity vis-à-vis the particular traditions of that nation could lead it to a doctrinal kinship with another Christian group engaged in a similar theological enterprise that was deeper than the kinship that either of them had with the mother church from which its missionaries had originally come. If such a younger church nevertheless continued to be a member of an international confessional fellowship with its mother church, the consequence appeared to be a double standard of doctrinal agreement by which those who already belonged to such a fellowship as a result of historical developments were held to a less strict requirement of agreement than those who sought to establish communion across confessional lines. Thus cooperation became essentially "a moral problem."

Similarly, as historical theology considered doctrinal movements of the recent past that had appeared in more than one church, affinities came into view that transcended the borders of the denominations. The orthodox Lutheran opponents of Lutheran Pietism in the eighteenth century had been quick to point out such affinities with Reformed Pietism and therefore to charge Spener and his followers with betrayal of the Lutheran confessions, but during the twentieth century the historical study of scholastic theology in the orthodox Lutheranism of the seventeenth century suggested that, for all its confessional rigidity, it had not only in turn manifested affinities no less profound with contemporary Reformed scholasticism but had even "reproduced the Thomistic [method of] distinction" on various points. Yet if there was some

K.S.Latourette ap.Rouse-Neill (1954) 353

See pp. 285-86 above

WMC.Co-Op.7 (1910:142-43)

See p. 38 above

See pp. 45, 58 above

See vol.4:336-50

Rtschl.DG.Prot.8.66 (1908-IV:302)

significant sense in which Lutheran confessional orthodoxy and Lutheran Pietism, or Reformed orthodoxy and Reformed Pietism, had both still been entitled to the names "Lutheran" or "Reformed," the question had to be asked whether the theological differences within the confessional denominations had not become deeper and more decisive than the traditional doctrinal differences between them, and whether therefore it had not become imperative to "make common cause in the search for the expression of that unity" which had made itself manifest beyond all those differences.

*Doc.Chr.Un.*277 (Bell 4:206)

Even the confessional differences that were still applicable, moreover, no longer appeared so automatically to prove doctrinal superiority. As this shift of perspective made itself especially visible in the reappearance of the Eastern Orthodox epiclesis and the Western eucharistic prayer within various Protestant liturgies, so, in the opposite direction, one concomitant of the biblical revival in Roman Catholic theology was the reinforcement of the requirement, made insistent already by the Council of Trent in response to the Protestant Reformation, that the centrality of the Mass in the worship and teaching of the church not overshadow the New Testament imperative to "preach the word, be urgent in season and out of season, convince, rebuke and exhort." "The preaching of the gospel" should have, the Second Vatican Council decreed, "a preeminent place among the duties of a bishop." As had happened after the legislation of the Council of Trent, so after that of the Second Vatican Council, this restatement of the practical duty of preaching set off a reconsideration not only of homiletics as a tool of the parish clergy and a course in the seminary curriculum, but of the theological content of the traditional Roman Catholic doctrine of the word of God as "the preaching of the gospel." Since that had been the central preoccupation of the Protestant churches from the beginning, both the practice and the theory of preaching within Roman Catholicism drew upon the resources of Protestant preaching and theology.

WCC.*Wys.Worsh.*4 (Edwall 33)

See p. 70 above

CTrid.24.*Can.*4 (Alberigo-Jedin 763)

2 Tim.4:2

CVat. (1962-65).3.*Lum.gent.* 3.25 (Alberigo-Jedin 869) See vol.4:290

See vol.4:167-82

Protestant liturgics and Roman Catholic homiletics were striking evidence for the awareness, reinforced by

Harn.*Red.Auf.* 2.2.3
(1904-II:253-54)

See vol.4:85-88
Hrom.*Th.crk.*3
(1949:217-31);
Hrom.*Csty.*2.1 (1927:48)

Goodall (1961) 159

Phds.*Ekk.hist.* (1973:258)

Rsch.*Chr.Soc.Cr.*4
(1907:176-79)

Flrv.*Chr.Cult.*6 (Nordland
2:131-42)

See pp. 9-10 above

Schlnk.*Th.Bek.*1 (1948:46)

the experience of contemporary life as well as by the researches of historical theology, that for both sides in every schism throughout Christian history there had been theological losses, not only gains, as even an heir of the Hussite Reformation had to acknowledge. Nothing made that point more dramatically than the sense of "enrichment" that came through the rediscovery of Eastern Orthodoxy by both Protestant and Roman Catholic theology during the twentieth century. Although the political catastrophes of the Orthodox Church throughout the century initially confirmed Western theologians, particularly the advocates of the social gospel, in their belief that the Eastern Church had been paralyzed by "sacramentalism" and "the dogmatic interest" and had therefore assumed a passive role in relation to the social order, the increasing participation of Orthodox theologians in ecumenical dialogue provided the churches and theologians of the West with the opportunity to see at first hand the resources in liturgy, dogma, and spirituality by which these "passive" churches had survived a whole series of political catastrophes in the nearly five centuries since the fall of Constantinople, and therefore to ask whether, in analogous crises, the theological vitality of the Western churches would in fact have proved itself to be any more capable of preserving the continuity and distinctiveness of the Christian witness.

Paradoxically, the deepening of doctrinal understanding and theological cooperation within the major confessions and confessional groups also contributed to the recognition of mutual needs and mutual strengths. In every group, therefore, some of the leaders of the reawakened confessional consciousness became at the same time spokesmen for an ecumenical definition of the doctrine of the church, because "the catholicity of the church and that of its confession have an essential connection." Organizationally as well as theologically, movements for reunion and intercommunion between (relatively speaking) closely related churches often preceded establishment of a broader fellowship. In addition to the historic losses that became visible from a restudy of the doctrinal charters formulated at the origin or during the development of the denomination, it likewise became evident that some of the principles of those charters, when pressed beyond a conventional or merely polemical reading, could lead to a more comprehensive interpretation of the unity among Christians and among churches.

One such principle was the Eastern Orthodox concept of "economy," which belonged to canon law as well as to doctrine. As a technical term in patristic Greek dogmatics, "economy" referred to the actions of God within human history, to be distinguished from "theology," the eternal being and action of God apart from time and history. From its application to divine action in the history of salvation, the principle of "economy" could be extended also to the actions of the church, and especially to such actions as were obliged to take account of ambiguities in the human predicament. In a "document of momentous importance," which "became at once, and still is, the basis of the ecumenical policy of the Greek Church," the study of *The Validity of Anglican Ordinations, from an Orthodox-Catholic Perspective* by the Greek Orthodox systematician Chrēstos Androutsos, "for the first time the concept of 'economy' was applied to ecumenical relations." While "this concept has never been clearly defined or elaborated," it was clear enough to make it possible that "for a solution based on theological principles some occasional practical arrangements were substituted." From that beginning at the level of "practical arrangements," in turn, deeper theological exploration of the doctrine of the church and of its unity could follow.

For Roman Catholicism as well, such "practical arrangements" could become a resource for definitions of church and church unity that went beyond the simplistic equation of the church with the ecclesiastical institution of which the pope was the visible head. One of these was baptism. While a valid ordination could be administered only by a bishop standing in the proper apostolic succession (though he might be in schism from the bishop of Rome) and a valid Eucharist in turn depended for its sacramental standing on a valid ordination of the consecrating priest, baptism had, since the controversies of the

See p. 198 above

See vol.2:8
See vol.2:193-94

Andrts.*Kyr.* (1903)

Flor.*Chr.Cult.*9 (Nordland ?·226 27)

Leo XIII.*Ap.cur.* (*ASS* 29:198-201)

CLater. (1215).*Const.*1 (Alberigo-Jedin 230)

See vol. 1:158-59
See vol. 1:308-13

Thos.Aq.*S.T.*3.67.3-5
(*Ed.Leon.*12:82-84)

CFlor. (1438-45).*Decr.Arm.*
(Alberigo-Jedin 543)

Pi.XI.*Div.il.mag.* (*AAS*
22:52)

CVat. (162-65).5.
*Unit.redint.*1.3
(Alberigo-Jedin 910)

See p. 271 above

See p. 272 above

Newm.*Art.XXXIX.*con.
(*Tr.Tms.*90:80)

*Conf.Aug.*II.1 (*Bek.*84)

bishop of Rome with Cyprian in the third century and of Augustine with the Donatists in the fifth century, been far less confined. At the Council of Basel-Ferrara-Florence, on the basis especially of the sacramental doctrine of Thomas Aquinas, it was officially affirmed that while baptism should ordinarily be administered by a priest, in an emergency literally anyone could baptize, so long as the form prescribed by the church was observed and there was the intention to do what the church does. Twentieth-century reaffirmations of that doctrine, as well as of the doctrine that the church could be defined as "the society in which through the washing of baptism human beings enter the life of divine grace," as Pope Pius XI put it, prepared the way for the Second Vatican Council to declare in its Decree on Ecumenism that "those who believe in Christ and have properly received baptism are brought into a certain, though imperfect, communion with the Catholic Church" and were therefore accepted by the church as brethren; this stopped just short of recognizing such baptized non-Roman Catholics as "members of the church," but it did point to the sacrament of baptism as a resource for church unity even if both the sacrament of holy orders and the sacrament of the Eucharist continued to be obstacles to it.

Renewed attention to the primary documents of the sixteenth century helped to reshape most of the body of Christian doctrine within the Anglican, Lutheran, and Reformed communions during the nineteenth and twentieth centuries, but no doctrine was more fundamentally affected by it than the doctrine of the church and its unity. Newman's methodological principle of reading the *Thirty-Nine Articles* and the *Book of Common Prayer*—as well as, by extension, the *Augsburg Confession*, together with the *Heidelberg Catechism*—"in the most Catholic sense they will admit," as a "duty which we owe both to the Catholic Church and to our own," was carried out, although in a way he may not have anticipated, when, as in the case of the *Augsburg Confession*, the asseveration that "our churches dissent from the church catholic in no article of faith" was pressed beyond "the initial emphasis on the spirituality of the church," on the basis of which "also its

Elrt.*Morph*.1.21
(1931-I:242-44)

Nsl.*Bek*.*KO*. (1938:137)

Shprd.*Comm*.pr. (1950:i)

See pp. 269-70 above

D.H.Yoder ap.Rousc-Neill
(1954) 240

universality or catholicity was to be found in the sphere of a nonempirical spirituality," to an emphasis on the empirically recognizable "common confession" in which all Christians shared. The twentieth-century editor of the *Heidelberg Catechism* published it as part of the total church order of the Palatinate, to provide "a significant indication that the confession of the church does not stand by itself, but is incorporated into the ordinances that regulate the worship life of the community." And a twentieth-century commentator similarly emphasized, in his remarks on the title of *The Book of Common Prayer*, that it "claims that the liturgy of the Prayer Book is that 'of the Church' as a whole, i.e. of the universal Catholic Church, continuous in time and spread throughout the world."

As the doctrinal decrees and confessions of the several churches could be exploited for their contribution to a deeper sense of the unity of the church, so from the other direction the opposition to the very notion of doctrinal decrees and confessions—an opposition that the confessional churches characterized as "sectarian"—was intended to contribute to that same end. The rejection of the Nicene and Athanasian Creeds and even of the Apostles' Creed as a divisive force by Alexander Campbell was an expression of the conviction that a divided church could be reunited only by a return to a precreedal "primitive Christianity," which had been characterized by theological liberty but not doctrinal chaos, by unity but not uniformity. Campbell strove to avoid not only any creed but any denominational label for his followers, identifying them simply as "Disciples of Christ," who "thought of themselves as a movement within the church seeking after the unity of the church" and who insisted "that their fundamental aim is still the same, namely to unite Christians." That aim was to become decisive for all the churches.

The Redemption of Society

In addition to all the other theological (and nontheological) reasons for renewing the faith and life of Christendom by pursuing with new vigor the vision of a reunited church, the late nineteenth and the twentieth century saw in this vision the possibility of making a contribution to the construction of a more humane and moral social order. Only if Christians could speak with a single voice could they expect to make such a contribution. The verse from the Gospels that was universally quoted as embodying, more than any other, the divine ecumenical imperative—the prayer of Christ for his followers on the night before his crucifixion "that they may all be one"—not only went on to articulate a doctrine that orthodox Christianity took as the trinitarian ground of church unity, "even as thou, Father, art in me, and I in thee, that they also may be [one] in us," but concluded with the goal that increasing numbers of Christians in all the churches took to be the church's evangelical significance, apologetic task, and social purpose: "so that the world may believe that thou hast sent me."

"The influence of doctrines on society," as a Spanish theologian had called it, and the deepening of the Christian commitment to the redemption of society could be seen already in the nineteenth century. The same William Wilberforce whose *Practical View of the Prevailing Religious System of Professed Christians* articulated the concern of evangelical Christians over the state of Christian doctrine and life took the lead in the campaign against slavery as "the greatest mass of guilt and misery which ever existed on earth." The same F. M. Dostoevsky who, as a Russian Orthodox thinker and man of letters, articulated what he and others took to be the abiding meaning of the Orthodox tradition of doctrine and spirituality also spoke about a historical process by which "the state is transformed into the church [and] will ascend and become a church over the whole world." The same Pope Leo XIII whose *Providentissimus Deus* of 1893 laid some of the most important foundations for modern Roman Catholic biblical study had also issued *Rerum Novarum* in 1891, a document that one of his successors on the throne of Peter, Pius XI, was to hail forty years later as the charter of Roman Catholic social teaching. And Albrecht Ritschl's critique of traditional Protestant doctrines such as reconciliation and justification proposed to make the recognition of the social responsibility of the Christian and the church a fundamental

*Doc.Chr.Un.*4 (Bell 1:16);
Söd.*Chr.Fell.*1 (1923:1);
Slp.*Posl.*14.vi.1970 (Choma 9:131)

Aug.*Trin.*4.9.12 (*CCSL* 50:177-78)

*Found.*7 (1913:355)

John 17:21

Blms.*Prot.*52 (Casanovas 4:559-79)

See p. 175 above

Wilb.*Ep.*30.i.1807 (Robert-Samuel 2:113)

See pp. 61-62 above

Dost.*Br.Kar.*1.2.5 (Černecova 69)

Leo XIII.*Prov.* (*ASS* 26:269-92)
Leo XIII.*Rer.Nov.* (*ASS* 23:641-70)

Pi.XI.*Quad.* (*AAS* 23:179-81)

See pp. 214-15 above

Rtl.*Recht*.2.1.5
(1882-II:26-34)

Mead (1963) 178

T.Smith (1957) 149

Piep.*Chr.Dogm*.
(1917-I:108-9)

Trlsch.*Soz*.conc.2 (Baron
1:967-68)

Doc.Chr.Un.app.3 (Bell
1:378)

Rsch.*Theol*.1 (1917:1)

Soc.*Crd*. (1912) (Ward 7)

See vol.1:39-41

See vol.4:171-74;217;244

Soc.*Crd*. (1912) (Ward 7)

constituent of the new and deeper understanding of what Jesus had meant by "the kingdom of God."

As that very catalogue of nineteenth-century names suggests and as the development of the movement for Christian social concern in the twentieth century was to confirm, "the theologies associated with the movement were many and . . . diverse"; and despite the "evangelical explanation of the origins of the social gospel," conservative theologians argued that the espousal of a particular social teaching was in itself an indication that its proponent shared the "undogmatic" position of others who took the same position on Christian social ethics. To some, this diversity was a reflection of "the dependence of the entire Christian intellectual system and dogma upon the fundamental sociological presupposition" of an established Christendom. To others, it promised the possibility of ecumenical cooperation on practical issues even where doctrinal disagreement remained. To yet others, it was proof that the conventional order of theological thought needed to be reversed. "We have a social gospel," declared the opening words of the most widely circulated restatement of doctrine in relation to the redemption of society, Walter Rauschenbusch's *A Theology for the Social Gospel*; "we need a systematic theology large enough to match it and vital enough to back it." And that was the kind of systematic theology the book proposed to articulate.

The social thought and the social strategy of the churches are important topics in the political and intellectual history of the twentieth century, with movements for world peace, human rights, and temperance as only some of their consequences. In any history of Christian social ethics, moreover, the account of the twentieth century would have to form a major chapter, rivaling in epoch-making significance those on the transformation of Roman society through the conversion of Constantine or on the capitalist challenge to feudal society in the age of the Reformation, also because it sought, in opposition to the excesses of both the Constantinian settlement and the rise of capitalism, to develop "a new emphasis on the application of Christian principles to the acquisition and use of property." For the history of Christian doctrine as such, however, the significance of modern social thought is considerably more complicated, both because of its subordination of doctrinal questions to questions of life and society and because of a theological heterogeneity, even when doctrinal questions did arise, that would have to include Walter Rauschenbusch and Pope Leo XIII. Yet like questions of polity (to which Christian social concern often related itself) and questions of liturgy (with which its relations were less consistent), questions of doctrine, though often receiving only implicit attention, inevitably arose in the debates over Christian social thought. And for our purposes here, it is these implicit questions of doctrine, rather than the explicit questions of social strategy or social-political programs, that must be central. Precisely because it claimed to be taking its start from a "social gospel" that was already in place as an unquestioned component of the life of the church, the sequence of doctrines discussed in Rauschenbusch's *A Theology for the Social Gospel* provides a convenient outline, though by no means the exclusive doctrinal content, for the present account as well.

Rauschenbusch felt able to make "The Challenge of the Social Gospel to Theology" the title of his first chapter, and yet according to his third chapter the social gospel was in fact "neither alien nor novel." The relation of the new interest in the redemption of society to the theological tradition was an issue that none of the advocates of this interest could evade, since they would all have agreed with the historical judgment "that the social task of the church in the present time is something new and is more urgent than it was in the past." Rauschenbusch professed to find in the social gospel "the old message of salvation, but enlarged and intensified," a message "as orthodox as the Gospel"; but for those who were more profoundly committed than he to the tradition represented by "the old message of salvation," such an "enlargement" or "intensification" required more elaborate justification from church dogma.

Therefore one of the first and most vital tasks of any theological justification in the church—any church—for the attention to the redemption of society was to clarify its doctrinal legitimacy within the structures of

Rsch.*Theol.*1 (1917:1)

Rsch.*Theol.*1 (1917:1-10)

Rsch.*Theol.*3 (1917:23-30)

Harn.*Red.Auf.*2.1.2 (1904-II:61)

Rsch.*Theol.*1 (1917:5)
Rsch.*Theol.*pr. (1917:vi)

traditional authority, whatever those might be for a particular church. As Rauschenbusch recognized, "doctrinal theology is in less direct contact with facts than other theological studies," because church doctrine "perpetuates an esoteric stream of tradition." Yet he had to argue that within this stream of tradition, whether "esoteric" or not, the social gospel could claim a proper place, indeed, could help to explain and justify traditional doctrines. That did not apply to "some of the more speculative doctrines," such as "the metaphysical problems involved in the trinitarian and christological doctrines"; on these "the social gospel has no contribution to make," or at any rate a relatively small one, but "the sections of theology which ought to express it effectively" were the doctrines of sin and of redemption.

Documentation of the theological genealogy for a direct consideration of the problems of society was clearer in some confessional and denominational groups than in others, the Roman Catholic and the Reformed traditions being able to draw upon doctrinal resources that were less immediately available to the Eastern Orthodox and the Lutheran traditions. Defensiveness about the historical record of the complicity of the Roman Catholic Church in persecution and repression, as symbolized by the Inquisition, and about its apparent connivance at slavery did not nullify the divine mission of the church to speak, and if need be to act, in the social and political realm; in so doing, it was speaking both as the voice of the revelation given in Christ and as the guardian of the "right given to man by nature [ius homini a natura datum]." Dismay over the way enemies of the gospel were using such appeals to natural knowledge and natural law as an alternate "source of the church's proclamation" did not prevent those who stood primarily in the theological lineage of Calvin from continuing to assert with him that the church "serves man and the nation, the state and culture" by faithfully following and speaking the word of God "in Christ's stead and thus in service to him and to his word."

While the study of history caused representatives of Eastern Orthodoxy to reexamine critically the patterns of "Caesaropapism" in Byzantine history and caused

Rsch.*Theol.*2 (1917:11-12)

Rsch.*Theol.*14 (1917:147-48)

Rsch.*Theol.*4 (1917:31)

See pp. 215-26 above

Blms.*Prot.*15-19 (Casanovas 4:140-202)

Leo XIII.*Rer.Nov.* (*ASS* 23:643)

See pp. 290-91 above

*Theol.Erkl.*1 (Niesel 335)

See vol.4:217;244

*Erkl.Bek.*3.3;4.1 (Niesel 331)

Andrts.*Ek.pol.*1.1.6 (1964-I:29-30)

Elrt.*Morph*.2.4.29
(1931-II:366-95)

Theol.Erkl.pr. (Niesel 335)

Krtšv.*Sob*.2 (1932:30-40)

Schmn.*Prav*.3 (1985:100-153)

See vol.4:313-22

Rsch.*Theol*.12 (1917:123)

See vol.1:313-18

Rsch.*Theol*.5 (1917:41)

Rsch.*Theol*.7 (1917:57)

Rsch.*Theol*.7 (1917:67)

the interpreters of Lutheranism to question much of their theological rationale for avoiding direct political involvement, their experiences during the twentieth century with authoritarian and totalitarian regimes intensified such criticism. Many German Lutherans took part in the (Second) *Barmen Declaration*, which was at pains to present itself as the voice not only of Reformed theology but of the mainstream of German Protestantism, across the usual lines of the confessions but in fidelity to each of them. Although the close identification of the Russian Orthodox Church with the Czarist regime evoked from Orthodox theology a vigorous defense of the church's tradition against the Russian Revolution, further reflection, both by exiles and by those with continuing responsibility within the new Russia, prompted some fundamental reconsiderations of the ambiguity of the "age of Constantine" as the ideal form for the church itself and for its relation to state and society. Free-church Protestantism had traditionally striven to avoid both Reformed or Roman Catholic "theocracy" and Lutheran or Eastern Orthodox "Caesaropapism," for the sake of securing the freedom and purity of the individual, and therefore of the church, in the gospel and the gospel alone; but now, as Rauschenbusch acknowledged, "a fresh understanding of the church is gaining ground today in [free church] Protestant theology in spite of the increasing knowledge of the past and present failures of the church," and many who, like Rauschenbusch, stood in this tradition were in the forefront of the new interest in the relation of the church to the social order. So it was that a variety of doctrinal traditions all led, through diverse ways, to that new interest.

Perhaps no traditional doctrinal formulation was, in Rauschenbusch's judgment, more relevant to it than the Augustinian doctrine of original sin; although "the traditional doctrine of the fall is the product of speculative interest mainly," the doctrine of original sin had been "one of the few attempts of individualistic theology to get a solidaristic view of its field and work," and it was therefore "an important effort to see sin in its totality and to explain its unbroken transmission and perpetuation." "Sin," he insisted, "is not a private transaction between the sinner and God. Humanity always crowds the audience-room when God holds court." From greatly divergent presuppositions, other exponents of Christian social ethics expressed the same insistence. The social solidarity of the human race in creation and in sin almost always formed part of the case set forth by the authors of the arguments against polygenism and for the historical descent of the entire human race from a single pair of parents.

The Protestant economist Richard T. Ely was speaking for a large and diverse constituency, therefore, when he declared that "nothing in that associated life of man which we call society is more remarkable than social solidarity." Although this doctrine was taught by history and the social sciences also apart from revelation, it was, theologically, the deeper meaning of the story of the fall of Adam and of the history of Israel; and the New Testament "taught, with even greater force, the law of social solidarity." From the theology of Ritschl, Rauschenbusch received corroboration for "this solidaristic conception of sin." It was necessary to keep this and other conceptions in mind "in order to realize the power and scope of the doctrine to which they all converge: the Kingdom of Evil." At a time when the received pictures of the devil were being replaced by a radical reinterpretation of "the demonic" and the conventional orthodoxy about hell was becoming unacceptable to many theologians, the theologians of the social gospel found themselves in agreement with those Roman Catholics and other Christians who recognized a permanent worth in these doctrines as an expression of the insight, expressed for example in the words of the familiar (if textually doubtful) pericope of the woman taken in adultery, that her accusers "went out one by one," which meant "that they all shared in the common guilt, for they had not done what might have been done to banish sin and to restore men to righteousness."

Together with the doctrine of sin thus reinterpreted, the doctrine of redemption was, for Rauschenbusch, the other of "the sections of theology which ought to express [the social gospel] effectively," be-

Rsch. *Theol.* 6 (1917:48)

See pp. 207-8 above

Fund. 8.6 (1910-VIII:84-85); Pi. XII. *Hum. gen.* (*AAS* 42:576)

El. *Soc. Lw.* 6 (*LPT* 235)

El. *Soc. Lw.* 6 (*LPT* 237)
See pp. 215-16 above

Rsch. *Theol.* 9 (1917:93)

Rsch. *Theol.* 9 (1917:78)

Tlch. *Syst. Theol.* 5.3 (1967-III:406-9)

John 8:9 (var.)

El. *Soc. Lw.* 6 (*LPT* 238)

Rsch. *Theol.* 4 (1917:31)

cause it, too, was, properly understood, "solidaristic" in its deepest meaning. Under the chapter headings, "The Social Gospel and Personal Salvation" and then "The Salvation of the Super-Personal Forces," he invoked the biblical definition of faith as "the substance of things hoped for"—a definition, as Augustine had said, "used by the enlightened defenders of the catholic rule of faith" throughout Christian history—in support of a rather non-Augustinian understanding of faith as "not so much the endorsement of ideas formulated in the past, as expectancy and confidence in the coming salvation of God," an emphasis of the social gospel through which, Rauschenbusch maintained, "the forward look of primitive Christianity is resumed." The principal objects of the redemptive action of God and the redemptive activity of the church, in the light of this forward look, were not the immortal souls of isolated persons, as Christian individualism had supposed, but the "super-personal forces," which would be "saved when they come under the law of Christ"; these included business, the state, and society itself.

As Rauschenbusch's use of the phrase "the law of Christ" to provide the content of "the salvation of the super-personal forces" suggests, a major doctrinal test for any Christian theory of the redemption of society would have to be its connection, or lack of connection, with the teachings of the churches about the saving power of the death of Christ; therefore the final chapter of *A Theology for the Social Gospel* bore the title "The Social Gospel and the Atonement." Rauschenbusch recognized that many Christians would regard the doctrine of the atonement as "the marrow of theology," although for him the doctrine of the kingdom of God was "the marrow of the gospel, just as the incarnation was to Athanasius, justification by faith alone to Luther, and the sovereignty of God to Jonathan Edwards"; in fact, however, each of these doctrines had been, for most of its defenders including the ones named, a corollary of redemption through the crucifixion and resurrection of Christ, which was therefore the ultimate "marrow of the gospel" for them as well. To link the social gospel to traditional conceptions of the atonement, its interpreters item-

Rsch.*Theol.* 10 (1917:95-109)
Rsch.*Theol.* 11 (1917:110-17)

Heb. 11:1

Aug.*Enchir.* 2.8 (*CCSL* 46:52)

Rsch.*Theol.* 10 (1917:101-2)

Rsch.*Theol.* 11 (1917:113)

See pp. 95-101 above

Rsch.*Theol.* 19 (1917:240-79)

Rsch.*Theol.* 19 (1917:240)

Rsch.*Theol.* 13 (1917:131)

See vol. 1:200-210;
vol. 3:155-67;vol. 4:155-67

Rsch.*Theol.* 19 (1917:248-58)

See p. 92 above

See vol.3:129

Rsch.*Theol.* 13 (1917:131)

Soc.Crd. (1908) (Ward 6)

See pp. 225-26 above

Matt. 16:18;18:17

Rsch.*Theol.* 13 (1917:131-32)

Gldn.*Ch.Kng.* 1 (*LPT* 10?)

Doc.Chr.Un. 6 (Bell 1:18)

Bnhfr.*Th.Gem.* 6 (Bethge 2:279-80)

Bnhfr.*Th.Gem.* 5 (Bethge 2:184-87)

ized the sins, "all of a public nature," that had been responsible for the crucifixion. That did not conceal the fundamental shift at work in the definition of the means of salvation, from the atoning work of Christ to the reforming teachings of Christ, or—employing the framework of the "threefold office" of Christ as prophet, priest, and king—from a Christ who was king through his sacrifice as priest, which could be seen as the consensus of the tradition, to a Christ who was king through his message as prophet.

"To those whose minds live in the social gospel," therefore, "the kingdom of God is a dear truth" and the central doctrine of the Christian message, calling as it did "for equal rights and complete justice" throughout society. It was even more than that: on the basis of the critical study of the Gospels that had been carried on especially since the beginning of the twentieth century, Rauschenbusch felt entitled to claim that in the Gospel accounts of the discourses of Jesus "only two of his reported sayings contain the word 'church,' and both passages are of questionable authenticity." What made their authenticity questionable was, he found it "safe to say," that Jesus had "never thought of founding the kind of institution which afterward claimed to be acting for him." Instead, as the Gospels made obvious, "Jesus always spoke of the kingdom of God." As Washington Gladden said, "the kingdom includes the church, but the church does not include the kingdom." Despite the ecumenical importance of the question, "What is the relation of the church to the kingdom of God?" so radical a disjunction between "church" and "kingdom"—or, for that matter, between "kingdom" and "state"—continued to be unacceptable to the main body of Christian teaching throughout the churches, also to the teaching of most of those who sought to address the concrete problems of modern society. Equally unacceptable to them was the reduction of the work of Christ to his prophetic message, or of that message to its ethical, even its social-ethical, content.

In addition, in spite of its rather tenuous relation to the body of doctrines or articles of faith, the idea of the kingdom of God became in twentieth-century

Christian thought an issue for at least two discussions that had vital significance not only for Christian political theory, but for doctrine as such, including the doctrine of the church: Roman Catholic social thought took as one of its historic starting points the medieval theory of the "two swords," while Lutheran social thought proceeded from a new attention to Luther's theory of the "two kingdoms." Neither formulation was altogether acceptable, and yet neither was avoidable either. These two theories are part of our subject matter here, too, but only for their decisive place in the history of twentieth-century ecclesiology.

The theory of two swords had arisen as an evident catachresis on the exchange between Christ and his disciples in the Garden of Gethsemane: "And they said, 'Look, Lord, here are two swords.' And he said to them, 'It is enough.' " It received wide currency through its incorporation in the bull *Unam Sanctam* issued by Pope Boniface VIII in 1302, where the doctrine of the church was defined more precisely than it had been in most earlier papal documents: there were "two swords, namely, the spiritual and the temporal," but both were in the power of the church, the former being wielded "by the church [ab ecclesia]" and the latter by the government but "on behalf of the church [pro ecclesia]." The theory of two swords belonged to the late medieval equation of the church with the kingdom of God, and as an "ex cathedra" papal pronouncement and thus a part of the deposit of the church's public teaching, *Unam Sanctam* was taken to be endowed with an authority binding on all times. The *Syllabus of Errors* of Pope Pius IX anathematized a series of propositions dealing with the position of the church within secular society, climaxing with the rejection of the heretical proposition that "the church should be separated from the state and the state from the church," and the *Syllabus* specifically condemned efforts to relegate its ecclesiology to the status of "a doctrine that prevailed [only] in the Middle Ages." Yet in the light of further historical reflection, and of the recognition that through religious pluralism "a new problem has been put to the universal Church," necessitating the application of the methodology of

Törn.*Reg.*2.1 (1940:23-27)

Luke 22:38

See vol.4:69

Bon.VIII.*Un.sanct.* (Lo Grasso 212)
See vol.4:81-85

Pi.IX.*Syll.*6.39-55 (*ASS* 3:172-74)

Pi.IX.*Syll.*6.55 (*ASS* 3:174)

Pi.IX.*Syll.*5.34 (*ASS* 3:172)

Mry.*Trths.*pr. (1964:11)

Mry.*Prob.Gd.*2 (1964:52-57)

CVat. (1962-65).9,
*Dign.hum.pers.*12
(Alberigo-Jedin 1009)

See pp. 333-34 below

See vol.4:174-75

Brth.*Rcht.* (1944:4)

Brth.*Ev.Ges.*2 (*TheolEx*
II-50:10-17)

Alt.*Eth.* (1965:137-41)

"development of doctrine" also to this ecclesiology, it became evident that the simple historical circumstance of its having "prevailed in the Middle Ages" did not make it permanently binding on the church. As the Second Vatican Council put it, "in the life of the people of God as it has made its pilgrim way through the vicissitudes of human history, there have at times been ways of acting which were less in accord with the spirit of the gospel and even opposed to it," including the persecution of those who did not accept the Christian faith. Reconsideration of the definition of the kingdom of God underlying the theory of "two swords" thus played a major part in the reconsideration and redefinition of church doctrine itself at the Second Vatican Council.

Originally formulated as a substitute for the medieval equation of the institutional church with the kingdom of God, Luther's distinction between the "two kingdoms [Regimente]" had been an effort to affirm that God exercised his rule both through "the kingdom of the left hand," the realm of law, power, and justice, and "the kingdom of the right hand," the realm of gospel, grace, and mercy: one God, but two realms. Therefore it was not legitimate for Christians to derive from the gospel the political principles that were to govern the state and the law courts; such principles came from history and from reason, not from the revelation in Christ. The political crises of the twentieth century raised profound questions not only about the social-ethical import of this theory, but about its doctrinal content. Evaluated from the central principle of the lordship of Christ over all, over the state no less than over the church, Luther's answer provided an "unsatisfactory" answer to the question of the relation between "justification" and "justice" and turned the distinction between law and gospel into a separation, endowing the "kingdom of the left hand" with a moral autonomy that opened the way to totalitarianism and tyranny and fundamentally distorting the New Testament picture of the church. Defenders of Luther's theory strove to reexamine the relation of "justification" and "justice" in his thought and insisted that his concept of a "kingdom of the right hand" stood in judgment upon all human

Törn.*Reg.*3.2 (1940:113)

institutions, including the human institutions of the church itself, and that it did impose "limits on the earthly kingdom." In a real sense, therefore, the church both was and was not the kingdom of God, but the kingdom of God extended far beyond the borders of the church to all creation.

See pp. 225-26 above

As the twentieth century had better reason to know than any previous century of Christian history, except perhaps the first, the term "kingdom of God," whatever its other meanings, carried unavoidable eschatological connotations. Although the spokesmen for the social gospel, with their quest for a "kingdom of God" on earth, did seem to be ignoring those connotations as often as had the spokesmen for the medieval equation of church and kingdom, the prominence of "consistent eschatology" as a method for interpreting the Gospels made it incumbent on anyone who now spoke about the kingdom of God to come to terms with them. Rauschenbusch set aside an entire chapter in his *A Theology for the Social Gospel* to "Eschatology," in which, addressing head-on the debate raging, as a consequence of historical criticism, over the so-called eschatological error of Jesus, he recommended the social gospel as a solution. "Historical science and the social gospel together," he proposed, "may be able to affect eschatology for good," in ways that neither had been able to do alone. For while "historical criticism by itself makes [eschatology] look imbecile and has no creative power," eschatology could be transformed by being combined with the social gospel, which "has that moral earnestness and religious faith which exerts constructive influence on doctrine."

Rsch.*Theol.* 18 (1917:208-39)

Rsch.*Theol.* 18 (1917:211)

See pp. 215-26 above

The interest of the nineteenth century in "the progress of the kingdom" was a warning of what such a "constructive influence on doctrine" could mean concretely in the reinterpretation of eschatology. Rauschenbusch acknowledged that he himself had once been so impressed by the notion of "the progress of civilization" that he adopted an "optimism . . . not warranted by the facts." The next generation of the pupils of the social gospel struck out at such easy optimism and at the identification of social progress with the kingdom of God, and it read the "eschato-

Rsch.*Miss.* (LPT 270-71)

Nbr.*Fth.Hist.* 1 (1949:1-13)

logical error" of the Gospels as an expression of transcendent divine judgment on every stage of human history. Where the church was seen as "the mystical body of Christ," the "fullness and completion of the Redeemer [plenitudo et complementum Redemptoris]" in the church, which was one with Christ as its head, was a "union of heaven and earth" and an expression of the realized eschatology that in the New Testament stood alongside futuristic eschatology in a tension of "already" and "not yet," a realized eschatology whose principal historical expression was the church and its celebration of the Eucharist. While the term "society," indeed "necessary society," was applicable to the family and to the state as well as to the church, only the church, as the sole "supernatural society," had a destiny beyond history and therefore a teaching function also in relation to these two "natural societies."

The political upheavals of the twentieth century, the practical experience of attempting to relate the Christian message of redemption to the structures of society, and the deepening recognition that, as Rauschenbusch put it, more extremely than many others would have, "our denominational divisions are nearly all . . . from a controversial age . . . [whose] real significance has crumbled away," all made the quest for the social significance of the gospel a major force toward Christian unity. What he said about the "social gospel" could have been applied as well to the "ecumenical gospel": "we need a systematic theology large enough to match it and vital enough to back it." And despite his vigorous polemic against Roman Catholicism, the most comprehensive attempt at such a "systematic theology" was to come, later in the century, from the decrees of the Second Vatican Council.

Lumen Gentium

On 3 July 1907 Pius X issued the decree *Lamentabili*, in which he condemned the effort of various theologians within the Roman Catholic Church to exempt themselves from the teaching authority of the church; and on 8 September of the same year, in the encyclical *Pascendi dominici gregis*, he extended and reinforced

Pi.XII.*Myst.corp.* (*AAS* 35:230)

Leo XIII.*Mir.car.* (*ASS* 34:642-43)

Pi.XI.*Div.il.mag.* (*AAS* 22:52-53)

Rsch.*Soc.Pr.Jes.* (1916:139-46)

Rsch.*Theol.* 1 (1917:1)

Pi.X.*Lam.* (*ASS* 40:470-77)

Pi.X.*Pasc.* (*ASS* 40:602)

Pi.X.*Sacr.ant.*(*AAS* 2:669-72)

J. Meyendorff ap.
Nichols-Stavrou (1978) 177

*Found.*int. (1913:vii)

See pp. 229-30 above

See vol.4:129

that condemnation, emphasizing "the origin of dogma and the very nature of dogma" as "the principal matter." In 1910 he added the requirement of an oath against these errors of Modernism to be taken by all professors of theology and other clergy. Within Eastern Orthodoxy, "with the exception of only four bishops, the entire Russian episcopate in 1905 demanded restoration of the patriarchate suppressed by Peter the Great," as a means of coping with the new situation of the Orthodox Church within the culture of twentieth-century Czarist Russia.

During 1909/1910 and following, Evangelical Protestants in the United States issued, in a total of more than three million copies, the twelve tracts entitled *The Fundamentals*, affirming the "five points of fundamentalism": the verbal inspiration and inerrancy of the Bible, the deity of Christ, the virgin birth of Christ, the substitutionary doctrine of the atonement, and the physical resurrection and bodily return of Christ. In 1912 a group of Anglican theologians from Oxford issued their "statement of Christian belief in terms of modern thought" under the title *Foundations*, in which they sought, without surrendering the essence of the Christian tradition, to reconcile historic Christian beliefs on those and other main points of doctrine with "science, philosophy, and scholarship," especially with the results of historical and biblical criticism.

Like the lectures of the liberal Lutheran historian Adolf Harnack on *The Essence of Christianity* in 1899/1900, these declarations at the beginning of the twentieth century by Roman Catholic, Eastern Orthodox, Evangelical Protestant, and Anglican spokesmen were all intended to formulate the essential meaning of the Christian tradition in its relations, whether positive or negative, to contemporary thought. All of them were, however, to be overshadowed in historical importance by the Second Vatican Council of the Roman Catholic Church convoked by Pope John XXIII, which met from late 1962 to late 1965. Most of the councils of the church, while considering tangentially a variety of disciplinary questions (penitential practice at the Fourth Lateran Council) or even theological questions (the relation among

See vol. 2:162-63

See vol. 1:200-210

See vol. 1:211-25

See vol. 1:256-66

See vol. 4:272-303
See vol. 4:276-77

CVat. (1962-65).5.*Or.eccl.*5
(Alberigo-Jedin 902)

CVat. (1962-65).5.
*Unit.redint.*3
(Alberigo-Jedin 910)

the patriarchates at the Council of Chalcedon), had concentrated on one burning doctrinal issue, as this had been raised in recent theological controversy: at Nicea, the relation of the Son to the Father; at Constantinople, the deity of the Holy Spirit and therefore the doctrine of the Trinity; at Ephesus and Chalcedon, the relation of the divine and human natures in the person of Christ. Occasionally, however, the recent theological controversy had been so comprehensive in its scope and so profound in its challenge that the council could not isolate one or two dogmatic questions, but felt obliged to address a wide (if never quite complete) range of doctrinal topics. Thus by the time the twenty-five sessions of the Council of Trent covering a period of eighteen years were over, very few doctrines had escaped at least some notice, although many had escaped definitive resolution.

Such comprehensiveness was, in seemingly unique measure, a characteristic of the Second Vatican Council. Also in unique measure, at least since the schism between East and West and the schisms of the Reformation, it deliberately strove to include the "separated brethren" in its purview. Not only did this give members of other communions a role, albeit an indirect one, in the discussions and deliberations of the council; even more pronounced and direct were the voices of the historic traditions represented by those communions, to which "the entire church was indebted." It was recognized that "some, even very many, of the most significant elements or endowments which together go to build up and give life to the church herself can exist outside the visible boundaries of the Catholic Church"; these "elements or endowments" included "the written word of God." Therefore Greek church fathers, Eastern liturgies, even Protestant Reformers and biblical scholars made themselves heard, if not always in the texts of the decrees, then in the historical footnotes to them. Those characteristics make the Second Vatican Council especially well-suited for this summation of the development of Christian doctrine—not only "the doctrine of the church" as an objective genitive, the doctrine about the church as set forth in the central declaration of the council, the Dogmatic Constitution on the

CVat. (1962-65).5.*Lum.gent.*
(Alberigo-Jedin 849-98)

See vol.1:1

See pp. 69-74, 241-52 above

See vol.4:276-77
See p. 261 above

See vol.4:277

CVat. (1962-65).8.*Dei
Verb.*2.9 (Alberigo-Jedin
974-75)

See vol.2:16-22

WCC.*Trad.* (Minear 12-51)

Church, *Lumen gentium*, but "the doctrine of the church" as a subjective genitive, in the more comprehensive sense as "what the church of Jesus Christ believes, teaches, and confesses on the basis of the word of God."

If only because of its prominence in every major doctrinal controversy of all the preceding centuries, the question of authority could not be avoided in any of the discussions at the Second Vatican Council. The very power and depth of *Lumen gentium* as an ecclesiological formulation stood in danger of seeming to subordinate both Scripture and tradition to the ongoing authority of the church. The Council of Trent, and then the First Vatican Council, had left unresolved the relation between Scripture and tradition as "the two sources [fontes] of revelation." The idea had been formulated in a preliminary draft at Trent that revelation was contained "partly [partim]" in the written books of Scripture and "partly [partim]" in tradition. Without an explicit condemnation of that idea, the tenor of *Dei Verbum*, the Dogmatic Constitution on Divine Revelation at the Second Vatican Council, stressed rather the mutual connection between "sacred tradition" and "Sacred Scripture," which had a single and common "source [scaturigo]" in divine revelation. Despite the opportunity to go on record regarding the question of whether all Christian doctrine was contained in Scripture or not, this decree in its explicit language left that question open, while implicitly, by its use of both Scripture and tradition, it affirmed that all doctrine came from Scripture, but from Scripture as it was continually being interpreted by authoritative tradition. In so doing, the council gave voice to a growing ecumenical consensus. For that had long been the historic teaching of Eastern Orthodoxy; and when the Commission on Faith and Order of the World Council of Churches, on which most Protestant, Anglican, and Orthodox churches were represented, created a study commission on "Tradition and Traditions," it set into motion a process of reflection and debate that would lead, if not to official dogmatic formulas, then to unofficial doctrinal formulations, that were strikingly similar to the language of *Dei Verbum*.

See vol.3:95-105;284-93
See pp. 183-84 above
CVat. (1869-70).3.2
(Alberigo-Jedin 806)

See pp. 290-91 above

*Theol.Erkl.*1 (Niesel 335)

See vol.1:27
Rom.1:19-20;
CVat. (1962-65).8.
*Dei Verb.*1.3
(Alberigo-Jedin 972)

CVat. (1962-65).8.*Dei
Verb.*1.2 (Alberigo-Jedin 972)

See vol.3:284-93

See pp. 241-52 above

Leo XIII.*Prov.* (*ASS*
26:286-87)

Pi.XII.*Div.affl.Spir.* (*AAS*
35:298)

One of the most urgent questions in the consideration of the doctrine of revelation in all the churches during the twentieth century had been "natural revelation," whose validity had been reaffirmed by the First Vatican Council against skepticism and rationalism. Yet to many, "natural theology" seemed itself to be a species of rationalism, as well as a device for erecting within the church another authority than that of Christ and his word. The first thesis of the *Barmen Declaration* condemned "the false doctrine that the church can and must acknowledge as a source of its proclamation, outside of and alongside this one word of God, also other events and powers, structures and truths, as the revelation of God." The answer of the Second Vatican Council to that critique of "natural theology" was, while repeating the traditional language of the Epistle to the Romans about the "testimony" of God "in created things," to do so only after articulating a complete confession of faith in "the economy of revelation" through the history of salvation climaxing in the incarnation of the Logos, which was, therefore, not to be seen as a supplement or even a completion of "the natural knowledge of God" but as the foundation for the entire dialogue of God with the human race. Without denying the philosophical validity or theological correctness of the standard Thomistic proofs for the existence of God, therefore, *Dei Verbum* expressed a growing doctrinal consensus of the twentieth century by shifting the emphasis from rationalistic arguments, whether heterodox or orthodox in their outcome, to the testimony of the word of God.

Yet the official statements of the Roman Catholic and Eastern Orthodox churches, no less than such promulgations as the Evangelical Protestant *Fundamentals*, had described the inspiration of Scripture as the guarantee of an inerrancy that excluded every error, not only in faith and morals but in history, archeology, and science. Application of the historical critical method to the study of Scripture continued to divide theologians, and entire churches, from one another. Although the encyclical *Divino afflante Spiritu* had clung to this definition of the inerrancy of Scripture, it had at the same time, with unprece-

Pi.XII.*Div.affl.Spir.* (AAS
35:314)

See pp. 246-47 above

Aug.*Doctr.christ.*3.18.26
(*CCSL* 32:93)

CVat. (1962-65).8.*Dei
Verb.*3.12 (Alberigo-Jedin
976)

Bltmn.*Jes.*int. (1964:11)

See p. 292 above

Bsst.*Kyr.Chr.*8
(1913:338-42)

See vol.1:256-66

Aug.*Trin.*2.1.2 (*CCSL* 50:81)
Aug.*Trin.*1.7.14;1.11.22
(*CCSL* 50:44-46;60-61)
Schmauch (1964) 24-33

dented force and clarity, given official recognition to the existence within Scripture of various literary forms and therefore to the need of paying attention to "the outlook [indoles] and condition of life of the sacred writer, and the age in which he lived." That recognition provided a justification at the council for a reconsideration of what was meant by "inerrancy" in the light of the way scientific and historical matters were treated in the Bible. Augustine had already spoken about the necessity in biblical interpretation of "making allowance for the condition of those times." Although he was referring not to science or history but to ethics, specifically to the polygamy of the Old Testament patriarchs, his words proved to be useful not only to several participants in the debate at the council, but to the text of the Dogmatic Constitution on Revelation itself in dealing with problems of chronology and cosmology as well. This development of the doctrine of biblical inerrancy was being played out also against the background of profound skepticism among some highly influential Protestant New Testament scholars about the possibility of knowing almost anything regarding "the life and the personality of Jesus," behind the kerygma of the early church. In a curious way, such Protestant skepticism could be used to confirm the Roman Catholic and Eastern Orthodox emphasis on the centrality of ecclesiology: neither Scripture nor Christ was accessible except through the tradition of the church—at any rate, the tradition of the primitive church, if not the church tradition of subsequent centuries.

As the research into that primitive tradition underlying the New Testament had shown, the distinctiveness of the Christian community had expressed itself in worship, which had then formed the basis for the development of doctrine. The title "Lord [κύριος]" for Jesus Christ was a cultic term before it became a creedal one; it was almost a consensus that Philippians 2:6-11, the primary proof text for the dogmatic Christology of "preexistence, kenosis, and exaltation," which provided the "canonical rule" for understanding the dual nature of biblical language about him, came not from metaphysics but from a hymn; the primary proof text for the deity of the Holy Spirit,

See vol.1.211-25
Matt.28:19-20

See p. 264 above

Eph.2:21-22
CVat. (1962-65).3.
*Sacr.Conc.*pr.2 (Alberigo-Jedin 820)
CVat. (1962-65).3.
*Sacr.Conc.*1.7 (Alberigo-Jedin 822)

See vol.1:156

See vol.4:85-98
CVat. (1962-65).3.*Sacr. Conc.*1.33 (Alberigo-Jedin 827)
CVat. (1962-65).3.
*Sacr.Conc.*1.9 (Alberigo-Jedin 823)

See vol.4:145-49
CVat. (1962-65).5.
*Lum.gent.*3.25 (Alberigo-Jedin 869);
CVat. (1962-65).9.
*Presb.ord.*2.4 (Alberigo-Jedin 1046)
CVat. (1962-65).5.
*Lum.gent.*3.21 (Alberigo-Jedin 865)

CVat. (1962-65).3.
*Sacr.Conc.*1.24 (Alberigo-Jedin 826)

See vol.4:175-76;272
CVat. (1962-65).8.
*Apost.act.*1.2-3 (Alberigo-Jedin 982-83);
CVat. (1962-65).3.
*Sacr.Conc.*1.14 (Alberigo-Jedin 824)

Ps.45:13 (Vulg.)
Leo XIII.*Or.dign.* (*ASS* 27:259)
*Conf.Aug.*7.3 (*Bek.*61);
*Art.XXXIX.*34 (Schaff 3:508);*Conf.Belg.*32 (Niesel 132)
*Conf.Helv.post.*23 (Niesel 267-68)

and thus for the dogma of the Trinity, had likewise been supplied by the worship practice of the church, as summarized in the baptismal formula. Far from being a later accretion to some supposedly nonliturgical status quo ante, then, the liturgy was that which "builds up those within the church into the Lord's holy temple," thus "manifesting the mystery of Christ and the genuine nature of the true church" as God's holy people. In this "work of making people holy," the liturgy of the church was the distinctive exercise of the priestly office of Christ.

The holiness of the church, which had been the earliest of its attributes to achieve creedal formulation, had also long been an occasion for misunderstanding. By defining the purpose of liturgical action as the praise of God but also the instruction of the church in holiness, and by thus grounding behavior in worship rather than worship in behavior, the council responded to Reformation critiques of medieval doctrine by avoiding the moralism that almost unavoidably attached itself to the term "holy." Therefore the council put the function of preaching and teaching first among the duties both of the episcopate and of the priesthood, citing the authority of "the tradition expressed especially in the liturgical rites and practice of the church both of the East and of the West." The reading, teaching, and preaching of Scripture was to be "of paramount importance [maximum momentum] in the celebration of the liturgy." This was in keeping with the council's emphasis, likewise a response to Reformation critiques of medieval sacerdotalism, on the universal priesthood of all believers in the church, as that priesthood, conferred through baptism, was expressed in the liturgy.

The ecclesiological import of the liturgy affected the understanding not only of holiness, but also and especially of unity amid diversity, as a mark of the church: the church, as the bride of Christ, was to be "surrounded with variety." The public statements of doctrine of all the churches asserted that diversity of ritual or of administrative structure as such did not negate unity, but those statements had long recognized that the special contribution of the churches of the East lay in making a theological point of the

Socr.H.e.5.22.57 (Hussey
2:635)

CVat. (1962-65).3.
Sacr.Conc.1.37 (Alberigo-Jedin
828)

CVat. (1962-65).5.Or.eccl. 6
(Alberigo-Jedin 902)

CVat. (1962-65).5.
Unit.redint.3 (Alberigo-Jedin
910)

CVat. (1962-65).9.Nostr.aet.1
(Alberigo-Jedin 1069)

CVat. (1962-65).9.Ad gent.5
(Alberigo-Jedin 1014)
See vol.1.321;325-27;
vol.4:237
1 Tim.2:4;see pp. 115-16
above
CVat. (1962-65).9.Ad gent.7
(Alberigo-Jedin 1017)

resistance to liturgical and organizational homogene-
ity. The Second Vatican Council explicitly declared
that "even in the liturgy, the church has no wish to
impose a rigid uniformity in matters which do not
involve the faith or the good of the whole community." This was the doctrinal foundation not only for
the approval of the use of the vernacular in the Mass
(which had far-reaching consequences for the life and
worship of the church, though not directly for its
doctrine), but for the reaffirmation of the right and
duty of Eastern churches, even if they were to achieve
(or recover) unity with the Holy See, to "preserve
their lawful liturgical rites and their established way
of life." The council added that even in churches
whose episcopate and priestly orders were not accepted by Roman Catholicism as valid, participation
in "the sacred actions of the Christian religion" could
"engender a life of grace" and even "provide access to
the community of salvation," although it could not be
said to provide "that unity which Jesus Christ wished
to bestow."

The affirmation of the universality or "sobornost"
of the entire church set forth in such language by the
Decree on Ecumenism, innovative or even revolutionary though it may have seemed, looked beyond the
borders of the church, of any church, in its vision of
the "one community of all nations." While continuing to affirm that "the mission of the church is
fulfilled by that activity which makes her fully present
to all" and that the will of God the Creator (in the
long-mooted words of the New Testament) for "all to
be saved" would not be completed until that missionary work had achieved its goal of converting the world
to the gospel of Christ, the council also moved to
consider the doctrinal meaning of the status of non-
Christians in their own right. In doing so, it sought
to articulate a Christian and Catholic alternative to
two prominent twentieth-century definitions of that
status. One of these, suggested in *Rethinking Missions*,
which had come out of the Protestant "laymen's
inquiry" into not only the practice but also the
theological presuppositions of the missionary enterprise, had proposed that "Christianity may find itself
bound to aid these [non-Christian] faiths . . . to a

Hckng.*Reth*.2.5 (1932:37)

John 1:9

Krmr.*Mssge*.3 (1938:75)

Acts 4:12

Nieb.*Rad.Mon*.4
(1960:49-63)

Söd.*Liv.Gd*.9 (1933:349)

Söd.*Liv.Gd*.10 (1933:378)

Nieb.*Rev*.3 (1960:132-37)

CVat. (1962-65).9.
Dign.hum.pers.15
(Alberigo-Jedin 1010)

truer interpretation of their own meaning"; this substituted complementarity and cooperation for the conventional view of the uniqueness and exclusivity of gospel revelation. Exponents of this view found support in the words of the prologue to the Gospel of John, which called the pre-existent Logos "the true light that enlightens every man who comes into the world." The other was the application to the relation with non-Christian religions of the new awareness of the primacy of revelation in Christ, the conviction that "God Himself can only make possible the impossible by His sovereign creative act of salvation in Jesus Christ." This sharpened, even more than earlier Protestant missiology had, the claim for the name of Jesus Christ summarized in the traditional exegesis of the words, "There is salvation in no one else, for there is no other name under heaven given among men by which we must be saved."

There was, however, another resolution of the problem that had also appeared in the twentieth century. It strove to combine a commitment to the particularity of Christian revelation with an affirmation of the universal salvific will of the God of Christian revelation. Nathan Söderblom stated the paradox in his Gifford Lectures when he spoke of "the uniqueness of Christ as the historical revealer, as the Word made flesh," but then went on to affirm that "God's revelation is not confined to the church, although the church has, in the Scriptures and in its experience, the means of interpreting God's continued revelation" past or present, wherever this might appear, whether within the church or beyond it. Theologically related to this concern with "progressive revelation" was one of the presuppositions underlying the Decree on Religious Liberty of the Second Vatican Council, *Dignitatis humanae personae*: the recognition that "all nations are coming into even closer unity" and that members "of different cultures and religions are being brought together in closer relationships." Doctrinally, this led to the combination of "the belief that God himself has made known to mankind the way in which men are to serve him, and thus be saved in Christ and come to blessedness," with an acceptance of the obligation of "all men to

CVat. (1962-65).9.
*Dign.hum.pers.*1
(Alberigo-Jedin 1002)

CVat. (1962-65).9.
*Dign.hum.pers.*9
(Alberigo-Jedin 1006)

seek the truth . . . and to embrace the truth they come to know, and to hold fast to it." But the acknowledgment that this insight, together with its implications for religious liberty, was not present in the ipsissima verba of the New Testament but had come only through the development of doctrine suggested that a deeper development in the church's understanding of revelation, through the experience of the centuries, could lead also to a further clarification of the relation between particularity and universality, and thus of the relation between Christianity and other religions.

That clarification was uniquely urgent in the relation between Christianity and Judaism, as in the course of the twentieth century both the development of Christian doctrine and the experience of the church in society had made abundantly evident. The Christian effort to come to terms with the unique and abiding place of the covenant with the people of Israel in the economy of divine revelation had always been a See vol.2:200-216 key to the nature of the Christian message; but just as the twentieth century witnessed the most traumatic wrench in Jewish-Christian relations since the primSee vol.1:12-27itive "de-Judaization of Christianity" in the first century, so it also produced, in the fourth article of *Nostra aetate*, the Declaration on the Relationship of the Church to Non-Christian Religions, the most forceful official Christian affirmation of the permanence of the covenant with Israel, at least since the See vol.1:23
CVat. (1962-65).7.*Nostr.aet.*4
(Alberigo-Jedin 970) ninth, tenth, and eleventh chapters of the Epistle to the Romans, upon which indeed it was based. Not only did the council begin its interpretation of the place of Judaism in the history of salvation by making this interpretation part of its reflection upon "the mystery of the church" rather than simply part of its discussion of non-Christian religions (despite its having eventually become part of the Declaration on the Relationship of the Church to Non-Christian Religions, rather than of the Decree on Ecumenism), but CVat. (1962-65).7.*Nostr.aet.*4
(Alberigo-Jedin 970) it affirmed "the spiritual bond linking the people of the New Covenant with Abraham's stock." Repudiating traditional observances that had provided an Bnl.*Diss.apol.* (1747) occasion for hatred and persecution, the council urged two "theological resources for unity" not only among Christians but also between Jews and Christians:

scholarship and dialogue. "Since the spiritual patrimony common to Christians and Jews is so great," it declared, "this sacred synod wishes to foster and recommend that mutual understanding and respect which is the fruit above all of biblical and theological studies and of brotherly dialogue."

CVat. (1962-65).7.*Nostr.aet.*4
(Alberigo-Jedin 970)

Although the relation of Christianity to faiths other than Judaism did not have the same doctrinal status and could not, except by a superficial analogy, be treated by making those faiths a "series of Old Testaments," the council did extend also to them the method of affirming the positive values in other traditions as evidence of "a certain perception of that hidden power which hovers over the course of things and over the events of human life" and which could be read as an expression of "the recognition of a supreme Divinity [numinis] and a supreme Father." Islamic monotheism was singled out as a special instance of that recognition, together with the Muslim veneration for the Virgin Mary. But instead of serving merely as the traditional proof from "the consensus of the peoples" had, this recognition provided the basis for declaring that "the Catholic Church rejects nothing that is true and holy in these religions," since Christ, as "the way, the truth, and the life," was "the true light that enlightens every man." The Father of Jesus Christ was "the Father of all," and the divine image was present in all. Like most of the decrees of the council, this was intended to have a pastoral and practical effect, but it both expressed and established a doctrinal foundation for the practice.

CVat. (1962-65).7.*Nostr.aet.*2
(Alberigo-Jedin 969)

See vol.2:227-42

CVat. (1962-65).7.*Nostr.aet.*3
(Alberigo-Jedin 969-70)

See p. 185 above

CVat. (1962-65).7.*Nostr.aet.*2
(Alberigo-Jedin 969)

John 14:6;John 1:9 CVat.
(1962-65).7.*Nostr.aet.*5
(Alberigo-Jedin 971);CVat.
(1962-65).9.*Gaud.sp.*1.2.29
(Alberigo-Jedin 1086)
CVat. (1962-65).9.
*Gaud.sp.*pr.2.
(Alberigo-Jedin 1069-70)

That doctrinal foundation, which the Second Vatican Council articulated for the church of the twentieth century, lay in the doctrinal development of all the centuries that had preceded it in all the churches— Roman Catholic, Eastern Orthodox, and Protestant. It defined the *unity* of the church both as a divine gift to be received with gratitude and as a task of "the restoration of unity [unitatis redintegratio] among all Christians," for them to carry out by fraternal dialogue between traditions and by the study of their common tradition. It affirmed with special vigor the centrality of worship as the "rule of prayer" through whose reform and renewal "the rule of faith" could be

CVat. (1962-65).5.
*Unit.redint.*pr.1
(Alberigo-Jedin 908)

CVat. (1962- 65).3.
Sacr.Conc.1.21
(Alberigo-Jedin 825)

CVat. (1962-65).5.
Lum.gent.2.13
(Alberigo-Jedin 859-60)

CVat. (1962-65).8.Dei
Verb.pr.1 (Alberigo-Jedin 971)

See vol.1:10

recovered and deepened, and the *holiness* of the church renewed. It looked beyond the needs and resources of any particular church to the vision of a genuinely *catholic* universality and "sobornost" within which the whole of humanity would be embraced. And it strove to speak as an authentic voice of the deposit of *apostolic* revelation, as this had been set down in Scripture and transmitted through apostolic tradition.

Therefore it is appropriate for this account of the development of Christian doctrine to conclude as it began: "Credo unam sanctam catholicam et apostolicam ecclesiam."

Selected
Secondary Works

GENERAL

Adeney, Walter Frederic. *The Greek and Eastern Churches*. New York, 1932.

Attwater, Donald. *The Christian Churches of the East*. 2 vols. Milwaukee, 1947–48.

Barth, Karl. *Protestant Thought: From Rousseau to Ritschl*. Translated by Brian Cozens. Introduction by Jaroslav Pelikan. New York, 1959. Although this book (in the original German) also appears in the list of primary sources for the present volume, it must, together with the corresponding book by Georges Florovsky, be listed here as well, as a profound introduction not only to the theology of the nineteenth century, but to the thought that preceded it.

Baumer, Franklin L. *Modern European Thought: Continuity and Change in Ideas, 1600–1950*. New York, 1977.

Benz, Ernst. *Geist und Leben der Ostkirche*. 2d ed. Munich, 1971.

Billington, James H. *The Icon and the Axe: An Interpretive History of Russian Culture*. New York, 1966. Especially valuable for its insights into the distinctively Russian style of bringing about the Enlightenment.

Blumenberg, Hans. *The Legitimacy of the Modern Age*. Translated by R. M. Wallace. Cambridge, Mass., 1983.

Chadwick, Owen. *From Bossuet to Newman: The Idea of Doctrinal Development*. Cambridge, 1957.

Elert, Werner. *Der Kampf um das Christentum: Geschichte der Beziehungen zwischen dem evangelischen Christentum in Deutschland und dem allgemeinen Denken seit Schleiermacher und Hegel*. Munich, 1921.

Florovsky, Georges V. *Ways of Russian Theology*. Translated by Robert L. Nichols. (See "Nordland" in "Editions and Collections," p. xlvii above.)

Franks, Robert S. *A History of the Doctrine of the Work of Christ in Its Ecclesiastical Development*. 2 vols. New York, 1918.

Frei, Hans W. *The Eclipse of Biblical Narrative: A Study in Eighteenth and Nineteenth Century Hermeneutics*. New Haven, 1974.

Fries, Heinrich, et al., eds. *Handbuch theologischer Grundbegriffe*. 2 vols. Munich, 1962–63.

Gass, Wilhelm. *Die Geschichte der protestantischen Dogmatik in ihrem Zusammenhange mit der Theologie überhaupt*. 4 vols. Berlin, 1854–67.

Gerrish, Brian A. *The Old Protestantism and the New: Essays on the Reformation Heritage*. Chicago, 1982.

Groff, Warren F., and Miller, Donald E. *The Shaping of Modern Christian Thought*. Cleveland, 1968.

Herzog, Johann Jakob, and Hauck, Albert, eds. *Realencyklopädie für protestantische Theologie und Kirche.* 3d ed. 22 vols. Leipzig, 1896–1909.

Hirsch, Emanuel. *Geschichte der neuern evangelischen Theologie im Zusammenhang mit den allgemeinen Bewegungen des europäischen Denkens.* 5 vols. Gütersloh, 1960.

Höfer, Josef, and Rahner, Karl, eds. *Lexikon für Theologie und Kirche.* 2d ed. 14 vols. Freiburg, 1957–68.

Lopuchin, Aleksandr Pavlovič, and Glubokovskij, Nikolaj Nikaronovič, eds. *Pravoslavnaja bogoslovskaja enciklopedija ili bogoslovskij enciklopedičeskij slovar* [Eastern Orthodox theological encyclopedia or theological encyclopedic dictionary]. 9 vols. in 12. Petrograd, 1900–1911.

Martinos, Athanasios, ed. *Ὀρησκευτικη καὶ ’Ηϑικὴ Ἐγκυκλοπαιδεία* [Encyclopedia of religion and ethics]. 12 vols. Athens, 1962–68.

Mead, Sidney Earl. *The Lively Experiment: The Shaping of Christianity in America.* New York, 1963.

Nichols, Robert, and Stavrou, Theofanis George, eds. *Russian Orthodoxy under the Old Regime.* Minneapolis, 1978. Particularly useful to the reader with access only to Western languages.

Pelikan, Jaroslav, ed. *Makers of Modern Theology.* 5 vols. New York, 1966–68.

———. *Jesus through the Centuries: His Place in the History of Culture.* New Haven, 1985.

Polnnj pravoslavnyj enciklopedičeskij slovar [Complete encyclopedic dictionary of Eastern Orthodoxy]. Reprint edition. 2 vols. London, 1971.

Smith, Page. *The Historian and History.* New York, 1964.

Stephan, Horst. *Geschichte der deutschen evangelischen Theologie seit dem deutschen Idealismus.* 2d ed. by Martin Schmidt. Berlin, 1960.

Turner, James. *Without God, without Creed: The Origins of Unbelief in America.* Baltimore, 1985. Covers most of the period dealt with in this volume.

Vacant, Jean-Michel-Alfred, et al., eds. *Dictionnaire de théologie catholique.* 15 vols. Paris, 1903–50.

1. THE CRISIS OF ORTHODOXY EAST AND WEST

Abercrombie, N. *The Origins of Jansenism.* Oxford, 1936.

Addy, George M. *The Enlightenment in the University of Salamanca.* Durham, 1966.

Allison, Henry E. *Lessing and the Enlightenment: His Philosophy of Religion and Its Relation to Eighteenth-Century Thought.* Ann Arbor, 1966.

Bahner, Werner. *Aufklärung als Periodenbegriff der Ideologiegeschichte: Einige methodologische Überlegungen und Grundsätze.* Berlin, 1973.

Barber, W. H., et al., eds. *The Age of the Enlightenment.* Edinburgh, 1967.

Baumer, Franklin L. *Religion and the Rise of Scepticism.* New York, 1960.

Berlin, Isaiah, ed. *The Age of the Enlightenment: The Eighteenth Century Philosophers.* Boston, 1956.

Beyer-Fröhlich, Marianne, ed. *Höhe und Krise der Aufklärung.* Leipzig, 1934.

Böhi, Hans. *Die religiöse Grundlage der Aufklärung.* Zurich, 1933.

Bolshakoff, Serge. *Russian Nonconformity.* Philadelphia, 1950.

Brunschwig, Henri. *Enlightenment and Romanticism in Eighteenth Century Prussia.* Translated by Frank Jellinek. Chicago, 1974.

Cassirer, Ernst. *The Philosophy of the Enlightenment.* Translated by Fritz C. A. Koelln and James P. Pettegrove. Princeton, 1951. A work of great learning, deep insight, and fundamental importance.

————. *Rousseau, Kant, Goethe.* Translated by James Gutman, Paul Oskar Kristeller, and John Herman Randall. New York, 1965.

Conybeare, Frederick Cornwallis. *Russian Dissenters.* Cambridge, Mass., 1921.

Cragg, Gerald Robertson. *Puritanism to the Age of Reason: A Study of Changes in Religious Thought within the Church of England 1660 to 1700.* Cambridge, 1950.

————. *The Church and the Age of Reason, 1648–1789.* New York, 1970.

Crocker, Lester G., ed. *The Age of Enlightenment.* New York, 1969.

Crummey, Robert O. *The Old Believers and the World of Antichrist.* Madison, Wis., 1970.

Denker, Rolf. *Grenzen liberaler Aufklärung bei Kant und Anderen.* Stuttgart, 1968.

Gay, Peter. *The Enlightenment: An Interpretation.* 2 vols. New York, 1966–69.

————. *A Loss of Mastery: Puritan Historians in Colonial America.* Berkeley, 1966.

Goyard-Fabre, Simone. *La philosophie des Lumières en France.* Paris, 1972.

Grabski, Andrzej Feliks. *Myśl historyczna polskiego Oświecenia* [The historical thought of the Polish Enlightenment]. Warsaw, 1976.

Greaves, Richard L. *John Bunyan.* Grand Rapids, Mich., 1969. A study of Bunyan as theologian.

Grossmann, Walter. *Johann Christian Edelmann: From Orthodoxy to Enlightenment.* The Hague, 1976.

Günther, Hansjürgen. *Das Problem des Bösen in der Aufklärung.* Bern and Frankfurt, 1974.

Hollifield, E. Brooks. *The Covenant Sealed: The Development of Puritan Sacramental Theology in Old and New England, 1570–1720.* New Haven, 1974.

Krauss, Werner. *Die Aufklärung in Spanien, Portugal und Lateinamerika.* Munich, 1973.

Krieger, Leonard. *An Essay on the Theory of Enlightened Despotism.* Chicago, 1975.

Kruse, Martin. *Speners Kritik am landesherrlichen Kirchenregiment und ihre Vorgeschichte.* Witten, 1971.

Laporte, J. *La doctrine de Port-Royal.* 2 vols. Paris, 1923.

Lauch, Annelies. *Wissenschaft und kulturelle Beziehungen in der russischen Aufklärung.* Berlin, 1969.

Marty, Martin E. *The Infidel: Freethought and American Religion.* Cleveland and New York, 1961.

Paquier, Jules. *Le Jansénisme: Etude doctrinale d'après les sources.* Paris, 1909.

Pascal, Pierre. *Avvakum et les débuts du Raskol: La crise religieuse au XVIIe siècle en Russie.* Liguge, 1938.

Patrides, C. A. *Milton and the Christian Tradition.* Oxford, 1966. Special attention to Milton's "Arianism."

Payne, Harry C. *The Philosophes and the People.* New Haven, 1976.

Plongeron, Bernard. *Théologie et politique au siècle des lumières (1770–1820).* Geneva, 1973.

Redwood, John. *Reason, Ridicule, and Religion: The Age of Enlightenment in England, 1660–1750.* Cambridge, Mass., 1976.

Rees, August Herbert. *The Doctrine of Justification in the Anglican Reformers.* London, 1939.

Schneiders, Werner. *Die wahre Aufklärung: Zum Selbstverständnis der deutschen Aufklärung.* Freiburg, 1974.

Scipanov, I. Ja. *Filosofija russkogo prosveščenija: Vtoraja polovina XVIII. v.* [The philosophy of the Russian Enlightenment in the second half of the eighteenth century]. Moscow, 1971.

Southgate, W. M. *John Jewel and the Problem of Doctrinal Authority.* Cambridge, Mass., 1962.

Stroup, John. *The Struggle for Identity in the Clerical Estate: Northwest German Protestant Opposition to Absolutist Policy in the Eighteenth Century.* Leiden, 1984.

Venturi, Franco. *Utopia and Reform in the Enlightenment.* Cambridge, 1971.

————. *Italy and the Enlightenment*. Translated by Susan Corsi. New York, 1972.

Voss, Karl-Ludwig. *Christian Democritus: Das Menschenbild bei Johann Conrad Dippel*. Leiden, 1970.

Willey, Basil. *The Seventeenth Century Background*. London, 1934.

2. The Objectivity of Transcendent Revelation

Aland, Kurt, ed. *Pietismus und Bibel*. Witten, 1970.

Bardon, Colette, et al., eds. *La pensée des lumières en Russie*. Lille, 1973.

Baumgart, Peter. *Zinzendorf als Wegbereiter historischen Denkens*. Lübeck, 1960.

Becker, Carl L. *The Heavenly City of the Eighteenth-Century Philosophers*. New Haven, 1932.

Boorstin, Daniel J. *The Lost World of Thomas Jefferson*. New York, 1948.

Bornkamm, Heinrich. *Mystik, Spiritualismus und die Anfänge des Pietismus*. Giessen, 1926.

Burns, Robert M. *The Great Debate on Miracles*. Lewisburg, Pa., 1980.

Burtt, Edwin Arthur. *The Metaphysical Foundations of Modern Physical Science*. Reprint ed. Garden City, N. Y., 1954.

Casel, Odo. "Zum Wort Mysterium." *Jahrbuch für Liturgiewissenschaft* 15 (1941):269–305.

Chadwick, Henry, ed. *Lessing's Theological Writings*. London, 1956. The "Introductory Essay" (pp. 9–49) is a concise examination of Lessing as theologian.

Cochrane, Eric W. *Tradition and Enlightenment in the Tuscan Academies, 1690–1800*. Chicago, 1961.

Cragg, Gerald. *Reason and Authority in the Eighteenth Century*. Cambridge, 1964.

Crocker, Lester G. *An Age of Crisis: Man and World in Eighteenth Century French Thought*. Baltimore, 1959.

Fascher, Erich. *Kritik am Wunder: Eine geschichtliche Skizze*. Stuttgart, 1960.

Greenslade, Samuel L., et al., eds. *The Cambridge History of the Bible*. 3 vols. Cambridge, 1963–70.

Greschat, Martin. *Zwischen Tradition und neuem Anfang: Valentin Ernst Löscher und der Ausgang der lutherischen Orthodoxie*. Witten, 1971.

Grossmann, Sigrid. *Friedrich Christoph Oetingers Gottesvorstellung*. Göttingen, 1979.

Heftrich, Eckhard. *Lessings Aufklärung: Zu den theologisch-philosophischen Spätschriften*. Frankfurt, 1978.

Hegel, Eduard. *Die katholische Kirche Deutschlands unter dem Einfluss der Aufklärung des 18. Jahrhunderts*. Opladen, 1975.

Hertzberg, Arthur. *The French Enlightenment and the Jews*. New York, 1968.

Hess, Hans-Eberhard. *Theologie und Religion bei Johann Salomo Semler: Ein Beitrag zur Theologiegeschichte des 18. Jahrhunderts*. Augsburg, 1974.

Hornig, Gottfried. *Die Anfänge der historisch-kritischen Theologie: Johann Salomo Semlers Schriftverständnis und seine Stellung zu Luther*. Göttingen, 1961.

Keller, Ernst, and Keller, Marie-Luise. *Miracles in Dispute*. Philadelphia, 1984.

Kiernan, Col. *Science and the Enlightenment in Eighteenth-Century France*. Geneva, 1968.

Knothe, Paul. *Siegmund Jakob Baumgarten und seine Stellung in der Aufklärungstheologie*. Gotha, 1928.

Körsgen, Siegfried E. *Das Bild der Reformation in der Kirchengeschichtsschreibung Johann Lorenz von Mosheims*. Tübingen, 1966.

Korshin, Paul J., and Allen, Robert R., eds. *Greene Centennial Studies*. Charlottesville, Va., 1984.

Koyré, Alexandre. *From the Closed World to the Infinite Universe.* Baltimore, 1957.

Kraeling, Emil G. *The Old Testament since the Reformation.* New York, 1955.

Lehmann, Hartmut, and Lohmeier, Dieter, eds. *Aufklärung und Pietismus im dänischen Gesamtstaat, 1770–1820.* Neumünster, 1983.

LeMahieu, D. L. *The Mind of William Paley: A Philosopher and His Age.* Lincoln, Neb., 1976.

Leube, Hans. *Orthodoxie und Pietismus: Gesammelte Studien.* Bielefeld, 1975.

Louth, Andrew. *Discerning the Mystery: An Essay on the Nature of Theology.* Oxford, 1983.

Lundsteen, A. C. *Hermann Samuel Reimarus und die Anfänge der Leben-Jesu-Forschung.* Copenhagen, 1939.

Mälzer, Gottfried. *Johann Albrecht Bengel: Leben und Werk.* Stuttgart, 1970.

Manuel, Frank Edward. *The Eighteenth Century Confronts the Gods.* Cambridge, Mass., 1959.

Marshall, Peter James, and Williams, Glyndwr. *The Great Map of Mankind: Perceptions of New Worlds in the Age of Enlightenment.* Cambridge, Mass., 1982.

May, Henry F. *The Enlightenment in America.* New York, 1976.

Mossner, Ernest Campbell. *Bishop Butler and the Age of Reason.* New York, 1936.

Normann, Carl E. *Enhetskyrka och upplysningsidéer* [The church of unity and the ideas of the Enlightenment]. Lund, 1963.

O'Brien, Charles H. *Ideas of Religious Toleration at the Time of Joseph II.* Philadelphia, 1969.

Pelikan, Jaroslav. "The Evolution of the Historical." Chapter 2 of *Historical Theology: Continuity and Change in Christian Doctrine*, pp. 33–67. New York, 1971.

―――. *The Excellent Empire: The Fall of Rome and the Triumph of the Church.* New York, 1987. Gibbon's *Decline and Fall* as a critique of patristic theories.

Peter, Klaus. *Stadien der Aufklärung: Moral und Politik bei Lessing, Novalis und Friedrich Schlegel.* Wiesbaden, 1980.

Philipp, Wolfgang, ed. *Das Zeitalter der Aufklärung.* Bremen, 1963. A collection of theological texts.

Ratschow, Carl Heinz. *Lutherische Dogmatik zwischen Reformation und Aufklärung.* Gütersloh, 1964–.

Reill, Peter Hanns. *The German Enlightenment and the Rise of Historicism.* Berkeley, 1975.

Rockwood, Raymond Oxley, ed. *Carl Becker's Heavenly City Revisited.* Ithaca, N.Y., 1958.

Rotermund, Hans Martin. *Orthodoxie und Pietismus.* Berlin, 1959.

Schian, Martin. *Orthodoxie und Pietismus im Kampf um die Predigt: Ein Beitrag zur Geschichte des endenden 17. und des beginnenden 18. Jahrhunderts.* Giessen, 1912.

Schloemann, Martin. *Siegmund Jacob Baumgarten: System und Geschichte in der Theologie des Übergangs zum Neuprotestantismus.* Göttingen, 1974.

Schmid, Hermann Alfred. *Die Entzauberung der Welt in der Schweizer Landeskunde.* Basel, 1942.

Schmidt, Julian. *Geschichte des geistigen Lebens in Deutschland von Leibnitz bis auf Lessing's Tod, 1681–1751.* 2 vols. Leipzig, 1862–63.

Schweitzer, Albert. *The Quest of the Historical Jesus: A Critical Study of Its Progress from Reimarus to Wrede.* Translated by W. Montgomery. Reprint edition. New York, 1961.

Sher, Richard B. *Church and University in the Scottish Enlightenment.* Princeton, 1985.

Strakoš, Jan. *Počátky obrozeného historismu v pražských časopisech a Mik. Ad. Voigt* [The beginnings of the historicism of national revival in Prague periodicals and Nicholas Adaukt Voigt]. Prague, 1929.

Sullivan, Robert E. *John Toland and the Deist Controversy: A Study in Adaptations.* Cambridge, Mass., 1982.

Titone, Virgilio. *La storiografia dell'illuminismo in Italia*. Milan, 1969.

Willey, Basil. *The Eighteenth Century Background: Studies on the Idea of Nature in the Thought of the Period*. London, 1940.

Wolterstorff, Nicholas. "The Migration of the Theistic Arguments: From Natural Theology to Evidentialist Apologetics." In: *Rationality, Religious Belief, and Moral Commitment*, ed. Robert Audi and William J. Wainwright. Ithaca, N.Y., 1986.

3. The Theology of the Heart

Aalen, Leiv. *Die Theologie des jungen Zinzendorf*. Hamburg, 1966.

Baker, E. W. *A Herald of the Evangelical Revival: A Critical Inquiry into the Relation of William Law to John Wesley and the Beginnings of Methodism*. London, 1948.

Bauch. Hermann. *Die Lehre vom Wirken des Heiligen Geistes im Frühpietismus*. Hamburg, 1974.

Benz, Ernst. *Emanuel Swedenborg: Naturforscher und Seher*. Munich, 1948.

Beyer-Fröhlich, Marianne, ed. *Pietismus und Rationalismus*. Leipzig, 1933.

Beyreuther, Erich. *Studien zur Theologie Zinzendorfs*. Neukirchen, 1962.

———. *Geschichte des Pietismus*. Stuttgart, 1978.

Bornkamm, Heinrich, et al., eds. *Der Pietismus in Gestalten und Wirkungen*. Bielefeld, 1975.

Blankenagel, W. *Tersteegen als religiöser Erzieher*. Emsdetten, 1934.

Cannon, William R. *The Theology of John Wesley*. New York, 1953.

Deschner, John. *Wesley's Christology: An Interpretation*. Dallas, 1960.

Dillenschneider, Clément. *La mariologie de S. Alphonse de Liguori*. 2 vols. Fribourg, 1931–34.

Elwood, Douglas J. *The Philosophical Theology of Jonathan Edwards*. New York, 1960.

Erb, Peter C., ed. *Pietists: Selected Writings*. New York, 1983.

Evenhuis, Rudolf Barteld. *De biblicistisch-eschatologische theologie van Johann Albrecht Bengel*. Wageningen, 1931.

Flew, R. Newton. *The Idea of Perfection in Christian Theology*. London, 1934.

Friedmann, Robert. *Mennonite Piety through the Centuries*. Goshen, Ind., 1949.

Goré, Jeanne Lydie. *L'itinéraire de Fénelon: Humanisme et spiritualité*. Grenoble, 1957.

Greschat, Martin. *Zur neuen Pietismusforschung*. Darmstadt, 1977.

Haillant, Marguerite. *Fénelon et la prédication*. Paris, 1969.

Haroutunian, Joseph. *Piety versus Moralism: The Passing of the New England Theology*. New York, 1932.

Heppe, Heinrich. *Geschichte des Pietismus und der Mystik in der reformirten Kirche*. Leiden, 1879.

Hildebrandt, Franz. *From Luther to Wesley*. London, 1951.

Knox, Ronald A. *Enthusiasm: A Chapter in the History of Religion, with Special Reference to the XVII and XVIII Centuries*. Oxford, 1950.

Lawson, John. *Notes on Wesley's Forty-four Sermons*. London, 1952.

Lerch, David. *Heil und Heiligung bei John Wesley*. Zurich, 1941.

Lindström, Harald. *Wesley and Sanctification*. London, [1946].

McNair, Alexander. *Scots Theology in the Eighteenth Century*. London, [1928].

Martens, Wolfgang. *Die Botschaft der Tugend: Die Aufklärung im Spiegel der deutschen moralischen Wochenschriften*. Stuttgart, 1968.

Mason, H. T. *Pierre Bayle and Voltaire*. Oxford, 1963.

May, James Lewis. *Fénelon: A Study*. London, 1938.

Mead, Sidney Earl. *Nathaniel William Taylor, 1786–1858: A Connecticut Liberal.* Chicago, 1942.

Meyer, Dietrich, ed. *Erweckungsbewegung.* Bonn, 1982.

Miller, Perry. *The New England Mind.* 2 vols. Boston, 1961.

Morgan, Edmund S. *Visible Saints: The History of a Puritan Idea.* Ithaca, N. Y., 1965.

Nordstrandh, Ove. *Den äldre svenska pietismens litteratur* [The literature of older Swedish Pietism]. Stockholm, 1951.

Nuttall, Geoffrey F. *The Holy Spirit in Puritan Faith and Experience.* Oxford, 1946.

Outler, Albert C., ed. *John Wesley.* New York, 1964.

Pelikan, Jaroslav. "Pietism." In *A Dictionary of the History of Ideas,* edited by Philip P. Wiener, 3:493–95. New York, 1968–73.

———. *Bach among the Theologians.* Philadelphia, 1986.

Peschke, Erhard. *Studien zur Theologie August Hermann Franckes.* 2 vols. Berlin, 1964–66.

———. *Bekehrung und Reform: Ansatz und Wurzeln der Theologie August Hermann Franckes.* Bielefeld, 1977.

Rückert, Georg. *Eusebius Amort und das bayrische Geistesleben im 18. Jahrhundert.* Munich, 1956.

Schmidt, Martin. *John Wesley: A Theological Biography.* Translated by Norman P. Goldhawk. Vol. 1. New York, 1962.

———. *Wiedergeburt und neuer Mensch: Gesammelte Studien zur Geschichte des Pietismus.* Witten, 1969.

———. *Der Pietismus als theologische Erscheinung.* Göttingen, 1984.

Stoeffler, F. Ernest. *The Rise of Evangelical Pietism.* Leiden, 1965.

———. *German Pietism during the Eighteenth Century.* Leiden, 1973.

Stout, Harry S. *The New England Soul: Preaching and Religious Culture in Colonial New England.* New York, 1986.

Wallmann, Johannes. *Philipp Jakob Spener und die Anfänge des Pietismus.* Tübingen, 1970.

4. Foundations of the Christian World View

Balthasar, Hans Urs von. *Die Gottesfrage des heutigen Menschen.* Vienna, 1956.

Blau, Joseph L., ed. *American Philosophic Addresses.* New York, 1946.

Bornkamm, Heinrich, ed. *Imago Dei: Beiträge zur theologischen Anthropologie.* Giessen, 1932.

Boulger, James D. *Coleridge as Religious Thinker.* New Haven, 1961.

Bury, John Bagnell. *The Idea of Progress: An Inquiry into Its Origin and Growth.* London, 1920.

Cairns, David Smith. *The Image of God in Man.* London, 1953.

Cassirer, Ernst. *The Problem of Knowledge: Philosophy, Science, and History since Hegel.* Translated by William H. Woglom and Charles W. Hendel. New Haven, 1950.

———. *Kant's Life and Thought.* Translated by James Haden. New Haven, 1981.

Collins, James Daniel. *God in Modern Philosophy.* Chicago, 1959.

———. *The Emergence of Philosophy of Religion.* New Haven, 1967.

Dampier, William Cecil. *A History of Science and Its Relations with Philosophy and Religion.* Cambridge, 1929.

Dillenberger, John. *Protestant Thought and Natural Science: A Historical Interpretation.* Garden City, N. Y., 1960.

Dilthey, Wilhelm. *Leben Schleiermachers.* Edited by Martin Redeker. 2 vols. Berlin, 1970. Far more than a biography, this remains the best introduction to Schleiermacher's thought.

Eucken, Rudolf. *Main Currents of Modern Thought: A Study of the Spiritual and Intellectual Movements of the Present Day*. Translated by Meyrick Booth. New York, 1912.

Flückiger, Felix. *Philosophie und Theologie bei Schleiermacher*. Zurich, 1947.

Frankel, Charles. *The Faith of Reason: The Idea of Progress in the French Enlightenment*. New York, 1948.

Furniss, N. F. *The Fundamentalist Controversy, 1918–1931*. New Haven, 1954.

Gillispie, Charles Coulston. *Genesis and Geology: A Study in the Relations of Scientific Thought, Natural Theology, and Social Opinion in Great Britain, 1790–1850*. Cambridge, Mass., 1951.

Greene, John C. *Darwin and the Modern World View*. Baton Rouge, La., 1961.

———. *Science, Ideology, and World View: Essays in the History of Evolutionary Ideas*. Berkeley, 1981.

Hartshorne, Charles, and Reese, William L., eds. *Philosophers Speak of God*. 2d ed. Chicago, 1963.

Hefner, Philip James. *Faith and the Vitalities of History: A Theological Study Based on the Work of Albrecht Ritschl*. New York, 1966.

———. ed. Albrecht Ritschl. *Three Essays*. Philadelphia, 1972.

Himmelfarb, Gertrude. *Darwin and the Darwinian Revolution*. Garden City, N.Y., 1959.

Jaki, Stanley L. *Lord Gifford and His Lectures: A Centenary Retrospect*. Edinburgh and Macon, Ga., 1986.

Kemper, Hans-Georg. *Gottebenbildlichkeit und Naturnachahmung im Säkularisierungsprozess*. 2 vols. Tübingen, 1981.

Kline, George L. *Religious and Anti-Religious Thought in Russia*. Chicago, 1968.

Korff, Hermann August. *Geist der Goethezeit: Versuch einer ideellen Entwicklung der klassisch-romantischen Literaturgeschichte*. 5 vols. Leipzig, 1923–57. Despite its subtitle, this massive work does not confine its insights to the history of literature, but has direct bearing on the history of Christian thought.

Kroner, Richard. *Kant's Weltanschauung*. Translated by John E. Smith. Chicago, 1956.

Krüger, Hans Joachim. *Theologie und Aufklärung: Untersuchungen zu ihrer Vermittlung beim jungen Hegel*. Stuttgart, 1966.

Le Guillou, Louis. *L'evolution de la pensée religieuse de Félicité Lamennais*. Paris, 1965.

Lotz, David Walter. *Ritschl and Luther: A Fresh Perspective on Albrecht Ritschl's Theology in the Light of His Luther Study*. Nashville, 1974.

Lovejoy, Arthur O. *The Great Chain of Being*. Cambridge, Mass., 1936.

Lütgert, Wilhelm. *Die Religion des deutschen Idealismus und ihr Ende*. 2d ed. 2 vols. Gütersloh, 1923.

Mackintosh, Hugh Ross. *Types of Modern Theology*. New York, 1937.

Merz, John Theodore. *A History of European Thought in the Nineteenth Century*. 4 vols. Edinburgh, 1896–1914. Intellectual developments of the nineteenth century as seen from the perspective of science.

Miller, Perry, ed. *The Transcendentalists*. Cambridge, Mass., 1950.

Niebuhr, H. Richard. *The Kingdom of God in America*. New York, 1937.

Ogden, Schubert M. *The Reality of God and Other Essays*. New York, 1966.

Pelikan, Jaroslav. "The Significance of *Nature*." Introduction to Ralph Waldo Emerson. *Nature*. Sesquicentennial edition. Boston, 1985, pp. 1-66.

Smith, Hilrie Shelton. *Changing Conceptions of Original Sin: A Study in American Theology since 1750*. New York, 1955.

Spiegler, Gerhard. *The Eternal Covenant: Schleiermacher's Experiment in Cultural Theology*. New York, 1967.

Tax, Sol, ed. *Evolution after Darwin*. 3 vols. Chicago, 1960. Includes several discussions of the theological implications of the issue.

Tice, Terrence N. *Schleiermacher Bibliography*. Princeton, 1966.

Turner, Frank. *Between Science and Religion: The Reaction to Scientific Naturalism in Late Victorian England*. New Haven, 1974.

Wagar, W. Warren. *Good Tidings: The Belief in Progress from Darwin to Marcuse*. Bloomington, Ind., 1972.

Walther, Ch. *Typen des Reich-Gottes-Verständnisses*. Munich, 1961.

Welch, Claude. *Protestant Thought in the Nineteenth Century*. 2 vols. New Haven, 1972–85.

West, Robert Frederick. *Alexander Campbell and Natural Religion*. New Haven, 1948.

Willey, Basil. *Nineteenth Century Studies*. New York, 1949.

―――. *More Nineteenth Century Studies*. New York, 1956.

5. THE DEFINITION OF DOCTRINE

Barth, J. Robert. *Coleridge and Christian Doctrine*. Cambridge, Mass., 1969.

Beckmann, Klaus-Martin. *Der Begriff der Häresie bei Schleiermacher*. Munich, 1959.

Birkner, Hans Joachim, et al. *Das konfessionelle Problem in der evangelischen Theologie des 19. Jahrhunderts*. Tübingen, 1966.

Bolshakoff, Serge. *The Doctrine of the Unity of the Church in the Works of Khomyakov and Möhler*. London, 1946.

Bouyer, Louis. *The Word, Church, and Sacraments in Protestantism and Catholicism*. Translated by A. V. Littledale. New York, 1961.

Brezik, Victor B., ed. *One Hundred Years of Thomism: "Aeterni Patris" and Afterwards*. Notre Dame, Ind., 1984.

Brose, Oliver J. *Frederick Denison Maurice: Rebellious Conformist*. Columbus, Ohio, 1971.

Butler, Cuthbert. *The Vatican Council*. 2 vols. New York, 1930.

Christensen, Torben. *The Divine Order: A Study in F. D. Maurice's Theology*. Leiden, 1973.

Congar, Yves M.-J. *Tradition and Traditions: An Historical and a Theological Essay*. Translated by Michael Naseby and Thomas Rainborough. New York, 1966.

Courth, Franz. *Das Wesen des Christentums in der liberalen Theologie*. Frankfurt, 1977.

Cross, Barbara M. *Horace Bushnell: Minister to a Changing America*. Chicago, 1958.

D'Arcy, Martin C. *The Meaning and the Matter of History*. New York, 1959.

Dupré, Louis K. *Kierkegaard as Theologian: The Dialectic of Christian Existence*. New York, 1963.

Fairweather, Eugene R., ed. *The Oxford Movement*. New York, 1964.

Faut, S. *Die Christologie seit Schleiermacher: Ihre Geschichte und ihre Begründung*. Tübingen, 1907.

Geiger, Wolfgang. *Spekulation und Kritik: Die Geschichtstheologie Ferdinand Christian Baurs*. Munich, 1964.

Geiselmann, Josef Rupert. *The Meaning of Tradition*. Translated by W. J. O'Hara. New York, 1966.

―――. ed. Johann Adam Möhler. *Symbolik oder Darstellung der dogmatischen Gegensätze der Katholiken und Protestanten nach ihren öffentlichen Bekenntnisschriften*. 2 vols. Darmstadt, 1958–61.

Gratieux, Albert. *A. S. Khomiakov et le mouvement slavophile*. 2 vols. Paris, 1939.

Groh, John E. *Nineteenth Century German Protestantism: The Church as Social Model*. Washington, 1982.

Heinecken, Martin J. *The Moment before God*. Philadelphia, 1956. A study of Kierkegaard's religion.

Hennesey, James J. *The First Council of the Vatican: The American Experience*. New York, 1963.

Herbigny, Michel d'. *Vladimir Soloviev, a Russian Newman (1853–1900)*. Translated by A. M. Buchanan. London, 1918.

Hocedez, Edgar. *Histoire de la théologie au XIXe siècle*. 3 vols. Brussels, 1947–52.

Hodgson, Peter Crafts. *The Formation of Historical Theology: A Study of Ferdinand Christian Baur*. New York, 1966.

Hök, Gösta. *Die elliptische Theologie Albrecht Ritschls nach Ursprung und innerem Zusammenhang*. Uppsala, 1942.

Kattenbusch, Ferdinand. *Die deutsche evangelische Theologie seit Schleiermacher: Ihre Leistungen und ihre Schäden*. 5th ed. Giessen, 1926.

Knudsen, Johannes. *Danish Rebel: The Life of N. F. S. Grundtvig*. Philadelphia, 1955.

Krieger, Leonard. *Ranke: The Meaning of History*. Chicago, 1977.

Küng, Hans. *Infallible? An Inquiry*. Translated by Edward Quinn. Garden City, N.Y., 1971.

Loetscher, Lefferts Augustine. *The Broadening Church: A Study of Theological Issues in the Presbyterian Church since 1869*. Philadelphia, 1957.

Løgstrup, Knud Ejler Christian, and Harbsmeier, Götz, eds. *Kontroverse um Kierkegaard und Grundtvig*. 3 vols. Munich, 1966–72.

Mackey, J. P. *The Modern Theology of Tradition*. New York, 1963. Includes a chapter on "the two sources" (pp. 150–69).

Meinecke, Friedrich. *Historism: The Rise of a New Historical Outlook*. Translated by J. E. Anderson. New York, 1972.

Marty, Martin E. *Modern American Religion*. Chicago, 1986–.

Neufeld, Karl H. *Adolf von Harnack: Theologie als Suche nach der Kirche*. Paderborn, 1977.

Nichols, James Hastings. *Romanticism in American Theology: Nevin and Schaff at Mercersburg*. Chicago, 1961.

Niebuhr, Richard R. *Schleiermacher on Christ and Religion: A New Introduction*. New York, 1964.

O'Connor, Edward Dennis, ed. *The Dogma of the Immaculate Conception: History and Significance*. Notre Dame, Ind., 1958.

Patterson, Robert L. *The Philosophy of William Ellery Channing*. New York, 1952.

Pelikan, Jaroslav. *From Luther to Kierkegaard: A Study in the History of Theology*. Saint Louis, 1950.

———. *Development of Doctrine: Some Historical Prolegomena*. New Haven, 1969.

———. *The Vindication of Tradition: The Jefferson Lecture for 1983*. New Haven, 1984.

Ratté, John. *Three Modernists: Alfred Loisy, George Tyrrell, William L. Sullivan*. New York, 1967.

Seeberg, Reinhold. *Die Kirche Deutschlands im neunzehnten Jahrhundert*. Leipzig, 1904.

Speigl, Jakob. *Traditionslehre und Traditionsbeweis in der historischen Theologie Ignaz Döllingers*. Essen, 1964.

Sponheim, Paul Ronald. *Kierkegaard on Christ and Christian Coherence*. New York, 1968.

Thomte, Reidar. *Kierkegaard's Philosophy of Religion*. Princeton, 1948.

Urementa, F. de. *Principios de filosofía de la historia . . . de Balmes*. Madrid, 1952.

Walgrave, J.-H. *Newman the Theologian: The Nature of Belief and Doctrine as Exemplified in His Life and Works*. Translated by A. V. Littledale. New York, 1960. Walgrave gives special attention to the development of the theory of development.

Welch, Claude. *In This Name: The Doctrine of the Trinity in Contemporary Theology*. New York, 1952.

————. *God and Incarnation in Mid-Nineteenth Century German Theology.* New York, 1965.

White, Hayden. *Metahistory: The Historical Imagination in Nineteenth-Century Europe.* Baltimore, 1973.

6. THE SOBORNOST OF THE BODY OF CHRIST

Anderson, Gerald H., ed. *Christian Mission in Theological Perspective.* Nashville, 1967.

Baillie, John. *The Idea of Revelation in Recent Thought.* New York, 1956.

Baum, Gregory. *That They May Be One: A Study of Papal Doctrine (Leo XIII–Pius XII).* Westminster, Md., 1958.

Beinert, Wolfgang. *Um das dritte Kirchenattribut: Die Katholizität der Kirche im Verständnis der evangelisch-lutherischen und römisch-katholischen Theologie der Gegenwart.* 2 vols. Essen, 1964.

Bennett, John C., ed. *Christian Social Ethics in a Changing World.* New York, 1966.

Berkouwer, Gerrit Cornelis. *The Second Vatican Council and the New Catholicism.* Translated by Lewis B. Smedes. Grand Rapids, Mich., 1965.

Calvez, Jean Yves, and Perrin, Jacques. *The Church and Social Justice: The Social Teaching of the Popes from Leo XIII to Pius XII, 1878–1958.* Translated by J. R. Kirwan. Chicago, 1961.

Carlson, Edgar M. *The Reinterpretation of Luther.* Philadelphia, 1948.

Congar, Yves M-J. *The Mystery of the Church.* Translated by A. V. Littledale. Baltimore, 1960.

Curtis, Charles J. *Söderblom: Ecumenical Pioneer.* Minneapolis, 1967.

Dillenberger, John M. *God Hidden and Revealed: The Interpretation of Luther's "Deus absconditus" and Its Significance for Religious Thought.* Philadelphia, 1953.

Dulles, Avery. *Models of the Church.* New York, 1974.

Fouilloux, Etienne. *Les catholiques et l'unité chrétienne du XIXe au XXe siècle.* Paris, 1982.

Glick, G. Wayne. *The Reality of Christianity: A Study of Adolf von Harnack as Historian and Theologian.* New York, 1967.

Goodall, Norman. *The Ecumenical Movement.* London, 1961.

Handy, Robert T., ed. *The Social Gospel in America.* New York, 1966.

Hebert, Gabriel. *Fundamentalism and the Church.* London, 1957.

Hoffmann, Georg. *Das Problem der letzten Dinge in der neueren evangelischen Theologie.* Göttingen, 1929.

Hopkins, Charles Howard. *The Rise of the Social Gospel in American Protestantism.* New Haven, 1940.

Jaki, Stanislas. *Les tendances nouvelles de l'ecclésiologie.* Rome, 1957.

King, John Joseph. *The Necessity of the Church for Salvation in Selected Theological Writings of the Past Century.* Washington, 1960.

Küng, Hans. *Structures of the Church.* Translated by Salvator Attanasio. New York, 1964.

————. *Justification: The Doctrine of Karl Barth and a Catholic Reflection.* Translated by Thomas Collins, Edmund E. Tolk, and David Granskou. New ed. Philadelphia, 1981.

Lelouvier, Yves-Noël. *Perspectives russes sur l'église: Un théologien contemporain, Georges Florovsky.* Paris, 1967.

Levie, Jean. *The Bible, Word of God in Words of Men.* Translated by S. H. Treman. New York, 1962. A study of *Divino afflante Spiritu.*

Lindbeck, George H. *The Future of Roman Catholic Theology: Vatican II—Catalyst for Change.* Philadelphia, 1970.

Lovejoy, Arthur O. *Essays in the History of Ideas.* Baltimore, 1948.

McNeill, John Thomas. *Unitive Protestantism: The Ecumenical Spirit and Its Persistent Expression*. Richmond, Va., 1964.

Minear, Paul S. *Images of the Church in the New Testament*. Philadelphia, 1960.

Müller, Reinhart. *Walter Rauschenbusch: Ein Beitrag zur Begegnung des deutschen and des amerikanischen Protestantismus*. Leiden, 1957.

Murray, John Courtney, ed. *Freedom and Man*. New York, 1965.

Neuner, Joseph. *Christian Revelation and World Religions*. London, 1967.

Outler, Albert C. *The Christian Tradition and the Unity We Seek*. New York, 1957.

Pauck, Wilhelm. *From Luther to Tillich: The Reformers and Their Heirs*. Edited by Marion Pauck. Introduction by Jaroslav Pelikan. San Francisco, 1984.

Pelikan, Jaroslav. *The Riddle of Roman Catholicism*. New York, 1959.

———. "Catholic Substance and Protestant Principle Today." In *Obedient Rebels: Catholic Substance and Protestant Principle in Luther's Reformation*. New York, 1964, pp. 159–206.

———. *Twentieth-Century Theology in the Making*. Translated by R. A. Wilson. 3 vols. New York, 1969–70. These three volumes of sources deal with, respectively, "Themes of Biblical Theology," "The Theological Dialogue: Issues and Resources," and "Ecumenicity and Renewal."

———. "Mary—Exemplar of the Development of Christian Doctrine." In *Mary: Images of the Mother of Jesus in Jewish and Christian Perspective*, pp. 79–91. Philadelphia, 1986.

Philippou, A. J., ed. *The Orthodox Ethos*. Oxford, 1964.

Rahner, Karl. *Theological Investigations*. Translated by Cornelius Ernst. Baltimore, 1961–. Every chapter in the present volume—and several in preceding volumes—can be said to show the influence of these wide-ranging historical and theological studies.

Röper, Anita. *The Anonymous Christian*. Translated by Joseph Donceel. New York, 1966.

Rouse, Ruth, and Neill, Stephen Charles, eds. *A History of the Ecumenical Movement, 1517–1948*. Philadelphia, 1954.

Rumscheidt, H. Martin. *Revelation and Theology: An Analysis of the Barth-Harnack Correspondence of 1923*. Cambridge, 1972.

Schlette, Heinz Robert. *Towards a Theology of Religions*. Translated by W. J. O'Hara. New York, 1966.

Schmauch, Werner. *Beiheft* to: Ernst Lohmeyer. *Die Briefe an die Philipper, an die Kolosser und an Philemon*. Göttingen, 1964.

Smith, Timothy L. *Revivalism and Social Reform: American Protestantism on the Eve of the Civil War*. Nashville, 1957. Origins of the social gospel in the nineteenth century.

Sundkler, Bengt. *Nathan Söderblom: His Life and Work*. Lund, 1968.

Tavard, George H. *Two Centuries of Ecumenism: The Search for Unity*. Mentor-Omega edition. New York, 1962. The historical background of the Second Vatican Council.

Theisen, Jerome P. *The Ultimate Church and the Promise of Salvation*. Collegeville, Minn., 1976.

Visser 't Hooft, W. A. *The Background of the Social Gospel in America*. Haarlem, 1928.

Watt, Louis. *A Handbook to Rerum Novarum*. Oxford, 1941.

Wellek, René. *Concepts of Criticism*. New Haven, 1963.

Zernov, Nicolas. *The Russian Religious Renaissance of the Twentieth Century*. New York, 1963.

Index

Biblical

General

(Like those in the preceding volumes, this is an index only to the text of the book, not to its marginal notes. The number of references in the text is therefore no indication of the frequency of citation in the notes.)

Jewel, John, d. 1571, bishop of Salisbury, 12–24

John, apostle, 99. *See also* Biblical Index

John XXII, d. 1334, pope, 20

John XXIII, d. 1963, pope, 326

John, d. ca. 749, native of Damascus, 203, 280

John Scotus Erigena, d. ca. 877, philosophical theologian, 200

Judaism, relation of Christianity to, 111–13, 191–92, 235, 292–93, 301, 334–35: on history, 233–34; images, 280; Jesus, 94, 96, 100, 102, 111, 293; monotheism, 186–87, 191–92; personal God, 188; tradition, 256, 260

Justice. *See* God; Justification; Law

Justification: and development of doctrine, 278, 306–7; as point of difference between Roman Catholicism and Protestantism, 215; in early church, 81; as essence of Christianity, 102; by faith or by faith and works, 139, 142–43; defined as imputation, 97, 212–13; relation to justice, 323–24; in Ritschl, 214; and sanctification, 132–33

Justin Martyr, d. ca. 165, apologist, 81

Kant, Immanuel, d. 1804, German Protestant philosopher, 61, 106–7, 117, 118, 153

Keble, John, d. 1866, Anglican theologian and leader of Oxford Movement, 176, 221–22, 223, 242, 266

Kierkegaard, Søren Aaby, d. 1855, Danish philosopher, 2, 186–87, 228

Kingdom of God, 135–36, 215–26, 314–15, 320–25. *See also* Christ, life of; Church; Eschatology

Lacordaire, Henri Dominique, d. 1861, French Dominican, 226

Lambeth Quadrilateral, Anglican proposal for church reunion in 1888, 284–86

Lamennais, Félicité Robert de, d. 1854, French apologist, 222, 254

Lange, Joachim, d. 1744, Pietist theologian, 144

Law. *See also* Christ; Church and state; Justification

—canon law, 19–20; law of Christ, 320–21; law and gospel, 140, 147, 155–58, 323–24; Mosaic law, 41–43, 113, 157–58; law as norm, 157; natural law, 317

Law, William, d. 1761, Anglican spiritual writer, 49–59, 149, 152, 154, 155

Leo I, d. 461, pope, 251

Leo XIII, d. 1903, pope, 314

Lessing, Gotthold Ephraim, d. 1781, German thinker and man of letters, 76, 111

Life and Work, 303

Light, uncreated, 23

Liguori, Alphonsus Maria de, d. 1787, Redemptorist, 144–45

Logomachy, 34–35

Luther, Martin, d. 1546, German reformer, and Lutheranism, 7–8, 83–84, 152, 236, 238, 294, 306

—as biblical scholar, 90–91; on bondage of will, 37, 205–6; on church and unity, 17, 294; abolition of confession, 52; on councils, 249; on creation, 202; on Eucharist, 52, 84, 297; on experience, 150–51; Judaism, 112; on law and gospel, 156–57; on original sin, 35, 42–43, 207

Lydda-Diospolis, synod of, in 415, 36

Maimonides, Moses, d. 1204, Jewish philosopher, 113

Man. *See also* Christ; Creation; Evolution; Grace; Justification; Salvation

—defined as: subject to bondage, 37, 205–6; endowed with conscience, 158–60, 163, 186, 293; special creation, 203–9; free, 116, 203, 205–6; image of God, 203–14, 335; immortal, 67–68, 107–10, 240; microcosm, 205; sinner, 35, 42–43, 206–8, 263, 280, 304; single in origin, 206–8, 256, 319; soul, 116, 130–46; will and intellect, 151

Manicheism, 40

Mary, 63, 136, 143–45, 279–80, 335. *See also* Christ; Salvation

—defined as: assumed into heaven, 26, 145, 265, 278–79; central to Christian life, 154; immaculately conceived, 26, 143–44, 208–9, 278–79, 283; model of development of doctrine, 274; mediatrix, 145, 230; Theotokos (Mother of God), 63, 144, 279–80; Virgin, 63, 240

Matrimony, 68, 205, 296

Maurice, Frederick Denison, d. 1872, Anglican theologian, 272

Mediation, historical, as principle, 230–41. *See also* Christ; Mary

Medieval, and Middle Ages, 177, 236

THE CHRISTIAN TRADITION, Volume 5

Designed by Joseph Alderfer
Composed by Carlisle Graphics
in Linotron Garamond 3.
Printed and bound by Maple-Vail
on 50# Glatfelter.
Bound in ICG Arrestox Vellum and
stamped in blue and gold.

The form of the Jerusalem Cross
shown on the jacket and binding is a
modern rendering of the medieval
"Crusaders' Cross" in the Church of the
Holy Sepulcher in Jerusalem. Its five
crosses, usually in red, represent the five
wounds of Christ.